SYDNEY & THE GREAT BARRIER REEF

ULRIKE LEMMIN-WOOLFREY

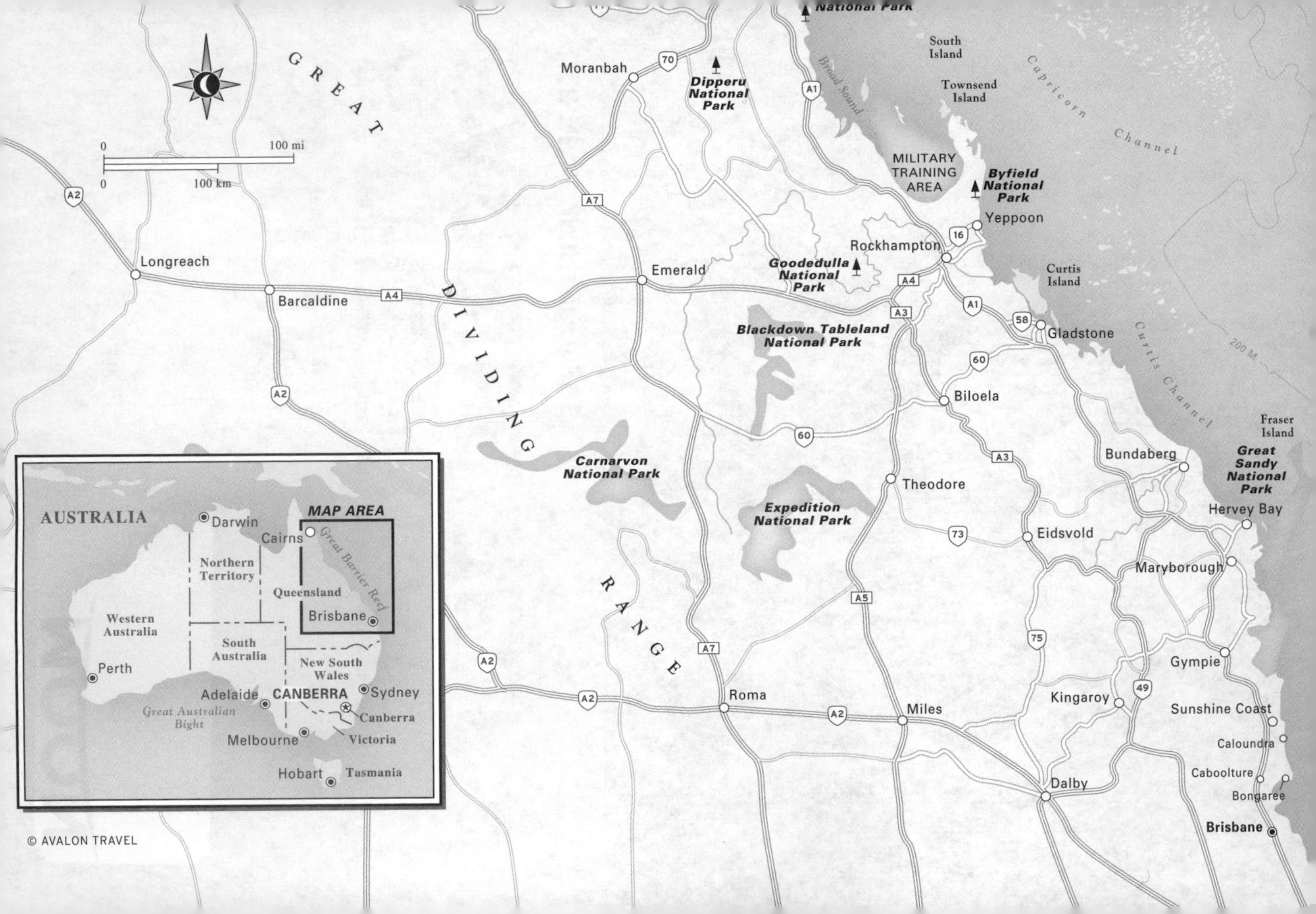

GREAT DIVIDING RANGE

0 100 mi
0 100 km

Longreach
Barcaldine
Emerald
Moranbah
Dipperu National Park
National Park
South Island
Townsend Island
Broad Sound
Capricorn Channel
MILITARY TRAINING AREA
Byfield National Park
Yeppoon
Rockhampton
Goodedulla National Park
Curtis Island
Blackdown Tableland National Park
Gladstone
Curtis Channel
200 M
Biloela
Carnarvon National Park
Theodore
Expedition National Park
Bundaberg
Fraser Island
Great Sandy National Park
Hervey Bay
Eidsvold
Maryborough
Gympie
Roma
Miles
Kingaroy
Sunshine Coast
Caloundra
Caboolture
Bongaree
Dalby
Brisbane

A1 A2 A3 A4 A5 A7 16 49 58 60 70 73 75

AUSTRALIA
MAP AREA
Darwin
Cairns
Great Barrier Reef
Northern Territory
Queensland
Brisbane
Western Australia
South Australia
New South Wales
Perth
Adelaide
CANBERRA
Sydney
Canberra
Great Australian Bight
Melbourne
Victoria
Hobart
Tasmania

SYDNEY AND THE GREAT BARRIER REEF

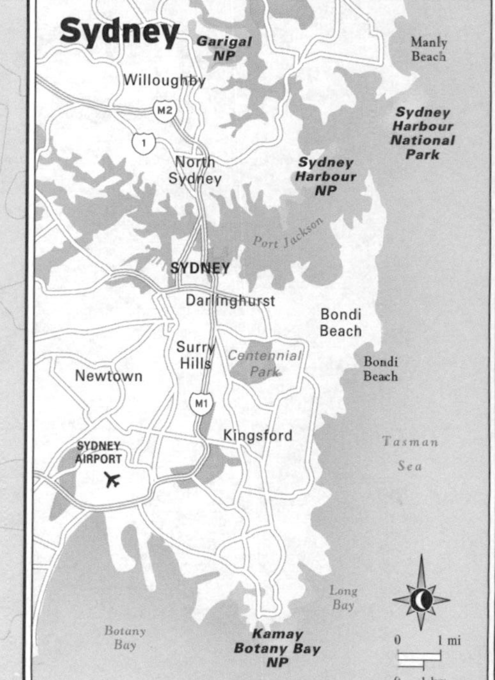

Lakefield National Park
PENINSULA DEVELOPMENTAL RD
Great Barrier Reef
200 M
1,000 M
Daintree National Park
MULLIGAN HWY
Port Douglas
BURKE DEVELOPMENTAL RD
44
81
Staaten River National Park
Cairns
Wooroonooran National Park
Grey Peaks National Park
Russell River National Park
Atherton
Mount Hypipamee National Park
Innisfail
Bulleringa National Park
1
Maria Creek National Park
Tully Gorge National Park
A1
GULF DEVELOPMENTAL RD
Hinchinbrook Island National Park
Georgetown
Undara Volcanic National Park
Girringun National Park
Ingham
62
Great Palm Island
Paluma Range National Park
Magnetic Island
63
Townsville
Cape Bowling Green
Blackbraes National Park
Ayr
Dalrymple National Park
A6
Cape Upstart National Park
A1
Bowen
Great Basalt Wall National Park
Charters Towers
Whitsunday Island National Park
Proserpine
Conway National Park
Hughenden
A6
A7
Eungella National Park
Mackay

Contents

DISCOVER

Sydney & the Great Barrier Reef

Sydney and the Great Barrier Reef: two of Australia's main attractions, and as different from each other as they come. Sydney, the capital of New South Wales, is Australia's largest city—cosmopolitan and modern yet full of history. For most visitors to Sydney, it is love at first sight. It doesn't take more than arriving for the first time at Circular Quay, seeing the Sydney Opera House on one side, the Sydney Harbour Bridge on the other, and in between the two the bustling harbor, all usually topped by glorious blue skies. It truly takes your breath away.

This bustling metropolis charts the beginnings of modern Australia; it all began here in the late 1770s, when the British settled the land down under. And just when you think Sydney has it all, it has more: stunning beaches, generous parks, and proximity to gorgeous countryside that ranges from mountains and valleys to farmed lands that undulate gently between world-famous wineries. What more could you want from a visit to Australia?

Ah, yes. The Great Barrier Reef, of course. The world's largest coral reef system, stretching over 2,600 kilometers and featuring some 900 islands, is a must-do for anybody who is even vaguely interested in what lies beneath the waves. In addition to

Clockwise from top left: koala at Wild Life Sydney Zoo; diving on the Great Barrier Reef; small boat moored up at the Great Barrier Reef; crocodile spotting on the Daintree River; surfing at Bondi Beach; a Sydney Harbour Tall Ships cruise arriving under the Harbour Bridge.

the colorful marine life, there are countless pristine beaches on the islands and along Queensland's endless coast.

But Queensland has not only the reef to boast about, but also the Daintree Rainforest, the world's oldest rainforest, which remains pretty much unchanged over the last few million years. It's stunning, eerie, and awe-inspiring—a bit like the reef, really.

So, you've got two extremely different destinations: a bustling city and a state full of breathtaking natural beauty. In Sydney and Queensland, you have choices that satisfy every need, from high-end shopping to soaking up history, from scuba diving among coral gardens to relaxing on deserted beaches, from hiking through truly wild nature to meeting some of the local animals that are just as enchanting as the rest of the country. And then some. Come see for yourself.

Clockwise from top left: view from Sydney's northern shore; Taronga Zoo; Luna Park; overlooking Coogee Beach.

LUNA PARK

Planning Your Trip

Where to Go

Sydney

Sydney is Australia's picture-postcard-perfect **signature city.** Visits to the iconic **Sydney Opera House** and the **Sydney Harbour Bridge** are a must, as is a ferry ride along the stunning natural harbor with its **accessible islands.** Combining history with modern flair, natural beauty with great restaurants and shops, the city also offers **Bondi Beach,** one of Australia's most loved beaches, just on its doorstep, making it an all-rounder.

The Southern Reef

Still a relative secret among travelers, the southern reef has a unique mix of **beaches, islands,** and **national parks,** with **stunning countryside** and sheer **seclusion.** If you like **road-tripping,** this section of Australia is for you, with easily managed day trips and sidetracks that offer **hiking, wildlife-watching,** lazing on beaches, and **snorkeling** on the **Great Barrier Reef,** and you'll hardly meet another soul.

Cairns and the Northern Reef

The diamond on the diadem of the Queensland coast, the tropical north is the place where two **natural wonders** come together: the ancient **Daintree Rainforest** and the breathtaking **Great Barrier Reef.** If you like nature to blow your mind, this is the place for you. Go **diving** among corals, gaze at lush forest, spot **crocodiles,** watch an incredible array of colorful **birds,** marvel at huge **lava tubes,** and explore picturesque **tablelands.** And with it all being contained in a relatively—for Australia—small area, you can fit a lot into a brief stay, using Cairns or Port Douglas as a base.

fire coral on the Great Barrier Reef

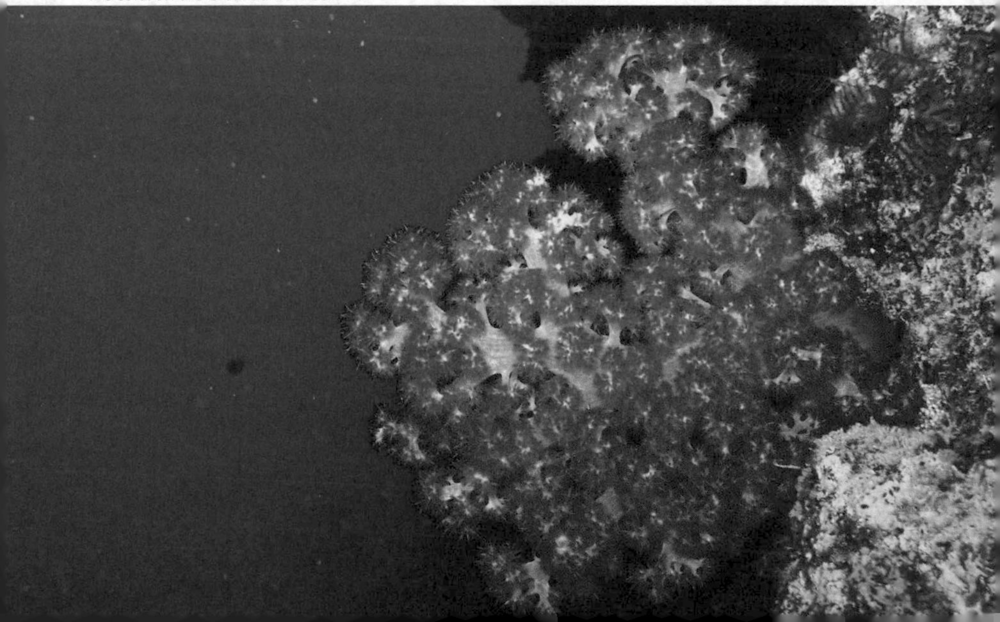

When to Go

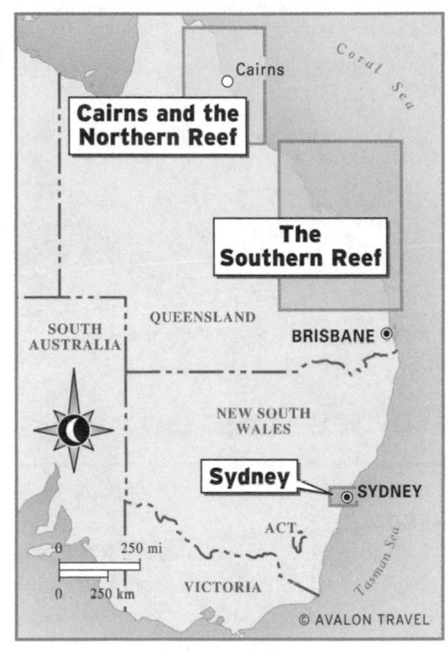

Sydney and the Great Barrier Reef are separated by the Tropic of Capricorn, with Sydney being temperate and the Queensland coast mostly tropical. So there are some differences in climate that could affect your travel.

Sydney has some of the best weather in Australia, with on average seven hours of sunshine a day, winter (July-Sept.) temperatures below 20 degrees Celsius, and summer (Nov.-Feb.) temperatures hovering around the high 20s to 30 degrees Celsius. It rains regularly; around a third of each month sees some precipitation. Spring and fall are the best months, when it's not too hot to walk along the city's pavements and not that cold that you can't sit outside and enjoy the views.

In the **tropical north,** temperatures do not change a great deal over the year, but the amount of rainfall does. Summer temperatures range between 24 and 33 degrees Celsius, while in winter they're between 14 and 26 degrees Celsius; the summer is the wet season, the so-called "green season" stretching from the onset of the monsoon, usually in November, and ending in May. The rain makes it hot and humid, at times quite uncomfortable. So, again spring and fall are the best options, avoiding the worst of the rain as well as the worst of the heat.

In Australia, the big **summer vacation** is between mid-December and early February, with all schools and universities breaking for nearly two months. This has an effect on number of people traveling as well as hotel prices, so be prepared to pay extra and see some crowds on the beaches.

For **diving, snorkeling,** and **swimming,** the ocean will be at its coolest in winter, dropping to around 24 degrees Celsius, but generally offers great visibility. In June and July, dwarf minke whales are commonly sighted. Between September and December the water warms up and many coral reef species breed, which can result in cloudy water around October. Manta rays are commonly spotted in the Coral Sea from April to October. The stinger (jellyfish) season is November to May/June, when it is advised to stay within stinger nets (provided on the most popular beaches) when swimming or to dress in stinger suits when out snorkeling on the reef. Taking it all into account, fall to winter is probably the best time for exploring the northern coastal regions.

If You Have . . .

- **FIVE DAYS:** Spend half in Sydney, seeing The Rocks and Circular Quay, taking a round-trip on the Manly ferry, and strolling along Macquarie Street. Then head to Heron Island for an intensive Great Barrier Reef experience with diving and snorkeling.
- **ONE WEEK:** Add Bondi Beach and a BridgeClimb in Sydney, and go to Cairns for a trip up to the Daintree Forest around Cape Tribulation.
- **TWO WEEKS:** Add the Blue Mountains from Sydney and an overnight trip to the Undara Lava Tubes, plus a day out in Kuranda from Cairns. Fly to Townsville for a brief stay on Magnetic Island and have breakfast with the koalas.
- **THREE WEEKS:** Add a few days of sailing the Whitsundays. Or explore the southern reef islands, such as Lady Musgrave from the Town of 1770, and learn to surf at neighboring Agnes Water.

Before You Go

Visas

All visitors, except those holding a New Zealand passport, require a visa to enter Australia. It is very easy to obtain an **electronic travel authority (ETA)** online from www.eta.immi.gov.au. It takes about five minutes to complete the details, pay, and get the confirmation online, and costs around $20, payable by credit card only. There will be no stamp in your passport, but the details are electronically logged and available to the immigration officers upon your arrival.

Booking Tours

Australia is well up to speed when it comes to tourism, and in addition to the designated visitors centers in the cities and towns, the **concierges** in most hotels can help you book tours in Sydney, while in Queensland the vast majority of hotels have dedicated **tour-booking desks** in every lobby. The main hubs have dedicated **booking offices,** all of which usually offer the entire range of what is available and mentioned in this guide. Prices tend to be set and are not open to negotiation.

Transportation

Within **Sydney** the **public transport system** is very good, relatively cheap, and easy to understand. Timetables are displayed at bus stops and train stations, with information booths also helping out and selling tickets. If the kiosks are closed, you can get one-way, daily, and weekly tickets via easy-to-use vending machines that take cash and credit cards. **Taxis** are easily recognized, and while not all are uniformly colored, they all display a taxi sign on the roof and are metered.

In **Queensland,** simply due to the sheer size of the state, public transport between cities and attractions is less common, but there are regular, if not necessarily daily, **trains** running up and down the coast. If you are on a budget and have a bit of time on your hands, one of the best ways is to travel by **Greyhound** buses, which tend to be economical and offer more stops than the trains. Most larger towns have small regional airports, and, due to the distances involved, **flying** is the most time efficient way to connect around Queensland. Most hubs, such as Hamilton Island, Townsville, and Cairns, are reached by low-cost airlines such as Tigerair and Jetstar, whereas some

the Daintree Rainforest

the Great Barrier Reef

of the more remote islands can only be reached by private local companies, making the prices a little higher.

Costs

The **average room** price in Australia at the time of writing was $177, with the most expensive room average found in the Whitsundays, ahead of Sydney. Budget accommodation, especially hostel beds, can be had from $20 per night, but in Sydney in particular, if you are not a backpacker keen on hostels, you'd better budget $150-200 per night—you stand a better chance to get something of a decent (and family-acceptable) standard.

The cost of **dining out** depends on where you go, but you can get a cup of coffee for $4, a substantial breakfast for $18, and a main course for dinner in a decent restaurant for around $30, accompanied by a glass of wine for $9.

Daily travel on a tram, bus, or other public transportation will set you back around $3 per trip for the shortest distance, with discounts if you buy passes. Air travel can be expensive, although domestic flights can be cheap on one of the low-cost airlines, such as Tigerair.

You can expect higher prices for **manufactured goods** as well as **clothing**—20 to 30 percent more than in the United States is a rule of thumb.

The Best of Sydney and the Great Barrier Reef

Dividing your time between Australia's greatest city and its greatest natural wonder presents an interesting challenge, given the embarrassment of riches they offer. Two weeks give you time to cover sights and activities that need to ticked off anybody's must-do list, along with some of my personal favorites.

Sydney

DAY 1

Arrive in Sydney, check into your hotel, and blow away the travel cobwebs with a first visit to **Circular Quay.** See the iconic **Sydney Opera House,** stroll past the ferries crisscrossing the harbor, and, depending on time, head for **The Rocks.** Amble through the lanes, pop into **The Rocks Discovery Museum,** and get a feel for Sydney's humble beginnings.

DAY 2

Head to **Sydney Tower Eye** to get your bearings, then spend the day exploring **Hyde Park Barracks** and walking down **Macquarie Street,** where each building offers a slice of Australia's history—stroll past or into the **Sydney Mint, Sydney Hospital,** the **State Library of New South Wales,** and **Government House.** Meander through the **Royal Botanic Gardens** to **Mrs Macquarie's Chair** for the best views of the city and the harbor. If you have time, have a look through the **Art Gallery of New South Wales.**

DAY 3

Take the bus to **Bondi Beach.** Spend the morning learning to surf or watching the pros take on the waves. After lunch, head off along the stunning **Bondi to Coogee coastal walk** toward Bronte Beach and Coogee Beach—the scenery is some of the best in the land. Head back to Sydney

the Royal Botanic Gardens

Best Beaches

Choosing the best beaches in Australia is like picking the best card out of a full deck. There are so many to choose from, and everybody has a different favorite number and design, but there are the face cards, which might just appeal more to everybody, if only by their extravagance when compared to others. Here are some of my personal favorites.

Four Mile Beach, alongside Port Douglas

- **Bondi Beach:** This iconic beach is famous for its surfing, its ever-vigilant lifeguards, and its stunning setting a mere 20 minutes from Sydney's CBD. Always bustling, Bondi is fringed by an esplanade filled with restaurants and quirky shops, has an old-fashioned bathers' pavilion and an exciting seawater pool, and is the start of the gorgeous coastal walk to Coogee. It's the perfect escape from the busy metropolis.

- **Manly Beach:** Which one is better, Bondi or Manly? It's a bit like potato and *patata.* Manly is on the north side of Sydney Harbour and is reached by the fantastic Manly ferry ride, so that is a plus. The waves, some say, are even better here for surfing, and the offerings of restaurants, ice cream parlors, and shops are similar to Bondi. The promenade is lined with tall pine trees, which add a different touch. See for yourself. Which one do you prefer?

- **Whitehaven Beach:** The best way to truly appreciate this stunning beach is from above. Flying over Whitehaven Beach and the associated swirls of the Hill Inlet takes your breath away. The pristine white of the sand and the turquoise to blue and green shades of the water look like they have been painted; there simply is no other beach like it. Seven kilometers of sand fringed on one side by palms and green bushland, on the other by the clear sea, it is a perfect spot for a luxury picnic and a snorkel. If you can splurge, take a luxury flight complete with champagne picnic to the beach; it will be one of the highlights of your trip.

- **Mission Beach:** An hour south of Cairns, Mission Beach sits alongside four other great beaches, stretching over 14 kilometers, but has the advantage of having a strip of little shops and restaurants, plus a few beach resorts for recreation and sustenance alongside. The beach looks out over Dunk Island and with its fringe of palms and bush offers plenty of secluded spots for utter privacy and relaxation.

- **Four Mile Beach:** Stretching alongside Port Douglas, this is a great beach for the whole family. You can hire sun loungers and umbrellas, take surf lessons, and even partake in yoga first thing in the morning. There are always throngs of people walking and running the length of the beach, but the white sand strip is large enough to accommodate fitness enthusiasts and those who simply want to relax. And there is still plenty of room to build sand castles.

for dinner at one of the little restaurants in trendy Paddington.

DAY 4

After a morning climb up the **Sydney Harbour Bridge,** take the **Manly ferry** in lieu of a harbor tour. Have lunch and upon returning double back toward **Taronga Zoo** to meet the local wildlife. In the evening, head back to The Rocks for dinner and the scenic views of the city at nighttime. If you have the budget, go straight to **Quay;** for a more affordable meal also with good views, try **Baroque.**

IF YOU HAVE MORE TIME

Spend a day exploring **Darling Harbour** and its attractions. Then amble down to the **Powerhouse Museum** and check out **Chinatown** and **Paddy's Market,** which offers a little bit of everything.

Head out of the city to the **Blue Mountains.** Ride the rails and cable cars at aptly named **Scenic World.** Learn about the environment, culture, and history of the region at the **Blue Mountains Cultural Centre** in Katoomba. Look at the **Three Sisters** rock formation from **Echo Point,** and maybe take a hike down into the valley before going back to Sydney for a late dinner.

Travel north to the **Hunter Valley.** Sample the wares at some **wineries,** enjoy a leisurely lunch, and explore the **Hunter Valley Gardens** in Pokolbin, and then head back to Sydney for dinner.

The Great Barrier Reef

DAY 5

Leave Sydney and head toward Queensland. Fly into Proserpine and travel onward to **Airlie Beach.** Spend the afternoon soaking up the relaxed atmosphere in the small town.

DAY 6

Take the morning boat to **Hamilton Island** and spend the day exploring this large Whitsunday island by buggy or free shuttle bus. Have lunch and beach time in the main resort center. In the evening, take the long way back on the ferry, returning via **Long Island** or **Daydream Island,** to enjoy the views and get a glimpse of other Whitsunday islands.

the Three Sisters rock formation in the Blue Mountains

ferry to Green Island

DAY 7

Take a day's sailing cruise to **Whitehaven Beach** with its swirly white sands for some snorkeling and swimming.

DAY 8

Sail to **Fantasea Reefsleep** and spend another day snorkeling and diving the Great Barrier Reef, then stay overnight on this floating hotel before heading back to the airport the next morning.

DAY 9

Fly into **Cairns.** Explore the ever-changing exhibits at the **Cairns Regional Gallery,** worth visiting just for its neo-Grecian-style building. Take a stroll along the sea on the **Esplanade,** with countless cafés, restaurants, and shops—it's a great place for people-watching and bird-watching. Enjoy a shady, restful walk at the **Flecker Botanical Gardens,** a lovely expanse of "tamed" rainforest.

DAY 10

Take a day trip to **Kuranda,** taking the **Skyrail cableway** over the rainforest's canopy. Shop till you drop at the town's **markets,** and pop into the **Australian Butterfly Sanctuary.** Return to Cairns by **Kuranda Scenic Railway,** sweeping past waterfalls and across gorges.

DAY 11

Take the ferry to pretty **Green Island,** the closest coral cay island to Cairns, for a refreshing day on the reef, swimming, snorkeling, and diving.

DAY 12

Do a day trip to **Cape Tribulation.** Go **crocodile spotting** on the Daintree River. Visit the **Daintree Discovery Centre** and head north through the ancient **rainforest** to one of the deserted beaches and one of the many boardwalks, learning about the Aboriginal history and local flora and fauna.

DAY 13

Take a trip inland today. Head past **The Boulders** in **Babinda** to the enchanting **Paronella Park.** Travel back past **Mission Beach,** trying to spot an elusive cassowary.

DAY 14

Relax on **Fitzroy Island,** covered by rainforest and fringed by reef. Top up the tan and get a last swim and snorkel in while reflecting on your trip before heading back tomorrow.

Best Diving Locations

hawksbill turtle

The Great Barrier Reef is synonymous with fantastic dive locations—it is pretty much one very large, perfect dive location. Wherever you stay, they will be able to recommend some great local spots and a tour to take you there, but if you have to choose, then these locations rank high.

- **Lady Elliot Island:** Gorgeous coral lagoons, perfect for snorkeling, line this coral cay island off the town of Bundaberg. Boats take you farther out to snorkel above manta rays, plate coral, and a variety of big fish. Divers can swim through the blowhole, 16 meters down, and see gorgonian fans, soft and hard corals, sharks, barracudas, and plenty of colorful reef fish.
- **Heron Island:** Scuba diving inventor and explorer extraordinaire Jacques Cousteau himself rated Heron island as one of his favorite dive spots on the globe. There are some 22 dive sites dotted around the island, including sites such as the Coral Cascades, featuring coral trout and anemones; the Blue Pools, favored by octopus, turtles, and sharks; Heron Bommie, with its rays, eels, and Spanish dancers; and so many more that you can stay under water for weeks and still not see it all. It's magical.
- ***Yongala* Wreck:** Acknowledged as the best wreck dive in Australia, the SS *Yongala* was sunk by a cyclone in 1911 and is now home to schools of trevally, kingfish, barracuda, and batfish, with giant Queensland grouper, lionfish, turtles, and plenty of hard and soft corals having settled here to the delight of the dive groups visiting the site.
- **Green Island:** If you like the idea of seeing what's underwater—after all, that is what the Great Barrier Reef is all about—but can't quite come to grips with the scuba diving, why not don a helmet, breathe normally, and "walk" down to the sea floor to get to know some rather friendly parrot fish? No experience needed, you barely get your hair wet, yet you can get an idea of what it's like under water.
- **Cod Hole:** One of Lizard Island's favorite dive sites, this is the home of a gigantic and quite friendly potato cod. You are even allowed to hand feed him. But that is not all: Nearby there are giant clams over 150 years old sitting among a stunning variety of dozens of species of coral in the so-called Clam Garden.

Destination: Queensland

You could spend years immersing yourself in Queensland's delights, but 11 days is enough time to sample the beauty and variety this state has to offer: Sail and snorkel in the Whitsundays, and then fly over the islands to get a different view of the reef. Make friends with koalas and other creatures over breakfast. Explore ancient forest and relax on secluded beaches. Indulge yourself at a luxurious island resort. You'll have memories to last you a lifetime.

Days 1-2

Fly into Proserpine and transfer to **Airlie Beach,** where you catch a two-day **Whitsunday sailing cruise** to start your vacation in a relaxing way, with daily snorkeling (diving perhaps on the second day after the flight) to ease you through the jet lag. Sail, swim, and simply enjoy the views.

Day 3

From Airlie Beach, go **flying over the reef.** Your flight over the Whitsunday Islands will give you a completely different perspective on the scenery you enjoyed over the last two days from sea level. Then head north to **Townsville.**

Day 4

In the morning, visit **Reef HQ** to learn about the species of fish and coral that live on the Great Barrier Reef, pop into the **Perc Tucker Regional Gallery,** and then catch the ferry to **Magnetic Island.** Hire a Mini Moke (open-top beach-buggy-type car) and explore the island and its gorgeous beaches.

Day 5

Start with the **Champagne Bush Tucker Breakfast** at Bungalow Bay Koala Village. Go on a self-guided snorkeling tour and take the **Forts Walk.** Later in the afternoon, head farther north up the coast to **Hinchinbrook Island,** with its quiet rainforest and pristine beaches.

Day 6

Hiking the entire **Thorsborne Track** takes several days, but schedule in at least one day to explore this wild and rugged island, maybe by kayak, if you don't want to walk.

Day 7

Head to **Port Douglas** and explore the small town's sights, such as the pretty **St. Mary's by the Sea** church. Laze on the **Four Mile Beach** and sample one of the many fine-dining restaurants in town.

Day 8

Explore **Mossman Gorge** and **Cape Tribulation** today. Savor the ancient forest, explore the deserted beaches (but be vigilant for saltwater crocs), and look out for cassowaries.

Days 9-11

Head to the Great Barrier Reef's northernmost island resort, **Lizard Island**—one of Australia's most exclusive resorts (although you can camp there, too). You can choose from more than 20 pristine beaches, secluded bays, snorkeling, diving, boating, fishing, being pampered in the spa, and enjoying fine dining. It's an expensive but exquisite way to end your Great Barrier Reef experience.

Wildlife Experiences

There is no denying that Australia has some of the most interesting and exotic creatures on earth. They are not just unique in the way they evolved, but they also tend to be either incredibly cute, and/or incredibly interesting. Even if you weren't an animal lover before you came to Australia, its critters are sure to turn you into one.

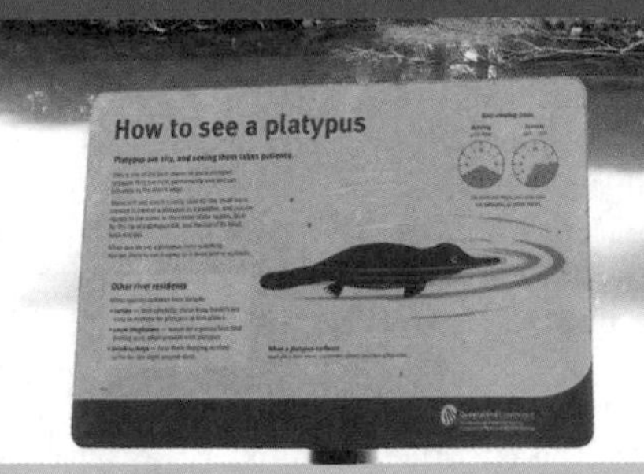

learning how to spot a platypus at Eungella National Park

KOALAS

Queensland is the only state in Australia where you can actually **hug a koala.** True, you might not agree that this is ethical, but the experience is nevertheless quite magical. Stand like a tree and an experienced wildlife warden will place a koala in your arms, and you can place a hand under his furry little behind and snuggle up close. Try the **Champagne Bush Tucker Breakfast** at Bungalow Bay Koala Village on **Magnetic Island,** where you'll get to meet koalas and all sorts of other inhabitants of the small wildlife sanctuary.

CROCODILES

The **Daintree River** is not just a majestic river winding its way through the ancient rainforest; it is also riddled with saltwater crocodiles. At the Daintree River Ferry crossing, hop onto the **Crocodile Express** and see some of these grumpy old reptiles up close.

KANGAROOS

You will see kangaroos pretty much everywhere as soon as you leave the city lights behind you. In the **Blue Mountains** they come out in the afternoon and tend to sit by the side of the road, watching the tourist buses go by. By the **Undara Lave Tubes,** a mob lives by the swimming pool, and wallabies and kangaroos are all around, even coming close to your cabin.

PLATYPUSES

For a reportedly "guaranteed" sighting of this shy and utterly unique creature, head straight for **Eungella National Park.** Be sure to be there really early in the morning (have breakfast later, but bring a coffee) or late in the afternoon. They are there—you just have to be patient and time it right.

TURTLES

It might sound pretentious of Australia, but you have a good chance to see a turtle when **diving** alongside most of the Great Barrier Reef. They are luckily still quite abundant along the coast. For watching little turtles hatch, try **Lady Elliot Island, Heron Island,** and the excellent **Mon Repos Conservation Park.**

WHALES

Even if you are not heading to the reef, you can go on **whale-watching cruises** from **Sydney,** and during the season you're pretty much guaranteed a sighting. If you'd like to **swim with minke whales,** between June and July special trips leave daily from **Cairns** and allow you to observe these friendly dwarf whales.

CASSOWARIES

Driving off the Bruce Highway toward **Mission Beach,** you will go through cassowary country. Winding roads have speed humps that ask you to slow down and look out for these rather large and elusive birds. The rare and unusual flightless birds tend to cross the road when you least expect it, so keep your eyes peeled. And if you see a large bird with a chick in tow, you'll know it is a father and child; they are temperamental parents, so do not approach them.

Cruising the Great Barrier Reef

Australia's Great Barrier Reef is a place that is overflowing with superlatives, and then breaks a few more records: Rated as one of the seven wonders of the natural world, it stretches for 2,300 kilometers along the Queensland coast, from Bundaberg to the Torres Strait, and comprises around 2,800 individual reefs, continental islands, reef islands, and sand cays—it would be impossible to cover them all in a single trip, or even a single lifetime. Due to time constraints many travelers choose one or two islands and enjoy those to the fullest. But if you want to try to see a few dozen islands and cays, even if only from the distance, then cruising is really the best option. And it doesn't have to be a gigantic hotel-on-the-sea. In the Great Barrier Reef, cruising can be as individual as you are.

Organized Cruises

There are organized cruises, usually on larger sailing or motor yachts, with often a dozen or more other people on board, and with set itineraries and scheduled stops and activities. You can book a cruise of two or three or more days in most of the towns along the coast—for example, with **Whitsundays Sailing Adventures** (www.whitsundaysailingadventures.com.au) in Airlie Beach. With departures every few days, you are bound to find something that suits you. On these cruises you usually have the option to learn to dive or snorkel (they show you the best grounds, reefs, and beaches), and you get fed in regular intervals and don't have to think at all. Just sit back and go with the flow, and you'll meet a few like-minded people from around the world on your trip as well.

The selection of half-day to full-day cruises is amazing, with companies such as **Ocean Freedom** (www.oceanfreedom.com.au). Usual departure times are around 7:30am to 8am. Go to reefs and islands to snorkel, dive (or learn to do so), swim, and explore. Most of these trips come with lunch, drinks, even open bars, and have all the equipment you'll need on board. They often stop at a purpose-built pontoon for a few hours, where you can be as active or lazy as you wish to be. There are plenty of activities for kids and they don't get stuck on a boat for days on end.

Bareboating and Private Charters

One of the most serene ways to cruise some of the islands is by bareboating—hiring a yacht and sailing it yourself. You will need to have sufficient experience and a large enough group to choose that option. Hiring a boat from an operator such as **SailFree** (www.sailfree.com.au), you can anchor in secluded bays, camp on some of the designated islands, snorkel wherever takes your fancy, and make your own agenda.

If that sounds lovely, but alas, you cannot sail a boat by yourself, hire a sailing boat with a crew. Charter companies such as **ISail Whitsundays** (www.isailwhitsundays.com) allow you to choose from a variety of yachts that come with a crew. Obviously it's not quite as private, but the crew does this for a living, and you can interact with them as much or as little as you wish.

Ferries

If time and budget are issues, one of the easiest and cheapest ways to get out onto the water for a "cruise" is to hop on an island ferry. Take **Cruise Whitsundays** (www.cruisewhitsundays.com), a commuter ferry that has a daily schedule and at least once an hour sets off from Shute Harbour near Airlie Beach to sail to Hamilton Island and some other islands along the way. There are direct ferries, and others take in two or three islands along the way. You can buy an island hopper ticket for the day and spend the day on the water, taking in the views and hopping on and off at various stops. It is a cheap, fun, and enjoyable way to see the Whitsundays on a budget.

Aboriginal Heritage

Aboriginal rock art

When you're rushing to see what the country has to offer, looking around The Rocks in Sydney and going through the museums, it is easy to forget that this is only the modern history of Australia. There is another history to explore that reaches far back into the past—the indigenous people of Australia are reportedly one of the oldest cultures in the world. Apart from the beautiful art, many visitors do not get any closer to learning about the Aboriginal peoples and their culture and tradition. Here are a few tips to experience a little more of Australia's true history.

- Australian Aboriginal art is the longest continuing art tradition in the world and an economic mainstay of the Aboriginal community. Galleries offer the typical dot paintings and other pieces of art. It is a souvenir that is truly unique to Australia, so go ahead and buy a piece, but try to go to galleries that are owned and run by Aboriginal people to ensure your money heads off into the right direction. Try the **Janbal Gallery** (www.janbalgallery.com.au) in Mossman, which is excellent and independently run by Aboriginal people.

- The knowledge of the flora and fauna of this country is what made the Aboriginal people so successful as a long-standing culture (until the Europeans came along, at any rate), and learning about the plants and animals goes a long way to understanding a little more about the culture. At Cooya Beach just north of Port Douglas, you can go walkabout with two local Kubirri Warra guides with **The Bama Way** (www.bamaway.com.au/KukuYalanji) and learn how to spear fish on the mudflats and mangroves; you'll also learn about the wildlife, their people, and their culture and heritage.

- If you are going to Kuranda by Skyrail, then make sure you stop off for the **Djabugay Aboriginal Guided Tour,** on which you go for a brief walk through the dense rainforest while your local guide points out specific plants and roots, telling you about their significance, healing properties, and other uses, all the while entertaining you with local stories and legends.

- The **Dreamtime Legend Walk** at Mossman Gorge starts with a traditional smoking ceremony and takes a small group to sacred sites on Kuku Yalanji land, where you see traditional huts and hear dreamtime stories.

- To enjoy some of the traditional dances, which all tell stories, have dinner at **Flames of the Forest** (www.flamesoftheforest.com.au) near Port Douglas, a thoroughly enchanting experience under the stars in the rainforest, with fire and pretty lights illuminating the tented venue and the forest and river behind it, creating a magical setting, a perfect setting for dances and music.

Sydney

Look for ★ to find recommended sights, activities, dining, and lodging.

Highlights

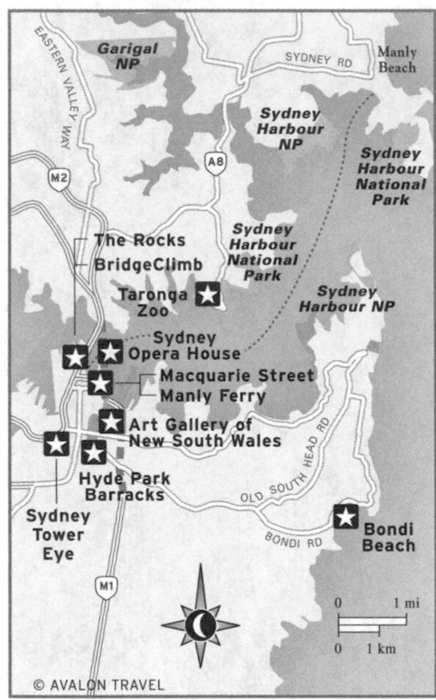

★ **The Rocks:** This is where it all started, where the First Fleet landed and the first settlers arrived, voluntarily or not. There is a great atmosphere of history in the air, the buildings are all wonderful, and the area is dotted with cafés, restaurants, and shops (page 29).

★ **Sydney Opera House:** It really doesn't get more iconic than the Sydney Opera House, one of the most widely recognized buildings in the world (page 29).

★ **BridgeClimb:** To get a view like no other, climb Sydney Harbour's iconic "coat hanger" bridge. It looks steeper than it is and the climb is slow with plenty of breaks, making it accessible for nearly everybody (page 33).

★ **Manly Ferry:** This commuter ferry goes past the opera house, all along the harbor, and past the islands to the entrance to the ocean at Manly. For a handful of dollars you get hundreds of dollars worth of views (page 36).

★ **Macquarie Street:** If you just see one street in Sydney, this must be it. Every building is historic, and the road stretches from the opera house, past the Royal Botanic Gardens, to Hyde Park. Take your time and pop into all the buildings along the way, and you'll have a great idea of Australia's history (page 39).

★ **Hyde Park Barracks:** This museum concentrates on Australia's first settlers, the workers that built the colony—how they lived, worked, struggled (page 40).

★ **Art Gallery of New South Wales:** Located in the beautiful Domain, with great views, the gallery is a fantastic collection of old European, contemporary, indigenous, and ancient Asian art (page 41).

★ **Sydney Tower Eye:** Get a good overview of this sprawling metropolis from up high. You can even do yoga or be daring and do a skywalk (page 44).

★ **Taronga Zoo:** Sydney is all about views—even the zoo has them. Stand by the giraffes and see the Sydney skyline, opera house, and bridge from there. Oh, and the animals, from near and far, are wonderful, too (page 55).

★ **Bondi Beach:** This is one of the best-known beaches on the globe. Curved along the bay, fringed by rocky outcrops and the "village," as the suburb proudly calls itself, the beach attracts surfers, bathers, and the famous lifeguards. And the stunning Bondi to Coogee walk starts here (page 59).

To call Sydney iconic is an understatement. The poster city for Australia is all about the harbor, with its natural beauty as well as the Sydney Opera House and the Sydney Harbour Bridge. One of the largest and most beautiful natural harbors in the world, the setting could not be more glorious if an entire conglomerate of top-notch town planners had tried.

Sydney's ancient history goes back to some 50,000 years ago, when anthropologists believe the Aboriginal people first reached Sydney's natural harbor, yet its more modern history does not start until 1770, when Captain James Cook landed at Botany Bay just south of Sydney and brought his tales of the long-sought and finally found Great Southern Land back to Britain. A few years later, with the American Revolution hampering the habit of transporting convicts from Britain to the Americas, it was decided that the land around Botany Bay would be suitable for future convict deportation. When the First Fleet of 11 ships landed on the southern coast, Captain Arthur Phillip deemed Botany Bay unsuitable due to its lack of fresh water, but he discovered a near perfect natural harbor a little farther up the coast, eventually deciding to settle at Sydney Cove, now Circular Bay.

Sydney Cove, and with it Sydney itself, was named after Captain Phillip's superior, Lord Sydney, and the day of the arrival of the First Fleet, on January 26, 1788, has gone down in history as the annually celebrated Australia Day. The first settlers were not terribly well chosen to establish a new colony in the land down under, with no carpenters, smiths, or even farmers among the officers or the convicts, but inroads were made due to teamwork, the need to survive, and sheer determination.

More and more voluntary settlers arrived together with regular supply ships from the homeland, trade routes were established with the Americas and Asia, and the wealth of the new world began to show in imposing buildings commissioned by Governor Lachlan Macquarie (governor of New South Wales from 1810 to 1821). The discovery of gold

Previous: Sydney Opera House; Sydney's Central Business District. **Above:** one of Paddington's little cafés.

Sydney

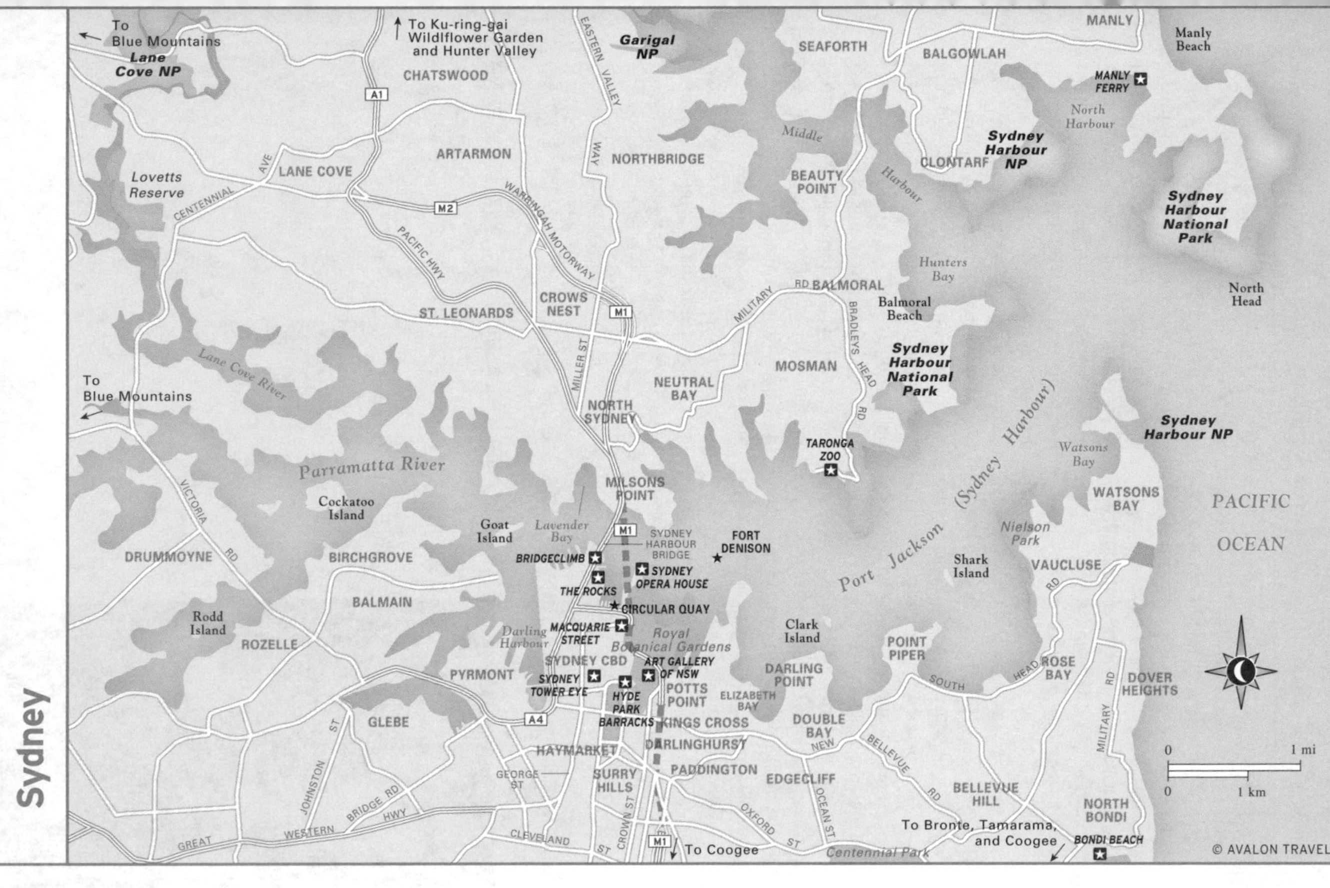
To Blue Mountains
Lane Cove NP
To Ku-ring-gai Wildflower Garden and Hunter Valley
CHATSWOOD
A1
EASTERN VALLEY WAY
Garigal NP
SEAFORTH
BALGOWLAH
MANLY
Manly Beach
MANLY FERRY
North Harbour
Middle Harbour
Sydney Harbour NP
CLONTARF
ARTARMON
LANE COVE
Lovetts Reserve
CENTENNIAL AVE
M2
WARRINGAH MOTORWAY
PACIFIC HWY
NORTHBRIDGE
BEAUTY POINT
Sydney Harbour National Park
Hunters Bay
BALMORAL
Balmoral Beach
North Head
CROWS NEST
ST. LEONARDS
M1
MILITARY RD
BRADLEYS HEAD RD
MILLER ST
Lane Cove River
MOSMAN
NEUTRAL BAY
Sydney Harbour National Park
To Blue Mountains
NORTH SYDNEY
Sydney Harbour NP
TARONGA ZOO
Parramatta River
MILSONS POINT
Watsons Bay
WATSONS BAY
PACIFIC OCEAN
VICTORIA RD
Cockatoo Island
Goat Island
Lavender Bay
M1
SYDNEY HARBOUR BRIDGE
FORT DENISON
Port Jackson (Sydney Harbour)
Nielson Park
DRUMMOYNE
BIRCHGROVE
BRIDGECLIMB
SYDNEY OPERA HOUSE
THE ROCKS
Shark Island
VAUCLUSE
CIRCULAR QUAY
BALMAIN
Rodd Island
ROZELLE
Darling Harbour
MACQUARIE STREET
Royal Botanical Gardens
Clark Island
POINT PIPER
SYDNEY CBD
ART GALLERY OF NSW
PYRMONT
SYDNEY TOWER EYE
HYDE PARK BARRACKS
POTTS POINT
ELIZABETH BAY
DARLING POINT
SOUTH HEAD RD
ROSE BAY
DOVER HEIGHTS
A4
GLEBE
KINGS CROSS
DOUBLE BAY
HAYMARKET
DARLINGHURST
NEW
BELLEVUE RD
MILITARY RD
0
1 mi
0
1 km
GEORGE ST
SURRY HILLS
PADDINGTON
EDGECLIFF
BELLEVUE HILL
NORTH BONDI
JOHNSTON ST
BRIDGE RD
HWY
WESTERN
GREAT
CLEVELAND ST
CROWN ST
OXFORD ST
OCEAN ST
To Bronte, Tamarama, and Coogee
BONDI BEACH
M1
To Coogee
Centennial Park
© AVALON TRAVEL

in the mid-1800s further drew more settlers and established the wealth and grandeur of Sydney.

Today, Australia's largest city has nearly five million inhabitants. Sydney spreads itself sumptuously along its sunken river valley, hemmed by some of the world's most expensive real estate. Being the financial capital of the country, the first stop for most visitors and would-be immigrants, the media hub, and the entrepreneurial engine of the entire continent, Sydney not only attracts money, it also demands it. Just recently, Sydney was named one of the most expensive cities of the world to live in.

Pricey or not, people come to Sydney and fall in love. The beauty of the harbor, the majestic buildings in the town center (Central Business District or CBD) harking back to prosperous times that started back in the early 1800s, and the proximity of some of the world's most famous and surfable beaches along the Pacific coast, together with the city being the hub from where to reach the rest of this rather large country, all make for a popular gateway to Australia and a stunning city in its own right.

More than a third of Sydney's population was born outside Australia, and most Australians descend from immigrants themselves, so the feeling in the city is one of a worldly cosmopolitan metropolis—a metropolis where at every turn you hear a different language, can enjoy a vast array of cuisines, and have great shopping. Still it is a very historic city, even if this is a relative term when you think how young the modern history of Australia is. Just as in Manhattan, it pays to look up and marvel at the variety of architecture: You have the imposing Victorian buildings, majestic Art Deco towers, and stunning modern high-rises.

Sydney is a great mixing and melting pot of people and styles. It is stunning and mostly sunny, offering beaches, pavements, history, and modernity. It captivates you. And often doesn't let you go again, as most of the recent immigrants to this Lucky Country can pay testament to.

PLANNING YOUR TIME

Like all of the world's great cities, Sydney is brimming with things to see and do, and demands time. With nearly five million people calling Sydney home, it is not only Australia's largest city, but also larger than the inner city of Los Angeles, and even if you would move here, you'd never get to see everything or experience it all. So you will just have to try to squeeze as much into your allocated time as possible. And it all depends on what your interests are.

If you are a history buff, numerous very good museums and heritage buildings could keep you busy, but you can get a good idea of Sydney's and Australia's history within a couple of days, taking in the main museums and sights, such as the Hyde Park Barracks, Macquarie Street, and The Rocks.

If you are a pleasure seeker, seek no further and head for the harbor and the beaches, then off into the city for some bar-hopping, excellent food, and great shopping. Depending on whether you want to learn to surf from scratch or if you are in need of a deep tan, then several days will be needed.

But most likely you are in Sydney because you have finally come to see the great continent down under and, while not the capital, Sydney is still *the* city to see when in Australia, and you will want to get a good idea of what it's all about, get a basic understanding of the history, see the iconic landmarks, and either see or sample Bondi Beach. In that case you should allocate around three days.

The handy thing in Sydney is the public transport. Yes, ask any local and they are likely to moan, but visitors can get a MyMulti card for either a day or a week (the weekly pass is worth it if you use it for more than two days) and literally hop on and off any bus, train, or ferry within the city limits and get everywhere easily. Download the public transport app on your phone. You can type in where you wish to go and it will tell you exactly how to get there with type of transport, directions if you will have to walk some, and time allowances.

And most likely you won't have to worry

about the weather too much. Sydney does have seasons, but depending on where you are from, even the winter (July-August) is still a lot more pleasant than in the rest of the world. According to the Australian Bureau of Meteorology, Sydney has, on average, seven hours of sunshine a day. Its temperature ranges from an average winter minimum of 9 and a maximum of 17 degrees Celsius to a peak summer maximum average of 26 degrees. Sydney's rainfall averages 1,213 millimeters a year, with an average of 11 wet days per month. More than 40 percent of this rain falls between March and June. But if you want to play it safe, then spring or fall are the best months, when it's not too hot to walk along the city's pavements and not so cold that you can't sit outside and enjoy the views. Spring generally has a little less rainfall than fall, but both have perfect temperatures for exploring.

Sydney does not have any great fluctuations in visitor numbers over the year, but bear in mind that the country's school summer holidays are across Christmas and New Year, so that is a bit of a hot spot. That said, there is no better place to be over New Year's Eve than Sydney, as long as you can cope with the crowds and the inflated prices. But that's only for a couple of nights and then it gets back to its normal—if pricey—self.

ORIENTATION

It is obvious from maps and just being there that Sydney is dominated by its harbor, which effectively splits the city in two. It's in a coastal basin, with the borders being the Pacific Ocean and its lovely Manly and Bondi beaches on either side of the harbor entrance to the east, and the formerly separate settlement of Parramatta being slowly swallowed up on the west side farther inland, where the broad harbor narrows into the mangrove-lined Parramatta River. On the northern side the sprawl continues through increasingly green suburbs up to the Hawkesbury River, while Botany Bay provides a natural border in the south.

The city's center, or **CBD,** with its towering skyscrapers and large colonial buildings, sits on the south side of the harbor and stretches from the busy ferry port of Circular Quay down to the railway hub of Central Station, bordering the chic residential areas of Woolloomooloo and Darlinghurst on the east and Darling Harbour on the west.

Sydney is quite hilly, increasingly so in the west toward the Blue Mountains, which can reach up to 1,215 meters (3,986 feet) above sea level. The hills allow tantalizing glimpses of water in the distance, even from the inner city suburbs, which adds to the attraction of most of Sydney's residential areas.

Sydney has some easy connections with major highways reaching out into the various suburbs: the **Pacific Highway** connects the CBD across **Sydney Harbour Bridge** with the north, indeed all the way to Brisbane and beyond. There is a toll fare charged when crossing Sydney Harbour Bridge southbound only, and the same system works for the Sydney Harbour Tunnel, with tolls charged each time. Once on the north side, **Military Road** gets you to most suburbs along the way to Manly.

Southbound, the **Southern Cross Drive** connects easiest to the airport, while **Parramatta Road** is a fast westward stretch to Parramatta past the docks and Sydney Olympic Park. Toward the east, **Oxford Street** winds itself through the suburbs; it's not fast, but it hits all the main suburbs along the way to Bondi Beach and is the route of choice for the buses, too.

Once you are heading out of the sprawling city limits, you may well encounter further **toll roads,** including the Eastern Distributor, which is only charged northbound, as well as the M5 East Freeway, the M5 South-West Motorway, the Westlink M7, the Hills M2 Motorway, and both the Lane Cove Tunnel and the Cross City Tunnel, which are all charged in each direction.

Sights

THE ROCKS AND CIRCULAR QUAY

★ The Rocks

The Rocks, on the west side of Circular Quay, the former Sydney Cove, is where Sydney began; indeed, where Australia began its modern history. The small lanes, cobbled streets, and historic buildings hark back to a time when this was not the atmospheric and friendly place it is now. The Rocks has a dark and sinister past, where rum was the currency, crime and prostitution were on the daily menu, and the living was not easy. This is where the first settlers, mostly convicts who had achieved their freedom, lived in ramshackle terraced houses (some still to be seen at Susannah Place Museum) and went out across the fast growing city to help build the soon to be magnificent and rich Sydney.

Today, apart from pretty much every building having a historic value, The Rocks nestle underneath the pylons of the grand bridge, and many tours, anything from ghost tours to pub crawls, tell their own story of this area, which started up around little Campbell's Cove, where you can now catch a tall ship to cruise the harbor and get a little bit of the feeling that the first settlers might have felt—just imagine the city without any buildings and houses, without the opera house and the bridge, just green bushland growing across the undulating hills. It must have been quite a sight.

The Rocks should really be your starting point, as it was then, but you may find it difficult to resist the lure of the Sydney Opera House. So start there, walk along Circular Quay, exhaust your memory card in your camera, and head to The Rocks. Soak up the atmosphere, get a feel for the history, imagine what it was like. Pop into one of the many cafés, have lunch, go out in the evening, and sit out on the pavement with a drink. Then move on to the rest of Sydney.

★ Sydney Opera House

The one building everybody associates with Australia, the **Sydney Opera House** (Bennelong Point, tel. 02/9250-7250, www.sydneyoperahouse.com, daily 9am-5pm, tours adult $35, child $24.50, family $90), was inscribed in the World Heritage List in June 2007 with the comments: "Sydney Opera House is a great architectural work of the 20th century. It represents multiple strands of creativity, both in architectural form and structural design, a great urban sculpture carefully set in a remarkable waterscape and a world-famous iconic building." Probably one of the most recognizable buildings in the world, the opera house is made up of two sets of three sail-shaped roofs facing the harbor and smaller ones facing the city. White tiles give it an ability to shimmer in different colors according to the angle of the sunlight and time of day, and also make it a perfect canvas for the annual Festival of Lights, which projects shapes and colors onto the roof. Although mostly likened to white sailboats due to its location by the water, the roof shapes have also been likened to shells and opening lotus leaves.

It was designed by Danish architect Jørn Utzon, whose design was nearly too ambitious for the times, with many redesigns necessary before the unique structure could be realized. Utzon resigned due to quarrels over design, schedules, and costs before he could see the entire project through. He was not in attendance for the grand opening in 1973, but he was rehired in 1999 to develop a set of design principles to act as a guide for all future changes to the building. The building is still a stunning example of the impossible possibilities of architecture, and it is a record-breaking accumulation of statistics: It cost $102 million to build (between 1957 and 1973), over one million tiles shimmer on the roof, some 1,000 rooms play host to 3,000 annual events

The Rocks

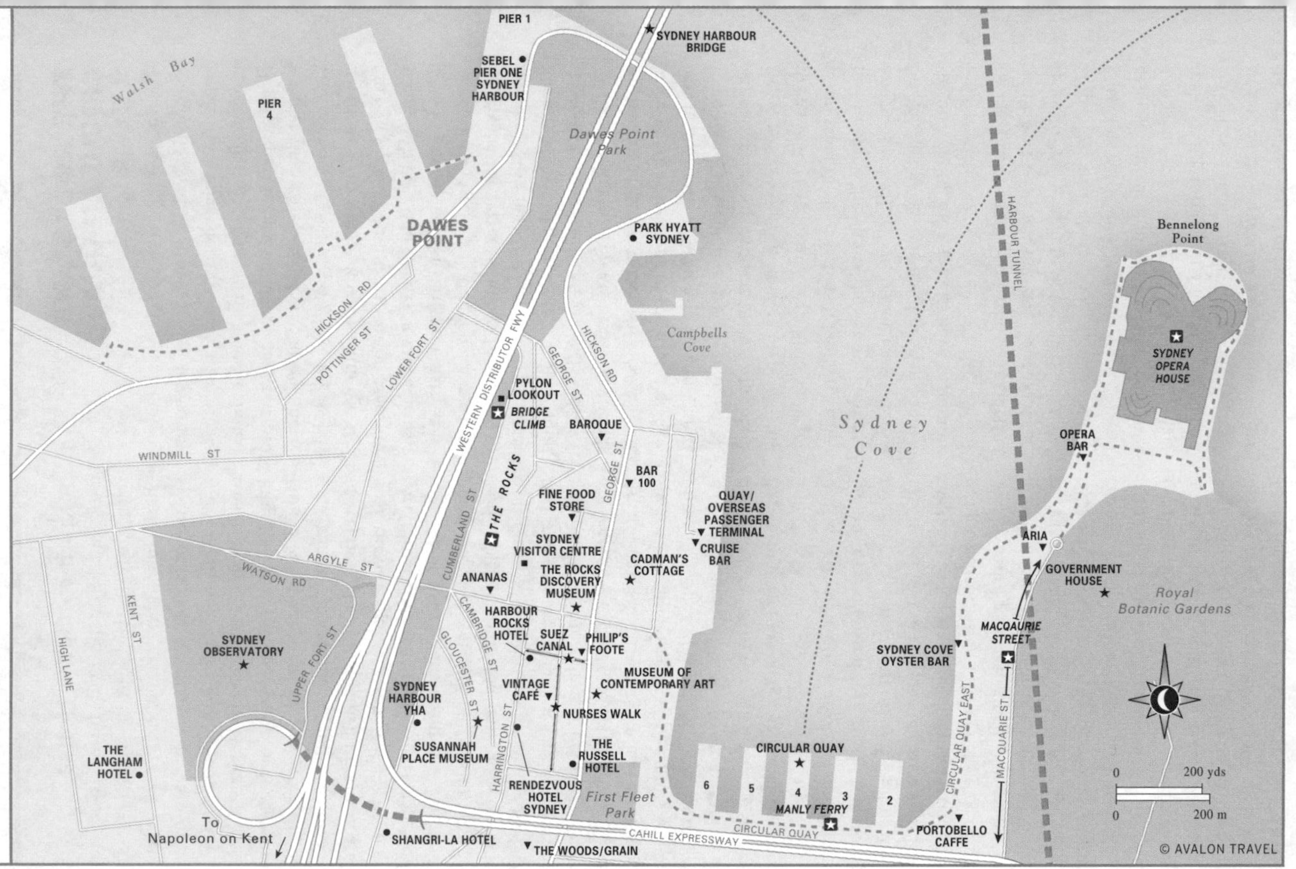
PIER 1
SYDNEY HARBOUR BRIDGE
Walsh Bay
PIER 4
SEBEL PIER ONE SYDNEY HARBOUR
Dawes Point Park
DAWES POINT
PARK HYATT SYDNEY
HICKSON RD
POTTINGER ST
LOWER FORT ST
WESTERN DISTRIBUTOR FWY
GEORGE ST
HICKSON RD
Campbells Cove
PYLON LOOKOUT
BRIDGE CLIMB
BAROQUE
WINDMILL ST
Sydney Cove
HARBOUR TUNNEL
Bennelong Point
SYDNEY OPERA HOUSE
OPERA BAR
BAR 100
THE ROCKS
FINE FOOD STORE
QUAY/ OVERSEAS PASSENGER TERMINAL
CRUISE BAR
CUMBERLAND ST
SYDNEY VISITOR CENTRE
CADMAN'S COTTAGE
ARGYLE ST
WATSON RD
ANANAS
THE ROCKS DISCOVERY MUSEUM
ARIA
GOVERNMENT HOUSE
Royal Botanic Gardens
KENT ST
HIGH LANE
SYDNEY OBSERVATORY
UPPER FORT ST
CAMBRIDGE ST
GLOUCESTER ST
HARBOUR ROCKS HOTEL
SUEZ CANAL
PHILIP'S FOOTE
MACQUARIE STREET
SYDNEY COVE OYSTER BAR
MUSEUM OF CONTEMPORARY ART
SYDNEY HARBOUR YHA
VINTAGE CAFÉ
NURSES WALK
HARRINGTON ST
CIRCULAR QUAY EAST
MACQUARIE ST
THE LANGHAM HOTEL
SUSANNAH PLACE MUSEUM
THE RUSSELL HOTEL
CIRCULAR QUAY
RENDEZVOUS HOTEL SYDNEY
First Fleet Park
6
5
4
3
2
MANLY FERRY
0
200 yds
0
200 m
To Napoleon on Kent
SHANGRI-LA HOTEL
CAHILL EXPRESSWAY
CIRCULAR QUAY
PORTOBELLO CAFFE
THE WOODS/GRAIN
© AVALON TRAVEL

watched by two million people, plus 200,000 tourists visit the opera house each year.

Several guided one-hour tours are offered daily 9am-5pm in various languages, and at noon there's one for visitors with limited mobility.

Writers' Walk

All around Circular Quay, from the opera house past the ferries to The Rocks, are metallic plaques set into the pavement celebrating journalists, poets, writers, and authors from Australia and around the world for their work celebrating Australia, its history, culture, and people. There are greats such as Charles Darwin, quoted as saying "This is really a wonderful colony; ancient Rome in her Imperial grandeur, would not have been ashamed of such an offspring" (letter from Charles Darwin, 1836). Another is Nevil Shute, with the quote "'It's a funny thing,' Jean said. 'You go to a new country, and you expect everything to be different, and then you find there's such a lot that stays the same'" (*A Town Like Alice*, 1950).

Each writer is named, with dates of birth and death where applicable, quotes from their works, and details about their lives and published efforts. Plaques commemorate other writers, such as Peter Carey, Germaine Greer, Robert Hughes, Clive James, Thomas Keneally, D. H. Lawrence, Jack London, Mark Twain, and many more.

The Museum of Contemporary Art

In a prime location on Circular Quay opposite the opera house, **The Museum of Contemporary Art** (140 George St., tel. 02/9245-2400, www.mca.com.au, daily 10am-5pm, Thurs. until 9pm, free) has constantly new and exciting exhibitions highlighting Australian and international art in its rooms. There are daily workshops, performances, talks, and ever-changing events that cover all aspects and dimensions of contemporary art. The large museum offers visitors an extremely wide array of modern art ranging from video installations to palm-front woven fishing traps (they are really quite individual pieces of art in themselves), from paintings to photographs and everything in between. It is a great place to hang out, stop off at the café on the top floor for a rest before taking in another room full of modern delights.

Cadman's Cottage

Built and cut into the natural rock shelf in

The Museum of Contemporary Art

1816, **Cadman's Cottage** (110 George St., tel. 02/9253-0888, Tues.-Sun. 10am-4:30pm, free admission) is one of only a handful of Sydney buildings that remain from the first 30 years of the colony. Over the years this sandstone cottage has been a coxswain's barracks, a sailors' home, and from 1845 the headquarters of the Sydney Water Police, among others. It used to be right beside the water, with its own sandy beach, but since the construction of Circular Quay, the water levels of the harbor have moved 100 meters away.

Suez Canal

The little alleyway between George Street and Harrington Street, opposite the Museum of Contemporary Art, was called the Suez Canal, allegedly after a colloquialism and pun on "sewers." Once a notorious stretch in The Rocks famed for drug abuse, prostitution, and a hangout for gangsters in the 19th century, it is a narrow passageway now decorated with images of "larrikins," a word that reportedly was first recorded in 1868, meaning a "young urban rough, a young hooligan or thug, especially one who is a member of a gang." Alight carefully onto bustling George Street, surprising unsuspecting passersby.

Nurses Walk

Today, Nurses Walk, between Suez Canal and Globe Street, is a bustling lane full of galleries and restaurants; historically it was the shortcut used by nurses to the young colony's first hospital, established together with numerous tent-like out buildings between 1788 and 1816. Formerly located on George Street, in the block bounded by Globe, George, Harrington and Argyle Streets, the hospital is today remembered with a plaque on the nearby former police station at 127 George Street, and the alleyway was renamed Nurses Walk in the 1970s as a tribute to the hospital.

The Rocks Discovery Museum

Housed in a restored 1850s building, **The Rocks Discovery Museum** (2-8 Kendall Ln., tel. 02/9240-8680, daily 10am-5pm, free) is informative, fun, interactive, and full of historical artifacts, pictures, and bits and pieces that bring the history of the surroundings to life. Whether broken rum bottles and glasses from 200 years ago, or shards of a family's crockery, or old toys, leftovers from a bygone era bring that era so much closer to the present. The rooms separate the time periods, which are Warrane (pre-1788), Colony (1788-1820), Port (1820-1900), and Transformations

Cadman's Cottage

(1900-present). The appeal of this little place is that it is certainly informative, but not overwhelmingly so, and it is right in the heart of the place it is telling the story about.

Dawes Point Park

Dawes Point Park is under the Sydney Harbour Bridge on the southern side of the harbor. The Southern Pylon is positioned in the park, and the park has a heritage and historical significance. Originally named Tar-ra by the indigenous people, the park was the site of Sydney's first fortification, built in 1788, although the fortification was removed when construction of Sydney Harbour Bridge began. The Dawes Point Battery was manned until 1916, and today five cannons remain on display in the park. Also a vantage point for the New Year's celebrations, the little park offers fantastic views and now is near the starting point for the BridgeClimb.

Sydney Harbour Bridge

The "coat hanger," as it is affectionately known, has dominated Sydney's harbor skyline since it was opened in 1932. Before then, to cross the relatively narrow gap between Dawes Point and Milsons Point, people needed to travel by one of the many ferries; with boatmen, who navigated smaller, often private, vessels across the harbor; or make an extended trip around the harbor foreshores toward Parramatta and back. To reduce the travel involved, the building of a bridge was proposed as early as 1815, but it was not until 1924 that work first began on the Sydney Harbour Bridge. For the construction of the pylons on both points, some 800 families living in its path, especially around the crowded Rocks, were displaced. Compensation was paid to the owners of the demolished houses, but the occupants, whose homes they were, received nothing.

On January 19, 1932, the first test train, a steam locomotive, safely crossed the bridge. About 90 others also crossed the bridge in the months that followed, as part of a series of tests to ensure the bridge's safety. After the bridge was deemed safe and finished, eventually the construction work sheds, which once occupied the land where you can now find Luna Park and the North Sydney swimming baths, were demolished, and the construction sites were tidied up.

When the Sydney Harbour Bridge was finally opened on March 19, 1932, it was the longest single-span steel-arch bridge in the world. The main span of 503 meters (1,650 feet) across used up more than 52,800 metric tons of silicon-based steel trusses, and the steel plates are held together by around six million steel rivets. From start to finish, the bridge and its approaches took eight years to complete, with a total financial cost of £10,057,170, in old money (roughly 500 times that in modern pounds sterling). This was not fully paid off until 1988.

The initial toll charged for a car was 6 pence while a horse and rider was charged 3 pence. Today the toll, only charged southbound, costs $4 maximum per day. More than 160,000 vehicles cross the bridge each day; before the Harbour Tunnel was opened this figure was as high as 182,000. The Sydney Harbour Bridge carries eight traffic lanes and two railroad lines. There is a pedestrian pathway on the eastern side of the bridge and a cycleway on the western side of the bridge. Pedestrians, horses, and nonmotorized bicycles are not allowed on the bridge roadways.

Located in the southeastern pylon is a **Pylon Lookout** (tel. 02/9240-1100, www.pylonlookout.com.au, daily 10am-5pm, closed Christmas Day, adult $13, child 5-12 $6.50, under 5 free) with 360-degree views and a museum covering the history of the Sydney Harbour Bridge.

★ BRIDGECLIMB

The best way to really appreciate the bridge is to climb it. There are about 200 steps to get to the top, but the views are some of the best in Sydney. **BridgeClimb** (3 Cumberland St., The Rocks, tel. 02/8274-7777, www.bridgeclimb.com.au, from $198 adult, $148 child midweek at night up to $308 adult, $208 child weekend at dawn or twilight) offers four "ways" to climb the bridge. There is really only one route, but the time of day creates four different experiences: You can go at dawn and maybe not quite catch sunrise (but close to it) or at twilight and catch the sunset. You can go in the middle of the day and be one of those strings of ants people point at from the ferries, or you can go up at night and watch magic happen over lit-up Sydney. Each time has its own advantages and disadvantages, so think what suits you and book ahead, as certain times, such as the night climb, have severely restricted numbers.

Once checked in, climbers are thoroughly briefed by the experienced staff about the possible dangers and dos and don'ts during the climb. You'll get suited up in a special "bridge suit" worn over your normal clothes, not only to protect you from the worst of the weather and from getting your clothing snagged, but also to protect the people crossing the bridge underneath you from falling debris. Then you get into a harness and will be wired up with communication equipment. You have to leave cameras and phones behind. Then you go on the climb simulator, to learn a little more about how to behave on the bridge before you are let loose on the real thing. Finally, you are attached to a static line for the duration of the climb, on which you follow a professionally trained climb leader to the top. It takes around three hours to get to the top and back, so you need a good head for heights and a bit of fitness. Be prepared for wind, too—you will be 134 meters (almost 420 feet) above sea level. You will get a photograph of yourself and the group at the top of the bridge.

Note: Climbers must be over 10 years old and more than 102 centimeters (40 inches) in height. If you are up to 24 weeks pregnant, you'll need a doctor's certificate to climb; if you are more than 24 weeks pregnant you can't participate. You will be tested with a Breathalyzer and only allowed up if your blood-alcohol reading is below 0.05. Bring sensible shoes, comfortable clothes, and a sense of adventure.

Susannah Place Museum

Built in 1844 by Irish immigrants, the four terraced houses at **Susannah Place Museum** (58/64 Gloucester St., tel. 02/9241-1893, tours adult $8, child $4, family $17) have been continuously lived in by working-class families and survived largely unchanged through the slum clearances of the early 20th century and the area's dramatic redevelopment in the

BridgeClimb

1970s. They did become increasingly uninhabitable, and in 1990 the museum was set up with the aim to save the buildings and tell the story of the "forgotten" working-class people who helped build Sydney and its wealth. The rooms were left as they used to be, or were restored to their former reality, complete with plates on the table, an old piano playing tunes, toys lying around. You can learn about the tenants of each of the houses, who they were, what they did, how they lived, down to the laundry and the outdoor toilet, and even their favorite brands of food items on sale in the shop.

Admission is by guided tour only, with one-hour tours daily starting at 2pm, 3pm, and 4pm. The tours tell you about the real people who lived in these very houses, and although the buildings are too small to offer actors re-enacting the realities of life then, there are points where you can hear the actual voices of the former tenants telling you about their daily lives in young Sydney.

Sydney Observatory

A beautiful historic building set in a beautiful historic spot, the **Sydney Observatory** (Watson Rd., Observatory Hill, tel. 02/9921-3485, www.sydneyobservatory.com.au, daily 10am-5pm, free daytime admission to gardens and observatory exhibition) offers not only the things you can do inside the observatory, but also the views across the entire harbor, the bridge, and all across Sydney. Built in 1858, the observatory is an astronomical observatory, a timekeeper, a signal station and meteorology center, and a museum with regular and changing exhibitions in keeping with its history. Amazing collections display early astronomical photos, including some of the first photos taken of stars in the southern hemisphere (dating back to 1890) as well as images of a lunar eclipse in 1906. Notice the great golden ball on the pole on the top of the tower. This ball has since 1858 been used as Sydney's timekeeper, being to this day raised at 12:55pm and lowered at 1pm, allowing the people of Sydney and ships' captains to set their chronometers accordingly.

There are daily telescope and planetarium sessions, and a 3-D theater shows both short films and interactive videos about space exploration and astronomy. Day charges for telescope and 3-D theater sessions are adult $10, child $8, family $26. Night telescope sessions are offered April-September at 6:15pm and 8:15pm, October-November at 8:15pm, December-January 8:30pm, and

the Sydney Observatory

February-March at 8:15pm (adult $18, child $12, family $50). An iPhone walking tour app ($1.99) guides you around the site of the observatory down to the Rocks Discovery Museum, past various historical points of interest.

★ Manly Ferry

It is not often that a commuter service is listed as a must-do sight in a guidebook—it is, after all, just a water bus, departing every 30 minutes on a 40-minute one-way trip. Yet the **Manly ferry** (departs from Wharf 3 at Circular Quay, $14.40 round-trip, free with a MyMulti daily or weekly pass) is so much more. Yes, in the morning and afternoon it carries workers between the northern beaches and the city, people who don't necessarily appreciate the views from the ferry, but in between rush hours and on the weekend, this ferry is a perfect way to get out on the water, see the islands, appreciate the view across the opera house and the bridge from the water, take in the mind-blowingly beautiful real estate along the coast, and sit back and enjoy being out on the harbor for a fraction of the price of a harbor cruise. And as a bonus, you get to go to Manly, with its bustling Corso, the partly pedestrianized shopping street connecting the ferry terminal with the beach, full of restaurants and shops, and its beach, which many say is a better surfing beach than the famous Bondi Beach. The jury is still out on that, but the beach is stunning and certainly should be on your list of day trips.

The ferry service runs roughly 6am-midnight. On weekdays, the first ferry leaves Circular Quay at 5:30am, leaves Manly at 6:10am; the last one leaves Circular Quay at 11:45pm, Manly at 12:20am. On weekends, the first ferry leaves Manly at 6:35am, Circular Quay at 6:20am; the last one leaves Manly at 11:40pm, Circular Quay at 11pm.

An alternative **fast ferry** ($9 each way, Wharf 6 at Circular Quay, Manly East Terminal, every 30 minutes) takes only half the time of the regular one but also has half as much character and enjoyment. It is, however, a great option if you need to rush back or the weather has turned.

For more information, check out the **NSW Transport Info** website, www.transportnsw.info, or call tel. 13/15-00.

CENTRAL BUSINESS DISTRICT (CBD)

The city's center, or Central Business District (CBD), with its towering skyscrapers and large colonial buildings, sits on the south side of the harbor and stretches from the busy ferry port of Circular Quay down to the railway hub of Central Station, bordering the chic residential areas of Woolloomooloo and Darlinghurst on the east and Darling Harbour on the west. The CBD is not, as the name might suggest, merely a business district, although most of the head offices of international and national companies can be found here. It is also the central shopping district, full of restaurants, cafés, and most of the museums. It's basically the center of the city, where everything happens during the day, but it gets a little quieter in the evening.

The Australian Museum

The Australian Museum (6 College St., CBD, tel. 02/9320-6000, www.australianmuseum.net.au, daily 9:30am-5pm, adult $12, child 5-15 $6, family $30) is on the corner of College Street and William Street, opposite St. Mary's Cathedral, across the road from Hyde Park. Founded in 1827, the museum is Australia's first and largest natural science museum, housed in an impressive sandstone building complete with Corinthian pillars. Permanent exhibits include a collection of Australian wildlife, including big (dead) spiders; a room on Aboriginal culture and art; a skeleton room; dinosaur displays; and a geology exhibit with replicas of some of the largest gold nuggets found in Australia (would you believe 71.06 kilograms/156 pounds?) and other earthly gems. Regular one-off exhibitions, set up in a separate room with additional entrance fees, have in the past included deep sea exhibits and treasures of Alexander

Free in Sydney

Sydney is expensive—there is no doubt about that. Yet there are a few excellent things to do that don't cost a thing.

- One of the best freebies is the free entry to the **Art Gallery of New South Wales** in the Domain. It is one of the country's, if not the world's, best art galleries, offering art from ancient China right through to modern Australia. The Yiribana Gallery downstairs focuses on Aboriginal and Islander art and offers free guided tours Tuesday-Saturday at 11am.
- The excellent **Museum of Contemporary Art** at The Rocks offers free entry, except for one-off special exhibitions and events that may have a separate charge.
- The free **Rocks Discovery Museum** tells the history of The Rocks from its Aboriginal origins up through today. There are interactive things to do for the kids, combining the teaching of history with the marvels of modern technology.
- **Government House,** the former residence of New South Wales governors in the Royal Botanic Gardens just off Macquarie Street, offers free guided tours every half hour Friday-Sunday 10:30am-3pm, showing you around the interior furnishings and art collections.
- Lovely **St. Mary's Cathedral,** by Hyde Park, offers free cathedral tours every Sunday at noon, and the crypt with its mosaic floor is open daily 10am-4pm.
- Check out the astronomy displays by day at Australia's oldest existing observatory, **Sydney Observatory,** in The Rocks. The Observatory exhibition, access to the building itself, and gardens are free during the daytime and are open daily 10am-5pm. Unfortunately, nighttime tours do have a fee.
- Interested in literature? Follow the **Writers' Walk** along the cobbled streets of The Rocks and along the promenade of Circular Quay, and read the 50 plaques celebrating Australian writers and critics such as Robert Hughes, Germaine Greer, Thea Astley, Peter Carey, Dorothy Hewitt, and James A. Michener.
- You can climb the famous **Sydney Harbour Bridge,** but that costs you. If instead you walk across it, for free (unlike the cars, which have to pay a toll), you get pretty much the same views and superb photo opportunities.
- **Customs House** is a grand historic building with an interesting interior, a library of more than 500,000 books, and a mini-Sydney under a glass dome downstairs. And free Wi-Fi throughout is an added bonus.
- The **Sydney Conservatorium of Music** invites you to listen to its Lunchbreak series during the academic year, with free classical music every Wednesday. See http://music.sydney.edu.au/event-listings for the schedule.
- Take a ride on **bus 555,** which is a free shuttle bus that will take you up and down George Street in the CBD between Railway Square and Circular Quay. It is not only a great way to see the grand buildings lining George Street but also saves time and money if you are shuttling between sights. Check the timetable and route at www.131500.com.au.

the Great. A permanent department offers hands-on science for kids on level two.

Hyde Park

Hyde Park (between Elizabeth, Park, and College Streets) is Australia's oldest park, and although a lot smaller than the original park in London, it is still an oasis within the bustling city, full of interesting sights and surrounded by splendid historical buildings. At the south end there is the **Emden Cannon,** erected to commemorate

Central Business District (CBD)

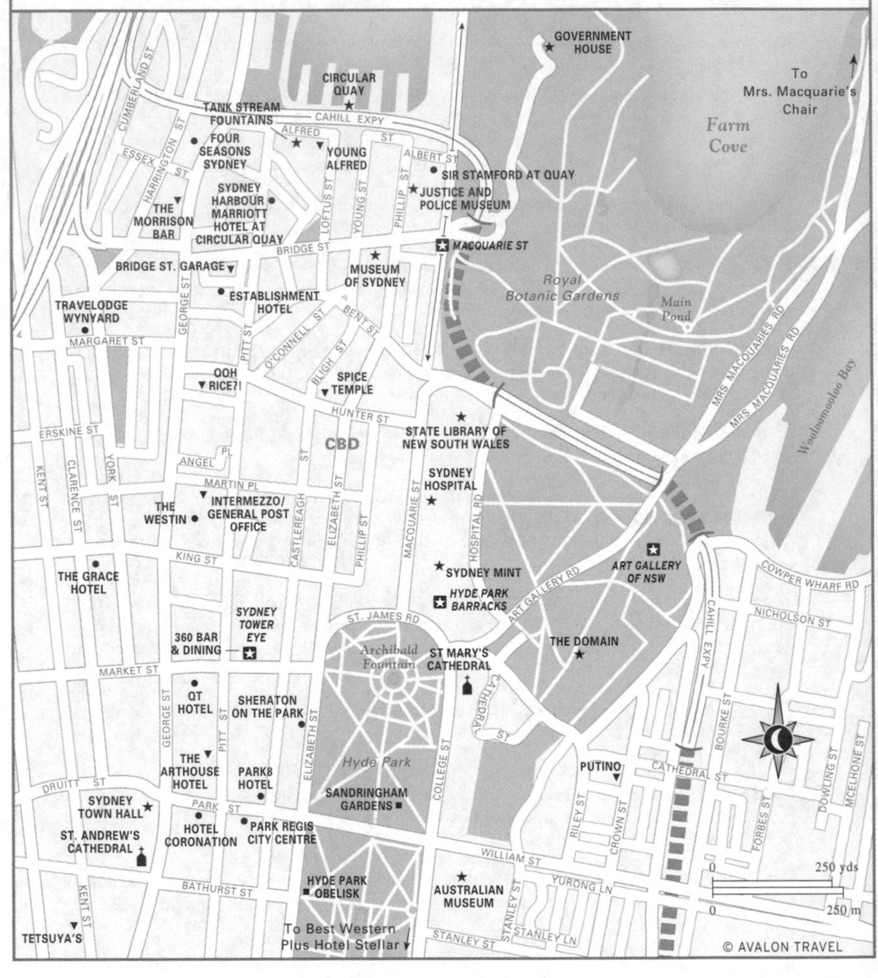

the destruction of the German raider *Emden* on November 9, 1914. The **ANZAC Memorial** is a stunning Art Deco shrine to those lost in the Great War, a peaceful, beautiful shrine that overlooks the Pool of Remembrance.

The **Hyde Park Obelisk,** by Elizabeth Street, was commissioned by the Mayor George Thornton and the Sydney City Council in the mid-1850s as a vent for the noxious gases from the sewer system. Modeled on Cleopatra's Needle in London, it was soon dubbed "Thornton's Scent Bottle."

Across Park Street are the **Sandringham Gardens.** Dedicated to both King George V and King George VI, these tiny sunken gardens, with terraces leading down to a reflecting pool in the center, have pergolas over the circular walk around the garden that, in spring, are cascading with wisteria. An avenue leads up to **Archibald's Fountain,** lined by ancient trees with grazing ibis scuttling through grass underneath. The stone fountain itself is a veritable zoo, with water-squirting bronze turtles, minotaurs being slain, horses, deer, and hounds looking on. It's a feast of 1930s style, conceived and erected by Parisian sculptor François Sicard. It was gifted by Australian journalist and publisher J. F. Archibald to commemorate the association of Australia and France in World War I.

St. Mary's Cathedral

St. Mary's Cathedral (St. Mary's Rd., tel. 02/9220-0400, www.stmaryscathedral.org.au, Sun.-Fri. 6:30am-6:30pm, Sat. 8am-6:30pm) is the seat of the Archbishop of Sydney. The largest cathedral in the city, it is a working church with traditional bell-ringers. A beautiful mass held at Christmas is attended by more than 1,000 worshippers.

The first St. Mary's foundation stone was laid by Governor Macquarie in 1821 and blessed by Father John Therry, one of Australia's first official priests. Work on extensions to the cathedral commenced in 1851 to designs by A. W. N. Pugin, a celebrated English architect and promoter of a more correct Gothic style. Sadly, the cathedral was destroyed by fire in 1865, and Archbishop Polding, the first Archbishop of Sydney, immediately commissioned William Wardell to design a new one. A temporary building was constructed but burned down in 1869.

Work began on the new cathedral in 1866 and took more than 30 years to complete. The incomplete northern section opened in 1882, and the entire church was finished in 1900. It's an outstanding example of Gothic Revival architecture, with the facade based on Paris's Notre Dame Cathedral.

Mary MacKillop, who in the 19th century established an order to educate Australia's rural poor, in 2010 became the first and only Australian to be canonized a saint. A statue of her stands on the city side of the building. St. Mary's does have the greatest length of any church in Australia and is famed for its colorful stained glass windows depicting numerous scenes relating to the life of Jesus, the saints, and, of course, Mary. The screen behind the altar is carved from Oamaru stone from New Zealand.

★ Macquarie Street

Macquarie Street (stretching between Hyde Park and the Sydney Opera House) is named after Lachlan Macquarie, who was governor of New South Wales between 1810 and 1821, and undoubtedly one of the most eminent and celebrated figures in Australian history. He had a vision for Sydney and carried it out: Macquarie Street was designed to be a ceremonial thoroughfare, on the eastern border of Sydney's CBD, and the border of the easy to maneuver grid system. Under Macquarie's guidance, many important historical buildings were located along this important street, starting with **St. James Church** (Sydney's oldest church, dating back to 1819, originally built as a courthouse, with an interesting copper dome inside), the **Hyde Park Barracks,** and **Sydney Hospital,** which were built when he was governor. **Parliament House,** the **State Library,** the **Sydney Conservatorium of Music,** and **Government House** followed later but are very much in keeping with the overall grandeur of the street, as is the **Sydney Opera House.**

Parliament House is still a working governmental building, housing the New South Wales Legislative Assembly; it's open to public (Mon.-Fri. 9am-5pm, free tour at 1pm on the first Thurs. of the month except when the assembly is in session).

Opposite the eminent state buildings, which are on the eastern side of Macquarie Street, are other architecturally important and beautiful buildings, such as the Old Colonial Regency-style Hornbury Terrace building (173 Macquarie St.), dating back to 1842, and the stunning Art Deco building housing the British Medical Association (135 Macquarie St.), just opposite the Palace Gates to the Botanic Garden. Many of the buildings are either private or used as offices, but the British Medical Association building has a tiny coffee shop on the ground floor, which allows you to peek into the building under the pretense of getting a sandwich: **Beans at Becs** (135 Macquarie St., tel. 02/9251-1137, weekdays 5:30am-3pm) has great made-to-order sandwiches for $7.

★ Hyde Park Barracks

Formerly an immigration depot, an asylum, and offices for various governmental departments, the **Hyde Park Barracks** (Queens Square, Macquarie St., tel. 02/8239-2311, www.hht.net.au, daily 10am-5pm, adult $10, child $5, family $20) started life as night lodgings for convicts who were laboring on public works in Sydney back in 1817. The Old Colonial Georgian-style building offered an alternative lodging and life for the working convicts away from the higgledy-piggledy living in The Rocks but also provided the government control over the convicts when they were not at work. The museum tells the story of those convicts very intimately—you can inspect the "ratacombs," the tunnels the rats were building under the floors and which were only discovered recently; learn about the convicts' meal rations; hear the story of the formidable Lucy Hicks, the live-in matron of the barracks, a woman who struggled to combine her intense work load with raising her 14 children in the 1870s; and find evidence of the elusive water source known as the Tank Stream. Ticket price includes a free audio guide. Allow around two hours for a self-guided tour covering most points.

Sydney Mint

Next to Hyde Park Barracks, the **Sydney Mint** (10 Macquarie St., tel. 02/8239-2288, www.hht.net.au, Mon.-Fri. 9am-5pm, free admission) was originally established to control the black market and prevent financial disaster after the discovery of gold in New South Wales. Operating between May 1855 and December 1926, the mint produced gold sovereigns and other coinage, over its 70 years processing more than 1,200 tons of gold and producing more than 150 million sovereigns. The elegant colonnaded colonial-style building, with a contemporary building behind it, is beautifully lighted at night and today serves as a library and houses a simple historical display. Notably, the Caroline Simpson Library holds the only public research collection dedicated to the history of the home and garden in Australia. Lovely little **Bullion Bar** (Wed.-Fri. 3pm-9pm) is perfect for a relaxing drink between cultural explorations.

Sydney Hospital

The oldest hospital in Australia, **Sydney Hospital** (8 Macquarie St., tel. 02/9382-7111) originally dates back to the arrival of the First Fleet in 1788, when it was dubbed "Rum Hospital." When the British government refused to provide money to build a hospital, Governor Macquarie entered into a business arrangement with three individuals who saw the opportunity to turn the governor's need for a hospital to their financial advantage. They reportedly undertook the building of the hospital if given a monopoly to import rum into the colony.

The hospital has been in the current location since 1811. A working hospital, it is not generally open to the public, but small parts, such as **The Little Shop** (Mon.-Fri. 10:30am-2:30pm), selling hand-made children's clothes and toys to the public, allow a small glimpse behind the facade. The Little Shop is staffed by volunteers and set up by the main entrance in the old gate house. There is also the lucky boar fountain, **Il Porcellino,** presented to the city in 1968 by Marchesa Torrigiani of Florence in memory of her father, Brigadier General Thomas Fiaschi. It's a replica of the original 1547 statue found in the Straw Market in Florence. Legend has it that it is lucky to rub the boar's nose and donate a coin toward the hospital. You'll find it just outside the main entrance on Macquarie Street.

The best view of the many architectural styles can be appreciated from the hospital's courtyard. The Nightingale Wing, home to the oldest nursing school in the country, is, after many reconstructions, the oldest part of the building now, dating back to 1868 and held in Gothic Revival style. It is joined by the main building, dating back to 1894, and other smaller wings, all of which are in distinctly different styles and surround the magnificent three-tiered cast-iron Robert Brough Memorial Fountain from the Colebrookdale, United Kingdom, factory, installed in 1907. **Courtyard Café da Capo** (tel. 02/9382-7359, Mon.-Fri. 7:30am-4pm), a quiet little Italian coffee shop in the courtyard, seemingly a million miles away from the bustle of Macquarie Street, allows you to savor the beauty of Sydney Hospital over a quiet drink.

State Library of New South Wales

The **State Library of New South Wales** (Bent St., corner Macquarie St., tel. 02/9273-1414, Mon.-Thurs. 9am-8pm, Fri. 9am-5pm, Sat. 10am-5pm, free) traces its origins to 1826, with the opening of the Australian Subscription Library. In 1869, the New South Wales government took over responsibility for the library and created the Sydney Free Public Library. In 1895 it was renamed the Public Library of New South Wales, and in 1975 it became the State Library of New South Wales.

The old part of the state library on Bent Street, looking like an ancient Greek temple, houses the Mitchell Library, opened in 1910. The foyer displays the marble copy of the original Tasman Map, which combines the results of Tasman's first (1642 to 1643) and second (1644) voyages with those of earlier Dutch navigators, showing a surprisingly accurate general outline of Australia. Princess George of Greece presented the original Tasman Map to the library in 1931, where it is kept under lock and key.

A quote from Thomas Carlyle in the entrance hall, "In Books lies the soul of the whole past time/The articulate audible voice of the past when the body and material substance of it has altogether vanished like a dream," gives a clue as to the importance of the library, and for book-lovers the Mitchell Reading Room in its understated elegance, lined with several stories of bookshelves concluding in a glass ceiling, is simply stunning.

The Domain

The Domain (Mrs Macquaries Rd., CBD) surrounds the Royal Botanic Gardens and was in colonial times the governor's buffer of privacy between his residence and the penal colony. Roads and paths were constructed throughout the Domain in 1831 to allow public access, somewhat ruining the governor's privacy, and the Domain has since been a place for the people. There is even a sign advising keen hobby gardeners on how to keep their own lawn green and healthy in times of drought. In the spirit of public enjoyment, this 34-hectare open garden space is a popular venue for concerts, festivals, open-air events, and, at Christmastime, the very popular **Carols in the Domain.** The manicured lawns invite you to picnic, take in the views, or use the expanse of walkways for exercise.

★ Art Gallery of New South Wales

Looking like a Greek temple from the front, sitting dominant on the Domain with lovely views across Woolloomooloo Bay, the **Art Gallery of New South Wales** (Art Gallery Rd., The Domain, tel. 1800/679-278, www.artgallery.nsw.gov.au, daily 10am-5pm, free) is a fantastic collection of art, stretching from old European collections to modern Australian works, ancient Asian art, and Aboriginal and Torres Strait Islander art. There are three permanent exhibitions: Australian, 15th to 19th century European, and Asian. Very aptly, the older works, such as those by Constable, Rubens, and Canaletto, are housed in the original building dating back to 1871, and the newer works are housed in the modern wing at the back. The old wing is a stunning space complete with vaulted ceilings, parquet flooring, and many historical features that do not take away from but instead enhance the art on display. The modern rooms are used perfectly to showcase installations, paintings, sculptures, and much more.

On the lower level, there is an incredible collection of ancient Asian art, showcasing a panorama of 7,000-odd years of Chinese and Asian art evolution, including ceramics dating to the period 206 BCE to 220 CE. Beautiful porcelains, examples of Japanese calligraphy, and day-to-day objects make for a stunning collection.

Regular traveling exhibitions (which may incur an entrance fee), talks and lectures by visiting artists, and workshops make this into one of the best museum/galleries in the country.

Admission Fees

You will find mention of **"family admission"** in most sights and attractions around Australia. This generally refers to a group made up of two adults and two children. Just to confuse the issue, some attractions, such as Tarongo Zoo, also offer a family ticket for two adults and three children, but generally speaking a family group is two adults and two children, and this group ticket always works out cheaper than separate tickets.

You will also see **"concession" tickets** on most signs. This refers to students, senior citizens, and those with disabilities. To be entitled to these reduced admission fees you will need to provide valid proof—a current card or pass, generally with a photograph on it—that you are, for example, a student.

The Royal Botanic Gardens

Not unlike Central Park in New York, **The Royal Botanic Gardens** (eastern edge of the CBD, bordered by Macquarie St., the Cahill Expressway, and Mrs Macquarie Rd., tel. 02/9231-8111, Nov.-Feb. daily 7am-8pm, Mar. and Oct. daily 7am-6:30pm, Apr. and Sept. daily 7am-6pm, May and Aug. daily 7am-5:30pm, June-July daily 7am-5pm, free) are the lungs of Sydney, a place to rest, relax, exercise, bring the family, grab some culture, and enjoy the surroundings. Signs actually encourage visitors to "walk on the grass," which is always a positive thing.

What started as a few paths cut through the native shrubby vegetation back in 1816 is now a 30-hectare parkland full of native and foreign plants and also is the oldest scientific institution in Australia, with research having continuously been carried out over the centuries. Not to be confused with the Domain (the parkland that surrounds the gardens), the Royal Botanic Gardens are a mix of manicured lawns, ancient trees, modern sculptures, and historic monuments placed to enhance the green surroundings and conveniently positioned to allow relaxation and views to come together. You can explore the rare and threatened plants from around the globe and learn about the Cadigal (the original inhabitants of Sydney's city center) and their relationship with this land at Cadi Jam Ora—First Encounters, a special garden display. Rose gardens and unique plants set among some of the best views in the world make this a great place to relax.

One of the best spots of all of Sydney is **Mrs Macquarie's Chair,** right at the tip of the Royal Botanic Gardens jutting out into the harbor, reportedly the place the governor's wife chose to retreat to to watch the world go by. A benchlike shape hewn out of the sandstone rock in 1810 by convicts, it's a great viewing point.

The gardens stretch around pretty Farm Cove, with the famous Fleet Steps, which have been taken even by Queen Elizabeth II, leading down to the water's edge. Within the botanic gardens are the historic Government House and the Sydney Conservatorium of Music, both situated along the border with Macquarie Street.

Government House

Architect Edward Blore of Buckingham Palace fame was heavily involved in the design of this impressive Gothic Revival castellated **Government House** (Royal Botanic Gardens/Macquarie St., tel. 02/9931-5222, grounds open daily 10am-4pm, house tours Fri.-Sun. 10:30am-3pm, free), which is still

part of the small Tank Stream exhibit in the basement of the General Post Office Building

a working state house and has been home to governors since it was opened in 1846, when it took over from the first Government House, remains of which can be seen at the Museum of Sydney. Inside, each governor has made changes according to their tastes, and the state rooms display a vast array of 19th- and 20th-century designs. Tours start every 30 minutes and last for around 45 minutes. They are the only way to look inside and learn about the history of the house and the governors, as well as the architecture and design of the house. You can wander around the gardens, taking in the house from the outside, and its general setting, but you'll get more insight through the tours.

Museum of Sydney

The **Museum of Sydney** (corner Bridge St. and Phillip St., tel. 02/9251-5988, www.hht.net.au, daily 10am-5pm, adult $10, child 5, family $20) stands on the site of the first Government House, which was the first major building to be constructed on the Australian mainland, started mere months after the landing of the First Fleet in 1788. The museum tells the story of that building with various paintings and tales. The exhibition moves on to the First Fleet, with details and replicas of each ship in the fleet, continuing with the city's trade history with examples of what was carried on the ships. One fantastic way of displaying various articles is in the great metal chest of drawers, each drawer being a miniature exhibition in its own right: full of broken china, letters, pieces of the life led by the early settlers, tempting you to spend hours looking at details lovingly displayed and allowing a certain intimacy with history. There are also changing exhibitions such as "Food," the story of Sydney told in numerous table settings complete with decor and food as it would have once been set up.

Justice & Police Museum

Located in three historic sandstone police courthouses dating back to 1856, the **Justice & Police Museum** (corner Albert St. and Phillip St., Circular Quay, tel. 02/9252-1144, www.hht.net.au, weekends 10am-5pm, adult $10, child under 15 years $5, family $20) tells the story of Sydney's rogues, vagabonds, and other perps, and the stoic police officers who brought them to justice and kept order in the growing city. Displays of weaponry, items that once belonged to infamous Australian outlaws (or bushrangers, as they are called locally, such as the Ned Kelly Gang), eerie photographs of criminals, and cells allow you to imagine what it was like in a late 1800s prison. You can even inspect real-life forensic evidence that related to two murders in the state.

Tank Stream

The **Tank Stream** (various locations) was one of the main reasons why the landing party from HMS *Supply,* ordered to explore the land by Governor Phillip on January 26, 1788, was deemed so successful. This small stream rising from the murky swamps that are now very civilized Hyde Park offered the vital source of fresh water needed to sustain the first colony.

Named after the four deep storage tanks that were dug into the sandstone base of the stream to ensure the fresh water collected could be used as and when needed, the stream was a precious commodity, appreciated and looked after by means such as 50-foot-wide greenbelts on either side of the stream.

By 1826 the Tank Stream was no longer the main water source, with a new vast reservoir being built in Centennial Park. The stream eventually got covered up, and ended up as a sewage and storm drainage system. But there are still many signs of the historic stream. Start the trail at Circular Quay, where several fountains celebrate the stream, then look for markers on the lanes and in buildings as to the former course. The markers are part of the Tank Stream installation created by artist Lynne Roberts-Goodwin in 1999 and can be found at various points throughout the CBD. Walk to Tank Stream Way, off Bridge Street, named after the bridge across the stream, and peek into 17 Bridge Street, an entrance to an office building where you can see two markers on the floor before the elevators. Go to the old General Post Office Building, now housing the Westin Hotel. In the basement among the bars and cafés, you will find a small, hidden away but publicly accessible exhibition showcasing sections of the brick structure that formerly enclosed the stream and numerous artifacts found in the stream. It is a secret history display that not many people find in the city, yet it pays homage to such an important part of Sydney's history.

Sydney Tower Eye dominating the city's skyline

★ Sydney Tower Eye

The **Sydney Tower Eye** (Level 5, Westfield Mall, Pitt St., tel. 02/9333-9222, www.sydneytowereye.com.au, daily 9am-10:30pm, from adult $18.20, child $10.50, family $54, combo deals available online) should be your first stop on your trip to Sydney. The 309-meter tower took six years and $36 million to build, was completed in 1981, and is still the tallest building in Sydney. Your journey begins with a surprisingly good 4-D cinema experience before you head up, giving you a 10-minute aerial tour of Sydney and surroundings, and the 360-degree viewing platform at the top allows you to get your bearings and appreciate the true beauty and sprawl of the harbor and city. Looking out all the way to the Blue Mountains on the horizon, Botany Bay, and the tiny entrance from the Pacific Ocean that the First Fleet thought worth investigating gives you an appreciation of the natural and man-made beauty of the surroundings. Seeing the parks and the magnificent buildings leaves you raring to go and explore.

If looking down through the glass is simply too boring for you, you can sign up for the Skywalk on the rooftop. Get dressed in blue coveralls, don a safety harness, and walk around the rim of the tower's roof for an hour, stopping off at two glass platforms looking out and down on the ant-like life below (adult $43, child $30, minimum age 8 years old, hourly from 10am). If serenity is more your thing, there are weekly yoga classes up in the tower every Wednesday morning at 7am ($25).

Sydney Town Hall

Sydney Town Hall

Constructed on the site of Sydney's first cemetery, which operated from 1792 to 1820 and was subsequently relocated, the grand **Sydney Town Hall** (483 George St., tel. 02/9265-9333, www.cityofsydneyvenues.com.au, Mon.-Fri. 8:30am-6pm) was built from honey-colored sandstone quarried from nearby Pyrmont. Built after the French Second Empire style, with some influences from Roman and Greek history, the town hall was conceived by architect J. H. Wilson, who, together with subsequent architects working on the project, died during construction, which stretched across the years 1868 to 1889, with the clocktower completed in 1873. Nevertheless, each seemed to have left quirky embellishments throughout the building, maybe trying to leave some of their ideas behind for history. Look for numerous lions on the facade, different styles of windows (some with stained-glass, others clear), and the bridges formed by the raised entrances, at the front and the side.

Inside, the town hall has a majestic vestibule and staircase, and an old-fashioned cage elevator. Inside the Centennial Hall, the Grand Organ was the largest and most magnificent in the world when it was installed in 1890, and regular performances showcase its prowess to the audience.

St. Andrew's Cathedral

Dating back to 1868, **St. Andrew's Cathedral** (corner George St. and Bathurst St., tel. 02/9265-1661, www.sydneycathedral.com, Mon.-Tues. 10am-4pm, Wed. 10am-7:30pm, Thurs. 10am-4pm, Sun. 8am-9pm) is Australia's oldest cathedral, complete with spiky spires and intricate stained-glass windows inspired by York Minster in England. The cathedral itself is not just beautiful but full of interesting bits of history: Near the entrance a copy of the Great Bible can be seen under glass, the original dating back to 1539, when Henry VIII decreed that a copy of the bible printed in English should be displayed in every parish church. Original foundations of the church were uncovered during restoration works to the cathedral in 1999, and a number of foundation plaques commemorate the laying of the foundation stone in 1819 by Governor Lachlan Macquarie. The organ, originally dating back to 1866, and since then updated and altered throughout the years, is still on display with its unusual wrought iron surrounds, and the church holds monthly organ recitals.

DARLING HARBOUR AND HAYMARKET

To the west of Sydney's CBD, Darling Harbour is a pedestrianized entertainment precinct located around Cockle Bay, a busy hub for ferries and pleasure boats. The area is ideal for families, with parks, museums, small trains taking you around the bay, and restaurants lining Cockle Bay Wharf. There is more than enough to keep you busy for an entire day.

Haymarket, just south of Darling Harbour, is home to Sydney's Chinatown, a bustling area full of restaurants, markets, and traditional shops. The neighborhood also features surprisingly quiet and serene parks and playgrounds (one even has an old-fashioned carousel), considering the nearby buzz.

Sea Life Sydney Aquarium

Highlights at **Sea Life Sydney Aquarium** (Aquarium Wharf/1-5 Wheat Rd., Darling Harbour, tel. 02/9333-9288, www.sydney-aquarium.com.au, daily 9am-8pm, last admission at 7pm, adult from $26, child $16, family $65, if booked online; combo deals available online) include turtles, sharks, sea horses, sea dragons, jellyfish, and even a dugong, a sister species of the manatees, among many other fresh- and seawater dwelling creatures from Australia and abroad. The displays are interactive, with plenty of Q&A stations for kids. An excellent display focuses on the Great Barrier Reef, which gives you lots of insight and knowledge about the reef and its critters. There are extra activities you can add onto your visit, such as a glass-bottom boat ride ($10), feeding the sharks ($15), and a behind the scenes look at 11:30am and 2pm daily ($25). Depending on your interests, you can spend easily spend two or three hours here.

Wild Life Sydney Zoo

Next door to Sea Life Sydney is **Wild Life Sydney Zoo** (Aquarium Wharf/1-5 Wheat Rd., Darling Harbour, tel. 02/9333-9288, www.wildlifesydney.com.au, daily 9am-6pm, adult from $26, child $16.80, family $79, if booked online; combo deals available online), where you are greeted by a koala munching on leaves right at the entrance. Go in and meet more of those near-mythical Australian animals: hopping kangaroos, wombats, even a cassowary. And you can get up close to a koala; although here in NSW you are not allowed to hug one, you can get very close and give him a little stroke. (The hugging you will have to leave until Queensland, where it is still legal.) There are snakes, lizards, spiders and nearly two of every creature that hops, crawls and wanders around this vast continent. A fun way to spend a couple of hours for all the family.

Double Up and Save

Sea Life Sydney Aquarium, Wild Life Sydney Zoo, Madame Tussauds, and **Sydney Tower Eye** are managed by the same company and offer reduced tickets if you want to visit two or more attractions. See any two of the attractions for adult $65, child $37, family $180; see three attractions for adult $70, child $40, family $195; or see all four for adult $80, child $50, family $240. The deal is well worth considering, especially if you have kids in tow.

Madame Tussauds

There are many museums telling the story of Australia, its history, and its people, and **Madame Tussauds** (Aquarium Wharf/1-5 Wheat Rd., Darling Harbour, tel. 02/9333-9240, www.madametussauds.com/sydney, daily 9am-8pm, last admission at 7pm, adult $40, child $28, family $136, save 30% online; combo deals available online) is doing the same, only it adds fun, modern history, current people you should know, and some gossip. Meet Australia's historic heroes, including Captain Cook and Trugernanner, the last Aboriginal woman to live and die in Tasmania; modern Australian heroes such as aviator Kingsford Smith; world leaders; and achievers and innovators from the fields of science, medicine, music, and film. And while you are learning about Australia, you can join in the fun and look behind the scenes and even have a hand cast done (one hand $20, two hands $25, four hands $40). Allow an hour to go through it all.

Australian National Maritime Museum

Australia's history is nothing if not linked closely with naval and maritime pursuits. Exhibits at the **Australian National Maritime Museum** (2 Martin St., Darling Harbour, tel. 02/9298-3777, www.anmm.gov.au, daily 9:30am-5pm, adult $7, child $3.50,

Darling Harbour and Haymarket

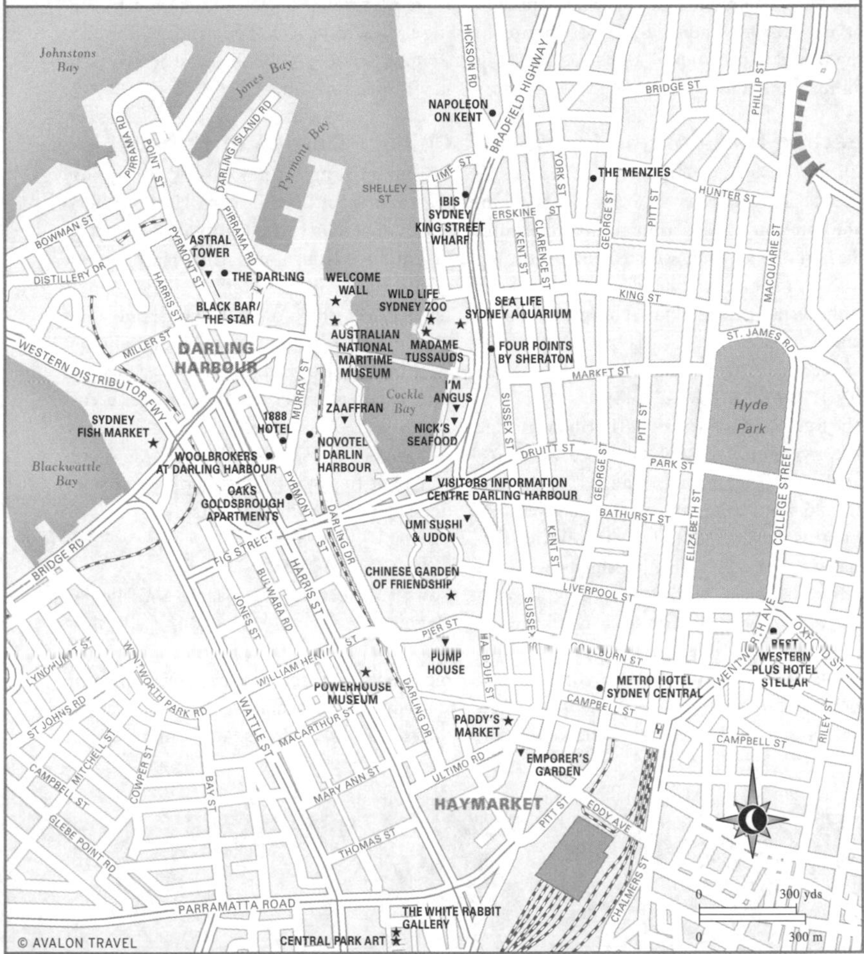

family $17.50, free first Thurs. of the month, extra fee for special exhibitions) go back to Aboriginal history, the First Fleet, explorations of the coast, and more recent wartime history, such as Gallipoli. The museum also has a historic fleet docked outside, and you can venture onboard a naval destroyer and marvel at other visiting vessels, such as a submarine that was in port during writing. Special exhibitions explore history such as that of the Vikings.

Welcome Wall

North of the Australian National Maritime Museum, between Darling Harbour and Pyrmont Bay is the Welcome Wall. Literally a wall, it is inscribed with the names of people who have migrated to Australia. To date there are more than 23,000 names listed, with countries of origin, which add up to over 150 different nations. Obviously this is a mere drop in the bucket where Australia's immigrants are concerned, but it makes interesting reading, whether you personally are looking for a name or not. If you have someone you'd like to be commemorated, you can apply to have your relative added to the list; inquire in the Australian National Maritime Museum for further details.

Darling Harbourside Fireworks

All across Darling Harbour, there are superb fireworks nearly every Saturday night at 9pm. You can watch them from anywhere around the harbor, but if you want to combine dining with the celebrations, you'd better book ahead as the restaurants tend to get busy around that time.

Sydney Fish Market

The **Sydney Fish Market** (Pyrmont Bridge Rd., Pyrmont, tel. 02/9004-1100, www.sydneyfishmarket.com.au, daily 7am until around 4pm, although some outlets and restaurants stay open until late) is a working fish market, so it is by definition smelly, wet, and at times slippery. But if you are interested in fish, be it on your plate or just to check out the variety landed off the Australian coast, a visit to the market is well worth it. With plenty of food stalls and restaurants around the market, you can sample the freshest catches of the day, and if you are inspired to become a seafood chef yourself but don't know where to start, there is even the option to take some cooking classes; just check the calendar for Sydney Seafood School and book ahead at www.sydneyfishmarket.com.au.

Chinese Garden of Friendship

Within bustling Sydney, just by all the busy restaurants south of Darling Harbour lies a haven of serenity, the **Chinese Garden of Friendship** (south of Darling Harbour, opposite the Sydney Entertainment Centre, tel. 02/9240-8888, daily 9:30am-5pm, adult $6, child $3, family $15), a step into another land and culture. The gardens bring together little pagodas, water features, bridges across gurgling streams, sculptures, and carvings. A lovely tea house has excellent scones, or if you'd like to stay with the theme order some dim sim (a dumpling-type dish).

Paddy's Market

Paddy's Market (Thomas St. and Hay St., Haymarket, tel. 02/9325-6200, Wed.-Mon. 9am-5pm) is a gigantic market space offering everything from fresh produce to cheap souvenirs, risqué underwear, makeup, accessories, clothes, toys, absolutely anything else

the Australian National Maritime Museum's mooring in Darling Harbour

you could possibly want, and then some. If you have dozens of friends to take souvenirs back to, then shop here for best deals.

Powerhouse Museum

The **Powerhouse Museum** (500 Harris St., Ultimo, tel. 02/9217-0111, www.powerhouse-museum.com, daily 10am-5pm, adult $12, child $6, family $30) really is a powerhouse of a museum that defies definition. In a vast space you will find entire trains, planes, cars, even space ships. But it is not a transport museum, even though it does have a transport display in one of its many rooms. There are science experiments but it is not a science museum. There are plenty of activities for children, but it is not a children's museum.

There are exhibits such as the "Steam Revolution," set in the original engine room of the Ultimo Powerhouse, where Sydney's first electric trams were generated. A beautiful bright red and brass NSW Fire Brigade water pump used to be pulled by horses and reportedly fought more than 1,000 fires in its time. Then there is the "Experimentations" exhibition, where your kids—and you—can get your hands busy experimenting with anything from smells and tastes to making your own fireworks. Move on and learn about costumes, the history of fashion and clothes-making, shopping habits in early Australian history, and even robots. You can try your hand at maneuvering a virtual Mars rover and try to collect some rock samples. Depending on how hands-on you will get in the museum, allow at least a couple of hours to marvel at all the exhibits.

The White Rabbit Gallery

The White Rabbit Gallery (30 Balfour St., Chippendale, tel. 02/8399-2867, www.whiterabbitcollection.org, Thurs.-Sat. 10am-6pm, free) is not strictly speaking in Haymarket, more on the edge of the district, but given that the gallery houses one of the largest and most important collections of modern Chinese contemporary art, it needs to be included near Chinatown attractions. The gallery not only has a great café and gift shop, but most importantly offers a glimpse into Chinese art and the psyche of some of the artists. Oppression and new-found freedom both rank high in the subject matter, with videos, paintings, and etchings being the typical media; there are also talking plants, traditional imperial clothes recreated from pages cut from a Chinese-English dictionary, and the moving rubble of a destroyed house. Certainly quirky,

modes of transport in the Powerhouse Museum

and a must for anybody interested in contemporary art.

Central Park Art

Just around the corner from the White Rabbit Gallery, **Central Park Art** (off Broadway, Chippendale, south of Central Station) is an amazing $8 million public art collection that has taken over this serene stretch of parkland. Integrated into the architecture surrounding the park, both modern and historical, the art is huge, such as the enormous jutting glass roof sheltering the park below, the animated Hula-Hoop, and the abstract red organic structure growing on the side of the old factory facade. It is impressive and there for everybody to enjoy and marvel at.

KINGS CROSS

Kings Cross is at best bohemian, colorful, and unconventional, and at worst, sleazy and suspect. The former red-light district is still a flamboyant place where pretty much everything goes, but it is also lively, bright, ethnically diverse, and exciting. Here it doesn't matter what your color, religion, gender, or sexual persuasion is—everybody mingles and comes to Kings Cross to have fun. The adjoining areas of **Potts Point, Woolloomooloo** (which surely must be the most intriguingly named suburb of Sydney, together with being the oldest), and **Darlinghurst** have been truly gentrified since the 1990s and now offer some of Sydney's most desirable real estate.

Reportedly, the name Woolloomooloo could have been derived from either *wallamullah,* meaning "place of plenty," or from *wallabahmullah,* referring to a young black kangaroo. In these suburbs, interesting history mingles with sedate suburbia; top restaurants live next to tattoo parlors; the clientele runs the gamut from genteel family to drug addicts and plenty of mostly backpacking overseas visitors. Seedy? Yes, in places. Fun? For sure, throughout. To experience the true diversity of Sydney, there is no better area. Once you see the large Coca-Cola sign, you know you are in the heart of Kings Cross and the vibrant Sydney mix.

Elizabeth Bay House

A lovely example of a former residence with incredible views across the harbor, **Elizabeth Bay House** (7 Onslow Ave., Elizabeth Bay, tel. 02/9356-3022, Fri.-Sun. 11am-4pm, adult $8, child $4, family $17) is hidden in a residential area, down steep lanes and hidden steps, and once you find it, you will probably also find it closed, as it is run by volunteers and on occasion the system fails, but like any good treasure hunt, it's actually the search that is fun. The area is full of incredible private residences.

The white Regency-style house with its colonnaded entrance and elegant features itself is lovely but tells a sad story: From 1826 Colonial Secretary Alexander Macleay had the dream to develop the current site overlooking the gorgeous Elizabeth Bay as a fine landscape garden and to build Elizabeth Bay House. It was widely dubbed "the finest house in colony," but he did not have the funds to see his project through. Macleay's life-long obsession with entomology plus the loss of his government post in 1837 required him to seek numerous loans from his eldest son William, and although this house looks grand, it is unfinished. A mere six years into his stay William foreclosed on his father, effectively forcing him to leave.

Today, when you enter, you can imagine the splendor of having lived here, with the grand spiral staircase winding its way up to the magnificent dome; the finely set dining table ready to host a dinner party; the magnificent library, reportedly once the largest room in any Australian house; and the grand views outside across the bay. The house is sometimes hired out for weddings because of its stylish interior, and you can just imagine a bride coming down the staircase with her dress's train sweeping down behind. For tours, please contact Elizabeth Bay House to arrange one convenient to you, as there are no set times. A tour takes around 45 minutes.

Kings Cross and Paddington

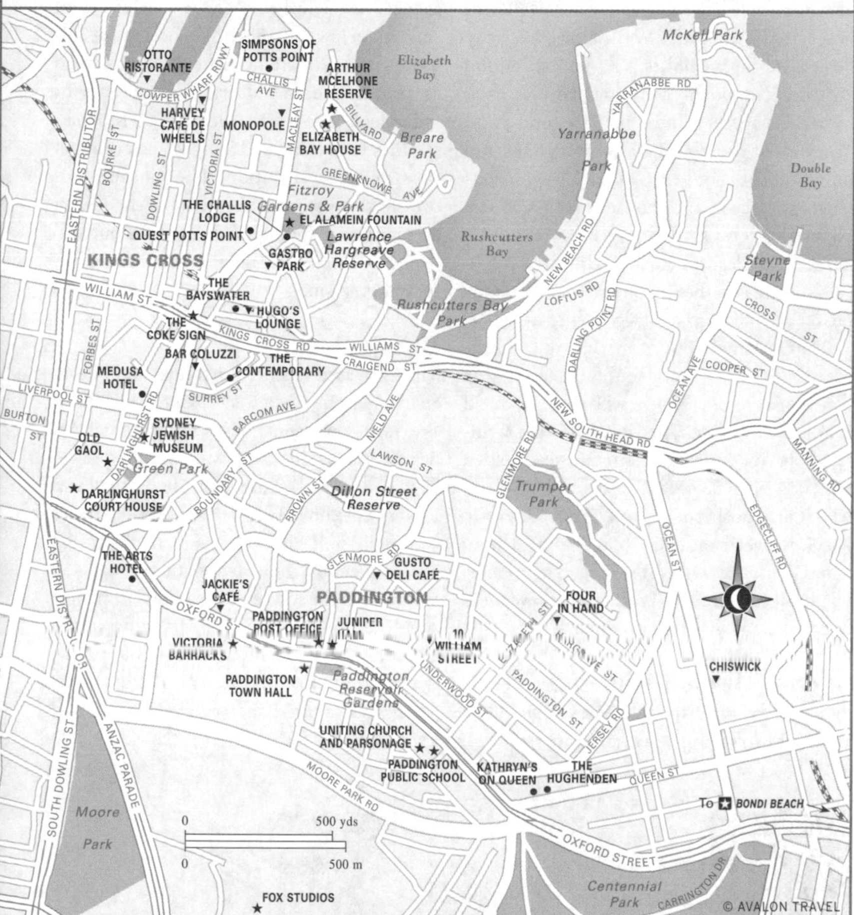

Arthur McElhone Reserve

On Elizabeth Bay House's doorstep lies the tiny hidden **Arthur McElhone Reserve** (Billyard Ave., Elizabeth Bay), a manicured little park with koi ponds and lily pads and stunning views across the harbor. Benches are provided to enjoy the views, and on a warm day, this is definitely the place to bring a sandwich and a book and enjoy the tranquil surroundings.

Breare Park

Breare Park (Ithaca Rd., Elizabeth Bay Marina) is a small but perfectly located park and one of the hot spots for New Year's Eve celebrations because of its stunning views across the harbor. Sailboats are twinkling away in the marina, a small island sits in the bay, and behind are some incredible real state gems. This is a perfect place to take a rest from sightseeing.

Macleay Street and Around

Coming back up from the bay, the varied architecture on display around Potts Point is worth a little look. Walk along Macleay Street, through Challis Avenue, and along Victoria Street before winding your way back to Macleay Street and you will get a good overview of the varied styles of architecture found house to house in Sydney. The gorgeous Victorian lace terrace houses along Victoria Street are set off by the imposing walls of St. Vincent's College for Girls, established back in 1858, whereas in the side streets you'll find interwar architecture and large Georgian villas.

The **El Alamein Fountain** (Fitzroy Gardens, Macleay St.) is an iconic fountain standing as a memorial to the soldiers who died in World War II in Egypt. Designed by Australian architect Bob Woodward, the fountain resembles a large dandelion flower and is set in a small park, which also hosts the **Kings Cross Organic Market** every Saturday (8am-2pm), where Kings Cross showcases fresh organic produce, home-baked sourdough bread, fresh flowers, exotic food stands, and entertainment.

Sydney Jewish Museum

The **Sydney Jewish Museum** (148 Darlinghurst Rd., Darlinghurst, tel. 02/9360-7999, Sun.-Thurs. 10am-4pm, Fri. 10am-2pm, adult $10, child $7, family $22) focuses especially on the experiences of Australian Jews during the Holocaust but also has regular non-Holocaust exhibitions, such as "Jewish Fashion and Art." Guided tours for individual visitors take place at noon Monday, Wednesday, Friday, and Sunday and are about 45 minutes in duration. The museum addresses the history and culture of the Jewish community in Sydney and Australia but also explains the culture, religion, and world history of Judaism.

Old Gaol

The **Old Gaol** (corner Burton St. and Forbes St., Darlinghurst, tel. 02/9339-8744, Mon.-Fri. 9am-5pm) now houses the National Art School, and its thick imposing walls hide a variety of historic buildings inside. The jail was used as a prison between 1840 and 1912. It was originally built for 732 prisoners, including 156 women, but reportedly at one stage 450 women were held there. A total of 79 people were executed there; the last hanging was in October 1908. Even though it's now a college, it is possible to walk around the grounds. There's also a coffee shop run by students and an art supply shop.

the El Alamein Fountain on Macleay Street

Darlinghurst Court House

Together with the Old Gaol next door, the **Darlinghurst Court House** (Forbes St., Darlinghurst, tel. 02/9368-2947, Feb.-Dec. Mon.-Fri. 10am-4pm) and its associated buildings make up an entire block representing the former justice system. The Greek Revival-style building was designed by architect Mortimer Lewis in 1844 and was the first purpose-built courthouse in New South Wales, becoming the template for courthouse design throughout the colony for the next 60 years. Still in use today, the main building was aligned to face directly onto Oxford Street, but the buildings stretch up to Taylor Square, where you can also find the Old Police Station. Check out the public toilet building for some historic background on the square and its buildings, as the bathroom building doubles as an information wall for the local area and its history.

PADDINGTON

Paddington, or "Paddo" as it is colloquially called, is a trendy suburb between Sydney's CBD and Bondi Beach. Developed in the 1820s, it was described by historian Max Kelly as "Sydney's first commuter suburb," because Paddington Village did not have any independent economic life to support its residents. Paddington is now known for its Australian designer fashion shops, the fashion walk (where local fashion icons are immortalized on numerous plaques on the sidewalk), its gorgeous residential homes, comfortable little cafés and bars, antiques shops, markets, and generally great atmosphere. It is an atmospheric place to come, away from the at-times overwhelming amount of history in The Rocks and the CBD, and just "be."

Saunter along the shops, buy some knickknacks, have a coffee, and grab a sneak peek of how Sydneysiders live in this part of the city. But there is also plenty of history, particularly around the main thoroughfare of Oxford Street, once a "walking track" used by the Aboriginal people, which runs along a ridgeline above most of Paddington. The land within Paddington was once the home of the Cadigal people, who spoke a Dharug dialect of the Aboriginal language, and many of their rituals and stories feature this distinct landscape of a ridge drawing alongside the natural harbor on one side and Botany Bay toward the other with what must have been sensational views to both sides.

Paddington's many historic buildings lining Oxford Street are really best viewed as part of a leisurely stroll down the bustling street, mixing pleasures of history with more modern shopping and culinary delights.

Victoria Barracks

The **Victoria Barracks** (Oxford St., between Greens Rd. and Oatley Rd., tel. 02/8335-5330, museum Thurs. 10am-12:30pm and Sun. 10am-3pm, free tour Thurs. by appointment, $2) were built out of local Hawkesbury sandstone between 1841 and 1849 in the Regency style, and were designed by Lieutenant-Colonel George Barney, who also built Fort Denison and reconstructed Circular Quay. Once located quite far from the city center, the barracks were initially occupied by British troops up until 1870 and then taken over by the New South Wales colonial forces. After the Australian Federation was established in 1901, Victoria Barracks housed the various headquarters responsible for administering and coordinating the military. Between 1931 and 1936 the barracks were home to the Royal Military College of Australia, and from July 1938 to July 1940 they also housed the Command and Staff School.

Today, the Victoria Barracks are home to the Headquarters of Forces Command. Inside, Australia's rich culture is prominently displayed, and parts of the building are open to visitors. You can view weapon displays, medals, and army uniforms from early colonial times through to World War II. And apparently, there is also a resident ghost, called Charlie the Redcoat.

Paddington Post Office

Still a working corner post office, **Paddington Post Office** (246 Oxford St., tel. 13/13-18, Mon.-Fri. 9am-5pm) dates back to 1885 and is associated with the NSW Colonial Architect's Office, which designed and maintained post offices across New South Wales between 1865 and 1890. The pretty Victorian Italianate building has numerous original architectural features, such as the colonnaded entrance, high ceilings, and the colorful emblem under the roof. It's as popular today as it was when first built.

Paddington Town Hall

The Victorian Italianate **Paddington Town Hall** (249 Oxford St., tel. 02/9265-9198), just opposite the post office, was completed in 1890. It towers over the Paddington skyline, the large clock tower reportedly symbolizing peace among nations. Today the town hall hosts a library, radio stations, and a cinema, and is often a venue for private functions.

Juniper Hall

Juniper Hall (250 Oxford St.) is the oldest standing example of a Georgian villa in Australia. Completed in 1824, it was built by convict settler Robert Cooper, who made his fortune as a gin distiller and legendarily had 28 children. The residence was saved from demolition in the 1980s and is now restored to its former glory and used as offices.

Uniting Church and Parsonage

The **Uniting Church and Parsonage** (395 Oxford St., tel. 02/9331-2646, 10:30am Sun. service) was built in 1877 on the site of the first church building in Paddington. The pretty sandstone church and its outbuildings are a bustling center of worship and community events but are probably now best known for the Paddington Markets held here every Saturday.

Paddington Markets

Paddington Markets (Uniting Church grounds, 395 Oxford St., tel. 02/9331-2923, Sat. 10am-5pm in summer, 10am-4pm in winter), Sydney's longest-running community market, began in 1973 in the Paddington Uniting Church. The market was always a place for artists and designers to mingle and flog their wares. It is home to an eclectic range of stalls offering a wide array of Australian goods plus foods. Top-notch cuisine is widely available, and fresh juices, barbecue, freshly made soups, Thai food, and cakes and other baked goods are available for purchase. The market is home to a host of local artwork and creative outlets. Fashion, in particular, is widely displayed, and emerging designers sell their merchandise at bargain prices. The impressive selection of Australian-made goods parallels the creative talent found in the city of Paddington.

Paddington Public School

Paddington Public School (399-435 Oxford St.) is another one of the string of gorgeous heritage buildings lining Oxford Street and one of the oldest continuously operating schools in NSW. Built in the Romanesque Revival architectural style, it is at once imposing as well as homely. The school dates back to 1856, when it started with a portable building brought over from England, designed for 200 pupils. It quickly grew and by 1892 some 1,400 students attended classes in the school. The school is still regularly named one of the top primary schools in Sydney.

Centennial Park

A little farther on toward Bondi Junction from Paddington Public School is **Centennial Park** (Oxford St.). Originally a large natural catchment area of creeks, swamps, springs, sand dunes, and ponds fed by groundwater, it was traditionally home to the Gadi people. But with a growing population to feed, in 1811 Governor Lachlan Macquarie designated the area as the second Sydney Common, making use of it for grazing, lime burning, and timber clearing. Sir Henry Parks dedicated the area as Centennial Park in 1888, and it played a key role in the inauguration of the Australian Federation, held in the park in 1901.

Although originally designed as a

traditional Victorian-style park with formal gardens, ponds, statues, and wide avenues for horse carriages and buggies, it also has a wide variety of Australian flora and fauna, grasslands, and woodlands. Many sculptures, statues, and heritage buildings and structures dot the park's paths, but the emphasis today is on recreation, and you can go horse-riding, play sports, and rent bicycles to explore the park.

Fox Studios

The **Fox Studios** (38 Driver Ave., Moore Park, tel. 02/9383-4200, www.foxstudiosaustralia.com) were built on the former grounds of Sydney's Royal Easter Show, a grand event full of agricultural competitions (best pig sort of thing), animal experiences, sheep sheering, exhibitions of all kinds of agricultural implements and produce, and lots of fun. It is the largest event of its kind in Australia, the sixth largest in the world, and has taken place regularly starting in 1869. In 1998 the show moved to new grounds, leaving the vast space open for Fox Studios to move in, building a full-fledged studio complete with sound stages, exterior filming locations, costume department, catering, and everything else a major film might need. It's not open to the public, but films such as *The Great Gatsby, Wolverine, Australia, Superman, The Matrix, Babe,* and many others were filmed here.

THE NORTHERN SHORE

The northern shore is mostly residential, although there are a handful of attractions worth visiting and some great views to be had.

Kirribilli Point

Admiralty House (Kirribilli, www.theaustralianafund.org.au) is the Sydney residence of the governor-general of Australia. Built in 1842 as a single-story Georgian-style home, it was originally named Wotonga. From 1885 to 1913, the property was the residence of the admiral of the British Royal Navy's Australian Squadron, and its name was changed to Admiralty House. During this period a second story and stone colonnades were added. Since 1913 Admiralty House has been used on and off as a residence for the governor-general when in Sydney. The colonial-style house, with wrap-around verandas on both floors, arched colonnades, and French windows opening to the views across the harbor, no longer quite commands as imposing a plot of land as Kirribilli House but is still prime Sydney real estate.

Near Admiralty House on Kirribilli Point, **Kirribilli House** (Kirribilli, www.theaustralianafund.org.au) is positioned in probably the prime real estate position in all Sydney—overlooking the harbor, the bridge, and the opera house. Built in 1854, the twin-gabled, Gothic-style house is the official Sydney residence of the prime minister of Australia.

Note: Once a year is **Open Day,** during which several normally private residences and governmental buildings are open for the public to buy limited tickets to gain entrance and have a look around. This usually happens around September, but exact dates are only released just before the event. Entrance tickets are typically around $10 per site (tel. 02/9285-9567, www.theaustralianafund.org.au).

Nutcote

Nutcote (5 Wallaringa Ave., Neutral Bay, tel. 02/9953-4453, www.nutcote.org, Wed.-Thurs. 11am-3pm, adult $9, child $3.50, family $20) was the home of May Gibb, whose *The Complete Adventures of Snugglepot & Cuddlepie* is still today one of Australia's best-loved children's books. The author and illustrator (1877-1969) built Nutcote house and gardens with her husband in 1925, and she lived there for 44 years. Today it is the gardens that draw visitors. Sloping down to the shore, the gardens are a riot of colors, with an attractive mix of local and imported plants and trees. Have a look at the adorable book before you go and you will see exactly how and where May Gibb got her inspiration.

★ Taronga Zoo

Even if you don't generally like the idea of

The Northern Shore

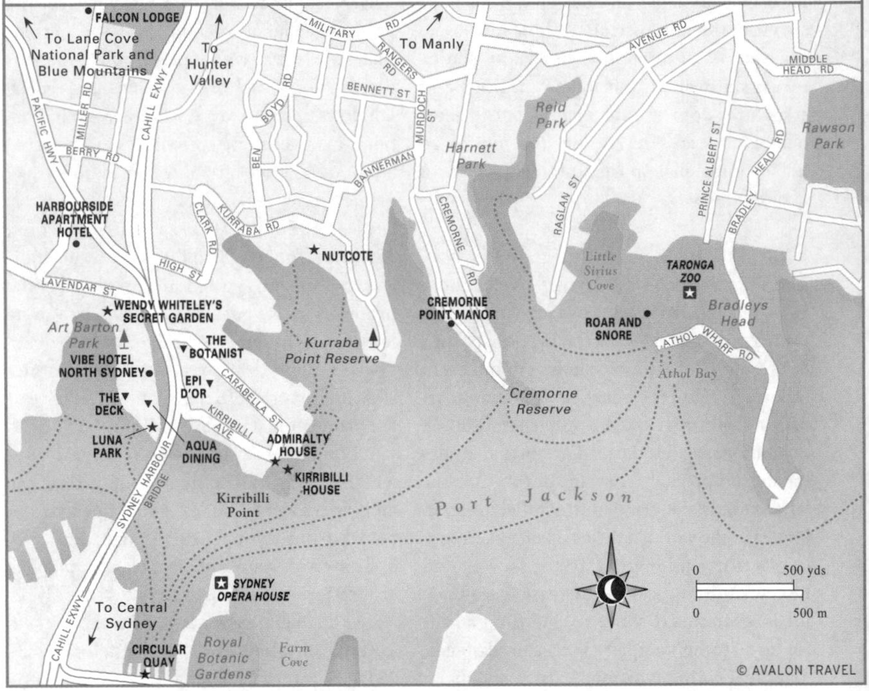

zoos, **Taronga Zoo** (Bradleys Head Rd., Mosman, tel. 02/9969-2777, www.taronga.org.au, daily 9am-5pm, May-Aug. closes at 4:30pm, adult $46, child $23, family $83-124) is a must-see in Australia. Undoubtedly the zoo with the best views in the world, overlooking the harbor, the bridge, the opera house, and the Sydney skyline, it is also arranged superbly to allow the animals plenty of space and make walking around a pleasant experience. Views are taken into consideration, and there are plenty of opportunities to get up close and personal with quite a few of the animals. Different sections specialize in African animals (with the giraffes having the best views in the house) or Australian animals, and there's even a farm where kids can hug a pet, learn about sheep shearing, meet the goats and pigs, and have plenty of fun. Encounters, feedings, and conservation talks are scheduled throughout the day, and there is a nighttime house where time is reversed so you can finally see all those nocturnal animals doing their thing. Inside, look out for the tiniest sugar gliders—tiny possums the size of a mouse, yet they can "float" between trees some 20 meters apart.

And even better? You can stay the night. See the website for details.

Wendy Whiteley's Secret Garden

Wendy Whiteley's Secret Garden (Lavender Bay) was created by the wife of the late Australian artist Brett Whiteley, after his death in 1992. Wendy channelled her grief and sorrow by transforming a previously neglected site into a secret garden full of sculptures, benches, and little hidden places, and continued to do so after the death of her only child, Arkie, from cancer. The ashes of Brett and Arkie are buried in the garden at an undisclosed location. Today the garden is open to everyone who is willing to find it, and is quite often used for blessing ceremonies and small weddings.

There are two ways to find the garden. The first option: Walk down from the North Sydney train station—aim for the Blue Street exit, turn right, and go up the steps toward Lavender Bay. Follow the road and then climb down the steps next to the little Indian Harbour Restaurant. On the left, the white house with the tower is the Whiteley House; the garden is just down a few steps also on the left. The second option: You can come from Lavender Bay, take the ferry to McMahons Point, walk left along the boardwalk in front of Luna Park, walk right under the arch and up steep steps and look for the house. It's a bit of a treasure hunt to find it, but it is a "secret garden," not found in many guides.

Step down from the garden through the railway bridge and walk along the **Art Barton Park,** a quirky display of miniature statues and sculptures celebrating the work of said Art Barton, who worked at Luna Park from 1937 to 1970, and who painted the scenes and created the huge smiling face that is the entrance to the park.

Luna Park

Dating back to the early 1930s, **Luna Park** (1 Olympic Dr, Milsons Point, tel. 02/9033-7676, www.lunaparksydney.com, hours vary, but generally weekdays 10am-6pm, weekends until 11pm) has not much changed over the years, offering good old-fashioned but nevertheless fun rides to kids of all ages, as well as food stalls, arcade games, slides, and excellent views. An Unlimited Rides Pass entitles you to unlimited rides for a full day. The cost of the pass depends on the height of the visitor: red (85-105 cm) $24.95, green (106-129 cm) $34.95, yellow (over 130 cm) $44.95. A single ride ticket is $10.

Lane Cove National Park

Some 10 kilometers north of Sydney, the 3.72-square-kilometer **Lane Cove National Park** (Lady Game Dr., Chatswood West, tel. 02/8448-0400, www.environment.nsw.gov.au, daily 9am-7pm during daylight savings, otherwise until 6pm, free) seems a million miles away from the bustling CBD. A pocket of bushland, this is a perfect place for walks or hiring a boat to meander along the peaceful

gondolas at Luna Park

river. The **Lane Cove Boat Shed** (Riverside Drive North Ryde, 4.5 km inside the park, www.lanecoveboatshed.com.au, weekends 10am-5pm) hires out boats (pedal boat 30 minutes $25, single kayak 1 hour $30). Take a picnic, or simply bring a book and relax. On occasions such as fire danger or severe weather the park may have to close at short notice.

ISLAND HOPPING IN SYDNEY HARBOUR

Within Port Jackson, more commonly known as Sydney Harbour, are six islands, all of them managed by **National Parks of NSW** (www.nationalparks.nsw.gov.au). Further information on any of the islands is available from the **Sydney Harbour National Park Information Centre** in Cadman's Cottage (110 George St., The Rocks, tel. 02/9253-0888).

Cockatoo Island

Cockatoo Island is west of Sydney Harbour Bridge, next to its smaller neighbor, Spectacle Island, a Royal Australian Navy Armament depot that is not open to the public. Named after the ubiquitous sulphur-crested cockatoos that frequented the island when it was still called Waremah by the native Eora people, in the early 1800s Cockatoo Island became a penal establishment to alleviate overcrowding on Norfolk Island, which between 1788 and 1814 functioned as an extension of the penal settlement in NSW. It stayed a prison on and off, interspersed with naval shipbuilding and other naval activities until 1908. Shipbuilding continued until 1992, when most buildings were demolished and the island lay abandoned for a decade. The Sydney Harbour Federation Trust realized the historical importance of the island, and after extensive restoration work, Cockatoo Island opened to the public in 2007.

In 2010 Cockatoo Island was placed on the UNESCO World Heritage List. Now the island is a hot spot of major events, such as the Biennale of Sydney in 2014; recreational activities such as tennis, kayaking, and fishing; and historical tours around the restored buildings. **Audio tours** can be arranged at the visitors center for $5 each, or $8 shared between two. You can even stay the night, with accommodation provided in **luxury apartments** (from $240 per night) or at a **campground** (from $40), with unique views across the harbor. Check www.cockatooisland.gov.au for information and online booking. To get to Cockatoo Island, take the **Cockatoo Island ferry** from Circular Quay (Wharf F, weekdays every 30 minutes, weekends every 15 minutes, round-trip tickets $7 pp).

Rodd Island

Rodd Island, southwest of Cockatoo Island, is a small island, previously used as a biological research institute under instruction from Louis Pasteur, a dance studio in the late 1800s/early 1900s, and a U.S. Army base during World War II. Two pretty summer houses make this a favorite spot for weddings and parties. The only way to get there is by water taxi, such as **Sydney Cove Water Taxi** (tel. 04/1470-8020), which costs around $150 round-trip for up to eight passengers.

Goat Island

Goat Island, lying just off the inner-western suburb of Balmain to the west of the Sydney Harbour Bridge, was used as a home for convict work gangs and as a gunpowder storage depot in the 1800s. The Queen's Gunpowder Magazine, which stands on Goat Island, was built in the 1830s by convicts using sandstone quarried from the eastern side of the island. It was used to store explosives, and beside it stand barracks, a cooperage, and a kitchen. Later, Goat Island was the site of the first water police station and harbor fire brigade. Following this, the island served as a shipyard, and in more recent years it has been a location for filming and concerts.

A handful of historical buildings make a walking tour interesting, but the main reason to come would be a picnic on the lawn with the stunning view of the bridge and Sydney's CBD. There usually is very restricted access to the island, but in 2013, limitations were relaxed a little and a Captain Cook Cruises ferry was operational. At the time of writing, the ferry is still available from Circular Quay. If in doubt, guided **tours** can be booked via www.sydney.com.au, priced at $69, including ferry and guided walking tour, with a duration of around 2 hours 45 minutes.

Fort Denison

Fort Denison is a tiny fortified structure on an even tinier island just off the Sydney Opera House. After the First Fleet arrived in 1788, the island was informally known to locals as Pinchgut (a skinflint person who starves himself), as it was believed convicts were sentenced to weeks at a time isolated on the island with little bread and water. The fort features the only Martello Tower to be built in Australia, and the final one ever constructed in the British Empire.

Today, there is no chance to starve, with a **restaurant** (reservations tel. 02/9361-5208, around $30 per main) offering a varied menu of classic dishes and Australian specialties for lunch and dinner and probably the best views in the city. Bookings are essential for the daily 30-minute **tours** (tel. 02/9253-0888, Mon.-Tues. at 12:15pm and 2:30pm, Wed.-Sun. at 10:45am, 12:15pm, and 2:30pm) around the small island. To get there, either use a **Captain Cook Cruises ferry** (tel. 02/9206-1111, www.captaincook.com.au, prices depend on tours available) from Circular Quay and/or Darling Harbour or take a water taxi, which can be ordered individually from **Sydney Cove Water Taxi** (tel. 04/1470-8020, around $65 one way for two people).

Clark Island

Clark Island, just off Darling Point, was named after Lieutenant Ralph Clark, who back in the late 1700s cultivated this 0.9-hectare island as a vegetable garden. Today there is no longer a veggie patch, but the island is popular with walkers and picnickers. It's limited to 150 people per day, so you will need to prebook a visit. It is even possible to rent the entire island for a private function. Call tel. 02/9253-0888 to find out more. To get to Clark Island, take a water taxi, which can be ordered individually from **Sydney Cove Water Taxi** (tel. 04/1470-8020, around $80 one way for two people from Circular Quay).

Shark Island

Shark Island in Rose Bay is overlooked by some of Sydney's best real estate and in turn has amazing views of the entire harbor down to the opera house and bridge, with the CBD as backdrop. Now a pretty parkland island, it used to be a quarantine facility for animals and a naval storage depot. It was named not for the presence of sharks but, as legend has it, for its shape resembling a shark. The island is difficult to access, but **Captain Cook Cruises' "Hop On Hop Off" ferry** (www.captaincook.com.au, from $40) will stop at the jetty.

THE BEACHES

Australia does beaches very well and Sydney is no exception. There are beaches within the harbor, on its islands, and all along the Pacific Ocean. Many are within a mere 10 kilometers of the city center, most at the end of a straight bus connection from the city and all of them gorgeous, sandy, and inviting. Sydney's status as one of the most livable—and visitable—cities in the world is due to the proximity of city and beach lifestyle. There are many beaches—too many, except the most famous ones, to mention here. But these are so good that they will suffice in showing you what a surfers' paradise Sydney is, and to give you a chance to top up your tan and have a quick swim in the sea. If you can't make it out of town and want to combine sightseeing or brunch with a quick visit to the beach, try **Balmoral Beach** on the northern shore, where you can enjoy a leisurely brunch or lunch in the Bathers' Pavilion right on the beach.

★ Bondi Beach

Bondi, or Boondi (an Aboriginal word meaning "the noise of water breaking over rocks"), hardly needs an introduction—its fame has spread beyond Australia's shores. Bondi, on the southern shore, is the iconic surfer beach where the lifeguards ply their trade, pulling out unsuspecting swimmers who have underestimated the riptides or swallowed a little too much water while off their surfboards. But it's all good, and the popularity of this beach speaks for itself. In the summer and on the weekends it is sometimes difficult to see the sand between the people, but the beach is wide enough to accommodate everybody, and there are dedicated parts of the beach for surfers and swimmers. Get changed into your swimming costume at the beach pavilion, and head off to learn to surf or play beach ball or even beach volleyball.

One thing that is a must-do, even if it will take you away from the beach, is the **Bondi to Coogee coastal walk.** Start off in Bondi, to the right if you are facing the sea, and start to ascend past the iconic **Bondi Icebergs** (1 Notts Ave., tel. 02/9130-3120, daily 11am-late, adult $5.50, child $3.50, spectator $3), a swimming club that has been in place since 1929 and has the fantastic location overlooking the entire beach and bay, while allowing you to swim both in a pool and the sea. (How, you might ask? There is of course the pool, a neatly laned rectangle of green water, but it is built so close to the rocks that in regular intervals the natural waves from the ocean crash into the corner of the pool, offering some refreshment.)

To continue on the walk, simply follow the coastal route and you will walk past stunning coastal views, with regular stop-off points. Each year in and around October-November the **Sculpture by the Sea** festival (www.sculpturebythesea.com) displays sculptures all along this first stretch of the walk, offering modern art set off beautifully by the natural surroundings.

Have a brief drink at the beach café on the quaint little **Tamarama Beach,** then continue on to beautiful **Bronte Beach** (maybe stop for lunch) and past the Waverley Cemetery, with the best views to be had anywhere, then finish up at the great sandy expanse of **Coogee Beach.** The entire walk should take you around two hours to complete. It is some six kilometers long, and the difficulty level is easy to medium, but it does undulate from steep inclines to softer hills, and there are a few steps along the way. You'll be rewarded with some of the most amazing coastal scenery Australia has to offer. You can then either walk back or take the bus back into

Bondi Icebergs swimming pool on Bondi Beach

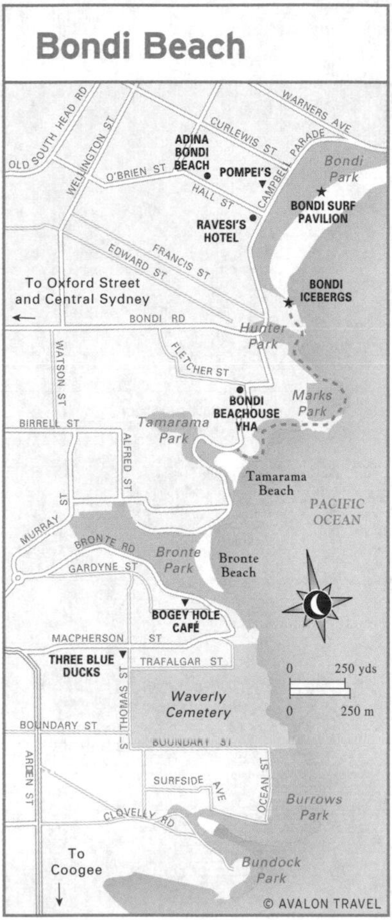

Sydney from Coogee. Be sure to bring some water and sunscreen.

Manly

Many say that Manly on the northern shore is a better beach than Bondi, but opinions are divided, and there is no right or wrong. Where Bondi is a beautiful curved beach in a bay setting with its village setting behind it, Manly is straighter and directly on the open ocean with tall Norfolk Island pine trees lining the beach. Both are stunning, with plenty of white sand, great surfing and swimming, and the beach esplanades offering everything from an ice cream to a glass of cold beer.

Manly stretches for some two kilometers, with beaches at either end, each offering a little walk and another scenic bay: **Queenscliff Beach** to the north just across the creek and little **Shelly Beach** to the south. If you are after a harder walk, a hike from Manly toward Sydney along the coastline of the harbor, the **Manly to Spit Bridge Walk,** offers one of the most beautiful walks in Sydney, but this is a three- to four-hour trek, which you can either take on in its entirety or split into smaller sections. Some of the section through the **Sydney Harbour National Park** can be quite steep and hard, whereas others are an easy saunter. Bus 143/144 follows roughly the same route, so you can catch that back at any time. For details of the various sections of the walk, have a look at www.wildwalks.com to plan ahead.

If jazz and beach are your perfect combination, then the annual **Manly Jazz** festival is for you. Having been a fixed occasion on the calendar since 1977, Manly Jazz has a rich history of dishing up some of the best live jazz performances from across Australia and around the world. Taking place usually over a long October weekend, this is an iconic event on the Australian music scene and is firmly positioned as Sydney's biggest celebration of all things jazz. Check the dates at www.manly.nsw.gov.au before you go.

Manly does not only beach and music, but also beach and art. Since 1994, the **Manly Arts Festival** (www.manlyartsfestival.com.au) has brought together art as diverse as the ocean and sky over a long weekend in September. From photography competitions and fine art exhibitions to dance demonstrations and drawing workshops, there are events to cater to all tastes.

To have a look past the beach and under the waves, check out **Manly Sea Life Sanctuary** (West Esplanade, Manly, tel. 02/8251-7877, www.manlysealifesanctuary.com.au, daily 10am-5:30pm, from adult $16.80, child $8.40, family $47). This is a lovely aquarium-cum-rescue center where the staff not only successfully breed animals in captivity, but also

Manly

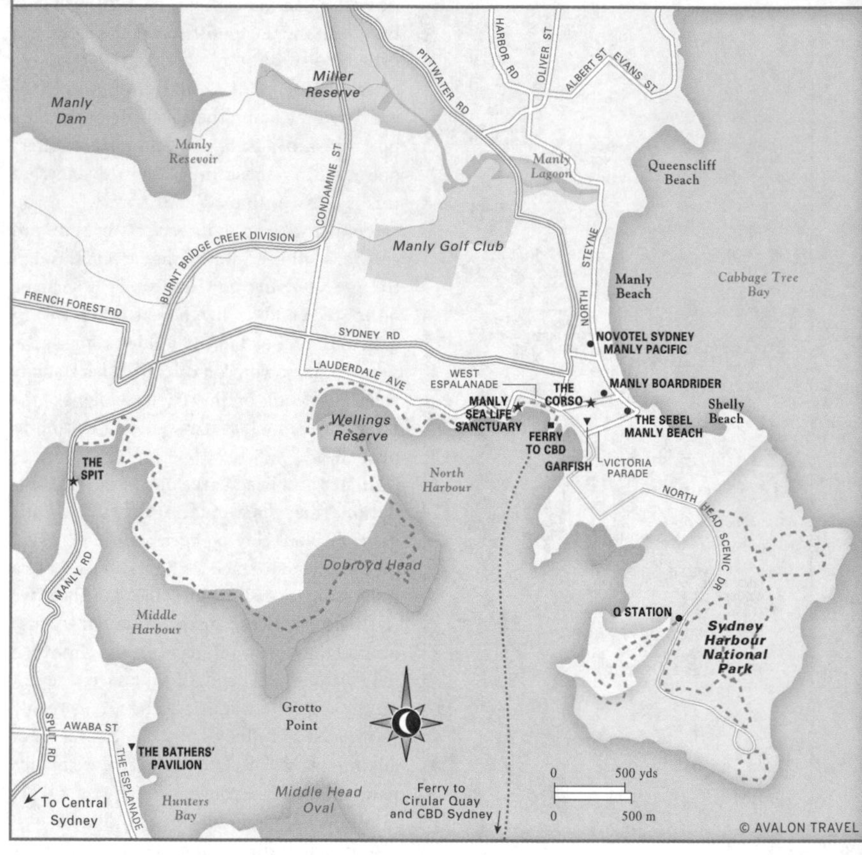

nurture sick wild animals back to health before releasing them again. There is a colony of little penguins (*Eudyptula minor*), an exhibit of everything that swims in Sydney Harbour (from sea horses to octopus to sharks), and an underwater shark tunnel. You can even jump into the aquarium and go for a shark dive (from $155 for a certified dive, $216 for an introductory dive, overall length 2.5 hours).

DAY TOURS

Walking Tours

The self-guided **City of Sydney's historical walking tours** (pick up a detailed map at any visitors center or print a PDF from www.cityofsydney.nsw.gov.au) include a tour of commercial and retail Sydney that is a must for lovers of architecture and shopping. The CBD is brimming with historic buildings, be they of Victorian or Art Deco heritage. Many either used to be old department stores or have evolved into modern shopping complexes in old shells. Explore the history of retail along Pitt Street and Martin Place, including the magnificent Queen Victoria Building, the Strand Arcade, and the Grace Hotel.

Explore Sydney's spooky side with **Ghost Tours** (meet outside Cadman's Cottage, opposite the Orient Hotel, 110 George St., The Rocks, tel. 02/9241-1283, www.ghosttours.

com.au, Apr.-Sept. daily 6:45pm, Oct.-March daily 7:45pm, 2 hours, $42). Hear true stories about murder, suicide, hangings, hauntings, recent ghost sightings, and strange phenomena, while you walk along through the cobblestone lanes of the historic Rocks. Special Halloween tours are also available. The tours are geared toward adults, though between Sunday and Thursday 13- to 17-year-olds may attend with a paying adult ($33 per teen). Teenagers cannot attend on Friday and Saturday evenings.

A pub crawl through The Rocks with **Sydney Pub Tours** (meet inside the Mercantile Hotel, 25 George St., The Rocks, tel. 04/1966-9832, www.sydneypubtours.com, Mon.-Fri. 6pm-9:30pm, $125 including drinks and dinner, must be over 18) will show you the Australian pub culture while informing you about the colonial history of the old pubs and the area. Stop at five historic pubs, get a complimentary wine/beer/soft drink at each location, have dinner in one location, get access behind the scenes, learn plenty of information, and have fun along the way.

Two Feet & a Heartbeat (tel. 1800/459 388, www.twofeet.com.au) offers walking tour options. The "Kings Cross Crime and Passion Tour" (from the Coke sign, corner William St. and Darlinghurst Rd., daily at 6pm, 2 hours, $40) explores the seedy and violent history of Kings Cross of the 1920s and 1930s; hear stories and see locations of murders, prostitution, gambling, and romance and try to imagine what it was like to live in this part of town in those darker times. Roughly following the Tank Stream, "Sydney with Conviction" (from Booking Centre, Wharf 6, Circular Quay, daily at 10am, 2 hours, $40) takes in the Sydney Harbour Bridge, The Rocks, Sydney Opera House, and the sights along the old Tank Stream route to Hyde Park.

I'm Free (Town Hall Square, 483 George St., CBD, www.imfree.com.au) offers free walking tours of Sydney: "Sydney Sights" (starting from the anchor on the Town Hall Square on George St., daily 10:30am and 2:30pm, 2.5-3 hours, free) heads up George Street, taking in sights such as Sydney Tower, the Talking Dog, Hyde Park Barracks, Martin Place, Sydney Opera House, and The Rocks. The tour ends at Circular Quay. "The Rocks" (meet in front of Cadman's Cottage, Circular Quay, daily 6pm, 1.5 hours, free) explores that area where Sydney began, including the lanes, Susannah Place, and Observatory Hill. You'll hear stories about the Rum Rebellion, Australia's largest bank robbery, evil murders, and the checkered history of the area.

The Rocks Dreaming Aboriginal Tour (from Cadman's Cottage, 110 George St., Circular Quay, tel. 02/8273-0000, www.therocks.com/therocksdreamingbookings, daily 10:30am, 1.5 hours, adult $42, child $32, children under 8 free) was developed by Margret Campbell, a Dunghutti-Jerrinjah woman, and is led by Aboriginal guides who have her permission to share her cultural knowledge. You will learn about the country before the settlers, hear the local language, experience cultural traditions, and even get your hands dirty with some ochre painting. Did you know that the Aboriginals were classed under "flora and fauna," not people, until 1967?

If you are interested in water features, be it fountains, following the old Tank Stream, drinking fountains, sewers, or even old-fashioned toilets, the self-guided **Walk on Water** (pick up a detailed map at any visitors center or print a PDF from www.cityofsydney.nsw.gov.au) is a quirky walk that you can pick up from anywhere and follow at your leisure, exploring a different side of Sydney's history.

Day Trips in and around Sydney

Sydney Boutique Tours (7 Campbell St., Artamon, tel. 02/9436-1333, www.sydneyboutiquetours.com.au, adult $250, child under 14 years $229) offers a boutique wildlife tour to the Southern Highlands, pristine bushland where Australia's iconic wildlife (such as kangaroos, wallabies, koalas, and emus) lives without the need for zoos or fences—just a 90-minute drive outside Sydney. This tour leaves at noon and does not return until later in the evening to ensure you have the chance to spot some of the nocturnal animals, such as possums and wombats. Travel in a small group with your own naturalist guide in a four-wheel-drive vehicle, stopping for lunch or afternoon tea and dinner while on "safari."

Take a tour to Canberra, Australia's capital city, with **Down Under Day Tours** (tel. 02/9251-7069, www.downunderdaytours.com.au, Mon., Wed., and Fri., hotel pickup around 7am, returning at 9pm, adult $125, child $63). You'll see the New and Old Parliaments, the Aboriginal embassy, the Australia War Memorial, the National Museum of Australia, Lake Burley Griffin, and Mount Ainslie. Tour cost includes a guided tour of parliament, entry to the war memorial, and entry to either the national gallery or the national museum.

Wachtl Australia (62/209 Harris St., Pyrmont, tel. 04/1208-6034, www.wachtlaustralia.com.au, from $198) offers a tour to Jervis Bay, where you can swim, go on dolphin trips, or simply relax and enjoy the unspoiled wilderness surroundings of Booderee National Park. Drive out of the city southward, and along the way see Botany Bay, where the first settlers arrived but did not stay; visit the impressive blowhole at Kiama; and spend some time on the pristine Hyams Beach, where you will hopefully be able to spot dolphins and maybe even humpback whales. A 10-hour round-trip, this tour gives you another impression of what's around the city.

EcoTreasures (tel. 04/1512-1648, http://ecotreasures.com.au, adult $145, child $99, hotel pickup 8am, around 5.5 hours, lunch included) takes you north of the city to explore Australia's Aboriginal heritage on the "Northern Beaches Cultural Heritage Tour." Walk with an expert cultural guide through Ku-ring-gai National Park and learn about the local peoples' art, culture, and traditions. Discuss Australia's native wildlife and ecosystems, search for tracks, and learn about bush tucker; then drive to West Head, which is home to culturally significant Aboriginal sites, including rock engravings, hand stencils, and midden sites.

Find the true essence of Australia in the rural Outback on the "Tobruk Sheep Station Outback Experience" tour offered by **Sightseeing** (tel. 1300/655-965, www.australiasightseeing.com, adult $149, child $75, around 6.5 hours). You will drive through NSW to a traditional farm, where you can watch the stockmen muster sheep and shear them, eat the typical "damper" (the soda bread prepared by campers in the Outback around a campfire), and maybe even try your hand at shearing or cracking a whip. Lunch is a typical steak followed by a lamington cake, and the experience feels a million miles away from modern Sydney. The return journey takes you past the majestic Hawkesbury River and through the Blue Mountains.

Looking for more than just a one-day trip? **Aussie Farmstay and Bush Adventures** (tel. 02/9660-3245, www.aussiebushadventures.com, adult $1,010, child $640) offers a four-day tour into the bush of Australia, experiencing the country and its ingrained traditions on a varied farm stay. On the way out of Sydney, you will visit the Koala Park Sanctuary and travel through the Blue Mountains to Mudgee for a wine tasting; the next day you will get into sheep shearing, bush craft, enjoying Australian bush tucker (food traditionally eaten and prepared by the Aboriginal peoples) around a campfire, and learning about the stars in the southern hemisphere sky. On day three, visit the country town of Canowindra, a fossil museum, and the Abercrombie Caves. Stay in the Megalong Valley in a log cabin. On day four you'll go horseback riding in the Jamison Valley, visit the Scenic Railway in Katoomba, and see Aboriginal rock art before heading back. All accommodations, meals, and activities are included.

Sports and Recreation

GARDENS AND PARKS

Ku-ring-gai Wildflower Garden

Ku-ring-gai Wildflower Garden (420 Mona Vale Rd., St. Ives, tel. 02/9424-0353, www.kmc.nsw.gov.au/kwg, daily 8am-5pm, free) is a mix of traditional bush land, heathland, fern tree gullies, ponds, and waterfalls spread across 123 hectares. Within the garden visitors can choose from a range of public access walking tracks, including the accessible Senses Track (15 minutes) or the more challenging Mueller Track (2 hours). Amenities include picnic areas with barbecues (some available for hire), on-site parking, toilet facilities, and a children's playground.

Nielsen Park

Found along the Rose Bay to Watsons Bay walk, **Nielsen Park** (Greycliffe Ave., Vaucluse, tel. 02/9253-0888, www.nationalparks.nsw.gov.au, daily sunrise-sunset but may close occasionally due to fire risk or severe weather, free) is part of the Sydney Harbour National Park, with stunning vistas across Sydney Harbour. It's a comfortable mix of open space and shady reserves, plus it features one of inner Sydney's best family beaches, Shark Beach, which is a great spot for snorkeling and swimming within the safe shark net. Amenities include a kiosk, toilet facilities, picnic tables with barbecues, and drinking water fountains.

Paddington Reservoir Gardens

The Paddington reservoir was a vital source of water for Sydney's rapidly growing population in the 19th century but eventually ceased supplying water in 1899. The site was neglected and fell into disuse until it was heritage-listed by the state and reinvented. Now an award-winning garden with parts of the original brickwork and timber and iron framework restored and incorporated in the design, **Paddington Reservoir Gardens** (251-255 Oxford St., tel. 02/9265-9333, daily sunrise-sunset, free) is an intriguing mix of ancient Roman-style baths and immaculate European gardens. This is a small secluded park, not necessarily a walking park, but perfect for a coffee and a book.

BIKING

Take in Sydney's historic sights and cycle across the Sydney Harbour Bridge with an experienced guide. There are several tours available with **Viator** (www.viator.com), ranging from a four-hour classic tour around all the main sights to a briefer highlight tour for 2.5 hours, as well as a Sydney Harbour Bridge ride (5 hours) and the Manly Beach sunset tour, which includes a ferry ride (4 hours, from $99 pp).

Life's an Adventure (tel. 02/9913-8939, www.lifesanadventure.com.au) also offers tour options. Bike around **Garigal National Park** (meet at P'Neenles Cafe, 6/5 Yulong Ave., Terrey Hills, hotel pickup $18, half day $145 pp, 10am-3:30pm), exploring the great trails. Or take a day trip to the **Blue Mountains** (hotel pickup from 7am or meet in Katoomba at 9:30am, finish 3:30pm, $185 pp, save $20 on Tues.). This is a fantastic guided mountain biking ride to Narrow Neck near Katoomba in the Blue Mountains, a plateau that stretches out into the wilderness dividing the Jamison and Megalong Valleys. The track provides a well-maintained undulating ride with four steep climbs and a couple of short, steep gullies, and breathtaking views throughout.

If you want to go it alone and just get some exercise in for a couple of hours, why not hire a bike in Centennial Park? You can go along the paths shared with pedestrians or the dedicated cycle paths, such as the Grand Drive, a 3.8-kilometer dedicated cycle lane. Rent bicycles from **Centennial Park Cycles** (50 Clovelly Rd., Randwick, tel. 02/9398-5027,

Sydney for Kids

- At the **Australian Museum** (6 College St., CBD, tel. 02/9320-6000, www.australianmuseum.net.au, daily 9:30am-5pm, adult $12, child 5-15 $6, family $30), you can get X-ray vision in the Hall of Bones, where you see the skeletons of people and lots of animals, including bats and even a snake.
- Bounce yourself happy at **Flipout Trampolines** (80 Mulgoa Rd., Penrith, www.flipout.net.au, Sun.-Thurs. 9am-10pm, Fri.-Sat. 9am-midnight, $10 for 30 minutes, $14 for 60 minutes).
- Cable cars and the world's steepest train rides are on offer at **Scenic World** (1 Violet St., Katoomba, tel. 02/4780-0200, www.scenicworld.com.au, daily 9am-5pm, adult $35, child 4-13 $18, family $88) in the Blue Mountains.
- Dodgems, roller coasters, and cotton candy are part of the all-day-long limitless fun at **Luna Park** (1 Olympic Dr, Milsons Point, tel. 02/9033-7676, www.lunaparksydney.com, hours vary, generally weekdays 10am-6pm during week, weekends until 11pm).
- Eat pancakes in all flavors, savory and sweet, in stacks and solo, at **Pancakes on the Rocks** (4 Hickson Rd., The Rocks, tel. 02/9247-6371, www.pancakesontherocks.com.au, daily 24 hours).
- Fly a kite at the **Bondi Beach Festival of the Winds** (www.waverly.nsw.gov.au, dates TBA, usually one Sunday in mid-September). Once a year there is an amazing display of kites in all shapes and sizes.
- Get your skates (and skateboards and BMX) on at the **Monster Skatepark** at Sydney Olympic Park (Grand Parade, Sydney Olympic Park, tel. 02/9763-7359, www.monsterpark.com.au, daily 9am-10pm, one-hour lesson from $30 including equipment).
- Hang out with Simba, Timon, and Pumba at *The Lion King*, the musical showing at Sydney's **Capitol Theatre** (13 Campbell St., Haymarket, tel. 1300/558-878, http://capitoltheatre.com.au, tickets from $50).
- Interested in science and looking for awesome cool toys, games, and experiments? Head to **Terrific Scientific** (51 Booth St., Annandale, tel. 02/9692-9206, www.terrificscientific.com.au, daily 10am-5:30pm).
- Join the fun at the newest water park in Sydney. There are countless slides, pipes and tipping buckets-of-fun for the whole family at **Wet'n'Wild** (427 Reservoir Rd., tel. 13/33-86, www.wetnwildsydney.com.au, summer daily 10am-5pm, from $54.99 for a day pass).
- **Koala Park Sanctuary** (84 Castle Hill Rd., West Pennant Hills, tel. 02/9484-3141, www.koalapark.com.au, daily 9am-5pm, adult $27, child $15) in the north of Sydney has koalas galore. Also meet kangaroos, dingoes, wombats, echidnas, emus, wallabies, and a large collection of birds in native bushland.
- Learn to surf at Bondi Beach. **Let's Go Surfing** (http://letsgosurfing.com.au, from $95 for 2-hour lesson) offers classes for beginners and near pros, as well as paddle boarding.
- Merrily go round on an old-fashioned carousel with beautiful horses, right next to the **Darling Harbour Playground** (www.darlingquarter.com/play). Other features include a giant 3-D swing, an Octanet, diggers, and messy water games.
- Need presents for friends back home? Get unusual souvenirs and toys at the **Australian**

Geographic Store (Westfield Bondi Junction, 500 Oxford St., Bondi Junction, tel. 02/9257-0060, http://shop.australiangeographic.com.au, Mon.-Wed. and Sat. 9:30am-6pm, Thurs. 9:30am-9pm, Fri. 9:30am-7pm). There are dinosaur eggs, magic kits, cuddly koalas, and more.

- Observe the sharks and the giant Japanese spider crab, which reaches 3.5 meters claw to claw, at **Sea Life Sydney Aquarium** (Aquarium Wharf/1-5 Wheat Rd., Darling Harbour, tel. 02/9333-9288, www.sydneyaquarium.com.au, daily 9am-8pm, last admission at 7pm, adult $26, child $16, family $65 if booked online).
- Pop into **Rip Curl** (98/100 The Corso, Manly) for some authentic Australian surfing gear.
- Question science, conduct some experiments, and find out for yourself at the **Powerhouse Museum** (500 Harris St., Ultimo, tel. 02/9217-0111, www.powerhousemuseum.com, daily 10am-5pm, adult $12, child $6, family $30).
- Reach to the stars at the **Sydney Observatory** (Watson Rd., Observatory Hill, tel. 02/9921-3485, www.sydneyobservatory.com.au), where night tours include a 3-D space session and you get to look at the sky through a gigantic telescope.
- Ships ahoy. Climb the mast on a tall ship in the harbor and get the best view of them all on a family pirate cruise with **Sydney Harbour Tall Ships** (tel. 02/8243-7961, www.sydneytallships.com.au, family pirate cruises $243 for family, mast climbing from 9 years old).
- Take the train along Darling Harbour. The little **People Mover** takes you from the Australian National Maritime Museum (2 Martin St.) past the playground to the Sea Life Sydney Aquarium and beyond, all for $5 adult, $4 child. It makes several stops all around the harbor basin.
- Upside down climbing and various rope challenges allow you to channel your inner Spiderman at Blaxland Riverside Park's **Urban Jungle Adventure Park** (Sydney Olympic Park Aquatic Centre, Olympic Blvd., Wentworth Point, tel. 02/9905-2559, www.urban-jungle.net.au, weekends 9:30am-6pm, weekdays by appointment only, $35 pp).
- Visit the red carpet at **Madame Tussauds** (Aquarium Wharf, 1-5 Wheat Rd., Darling Harbour, tel. 02/9333-9240, www.madametussauds.com/sydney, daily 9am-8pm, last admission at 7pm, adult $40, child $28, family $136, save 30% online), mingle with the stars, and get yourself an Oscar.
- What do will.I.am and Michael Jackson have in common? They left some of their stuff at the **Hard Rock Café** (Harbourside Centre, Level 2/2-10, Darling Dr., tel. 02/9280-0077, www.hardrock.com, Mon.-Fri. noon-late, Sat.-Sun. 11:30am-late, burger and fries $20) on Darling Harbour.
- Xmas displays at **Myer** (436 George St.) and **David Jones** (86-108 Castlereagh St.) in the CBD: If you happen to be in Sydney between late November and Christmas, don't miss the magical window displays at these two department stores.
- Yeehaw! Go horse riding in **Centennial Park** (www.centennialparklands.com.au, Sat.-Sun. 10am-2pm, pony rides child 2-11, $15).
- Zzzs at the zoo. Grab some Zzzs with the lions at **Taronga Zoo** (Bradleys Head Rd., Mosman, tel. 02/9969-2777, www.taronga.org.au, daily 9am-5pm, May-Aug. closes at 4:30pm, adult $44, child $22, family $270). Camp in the zoo and meet some animals behind the scenes.

daily 8:30am-5:30pm, children's bike from $10/hour, adult road bike from $20/hour).

HIKING

Harbour Walk (meet at Wharf 4, Circular Quay, tel. 04/0496-8968, daily 9am, from $89 pp, discounts for children) is an all-day walking tour with ferry rides to the starting point and returning. Take the ferry to Rose Bay, walk for around 3.5 hours at a leisurely pace along the coastline of the harbor, past Sydney Harbour National Park, along the bays to the prestigious suburb of Vaucluse. Have tea along the way, then fish and chips for lunch at Watsons Bay, and return to Circular Quay by ferry.

The walking enthusiasts at **Sydney Coast Walks** (tel. 02/8521-7423, www.sydneycoastwalks.com.au, from $75) know the best walks in and around Sydney's coast and offer half-, full- and two-day treks showing you the best of the scenery, bush, and national parks. They take out groups of like-minded people on a variety of walks catering to all fitness levels, and also offer personalized tours. Try the "Marley Walking Tour" (adult $145, child $135)—you'll get picked up at around 7am from your hotel and enjoy a roughly seven-hour walk through national parkland, with coastal views, cave exploration, wildlife sightings, and viewing Aboriginal engravings on the sandstone. Lunch is provided (and carried!), and you'll also enjoy a ferry round-trip.

Short Walks (http://short-walks.com.au) is a great website that allows you to search for walks according to location or duration. There are plenty of hikes in and around Sydney and New South Wales, including the Blue Mountains and the Southern Highlands, both of which offer a huge variety of walks. Each walk gives you an idea of difficulty level, duration, and length, and a reasonably detailed map, plus a weather forecast.

SNORKELING AND DIVING

Even though it is a harbor, there are more species of fish in Sydney Harbour than in the entire Mediterranean. For example, did you know there are numerous different species of seahorse found in the harbor? **EcoTreasures** (Q Station Wharf, Quarantine Beach, Manly, tel. 04/1512-1648, http://ecotreasures.com.au, group tours from adult $55, child $35) takes you out into the harbor to discover the myriad marine life. The 90-minute tour includes a marine eco talk, wet suits, noodles, snorkeling gear, and a guide.

If you want to go deeper, there is always scuba diving. **Pro Dive Experience** (169 Pittwater Rd., Manly, tel. 02/9977-5966, and 27 Alfred St., Coogee, tel. 02/8116-1199, www.prodive.com.au, from $69, including equipment) organizes shore and open-water dives, including night dives. They also offer a weekend openwater course for beginners (from $499) and advanced courses at two sites in Sydney (from $299).

Dive Centre Manly (10 Belgrave St., Manly, tel. 02/9977-4355, www.divesydney.com.au, from $95 one dive, $125 for two shore dives, including equipment) offers shore dives at Shelley Beach, where sightings of wobbegongs (carpet sharks) are common, and at other nearby sites that are not deep and are ideal for beginners. Boat dives include a shark dive to see gray nurse sharks, the South Head Sponge Gardens, and the Gap Cave, which offers a great variety of local fish, sponges, and underwater geology.

SURFING

If you would like to get into the surf culture, then Sydney is one of the best spots in Australia to try your hand at this sport. Both **Bondi Beach** and **Manly Beach** are world-renowned for all-year-round waves that lend themselves to world-class surfing. There are plenty of other beaches around and outside Sydney, but there you will have to bring your own gear and know where you are going and what you are doing. If you need to hire your equipment and are looking for a lesson or two, Bondi and Manly are the perfect spots to do both. The schools also hire out boards if you are already accomplished. At **Manly**

Beach Hire (www.manlybeachhire.com.au), directly on the sand, you can hire a surf- or bodyboard from $10 per hour; in Bondi Beach, **Let's Go Surfing** (http://letsgosurfing.com.au, 128 Ramsgate Ave., North Bondi, tel. 02/9365-1800) hires out surfboards from $20 per hour.

Let's Go Surfing also offers the "Bondi Surf Experience" (from $99), great for beginners or those needing to refresh their skills. It's a two-hour lesson on Australia's most famous beach, and you'll be in a small group. Or get a private lesson ($140/hour, with board, wet suit, and sunblock included) with a professional, either learning the basics or improving on the skills you have.

Manly Surf School (North Styne, Manly, tel. 02/9932-7000, http://manlysurfschool.com.au, tours from $120, lessons from $70 adult, $55 child) offers not only lessons for beginners and advanced surfers, but a day-long "Surf Tour." Be picked up at 9:30am in the city, learn about surfing (including the history and local importance), then drive to one of the nearby northern beaches for a 90-minute lesson. Have a typical Aussie pie for lunch, another lesson, and head back around 4pm. They also do paddleboard lessons (from $35, all gear included).

KAYAKING

Life's an Adventure (tel. 02/9913-8939, www.lifesanadventure.com.au) gives you a chance to watch Sydney wake up during a great morning kayak tour through Sydney Harbour (Woollahra Sailing Club, Vickery Ave., Rose Bay, adult $99 pp, child 8-16 years $65, pickup from hotel $10). Go past the opera house and the bridge, and explore the coves around the inner harbor. Meet with your guide at Rose Bay at 7am, tour the harbor, and be back by 9:30am, ready for a day's sightseeing. Another option is the biking, hiking, and kayaking experience (Craig Avenue Boat ramp, Little Manly Beach, Manly, 9:30am-5pm, adult $199, child 10-16 $179, save $20 pp on Mon.). For a sporting day out taking in the northern beaches, this adventure involves an entire day of biking, hiking, and kayaking. Start with cycling to Manly's beautiful North Head (the northern end of the entrance from the Pacific Ocean into Sydney Harbour), exploring the natural beauty and military history of the North Head national park. You then kayak around the secluded sandy coves and oceanic waters of Manly, stopping for lunch on a remote picturesque beach not accessible by road. Finish the day with a guided walk from Manly to The Spit, a point of coast

sailing yachts in Sydney Harbour

jutting out into the harbor, along the dramatic coastline and rugged bushland of the Sydney Harbour National Park, complete with photo opportunities and great views.

Natural Wanders (Milsons Point, tel. 04/2722-5072, www.naturalwanders.com.au, from $120 pp including photographs) offers custom **VIP Paddle** tours, which start early on weekdays, and you can suggest a route, the difficulty of the tour, and length. The "Bridge Paddle" route is a possibility for beginners on these trips, while on weekends this is for experienced sea kayakers only. Starting off at Lavender Bay on the north side of the Sydney Harbour Bridge, the Bridge Paddle takes you under the bridge, past Kirribilli Point opposite the opera house, paddling into bays and along beaches and past a bushland setting, giving you a whole new perspective of the harbor. This is quite an adventurous paddle combined with stunning scenic views, and will put your paddling skills to good use as well as improve your knowledge of Sydney's northern shore. Total distance is around 14 kilometers, and as tours are small and private, the timing can be set around your schedule and abilities.

SAILING

Bareboat Yacht Charter (yachts moored at d'Albora Marina, Rushcutters, tel. 02/9327-1166, www.eastsail.com.au, contact for charter prices) has a selection of yachts available for bareboat sailing charter on Sydney Harbour, including Beneteau 33.7, 40.7, First 40, Oceanis 40, Dufour 335, and Sydney 36 yachts. All come with well-equipped galley with gas oven, crockery and cutlery, fridge/icebox, private bathroom with hot water, CD stereo with iPod jack, and full safety inventory. You can also day-charter skippered private yachts, which come with a crew and hostess upon request, or join a "Morning Adventure Sail" (10am-12:30pm, adult $119, child $89, minimum of four adults) or a "Sunset Cruise" (6pm-8pm, $596 for four guests, including drinks and snacks).

Sydney by Sail (Festival Pontoon, National Maritime Museum, Darling Harbour, tel. 02/9280-1110, www.sydneybysail.com.au, $1,395 per couple) offers a romantic overnight sailing experience on a Hunter 39 yacht. Set off from Darling Harbour, sail around Sydney Harbour taking in the sights and early sunset, and then anchor for the night. The hired skipper will leave you on our own, securely anchored. Dinner and breakfast are provided and in the morning the skipper will return you to Sydney.

Want to sail on an Americas Cup Yacht? **Adrenalin** (20 Burton St., Darlinghurst, tel. 1300/791-793, www.adrenalin.com.au, from $79) will take you on a 2.5-hour cruise on the 75-foot racing yacht. It departs King Street Wharf, Darling Harbour and then takes in the sights and thrills of Sydney Harbour, with an experienced crew allowing you to pitch in along the journey. There are usually up to 30 guests, and only selected dates are available.

CRUISES AND RIDES

Sydney Harbour Tall Ships cruises (book at Kiosk 3, Wharf 5, Circular Quay, tel. 02/8243-7961, www.sydneytallships.com.au, from adult $99, child $45) depart from Campbell's Cove, The Rocks. They give you an opportunity to go out into the harbor on a tall ship—not quite the size of ship the first settlers came on, but more authentic than a modern motor yacht any day. Lounge around on the deck, or maybe climb up into the mast to get an even better view and savor the history. When the sails are set and you look back into the harbor, you'll get a much better feeling for how it must have been in the early days. On the "Convicts, Castles & Champagne Tour" (Thurs.-Mon. at 1pm, additional cruises weekends 11:30am and 2:30pm, 2.75 hours, adult $89, child $39), you'll cruise along the harbor, stop off at Goat Island, tour the 1800s gunpowder magazine, learn about convict history, and sail past some of Sydney's best real estate and the government houses, while enjoying an open bar, including free local bubbles. There are even special "Family Pirate Tours" (usually 1.5 hours long; departure times and dates vary seasonally and according to school

Sydney Harbour Tall Ships cruise

holidays), or you can opt for the more sophisticated "Wine and Canapés Tour" at sunset (3 hours, adults only, $149 includes finger foods and unlimited wine, beer, and soft drinks; mast climb $25).

Captain Cook Cruises (tel. 02/9206-1111, www.captaincook.com.au) offers a "Coffee Cruise" (departs Jetty 6, Circular Quay, daily 10am and 2:15pm, 2 hours, adult $39, child $10) that runs along the harbor, taking in all the sights, islands, beaches, cliffs, and real estate on the waterfront, while you enjoy morning or afternoon tea and coffee and listen to the personalized commentary. Captain Cook also offers "Hop On Hop Off" (from adult $45, child $24, family $90), a 24-hour pass allowing unlimited access to the hop-on, hop-off ferry that takes in eight main sights on the harbor, including Taronga Zoo, Fort Denison, Shark Island, Manly, Luna Park, and others. You can pay extra and have entrance fees to other sights, such as the Sea Life Sydney Aquarium, Madame Tussauds, Wild Life Sydney Zoo, Sydney Tower Eye, Fort Denison, and Shark Island included in the price. Prices vary according to how many attractions you opt for. On the "Dinner Cruise" (departs Jetty 6, Circular Quay, or Jetty 1, King Street Wharf, Darling Harbour, daily 7pm, 2.5-3 hours, from $89, adults only), you'll enjoy sparkling nighttime Sydney views from the water during a three-course contemporary Australian à la carte dinner with live music and dancing.

TourChief (tel. 02/8296-7233, www.tourchief.com) offers a simple harbor sightseeing cruise (code AUS1511; departs daily every two hours from the following: Darling Harbour, Circular Quay, Taronga Zoo, Watsons Bay, Manly, Q Station, Milson's Point, two hours, adult $28, child $15, family $71) with running commentary, taking in all the sights along the harbor from the bridge to the opera house, going past some of the many islands and allowing you to enjoy the city skyline and unusual perspective of sights from the water.

See Sydney Harbour at breakneck speeds on a powerful jet boat with **OzJetBoating** (depart from the east side of Circular Quay, tel. 02/9808-3700, www.ozjetboating.com, hourly departures daily 11am-4pm, 30 minutes, adult $70, child $45, family $195). Get wet (coveralls provided) and thrilled while splashing along past the opera house to Shark Island, Taronga Zoo, and the Sydney Harbour Bridge.

To get a whole new perspective of Sydney and the scenic harbor, try flying over it with **Sydney by Seaplane** (tel. 02/9974-1455, www.sydneybyseaplane.com, daily 7am-10pm, departures from Rose Bay). Flights include a 15-minute trip (from $185 pp) across the bridge and opera house to Manly and Bondi Beach, as well as dinner flights (from $365 not including dinner and drinks), where the plane takes you to the northern beaches or the Hawkesbury River, drops you off for a romantic dinner, and then flies you back home. Alternatively, opt for the "Gourmet Beach Picnic with Champagne" (from $890 pp, 3.5 hours, food and drinks included).

WHALE-WATCHING

The whale-watching season along NSW's east coast runs from May to November, and humpback and southern right whales migrate from the Antarctic up to the Great Barrier Reef for breeding. More than 50 percent of the planet's cetaceans, whales, dolphins, and porpoises can be found in Australia, with nine species of baleen whales and 36 species of toothed whales living in the local waters. Thousands of whales swim past, and sometimes into, Sydney Harbour, and there are plenty of cruises to take advantage of the annual spectacle.

Whale Watching Sydney (from Darling Harbour, Cockle Bay Marina, tel. 02/9583-1199, www.whalewatchingsydney.net) offers a half-day "Photo Safari" (daily 2pm, $199 pp), limited to 20 passengers. This is a specialist photography trip, not a leisure cruise, guided by a professional photographer who will ensure keen amateur photographers get the best pictures they can from this trip. The boat returns after sunset, allowing for some atmospheric sunset pictures. Just in case, the photographer will also provide you with a USB drive loaded with pictures. Whale Watching Sydney also offers Sydney's fastest whale-watching trip, an "Adventure Cruise" (daily 10:30am and 2pm, adult $54, child $36, 2 hours) on the speedboat *Totally Wild*. The boat will get beyond the headlands and into the ocean within 20 minutes of departure from Darling Harbour, and due to the small size and better maneuverability of the boat, you can get closer to the animals. Do bring a waterproof jacket, as they do sometimes get very close!

Captain Cook Cruises (tel. 02/9206-1111, www.captaincook.com.au) runs "Whale Watching AM" (Aquarium Wharf, Darling Harbour, adult $90, child $57), a three-hour morning cruise with coffee and tea and live commentary throughout. They give a whale sighting guarantee, with you being able to get onto another cruise if you did not spot a whale on your trip. This is a family-friendly trip, taking it easy and slow, although the waves on the ocean can still be unpredictable.

SPECTATOR SPORTS

Stadium Tours

ANZ Stadium (Sydney Olympic Park, tel. 02/8765-2300, www.anzstadium.com.au) is a multipurpose stadium, mostly famous for the 2003 Rugby World Cup and the Olympic Games. Take the **stadium tour** (from adult $28.50, child $18.50, family $70, one hour,

whale-watching

daily except for bank holidays and special event days) and go behind the scenes, run through the players' tunnel onto the pitch, visit the changing rooms, stand on one of the Sydney Olympic medal stands, and spot your hero's autograph on the signature board.

If cricket is your passion, touring the **Sydney Cricket Ground and Allianz Stadium** (Driver Ave., Moore Park, tel. 1300/724-737, www.sydneycricketground.com.au) is a must. This **tour** (Mon.-Fri. 11am and 2pm, Sat. 11am, adult $30, child $20, family $78) takes approximately half a day, depending on the individual group's requests. It's a three-in-one tour of the Sydney Cricket Ground, the SCG Museum, and the Allianz Stadium that gives you a behind-the-scenes look at the place where plenty of sport history was written. You can see the dressing rooms, the pitch, and the members pavilion; explore the museum; experience the Allianz Stadium's field of play and players' tunnel; and learn about the sport's history.

Australian Rules Football

The season for the AFL is between March and July, and games are played across Australia. The local team is the **Sydney Swans** (www.sydneyswans.com.au). Their home ground is the **Sydney Cricket Ground** (Driver Ave., Moore Park, tel. 1300/724-737, www.sydneycricketground.com.au) and also **ANZ Stadium** (Sydney Olympic Park, tel. 02/8765-2300, www.anzstadium.com.au). For games played in Sydney, please check the website.

Cricket

Cricket is one of Australia's favorite sports. In the rest of the world, such as the cricket-mad United Kingdom, the season for this summer sport runs mid-April to September, whereas in Australia the season starts in October and ends in February or early March. During the season, all games played will be listed on the website for the **Sydney Cricket Ground** (Driver Ave., Moore Park, tel. 1300/724-737, www.sydneycricketground.com.au), together with times and prices. On game days there are food and merchandise stalls outside the stadium, making for a pleasant day out and fun for the entire family.

Soccer

The season for football (soccer) is during the Australian summer. This being the home ground of the **Sydney Football Club** (www.footballaustralia.com.au/sydneyfc), there are always plenty of games on at **Allianz**

soccer game in Sydney

Stadium (Driver Ave., Moore Park, www.scgt.nsw.gov.au). Check online for dates and tickets.

Rugby

Warathas (www.warathas.com.au) are the professional Rugby Union team of NSW and play in the Allianz Stadium. The season is during the Australian winter, and while games are played across the nation, you might be able to catch a home game.

Surfing

Held on Manly Beach in late summer (February), the nine-day **Hurley Australian Open of Surfing** (www.australianopenofsurfing.com) brings together national and international competitions from the world of surfing and skateboarding. There are also arts and live music venues set up throughout the event, making it into an all-round festival.

Yachting

Filling the harbor with sails large and small, the **Sydney to Hobart Yacht Race** (from Sydney Harbour, every Boxing Day, December 26) is a spectacle not to be missed if you are in the city. Setting off from near the Royal Botanic Gardens, scores of yachts prepare to battle against the treacherous Tasman Sea to reach Hobart, Tasmania, some 630 nautical miles away, in one of the world's most difficult races.

Horse Racing

Located relatively close to the city, **Royal Randwick Racecourse** (77-97 Alison St., Randwick, tel. 02/9663-8400, www.randwickraces.com.au) is a convenient race course to see some local and international thoroughbreds run. Races are held throughout the year, although the most famous is probably the Autumn Carnival, which is one of the richest racing carnivals in the world, held in February and March. Alternatively, there is the Spring Carnival, held in September and October each year, which is another racing—and fashion—highlight of the year's events calendar.

Dog Racing

Since the 1930s, **Wentworth Park** (Wentworth Park Rd., Glebe, tel. 02/9552-1799, www.wentworthparksport.com.au) has been the place to come to see greyhounds race. Twice a week, every Friday and Saturday night starting from 7:15pm, these sleek hounds chase the ever elusive hare around the track.

Entertainment and Events

NIGHTLIFE

Sydney is a city that can party hard, but walking around the CBD on a Saturday night, you'd be excused for thinking everybody has gone to bed early. Hot spots such as King's Cross and Darlinghurst attract the most raucous and eclectic crowds, making the most noise, but in the CBD you will have to know where to go if you want to party past midnight.

Bars

If you only go to one bar in the city, make it the **Opera Bar** (Lower Concourse Level, Sydney Opera House, tel. 02/9247-1666, www.operabar.com.au). The location is just below the opera house, on the tip of Circular Quay, opposite the bridge. Basically, the location does not get any better, and that is why this venue is *the* place for New Year's in Sydney, booked out months in advance. But NYE or not, this is simply the best place to "be" in Sydney. A little nondescript during the day, with tables and benches taking over the pavement that winds its way toward the opera house, it is the lighting and sheer atmosphere at night that makes this into a bar. The decor is the view—the furniture is comfortable enough but nothing special. This place relies fully on ambience, and that it has in spades. Sit back and soak it all up; it really is a fantastic city to watch at night over drinks. Yes, you share with the tourists, but there are also plenty of local pre-show guests. Despite that, it's relaxed and laid-back.

Near the Opera Bar is **Cruise Bar** (West Circular Quay, tel. 02/9251-1188, www.cruisebar.com.au), with another vantage point looking out across Circular Quay, the opera house, and the twinkling lights of the CBD. Relax on one of the white sofas or padded leather armchairs and enjoy the setting. On the weekend there's a DJ livening things up a little, but generally this is a relatively low-key place to have a drink or two off the cocktail list before moving onto dinner, a show, or a club. It is open in the daytime, but at night the lights of the city make it really special.

Just opposite Circular Quay in The Rocks is **Bar 100** (100 George St., The Rocks, tel. 02/8070-9311, www.bar100.com.au). Bar 100, strictly speaking, is a cocktail bar in a stunning historic building (the Mariners' Church, established in 1856), but in reality it is several venues in one, ranging from the heritage-look setting to a modern rooftop bar to a dining room and an old-fashioned lounge. Drifting from venue to venue is a great way to spend a night on The Rocks. You can get a wide selection of drinks plus bar snacks and other food (pizza $22, kangaroo burger $20).

Around the corner from Bar 100 is **Eric's Bar—Searching for Scarlett** (34 Harrington St., The Rocks, tel. 02/8220-9999, www.scarlettrestaurant.com.au). A lovely little bar on the ground floor of the Harbour Rocks Hotel, it is reportedly named after Eric, a merchant sailor in the late 1800s who was in love with Scarlett, a madam who ran the brothel next door. It's a romantic setting, full of character, incorporating modern furniture into the historic setting, with quirky decor, such as the lovely map mural of old Sydney Cove. The bar offers a great choice of grapes as well as bar snacks to share, such as edamame or potato wedges ($7 per plate).

On the way into the CBD from The Rocks is **Grain** (Four Seasons Hotel, 199 George St., CBD, tel. 02/9250-3100, www.fourseasons.com/Sydney), a small, comfortable bar on the ground floor of the Four Seasons Hotel that is also accessible from the outside. The Grain moniker refers not just to the drinks but also to the smooth wood decor. Dotted with beautiful pieces of art, this is a quiet place to have a beverage before contemplating the night out.

The ArtHouse Hotel (275 Pitt St., CBD, tel. 02/9284-1200, www.thearthousehotel.com.au) lies in the heart of the CBD. Dating back to 1836, this heritage-listed building right in the heart of the city center originally was Sydney's School of Arts and later served as a theater, a library, and even a chapel before reinventing itself as a bar—or bars, as there are three venues in one. True to its name, the bar doubles as a gallery, and the ArtHouse hosts a few dozen exhibitions every year, plus it regularly stages creative arts events such as life drawing, burlesque and cabaret variety nights, and photography workshops. It is an impressive venue in a great location and a place to hunker down and stay awhile.

The elegant decor of **Black Bar** (Harbourside Entrance, The Star, Pirrama Rd., Pyrmont, tel. 02/9777-9000, www.star.com.au), in the entertainment complex of The Star just off Darling Harbour, evokes the 1920s with stylish surroundings and bartenders wearing crisp white shirts and suspenders. The twirling and whirling young men are reviving pre-prohibition cocktails and some long forgotten drinks. Look out for the hand-chiseled, diamond-shaped ice cubes and the Brunch Cocktail, the signature orange drink on everybody's lips.

While Kings Cross can be a little seedy, **Hugo's Lounge** (33 Bayswater Rd., Kings Cross, tel. 02/9357-4411, www.hugos.com.au) is chic personified. All the cool people of Sydney seem to mingle here sipping their champagne or trying out new cocktails, adding a touch of sparkle to the black stone walls, black couches, black floors, and cream ottomans. It's very stylish, very elegant, and from the rooftop you have great views out and over the seedier life below.

Down the road from Kings Cross in Woolloomooloo is the **Water Bar** (6 Cowper Wharf Rd., Woolloomooloo, tel. 02/9331-9000, www.waterbaratblue.com). Continuously winning awards and having been named "Bar of the Year" by numerous magazines—and even notching up a "Top Ten Bars in the World" accolade from *Condé Nast Traveler*—the Water Bar is huge and swanky, combining industrial warehouse heritage with sparkling Swarovski crystal water-drop curtains. Inside the BLUE Sydney Hotel on Woolloomooloo Wharf, you are surrounded by top-notch restaurants, such as Otto Ristorante, so a pre- or après-dinner drink is certainly called for.

If you are in Bondi, look no further than the **Neighbourhood** (143 Curlweis St., Bondi, tel. 02/9365-2872, http://neighbourhoodbondi.com.au). Bare brick walls, retro lighting, and shabby-chic leather armchairs add to the general laid-back Bondi beach atmosphere. The broadcasting studio of the since-departed Bondi 88.0 FM radio station in the bar has been taken over by new Bondi Radio, promising 24-hour entertainment and broadcasting from right there. The bar prides itself on innovative and seasonal drinks, always offering something out of the ordinary.

Dance Clubs

If you want to go clubbing in Sydney, it's easy to catch up with a few clubs right in the CBD and nearby neighborhoods. **Chinese Laundry** (111 Sussex St., CBD, tel. 02/8295-9999, http://chineselaundryclub.com.au, cover $25, varies), colloquially known simply as the "Laundry," is one of Sydney's biggest and most popular dance clubs. The professional sound system in the "Cave," another chill-out room in the club, has attracted heavyweight internationals such as James Holden, Gui Boratto, and Sasha, with local and visiting DJs hosting nights every weekend, and the outdoor dance floor is the place for summer clubbing.

Ivy (1/330 George St., CBD, tel. 02/9254-8100, http://merivale.com.au/ivy, cover Saturday nights minimum $20) is a truly mammoth complex, boasting 13 venues, right in the center of the city. Venues include restaurants, secluded lounges, the exclusive but not members-only rooftop Pool Club, and bars. Most importantly, there is **Pacha,** the huge dance venue with sky-high ceilings and a packed floor hosting DJs and pool parties. It was voted "Dance Club of the Year" in 2013. Then there is the Changeroom, with actual lockers and changing rooms. It reportedly is the city's most popular hetero pseudo sex-club with a dance floor, so be careful of which floor you step out of the elevator.

Less overwhelming than Ivy is **The Spice Cellar** (58 Elizabeth St., CBD, tel. 02/9223-5585, http://thespicecellar.com.au, $10 to $20 for events). Sydney DJ Murat Killic teamed up with club promoters Warren Faulkner and Rebecca Alder to create a much-needed halfway point between bar-hopping and clubbing for the city's nightlife enthusiasts. There is a cocktail lounge for late afternoon drinks, a tapas bar for sustenance, and on weekends the Spice Cellar hosts local and visiting DJs and stays open until 10am.

Just slightly out of the CBD toward Ultimo is **Abercrombie** (corner Broadway St. and Abercrombie St., Broadway, tel. 02/9280-2178, free). This is a hotel (a.k.a. pub) turned techno den, with the Strange Fruit parties on Saturday nights bringing in the crowds, probably mostly owing to the free entry. Featuring plenty of regular DJs, this place is popular with students due to its proximity to TAFE (Training and Further Education) Ultimo College.

In the bustling alternative nightlife scene that is Darlinghurst's Oxford Street, **The Exchange Hotel** (44 Oxford St., Darlinghurst, tel. 02/9331-2956, http://exchangesydney.com.au, cover varies) features several venues, such as the **Q Bar,** the dance hot spot with plenty of funk and house; **Spectrum,** hosting mostly live music in an intimate 250-capacity venue; subterranean **Phoenix,** hosting a slightly older crowd with an eclectic mix of dance music; and **34B,** the burlesque venue with regular shows on the roster.

GLBT

Darlinghurst's Oxford Street has a heavy dose of gay and lesbian bars, clubs, shops, and general scene. Start the night at **The Midnight Shift** (85 Oxford St., Darlinghurst, tel. 02/9358-3848, daily 2pm-late, Fri.-Sat. even later), Sydney's oldest gay venue, which is packed with full shows, featuring entertainment every night.

Arq (16 Flinders St., Darlinghurst, tel. 02/9380-8700, Thurs.-Sun. 9pm to early morning) is one of Sydney's largest clubs, with an enormous dance floor, light and laser shows, and a bustling mezzanine floor overlooking the dancers. Four nights a week entertainment features Drags to Riches dance competitions, Drag'n'Fly shows, go-go boy strippers, dancers in cat outfits, and so much more.

A (formerly) traditional pub, **The Oxford Hotel** (134 Oxford St., Darlinghurst, tel. 02/8324-5200, daily 10am-4am) is a mix of gay and straight, open-minded and eclectic. Downstairs in the Underground Bar with its brick arches, you can find music, lasers, inner sprung dance floor, pinball machines, and plenty of unconventional people.

Live Music

There are plenty of live music venues throughout the city, although you might have to jump into a taxi to get to some of them. Right in the CBD is **The Basement** (29 Reiby Place, Circular Quay, CBD, tel. 02/9251-2797, www.thebasement.com.au). This little basement (literally) is primarily a jazz venue with the likes of Dizzy Gillespie having played here in its 40-year history. There is a steady list of local and international contemporary musicians and jazz bands playing here nearly daily, with special events held on certain occasions. It's a great venue in a bustling location.

The historic **Marble Bar** (Level B1, 488 George St., CBD, Hilton Sydney, tel. 02/9266-2000, http://marblebarsydney.com.au) is also conveniently located in the city's center. It would be worth seeing, even if you weren't heading there for live music. Built in 1893, this high-ceilinged Victorian bar was not originally raised in the place it is now but was painstakingly dismantled and re-erected in the current site. With marble columns, fireplaces, and over-the-top but well-suited pastage decor, this place is a piece of history and hosts live music every Wednesday to Saturday evening, with bands ranging from R&B and soul to '80s mixes, from jazzy to cover versions of rock classics.

In bustling Kings Cross and Darlinghurst you can find more venues, such as **FBi Social** (Kings Cross Hotel, 244-248 William St., Kings Cross, tel. 02/9331-9900, www.kingscrosshotel.com.au), which lines up some of the best local bands and DJs alongside a carefully selected lineup of international acts. During the week you'll find a variety of shows to supplement the music on the weekends, such as open mic nights, comedy fixtures, and even some poetry.

The World Bar (24 Bayswater Rd., Kings Cross, tel. 02/9357-7700, www.theworldbar.com) can be found in the unlikely location of a three-story Victorian terrace house. This venue is an odd combination of historic club lounge (complete with leather settees, chandeliers, old dials, and knickknacks), tea room, and trendy bar. This strangely likable setup is a mix of bar, club, and live music venue, and offers something different at every turn.

The **Oxford Art Factory** (38-46 Oxford St., Darlinghurst, tel. 02/9332-3711, www.oxfordartfactory.com) offers visual art, performance art, and live music. The concept is based on Andy Warhol's New York Factory, providing an edgy venue and myriad performance spaces. Most of the live music performances are local bands that play for free.

A little farther out toward the city's southwest is the **Lazybones Lounge** (Level 2, 294 Marrickville Rd., Marrickville, tel. 04/8875-9548, http://lazyboneslounge.com.au), but it is well worth the trip. Set up like someone's living room complete with bookshelves, old couches, chandeliers, and knickknacks, this venue is a music lounge with live music seven nights a week, ranging from jazz to DJs on Saturday nights. Local beers and ciders are on tap. The atmosphere is relaxed, with comfort food coming from the kitchen, including South African street food such as the famed Bunny Chow, a type of curry served in hollowed-out bread. Sit back, relax, enjoy the music.

Shows

Sydney has some great dinner shows, some burlesque, some magic, all in great venues and fun. Try the **Crystal Boudoir** (GPO, 1 Martin Place, CBD, tel. 02/9229-7799, www.gposydney.com, Sat. 8:30pm-2am, $85 for a two-course meal). Right in the heart of the city, in the gorgeous old General Post Office building, this is a glamorous bar, restaurant, and show venue. In the dimly lit yet sparkling room there are choreographed dancers performing a variety of acts, from flamenco to burlesque to contortions. It has a distinctive Parisian 1920s nightclub atmosphere in historical surroundings.

El' Circo (41 Oxford St., Darlinghurst, tel. 02/8915-1899, http://slide.com.au, selected Fri. and Sat. nights 7pm, $109 pp) is hidden away from hopping Oxford Street. You come in through a door you'd nearly walk past and enter a cave of fun. Enjoy a nine-course degustation menu combined with nine circus acts. Created by French-born Marc Kuzma, El' Circo features circus acts influenced with the mysterious charm and flavor of Parisian or Berlin cabaret.

Or why not hop on a boat? Sydney is all about the harbor, after all. Set sail with **Sydney Showboats** (32 The Promenade, King Street Wharf 5, Darling Harbour, tel. 02/8296-7200, www.sydneyshowboats.com.au, from $120 pp) on an old-fashioned showboat and sail past the Sydney Harbour Bridge, Sydney Opera House, and the various islands while enjoying a three-course dinner on board. Then watch the one-hour show full of cancan dancing, sequins, feathers, and fishnet stockings—lively and fun.

THE ARTS

There is a thriving arts scene in Sydney. Be it visual art, performance art, music, or dance, Sydney offers many venues and events, but dates change and it is best to check what's on when you know your dates of travel. Certain organizations always showcase something interesting, however. This is a selection of permanent venues.

The Archibald Prize is Australia's most prestigious and controversial art award and has been going strong since 1921. It is awarded to the best portrait painting. Each year the trustees of the Art Gallery of NSW judge the Archibald and Wynne Prizes (awarded to best Australian landscape painting or figure sculpture) and invite an artist to judge the Sulman Prize (awarded to best subject painting, genre painting, or mural project in oil, acrylic, watercolor, or mixed media). The **Archibald Prize** (Art Gallery of NSW, The Domain) is held usually in fall or winter, but dates vary. All contenders for the prizes are shown and you're allowed to vote for your favorite portrait in the People's Choice award.

Bangarra (Pier 4, 15 Hickson Rd., Walsh Bay, tel. 02/9251-5333, www.bangarra.com.au) is Australia's leading Aboriginal performing arts company, weaving traditional and modern cultures seamlessly into its award-winning contemporary dance theater productions. Stunning, modern, challenging, and thought-provoking, the performances and productions are a new way of telling the indigenous stories. There are always several productions ongoing throughout the year, at different venues, such as the Sydney Opera House, and the company travels throughout Australia, so please check the calendar for dates.

The **Belvoir** (18 & 25 Belvoir St., Surry Hills, tel. 02/9699-3444, http://Belvoir.com.au), one of Australia's most pioneering and celebrated theater companies, has continuously made landmark productions available to the public and has over the years earned a myriad of prize nominations, and subsequent wins. Some have since been staged in New York, such as the 2013 production of *Peter Pan*. Both the Upstairs and Downstairs stages at the Belvoir have fostered the talents of prominent Australian artists, such as actors Geoffrey Rush and Cate Blanchett.

In the brick-and-iron buildings of the old Eveleigh Railyards, built between 1880 and 1889, **Carriageworks** (245 Wilson St., Eveleigh, tel. 02/8571-9099, http://carriageworks.com.au) hosts a diverse lineup of experimental music, theater, film, and fine art exhibitions. The largest multi-art venue in the country, it is home to contemporary arts organizations.

Sydney Theatre Company (The Wharf, Pier 4, Hickson Rd., Walsh Bay, tel. 02/9250-1700, www.sydneytheatre.com.au) is the premier theater company in Australia, and a major force in Australian drama since its establishment in 1978. The company presents an annual 12- to 13-play program at its home base, The Wharf; at the nearby new Sydney Theatre (22 Hickson Rd., Walsh Bay, tel.02/9250-1999), which Sydney Theatre Company also manages; and as the resident theater company of the Sydney Opera House.

The **Sydney Conservatorium of Music** (corner Bridge St. and Macquarie St., tel. 02/9351-1438, http://music.sydney.edu.au, Mon.-Sat. 8am-6pm, free) is open to visitors to inspect the eclectic architecture of its buildings, made up of a colonial main building, stables, and modern additions, making for a seemingly fortified structure reminiscent of a European castle. Bear in mind that it is a working school and performance venue, so access to some areas is not permitted. Regular concerts by students and visiting artists are held in the venue. For a schedule of events check the website.

FESTIVALS AND EVENTS

Australians love nothing better than a good party, and any excuse will do. The main annual events are listed here. For a detailed and up-to-date calendar of what's on when you are in the city, check www.visitnsw.com/events.

January

- **Australia Day** (www.australiaday.com.au): On January 26, Australians celebrate the spirit of Australia Day, which commemorates the arrival of the First Fleet, always making it into a long weekend filled with parades, music, events, barbecues, and lots of fun all across the city and the entire country.

- **Sydney Festival** (www.sydneyfestival.org.au): The city erupts into a frenzy of performing arts with over a fortnight of concerts, plays, circuses, and dance. There are some 300 performances in 100 events executed by more than 1,000 artists at various venues. The festival usually runs between January 8 or 9 until the 26th, depending on the days of the week.

February

- **Chinese New Year** (www.sydneychinesenewyear.com.au): Celebrate the Lunar New Year in late January or February, together with Sydney's large Chinese population. Numerous events, markets, and parades are held in Chinatown and throughout the city.

- **Sydney Gay & Lesbian Mardi Gras** (www.mardigras.org.au): Ongoing throughout the month, this is undoubtedly the biggest and most colorful parade and party in town. It attracts more than 20,000 visitors each year. Festivities are held on Oxford Street and at various venues.

March

- **Sydney Harbour Regatta** (www.shr.mhyc.com.au): Watch beautiful boats in a beautiful setting. More than 300 yachts and

Welcoming the New Year

There is no doubt that Sydney is naturally one of the most stunning cities on this Earth, but when it wants to, it can even improve on its natural beauty. Being one of the first cities to welcome a New Year, its fireworks spectacular has been watched by millions around the world, usually on television. But if you are in Australia, a visit to Sydney at New Year is an absolute must. There simply is no better celebration to watch live.

One of the first things to remember is that New Year down under falls in the middle of the summer holidays, so there is no need to wrap up warm—just put on your summery glad rags. Then, whatever you are planning to do, book early—organized venues and events places are limited and very sought-after.

The main focus of the celebrations is the **Sydney Harbour Bridge,** or the "old coat hanger," as it is affectionately known. A view of the opera house and the bridge are preferable, but fireworks are let off throughout the harbor, and a star-spangled flotilla of boats parades through the length of the harbor between the **two main fireworks events.** Yes, there are two occasions to see the magic happening in the sky: Traditionally Sydney sends off the first volley of fireworks at 9pm for the younger generation, and then the proper full works go off at midnight. The 9pm version is a smaller teaser-version of the fireworks to follow later on, but it's designed for the children, who can then be safely sent off to bed.

The **best place** to enjoy the night is on a **boat in the harbor,** and it is amazing how by midnight the water seems to have pretty much disappeared beneath the sea of boats. All types and sizes are puttering around the waterways, full of revelers and merry-makers. Many are private vessels, but plenty are ferries and cruise ships on which tickets for the night can be secured. Tickets usually include dinner, dancing, and a glass of bubbly at midnight, and prices range from 200 to several hundred dollars. Try the following companies: **All Occasion Cruises** (www.aocruises.com.au), **Sydney Harbour Cruises** (www.sydneyharbourcruises.com.au), **Stars Cruising Nightclub** (www.starscruisingnightclub.com.au), **Bass & Flinders Cruises** (www.newyearsevecruise.com.au), **Vagabond Cruises** (www.vagabond.com.au).

The **cheapest way** to enjoy the night is by **coming early,** and I mean early: Surprisingly, many camp overnight, and by 10am the really good spots are already taken, especially those by the opera house, at Mrs Macquarie's Chair in the Royal Botanic Gardens, or on any of the north shore beaches overlooking the bridge. This obviously takes planning and dedication, especially as numbers admitted and items taken are limited and scrutinized by security, ensuring that people don't get too squashed.

2,500 crew compete inshore and offshore, over two days of racing, on eight course areas and over 24 divisions. It's usually held the second weekend of the month.

- **Royal Easter Show** (www.eastershow.com.au): Since 1823 this nearly two-week-long event has celebrated Australia's best produce by showcasing animals, agricultural produce, free entertainment, and lots of fun. It's held at Sydney Olympic Park at the end of the month, running into April.

- **Opera on the Harbour** (http://operaonsydneyharbour.com.au): Once a year for a stretch of around six weeks, Sydney Opera moves to Farm Cove and performs under the stars in the most magical setting, overlooking the Sydney Opera House and Sydney Harbour Bridge with the Domain behind you.

April

- **Biennale of Sydney** (www.biennaleofsydney.com.au): Australia's largest contemporary visual arts event, presenting artist talks, performances, forums, exhibitions, and tours at various venues. It's held every two years, usually from the end of March until June.

New Year's Eve fireworks in Sydney Harbour

If you can afford a **splurge,** then being squashed need not be an issue and you can enjoy dinner and drinks in one of the many **hotels and bars** overlooking the harbor. But you will need to book early and be prepared to part with several hundred dollars per person for the privilege. Some of the best and priciest hot spots for the night are the **Shangri La** (www.shangri-la.com), with its suites overlooking the harbor and restaurants putting on special menus; the bar at the top of the Sydney Tower, **360 Bar & Dining** (www.trippaswhitegroup.com.au); or indeed the **Opera Bar** (www.operabar.com.au) below the opera house, where an entrance fee of some $300 is charged, excluding drinks.

Either way, it is a night not to be missed, and whatever your budget, Sydney does its best not to disappoint, and you will certainly welcome the New Year in a spectacular fashion. Check out www.sydneynewyearseve.com for planning tips and a program of events.

- **Mercedes-Benz Fashion Week Australia** (www.mbfashionweek.com.au): Usually held in mid-April for a week, this fashion extravaganza showcases Australia's emerging and established talent.

- **ANZAC Day:** On April 25, Australia remembers those who gave their lives in service to the country. Parades, memorial services, and celebrations are held throughout the city and country.

May

- **Vivid Sydney** (www.vividsydney.com): See the opera house lit up in psychedelic colors during this unique annual event of light, music, and ideas. Public exhibitions of outdoor light sculptures and installations, creative forums, concerts, and performances are held over a fortnight, usually at the end of the month into June.

June

- **Sydney Film Festival** (www.sff.org.au): Since 1954 (making it one of the world's longest running film festivals), this 12-day event held in mid-June has celebrated the best in Australian and international film, shorts, and documentaries.

July

- **Splendour in the Grass** (http://splendourinthegrass.com): One of Australia's biggest outdoor music festivals, this event stretches over three days with always great lineups. It's held at Byron Bay, just south of the city, at the end of the month.

August

- **City to Surf** (www.city2surf.com.au): In mid-August is Sydney's favorite sporting event and the world's largest run, with around 85,000 registered participants each year. The 14-kilometer course takes runners from Hyde Park to Bondi Beach.

- **Sydney Spring Racing Carnival** (www.australianturfclub.com.au): Held at Royal Randwick and Rosehill Gardens, this important day in horse racing is also a great excuse to get that hat out. Dates vary.

September

- **Festival of the Winds** (www.waverley.nsw.gov.au): Is there anything more beautiful to see in a beach setting and on a blue sky than colorful kites? The festival is held at Bondi Beach, along with markets, music, and lots of fun, usually from mid-September until early October.

October

- **Opera in the Vineyards** (www.operainthevineyards.com.au): Since 1995, this annual celebration of food, wine, and opera has been held in the beautiful Hunter Valley.

November

- **Sculpture by the Sea** (www.sculpturebythesea.com): Stretching along one of Australia's most scenic walks from Bondi Beach to Tamarama Beach, stunning sculptures are placed to enhance the already stunning views. It's usually held from late October to mid-November.

December

- **Carols in the Domain** (www.carolsinthedomain.com): Get into the Christmas mood even though the sun is shining by attending this traditional carol singing event in the Domain, usually held on December 21 or 22.

- **Rolex Sydney to Hobart Yacht Race** (www.rolexsydneyhobart.com): Held since 1945, this is the most iconic of yacht races down under. Participants from maxi yachts to weekend racers take part in this event, which starts from Nielsen Park in Sydney Harbour and takes the international fleet 628 nautical miles to the finish line in the Derwent River, Hobart. The race starts in Sydney on Boxing Day, December 26, and usually takes four days, but arrivals vary.

- **New Year's Eve** (www.sydneynewyearseve.com, www.new-years-eve-in-sydney.com): Sydney is the place to be at New Year's. On December 31, countless venues across the city hold celebrations, and fireworks can be seen.

Shopping

SHOPPING DISTRICTS AND SHOPPING CENTERS

Paddington is the hub of chic and contemporary Australian fashion and then some. Saunter along Oxford Street and find trendy fashion boutiques, quirky accessory shops, and the walk of fashion, a stretch of sidewalk dotted with plaque celebrating Australia's fashion-influencers, where you can test your Australian fashion knowledge. To see what shops are where, pick up an *Urban Walkabouts* booklet in any visitors center, or download the map at www.urbanwalkabout.com/paddington.

The **Queen Victoria Building (QVB)** (455 George St., CBD, tel. 02/9265-6800, www.qvb.com.au, lower ground and ground floors open Mon.-Sat. 9am-6pm, Sun. 11am-5pm; Level 1 and Level 2 open Mon.-Sat. 10am-6pm, Sun. 11am-5pm) is possibly the prettiest and grandest shopping mall in the world. First opened in 1898, the building replaced the old Sydney Markets and housed a hotel, a concert hall, numerous shops, warehouses, and markets in the basement. The Romanesque building, which was remodeled in the 1930s and then again restored in the mid-1980s, now houses numerous shops, cafés, and restaurants. Very generally speaking, it gets more expensive the higher up you go, with many designer stores such as Ralph Lauren on the upper levels and high street shops, services, and food courts in the basement. However, it's not just the shopping you come here for but the building itself: At Christmas the mid-entrance is literally filled with a gigantic Christmas tree, the toilets are well worth a visit for their heritage beauty, and even the staircases are pretty.

Built in the 1880s, the Victorian building housing the **Strand Arcade** (412-414 George St., CBD, tel. 02/9232-4199, www.strandarcade.com.au, Mon., Tues., Wed., Fri. 9am-5:30pm, Thurs. 9am-8pm, Sat. 9am-4pm, Sun. 11am-4pm) was one of the first in Sydney designed to take into account the harsh Australian climate. The roof was to be made of glass, specially tinted to reduce glare, and the access gallery of the top floor was projected to shade the lower levels. This is a lovely old shopping arcade in the vein of the Burlington Arcade in London, and then as now it is a refuge from the bustling George and Pitt Street shops, a collection of classy, high-quality select individual shops that reflect a bygone era. Stop for a hot chocolate and watch people saunter past. No rushing here—take your time and spend lots of time window shopping and browsing. It's part of the fun.

Westfield Sydney (188 Pitt St., CBD, tel. 02/8236-9200, www.westfield.com.au/sydney, Mon.-Sat. 9:30am-7pm, Sun. 10am-6pm) is a fantastic inner-city mall that offers anything and everything from luxury designer goods to home decor and gifts. Think Gucci and Prada, and think Zara and Gap—it's all under one roof. Spread over six shopping levels, it also allows access to Sydney Tower Eye and the 360 Bar & Dining restaurant and offers valet parking and a concierge desk, should you need help deciding.

CLOTHING AND ACCESSORIES

Nearly every big city has a **Burberry** (343 George St., CBD, tel. 02/8296-8588, http://au.burberry.com, daily 10am-6pm), Sydney being no exception. What makes this one special is the building. A former bank building, it is huge, with high ceilings and marble columns throughout. The sheer glamour of the surroundings making shopping here either better or quite unnecessary—just go for a look around.

When in Australia you'll find yourself needing a hat to protect you against the fierce

Stylish Sydney

Sydney is Australia's fashion capital and is flash, modern, rich, and stylish. The country's best designers have their seats here, and shopping has evolved to an art form. Here's where to stay, eat, shop, and, of course, be seen.

HOTELS

QT Hotel is part film set, part art gallery, part Las Vegas showgirls, with a dash of luxury bordello thrown in the mix. The hotel has taken over an old theater and has kept the grandeur, illusion, and eccentricity of that world. See and be seen.

Smaller but just as trendy, **Establishment Hotel** offers a fashionable stay in a former warehouse. Exposed brick balances the understated elegance; cushions offer a splash of color against sophisticated minimalist hues; and the heritage-meets-fashion theme is carried throughout.

SHOPS

Head for the **Queen Victoria Building (QVB)** to experience what is probably the chicest mall there is: This late-1800s structure is magnificent in its own right, with stunning architecture and intricate decor details. The great old building has been filled with myriad shops that have been selected to enhance the experience. Down below, you'll find the quite literal bargain basement. The higher up you go, the pricier and classier the shops, selling designer clothing, exquisite modern as well as antique jewelry, and accessories.

The Victorian **Strand Arcade** is great for browsing shops in the old-world style, complete with old-world service. Shops offer anything from cufflinks to hand-made shoes, from superb leather wares to beautiful straw hats.

To sample some of Australia's finest fashion, head straight for **Paddington.** Follow the fashion walk, with stars given to the local design talent. Snoop around the quirky individual boutiques for the latest trends and scoop up some unique accessories and decor items before relaxing in one of the many little cafés.

FOOD AND DRINK

Take pre- or après-dinner drinks at the **Opera Bar,** with its stunning views and eclectic clientele.

sun. **Hatworld** (81 George St., The Rocks, tel. 02/9252-3525, daily 9:30am-7:30pm) not only sells the iconic Outback Akura hats, worn by the truly rugged types, but also great straw hats, panamas, fedoras, and all sorts of head coverings, in a good range of sizes. Here you can go for quality rather than a last-minute purchase at the airport.

If you are looking for a good quality bag, suitcase, or any type of leather accessory, **Hunt Leather** (412 George St., CBD, tel. 02/9233-8702, www.huntleather.com.au, Mon.-Wed. 9am-6pm, Thurs. 9am-8pm, Sat. 9am-5pm, Sun. 11am-5pm) is the shop to look for it. Elegant, understated, timeless, yet modern, the items are lovely and you won't find them dangling from every other arm.

Originally started in Melbourne, **Shag** (34 Oxford St., Paddington, tel. 02/9357-2475, daily around noon-6pm) is a great vintage store stocking clothing (including pretty petticoat dresses and men's tuxedos), costume jewelry, bags and accessories from the 1920s to the 1970s, leather jackets, and tweeds, and you might even find the odd luxury designer treasure. It takes time to look through all the offerings, but the staff is knowledgable and can find things for you, even if you don't know what you want.

The Intersection (corner Oxford St. and Glenmore Rd., Paddington, tel. 02/4888-2359, www.theintersectionpaddington.com.au) is a fashion shopping destination developed with the clear vision to create a unique

shopping in the Queen Victoria Building

Anything goes, from long dresses prior to an opera event to touristy sneakers and backpacks, but you still can't beat the style and location.

Then move along to **Quay,** one of Sydney's best restaurants, where you might know the ingredients on the menu, but you'll be surprised by what the celebrity chef does with them. The inside is just as fashionable as the views across to the opera house, and you'll probably spot a celebrity or two as well.

FASHION

The annual **Mercedes-Benz Fashion Week Australia,** usually held around April, lures international fashion buyers, media, and celebrities to the city, which in turn dresses the part with many store windows designed to showcase participating designers.

retail environment focused exclusively around Australian designers. Numerous individual boutiques showcase the latest designers, high fashion but wearable and varied. Brands include Willow, Scanlan & Theodore, Jac + Jack, Ginger/Smart, and Ksubi. Hours vary per boutique, but most are open between 10am and 5:30pm.

Vanishing Elephant (Shop 3022, Westfield Bondi Junction, Bondi Junction, tel. 02/9389-4138, Mon.-Fri. 9:30am-6pm, Thurs. 9:30am-9pm, Sun. 10am-6pm) is a men's clothing store where you can get the perfect white shirt or checked shirt, cords, khakis, and more—stylish and modern yet classic outfits for work and leisure, designed by men for men.

GIFTS

With 95 percent of the world's opals being mined in Australia, it seems to be an obvious souvenir and gift, but there are so many different varieties and range in quality that expert advice is needed. **Australian Opal Cutters** (3/295-301 Pitt St., CBD, tel. 02/9261-2442, www.australianopalcutters.com, Mon.-Fri. 9am-6pm, Sat. 9am-5pm, Sun. 10am-5pm) has one of the largest selections of opals in Australia and knowledgable staff who can advise you.

Gannon House Gallery (45 Argyle St., The Rocks, tel. 02/9251-4474, www.gannonhousegallery.com, daily 10am-6pm) offers a great selection of Aboriginal and contemporary Australian art pieces for sale, ranging from lantern domes painted in the naive style that depict the Sydney cityscape to huge dotted paintings. While the vast Aboriginal paintings often cost a small fortune, smaller pieces are also typically Australian, and they make great gifts or souvenirs.

The museum shop **MCA** (Museum of Contemporary Art, 140 George St., The Rocks, tel. 02/9245-2458, Thurs. 10am-9pm, Fri.-Wed. 10am-5pm) is the place to find gifts that are a little out of the ordinary, including handcrafted jewelry, bags, unique home wares, limited edition artists' books (often signed), stationery, coffee-table books, and prints.

If you are looking for something quirky, **OPUS** (344 Oxford St., Paddington, tel. 02/9360-4803, Mon.-Sat. 10am-6pm, Sun. 11am-5pm) is your store, with lovely journals, select travel guides, assorted Sydney walks on playing cards, small home decor items, kitchen wares, gadgets and novelty items for the office, and more. It is impossible to leave without a little something.

Victoria's Basement (Queen Victoria Building, George St., tel. 02/9261-2674, Mon.-Sat. 9am-6pm, Sun. 11am-5pm) is a cheap, fun place to rummage for home items and great, lightweight souvenirs such as linen tea towels imprinted with Australian themes or Sydney cityscapes. It's definitely worth a look while you're in the QVB.

ANTIQUES AND CURIOS

Sydney Antique Centre (531 S. Dowling St., Surry Hills, tel. 02/9361-3244, www.sydantcent.com.au, daily 10am-6pm) is one of Australia's largest and oldest antiques centers, complete with café. With Australia being home to immigrants from all across the globe, the finds here can range from Art Deco French glass to Japanese netsuke, from Australiana to German china. With collectibles, jewelry, and even vintage clothing, this is a haven for treasure hunters.

Located in the basement of the Metcalf Arcade in The Rocks, **Bottom of the Harbour** (Metcalfe Arcade, 80 George St., The Rocks, tel. 02/9427-8107, Tues., Wed., Sat., and Sun. 9:30am-5:30pm, Mon., Thurs., and Fri. 9:30am-3:30pm) specializes in maritime antiques, curios, and trinkets. You can find anything from ship's steering wheels to glass floating devices and old coins. It's fun to rummage through, and maybe you'll find a pirate's treasure.

BOOKS

Ariel Booksellers (103 George St., The Rocks, tel. 02/9241-5622, www.arielbooks.com.au, daily 9am-late) is a lovely little bookshop specializing in coffee-table books covering architecture, art, design, and photography. It also sells the latest novels and a great assortment of kids' books. Together with its sister shop in Paddington (42 Oxford St., tel. 02/9332-4581, daily 9am-late), this is an independent venture and staffed by knowledgable and interested employees.

Probably Australia's best-loved book store, **Dymocks** (The Dymocks Building, 428 George St., CBD, tel. 02/9235-0155, Mon.-Fri. 9am-7pm, Thurs. till 9pm, Sat. 9:30am-5pm, Sun. 10am-5pm) is the Dymocks flagship store, going back to 1879 when young William Dymock commenced business as a bookseller in nearby Market Street. In 1922, the Dymock family started to build the historic, Art Deco landmark Dymocks building, completed in 1930. The store is very pretty, with an open mezzanine floor and wooden banisters keeping readers from toppling down. Dymocks has a great selection of books, some special offers, an assortment of great gifts, and a coffee shop in the back.

What goes together better than coffee and books? The cozy little **Gertrude & Alice Café Bookstore** (46 Hall St., Bondi Beach, tel. 02/9130-5155, weekdays 7:30am-11pm, weekends 7:30am-noon), lined with vintage books, was named after Gertrude Stein and Alice B. Toklas, and is always busy with people taking their time over their steaming cup of chai and browsing the shelves. There are some truly beautiful old editions of Australian kids' stories and many books paying homage to the owners' love of the 1920s and 1930s Paris literary circles.

Elizabeth's Books (343 Pitt St., CBD, tel. 02/9267-2533, www.elizabethsbookshop.com.au) sells both new and used books. An independent small bookstore, it offers little quirks the giant stores simply don't, such as a shelf full of books wrapped in brown paper, with merely two clues on the front as to what the story is about: "marooned on island" and "thriller," says one; "Australia" and "romance" says another. A great way to be a little more adventurous and discover new authors.

The Singaporean bookstore giant **Kinokuniya** (Level 2, The Galleries, 500 George St., CBD, tel. 02/9262-7996) is not quite as gigantic here in Sydney as elsewhere in the world, but it still has a fantastic selection of all current and classic books, with a nice travel corner. There's a good Asian selection, too, covering books about Asia, by Asian authors, and various Asian-language titles.

Accommodations

Sydney is a large, cosmopolitan city, and you can find a vast variety of accommodation options here. But it is expensive. As a general guideline, although there are youth hostels and budget options, you should allow around $200 per night for a basic room. Anything below that is a bonus. That said, if you book well in advance and take advantage of special offers, you should hopefully be able to secure something central and budget-friendly. The local transport system is fantastic, with trains easily accessed and taking you all across the city for a good price, but while you might save some money by staying a little farther out of town, finding accommodations near the center and paying a little extra is often worth it for the time and effort saved. Being able to walk back to your hotel for an afternoon rest is often the traveler's savior when sight-seeing. Room prices quoted are usually for the most basic double room, low-season, without breakfast unless mentioned.

THE ROCKS AND CIRCULAR QUAY

Under $150

Located at the south end of The Rocks toward the CBD, **The Menzies** (14 Carrington St., tel. 02/9299-1000, www.sydneymenzieshotel.com.au, from $149) offers basic but clean and comfortable standard rooms in single, double, and triple configuration. They are spacious enough to accommodate a family with up to two kids, while the superior rooms and suites offer separate living areas and more space. There is a breakfast restaurant, and three bars offer bar snacks, coffees, and wines. The hotel is a 1960s build, once a sought-after address that now has lost some of its initial accolade of being the first international hotel built after World War II. Despite its now quite stark exterior, it is a good value place to stay.

Napoleon on Kent (219 Kent St., tel. 02/9299-5588, http://napoleononkent.etourism.com.au, studio from $104) has very basic apartments in a modern-build block right underneath a thundering flyover along a relatively busy road, but the facilities are all there, and the rooms are modern and comfortable, with private baths and coffee-making facilities. The larger apartments have separate dining areas and kitchenettes. Not necessarily somewhere to linger, but if you're out all day and want somewhere cheap (for Sydney) to sleep, you could do a lot worse.

★ **Sydney Harbour YHA** (110 Cumberland St., tel. 02/8272-0900, www.yha.com.au, dorm beds from $39 pp per night, double rooms from $133 per night, four-person family rooms from $165 per night) is the only backpacker place within the historic Rocks district—a modern build alongside the historic setting. Views from the roof terrace (and some of the rooms) rival those of any five-star hotel. This is a gem many would forgo simply because it is a hostel, but the location and facilities are first class and offer dorm rooms as well as private doubles with en suite bathrooms.

$150-250

On a pier underneath the Sydney Harbour Bridge, the **Sebel Pier One Sydney Harbour** (11 Hickson Rd., tel. 02/8298-9999, www.sebelpierone.com.au, from $221) offers some of the best views in town. Minimalist rooms, decorated mostly in white with comfy couches and select art work, mostly photography, are designed to make the most of the views either across the harbor and Luna Park or of the bridge and The Rocks. The Sebel Suite even features an egg-shaped free-standing bath overlooking the harbor.

Dating back to the early 1800s, **The Russell Hotel** (143A George St., tel. 02/9241-3543, www.therussell.com.au, from $154) just off Nurses Walk is an attractive historic hotel full of character and history. Located on a street corner with a small turret above the entrance, it has many period features and quirky room layouts to accommodate its shape. Accommodations vary from a tiny single room with shared bathroom to a family-sized room with en suite facilities, with each room furnished uniquely, suiting its shape and with plenty of architectural and decoration features, from window seats to ceiling plaster roses. It all makes for a charming home away from home in a handy location.

Opposite Harbour Rocks Hotel, **Rendezvous Hotel Sydney The Rocks** (75 Harrington St., tel. 02/9251-6711, www.rendezvoushotels.com, from $230, terraces $360) is a little gem, offering basic and compact studios and larger apartments with and without harbor views. The modern glass entrance belies the fact that the hotel also includes small historic terraced houses next door to the main hotel with a living and entertaining area on the ground floor and bedroom and bathroom upstairs. The decor is modern, the views amazing, and the hotel has a small but enjoyable pool.

Over $250

With understated elegance, luxury, and some of the best views to be had in Sydney, the ★ **Park Hyatt Sydney** (7 Hickson Rd., The Rocks, tel. 02/9256-1234, www.sydney.park.hyatt.com, from $910) delivers and makes the most of all of it. The building itself is modern and not necessarily special, but the location cannot be beaten. You can get an Opera View room that would make pulling the curtains closed a crime. Swim in the stunning rooftop pool overlooking the harbor, the bridge, and the opera house, or enjoy an iconic afternoon tea with champagne, feeling part of Sydney high society. And you'll probably bump into some celebrities in the gym. This is a gorgeous property in a gorgeous location.

The views at the **Shangri-La Hotel** (176 Cumberland St., tel. 02/9250-6000, www.shangri-la.com/sydney, from $355) could hardly get any better. This large skyscraper on Sydney's skyline overlooks The Rocks as well as the harbor, the bridge, and the opera house. Add to that elegant understated hues of brown, tasteful interior decor, spacious rooms with dark-wood furnishings and marble bathrooms, and attentive staff, and you really feel special staying here.

In a beautiful historic Georgian-style building brought back to life, the stunning lobby at the **Harbour Rocks Hotel** (34 Harrington St., tel. 02/8220-9999, www.harbourrocks.com.au, from $349), with its high atrium, welcomes you with soft couches and a wall full of books. The rooms are decorated in elegant browns and have painted brick walls, with exposed brick also featuring in the restaurants. History is palpable throughout the building, built in 1887 on roughly the site of Sydney's first hospital. It's a perfect fit for its perfect location in the heart of The Rocks.

Plush luxury with chintz curtains and comfortable chairs and couches marks **The Langham Hotel Sydney** (89-113 Kent St., tel. 02/9256-2222, http://sydney.

langhamhotels.com.au, from $285) as a traditionally indulgent stay. The colonial-style modern building is decorated with plush luxury in mind. Rooms feature big soft beds and plenty of frilly cushions, linen chests, and all things comfy. The bathrooms and expansive indoor pool, though, are all modern marble, large and extravagant.

CENTRAL BUSINESS DISTRICT (CBD)

Under $150

On the western side of the CBD's main drag, George Street, the ★ **Travelodge Wynyard** (7-9 York St., tel. 02/9274-1222, from $129) is close to the attractions of The Rocks, Circular Quay, and the shops on George Street, and near the train stop of Wynyard, which connects you to the rest of Sydney with ease. Rooms are in understated hues with an abstract print as a splash of color, and they feature a small desk and coffee- and tea-making facilities. As compared to some lower budget stays, this hotel offers a number of amenities: a gym, in-house breakfast, lunch and dinner options, a lobby bar, and in-house laundry.

The **Park Regis City Centre** (27 Park St., tel. 02/9267-6511, www.parkregiscitycentre.com.au, from $144) is a functional hotel without frills, but it boasts a great location and is perfect for simply crashing at night and saving the travel budget for more exciting things. Rooms range from extremely compact (don't opt for the Express Room unless you are a tiny person who travels extremely light) to rather nice, spacious with colored feature walls decorated with modern abstract prints, and views across the city. Amenities include a rooftop pool and a gym, and the hotel delivers well for the price.

Although first impressions may not necessarily be the best, judging by the drab and nondescript outside and the small lobby, the rooms in the ★ **Best Western Plus Hotel Stellar** (4 Wentworth Ave., tel. 02/9264-9754, www.hotelstellar.com, from $130) are spacious, clean, and decorated in an attractive modern style. Small kitchenettes offer the ease of making a coffee in the room or reheating a take-out meal in the microwave, and you simply cannot beat the location. On the corner of Hyde Park and Oxford Street, it's 1.6 kilometers (a 10-minute walk) from Circular Quay and within skipping distance of the shops and sights of the CBD, and 2.1 kilometers from trendy Paddington. There is a bar downstairs.

The **Hotel Coronation** (7 Park St., tel. 02/9266-3100, www.hotelcoronation.com.au, from $109) is basic and simple, with rooms that (apart from the suites) are on the compact side. Being a skip away from the city's shops and sights, this hotel offers location over luxury, and for the location, the prices are great. The large and popular bar downstairs could be a positive or negative point, depending on when you are staying and your demographic, with sleep bound to be somewhat disrupted during weekend nights but much quieter midweek.

$150-250

The fashionable ★ **Establishment Hotel** (5 Bridge Ln., tel. 02/9240-3100, http://merivale.com.au, from $249), in a former warehouse, has 31 sleek and contemporary rooms, all with high ceilings and marble or bluestone baths. Interiors are a mix of colonial heritage and modern with two design schemes: one Japanese-influenced with dramatic black-stained wooden floors, the other decorated in bleached oak and muted fabrics. It is part of a small entertainment complex that is a hub for cool Sydneysiders; the **Hemmesphere Lounge, Tank Club,** and **Gin Garden** are always busy, and chef Peter Doyle has won plenty of accolades for his innovative take on modern Australian cuisine at **Est.** restaurant.

Right on Hyde Park, along chic Elizabeth Street with the museums and Macquarie Street historic sites a brief saunter away, the **Sheraton on the Park** (161 Elizabeth St., tel. 02/9286-6000, www.sheratononthepa-rksydney.com, from $199) is perfectly placed. Rooms range from simple rooms city-side (no views to speak of) to suites overlooking the park and the harbor in the distance. All are spacious, modern, and comfortable, and the hotel, for a worldwide chain, is individual and inviting. A rooftop pool, health spa, gym, bars and restaurants, plus the Sheraton Club level, make it a great stay at a really convenient location.

With only 36 rooms, the **Park8 Hotel** (185 Castlereagh St., tel. 02/9283-2488, www.park8.com.au, from $209) feels like a private residence rather than an inner city hotel. A Victorian multistory on a corner just by Hyde Park, this little boutique hotel is within easy walking distance of the city shops and sights. Rooms are small but comfortable, with a modern understated decor in hues of gray with the splash of color being a rug or cushions, and there is the option of a split-level two-bed apartment with kitchenette and separate living area.

If you are an Art Deco fan, ★ **The Grace Hotel** (77 York St., tel. 02/9272-6888, www.gracehotel.com.au, from $189) is for you. Located in the iconic Grace Building, designed by Morrow & Gordon and built by Kell & Rigby during the late 1920s, it was opened in 1930 by Grace Brothers, the Australian department store magnates, as their headquarters, and the exterior and the grand lobby are fine examples of the period. The rooms themselves have been renovated in elegant hues of brown and olive, with clean modern furniture befitting the building.

The Grace Hotel

Over $250

Right in the center of the city, the flamboyant, quirky, and thoroughly decadently modern **QT Hotel** (49 Market St., tel. 02/8262-0000, www.qtsydney.com.au, from $450) does not fit into any general hotel category. Entering the hotel feels like stepping into a movie full of props and dressing up. The building used to be a theater, and the general idea of it is still very much alive. Glitzy and glam Las Vegas meets theatrical Sydney—perfect for those who want to make a short stay in Sydney a unique experience.

The **Sir Stamford at Quay** (93 Macquarie St., tel. 02/9252-4600, www.stamford.com, from $275) offers accommodations brimming with old world luxury in the form of antique furniture, crystal chandeliers, and open fireplaces, and even a Steinway grand piano in the Presidential Suite, together with modern amenities of pool and gym and a superb location. Most Deluxe rooms have French doors opening up to balconies, and even the slightly smaller Superior rooms have antique executive desks. All have superior and elegant but comfortable decor. It all makes for a memorable stay. The well-dressed staff and enormous collection of art are reminiscent of a grand hotel in London, and it might be a little much if you are more the flip-flop type.

Imagine a corner window with views across the Sydney Opera House, Circular Quay, and Sydney Harbour Bridge—it does not come much better than that. The ★ **Four Seasons Sydney** (199 George St., tel. 02/9250-3100, www.fourseasons.com/sydney, from $250) offers a variety of rooms with a variety of views: city view (over George Street), city/harbor views (part city, some harbor), and harbor views (all harbor with both opera house and bridge). The rooms themselves are held in understated muted hues, with sleek furniture, but comfortable and homey. Add to that the Endota spa, the liveried staff holding the doors open for you, and the perfect setting at the end of George Street, just across from Circular Quay by The Rocks, and you have a treat of a stay, which is also great for families. Not only can they use Sydney's largest heated outdoor pool, but the concierge has specialized knowledge of family activities around the city, and the room service menu's kids' selection has been developed with the help of the executive chef's daughter, who chose a few of her favorites. Another great addition is the Executive Club Access to the club lounge, which you can opt for daily, whichever room type you are staying in: For $70 for a single person or $105 per couple per day, you get breakfast, Internet access, all day access to coffee, tea, beautiful savory and sweet snacks, soft drinks, and peace and quiet, making the investment a definite saving if you were considering paying for it all separately.

In the old General Post Office building right in the center of the city, steps from the shops, restaurants, and sights, **The Westin** (1 Martin Pl., tel. 02/8223-1111, www.westin.com, from $246) gives you the best of two worlds: rooms located in the old post office building, and rooms in the modern tower above the old GPO, offering you the choice of either super modern luxury rooms or heritage rooms with high ceilings, rounded windows, and older decor and features. It is a large hotel, but well organized with plenty of great restaurants and bars on the premises and even a small museum exhibit of the old Tank Stream in the basement. Whichever you opt for, all rooms are comfortable, with modern amenities, and some of the ones higher up have great views.

At the Circular Quay end of bustling Pitt Street, steps away from the ferries and train connections across Sydney and the restaurants and bars along Bridge Street, the **Sydney Harbour Marriott Hotel at Circular Quay** (30 Pitt St., tel. 02/9259-7000, www.marriott.com.au/Sydney-Hotel, from $279) is a large, comfortable, and perfectly positioned option. The guest rooms are elegant and stylish, more so than the lobby would suggest, and the higher rooms have stunning views across the harbor.

DARLING HARBOUR AND HAYMARKET

Under $150

★ **Metro Hotel Sydney Central** (431-439 Pitt St., Haymarket, tel. 02/9281-6999, www.metrohotels.com.au, from $130) is within walking distance of the CBD, Haymarket, and Darling Harbour, and a stone's throw from the central train station, making it a perfect hub for the city and surroundings. The hotel is also on the pickup list for most bus tours around and out of Sydney. The rooms are spacious, clean, and comfortable and surprisingly quiet considering the closeness of the Capitol Theatre opposite and the many bars and little Asian eateries nearby. This is a great, affordable option for inner Sydney.

Simple and basic, but in a location surrounded by the Darling Harbour restaurants, **Ibis Sydney King Street Wharf** (22 Shelley St., King Street Wharf, Darling Harbour, tel. 02/8243-0700, from $111) is a place to sleep after a day's worth of sightseeing, not necessarily a place to spend hours in your room. Functional and modern, the rooms offer tea- and coffee-making facilities and a small refrigerator, plus there's a bar downstairs.

With a bustling location, **The Woolbrokers at Darling Harbour** (22 Allen St., Pyrmont, tel. 02/9552-4773, standard single rooms from $69, double from $85) is an old-fashioned hostel, with old-fashioned furniture making it much cozier than most. Room options range from single with shared baths, en suite rooms, and family rooms to group rooms sleeping up to eight with bunks included. The accommodations are basic, but all rooms are outfitted with TVs, tea- and coffee-making facilities, and a fridge. Features include breakfast rooms (breakfast $7.50), a courtyard, and guest laundry.

$150-250

The large 525-room **Novotel Darling Harbour** (100 Murray St., Darling Harbour, tel. 02/9934-0000, www.novoteldarlingharbour.com.au, from $209) dominates the harbor's skyline and offers everything you'd expect from a global chain. There are various restaurants, a gym, pool, tennis courts, and a wide selection of rooms from single to spacious two-level loft suites with a variety of views, with the one across Darling Harbour being so good that you won't want to go out at night. The rooms themselves are of clean modern decor, hues of beige, brown, and orange, with a small desk and comfy chair. Within a two-minute walk of all the nearby attractions and a mere 10 minutes from the city center, this is a family-friendly (with regular family discounted offers) and comfortable stay.

Australia's largest hotel, with 683 rooms, the **Four Points by Sheraton Sydney** (161 Sussex St., Darling Harbour, tel. 02/9290-4000, www.fourpointssydney.com, from $175) is located between Darling Harbour and the CBD, making it easy to access both within minutes. And it being the large hotel and chain it is, you get all the conveniences only a hotel that size can offer, barring perhaps the personal touch. Rooms are simply furnished with a lot of wood veneer and fresh turquoise accents—simple and functional, nothing plush. It's a business and leisure hotel, so you also get large meeting and conference venues, a pub, a bar, and a buffet-style restaurant, plus a leisure center, slick service, contemporary rooms, and location.

The self-contained ★ **Oaks Goldsborough Apartments** (243 Pyrmont St., Darling Harbour, tel. 02/8586-2500, www.oakshotelsresorts.com, $109 for a studio to $315 for a two-bed executive apartment with harbor view) are located very conveniently next to Darling Harbour, a five-minute walk into the CBD. The vast historic red-brick building, built in 1883, is an old wool store that has been converted into modern apartments with kitchens fully equipped with all utilities, making this a great option for longer-term stays and families.

Over $250

The Darling (The Star, 80 Pyrmont St., Pyrmont, tel. 02/9777-9000, www.thedarling.com.au, from $309), named one of the 60 best new hotels in the world in 2012 by *Condé Nast Traveler*, is part of The Star, a luxury development with shopping, casino, spa, restaurants, and accommodations at the end of Darling Harbour. The modern glass building sits just off the residential area of Pyrmont, and the understated exterior belies the sumptuous interior. Accommodation options range from the standard 35-square-meter Darling rooms upwards to the penthouse, each with distinctive designs and decor, all luxurious. The penthouse is simply mind-blowing, with amazing views through the floor-to-ceiling windows. Very modern in-room technology operates everything from the blinds to the TV to the wake-up calls. Features include adult-only floors, Molton Brown cosmetic goodies, and a level of service that puts many other top hotels to shame.

Also part of The Star development, in the same shiny glass tower, the **Astral Tower** (The Star, 80 Pyrmont St., Pyrmont, tel. 02/9777-9000, www.star.com.au, from $309) offers one- to three-bedroom apartments, easy access to all The Star facilities, and a choice of views across the harbor or the city. The rooms are in understatedly elegant brown and gray hues with natural wood accents and plush carpets; many have window seats to make the most of the views. Considering the closeness to restaurants and the casino, the hotel has a strict no-party policy and monitors alcohol consumption, to ensure guests get the rest they deserve.

The ★ **1888 Hotel** (139 Murray St., Pyrmont, tel. 1800/818-880, www.1888hotel.com.au, from $179) has reached some fame as reportedly the first Instagram hotel in the world, encouraging guest to post pictures of the chic interior and offering a "selfie" space. The hotel is certainly modern and combines the heritage setting well with its trendy outlook. The imposing brick building still has many of the original 1888 features, such as three-meter-high ceilings in the rooms, large exposed beams and bare brickwork, and large old windows; even the sign 1888 on the outside had to remain in place, as it is a listed building. Add to that minimalist modern furniture and artwork, and the combination works surprisingly well. Rooms range from tiny (Shoebox, 15 square meters) to relatively roomy (The Attic, 30 square meters inside and 17 square meters on an outdoor patio), but all have smart interiors and are equipped with free Wi-Fi, media hubs, and free access to the large swimming pool at the Ian Thorpe Aquatic Centre across the road. A great and unusual place.

KINGS CROSS AND DARLINGHURST

Under $150

Next door to the popular celebrity-chef-owned Hugo's Restaurant in Kings Cross, **The Bayswater** (17 Bayswater Rd., Kings Cross, tel. 02/8070-0100, www.sydneylodges.com, from $130) offers chic, clean-cut accommodations in a bustling hub, just around the corner from the big Coke sign. It might be a little noisy on weekends, but you're probably joining the revelers anyway.

The Challis Lodge (21-23 Challis Ave., Potts Point, tel. 02/9358-5422, www.sydneylodges.com, from $65) is a basic guesthouse that offers simple and modern rooms with an option of shared or en suite bathroom facilities, a communal kitchen, and laundry facilities, in a lovely period building in the colonial style, complete with arched and columned wrap-around verandas.

$150-250

Formerly The Storrier, **Quest Potts Point** (15 Springfield Ave., Kings Cross, tel. 02/8988-6999, www.questapartments.com.au, petite studio from $150) was inspired by contemporary Australian artist Tim Storrier. This little apartment hotel is tucked in a lane a couple of hops from Macleay Street, the bustling Kings Cross main thoroughfare. The snazzy interior includes monochrome upholstery, striped lampshades, and unusual pieces of art, and a rooftop terrace has great views across the city. The studios are small but adequate—a good value.

In a renovated heritage building dating back to 1892, **Simpsons of Potts Point** (8 Challis Ave., Potts Point, tel. 02/9356-2199, www.simpsonshotel.com, from $235) was originally known as Killountan and consists of two adjoining buildings: the main house at the front and a servants' wing at the rear. A meandering big brick and timber house with myriad gables, nooks, and crannies, its style is Victorian cum Arts and Crafts. In the heart of chic residential area Potts Point, yet a mere five-minute walk from bustling Kings Cross, this is an accommodation option that is secluded and private. Homey rooms have a personal touch, each one decorated individually and cozy, with bedspreads, armchairs, and heritage-style decor, and you won't want to leave the old-fashioned library/drawing room, which has an open fire in winter.

Over $250

A Victorian townhouse in a quiet residential area, the historic exterior of the ★ **Medusa Hotel** (267 Darlinghurst Rd., Darlinghurst, tel. 02/3991-1000, www.medusa.com.au, from $310) belies its funky and luxurious interior. The little boutique hotel's 18 rooms range from Grand Rooms in the old part of the building, with high ceilings and larger sizes, to more compact rooms in the back. Either way, the rooms are a mix of contemporary and historic, with great pieces of colorful, modern furniture coupled with the architectural character of the original building. Individual, artfully designed, and full of character, the Medusa offers an individual stay close to the city and the hub of Kings Cross.

The Contemporary (Surrey St.,

Darlinghurst, tel. 02/9698-4661, www.tct-sydneyaccommodation.com.au, from $295 per night for a three-night stay) is one of three properties dotted throughout Sydney's central suburbs developed by the so-called "tastemaker of Sydney," Geoff Clark. The one-off boutique one-bedroom apartments are designed individually and tastefully, like someone's private home. Rooms are available on a three-night-minimum basis, unless you are willing to pay an inflated price for one night (from $475). The Contemporary has charcoal painted walls full of quirky artwork, and rooms are accented with wooden tables, seedpod-like lamps, earthy African-style rugs and cushions, and even the odd trunk and suitcase to complete the tasteful "travel-the-world" theme of its decor. Small, but big enough to sleep two, each apartment has a tiny kitchen and amenities in the bathroom. Even a beach towel and picnic basket are provided. This is a home away from home with restaurants and cafés within easy walking distance.

PADDINGTON

Under $150

The Arts Hotel (21 Oxford St., tel. 02/9361-0211, www.arthotel.com.au, from $134) is perfectly located for access to Paddington, Darlinghurst, and, via bus, the CBD and Bondi. Small, modern, and simply decorated, this hotel is affordable and handy for a brief city break.

Paddington is a mostly residential area, and the charm lies often behind the individual buildings you normally can't get access to, so why not rent a vacation property and stay right among those who live here? **HomeAway** (www.homeaway.com.au, from $100 per night) offers properties ranging from studio apartments to gorgeous Victorian terraces, sleeping between two to more than 10 people, depending on the property.

$150-250

★ **Kathryn's on Queen** (20 Queen St., 02/9327-4535, www.kathryns.com.au, from $180) is a lovely little boutique bed-and-breakfast in a heritage-listed Victorian terrace, situated a stone's throw from the fashion district in Paddington. The rooms are light and airy, decorated in the shabby chic style: comfortable, stylish, and lovingly worn furniture that complements the setting. Le Attic overlooks the city's skyline and the harbor bridge from the top of the building, while Le Grand looks out on Queen Street and has its own balcony and marble fireplace. Both have private bathrooms.

★ **The Hughenden** (14 Queens St., Woollahra, tel. 02/9363-4863, www.thehughenden.com.au, from $158) is in a rambling white Victorian villa built in the 1870s, and it embraces both the antique features and the slight shabbiness that comes with old buildings. Many rooms, however, have been renovated, so fear not. Antique furniture, matching curtains and bedcovers, cushions, and old-fashioned bedside lamps make the rooms cozy and in keeping with the style of the house. This is a pet-friendly hotel, so if you don't want to risk hairs in your room, ask for a non-pet room. The location is fantastic for Paddington and Centennial Park, and the buses into the CBD and Bondi depart a few steps away.

THE NORTHERN SHORE

Under $150

Falcon Lodge (182 Falcon St., North Sydney, tel. 02/9955-2358, www.falconlodge.com.au, from $41), in a terrace of Federation buildings, offers a range of very simple rooms, some with shared bathroom facilities, others en suite. Select rooms have a small kitchenette where you can prepare basic meals. A shared kitchen, laundry facilities, weekly linen service, and free Wi-Fi make this popular with longer-stay guests and families on a budget.

A campsite/caravan park, **Lane Cove River Tourist Park** (Plassey Rd., Macquarie Park, tel. 02/9888-9133, lccp@environment.nsw.gov.au, from $37 for an unpowered site), right in the heart of Lane Cove National Park, is shady and restful and offers the usual amenities, such as shared bathroom blocks, laundry facilities, camp kitchen, a recreation room with a TV, and a pool. A kiosk sells basic supplies, and there's public transport from North Ryde Station, some 700 meters from the site.

$150-250

Vibe Hotel North Sydney (88 Alfred St., North Sydney, tel. 02/8272-3300, www.vibehotels.com.au, from $143) is just a skip away from Milsons Point train station and a brief stroll from the ferry stop, connecting you with Sydney's CBD and its attractions within easy public transport reach of 5-10 minutes, yet the prices at this sleek modern hotel seem much farther away from the city center. The rooms all offer reasonable space with a small seating area, and many have a view across the harbor. The hotel has its own pool (overlooking pretty Lavender Bay) and a sauna, and also offers free access to the Olympic swimming pool nearby and packages to Luna Park.

Near the ferry point, allowing you access to Sydney within a 10-minute ride, the modern **Harbourside Apartment Hotel** (2a Henry Lawson Ave., McMahons Point, tel. 02/9963-4300, http://harboursideapartments.com.au, studios from $209) offers a variety of accommodations, from studio apartments to one- and two-bedroom apartments. Each can be had without a view or with views across the bridge toward the opera house. All apartments are in neutral earthy tones with light blue accents, modern and elegant furnishings, and, if you opt for a larger apartment, comfy couches and chairs. Except for the studios, the apartments come with full kitchens. A harborside pool, barbecue facilities, guest laundry and dry-cleaning service, a daily paper, and access to the popular **Sails on Lavender Bay** restaurant make this a family friendly and comfortable place to stay, with rates becoming more budget friendly if you are staying a longer term, such as 10 days.

In the suburbs, ★ **Cremorne Point Manor** (6 Cremorne Rd., Cremorne Point, www.cremornepointmanor.com.au, tel. 02/9953-7899, from $75 for single room with shared shower to $259 for en suite King Spa suite) is a fully restored late 1800s federation-style double-story villa with balustrade balconies and verandas, less than a 10-minute ferry ride from the CBD, with great views from some rooms and the roof terrace. Rooms are simply furnished but with nice touches such as cushions and bedspreads; it's not high quality furniture, but it's functional. At this family-run boutique place, it is the small details that make this special: a robe and slippers, little toiletries in the bathrooms, and lovely art collected from around the world set in beautiful frames. Nooks and crannies where you can sit with a cup of tea and a book make this a great place away from Sydney, yet near to Sydney.

Over $250

★ **Roar and Snore** (Bradleys Head Rd., Mosman, tel. 02/9978-4791, www.taronga.org.au/roarandsnore, weekdays from $288 adult, $184.50 child, weekends from $320 adult, $205 child, includes all meals and drinks, strictly no BYO) is the best place to sleep for a night, if you have kids or you are one at heart. You're right in the zoo, with amazing views across the harbor to the bridge and opera house with the Sydney skyline on the horizon, and the animals are just outside the (small) fence surrounding the camp. And it *is* camping. The tents are spacious, with two or three beds in them, but that is pretty much it, although the site offers everything you'll need (all amenities, beds, linens, etc., are provided). You obviously have access to the zoo, and you will meet a "creature" (depending on whose turn it is) and get a behind-the-scenes look. Plus there's tea and nibbles upon arrival, dinner, and a light breakfast before you leave.

THE BEACHES

Bondi

On the hill behind the Iceberg swimming pool, halfway to Tamarama Beach, the clean and friendly ★ **Bondi Beachouse YHA** (63 Fletcher St., Bondi Beach, tel. 02/9365-2088, www.yha.com.au, beds from $30) is still within easy walking distance of the two beaches and all the action down on Bondi. The accommodations are mostly shared rooms, but there are also some double rooms with private bathrooms (from $90). The hostel has a communal kitchen, barbecue, free snorkeling gear, and surfboards for hire. A small supermarket is just round the corner, and there are plenty of backpacker pubs and eateries nearby.

Two minutes from the beach and the shops, the spacious apartments at **Adina Bondi Beach** (69-73 Hall St., Bondi Beach, tel. 02/9300-4800, www.adinahotels.com.au, studio from $249) are decorated in sandy tones, complemented by light turquoise and blues and timber accents, reflecting their famous location. Ranging from studios to one- to three-bedroom apartments, all have balconies, kitchens, and laundry and living areas, and the hotel offers a grocery delivery service. Interconnecting rooms make it easy to expand the apartments to a size you need.

You can't get any more central than **Ravesi's Hotel** (118 Campbell Parade, Bondi Beach, tel. 02/9365-4422, www.ravesis.com.au, from $269). Overlooking the beach and promenade, Ravesi's Hotel is mostly a restaurant plus wine and cocktail bar on two levels. But 12 individual rooms have stylish half-rounded windows (alas, only a couple overlook the seafront), with modern and quite masculine decor: walls in dark chocolate hues and golden-brown accents set with pieces of art and cushions. The rooms offer a more urban than beach experience, but if you want to be where Bondi is happening, this is it.

Coogee

A large hotel resort overlooking lovely Coogee Beach, the **Crowne Plaza Coogee Beach** (242 Arden St., Coogee, tel. 02/9315-7600, www.crowneplaza.com, from $208) offers all the amenities and facilities you'd ask for in a well-known chain hotel. There are several dining options, a health club, and access to several nearby pools, and the beach is just across the road. Contemporary in design, the rooms are open and airy, and all offer a comfortable chair and desk area, as well as in-room dining. Guests in the ocean-view rooms have been known to see whales from their balcony.

Tamarama

The **Tama Beach House** (22 Deliview St., Tamarama, tel. 02/9365-0259, http://tamabeach.com, from $98) is divided into four separate apartments, which offer a private self-contained vacation experience. The house itself is a large white modern building with the pool, and the inside is fresh and beachy, with lots of white and turquoise and wood befitting the summery location. A good-size pool-view studio on the ground floor opens to the paved pool area and has a kitchen, living area, and free Wi-Fi. The ocean-view apartment (from $150) has two bedrooms and offers stunning views across the little Tamarama Beach, just a 20-minute walk from Bondi along the gorgeous beachfront walk. A small but airy pool-view studio has the shower in the kitchen area, and a pool-view apartment includes a separate bedroom, living and dining area, plus outside seating.

Manly

From dorm rooms to private en suite rooms, the **Manly Boardrider** (63 The Corso, Manly, tel. 02/9977-6677, www.boardrider.com.au, from $30 for a dorm bed, $125 for deluxe room with bathroom) is a hostel cum motel, but a place to party rather than sleep. Modern, basic, and clean, it is the destination for backpackers in Manly. It's right there on the Corso, among the pubs, nightclubs, and all the action. There are daily organized activities ranging from beach volleyball to pub crawls, from quiz nights to barbecues. Never a dull—or quiet—moment.

Right out on the point where Sydney Harbour meets the Tasman Sea, ★ **Q Station** (1 North Head Scenic Dr., Manly, tel. 02/9466-1500, www.qstation.com.au, from $133) is an idyllic spot right in the Sydney Harbour National Park. This former quarantine station dates back to 1832, with original historic buildings still dotted around the site. A selection of colonial-style, beautifully restored, and in places modern main buildings, together with a handful of renovated historic cottages, nestle in the green surroundings. Wrap-around verandas and balconies, together with a lot of decking, and wood used in the interior give the space a light and airy atmosphere. This hotel resort is a destination in itself, with Sydney being a place you visit on day trips. Here you go for walks, snorkel, kayak, or simply enjoy sitting on the terrace and watching the myriad boats on the harbor. It offers a good deal of variety—heritage rooms, deluxe harbor-view rooms, private and secluded retreat suites, and the separate historic cottages in the national park. There are restaurants and bars, and a concierge service organizes your day trips for you, should you really want to leave.

The Sebel Manly Beach (8-13 S. Steyne, Manly, tel. 02/9977-8866, www.accorhotels.com, from $233) is on the beachfront at Manly, 30 minutes from Sydney's CBD by fast ferry. The 83 spacious rooms in the light and modern building dominated by large windows have private balconies to make the most of the views. The rooms are simply and tastefully decorated, in light earthy colors. A casual beachside restaurant offers anything from breakfast through to a glass of wine over dinner. There is a pool and sauna, and the hotel offers baby-sitting on request.

The beachfront **Novotel Sydney Manly Pacific** (55 N. Steyne, Manly, tel. 02/9977-7666, www.novotelmanlypacific.com.au, from $242) is a sister to the Novotel Darling Harbour, but on a smaller scale. The modern building is functional, with 213 guest rooms ranging from single rooms to family rooms and two-bedroom suites. The rooms are spacious, in beige and brown tones—simple but comfortable. This is a modern "all singing and dancing" hotel of a chain that knows what it's doing when it comes to around-the-world guest services and facilities, with several bars and restaurants and a pool. There's also a play center for the kids and plenty of special family-friendly offers.

Food

THE ROCKS AND CIRCULAR QUAY

Often voted the best restaurant in Australia, ★ **Quay** (Upper Level, Overseas Passenger Terminal, The Rocks, tel. 02/9251-5600, www.quay.com.au, lunch Tues.-Fri. noon-2:30pm, dinner daily 6pm-10pm, three-course lunch menu from $130, four-course dinner menu from $175) also comes with the best views. Next to Sydney Harbour Bridge, looking across to the Sydney Opera House, this modern glass-encased eatery by celebrity chef Peter Gilmore delights with simply stunning dishes. You will recognize the names of most of the ingredients, but what the chef does with them is pretty much out of this world. Your steak, for example, is prepared with grains and miso, your fish would be a Tasmanian trumpeter with smoked oyster crackling, and for dessert you must have the snow-egg, which you crack open to reveal custardy goodness inside. This treat for all the senses, while expensive, is truly worth it.

On a corner plot in the heart of The Rocks, ★ **Baroque** (Bushells Pl., 88 George St., tel. 02/9241-4811, www.baroquebistro.com.au, daily 8am-3pm, fine dining Thurs.-Sat. 6pm-late) is a great place to sit outside and watch the bustling life around you while munching on pan-roasted barramundi, Australia's best-loved fish, with globe artichoke and zucchini ($26). If you are less hungry, a simple croque monsieur might do ($17). Baroque is split into a daytime bistro and a nighttime fine dining restaurant and wine bar. Come for dinner in the copper-accented modern indoor setting with open kitchen, and be wowed by the French chef's beautifully constructed and prepared plates, a fusion of French and modern Australian cuisine. The dishes usually look too pretty to eat, but if you have to, try something innovative, such as the beetroot starter with hay and goat curd, followed by the quinoa-encrusted lamb loin with onion puree and olive jus (mains $38).

Step out of Sydney and straight into Paris at **Ananas** (18 Argyle St., The Rocks, tel. 02/9259-5668, www.ananas.com.au, lunch Mon.-Fri. noon-3pm, dinner Mon.-Wed. 6pm-midnight, Thurs.-Sat. 6pm-3am, bar open Mon.-Fri. from noon, Sat. from 4pm, mains $37). The Art Deco interior is as chic as the exposed brick of this heritage building, and the food is *délicieuse,* including traditional steak frites, oysters shucked to order, a superb wild mushroom pappardelle, and a hint of truffle lingering in the air. Dress up, grab a champagne flute, and enjoy being with the young and beautiful of Sydney. Stay until the morning. Reportedly the urinals are somewhat scandalous—red-lipped, like an open mouth (the author apologizes for not being allowed a close look to check that statement).

Australia is known for its steaks on the barbecue, and at **Phillip's Foote Restaurant** (101 George St., The Rocks, tel. 02/9241-1485, www.phillipsfoote.com.au, Mon.-Sat. noon-midnight, Sun. noon-10pm) that is exactly what you get. You buy your steak at the counter, take it to the communal barbecue outside in the yard by the little lane called Suez Canal, and you cook the steak to your liking. Help yourself from the salad bar, top up with sauces and bread, and that's that. If you think $32 for a steak, salad, potatoes, and bread is a lot considering you are doing the cooking and serving yourself, maybe you're right, but it is fun, and you'll have a new experience—and a decent steak. There are also fish and chicken options. The restaurant itself is an unpretentious old-fashioned pub, absolutely no frills, but cooking a steak on the barbie with some mates—you don't get more Aussie than that.

The Vintage Café (3 Nurses Walk, The Rocks, tel. 02/9252-2055, www.vintagecafe.com.au, Mon.-Wed. 10:30am-4:30pm, Thurs.-Fri. 10:30am-9:30pm, Sat.-Sun. 9am-9:30pm) is ideal for a lunchtime snack. You can choose from tapas or various sharing plates, with mostly Mediterranean food options. Tapas are around $11 per plate; paella for two is $58. The café is in a great building with exposed bricks and beams, quirky roofing, and a historic setting. The lovely wood balcony is perfect for dining alfresco.

Pony Dining (corner Kendall Ln. and Argyle St., The Rocks, tel. 02/9252-7767, www.ponydining.com.au, daily noon-3pm) is a contemporary and relaxed place famed for its "butchers block" food, such as steaks (800-gram T-bone to share, $85) and its Pony on a Bun burgers ($18.50). The decor of exposed brick and pony-skin wall coverings, together with the gleaming kitchen busy with chefs plying their trade, is a great setting. Sitting outside on the wooden deck allows you to people-watch while you eat.

Guylian Belgian Chocolate Café (91 George St., The Rocks, tel. 02/8274-7500, Sun.-Thurs. 8am-11pm, Fri.-Sat. 8am-midnight) offers lunchtime specials for $12.50 for a baguette sandwich and a glass of wine—but really you'd come here for the hot chocolate ($7.50) and the Belgian waffles that indulgently come with chocolate dip and ice cream ($15). And you can indulge nearly all night long, too. Just add a glass of wine to your waffle and enjoy the charming heritage building and surroundings.

Hidden downstairs from Sydney Visitor Centre and opposite The Rocks Discovery Museum, ★ **The Fine Food Store** (The Rocks Centre, corner Kendall Ln. and Mill Ln., tel. 02/9252-1196, Mon.-Sat. 7am-5pm, Sun. 7:30am-5pm), a deli-cum-coffee shop, serves seriously delicious salads and sandwiches. The setting is relaxed, the staff lovely, and if you sit by the table benches at the window you can peek out on the cobbled lane and watch the people go by. Don't leave without trying the toasted beetroot, walnut, and cheese sandwich ($9.50)—have it with an iced tea for perfection.

CENTRAL BUSINESS DISTRICT (CBD)

The award-winning, highly acclaimed ★ **Tetsuya's** (529 Kent St., tel. 02/9267-2900, www.tetsuyas.com, dinner Tues.-Fri. from 6pm, lunch Sat. from noon, dinner Sat. from 6:30pm, 10-course degustation menu without drinks $220 pp) is a true treat, one that comes with a price tag but also provides a priceless experience. The restaurant itself is a cross between a Japanese shrine and an art gallery, complete with zen garden, and chef Tetsuya is known for his philosophy of using natural and in-season ingredients, enhanced by traditional French cuisine techniques, and his degustation menu is a journey through the world's best ingredients, with a leaning toward the Japanese cuisine, but with plenty of courses that are fusion or truly international. Try the tea-smoked quail breast or confit of ocean trout, along with the white peaches with almond milk ice cream for dessert.

Modern and glass-encased with a simply elegant interior, **Aria** (1 Macquarie St., tel. 02/9252-2555, www.ariarestaurant.com, Mon.-Fri. noon-2:30pm and 5:30pm-11pm, Sat. 5pm-11pm, Sun. 6pm-10pm, pre-theater menu 5:30pm-7pm, one-course lunch $46, two-course lunch $74, two-course dinner from $105) boasts an award-winning celebrity chef. The views will make you forget the food in front of you. At probably the most memorable address in the city, right at the beginning of historic Macquarie Street, by the opera house, Circular Quay, and the bridge, Aria produces plates of food that look as if they come straight from an art gallery. Even if you think you know the ingredient, you'll be surprised at the new take on it, so even if you go for an old favorite, you'll be trying something new. The modern Australian cuisine offers tidbits such as spanner crab mayonnaise with pine nuts, nasturtium, and persimmon; truffled baby cabbage with king brown oyster mushrooms and chestnuts; and black sesame parfait with passionfruit jelly. Tempted?

As the name suggests, the main ingredient at ★ **The Woods** (199 George St., Four Seasons Hotel, tel. 02/9250-3160, lunch Mon.-Fri. noon-2:30pm, dinner Mon.-Sat. 5:30pm-10:30pm, coffee, drinks, and snacks Mon.-Fri. all day, Sat. from 5:30pm, $38) is wood. Not to eat, but to cook with. Large wood-burning ovens and grills feature different woods each week, anything from olive, grapevine, lemon, orange, apple, or peach wood, all giving special flavors to the ingredients. And it is not just meat that is smoked or cooked over wood. The starter of smoked beetroot with labne and hazelnut is great, and daily specials, such as lamb, are simply gorgeous. The setting, although in the hotel lobby, is discreet and relaxing. The ceiling is scribbled with recipes, there is a herb wall, and little anecdotes are framed between the bottle displays, giving the restaurant an elegant yet quirky feel. The spacious low-benched open kitchen adds to the theater. There is a separate vegetarian menu, with some vegan options, in addition to the daily menu.

Spice Temple (10 Bligh St., tel. 02/8078-1888, www.spicetemple.com.au, lunch Mon.-Sat. noon-3pm, dinner 6pm-11pm, mains $40) is celebrity chef Neil Perry's offering to all things Asian, but without a red-tasseled light shade in sight. Instead you have stylish understated Asian decor, plenty of hanging lights, and terribly chic beaded curtains. This restaurant does stylish, spicy, tasty, beautiful food "with a twist" incredibly well, focusing mostly on regional Chinese cuisine. In the main restaurant opt for delicacies such as a seriously spicy and crispy duck, or the poached chicken and noodle salad. At the bar, however, you've got to try the "burger," a dumpling with pork, pickles, and chili that is positively addictive.

Way up high above Sydney's CBD you can find the **360 Bar & Dining** restaurant (Sydney Tower, Sydney Westfield Centre, between Pitt St. and Castlereagh St., tel. 02/8223-3883, www.360dining.com.au, access via lift on level 4, lunch Mon.-Fri. noon-2pm, dinner daily 5:30pm-9pm, two-course dinner from $75). The 360-degree views are magnificent, especially of the sparkling city at night, which complements the sparkling and showy restaurant setting. The food is stylish modern Australian with all the favorites, such as confit of duck, roasted lamb, and an impressive selection of steaks, plus local fish choices such as hapuka and Tasmanian salmon.

Don't let the name of ★ **The Morrison Bar and Oyster Room** (225 George St., tel. 02/9247-6744, http://themorrison.com.au, Mon.-Fri. 7:30am-late, Sat.-Sun. 11:30am-late) put you off. Yes, there are plenty of fresh oysters, especially at Wednesday's happy hour, when they go for $1 apiece, and you can choose from an oyster library listing the mind-blowing array of the critters. But there are also plenty of other options, such as the fish of the day (for example, a whole John Dory to share, $45), and the duck-fat fries are superb. This wood-paneled, partly old-fashioned, partly hypermodern eatery is a great place to grab a drink and a bite to eat. It's always busy, but not overwhelmingly so, and it makes for a good atmosphere.

A trendy restaurant in the grand setting of Customs House, **Young Alfred** (Customs House, 31 Alfred St., Circular Quay, tel. 02/9251-5192, www.youngalfred.com.au, Mon.-Fri. 7am-late, Sat. noon-10pm) has a mostly modern Italian menu. Try the roasted chicken salad ($18) or the gnocchi with basil, or the delectable fungi risotto ($24) for a treat. It's a popular spot with the workers from the CBD for lunch and after-work drinks, but the buzz adds to the atmosphere.

The tiny little ★ **Portobello Caffe** (East Circular Quay, tel. 02/9247-8548, daily for breakfast, lunch, and dinner) undoubtedly occupies the best spot in the city, right on Circular Quay, on the way to the opera house and overlooking the quay with its busy ferries and the bridge. You'll want to linger here forever. But alas, it is only a place to sit outside and grab a panini ($15) or gelato, while enjoying the views. There's good coffee, too. Next door is the **Sydney Cove Oyster Bar** (East Circular Quay, tel. 02/9247-2937, daily 9am-9pm), like Portobello also a small hut (maybe once a ticket office or security hutch?) with outside seating. Here you get said oysters, chilled lobster (half for $59, whole for $120), caviar, and champagne—appropriate food to accompany the million-dollar view.

Bridge St. Garage Bar and Diner (17-19 Bridge St., CBD, tel. 02/9251-9392, www.bridgestgarage.com.au, Mon.-Tues. noon-5pm, Wed.-Sat. noon-late, burger $19.50, sticky pork ribs $36) is an American style bistro where decadent fare like burgers, fries, and ribs is served on rustic wooden boards. It also offers a huge beer list. A nice combination of chic and comfort, the setting is fantastic, with tiles and open brick, set off by wall murals and large globe lights.

Within the gorgeous renaissance interior of the General Post Office, surrounded by marble, wood, and colonnades, the grand Italian restaurant **Intermezzo** (GPO, Martin's Place, tel. 02/9229-7788, lunch Mon.-Fri. noon-3pm, dinner Mon.-Sat. 6pm-10pm, mains $32) offers style and elegance, together with an award-winning wine list and food experience. There's no pizza here, but instead traditional dishes such as veal roll filled with smoked bocconcini (a mozzarella-like cheese) and pine nuts, and handmade meatballs of pork and veal.

Just one of the food outlets in Hunter Connection, an Asian food court, **Ooh Rice?!** (7-13 Hunter St., CBD, tel. 02/9223-9962, Mon.-Fri. 11am-3pm, dishes around $8.50) specializes in Japanese curry, and it's delicious. If you like Japanese food but are bored with all things sushi and crave something a little more hearty, this is a really cheap and tasty lunch option.

DARLING HARBOUR AND HAYMARKET

At **Zaaffran** (Level 2, 345 Harbourside Shopping Centre, Darling Harbour, tel. 02/9211-8900, www.zaaffran.com, daily noon-9:30pm), on the second level of the Darling Harbour Harbourside complex, the crowd usually is a good mix of tourists and Indian families, always a good sign when you're eating at an Indian restaurant. Established in 1998, this is not your typical Indian restaurant when it comes to looks—it is modern, open, with great views across the harbor—but the food is just as it should be. There are lassis, paneers, curries, nan, and tandoor-cooked meats, and the portions are ample. There is even a biryani pie, which is somewhat unusual, and a Zaaffran specialty.

If only a good steak will do, look no further than **I'm Angus** (The Promenade, Cockle Bay, Darling Harbour, tel. 02/9264-5822, Mon.-Sat. 11:30am-3pm and 5:30pm-10pm, Sun. 11:30am-10pm, steaks around $25). This is a huge and bustling steak house, right on the water's edge, and while it does token foods of other types, steak is the thing you come here for. No excuses. It's what they do best.

Sit by the wharf at **Nick's Seafood Restaurant** (The Promenade, King Street Wharf, tel. 1300/989-989, www.nicks-seafood.com.au, Sun.-Thurs. 11:30am-10pm, Fri.-Sat. 11:30am-11pm, mains $38) and watch the myriad day-tripping boats come and go and visitors from around the world saunter past, all while enjoying the freshest catch of the day prepared to your liking. The interior spills across the wide open sliding doors, merging the restaurant's indoor and outdoor seating and making for an airy atmosphere. Have a huge platter with a variety of seafood to share for the table, or try a grilled fish with a salad. For lunch or dinner, this is a great place to sit and enjoy what the sea around Australia dishes up.

★ **Pump House** (17 Little Pier St., Darling Harbour, tel. 02/8217-4100, www.pumphousebar.com.au, daily noon-11pm, pizza $19) is a microbrewery in a fantastic old building, originally designed and built as a pumping station in 1890 for the Sydney & Suburban Hydraulic Power Company, before times of electricity. Apart from the rather impressive beer and drinks list, the food is simple: pizza, lunch specials such as pumpkin pasta, and steaks, catch of the day fish, and fresh local produce on the dinner menu. An interesting option is the skilled matching of beers to your food to get the most out of both, as recommended by your beer sommelier.

Need a quick and easy Japanese food fix? **Umi Sushi & Udon** (Shop 10/1-25 Harbour St., Darling Harbour, tel. 02/9283-2006, daily 11:30am-10pm) is a large setup with long sushi bars around the preparation areas, but also some tables for a more intimate setting, and outside there's plenty of seating near the Chinese Garden of Friendship. There's excellent miso soup for only $2.50, chicken udon ($11), and sushi such as tuna nigiri at $4.60 each, and even kids' bento boxes ($9.80).

The large **Emperor's Garden Restaurant** (96-100 Hay St., Haymarket, tel. 02/9211-2135, www.emperorsgarden.com.au, daily 7:30am-1:30am) serves decent Cantonese food, but the main draw is the little window to the side of it, on Dixon Street. This is where you get the Emperor's Puffs: delicate small warm puffs of dough filled with custard, sold in a bag at $0.30 each, or four for $1. Just look for the line of patiently waiting people, all day and night—you can't miss it.

KINGS CROSS

★ **Otto Ristorante** (Area 8/6, Cowper Wharf Roadway, Woolloomooloo, tel. 02/9368-7488, www.ottoristorante.com.au, daily noon-10:30pm, mains $35) offers a spectacular setting, by the water underneath the Royal Botanic Gardens and the Art Gallery of NSW, and serves up Italian food with a twist. The restaurant is modern and elegant, yet also relaxing and perfect for an evening out, be it summer or winter (in winter the outside heaters warm the atmosphere to comfortable levels). The food really shines: Try the *crudo di tonno*, butter-soft, thin yellowfin tuna served with miniature pickled cucumber balls and crispy pork crackling; the *pici*, porcini pasta with wild-boar ragout; or play it safe with the fish of the day special. Then end with the rich-but-worth-it white chocolate and hazelnut mousse with peanut butter wafers. Savor the little quirky additions to every meal and the superb presentation, but don't forget to look around you occasionally.

Awarded two hats by the *SMH (Sydney Morning Herald) Good Food Guide 2012-2013*, **Gastro Park** (5 Roslyn St., Kings Cross, tel. 02/8068-1017, www.gastropark.com.au, lunch Thurs.-Sat. from noon, dinner Tues.-Sat. 6pm-late, mains $45) is a self-confessed playground for the tastebuds. You might not expect to find a little gem like this in the backstreets of Kings Cross, but people have been discovering this restaurant with its simple but elegant decor that is at odds with the somewhat eclectic life playing out on the streets nearby. The food (modern Australian) is whimsical, risk-taking, and delicious. The menus change daily, always offering what is fresh and in season. You might have steamed Murray cod with charred white asparagus, or even suckling pig with endive, grapes, carrot, and plum with some caramelized apple skins for dessert.

The restaurant and wine bar **Monopole** (71a Macleay St., Potts Point, tel. 02/9360-4410, www.monopolesydney.com.au, dinner daily from 5pm, lunch Sat.-Sun. noon-around 3pm) is casual yet classy. Sit by the bar or along the long leather couch lining the opposite wall, or indeed grab, if you can, the window seat and watch life go by outside. Monopole's food is modern Australian with a twist, and beautiful. The baby corn on the cob is still dressed in leaves but chargrilled to perfection, and the cress salad is decorated with edible flowers, making it nearly too pretty to eat. Plates to share are around $26 for a selection of various starters, such as cured meats; mains are around $20.

The family-run Italian restaurant **Puntino** (41 Crown St., Woolloomooloo, tel. 02/9331-8566, www.puntino.com.au, lunch Tues.-Fri. noon-3:30pm, dinner Tues.-Sat. 6pm-10:30pm), complete with wooden tables and red-checkered napkins adding to its homey atmosphere, is a perennial favorite of Sydneysiders. Mozzarella *degustazione* platters ($15.50 pp, to share) and black-truffle-infused pasta ($24) make it difficult to leave enough space for the Nutella pizza for dessert.

On first glance it's a mere hot-dog stand by the harbor, but ★ **Harvey Café de Wheels** (corner Cowper Wharf Roadway and Brougham Rd., Woolloomooloo, tel. 02/9357-3074, www.harryscafedewheels.com.au, daily 8:30am-2am, pie $6.20) is really a Sydney legend. Sydney's best hot dogs and savory pies are served up all day until late in the night, making it perfect for snacks, lunch, something on the run, or, especially, a perfect midnight snack after a few drinks in the nearby bars.

Bar Coluzzi (322 Victoria St., Kings Cross, tel. 02/9380-5420, daily 10am-2pm) is a tiny roadside coffee shop easily overlooked if it weren't for the assortment of people sitting on wooden stumps and crates on the pavement slurping their coffees. Typically Italian, this little place oozes the kind of atmosphere you have in a side alley of Rome: crowded with coffee drinkers, all talking at once, yet somebody will be sitting quietly reading a book, with no thought given to the decor of the place bar the stools and tables. Nobody cared about interior design here, and people gladly share their wooden pallets and stools with other people stopping for a brief interlude. Stay for breakfast or lunch (they do a nice home-made lasagna), but definitely have a coffee.

PADDINGTON

Hidden in a quaint backyard, little **Jackies Café** (1c Glenmore Rd., off Oxford St., Paddington, tel. 02/9380-9818, www.jackies-cafe.com.au, daily 8am-3:30pm, breakfast $18) is perfect for a lazy breakfast or a light fresh lunch and a glass of bubbles after shopping on trendy Oxford Street. The café offers outdoor and indoor seating, from cozy tables to communal benches where you might have to share the Sunday papers with your neighbor. The food has more than a hint of Italian in it, with fresh salads, open sandwiches, and daily specials of pasta, but it also offers a sushi bar for those wanting to mix it up a little.

A tiny little place with a few benches seating just about two people at a time, **Gusto Deli Café** (corner of Five Ways, Broughton St., Paddington, tel. 02/9361-5640, daily

7am-7pm, croissant $3, sandwich $11) is frequented by people snuggled in the corner with a book or a newspaper, taking their time over coffee. A great selection of sandwiches and not-run-of-the-mill salads (think quinoa and beetroot) are all on tempting display, and you simply cannot have a coffee without accompanying it with a fresh *pain au chocolat.* This is the perfect place to rest your weary feet after traipsing through picture-perfect Paddington.

★ **Four in Hand** (105 Sutherland St., tel. 02/9326-1999, www.fourinhand.com.au, Tues.-Sun. noon-2:30pm and 6pm-late, bar mains $24) is a gastro pub hidden away in the residential streets of Paddington, and a gem at that. It's not cheap, but the atmosphere and the food make up for that. While there is fine dining in the main restaurant, try the bar instead—the setting is more relaxed, decorated in black and white with chrome bar stools around the finely tiled floors of the bar hub, and solid wooden tables and chairs make it classy and cozy at the same time. The bar menu gives you a good idea of the type of food Four in Hand offers, with salt cod and chorizo croquettes, and more offbeat items such as pig's-ear schnitzel. The beef burger with beetroot is excellent.

Rather than going to the Italian restaurant **10 William Street** (10 William St., Paddington, tel. 02/9360-3310, weekdays 5pm-late, Fri.-Sat. noon-midnight, no reservations, share plates and light lunch from $14, dinner mains $42) for dinner, which is delicious but can be pricey, try a late breakfast/early lunch on Friday or Saturday, which will give you a perfect excuse to have the English muffin with egg and sausage, listed under antipasti. The atmosphere is bustling, very much French café, lending itself to a lazy lunch, with the menu on the blackboard and different sized tables to linger at.

A sister restaurant to celebrity chef Matt Moran's Aria Restaurant, **Chiswick Restaurant** (65 Ocean St., Woollahra, tel. 02/8388-8688, www.chiswickrestaurant.com.au, Mon.-Thurs. noon-2:30pm and 6pm-10pm, Fri.-Sat. noon-3pm and 5:30pm-10pm, Sun. noon-3pm and 6pm-9:30pm, mains $30) is more relaxed and affordable, and the food is still fantastic. The large windows and French doors allow views to the garden behind the restaurant while watching the chefs, maybe even *the* chef, do their thing inside in the open kitchen. The fresh, seasonal modern Australian cuisine is locally sourced, often from the chef's own farm. Try the fish and prawn pie, or the wood-roasted lamb (from the chef's farm) to share.

THE NORTHERN SHORE

If you are looking for great views, you'll find them at **The Deck** (1 Olympic Dr., Milsons Point, tel. 02/9033-7670, www.thedecksydney.com.au, bar Wed.-Thurs. 11am-11pm, Fri.-Sat. 11am-late, Sun. 11am-9pm; restaurant Wed.-Sun. noon-8pm). By Luna Park, looking through the bridge at the opera house, with ferries bustling past, this is a great setting. With Luna Park in the background, it is not necessarily a quiet setting for a romantic dinner, but it's perfect for drinks and a plate of food to share: The confit rabbit pappardelle ($26) is great, and there is a children's menu. The menu offers an eclectic mix of world cuisine with, for example, Moroccan salad, Turkish fritters, paella, bouillabaisse, and Australian steak. Something for everybody.

In the lovely Art Deco swimming pools above the Olympic-length lanes, and nearly under the bridge, with views across the harbor, **Aqua Dining** (North Sydney Olympic Pool, corner Paul St. and Northcliff St., Milsons Point, tel. 02/9964-9998, www.aquadining.com.au, daily noon-9pm) has an unusual but great setting. The fine dining restaurant also has lounges outside, where you can enjoy a pre-dinner drink before indulging in this fine Italian menu and the very extensive wine list. The menu offers typical Italian fare brought up to an elegant fine-dining level, with an Australian twist, such as the emu fillet with broccolini and truffled honey ($39). Try to be on the outside veranda around sunset—it's quite magical.

Epi d'Or (Shop 11, Bligh St., North Sydney,

tel. 02/9922-5613, Tues.-Sat. 7:30am-5pm, Sun. 7:30am-2pm) is a tiny little café bursting with French charm, wicker chairs, walls full of picture frames, and some of the best fresh bread and croissants in town. Bring a paper or a book and linger over coffee and pastries.

Named after the botanist Gerard Fothergill, who once occupied the building, ★ **The Botanist** (17 Willoughby St., Kirribilli, tel. 02/9954-4057, http://thebotanist.com.au, Wed.-Sun. 11am-midnight, Mon. and Tues. 4pm-11pm) is botanically inspired in its decor, mix of cocktails, and fresh seasonal food ingredients. It's famous for its sliders, a cross between a mini-burger and a sandwich, which come in several varieties, such as pulled pork and crab—perfect for sharing or as light snacks ($20 for four pieces). There are other sharing options, such as grilled haloumi with pomegranate, lamb skewers, or braised beef cheeks with polenta. They also do great brunch every weekend.

★ **The Bathers' Pavilion** (4 The Esplanade, Balmoral, tel. 02/9969-5050, www.batherspavilion.com.au, café daily 7am-10pm, breakfast $18, lunch $20, dinner $22; restaurant daily noon-3pm and 6pm-10pm, mains $50, degustation menu $145) is a stunning old pavilion overlooking the lovely Balmoral Beach, in a little cove just along from Mosman and Taronga Zoo. The building has been divided into a relaxed café and a more fine-dining restaurant, both absolutely lovely. The café is accented with stylish colorful napkins and cushions, reflecting the sunny attitude of the whole place. This is the perfect place to relax over a lazy brunch on the weekend, maybe before or after taking a dip off the beach or walking in the parkland. The Big Balmoral Breakfast, served in the café, complete with eggs, toast, mushrooms, and hash browns, will set you back $25, but it will last all day.

THE BEACHES

★ **El Topo** (Level 3, The Eastern Hotel, Bondi Junction, www.eltopo.com.au, Mon. 6pm-10pm, Tues.-Sun. noon-3pm and 6pm-10pm, mains $15) is not your average Tex-Mex restaurant, but a Mexican restaurant specializing in the cuisine of the Oaxaca region. El Topo not only sourced all its colorful typical-for-the-region interior decor, complete with grinning skulls, bright tiles, and dancing skeletons, in the Oaxaca region, but it also serves a mean taco and well-aged vintage tequila, recommended by the in-house tequila and mescal "sommelier." On the "share with friends" menu you'll find fried crickets, which incidentally taste nutty with a hint of lime. The best dishes include the charred corn side dishes and the mushroom quesadilla, followed by the coconut flan, but you could also easily go with the kingfish ceviche, which is feather-light, and the spicy chorizo with slow-cooked egg and turtle beans. The atmosphere is part of the deal—colorful, busy, festive—so grab some friends and plan to spend a long evening.

Recently voted one of the best pizzerias in Sydney, **Pompei's** (126-130 Roscoe St., Bondi, tel. 02/9365-1233, www.pompeis.com.au, Fri.-Sun. 11:30am-11pm, Tues.-Thurs. 4:30pm-11pm, pizza $24) not only makes great pizza, but also their own gelato—a prize-winning combination just a stone's throw from the beach, complete with beach atmosphere—open, modern, and relaxed. Try the popular *speck e funghi trifolati* pizza with smoked prosciutto and a variety of wild mushrooms.

At ★ **Three Blue Ducks** (143 Macpherson St., Bronte, tel. 02/9389-0010, www.threeblueducks.com, daily 7:30am-11:30am and noon-2:30pm, Wed.-Sat. 6pm-11pm), a lovely small restaurant café where you can sit and people-watch, enjoying the simple but delicious food, which has recently been immortalized in a cookbook by the young owners. Try the famous steak sandwich ($10), the beetroot and haloumi salad with spiced pistachio praline ($21), or steamed mussels with herb, coconut sambal, and chili toast ($28), all served in easy comfortable surroundings.

Located by the park next to the beach, the **Bogey Hole Café** (473 Bronte Rd., Bronte, tel. 02/9389-8829, www.bogeyholecafe.com, daily 7am-4pm and 5:30pm-8:30pm) is perfect for lunch after a dip in the sea, which is very apt, as the café was named for a local rock pool (*bogey* in the local Aboriginal language denotes a place that is safe for swimming). The food is simple and healthy—try the cauliflower, quinoa, and chickpea salad ($17), or indulge in the all-day breakfast. Daily specials can be found on the large blackboard.

If you like seafood, ★ **Garfish** (1/39 East Esplanade, Manly, tel. 02/9977-0707, www.garfish.com.au, daily noon-3pm and 5:30pm-10pm) is the best place to come to. The decor is simple and stylish, with a large blackboard over the open kitchen and large windows allowing views across the water and the bustling ferry wharf. The menu is brimming with local and international fish. The signature dish is a snapper pie ($34), which is simply gorgeous. But there are also grilled options, catch of the day, and a couple of choices for meat-eaters, plus fresh oysters. And for dessert try the Belgian waffles. Overlooking Manly Bay, this is a definite favorite, if you are into fish.

Information and Services

TOURIST INFORMATION

There are two main branches of the **Sydney Visitor Centre,** one in The Rocks (corner Playfair St. and Argyle St., tel. 02/8273-0000, www.therocks.com.au, daily 9:30am-5:30pm) and another at Darling Harbour (33 Wheat St., behind Starbucks and IMAX Cinema, tel. 02/9211-4288, www.darlingharbour.com, daily 9:30am-5:30pm), with three additional kiosks: outside the Town Hall (George St.), at Circular Quay (corner Pitt St. and Albert St.), and in Haymarket (Dixon St. near Goulburn St.).

HOSPITALS, EMERGENCY SERVICES, AND PHARMACIES

Sydney has some of the country's best hospitals within its city limits. **Sydney Hospital** (6 Macquarie St., CBD, tel. 02/9382-7111), **Royal North Shore** (Pacific Highway, St. Leonards, tel. 02/9926-7111), and **St. Vincent's Hospital** (390 Victoria St., Darlinghurst, tel. 02/8382-1111), as well as the country's best children's hospital, **Sydney Children's Hospital** (High St., Randwick, tel. 02/9382-1111), are all equipped for around-the-clock emergencies.

There are countless pharmacies in the city, such as **CBD Pharmacy** (92 Pitt St., CBD, tel. 02/9221-0091, daily 7:45am-6:30pm). Some have extended hours, such as **Bondi Day and Night Pharmacy** (132 Campbell Parade, Bondi Beach, tel. 02/9130-4566, daily 8am-10pm) or **PriceLine Pharmacy** (Ground Level 9, World Square Retail, 644 George St., CBD, tel. 02/9268-0042, Mon.-Fri. 8:30am-10pm, Sat. 10am-8pm, Sun. 11am-6pm)

MONEY

There are branches of most larger banks throughout the inner city, on most main streets and shopping centers. Banks are generally open Monday to Friday from 9:30am to 4:30pm or 5pm depending on the bank. There are automated teller machines (ATMs) in and outside most branches, in malls, around travel hubs such as train stations, and even in some pubs and convenience stores. Most ATMs accept major international credit cards, which are also accepted in all major shops, cafés, and restaurants, except for maybe at market stalls. Foreign money exchange kiosks can be found along George Street, Circular Quay, and all major tourist areas.

Main bank branches are **HSBC** (570 George St., Town Hall, CBD, tel. 02/8113-2753), **Westpac** (283-285 Kent St., CBD, tel. 02/8254-2750), and **Citibank** (2 Park St., Ground Floor, Citigroup Centre, CBD, tel. 02/8225-1860).

POSTAL SERVICES

The **Sydney GPO Shop** is at 1 Martin Place in the CBD (tel. 13/13-18, Mon.-Fri. 8:15am-5:30pm, Sat. 10am-2pm), and there's another at 264a George Street, CBD (tel. 13/13-18, Mon.-Fri. 8:30am-5:30pm). Most newsagents and many postcard sellers also sell stamps.

INTERNET AND TELEPHONE

If you have a laptop or a smartphone, you can get free Wi-Fi connections at the following locations: Customs House, Town Hall, Ultimo, Haymarket, Kings Cross, and many cafés and restaurants in the city. The public libraries throughout the city also provide computers and Internet access for a nominal fee, and around the TAFE (Technical and Further Education) colleges in Ultimo, Haymarket, there are plenty of printing places that allow you to print from the Internet or a USB drive for a few cents per page.

Cell phones' compatibility with U.S. phones can be a problem, but even if yours is working abroad, the costs of international roaming can easily spiral out of control. If you feel you will absolutely need a cell phone, stop off at the Optus shop in the airport, or any mobile phone shop in the city, and get yourself a local SIM card or an Australian starter kit. Telstra, Optus, and Vodafone all have prepaid mobile systems that are easily available and quick to set up. The kits start from around $30. Alternatively, there are still public call boxes in the city, taking coins and international calling cards.

Getting Around

Trains, light rail, buses, ferries—Sydney has it all. The public transport system is so extensive and reliable that it makes a car pretty much unnecessary, and you can generally save yourself a taxi fare.

GETTING TO AND FROM THE AIRPORT

Sydney's **Kingsford Smith Airport** (SYD, Airport Dr., tel. 02/9667-9111, www.sydneyairport.com.au), named after a local pioneer in flying but often and confusingly called Mascot Airport, is roughly a 20-minute taxi ride ($30), airport express train (every 6-7 minutes, $17.20 one way), or bus ride (Sydney Airporter, www.kst.com.au, online pre-booking service to and from the airport, regular departures, adult $15, child $10 each way) from your hotel. Unless you are traveling on your own, a taxi works out cheapest and probably is most convenient. The train is fast and easy but won't drop you off right by your hotel. Because the airport is on the south border of Sydney's sprawl and the runway extends into Botany Bay, the approach over Sydney is one of the most beautiful in the world, giving you views over the harbor, the opera house, and the bridge—if you are in the right seat and the weather is in your favor, of course.

Security is pretty much the same as everywhere in the world upon departure, though upon arrival, the checks are intense due to Australia's strict import laws. No food, plant, or animal items, dead or alive, not even an apple left over from the journey, are allowed into the country, and getting caught inadvertently "smuggling" something in can lead to serious delays and inconvenience after a long flight. Make sure there is nothing in your checked luggage, and double-check your hand luggage before leaving the plane.

Three terminals, including international (T1), domestic (T2), and domestic Qantas only (T3), serve Sydney well, and the airport is spacious and comfortable and has plenty of shops and cafés to while away any waiting time.

PUBLIC TRANSPORT

The main hubs are the Central Railway Station to the south of CBD, and Circular

Quay to the north. From either of those you can connect to anywhere in the CBD and surrounding suburbs, with buses having the widest reach into the depth of the suburbs. The train system is extensive and is best for quick connections between north and south of the harbor, or from the CBD west and east, but the reach is not as comprehensive as those of the buses. For timetable and connection information access www.sydneytrains.info.

The Sydney buses run nearly 24 hours a day, charging from $2.20 to $4.60 for a single adult fare, depending on distance traveled. Trains and ferries start from around 5am or 6am and run until past midnight. The Sydney Trains and NSW TrainLink networks run hand-in-hand (fares from $3.60 for rides of less than 10 km, increasing with distance to $8.40 for a single adult fare). Ferry fares run $5.80 to $7.20 for a single adult fare depending on distance traveled. Most local commuters use a mix of public transport options (such as ferry and bus or train and bus) to reach their destination, and even the ticketing options are set up for individual options. The same goes for travelers, although access to most major sights is quite streamlined and easy.

The **MyMulti tickets** issued from **Transport for NSW** (www.transport.nsw.gov.au, tel. 13/15-00) encompass travel by train, bus, ferry, and light rail, and an adult one-day ticket costs up to $24, including all zones and modes of transport. Notable exceptions are some private ferry companies, which run a handful of express ferries. The MyZone fare system allows you to choose tickets that are just bus, train, or ferry or more than one mode of transport. Selecting which zones you will travel within and which mode of transport you will use will give you the best and cheapest option. These tickets come in passes lasting from one single trip to one-day, weekly, monthly, quarterly, or annual passes, with student and pensioner (senior) discounts available, too. If you are in Sydney for any longer than two days, the weekly MyMulti ticket for $46 covers all eventualities, and you can hop onto buses, trains, and ferries within Zone 1, which is pretty much all of Sydney, as many times as you need to.

On Sundays you can purchase a Family Funday Ticket at $2.50 per person as long as the traveling group includes one child and one adult. These tickets allow you to go anywhere in Sydney, on the entire Sydney Trains and NSW TrainLink networks, plus all government ferries and buses. This means you could go all the way up to Newcastle or to the Blue Mountains for $2.50 each.

To find your way around the city's extensive public transport options, load the **NSW Transport Info** app onto your smartphone. This app allows you to put in your current location and your destination, giving you details of all the modes of transport available to get you there. It even gives you directions if there is some walking involved. Alternatively, log on to www.transportnsw.info, the NSW Transport Info website, which gives you all the information you will need to find the best way to your destination.

TAXIS

Taxis are all regulated and metered, and can be hailed at taxi ranks, off the street, and by telephone. Some of the most popular taxi companies are **ABC Cabs** (tel. 13/25-22), **Manly Cabs** (tel. 13/16-68), **Premier Cabs** (tel. 13/10-17), **Silver Service** (tel. 13/31-00), and **Taxis Combined** (tel. 13/33-00). For a rough estimate of taxi fares across the city, try www.taxifare.com.au; if you have your set-off point and destination, it will give you an estimate.

Aussie Water Taxis (tel. 02/9211-7730, www.aussiewatertaxis.com) can be booked by phone or online and take you wherever you want to go in Sydney Harbour. One-way trips from Darling Harbour to Taronga Zoo, for example, would cost you $25 per adult and $15 per child, with a round-trip usually saving you $5.

DRIVING

If you intend to drive, Sydney's roads are safe, comfortable, and get you where you want to go without too much scope for getting lost. Commuter traffic is, like in all cities around the world, a major pain, with delays exactly where you don't want them. Here as everywhere in the world, try to avoid the roads 7am-9:30am and 5pm-6:30pm. So, if you have a choice, opt for public transport to get around.

Sydney has some easy connections with major highways reaching out into the various suburbs: The Pacific Highway connects the CBD across Sydney Harbour Bridge with the north, indeed all the way to Brisbane and beyond. There is a toll fare charged when crossing Sydney Harbour Bridge southbound only, and the same system works for the Sydney Harbour Tunnel, with tolls charged at $4 each time. Once on the north side, Military Road gets you to most suburbs along the way to Manly.

Southbound, the Southern Cross Drive connects easiest to the airport, while Parramatta Road is a fast westward commute to Parramatta past the docks and Sydney Olympic Park. Toward the east, Oxford Street winds itself through the suburbs; it's not fast, but it hits all the main suburbs along the way to Bondi Beach and is the route of choice for the buses, too.

Once you are heading out of the sprawling city limits, you may well encounter further toll roads, including the Eastern Distributor, which is only charged northbound; the M5 East Freeway and the M5 South-West Motorway, both charged in each direction; the Westlink M7, the Hills M2 Motorway, and both the Lane Cove and the Cross City tunnels, which are all charged in each direction.

Parking is a continuous bugbear with all Sydneysiders, as it is limited and expensive. Rates vary with location and peak hours, but in the CBD parking meter tariffs are $7 per hour weekdays 8am-6pm and $3 per hour on weekends. Secure parking can be even more pricey.

Blue Mountains

Some 50 kilometers west of Sydney, the Blue Mountains are a range of geological sandstone plateaus, escarpments, and gorges, covering an area of some 10,300 square kilometers, around 1,150 meters high. Originally named by Governor Arthur Phillip in 1788 as the Carmarthen Hills (for the northern section near Sydney) and the Lansdowne Hills (for the southern), the Blue Mountains soon got their current name due to the blue color the mountains seem to shimmer in due to the haze of eucalyptus oils from the more than 90 different species of eucalyptus tree found in the region.

Although officially called the Blue Mountains, the region really is all about the valleys and gorges, not the mountains. You will not see a rugged mountainscape as you approach, but rather find the beauty when climbing down from the plateaus into the eroded gorges of up to 760 meters depth.

Added to the UNESCO World Heritage list in 2000 because of their diversity and geological uniqueness, the Blue Mountains cover seven national parks and a conservation reserve. The main center is **Katoomba,** a bustling town on the edge of the Jamison Valley, from where most tours, attractions, and hikes start.

SIGHTS

Blue Mountains Cultural Centre

Opened in November 2012, the **Blue Mountains Cultural Centre** (30 Parke St., Katoomba, tel. 02/4780-5410, www.bluemountainsculturalcentre.com.au, Mon.-Fri. 10am-5pm, Sat.-Sun. 10am-2pm, adult $5, child under 18 free) features the Blue Mountains City Art Gallery, showcasing local artists, and the World Heritage Exhibition, devoted to education about the distinctive

Blue Mountains

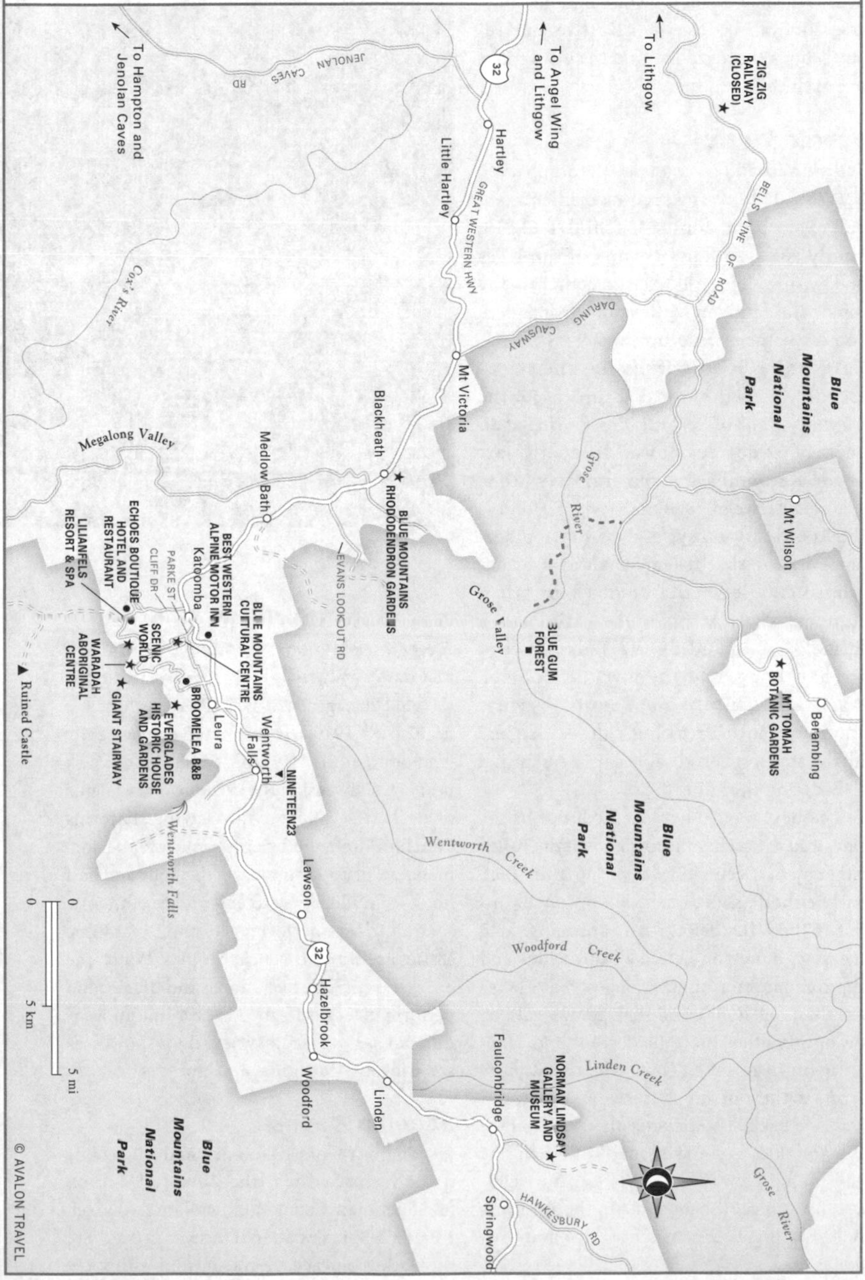

To Hampton and Jenolan Caves
JENOLAN CAVES RD
To Angel Wing and Lithgow
To Lithgow
ZIG ZIG RAILWAY (CLOSED)
32
Hartley
Little Hartley
GREAT WESTERN HWY
BELLS LINE OF ROAD
DARLING CAUSWAY
Cox's River
Mt Victoria
Blackheath
Blue Mountains National Park
Megalong Valley
Medlow Bath
BLUE MOUNTAINS RHODODENDRON GARDENS
EVANS LOOKOUT RD
Grose River
Grose Valley
BLUE GUM FOREST
Mt Wilson
MT TOMAH BOTANIC GARDENS
Berambing
BEST WESTERN ALPINE MOTOR INN
BLUE MOUNTAINS CULTURAL CENTRE
Katoomba
PARKE ST
CLIFF DR
ECHOES BOUTIQUE HOTEL AND RESTAURANT
LILIANFELS RESORT & SPA
SCENIC WORLD
WARADAH ABORIGINAL CENTRE
GIANT STAIRWAY
BROOMELEA B&B
EVERGLADES HISTORIC HOUSE AND GARDENS
Leura
Wentworth Falls
NINETEEN23
Ruined Castle
Wentworth Falls
Blue Mountains National Park
Wentworth Creek
Lawson
Woodford Creek
Hazelbrook
Woodford
Linden
Faulconbridge
NORMAN LINDSAY GALLERY AND MUSEUM
Linden Creek
Springwood
HAWKESBURY RD
Grose River
Blue Mountains National Park
0 5 km
0 5 mi

environment, history, and culture of the Blue Mountains region. The Cultural Centre also houses the new Katoomba Library and showcases innovative, diverse, distinctive, and creative cultural programs. And the gift shop is one of the best around.

Scenic World

Scenic World (1 Violet St., Katoomba, tel. 02/4780-0200, www.scenicworld.com.au, daily 9am-5pm, adult $35, child 4-13 $18, family $88) is a fantastic mix of fun rides and nature. There is a large center at the top of the Jamison Valley, and from there you have three ride options: First is the **Katoomba Scenic Railway,** the steepest railway in the world according to the *Guinness Book of Records,* descending at an angle of 52 degrees; it was originally part of the Katoomba mining tramways constructed between 1878 and 1900. Second is the **Scenic Skyway,** a glass-bottom aerial cable car that traverses an arm of the Jamison Valley at Katoomba and offers stunning views across to the various rock formations, including the Three Sisters, Orphan Rock, and the lovely Katoomba Waterfalls. Third is the **Scenic Flyway,** another record-breaking ride—this time it's the steepest aerial cable car in Australia, showcasing the valley below.

The best way to get the most out of the rides and the scenery is to go down the valley either by the Scenic Flyway or the train, then enjoy either a short bushwalk or longer option in the valley below (there are maps along the way giving you details of directions and approximate timing; the longest walk takes less than one hour), and then go up again by the option other than the descent one. Do it all again in reverse. Then take the Skyway across to the lookout platform, take pictures, and ride back. The tickets allow you to take as many rides as you wish, and with each ride only taking a few minutes, you can have endless fun and get the most out of the stunning valley setting. Estimate at least two hours for this stop.

Katoomba Scenic Railway in Scenic World

Waradah Aboriginal Centre

A proud celebration of Aboriginal culture, art, and dance, **Waradah Aboriginal Centre** (World Heritage Plaza, Echo Point, Katoomba, tel. 02/4782-1979, www.waradah.com.au, daily 9am-5pm, adult $10, child $5) is a landmark product, showcasing the extraordinary talents of local artists. Next to the viewing platforms at Echo Point, the brief (30-minute) performance, every 30 minutes on the hour and half hour, is an ideal way to experience authentic song and dance performances and Dreamtime stories as told by the local peoples. Watch the energetic corroboree (dance) and didgeridoo performances performed in costume and traditional paint. A gallery next door showcases some lovely Aboriginal art.

Jenolan Caves

Just an hour from Katoomba and a 2.5-hour drive from Sydney, the **Jenolan Caves** (4655 Jenolan Caves Rd., Jenolan Caves, tel. 1300/763-311, www.jenolancaves.org.au) are the world's oldest cave system, and with some

10 different caves to explore, they're some of the world's most spectacular, too. Legend has it that it was an outlaw who was hiding from his potential prosecutors who happened upon the first cave, only to get deeper and deeper, uncovering a truly magical underground system that stuns with its 340-million-year-old history.

There are tours for all fitness and adventure levels available. The basic option ($32 adult, $22 child, and $75 for families) allows you to choose Chifley Cave, Imperial Cave, or Lucas Cave, and tours range 60-90 minutes. There are many additional caves, and tour prices vary.

One of the most stunning caves is probably **Lucas Cave,** which contains one of Jenolan's highest and largest chambers. The internal chambers are connected with some 910 steps, at times very steep but manageable, giving it a level three difficulty rating. **Imperial Cave,** a level one cave with 258 steps, follows an underwater river passage. **Chifley Cave,** with its examples of special spar crystal, is a level two with 421 steps.

If you're after more excitement, try one of the **Adventure Caving** tours, where you can go properly caving, suited up in coveralls, helmets, and ropes, needing to squeeze through tight spaces, rappel, and challenge yourself in the dark. The "Plughole Adventure" does not require previous experience and takes approximately two hours ($90 pp, minimum age 10, all equipment provided). The slightly more advanced "Aladdin Cave Adventure" takes three hours (all equipment provided, $100 pp, minimum age 12).

There are, in addition to the caves, many other reasons to spend time at Jenolan Caves. Many self-guided nature trails of various lengths meander through the caves' beautiful surroundings, including a walk to **Blue Lake,** which is a habitat of the shy platypus. The historic **Caves House** (tel. 1300/763-311, www.jenolancaves.org.au, from $135), a hotel on the heritage register, is right next to the caves' entrance. It's a perfect place to spend a night, giving you more time to explore.

Everglades Historic House and Gardens

At **Everglades Historic House and Gardens** (37 Everglades Ave., Leura, tel. 02/4784-1938, www.everglades.org.au, fall and winter daily 10am-4pm, spring and summer daily 10am-5pm, adult $10, child $4), a beautiful heritage garden is set around a historic home from the 1930s. But here you

the fantastic formations inside the Jenolan Caves

get not only the lovely gardens, flowers, and sculpted hedges, but also stunning views across Jamison Valley and the surrounding area. Features include various follies and water features, a gift shop, and tea rooms, and depending on when you are visiting, there can be a riot of color of the seasonal flowers, with tulips and bluebells demanding attention at times. The house itself is well worth seeing, especially the Art Deco bathrooms.

The Zig Zag Railway

Unfortunately, this scenic and historic railway was completely destroyed in the November 2013 bushfires with no immediate plans of reopening.

RECREATION

The **Blue Mountains Adventure Company** (84a Bathurst Rd., Katoomba, tel. 02/4782-1271, www.bmac.com.au) offers rappelling, rock climbing, caving, and bushwalking to fully appreciate the challenges the mountains and gorges can throw at you. Even if you are a novice, you could challenge yourself and take part in a day's introductory rappelling, learning the skill and practicing at various terrains, working your way up to the final rappel down a 55-meter rock face ($195 pp).

Hiking is one of the best ways to see the Blue Mountains and its valleys. Try the **Giant Staircase Walk,** which kicks off at **Echo Point** lookout point and covers a distance of 3.5 kilometers. It takes roughly three hours one way. It does, as the name suggests, include a 900-step staircase, made from steel and with handrails. The really good news is that at the bottom, there is a scenic easy walk and a potential ride on the world's steepest railway back up the slope (run by Scenic World, adult $14, child $8)—although you could climb back up. For directions, check in the **Blue Mountains Visitor Information Centre** at Echo Point (Echo Point Rd., Katoomba, tel. 1300/653-408, www.bluemountainscitytourism.com.au). There are several other walks of varying length and difficulty; choose something that suits you at www.bluemts.com.au and find detailed maps at Echo Point.

Centennial Glen Stables (Kanimbla Dr. via Shipley Rd., Blackheath, tel. 02/4787-1193, www.centennialglenstables.com, from $110) offers **sulky driving**—basically driving a two-wheel horse carriage across a farm track in the mountains. The sulky carries two people and the ride is a little more sedate than riding the horse itself. You can take a picnic and extend the one-hour ride, if you wish, to take in more of the scenery. You can also combine the sulky tour with horse riding, with two on the carriage and someone else alongside on the horse.

Trail ride and wine tasting tours are offered by **Adrenalin Tours** (www.adrenalin.com.au, tel. 1300/791-793, from $89). Visit the only winery in the Blue Mountains, the Dryridge Estate, and enjoy a cheese platter, some of the home-grown Cabernet Sauvignon or Riesling, and then head back on your horse. It's a lovely way to enjoy the surroundings, but make sure you don't overdo the drinking and riding.

ACCOMMODATIONS

Stay in a home called **Angel Wing** (Jenolan Caves Rd., www.contemporaryhotels.com.au/blue-mountains/angel, tel. 02/9331-2881, $1,100 per night, minimum stay two nights), perched high on a hill near the Jenolan Caves with stunning views across the valleys. The open-plan house is a treat in itself, with floor to ceiling windows, an open fire, contemporary furnishings, and superior linens and toiletries. It sleeps up to eight persons. Or try the **Echoes Boutique Hotel & Restaurant** (3 Lilianfels Ave., Katoomba, tel. 02/4782-1966, www.echoeshotel.com.au, from $319). Overlooking the Jamison Valley, Echoes is a small hotel that evolved from a B&B yet retained its personal touch, with some added luxuries, such as its fine-dining restaurant. The rooms are spacious and comfortable, with the suites offering sitting areas with amazing views, and the terrace of the restaurant must surely be one of the best places to enjoy vistas of the Blue Mountains.

The fabulous **Lilianfels Resort and Spa** (Lilianfels Ave., Katoomba, tel. 02/4780-1200, www.lilianfels.com.au, from $249) is a gorgeous old villa overlooking the valleys, with a traditional old-world atmosphere about it. You can just imagine tourists in the early 1900s staying here. Plush furniture, pretty curtains and wallpaper, and a chandelier in the restaurant all add to the charm. Perfectly located within a five-minute walk to the iconic Three Sisters rock formation and the town center, this is a lovely place to stay. On a smaller scale, try the **Broomelea Bed & Breakfast** (273, The Mall, Leura, tel. 02/4784-2940, www.broomelea.com.au, from $175), a rustic little bed-and-breakfast place offering rooms, suites, and one self-contained cottage. There are four-poster beds, roaring open log fires, and timber beams, making it a very cozy place to stay, especially if it's chilly outside.

If you are on a budget, you could do a lot worse than the **Best Western Alpine Motor Inn** (Great Western Highway, corner Camp St., Katoomba, tel. 02/4782-2011, www.alpine.bestwestern.com.au, from $143). It's a no-frills but clean and roomy motel accommodation in a central location, offering an easy family stay with the option of interconnecting rooms, within easy reach of all the Blue Mountains attractions. If you are out all day and just need a budget-friendly place to crash at night, this ticks the boxes.

FOOD

Step back in time to the early 1900s at the **Paragon Cafe and Restaurant** (65 Katoomba St., Katoomba, tel. 02/4782-2928, Sun.-Fri. 10am-4pm, Sat. 10am-10:30pm). This little café/restaurant offers a time capsule with decor, furniture, and even the music in the style of the 1920s, with diners sitting in little wood-fitted alcoves, enjoying the coffee and hand-made chocolates. Come for coffee and scones, a light lunch of toasted sandwiches ($13.50), or a large portion of fish and chips ($18.50). And do go and explore the two back rooms, one a stylish cocktail lounge, the other a private dining room. There is also a display of old cash registers.

Nineteen23 (1 Lake St., Wentworth Falls, tel. 04/8836-1923, www.nineteen23.com.au, Thurs.-Sun. 6pm-late, lunch Sat.-Sun. noon-late, five-course menu $55) is, as the name suggests, also set in a 1920s heritage building, and offers fine dining in beautiful surroundings. The head chef comes from having headed a celebrity restaurant back in Melbourne and offers a seasonal menu that changes regularly, literally keeping things fresh. If the weather plays ball, reserve a table on the veranda overlooking the mountains. It's stunning.

The **Leura Garage** (84 Railway Parade, Leura, tel. 02/4784-3391, www.leuragarage.com.au, Sat.-Thurs. 12:30pm-late, closed Fri.) is a rustic and bustling place where the food is served on wooden boards. Look around at the displays of interesting materials, covering anything from twigs to leather and stones, used for the decor as well as the art installations. The corn on the cob with smoked paprika butter ($14) and the sticky pork ribs ($24) are definite favorites.

Pop into **Sassafras Creek** (83 Old Bells Line of Road, Kurrajong, tel. 02/4573-0988, www.sassafrascreek.com.au, Tues.-Thurs. 9am-4pm, Fri.-Sun. 9am-5pm, Fri.-Sat. dinner from 6:30pm), a lovely mix of gallery, florist, and café, with great simple yet tasty options. Try the soup of the day with crusty bread ($15) or the tarragon chicken breast with pancetta salad ($23), and then check out the offerings in the gallery. It's a destination in itself.

INFORMATION AND SERVICES

The superb **Blue Mountains Visitor Information Centre at Echo Point** (Echo Point Rd., Katoomba, tel. 1300/653-408, www.bluemountainscitytourism.com.au, daily 9am-5pm) is where to get information on things to do and where to stay and book tours. The staff also have intimate knowledge of all the hikes in the region and can give you

A Drive to Canberra

A mere three-hour drive from Sydney is Australia's very underrated capital city, Canberra, which celebrated its centenary in 2013. The city is a perfect place to spend a day or two with the entire family, taking in the museums, shopping, and seeing where Australia is ruled from.

In 1913, Australia's capital was established amid the rolling countryside at supposedly the halfway point between the ferociously competitive cities of Sydney and Melbourne, who both wanted the glory for themselves. The alleged halfway point is actually 287 kilometers from Sydney and 676 kilometers from Melbourne, but that is only good if you're coming from Sydney.

Depart Sydney via the M5 tollway heading south, connecting to Hume Highway 31, and after you've spotted the gigantic merino sheep sculpture in Goulburn, one of Australia's iconic "Big Things," turn onto the Federal Highway to Canberra. It's easy and scenic all the way.

If you are there during the week, don't miss the open-to-the-public question time at 2pm weekdays at the **Parliament House** (Parliament Dr., tel. 02/6277-7111, www.aph.gov.au, open on non-sitting days 9am-5pm) dominating Canberra's many traffic circles. Question time tickets for the House of Representatives can be booked during office hours by telephoning the Serjeant-at-Arm's Office (tel. 02/6277-4889) up until 12:30pm on the day required.

Once you've seen where Australia's laws come from, go and see where its coins are made. The **Royal Australian Mint** (Denison St., Deakin, tel. 02/6202-6999, www.ramint.gov.au, Mon.-Fri. 8:30am-5pm, Sat.-Sun. 10am-4pm, free) produces every single coin in circulation in Australia and has a great exhibition of the evolution of money throughout the years.

If you have kids to keep happy, head straight for the **Questacon** at the **National Science and Technology Centre** (King Edward Terrace, Parkes, tel. 02/6270-2800, www.questacon.edu.au, daily 9am-5pm, adult $23, child $17.50, family with three children $70), where there are interactive exhibits such as the earthquake house, moving magma, caged lightning, and much more. Plan to be here at least a couple of hours.

Just around the corner lies the **National Gallery of Australia** (Parkes Place, Parkes, tel. 02/6240-6411, www.nga.gov.au, daily 10am-5pm, free, but fees for special exhibitions), holding more than 120,000 pieces of artwork and sculptures, including many pieces of Aboriginal and Torres Strait Islander art. The gallery is always holding special exhibitions, many of which are unique to Australia.

Just 35 kilometers southwest of Canberra lies the fascinating **Canberra Deep Space Communication Complex** (421 Discovery Dr., Paddys River, tel. 02/6201-7880, www.cdscc.nasa.gov, daily 9am-5pm, free), a ground station that is part of the Deep Space Network run by NASA's Jet Propulsion Laboratory and is one of just three in the world. You can see a real moon rock weighing in at 142 grams, which is the largest piece of moon rock outside the United States, and can track flight paths of manned missions and satellites that are currently ongoing.

Stay at **East Hotel** (69 Canberra Ave., tel. 02/6295-6925, www.east.com.au, from $180), a trendy aparthotel full of art and stylish quirkiness, with a great restaurant downstairs. Centrally located near the parliament, it is within walking distance of the swanky suburbs of Kingston and Manuka Village, both with great individual boutique shops and cafés. If you are in town on a Sunday, go to the **Old Bus Depot Markets** (21 Wentworth Ave., Kingston, tel. 02/6295-3331, Sun. 10am-4pm) which offer food stalls, handicrafts, jewelry, collectibles, and pretty much something for everybody.

detailed advice on where to go and how long it will take, sign you in and out, and provide detailed maps of each walk.

GETTING THERE AND AROUND

The easiest and most flexible way to travel the Blue Mountains is by car. The entrance to the Blue Mountains at Glenbrook/Lapstone is only around a 50-minute drive west from Sydney. From the city, take the A4 (City West Link) and follow the signs to Parramatta; the M4 Motorway starts at Strathfield and takes you through to Lapstone in the Blue Mountains. Signs to Katoomba and the various attractions are easily followed from there.

Alternatively, you can travel to Katoomba by rail: **Sydney Trains** (www.sydneytrains.info) and **NSW TrainLink** (www.nswtrainlink.info) offer an extremely efficient service to the Blue Mountains (from $11.40 off-peak). If you are flying into Sydney, you can connect directly from Sydney Airport to Central Railway Station by CityRail, or take one of the many shuttle buses. From Central Station, you can catch the air-conditioned double-decker Mountains train, which will get you into Katoomba within two hours. It leaves every hour. If you have a three-zone multiday or weekly public transport pass (from $22 per day), you can use that without having to pay extra.

Several coach tours pick you up from your hotel in the morning, take you to the Blue Mountains, and include many attractions, such as the Jenolan Caves. Try **AAT Kings** (www.aatkings.com, Blue Mountains and Jenolan Caves $149), or **Life's an Adventure** (www.lifesanadventure.com.au, from $299 for personalized 4WD tour), which offers hiking and four-wheel-drive tours to the mountains. Generally, all these tours pick you up from your hotel early in the morning, around 7:30am, and deliver you straight back for dinnertime, although timing may vary slightly.

Once you are in Katoomba, there are a couple of easy ways to see what's on offer: **Blue Mountain Trolley Tours** (76 Main St., Katoomba, tel. 02/4782-7999, www.trolleytours.com.au, $25 per adult, $15 per child, $70 for a family) has 29 stops on a hop-on/hop-off basis covering the main region. The trolley bus departs hourly from Katoomba, and the company also offers packages that include entry tickets to Jenolan Caves and/or rides at Scenic World. The **Blue Mountains Explorer Bus** (Katoomba Railway Station, tel. 1300/300-915, www.explorerbus.com.au, adult $38, child $19, family $95) also follows the hop-on/hop-off system along the 29 stops across the Blue Mountains and offers live commentary. The bus departs every 30 minutes in the mornings and afternoons, with an hour's lunch break between 12:35pm and 1:35pm.

Hunter Valley

The Hunter Valley is Australia's oldest and New South Wales's largest wine-growing region. The first vines were planted around 1830 on the fertile flats of the undulating Hunter River and its many tributaries, and some 150 wineries produce over 39 million liters of premium wine annually, with favored grape varieties including Semillon, Chardonnay, Shiraz, and Cabernet Sauvignon. Since the first road was cut between Sydney and Newcastle, reaching inland to Willombi back in 1826, the region has expanded to cover 6,000 hectares of vineyards and has become a major weekend destination, with some 2.8 million annual visitors from Sydney and afar. The visitors are drawn not only by the fine wines, but also by the many resultant attractions that have sprung up around the wineries, offering anything from ballooning to spectacular gardens, from afternoon tea to fine dining, from carriage rides to cycling across the imposing Brokenback Range.

If you are driving (the best way to experience this part of NSW), the acknowledged hub for basing yourself is the tiny "village" of **Pokolbin,** with most attractions and events in the vicinity. Village may be the incorrect term to use, as both Pokolbin and Hunter Valley villages are a mere assortment of shops and amenities. **Hunter Valley Village** can be found within the locale of Hunter Valley Gardens and offers all the necessities of a village: a pharmacy and a general store together with numerous shops selling pretty knickknacks, pieces of arts and crafts, chocolates, wine, and many handsome souvenirs, plus a

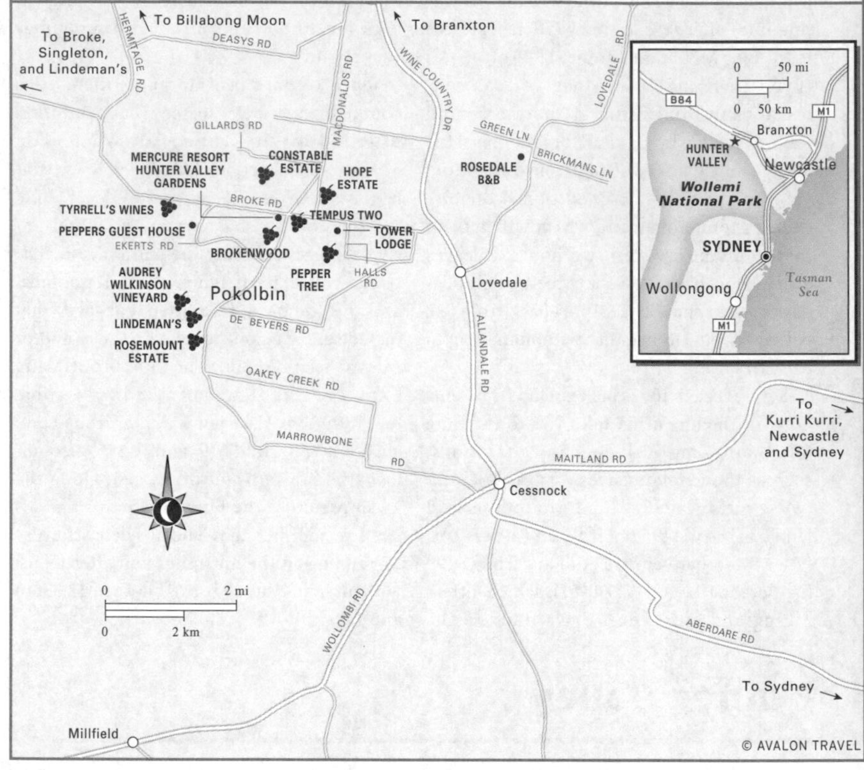

generous assortment of restaurants and cafés. It's a perfect village, inviting visitors to leisurely stroll through it before exploring the gardens and tasting some wine.

The Hunter Valley is synonymous with festivals. There is always something going on in the Hunter Valley, with a fine array of events spread throughout the year. From operatic festivals to pop, there is something for every interest, something every month. Check www.winecountry.com.au before you set off.

WINERIES

With so many wineries, from large and established for generations to quirky, boutique, and relatively new, it is impossible to choose which ones to recommend, as wine is such a personal thing. However, some vineyards keep cropping up in conversation, keep winning awards, and are on the lips of most people in the know. Here is a selection.

In the business since 1866, the **Audrey Wilkinson Winery** (Debeyers Rd., Pokolbin, tel. 02/4998-7411, www.audreywilkinson.com.au, daily 10am-5pm) is widely regarded as the first wine vineyard in the Pokolbin area. Known for its Semillon, Verdelho, Gewürztraminer, Chardonnay, Shiraz, Merlot, Malbec, Tempranillo, Cabernet, and Muscat, and boasting spectacular views across the Hunter Valley, the vineyard was rated by *Gourmet Traveller Wine* as one of the "Top 10 Cellar Doors" in the country, and the only one in NSW.

Founded only some 40 years ago, **Brokenwood** (401-427 McDonalds Rd., Pokolbin, tel. 02/4998-7559, www.

brokenwood.com.au, daily 9:30am-5pm) has grapes that are consistently praised and have produced an award-winning Shiraz.

At **Constable Estate** (205 Gillards Rd., Pokolbin, tel. 02/4998-7887, www.constablevineyards.com.au, daily 10am-4pm) the draws, apart from the wine (Cabernet Sauvignon, Verdelho, Semillon, Shiraz, and Chardonnay), are the beautiful rose and camellia gardens, the sculpture park, and the various walks across the large estate. A small boutique estate with only 3,000 cases produced each year, it is, however, one of the most entertaining and pretty.

The immense tasting room at **Hope Estate** (2213 Broke Rd., Pokolbin, tel. 02/4998-7363, www.hopeestate.com.au, daily 10am-5pm), with 59 huge wooden casks (each holding 4,500 liters) and beamed ceilings, looks like an opera set and is popular as a wedding venue. Outside, there always seems to be a mob of kangaroos lazing on the lawn. Hope specializes in Verdelho, Semillon, Chardonnay, Shiraz, and Merlot.

Lindeman's (119 McDonalds Rd., Pokolbin, tel. 02/4998-7684, www.lindemans.com, daily 10am-5pm) is one of the oldest continuous Australian wineries, famous especially for its Shiraz, having been founded in 1843 by Dr Henry Lindeman with his wife Eliza at their property, Cawarra, in the Hunter Valley. Apart from the wine, a new drawing card to the vineyard is the 1843 Harvest Café, which offers seating inside and outdoors overlooking the valley.

In the Mount View area of the valley, **Pepper Tree** (Abbotsbury, Pokolbin, tel. 02/4909-7100, http://peppertreewines.com.au, daily 9am-5pm), winner of the Hunter Valley 2011 Cellar Door of the Year, is a benchmark for quality. Set among pristine gardens, a short walk from a historic convent building, Pepper Tree's vast vineyards are perfect for both sight and palate. Apart from its Chardonnay, Verdelho, Semillon, Shiraz, Viognier, Sauvignon Blanc, Merlot, Cabernet, Grenache, and Pinot Noir, the estate has also branched out into coffee blends.

Rosemount Estate (Rosemount Rd., Denman, tel. 02/6549-6400, www.rosemountestates.com, Mon.-Sat. 10am-5pm, Sun. 11am-5pm) was established by Robert Oatley and family in the Upper Hunter Valley in 1969. By 1976, Rosemount wines had won gold medals in Paris, Montpellier, Calcutta, and America, and today it's one of Australia's leading wine companies, with the Rosemount Estate Balmoral Syrah as the brand's flagship wine. They produce a wide range of wine, with something to suit both sophisticated tastes and everyday drinkers.

Tempus Two (corner Broke Rd. and McDonalds Rd., Pokolbin, tel. 02/4993-3999, www.tempustwo.com.au, daily 10am-5pm) is a boutique winery with a spaceship-like tasting room. The architect-designed cellar door features a Japanese restaurant with a sizzling teppanyaki grill and a trendy bar where you can learn to pour the perfect cocktail. The winery specializes in blending a distinctive range of wines from Australia's premier winegrowing regions.

Family-owned since 1858, and now headed up by fourth-generation family member Bruce Tyrrell, **Tyrrell's Wines** (1838 Broke Rd., Pokolbin, tel. 02/4993-7000, www.tyrrells.com.au, Mon.-Sat. 9am-5pm, Sun. 10am-4pm) is home to some of Australia's most acclaimed wines, including the iconic Vat 1 Semillon. Since 1971, Tyrrell's has been awarded over 5,000 trophies and medals and in 2010 was named "Winery of the Year" in James Halliday's *Australian Wine Companion.*

RECREATION

Barrington Tops National Park (Chichester, tel. 02/6538-5300, daily 24 hours, except in severe weather and fire events, free) is a rainforest reserve carved out of volcanic flows and is ideal for bushwalks, picnics, and fishing. The **Barrington Outdoor Adventure Centre** (www.boac.com.au, tel. 02/6558-2093, daily 9am-5pm) offers a range of exciting white-water kayaking, canoeing, and downhill mountain-biking adventures.

Hunter Valley Carriages (917 Hermitage

Rd., Pokolbin, tel. 04/3133-7367, www.huntervalleycarriages.com.au) offers horse riding ($45 for 30 minutes), pony rides (from $20), and two-hour trail rides ($55 pp). It also offers carriage rides ($160 pp, minimum three people) through the valley, taking in several wineries and lunch along the way—a great way to experience the beauty of the valley.

If you want to tour the region under your own steam, why not have a bike delivered right to your door? With **Hunter Valley Cycling** (tel. 04/1828-1480, www.huntervalleycycling.com.au, mountain bike $35/day, children's bike $20/day), you get all the gear, including bike, helmet, and maps, delivered to your accommodations.

Set on 25 hectares, **Hunter Valley Gardens** (2090 Broke Rd., tel. 02/4998-4000, www.huntervalleygardens.com.au, daily 9am-5pm, adult $26, child $15, family $57) has 12 themed gardens and eight kilometers of paths, making this a haven for garden lovers. Choose favorites such as the Rose Garden or Chinese Moongate Garden, or try the unique Indian Mosaic Garden, the enchanting Storybook Garden, or the Formal Garden. Or see them all, if you have enough time.

Hunter Valley Zoo (138 Lomas Ln., Nulkaba, tel. 02/4990-7714, www.huntervalleyzoo.com.au, Thurs.-Tues. 9am-4pm, adult $19, child $11, family $55) is a small zoo, but it has all the iconic Australian animals in residence. You can get close to a koala, nuzzle a kangaroo, pat a wombat, and stroke a reptile. There are dingoes, crocodiles, and Tasmanian devils, all on a manageable scale.

The Golden Door Health Retreat—Elysia (Thompsons Rd., Pokolbin, tel. 02/4993-8500, www.goldendoor.com.au) is a beautiful spa that overlooks the mountains and valleys, offering massages, facials, and more unique experiences, such as the watsu treatment, moor mud baths, and steam infusions.

Wine Country Ballooning (332 Lovedale Rd., Lovedale, tel. 02/4991-7533, from $239) gives you a whole new perspective of the lovely countryside. Glide over wineries and mountains, and maybe even enjoy champagne and chocolates while in the air.

ACCOMMODATIONS

If you prefer smaller and more personal accommodations, stay at **Rosedale B&B** (377 Lovedale Rd., Lovedale, tel. 02/4990-9537, http://rosedalebnb.com.au, from $150 weekdays, $250 weekends), a family B&B with just three rooms. Enjoy their beautiful gardens, the book and DVD library, and the substantial breakfast.

To get away from it all, why not stay in a cottage by a billabong (watering hole) or even in the trees? The lovingly decorated cottages at **Billabong Moon** (393 Hermitage Rd., Pokolbin, tel. 02/6574-7260, www.billabongmoon.com.au, cottages from $230) are set among large wood- and grassland areas frequented by kangaroos. They even come with breakfast provisions, although you'll have to do the cooking yourself in your own kitchen.

Peppers Guest House (Ekerts Rd., Pokolbin, tel. 02/4993-8999, www.peppers.com.au, rooms from $179 including full buffet breakfast, homestead from $790) offers beautifully appointed rooms in an elegant country-heritage-style house nestled among the vineyards. You can stay in the main house or, if traveling in a group, share the homestead, a separate house that sleeps up to 11 guests and feels like a step back in time. You can even hold your own dinner party—with help from the staff.

Right by the Hunter Valley Gardens and the local golf course, **Mercure Resort Hunter Valley Gardens** (2090 Broke Rd., Pokolbin, tel. 02/4998-2000, www.mercurehuntervalley.com.au, from $179) is a superior motel-style accommodation with elegantly furnished modern rooms but a rustic country-style lobby and bar. It also has a pool, spa, and steakhouse restaurant.

A gorgeous luxury boutique stay, **Tower Lodge** (6 Halls Rd., Pokolbin, tel. 02/4998-4900, www.towerestatewines.com, from $490, two-night minimum stay) looks a little like a convent, with stone floors and columns outside in the secluded courtyard, yet inside it is comfort and coziness all the way. Spacious rooms come with round-the-clock room service and the feeling of being pampered throughout. It's perfect for an indulgent adult weekend.

FOOD

Whether you're sitting on an outdoor terrace overlooking the valley, winery, and lake, or inside next to a roaring fire, dining at **Chez Pok** (Peppers Guest House, Ekerts Rd., Pokolbin, tel. 02/4998-8999, www.peppers.com.au, breakfast Mon.-Fri. 7am-10am and Sat.-Sun. 7:30am-10:30am, lunch Fri.-Sun. 12:30pm-3pm, dinner daily 6:30pm-9:30pm, dinner mains $35) is a treat, especially considering that Chez Pok has a longstanding association with the region; roughly translated it means "among the Pokolbin people." A small but choice menu offers regional ingredients and is inspired by the French chef.

Cafe Enzo (1 Broke Rd., Pokolbin, tel. 02/4998-7233, www.enzohuntervalley.com.au, daily 9am-5pm, breakfast $20, lunch $27) is a rustic and easy-going yet stylish place, where you can sit in the courtyard at wooden tables and enjoy a breakfast or lunch of common staples made fancier: the fish and chips is beer-battered John Dory, the burger is wagyu with beetroot, and the tiger prawns come with shaved parmesan.

Being part of a winery, much of the Bimbadgen Estate's wine is incorporated into the food at **Esca Bimbadgen** (Bimbadgen Estate, 790 McDonalds Rd., Pokolbin, tel. 02/4998-4666, www.bimbadgen.com.au, lunch daily from noon, dinner Wed.-Sat. from 6pm, tasting plates $38) in the form of syrups, caramels, sauces, and, of course, in the accompanying wine list. The setting is sensational, on a hill above the valley, and the tasting plates offer a selection of choice modern Australian cuisine with matched wines.

If you find yourself fancying a beer among all that wine, head to the **Matilda Bay Brewhouse Hunter Valley** (Hunter Valley Resort, Hermitage Rd., Pokolbin, tel. 02/4998-7777, ext. 249, www.hunterresort.com.au/beer-table, daily noon-4pm and 6pm-9pm, bar food $20) and sample some local brews while enjoying some bar snacks in relaxed surroundings. There are no white tablecloths, but there is plenty of music, and even a pool table.

You'll find great food in an unusual indoor garden setting at **The Cellar Restaurant** (Hunter Valley Gardens, 2090 Broke Rd., Pokolbin, tel. 02/4998-7584, www.the-cellar-restaurant.com.au, Mon.-Sat. noon-3pm and 6:30pm-9pm, mains $39, "morsels" $5.50 each). You can dine on great mains, such as deboned spatchcock (a poussin chicken favored in Australia) with Italian sausage; share several "morsels" (the zucchini flowers, meatballs, and calamari are great); or enjoy a charcuterie plate. It's a nice varied menu.

INFORMATION AND SERVICES

The Hunter Valley Wine Country Tourism Centre (455 Wine Country Dr., Pokolbin, tel. 02/4990-0900, www.winecountry.com.au, Mon.-Sat. 9am-5pm, Sun. 9am-4pm) can tell you about all the wineries and restaurants, book accommodations, and get you tickets to local events.

There is also a Hunter Valley iPhone and iPad app, which is free and gives up-to-date information on events, restaurants, accommodations, and everything wine-related. Pick up the annual *Hunter Valley Visitors Guide* from any tourism information bureau in the region—it comes with an excellent touring map in the back.

GETTING THERE AND AROUND

If you are driving, allow a comfortable two hours for your drive. Leave Sydney's CBD via Sydney Harbour Bridge heading north, and follow the Pacific Highway toward Hornsby. Before Hornsby, at Wahroonga, take National Highway 1 (F3 Freeway) north toward Newcastle. After 100 kilometers, around one hour's driving, exit at the Cessnock/Hunter

Valley Vineyards exit sign. Follow the signs to Cessnock/Vineyards. On the way back you could take the scenic route: Head along Tourist Route T33 through Wollombi and the mountains before returning to the National Highway 1 (F3 Freeway) heading south to Sydney.

If you are not driving, there are several day trips up to the Hunter Valley. **Hunter Valley Wine Tasting Tours** (tel. 02/9357-5511, www.huntervalleywinetastingtours.com.au, pickup from hotel around 7am, return 6:30pm, from $100) offers a number of tours, all in smaller 14-seater buses, with stops for coffee, along with taster sessions at five wineries, a cheese shop, and a local chocolate manufacturer, with optional lunches. **AAT Kings** (tel. 1300/228-546, www.aatkings.com.au, depart 8am, return around 7pm, adult $165, child $85) offers a day tour that includes not only visits to a handful of wineries, but also lunch, a taster session at the local beer brewery, and a stop at the famous Hunter Valley Gardens.

The Southern Reef

Look for ★ to find recommended sights, activities, dining, and lodging.

Highlights

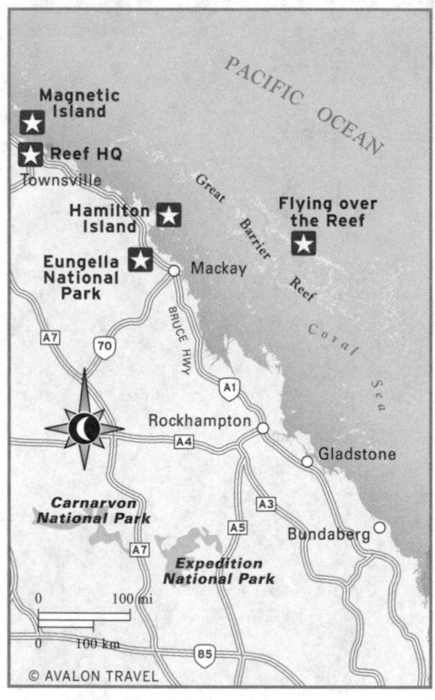

★ **Eungella National Park:** Australia's largest national park is one of its most stunning, featuring hills and valleys covered in dense forest, gurgling streams and rivers, amazing views over the surrounding countryside, and maybe even a chance to spot an elusive platypus (page 160).

★ **Flying over the Reef:** The Great Barrier Reef is amazing under water, but unless you've seen it from above, you can't appreciate the true size and beauty of it. And this is also the only way to see the famed Heart Reef. There are lots of flying options, from expensive luxury flights to short and relatively affordable hops (page 166).

★ **Hamilton Island:** The most accessible of the Whitsunday Islands, this is also the one with the most accommodation options and activities. From snorkeling above the corals to hiking through the dense bush of the national park, from fine dining to sailing the neighboring islands, it's all there (page 170).

★ **Reef HQ:** Townsville's number one attraction, this aquarium brings the denizens of the reef onto dry land. You don't have to get wet to see a living, breathing coral reef (page 188).

★ **Magnetic Island:** A brief ferry ride from Townsville, Magnetic Island is the city's playground. Hug a koala and spot wallabies on the nature walks. Dive the famed SS *Yongala* wreck, or take yourself on a self-guided snorkel tour (page 195).

With the Great Barrier Reef stretching over 2,000 kilometers and covering an area of around 348,000 square kilometers, to go to Australia and "see" the entire Great Barrier Reef is practically impossible. Even marine biologists who live and work on the islands will never get to experience it all. So, where to start? Begin at the beginning: The reef officially starts near Bundaberg, with some small islands around Lady Elliot and Heron Islands, and that is a mere four hours' drive north from Brisbane, or a couple of hours' flight from Sydney.

The southern reef region, on land, is still unexploited by visitors. It is mostly arable land (sugarcane and fruit, together with cattle, are the farming mainstays), and there are plenty of national parks—wild, uninhabited, and rarely visited bushland and forest that is home to an amazing variety of unique flora and fauna.

The cities and towns dotted along the coast are mostly industrial and not geared up for mass tourism, although superb visitors centers guide you to nearby attractions and book visits to the reef. North of the Tropic of Capricorn, tourism becomes more of an industry, and you'll find proper, if small, beach resorts bustling with activities that suit the entire family. But on the whole, the region of the southern reef is a combination of excellent and not overrun access to some spectacular islands along the reef and a coastline that is very quiet and laid-back, with touristy attractions far and few between, spaced out along quite considerable distances.

PLANNING YOUR TIME

It can't be stressed enough just how large a country Australia is. Trying to even make a dent in all its attractions requires intensive planning and time. While you can do things on a budget, when time and budget are limited the planning is even more important, and you have to accept that you simply will not be able to see it all.

The key is to figure out your priorities. Queensland and the reef offer such a huge variety of activities that you will probably have to choose and, again, set priorities.

Previous: train carrying sugarcane in Queensland; Catseye Beach on Hamilton Island. **Above:** Tully's Big Golden Gumboot, designed, fabricated, and installed by Brian Newell.

The Southern Reef

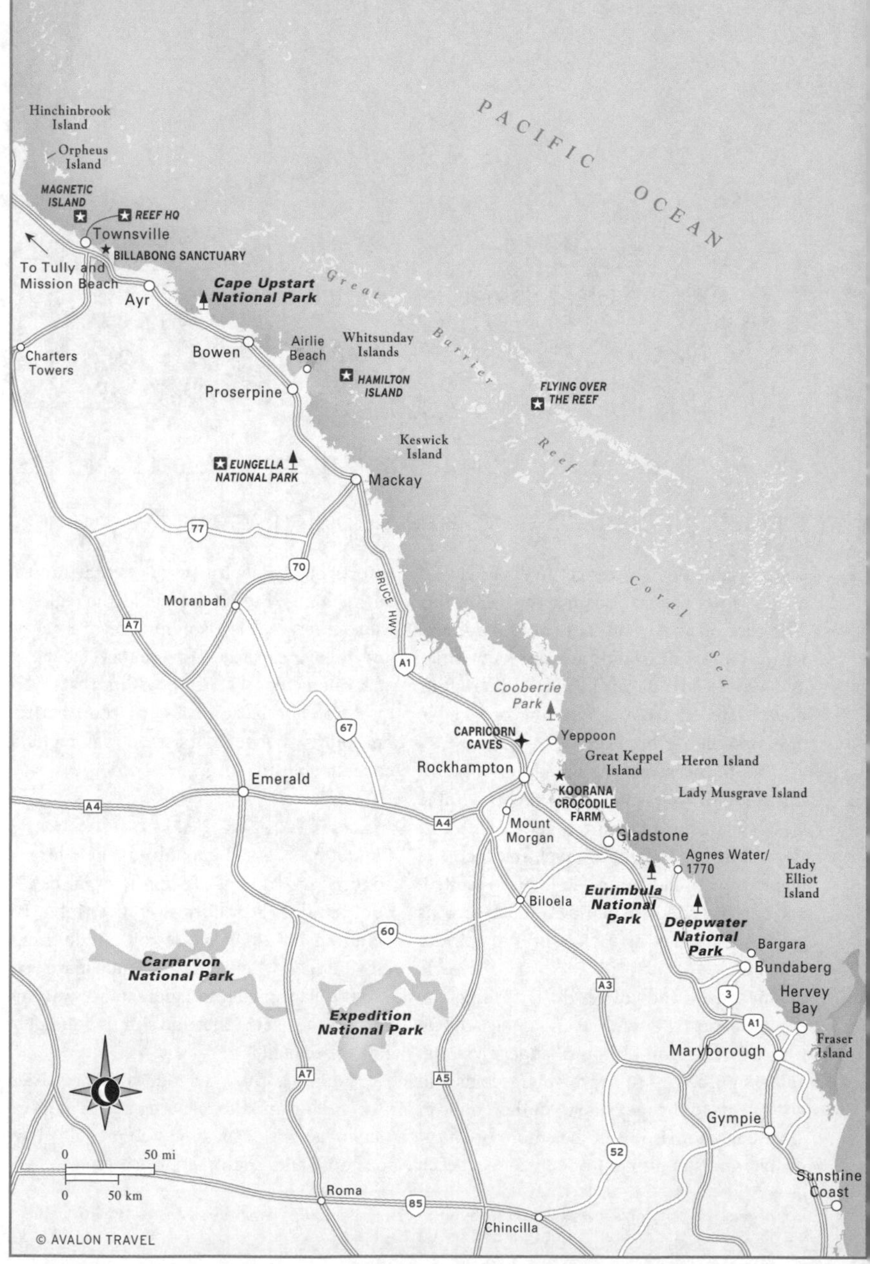

If you are an avid hiker, then the southern reef region is a great place for you, especially if you combine the hiking with bird-watching. You'll never want to leave. The national parks all offer nature walks, tracks that are well signposted at every parking spot along the road, and they often come with picnic facilities. If you are a serious hiker, then maybe the Thorsborne Track on Hinchinbrook Island is for you; you will get dropped off on the island and walk for four or five days, camping as you go. You can fly from Sydney up to Cairns or Townsville and reach the island from there.

Are you a keen diver or a closet marine biologist? Then opting for a secluded and not too expensive island resort where you can spend most of your time and money underwater would be best. Fly out to Heron Island and book a set of dives. You can fly in and out via Gladstone and need not set foot on the mainland for long.

If, however, you are a couple or family with a variety or even a clash of interests, then either make camp in a more bustling resort such as Airlie Beach and take day trips from there, or, quite honestly, move on to the northern reef region and place yourself in Cairns or Port Douglas, from where you can reach many more activities and sights in a shorter space of time than is possible anywhere along the southern reef.

The best way to get around the various places along the southern reef is either by flying in and out (most places do have small regional airports) or driving. To drive the entire coast, from Bundaberg to Mission Beach, visiting all the points covered in this chapter, would take a bare minimum of two weeks, as the distance is around 2,500 kilometers and excursions to islands always take at least one entire day, so depending on your stops, calculate around three or four weeks to do it all.

Bear in mind that the drive crosses the Tropic of Capricorn and the tropics, so the weather is good pretty much all year round, but the rainy season in the southern summer (November to February) is quite humid, and some of the national parks get blocked off due to flooding. The dry and more popular season, roughly between May and October, often sees inflated accommodations prices and more visitors. You can swim in the sea all year round, although you may have to stay within the stinger nets during jellyfish season (October to May). If you come for the hiking, you may want to opt for the cooler in-between months of August or March.

Capricorn Coast

At 23.5 degrees south of the equator sits the Tropic of Capricorn. The region is generally known as the "tropics," meaning the region does not experience dramatic changes in seasons as the sun remains consistently high in the sky all through the year. Unlike the Tropic of Cancer (23.5 degrees north), which passes through many areas of land in the northern hemisphere, the Tropic of Capricorn passes mainly through water, simply because there is less land for it to cross in the southern hemisphere. But it does cross Australia, making land around the Yeppoon area of the coast—hence the name Capricorn Coast.

Strictly speaking, the Capricorn Coast does not have set geographic boundaries, but it is generally agreed to stretch between Thompson Point on the Fitzroy River, some 30-odd kilometers north of Gladstone and just short of Rockhampton in the south, and Shoalwater Bay, some 20 kilometers north of Yeppoon, in the north. Yeppoon is the largest town literally on the Capricorn Coast.

That means that, geographically speaking, it is a tiny stretch of coast, full of coves and bays, mostly rocky and quite deserted where residents and even visitors are concerned. The main attractions along this stretch of coast are the Keppel Islands and the towns of Rockhampton and Yeppoon. But with it being such a lovely name, and crossing such an important, if imaginary, line on the globe, we stretch it a little and include the entire coast from Bundaberg to Mackay in this section, with the Capricorn Coast lying somewhere in the middle between the two cities.

BUNDABERG

The name "Bundaberg" is a combination of "Bunda," the name of the local Aboriginal tribe, and "burg," the Saxon word for town. It is not certain whether the first European explorer of the area by the Burnett River, Henry Russell, who arrived in 1842, was of Saxon origin, but we know that he was not impressed with the region and left again soon enough. So, it wasn't until 1866 that the first white settlers, the timber-cutting Steuart brothers, moved into the area. Settlement rapidly progressed thereafter, and in the 1870s German and Danish migrants were joined by immigrants from around the world who started to cultivate the fertile river soils. Soon several stores, hotels, a sawmill, and some factories began to appear along the banks of the Burnett River, and in 1880s the railway reached the town.

Today Bundaberg is a thriving little city spanning a calm, if prone to flooding, river, and is supported by the growth of beef and dairy cattle, tropical fruit, and tomatoes, but dominated by the sugarcane industry that surrounds it. The area provides nearly 20 percent of Australia's sugar and is probably best known for its potent drinks: It is the country's largest producer of brown rum and also brews other concoctions, such as ginger beer, sarsaparilla, and root beer. Not surprisingly, the rum and its distillery are one of the most visited and duly sampled attractions nearby.

That said, Bundaberg is mostly ignored by visitors, and the town is really set up for through traffic, the majority of visitors coming to town on business rather than tourism. There are enough attractions in town to keep you busy for a day, but then it's usually onward to the sea and the reef, and Bundaberg does reflect the merely fleeting interest in it by being a quiet little town concentrating its business more on the local residents and business visitors as compared to tourists.

Sights

BUNDABERG RUM DISTILLERY

The skyline and river landscape are dominated by the hulking **Bundaberg Rum**

sugarcane fields in Bundaberg

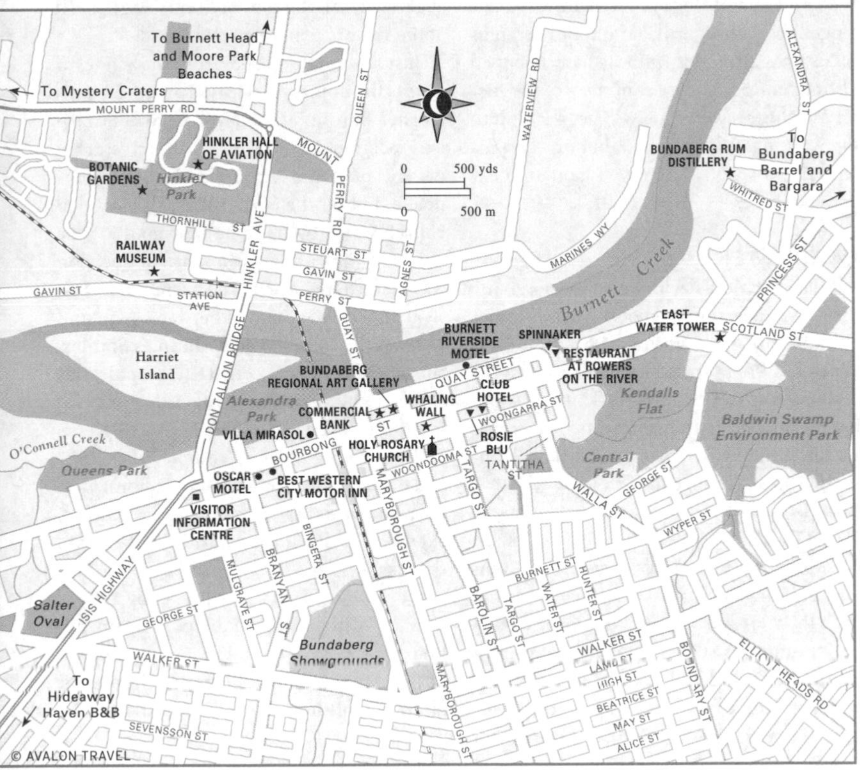

Distillery (Whittred St., tel. 07/4131-2999, www.bundabergrum.com.au, hourly tours Mon.-Fri. 10am-3pm, Sat.-Sun. 10am-2pm). A metal shack puffing huge white clouds into the blue sky, the distillery, founded back in 1888, is not only what spreads Bundaberg's fame countrywide, but also is the best attraction in town. Using the ubiquitous sugar from around the region to make rum, the Bundaberg Distillery has a white bear logo that is known to every Australian worth his spirit measure. You can visit the distillery itself, with guided tours leaving every hour on the hour and lasting one hour, and learn all there is to learn about this famous drink (adult $25, child $12.50, family $62.50); note that you must wear enclosed shoes as you will be entering the workspace. Alternatively, go on a shorter self-guided tour, which will give you the history of the place but no access to the distillery itself (adult $15, child $7.50, family $37.50, same opening hours as distillery). The self-guided audio tour takes you through a small exhibit of the history of the distillery, displays of bottles, the Bundaberg Bear, machinery involved in the process of making rum, and the grounds. Both tours allow you to sample the product, if you haven't been overcome by the fumes already.

BUNDABERG BARREL

Bundaberg Barrel (147 Bargara Rd., tel. 07/4154-5480, www.bundaberg.com, Mon.-Sat. 9am-4:30pm, Sun. 10am-3pm, adult

$12.50, child $5.50, family $28.50) is the lesser cousin of the distillery. Founded in 1960 and famous for brewed drinks such as ginger beer, sarsaparilla, and root beer, plus sodas, this attraction with its barrel-shaped visitor center is a mere summary of the history of this brewery; you will get a look into the workings of the factory, but only via interactive displays. There's no hands-on experience here.

EAST WATER TOWER

Bundaberg is dotted with water towers, giving the city's water supply a boost when it comes to water pressure. Built in 1902, the **East Water Tower** is a masterpiece of bricklaying with walls up to 1.4 meters thick in places and has recently been given a facelift. The prettiest tower in town, it's worth a quick look, although you cannot go inside.

HERITAGE TRAIL

The **Heritage Trail** covers several lovely heritage buildings in town, with the old (dating back to 1890) and still working **Post Office** (157 Bourbong St.) with its 30-meter-high clock tower and the double-story colonnaded Victorian Italianate design dominating the city skyline. The **School of Arts** (184 Bourbong St.) is a lovely arch-studded heritage building dating back to 1888, listed on the suggested walking tour of Bundaberg, issued at the visitors center down the road.

Just around the corner from the School of Arts is the impressive **Holy Rosary Church** (corner Barolin St. and Woongarra St.). In this location since 1875, the church started off as a small timber church, like the one opposite, but by the early 1880s, the wooden church was proving to be too small for the needs of the congregation, and a decision was made to replace it. The current neoclassical church was erected between 1886 and 1888, and was designed by Francis Stanley, the 19th-century architect of colonial Queensland. The stunning **Commercial Bank** building (corner Maryborough St. and Bourbong St.) was completed in 1891 and displays grand examples of colonnades, a cast-iron balustrade, French windows, excellent cedar joinery, and an elaborate staircase.

Of more modern times (the early 1990s), the **Whaling Wall** (Suncorp Building, Bourbong St.) is a mural of a pod of gigantic humpback whales, celebrating the annual migration of those whales along the nearby coast.

Bundaberg Rum Distillery with its iconic Bundaberg Bear

BUNDABERG REGIONAL ART GALLERY

The **Bundaberg Regional Art Gallery** (1 Barolin St., corner Quay St., tel. 07/4130-4750, Mon.-Fri. 10am-5pm, Sat.-Sun. 11am-3pm, free) started life as a Customs House in 1902, and from 1921 to 1978 it was occupied by the Commonwealth Bank. During that time, distinctive changes were made to the building's architecture, including the installation of two concrete bank vaults armed with heavy combination locks, which today take center stage as the gallery's collection storage facility and the vault installation space. The gallery has regular exhibitions that change every month or so, but also houses a permanent collection comprising four sub-collections amounting to some 400 pieces across all art forms, from 19th-century paintings to modern Aboriginal art.

BUNDABERG BOTANIC GARDENS

Bundaberg Botanic Gardens (Mount Perry Rd., tel. 07/4130-4400, Sept.-April daily 5:30am-6:45pm, May-Aug. daily 6:30am-6pm, free) are not only beautiful gardens inviting you to saunter and maybe have a picnic, they are also home to several main attractions in Bundaberg, such as the **Bundaberg & District Historical Museum** (daily 10am-4pm, adult $5, child $2, family $11). A working venue for the local history society, the museum houses plenty of artifacts and photographs chronicling the region's history, and also has working archives, which are open to the public upon request.

Then there is the excellent **Hinkler Hall of Aviation** (Bundaberg Botanic Gardens, corner Mount Perry Rd. and Young St., tel. 07/4130-4400, http://hinklerhallofaviation.com, daily 9am-4pm, public holidays 10am-3pm, adult $18, child $10, family $38), a celebration of the life of locally born aviator and inventor Bert Hinkler. An aviation pioneer and war hero, he was famous for his record-breaking long-distance flight from Sydney to Bundaberg in 1921. Sadly, he died in 1933 while attempting another solo flight from England to Australia and is buried in Italy. The hall teaches everything about aviation, aeronautical technology, and the dream of flying, complete with aircraft, gadgets, and models, some items once belonging to Hinkler himself, others relating to aviation records. Much of Hinkler's memorabilia is also housed in the **Hinkler House,** his old home, which originally stood in Southampton, in the U.K., but was painstakingly dismantled and rebuilt here in the botanic gardens. Self-guided tours of the house are included in your Hinkler Hall of Aviation ticket.

BUNDABERG RAILWAY MUSEUM

A little treasure for train enthusiasts and all kids, large or small, the **Bundaberg Railway Museum** (28 Station St., corner Wilmot St., tel. 07/4154-2170, Tues., Fri., and Sat. 9am-3pm, adult $2, child $1), just down the road from the botanic gardens, is full of photos from the first railway reaching the region, old uniforms, office records, manuals, timetables, all sorts of train machinery and tools, and whatever floats your boat, or rolls your train. The museum is in the first, very pretty railway station built here in 1881, although it's not quite in its original place but some 500 meters down the track. This is a picturesque and interesting outing and offers an account of the railway's past and a slice of history for the entire region.

MYSTERY CRATERS

Discovered only in 1971, the **Mystery Craters** (15 Lines Rd., off Bundaberg Gin-Gin Rd., South Kolan, tel. 07/4157-7291, daily 9am-5pm, adult $7.50, child $5, family $20) are steeped in the unknown. In all, there are 35 craters, some up to 60 meters deep and all reportedly around 25 million years old. Undoubtedly natural and old, some are water-filled, others dry. Whether they are made by meteor hits, are footprints of some gigantic animals, or were made by aliens—that's the mystery. A small wooden tower with commentary at the push of a button allows you a view from above. Together with a chubby replica of a *Tyrannosaurus rex*, an odd shed full of mostly agricultural but also hodgepodge machinery and tools, and another display of artifacts, rocks, and fossils, plus a coffee shop, this is indeed a mysterious attraction.

Beaches

Along the coast there is a succession of beaches and coastal communities, such as **Moore Park Beach** (21 kilometers north of Bundaberg, on the northern side of the Burnett River), which is a 17-kilometer-long pristine beach, with only residential buildings nearby. Not developed much beyond a campground just by the beach and a lifeguard hut, with a small shopping center at the entrance of the community, this is a beautiful place to spend a day just swimming or surfing (as long as you bring your own gear). Or you could stay a night or two at **Moore Park Beach Holiday Village and Kiosk** (2 Park Dr., tel. 07/4145-8388, cabins from $75) or at a very basic motel, **Moore Park Beach Motel** (29 Club Ave., tel. 07/4159-8332, from $95). Once a year Moore Park plays host to the annual Festival of Arts, usually mid-August, when the beach area comes alive.

On the southern side of the Burnett River lies **Burnett Head,** the headland by the Burnett estuary. Not a beach as such, it is still a lovely spot by the coast. The place where the old Burnett Lighthouse served the community faithfully between 1873 and 1972 (when it was replaced with a more modern construction) is the start of a very scenic coastal walk. You can still visit the original small wooden lighthouse just down the road, where it was moved in its entirety to preserve the historically important structure. The walk, starting at the new lighthouse, is the **Coral Coast Pathway,** which leads along the coast taking in several of the beaches along the way. The first stop along the path is secluded Oaks Beach, some 1.2 kilometers and around a 12-minute walk along, followed by Mon Repos Beach (5.1 kilometers, 50 minutes), Bargara (8.9 kilometers, 90 minutes), and pristine Kellys Beach (10.8 kilometers, 108 minutes).

Mon Repos Conservation Park, some 15 kilometers north from Bundaberg, is home of the largest and most accessible **loggerhead turtle rookery** in the South Pacific. Mon Repos Beach itself is secluded and quite unspoiled, but it is mostly famed for its turtles. The beach is closed between October 15 and April 30 for the turtle breeding season, and there is no overnight camping allowed at all in the area in order to protect the turtles. You can, however, get to learn more about them and even see them. Guided tours during turtle season provide a unique opportunity to see adult female turtles come ashore to lay their eggs from November to January. Eight weeks later (from January to March), the young hatchlings emerge and race to the ocean. From the Mon Repos Conservation Park information center (follow the signs to the Turtle Rookery), there are **ranger-guided tours** (adult $10.55, child $5.55, family $25.15) operating nightly between 7pm and 2am from November until late March. The tours are flexible, in both start time as well as duration, depending on turtle activity and sightings. Book through **Bundaberg Visitor Information Centre** (tel. 07/4153-8888, www.bookbundabergregion.com.au).

Bargara, overlooked by the so-called Hummock, an extinct volcano cone allowing views over the flat land and toward the coast, is the largest community along the coast near Bundaberg and is well appointed with all sorts of accommodations, plus a few restaurants, shops, and amenities. Two beaches straddle the small headland, and the Esplanade is busy with playgrounds and park benches and is generally a place to hang out and enjoy the coast. Just a 10-minute drive toward the coast from Bundaberg, this is a very nice alternative to staying in the city itself.

Reef Tours

Reef Free tours (tel. 07/3852-2575, www.reef-free.com.au, tours from $210) offer a great way of enjoying the reef and various activities on a whole day out from Bundaberg. Pickups are provided from Bargara and Bundaberg, then your bus will take you to the Town of 1770, and you'll take the catamaran out to Lady Musgrave Island. Once there, after a roughly two-hour sail, you can go snorkeling, ride the glass-bottom boat, or feed the fish (all included). After lunch there is a guided nature walk, more snorkeling, and plenty of time for extra activities, such as fishing ($40), an introductory dive ($95), or one or two certified dives (from $60). This tour is a nearly 12-hour extravaganza, starting with pickups at 6:30am, a long day out on the water, and then drop-off around 7pm.

Alternatively, you can take a day trip out to Lady Elliot Island, organized by the **Lady Elliot Island Eco Resort** (tel. 1800/072-200, www.ladyelliot.com.au, from $335 adult, $185 child). This is not a cruise but a day trip out by plane; you leave Bundaberg around 8:40am, take the short 30-minute hop to the island, and stay there until departure at around 4pm. You will be given a welcome drink and orientation tour of the island, snorkeling equipment and a guided tour of the reef, a glass-bottom boat tour, hot and cold buffet-style lunch, and even towels and reef walking shoes for your comfort.

Recreation

Coral Cove Golf Club (1 Pebble Beach Dr., Coral Cove, tel. 07/4132-5600, www.coral-coveresort.com.au, greens fees Mon.-Fri. $40 for 18 holes, $22 for 9 holes, Sat.-Sun. $50 and $25) is a picturesque golf club with stunning views across the sea, with accommodation packages available. Overlooking the rocky headland just south of Bargara, some 15 minutes' drive from Bundaberg, this course makes for a lovely day out. Coral Cove Golf Club is renowned for having the longest hole in Australia, measuring 635 meters, and is one of only two courses in Australia with a par 6 hole.

Enviro Reefs Paddle & Surf School (tel. 07/4159-0030, www.enviro-reefspaddleand-surf.com, private lessons from $30 pp) teaches you how to paddle board and how to surf. Various levels of skills are accommodated, and the location can be chosen to suit you (Mon Repos Beach and Kellys Beach are among the options).

Inland there is some great fishing to be had. Since no tours are currently operating to the reef, try fishing at inland Lake Monduran. **Rob Wood Game and Sports Fishing Charters** (tel. 04/2759-0995 or 07/4157-4342, www.bundabergfishing.com.au) offers various tours (from around $120 pp, tackle provided), even with accommodations, depending on what you need. One of the most popular is going out for an entire day to catch Australians' favorite fish, the barramundi, which average around 106 centimeters.

Accommodations

In Bundaberg itself, the accommodations are limited to mostly motels. Spread along the main drag of Bourbong Street, steps away from the river and the city center, these are basic and easy places to stay, especially if you are on a driving vacation and will be heading onward soon enough. Slightly more luxurious stays can be found at the beaches, mostly in Bargara, where you get a beach resort and vacation atmosphere.

On the outside, **Alexandra Apartments** (124 Dr Mays Rd., Bundaberg, tel. 1800/65-8565, www.alexandraapartment.com.au, two-bedroom apartments from $210) looks more like a suburban terraced house, with garages out front. Inside, the apartments are spacious, modern, and have plenty of amenities, such as a kitchenette, dishwasher, free Wi-Fi, large TV, CD and DVD players, private courtyard with barbecue, large bathrooms, and living, dining, and sleeping areas. There is also a pool.

More a hotel than a motel, **Burnett Riverside Motel** (7 Quay St., Bundaberg, tel. 07/4155-8777, www.burnettmotel.com.au, room from $150, two-bedroom apartment from $260) offers accommodations ranging from standard rooms to two-bedroom apartments, and even a honeymoon suite. There is an in-house restaurant and bar, and the location couldn't be more central, being steps away from the city center.

Colorful little **Oscar Motel** (252 Bourbong St., Bundaberg, tel. 07/4152-3666, www.oscarmotel.com.au, from $102) is simple, basic, and comfortable and is handily located on the main road of Bundaberg. Rooms are spacious and have a small kitchenette. The owners are lovely people who make you feel welcome and will help you make the most of your stay. Try to stay in room 8, 9, or 10, as next to the reception it can get noisy.

Best Western City Motor Inn (246 Bourbong St., Bundaberg, tel. 07/4152-5011, from $135) is one of the series of motels sitting next to each other on Bourbong Road. Clean, spacious, with a tiny pool by the main road, this is a comfortable and easy option to stop off along your way.

Villa Mirasol (225 Bourbong St., Bundaberg, tel. 07/4154-4311, www.villa.net.au, from $145) is a little piece of Mexico on Bundaberg's busiest street. The terra-cotta rooms are cheerful and basic, but clean and comfortable with free Wi-Fi, and the breakfast is not included but is recommended. Villa Mirasol is just a little closer to the CBD than the other motels on Bourbong Street, making walking easy.

Some 15 minutes southwest out of Bundaberg, in the middle of a forest lies ★ **Hideaway Haven Bed and Breakfast** (72 Tysons Rd., off Isis Highway, Bundaberg, tel. 07/4155-0448, www.hideawayhaven.com.au, from $120), a little gem of a B&B. Full of collectibles and personal trinkets, the four rooms have been lovingly decorated, including a teddy bear in each room, and you could not be made to feel more welcome. Very quiet, apart from bird sounds, it is utterly peaceful, and you can sit on the veranda watching the kangaroos and wallabies graze in the afternoon, maybe even spot a platypus in the nearby dammed lake. Rates include a very generous breakfast.

Selling itself as the only five-star accommodation in Bargara, **Manta Bargara Beachfront Resort** (95-97 The Esplanade, Bargara, tel. 07/4159-2266, www.mantabargara.com.au, from $250) is not a beach resort as such. The modern apartment block is a mix of vacation rentals, hotel rooms, and private units, complete with pool, tennis court, and gym. Accommodations vary from spacious one-bedroom to three-bedroom apartments, with balconies mostly overlooking the sea. While walk-in rates apply and one-night stays are available, these apartments are aimed at longer stays and get slightly cheaper the longer you stay.

A small apartment block with only 39 rooms, **Hotel Grand Mercure Apartments Bargara** (83-87 The Esplanade, Bargara, tel. 07/4130-1600, www.accorhotels.com, from $175) has the advantage of being on the seaside, with each good-size room and apartment featuring a huge balcony overlooking the ocean. The space in the apartments, the relaxed poolside, and great setting make this perfect for a slightly longer stay in the area; the incredibly spacious three-bedroom apartment, sleeping up to six persons, is perfect for a large family.

Family-friendly **Kellys Beach Resort** (6 Trevors Rd., Bargara, tel. 07/4154-7200, www.kellysbeachresort.com.au, from $155) has 40 self-contained stand-alone units, a large pool, restaurants, game room, tennis court, and gardens and offers proximity to the beach, making this an inexpensive relaxed and fun place to stay and enjoy the area. The units have two bedrooms, a kitchen, large lounge, and private deck. Rates get cheaper the longer you stay.

With accommodation options ranging from pool-view rooms with private terrace to family-sized apartments with large balconies and sea views, **Kacy's Bargara Beach Motel** (62 The Esplanade, Bargara, tel. 07/4130-1100, www.bargaramotel.com.au, from $139) is an affordable option just steps away from the beach and the Bargara shops and restaurants.

Just by the popular surfing beach, a couple of minutes out of main drag Bargara, the extensive campground **Bargara Beach Caravan Park** (25 Fred Courtice Ave.,

Nielson Park, tel. 07/4159-2228, www.bargarabeach.com.au) offers anything from unpowered tent sites to places to park your RV, to separate cabins ranging from studio to two bedrooms with private terraces (sites from $28, powered sites for RVs from $35, cabins from $96 per night, all prices for two people). There are plenty of things to do, including tennis, basketball, skating, playground, and numerous barbecue and picnic spots. A small shop and gas refill station looks after your worldly needs.

Food

Bundaberg is not necessarily the place you'd go expecting fine dining. Or even semi-fine dining. Just as the accommodations are mostly motels, the food is mostly fast. All the big chain names are snuggled near the motels along Bourbong Street, with a few individual places thrown in the mix. A handful of large hotels (a.k.a. pubs) offer food alongside plenty of beer and rum, plus usually the "pokies" (poker machines), and they are fine for an easy casual meal, such as the **Club Hotel** (50 Bourbong St., tel. 07/4151-3262, Sun.-Fri. 10am-10pm, Fri.-Sat. 10am-3am, daily specials from $12), a typical Australian corner pub with wood decor, large bar area, and TV sets in the corners. It offers themed nights with specials on the menu, such as steak night on Wednesday and chicken parmesan on Monday.

★ **Spinnaker Restaurant & Bar** (1A Quay St., Bundaberg, tel. 07/4152-8033, Tues.-Fri. noon-2pm and 6pm-9pm, Sat. 6pm-9pm, Sun. 9am-2pm, mains $30) has probably the best location in the town. Perched on the side of the Burnett River, this modern, open-plan venue overlooking the pretty bridges is all about location, location, location. Cuisine is modern Australian with a sprinkling of perennial favorites, and this is one of the best Bundaberg options.

Restaurant at Rowers on the River (corner Quay St. and Toonburra St., tel. 07/4154-4589, Tues.-Sat. 6pm-midnight, mains $25) is next door to Spinnaker, with the same spectacular river views, but it's a little more family oriented with a retro brown interior decor. It's one of the top choices for weddings on weekends, offering modern Australian food.

Rosie Blu (90 A Bourbong St., tel. 07/4151-0957, Mon.-Sat. 8:30am-4pm, mains $15) is right in the CBD of Bundaberg, a nice little healthy alternative to all the fast food outlets. Homemade sandwiches, fresh salads, and also some nice pizzas make for a great place to stop for brunch, lunch, or an early dinner.

In Bargara, whether you're after a lovely breakfast, a light lunch, or a more substantial dinner, ★ **Salt** (corner Bauer St. and Esplanade, Bargara, tel. 07/4159-0022, Sun.-Wed. 7:30am-10pm, Thurs.-Sat. 7:30am-5pm, mains $25) is a great place with huge French windows, allowing even the tables inside to enjoy the outside ambience. Modern and with beach views, it is also perfect for people watching. It serves fresh, seasonal, modern Australian cuisine; do try the grilled fish and chips option, which is tasty and healthy at the same time.

The other Bargara favorite is **Kacy's** (62 Esplanade, corner of Bauer St., Bargara, tel. 07/4130-1100, Tues.-Sun. 7am-9:30am, Thurs.-Sun. noon-2pm, daily 5pm-late, mains $35), across the street from Salt. With a huge menu for breakfast alone, this is a great place to start the day, but also check out the specialties like the garlic prawn and scallop hotpot, or the New Orleans-style gumbo. Both Salt and Kacy's have great indoor and alfresco options just a stone's throw from the beach.

Just a little farther up on Bauer Street is the **Bargara Beach Hotel** (corner Bauer St. and See St., tel. 07/4159-2232, daily 10am-midnight, mains $18), where a sports bar is perfect for stopping for a beer and/or a game on the pokies or pool table or just watching sports on the TV. Food served is typical Aussie comfort food with steaks and burgers and shrimp the favorite options.

Information and Services

The **Bundaberg Information Centre**

(corner Mulgrave St. and Bourbong St., tel. 07/4152-2333, www.bundabergregion.info, daily 9am-5pm) is a treasure trove of information on the entire region, with the staff being extremely lovely and helpful.

Farther down Bourbong Street near the post office are several **banks** (usually Mon.-Thurs. 9:30am-4pm, Fri. 9:30am-5pm), with ATMs taking most cards, and a couple of separate money exchanges. The main **post office** (corner Bourbong St. and Barolin St., Mon.-Fri. 9am-5pm, Sat. 8:30am-noon) sells anything from stamps to stationery.

There are three hospitals in town: **Bundaberg Base Hospital** (Bourbong St., corner Hinkler Ave., tel. 07/4152-1222), **Mater** (313 Bourbong St., tel. 07/4153-9539), and **Friendly Society Private Hospital** (19-23 Bingera St., tel. 07/4153-0666). Bundaberg has several pharmacies, such as **Friendly Society Pharmacy** (9 Bingera St., tel. 07/4154-0540, Mon.-Fri. 8:30am-5:30pm, Sat. 8:30am-12:30pm) and **West Bundaberg Pharmacy** (3/290 Bourbong St., tel. 07/4153-4133, Mon.-Fri. 8am-6pm, Sat.-Sun. 8am-noon).

Getting There

Bundaberg is served by the small **Bundaberg Airport** (BDB, Airport Dr., tel. 1300/883-699) six kilometers south west of Bundaberg. There are connections from Sydney, with both **Virgin Australia** (www.virginaustralia.com) and **Qantas** (www.qantas.com) flying into the town via Brisbane with around 35 services per week. All the major car rental companies are located at the airport, and there is a bus shuttle, operated by **Bundaberg and Wide Bay Shuttle Service** (tel. 04/2141-3446, 20-minute drive into the city center, $16.50 one way, service runs 7am-5pm and according to arrivals of flights), but that needs to be pre-booked.

If you are driving, follow the Airport Drive onto Isis Highway, turn right toward Bundaberg, following the road toward the right before the river, and you'll end up in the center. Isis Highway turns into Bourbong Street, where most of the accommodations, shops, and restaurants are.

The **Greyhound** coaches (tel. 1300/473-946, www.greyhound.com.au, one-way from $193) have a twice-daily service that stops in Bundaberg en route from Sydney to northern Queensland, taking around 27 hours for the trip. Trains are far and few between, but **Queensland Rail** (tel. 07/3235-7322, www.queenslandrailtravel.com.au, one way $89) has a once-a-day service that connects you from Brisbane's Roma Street to Bundaberg within 4.5 hours. This train terminates in Cairns.

Getting Around

As anywhere in Australia, and especially Queensland, distances are vast and the easiest way to get around to really experience the nooks and crannies of the region, and have flexibility, is driving. That said, **Duffy's Buses** (tel. 1300/383-397, www.duffysbuses.com.au, fares calculated depending on how many zones you cross, from around $0.90 in the inner city) take you around town and to Bargara (service 4) and Burnett Head (service 5) from Bundaberg Plaza (19 Mayborough St.). A local taxi service (**Bundaberg Cab Company,** tel. 13/10-08, www.131008.com.au) allows you to call taxis in the area. A trip between Bundaberg and Bargara takes around 17 minutes and costs approximately $30 one way.

LADY ELLIOT ISLAND

The southernmost coral cay of the Great Barrier Reef, only 46 nautical miles from Bundaberg and an hour's flight from major hubs such as Brisbane, Lady Elliot Island is relatively easy to reach and offers the whole shebang when it comes to the Great Barrier Reef. The picture-perfect island, with its hem of white sand and frill of reef, offers clear water teeming with life, from turtles to manta rays, from colorful reef fish to barracuda and some sharks (mostly harmless ones). On land, life is teeming, too. Countless sea birds come here to roost, leaving their rather pungent and omnipresent guano behind. It was the guano mining that razed Lady Elliot's vegetation to the ground back in the 19th century, when expatriate Malay and Chinese workers excavated the meters-deep bird droppings. Since then reforestation has seen a lush covering of casuarina and pandanus trees, enough to hide the island's small resort at any rate.

The elegant lighthouse, completed in 1873, was decommissioned in the 1980s and was recently included on the Commonwealth Heritage List. It stands as a marker for the ubiquitous ships that crash into cay's reefs at a legendary rate of one wreck per year. Tellingly, it was a ship wrecked on the island that gave it its name: the *Lady Elliot,* named after the wife of India's colonial governor, crashed onto the island's reefs one evening in 1816 and passed on its name.

Recreation

There are 14 recommended **dive sites** near the island, including a wreck site and the famous Blowhole, which lies within a cavern whose residents include lionfish, manta shrimp, wobbegongs (carpet sharks), and rare gnome fish. Divers must produce qualifications and log book before diving, and allow a minimum of 12 hours surface time between diving and flying. All gear is available for hire at the PADI shop, which is part of the resort. Boat dives cost $65.

Accommodations and Food

Accommodations on the island are through its one and only resort, the **Lady Elliot Island Eco Resort** (tel. 1800/072-200, www.ladyelliot.com.au). It's no luxury resort, but a true eco resort instead: an advanced Ecotourism Certified destination, operating almost entirely on solar power. The certification program, operated by Ecotourism Australia, requires resorts like that of Lady Elliot to contribute to environmental conservation, help local communities, and use resources wisely. As such, they are supporters of Project Manta, which collects data about island manta ray populations; and owner Peter Gash regularly speaks in favor of alternative energy initiatives. The resort also desalinizes seawater and collects rain for drinking. Visitors on Lady Elliot are limited to 150 people at any one time, including overnight and day guests, so it will feel like you have the island to yourself. Accommodations come in various units, from a Garden Unit, which sleeps four (from $204), to a two-bedroom Island Suite, which also sleeps four but is slightly more upmarket (from $291). The suites are in basic one-story cabins, pretty much no decor, but functional furniture and amenities. The resort itself is left as wild as possible—no manicured gardens, but simple sandy walkways. The restaurant is buffet-style, with plastic chairs and tables. All clean and usable, but highlighting the fact that you don't go to Lady Elliot Island for a resort stay, but for the environment.

And if you are not in or under the water, other amenities include a tennis court, playground, reef education center, saltwater pool, and numerous beaches.

There is a restaurant and bar on the island, plus a beachfront café, all of which are open throughout the day. Breakfast and dinner are included in the room rate.

Getting There and Around

The only way in and out of the island is by plane with **Seair Pacific** chartered by the resort, which has a fleet of 12-seater Cessna Caravans. Bookings go through the resort website (www.ladyelliot.com.au). There are two daily 40-minute flights from Bundaberg (8:40am and 1:10pm, returning at 11am and 4pm). Round-trips cost from $269. Luggage is limited to 10 kilograms per person, although divers can purchase an extra 10 kilograms for $100.

THE TOWN OF 1770 AND AGNES WATER

Hailed as the birthplace of Queensland, the tiny Town of 1770 is built on the site where James Cook (then lieutenant, later promoted to captain) first landed on the Queensland coast in May 1770, and the town has been stuck with the date ever since. The Town of 1770 and its twin town, Agnes Water, are snuggled between two national parks, and with its little sandy coves and calm Bustard Bay, 1770 was not a bad place for a first landing at all.

Legend has it that the local tribes watching the landing of Cook and his naturalist, Joseph Banks, said: "The tall leader [Cook] was clever as he directed the canoe and had a good look at two of their [sic] food trees [fig and Burdekin plum]. The short leader [Banks] was not clever as he was stung by the ants and caterpillars and took away plants that were useless for food or medicine." But they did find decent food: a turkey or bustard weighing a precise 17.5 pounds—how reliable the recordings are I cannot promise, but they seem rather specific. After enjoying their bird, Cook named the tranquil bay Bustard Bay.

Although Bustard Bay is straightforward enough, being stuck with a number for a name can get confusing. On most maps the town's name is written as Seventeen Seventy, yet it calls itself the Town of 1770, and this is how it's identified on quite a number of publications, but as Australians like to shorten everything, it often gets stuck with being called simply 1770.

Barely more than a fishing village, 1770 is surrounded on three sides by Coral Sea and Bustard Bay, and it boasts a couple of restaurants, a general store, and a marina from where you can hitch a ride to Lady Musgrave Island. For other amenities, you'll need to pop down the road, just eight kilometers south, to the town of Agnes Water.

Agnes Water was named after a ship, the coastal schooner *Agnes,* which was lost on its way between Bustard Bay and Mackay, and is a popular if small beach resort. Agnes Water is mostly residential, with roughly 1,500 people, and the 5.5-kilometer beach is the main draw of the town.

The slightly curved 1770 beach is not as impressive, although its picturesque sandbanks are visible at low tide, making it tranquil and safe. People are busy sailing or learning to paddle board, or simply casting a line, trying to avoid the ubiquitous pelicans. Agnes Water beach is a longer and wider beach with rolling waves, and as such is more suited to learning how to surf, with the waves crashing in and tossing any newcomers around a little.

Sights and Festivals

The little **Discovery Coast Historical Society Museum** (69 Springs Rd., Agnes

landing point of Captain Cook during his exploration of Australia in 1770

Water, tel. 07/4972-9000, weekdays except Tues. 1pm-4pm, Sat. 10am-4pm, adult $3), just opposite the visitors center in Agnes Water, offers plenty of information on what happened when in this region, with copies of Captain Cook's journals, Aboriginal artifacts, maritime displays, and a few historic photos of the area.

The Town of 1770 comes out to celebrate the 1770 occasion with its annual **Captain Cook 1770 Festival,** complete with reenactment of the historic events. It's held on a weekend in May close to May 24, the date of the first landing.

National Parks

Two lovely national parks flank 1770 and Agnes Water on either side. While both are gorgeous and well worth visiting, please note that they are only accessible by four-wheel drive, as most of the ways into the parks are mere tracks of sometimes dubious condition, which may leave smaller cars stranded in remote locations without decent cell phone coverage. Even if you are renting a four-wheel-drive vehicle, please check with park authorities about road conditions before you head out, through the **Department of National Parks, Recreation, Sport and Racing** (www.nprsr.qld.gov.au).

DEEPWATER NATIONAL PARK

Deepwater National Park has diverse vegetation of coastal scrubs, eucalyptus woodlands, wet heaths, and sedgelands surrounding Deepwater Creek and its tributaries. The creek is brown, not necessarily healthy looking, but the color is naturally derived from tannins and other substances leached from surrounding heath plants. Fringed by tall forests of swamp mahogany, paperbark, and cabbage palms, the creek is broken in places by shallow sections of reed bed and paperbark forest. With this diverse flora, Deepwater supports an equally diverse birdlife, including emus, red-tailed black-cockatoos, honeyeaters, kites, and various water birds. From January to April, turtle hatchlings emerge from the nests on the beaches, and not all beaches are patrolled by volunteers, so please be sensible and do not disturb the natural cycle.

Vehicle-based **camping** is permitted at Wreck Rock and Middle Rock camping areas, with camping fees $5.60 per person per night. Basic facilities such as compost toilets and picnic tables are provided at Wreck Rock camping area, but Middle Rock camping area has no facilities. Obtain a camping permit before you head into Deepwater through www.nprsr.qld.gov.au.

EURIMBULA NATIONAL PARK

Eurimbula National Park is to the north of 1770, and is famous for Captain Cook's naturalist Joseph Banks having collected plant specimens here on their first landing on the coast. He found a rich botanical habitat that exhibits both tropical rainforests and coastal mangroves. Not much is changed today, and the park is perfect for bushwalkers, boat lovers, and anglers, as long as you bring all your own equipment. There are no facilities, rentals, or shops. There are numerous walking tracks of differing length and fitness level; for example, the short and easy few minutes' walk to Ganoonga Noonga lookout offers views along the coast and across swamps and heathlands. Signposts are everywhere, offering you guidance on where to head and how long it will take you.

You can **camp** at Bustard Beach, where basic facilities are provided, with camping fees $5.60 per person per night. In dry weather conditions, you can get through to Bustard Beach in a non-four-wheel-drive vehicle, but do check the conditions before you set off. The track is unsuitable for caravans. Obtain a camping permit via www.nprsr.qld.gov.au.

Reef Tours

Lady Musgrave Cruises (1770 Marina, tel. 07/4974-9077, www.lmcruises.com.au, adult $190, child $90, family $495) takes you on a 75-minute ride across the bay to **Lady Musgrave Island;** you spend some five hours on the coral island snorkeling and diving, enjoying glass-bottom boat rides and guided island nature walks, swimming with turtles, and hanging out on the pontoon with its underwater observatory. All equipment is included, as is lunch, tea and coffee, and drinking water throughout. Departures are daily at 8:30am (8am check-in), returning at around 5pm.

Setting out on a gigantic amphibious contraption with **1770 LARC Tours** (1770 Marina, tel. 07/4974-9422, www.1770larctours.com.au) is an adventure in itself. A LARC (which stands for Lighter Amphibious Resupply Cargo) is at home on land and in the water, and there are two tours you can choose from. The "Paradise Tour" (leaves Mon., Wed., Sat. at 9am, returns at 4pm, adult $153, child $93) is a daylong land tour, taking in the coastline of the Eurimbula National Park and the Bustard Bay Lighthouse and even allowing you to sand-board across the dunes, if you are so inclined. With nature commentary, a tour through the lighthouse keeper's cottage and the station itself, tea and lunch, and the unusual aspect of the stunning coastline, this makes for a great day out. The "Afternoon Cruise" (departs daily at 4:30pm, returns 5:30pm, adult $32, child $17) takes in the coastline around sunset time, when the light is at its best and the coastline looks even prettier than usual.

Recreation

See the coast and the reef from above with **1770 Air Charters** (Captain Cook Dr., tel. 04/2866-1434, www.1770aircharters.com.au, from $80 pp). You can choose from four different scenic flights of differing lengths of time. Do a loop around the headland and across Bustard Bay Lighthouse (30 minutes, $80); fly out to Lady Musgrave Island (60 minutes, $125); take a tour of the reef and Lady Musgrave Island (60 minutes, $150); or loop across 1770, the headland, One Tree Island, Heron Island, and several reefs (75 minutes, $175).

Fishing Offshore 1770 Charters (1770, tel. 07/4974-9686, www.1770fishing.com, half day from $150 pp) takes you out for a cruise on the 10-meter Cougar Cat, and hopefully you'll be bringing home some fresh fish for dinner.

Learn **stand-up paddle boarding** with **1770 SUP** (1770, tel. 04/2102-6255, www.1770sup.com.au, from $20 per hour for board rental, $45 for a lesson). Paddle boarding is the best way to spend some time in Bustard Bay and 1770 beach. Learn how and

one of 1770 LARC Tours' Lighter Amphibious Resupply Cargo vessels

then hire a board and paddle with these guys. They even do tours along the coastline.

Alternatively, learn to **surf** with the **Lazy Lizard Surf School** (1770 and Agnes Water Beach, tel. 04/8817-7000, www.lazylizardsurfschool.com.au, special offers from $22 for a lesson, board rental from $20), right on the beach in Agnes Water, where the waves are perfect for beginners as well as accomplished surfers. Either learn the ropes or rent a board for a few hours.

Kayak tours are offered by **1770 Liquid Adventures** (1770, tel. 04/2895-6630, www.1770liquidadventures.com.au, from $55 pp). Go on a sunset tour, a family tour, or a creek exploration, or simply hire a kayak ($20 per hour) and choose your own route.

On land, why not go on a **motorbike tour** of the headland? Operators at **Scooter Roo Tours** (21 Bicentennial Dr., Agnes Water, tel. 07/4974-7697, www.scooterrootours.com, from $75 pp) provide you with training and a bike, as long as you have a valid car driving license. They even throw in flamed leather jackets, helmets, and fake tattoos to make the tours more authentic.

Accommodations

One of the original beach shacks built along the Esplanade, the family-friendly **Sunset Villa** (The Esplanade, 1770, tel. 07/4974-9990, www.1770beachaccommodation.com.au/sunset-villa.htm, from $230 per night, $600 per week) offers plenty of beach charm, with its blue and white hues and airy interior. There are two self-contained, open-plan apartments, each sleeping four guests. Overlooking Bustard Bay, the villa is secluded from other properties and surrounded by bushland; wallabies and black cockatoos live in the surroundings. The beach is around 150 meters away.

The ★ **Town of 1770 Beach Shacks** (Captain Cook Dr., 1770, tel. 07/4974-9463, www.1770beachshacks.com, from $188 per couple) is steps from the beach with great views and next to the couple of restaurants in 1770—location is everything, and this one is great. The "shacks" are a few beautiful, tropical Bali-esque houses, ranging from a tree house for two to accommodations sleeping up to six. The style of each shack is relaxed, with hammocks and decks, colorful linens, and wooden floors and beams. All have outdoor areas, couches, cushions, kitchens, and great views.

Right on the beach toward the residential end of 1770, the **1770 Camping Ground** (Captain Cook Dr., 1770, tel. 07/4974-9286, www.1770campingground.com.au, sites from $33) is the perfect way to enjoy all 1770 has to offer. Literally steps from the water, the location could not be any better. There are no cabins, just sites for tents and caravans, but amenities include a camp kitchen, showers and toilets, laundry, and a kiosk for daily necessities.

Agnes Water Beach Club (3 Agnes St., Agnes Water Beach, tel. 07/4974-7355, www.agneswaterbeachclub.com.au, from $200) offers spacious apartments from one to two bedrooms set around a large pool, giving a proper resort feeling, just minutes from the beach.

★ **Agnes Water Caravan Park** (Jeffrey Court, Agnes Water Beach, tel. 07/4974-7279, www.agneswaterbeach.com.au, sites from $30, breakers from $150) has private access to the beach, making it easy to carry your surfboard to the waves. Bring your own tent or caravan, or rent one of the amazing tents on stilts, called "breakers," which give meaning to the word "glamping," with wooden floors and decks overlooking the beach, en suite bathrooms, comfortable beds and seating. They sleep up to four and include cooking equipment, fridge, barbecue, and even a TV. Amenities on the campsite include camp kitchen, toilets and showers, laundry, and a café.

Food

Both 1770 and Agnes Water are tiny communities and food options are limited.

In 1770, right by the beach, is **The Tree** (576 Captain Cook Dr., 1770, tel. 07/4974-7446, daily for breakfast, lunch, and dinner, breakfast $15, burger $16, dinner mains $30), where you can enjoy bar foods ranging from anything from cake during the day to burgers and fries at night. The food is simple and filling, and the restaurant is in a great location.

The **Deck Bistro** (384 Captain Cook Dr., 1770, tel. 07/4974-9157, mains $25) is part of the 1770 Camping Ground and is open daily all day. It offers not only local fare but also a decent curry, if you are in the mood for Indian food.

In Agnes Water, try **Bustards Restaurant** (7 Agnes St., Agnes Water, tel. 07/4974-7675, daily 7am-8:30pm, mains $30), which is at the main beach entrance and offers modern Australian food with plenty of local ingredients. This is a relaxed place that is happy for you to linger over your food. They also do fresh ice cream and takeout.

The ★ **Garden Café** (303 Bicentennial Dr., Agnes Water, tel. 07/4574-9323, Sun.-Fri. 8am-4pm, dinner bookings Wed. and Sun., mains $20) hides behind an impressive entrance of wooden Balinese doors and lush gardens. The interior stays with the theme with hardwood floors, wooden tables, open window-walls, and simple decor that allows the gardens and the setting to shine. Apart from the tropical atmosphere, it's the freshly brewed coffee, hand-squeezed juice, traditional wood-fired pizzas, and vanilla slices (a creamy cake slice) that are the true crowd pleasers.

Information and Services

The **Agnes Water Visitor Information Centre** (71 Springs Rd., Agnes Water, tel. 07/4902-1533, Mon.-Fri. 9am-5pm, Sat.-Sun. 9am-4pm) has a wealth of information for 1770, Agnes Water, and the national parks, including safety, accessibility, and suggestions of walks and itineraries. There are a couple of banks with ATMs, a pharmacy (tel. 07/4974-9700), and medical center (tel. 07/4974-7265), along with a post office and Internet café in the **Caltex Centre** at the entrance to Agnes Water (corner Round Hill Rd. and Captain Cook Dr.).

Getting There and Around

The closest airports are at Bundaberg and Gladstone, and both have all the major car rental companies represented.

Queensland Rail (tel. 07/3235-2222, www.queenslandrail.com.au) operates services to Miriam Vale, some 50 kilometers inland, with connecting coach links with **TQ Tours** (14 Webster Ct., Agnes Water, tel. 04/3782-9277) to the Town of 1770 and Agnes Water.

There is a **Greyhound bus stop** (www.greyhound.com.au) at the **Caltex Centre** (tel. 07/4974-7557) at the entrance to Agnes Water. From there, regular local buses run between Agnes Water and 1770, or you could hire a bicycle or scooter at the Caltex Centre.

By far the easiest option to get to 1770 and Agnes Water is by driving. The communities are between Bundaberg and Gladstone; Agnes Water is some 60 kilometers off the Bruce Highway at the Lowmead turnoff, with 1770 six kilometers farther north.

LADY MUSGRAVE ISLAND

Named after Lady Jeannie Lucinda Musgrave, the American-born wife of Sir Anthony Musgrave, governor of Queensland in the late 1880s, Lady Musgrave Island has had a number of incarnations. As on Lady Elliot Island, guano "mining" was the island's bounty from the early 1900s. When the miners finally left, they abandoned their goats. Legend has it, they did it for the good of shipwrecked sailors, but instead of feeding starving sailors, the goats instead stripped the island of its undergrowth, nearly destroying the delicate ecosystem. In the 1930s, a couple of simple cabins on the island attracted the rich and famous for a while before World War II put an end to such indulgences. Since then, the island has been left to its own volitions, apart from the myriad day-trippers and handful of campers who come to be marooned for a few hours on a near-perfect desert island.

The island is surrounded by a picturesque kidney-shaped lagoon, which changes the look of, and the views and experiences from, the island, depending on whether it is high or low tide. While at high tide the lagoon offers navigable anchorage for boat owners, at low tide the fringing reef pops above the surface, offering a new set of explorations.

Recreation

With its sheltered lagoon, Lady Musgrave is ideal for **snorkeling** beginners, offering calm and clear waters and a plentitude of colorful reef fish, with turtles often coming to play as well. Look out for the amazing blue starfish and anemone fish, but stay away from the infamous cone shells, which are poisonous. **Diving** is a little more exciting outside the lagoon, with larger fish sightings.

Above land, this island, as you can guess from the amount of bird poop, is a haven for **bird-watching** enthusiasts: white-capped noddy terns can be found nesting in the pisonia trees, while the silver gulls, bridled terns, and black-naped terns nest nearer the beach on more open ground areas. Plenty of visiting wading birds, such as ruddy turnstones, Mongolian plovers, bar-tailed godwits, whimbrels, and grey-tailed tattlers, can be seen foraging on the reef from September to March.

You will probably see some distressed small birds covered in sticky pisonia seeds and debris. While it is natural to want to help, unfortunately this is part of life here, and you are asked not to interfere with nature.

Accommodations

Bush camping (from $5 per night) is permitted on the island, but there are few facilities (three composting toilets and an emergency VHF radio) and no other amenities or shops, so campers will have to come prepared for self-sufficiency, with plenty of fresh water and all other necessities, and are also required to leave nothing behind. Spaces are limited to 40 people, and bookings are required. Open fires are prohibited. The island is closed to campers from Australia Day weekend (January 26) through to Easter to avoid interference with nesting wildlife. Bookings can be made through **Capricorn Cays National Park** (tel. 13/74-68) or through **Lady Musgrave Cruises** (tel. 07/4974-9077).

Getting There and Around

Daily, **1770 Great Barrier Reef Cruises/ Lady Musgrave Cruises** (1770 Marina, tel. 07/4974-9077, www.lmcruises.com.au, adult $190, child $90, family $495) takes day-trippers as well as campers to the island from Town of 1770. The fast catamaran *Spirit of 1770* moors alongside a private floating pontoon, some 300 meters from the island. From there you can go snorkeling, watch the reef fish through the glass-bottom boat, take a guided island walk and learn about the birds and wildlife, and maybe, if it's the season (Nov.-Feb.), watch the turtles and whales from the beach. The price includes snacks and lunch, all snorkeling equipment, and even sunscreen. Optional extras include reef fishing ($20), scuba diving ($60), and transfers from Bundaberg (adult $20, child $10). Departures are daily at 8:30am, and it takes 75 minutes to get to the island, allowing five hours of snorkeling and diving when there, followed by a 75-minute trip back, depending on weather conditions.

GLADSTONE

The Gladstone area was first explored in 1770 by Captain Cook, who named Bustard Head south of the city. Other explorers followed: In 1802 Captain Matthew Flinders, the English navigator and cartographer, named Port Curtis, in 1823 explorer and surveyor John Oxley traveled the coastline, and in 1848 British Royal Navy officer and surveyor Owen Stanley charted the entrance to the port. The city of Gladstone itself was founded in 1847 as a minor penal colony, and named after the then British colonial secretary, William Ewart Gladstone, who later went on to become prime minister of Great Britain. The port's first wharf was built at Auckland Point in 1885, and the railway finally reached the town in 1897. Gladstone remained a relatively small port serving the local cattle industry

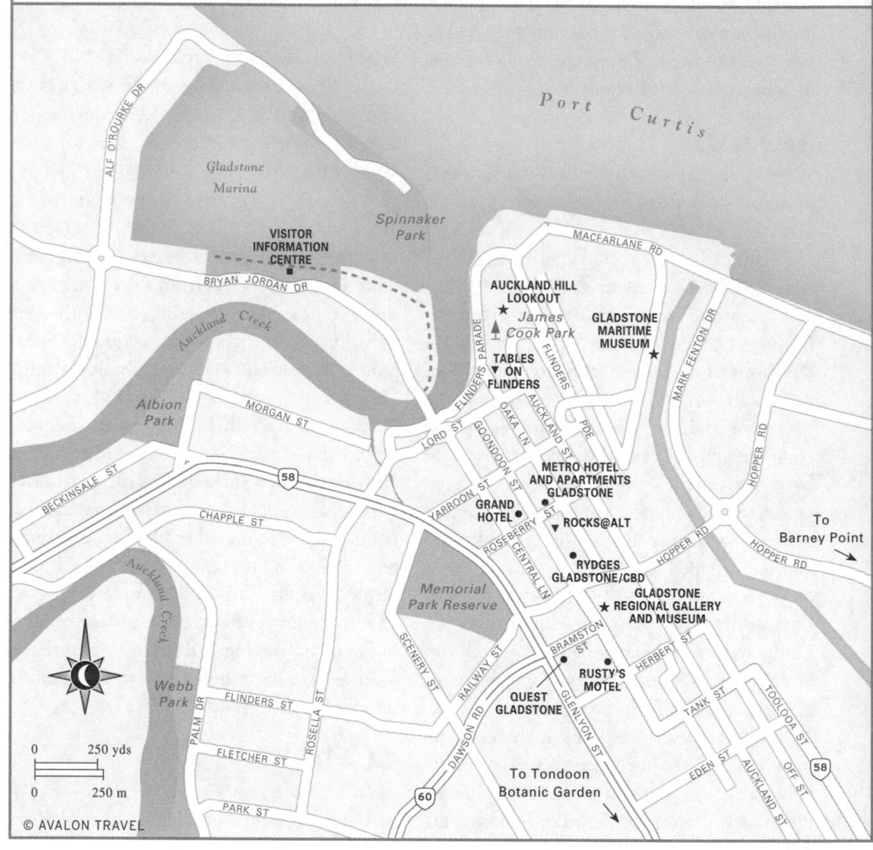

until 1961, when the export of coal resulted in a huge increase in both population and port activity.

Today, located 540 kilometers north of Brisbane and 107 kilometers south of Rockhampton, Gladstone is one of the most substantial and commercially successful ports in Australia, with some of the most sophisticated loading facilities in the country. It's also home to the world's largest aluminum refinery, the state's largest power station, and Australia's largest smelter.

Although Gladstone is an industrial city through and through, the area around the marina is relatively pretty, and this is also the place from where to get to Heron and Wilson Islands, the islands denoting the southern end of the Great Barrier Reef. But, quite honestly, that is pretty much it where Gladstone is concerned.

Sights

A good place to get an idea of what Gladstone is all about is the **Auckland Hill Lookout** (James Cook Park, off Endeavour St.), offering views across to the islands, across the city and marina.

Hidden in the industrial area surrounded by port activity and railway tracks, the **Gladstone Maritime Museum** (1 Francis

Dr., tel. 07/4972-0810, Thurs. and Sun. 10am-4pm, adult $6, child $3, family $15) is quite difficult to find. It is a shame this museum isn't open every day, as it is a little trove of maritime treasure. The grounds hold a small lighthouse, and there's a map of shipwreck locations in the region. Another feature is the *Jenny Lind* figurehead, which was found washed ashore at Great Keppel Island after the *Jenny Lind* fell afoul of the Kenn Reef in 1850. Luckily, all aboard the *Jenny Lind* survived the shipwreck, due to resourceful crew members distilling drinking water from seawater and building a rescue vessel from the ship wreckage, which carried passengers safely to Moreton Bay. There are also lots of models of ships and boats, illustrating the history of early sailing vessels, naval vessels, and even a model of the paddle steamer *Premier,* which provided the passenger link from the end of the railway at Gladstone through the narrows to Rockhampton at the turn of the 20th century.

The **Gladstone Regional Gallery and Museum** (Goondoon St. corner Bramston St., tel. 07/4976-6766, Mon.-Sat. 10am-5pm, free) is in the former Gladstone Town Hall, a lovely heritage building with rounded windows and a grand columned entrance, with a modern annex. The mix of old setting and modern gallery, linked by a glass "bridge," is a nice setting for the various, ever-changing exhibitions focusing on the regional arts and culture, plus the occasional exhibition of local school kids' work, which can be surprisingly good. A statue of the city's namesake, William Ewart Gladstone, is housed in the new part of the gallery and, through the glass, is on show for all passersby to see.

Spinnaker Park (Alf O'Rourke Dr., across the creek) stretches along the breakwater opposite the marina, sheltering the boats while offering a manicured park with paths, making it perfect for walks, jogging, rollerblading, and all sorts of outdoor fitness pursuits, all with industrial views seaward and the marina inland. It's also popular with families, who are drawn here by the tamed bushland and the seating areas, complete with barbecues that are regularly used for parties and picnics.

Gladstone Marina (Bryan Jordan Dr., tel. 07/4976-1396) is home to the ferries to the islands, as well as the excellent **Gladstone Visitor Information Centre** (Mon.-Fri. 8:30am-4:30pm, Sat.-Sun. 9:30am-4:30pm).

At **Tondoon Botanic Gardens** (Glenlyon Rd., tel. 07/4977-6899, Oct.-Mar. weekdays 7am-6pm and weekends 9am-6pm, Apr.-Sept. weekdays 7am-5:30pm and weekends 8:30am-5:30pm, free), self-guided trails highlight some of the gardens' varied planted areas, including: the Native Wildflower Walk (20 minutes); the Useful Wild Plants Walk (30 minutes); and the Dry Rainforest (20 minutes), Wet Rainforest (20 minutes), and Queensland Rainforests Walks (30 minutes). The Mount Biondello Circuit Trail (3 km, about 1.5 hours) is a medium-difficulty, steadily climbing bushwalk taking you through eucalyptus forest and pockets of dry vine scrub, with views of Gladstone Harbour and the city from the summit. A map for all the walks can be obtained at the Tondoon Visitor Centre at the entrance to the gardens.

Beaches and Islands

Barney Point is the only official swimming beach near Gladstone and is one kilometer east of the city center. The beach is made up of coarse sand and pebbles, with calm waters and wide tidal flats. It is backed by a reserve that commemorates the founding of Gladstone, together with a picnic area, playground, and barbecue site. That said, it is flanked by a refinery and coal store (you even find bits of coal on the beach) and has large ships going past, reminding you that essentially Gladstone is an industrial city, not a beach resort.

You are better off ignoring this beach, unless you are desperate, and heading a little farther south to **Tannum Sands,** just 20 kilometers from the city. This one is a gorgeous, long, white-sand beach overlooking Facing Island. Recently awarded "Queensland's Friendliest Beach" and "Central Queensland's Tidiest Beach," the main beach has beautifully landscaped parklands ideal for picnics and barbecues but is backing onto residential areas, forgoing any touristy development. Queensland Lifesavers patrol the main beach each weekend and during summer holidays, adding to the safe and relaxed holiday atmosphere. Tannum Sands is a popular spot for kite surfing and paddle boarding, both organized by **In the Loop** (48 Gregory St., Townsville, tel. 04/1583-7484, www.intheloopkiteboarding.com, kite-boarding lesson $100, paddle-board lesson $90; lessons only, no board rental).

Curtis Island offers surprisingly unspoiled beaches, small bays, clean water, wilderness, and wetlands as well as an outback-style cattle station. Being partly industrialized, it also has its own airstrip. **South End Campground** is 1.2 kilometers from the jetty on the northeast side of the South End township on Curtis Island. The campground is an open grassy area with 20 sites and with large eucalyptuses providing some shade. No facilities are provided, campers will need to be self-sufficient. Permits can be organized through the **Gladstone Visitor Information Centre** (tel. 07/4972-9000, from $5.60 pp per night to $22.40 per family of two adults, three children per night). **Curtis Island Ferry** (tel. 07/4972-6990, www.curtisferryservices.com.au, adult round-trip $30, child $22, family $84) leaves Gladstone Harbour five days per week (Mon. 12:30pm, returning 3:30pm; Wed. 8am and 2:30pm, returning 9am and 3:30pm; Fri. 8am and 5:30pm, returning 9am and 6:30pm; Sat. and Sun. 8am and 2:30pm, returning 9am and 3:30pm.

Facing Island boasts long sandy beaches and a lot of privacy, as it is only accessible by private boat or barge service, allowing you to bring your four-wheel-drive to the island (just catch the Curtis Island ferry—it stops at Facing Island along the way). Located some 12 kilometers from the Gladstone mainland, the island offers designated camping areas, perfect for those who come organized with a fishing rod or a surfboard, or who simply want to relax and explore the unspoiled bushland and coastline. The **Oaks camping grounds** are on the northwest side of Facing Island, a short distance from the ferry drop-off point at the Oaks beach. Oaks is solely suitable for self-sufficient campers, as there are no facilities provided. Bookings and permits are required and can be made through the **Gladstone Visitor Information Centre** (tel. 07/4972-9000, from $5.60 pp per night to $22.40 per family of two adults, three children per night).

Helicopter Tours

Gladstone Helicopters (1 Callemondah Dr., tel. 1300/761-907, www.gladstonehelicopters.com.au) offers scenic flights across the nearby islands (Curtis and Facing Islands, and tiny islands farther away that you can see from on the flight) and also inland to Lake Awoonga. Flights range from 15 minutes ($145 pp) to 90 minutes ($850 pp).

Accommodations

Rydges Gladstone (100 Goondoon St., tel. 07/4970-0000, www.rydges.com, from $145) is a business and leisure hotel with great (industrial) harbor views from some of the rooms, plus a big pool; it is also right on Goondoon Street, the main street full of shops and restaurants. Accommodations from single rooms to suites are available, with the rooms all very large and airy, with modern furniture, funky retro carpets, coffee/tea-making facilities, and free Wi-Fi. The relaxed CBD Restaurant offers alfresco and indoor dining, and the menu emphasizes the region's meat products.

Options range from studios up to three-bedroom apartments, making **Quest Gladstone** (39-43 Bramston St., tel. 07/4970-0900, www.questapartments.com.au, studio from $179) one of the more family-friendly places to stay in Gladstone. Features include balconies, a swimming pool, and a barbecue area. Although there is no on-site restaurant, the kitchens are fully equipped, and a pantry shopping service is available, where you complete your shopping list and find the items in your room when you return. The apartments are quite plain, but modern and functional, with even the studio offering a desk and dining table.

On top of one of the many hills in the city, just off the main shopping on Goondoon Street, ★ **Metro Hotel and Apartments Gladstone** (22-24 Roseberry St., tel. 07/4972-4711, www.metrohotels.com.au, from $145) is perfectly placed between the city center and the inlet and harbor for exploring the city and marina. The views are pretty much as good as they come in Gladstone, and the apartments are very spacious, with balconies, all amenities, even washing machine and dryer. The decor is airy and light, and you get a comfy sofa, which folds into a bed should you need to fit more than two people into the apartment. Downstairs is the excellent Rocks@lt Restaurant, and any food and drink had at the **Grand Hotel** (79 Goondoon St., tel. 07/4972-2422, daily 10am-midnight), just around the corner, can be charged to your room, too.

Already an icon in Gladstone, centrally located **Rusty's Motel** (167 Goondoon St., tel. 07/4971-6000, www.rustysmotel.com.au, from $120, apartment from $350) has basic if comfortable and clean rooms and one self-contained executive apartment, which sleeps up to five in two en suite bedrooms, with dining room, kitchen, and outdoor space. It also offers a palm-fringed pool, easy parking, and a popular restaurant and café, which serves staples such as garlic prawns, steak, pasta, and local fresh fish (mains $28).

Food

There are two good fine-dining restaurants in Gladstone, neither cheap, but offering a nice experience in otherwise quite grim Gladstone: **Rocks@lt** (Metro Hotel, 22-24 Roseberry St., tel. 07/4972-9884, www.rocksaltgladstone.com.au, Mon.-Fri. 6am-late, Sat.-Sun. 11:30am-late, mains $40) is open for breakfast, lunch, and dinner. Plenty of pastas and tapas are on the menu, but it's difficult to beat the sizable steak with potato mash and fresh salad on the side. ★ **Tables on Flinders** (2/3 Oaka Ln., tel. 07/4972-8322, http://tablesonflinders.net, lunch Fri.-Sun. 11:30am-2pm, dinner daily from 6pm, mains $47) is a lovely place by the creek, open for lunch and dinner. The atmosphere is all white tablecloths and clinking wine glasses, yet it is small enough not to be daunting, and perfect for a night out for two. This is the place to try the famed Gladstone mudcrab, with modern Australian dishes and local, seasonal ingredients leading the seasonally changing menu.

Scotties Bar and Restaurant (46 Goondoon St., tel. 07/4972-9999, Mon.-Sat. 6pm-midnight, mains $38) is a favorite with locals, offering à la carte, indoor and alfresco dining in the evenings, with popular dishes including fresh oysters, steaks, and lamb shanks. The **CBD Restaurant and Bar** (Rydges Hotel, 100 Goondoon St., tel. 07/4970-0025, breakfast Mon.-Fri. 6am-9am, Sat. 7am-9:30am, Sun. 7am-9:30am, dinner Mon.-Sat. 6pm-9pm, mains $33) is modern and stylish, offering great modern Australian food.

Information and Services

The **Gladstone Visitor Information Centre** (Marina Ferry Terminal, 72 Bryan Jordan Dr., tel. 07/4972-9000, Mon.-Fri. 8:30am-4:30pm, Sat.-Sun. 9:30am-4:30pm) is at the ferry terminal and offers not only cruises but information on the region, complete with booking service.

For all other services, Goondoon Street has it all: the **post office** (190 Goondoon St., tel. 13/13-18, Mon.-Fri. 9am-5pm) and several **banks** with ATMs accepting all major cards. **Gladstone Hospital** (Park St., tel. 07/4976-3200) has an accident and emergency department, and there are several pharmacies along Goondoon Street, such as **Family Chemist** (83-85 Goondoon St., tel. 07/4972-8400, Mon.-Fri. 8:30am-5:30pm, Sat. 8:30am-noon).

Getting There

There are several daily links between Sydney, Brisbane, and Gladstone, with Qantas and Virgin Australia flights being a quick 50-minute hop between Gladstone and Brisbane. The **Gladstone Airport** (GLT, Aerodrome Rd.,

Clinton, tel. 07/4977-8800, www.gladstone.qld.gov.au/gladstone-airport) is also the departure point for aerial services to Heron and Wilson Islands, and it lies about five kilometers inland, southwest of the city center. All major car hire companies are represented within the Gladstone Airport Terminal or close by. If you are driving, follow the Aerodrome Road onto Dawson Highway, turning left toward the city center; at the junction with Glenlyon Street, go straight across onto Bramston Street and turn left onto the main CBD drag of Goondoon Street.

Gladstone Airport Transfer (tel. 04/3790-2302, http://gladstoneairporttransfer.com.au, booking essential 24 hours in advance, one way $19, timings coincide with arrivals) is a shuttle that takes you directly to your hotel. There is a taxi rank for **Blue and White Taxis** (tel. 13/10-08, www.gladstonetaxis.com.au); the ride takes around 15 minutes and costs roughly $25 one way.

Queensland Rail (tel. 07/3235-2222, www.queenslandrail.com.au) operates regular services to the Gladstone region on many Travel Train services, the main being the Tilt Train, which services the Gladstone region regularly, stopping at Gladstone and Miriam Vale. **Gladstone Railway Station** (corner Tank St. and Toolooa St., tel. 07/4976-4324) is a 20-minute walk from Goondoon Street, near which most of the hotels are found. Alternatively, bus route 501 of **Buslink Gladstone** (tel. 07/4972-1670, www.buslinkqld.com.au/gladstone, adult one way $2.40) takes you from the station into the center, but note that the bus only runs roughly once every two hours.

Greyhound Australia (www.greyhound.com.au, tel. 1300/473-946) runs bus services that call in to various coastal and country spots throughout the Gladstone region. Daily services to Gladstone stop at the BP service station on Dawson Road.

Driving yourself to Gladstone from Sydney following the Bruce Highway is around 1,400 kilometers, with an estimated driving time of around 28 hours. From Bundaberg it is around 185 kilometers, an easy drive along the Bruce Highway.

Ferries to Heron and Wilson Islands depart from **Gladstone Marina** (Bryan Jordan Dr., tel. 07/4976-1396).

Getting Around

Buslink Gladstone (tel. 07/4972-1670, www.buslinkqld.com.au/gladstone, adult one-way tickets from $2.40) operates several buses that do loops around the city, but this is a working industrial town, not a touristy city, so the buses tend to run more often during commuting hours and don't take in the few sights. Taxis (such as **Blue and White Taxis,** tel. 13/10-08, www.gladstonetaxis.com.au) are an easier option, while in the city center, you can easily get around on foot.

HERON ISLAND

Strangely enough, both Captain Cook, who sailed past the tiny island around 1770, and Matthew Flinders, who by passed it in around 1802, failed to actually locate Heron Island. It wasn't until January, 12, 1843, that the HMS *Fly* anchored off the island. Noting the reef herons, the ship's naturalist, Joseph Bette Jukes, named it after the birds, which are part of the rich feathered wildlife that inhabits the island. That said, local folklore insists that Heron Island was erroneously named such by a geologist, not an ornithologist, who had spotted an egret, not a heron, but the name stuck.

Either which way, Heron Island is part resort, part national park, and part research center, and only those lucky few with booked accommodations at the Heron Island Resort, or invited marine biologists, have access to the island, so day-tripping is unfortunately not an option. But some cruises do go to the nearby Heron and Wistari reefs for diving and snorkeling. Indeed, Jacques Cousteau declared the island and its pristine waters one of the top 10 dive spots in the world; after all, the reefs around Heron Island boast 60 percent of the 1,500 species of fish and about 70 percent of the hard and soft coral varieties of the Great

Barrier Reef, making the underwater world a riot of color.

Only less than one kilometer in length and 300 meters wide, this tiny island used to boast two time zones: Queensland time and a time zone established by General Douglas MacArthur in World War II. But that changed in 2014, to be in line with the mainland.

Recreation

Heron Island is exclusive to resort guests (no day-trippers allowed), and all activities are arranged through the **Heron Island Resort** (tel. 03/9426-7550, www.heronisland.com).

Head out for a **Wilson Island Day Trip** ($175 pp) to enjoy a desert island lifestyle, even more so than on Heron Island. Carrying only 8-12 guests, the boat to Wilson Island departs Heron Island every Monday, Wednesday, and Friday at 9am, returning around 5pm. The trip includes morning tea, lunch, and afternoon tea while snorkeling and exploring the island.

The **Great Barrier Reef Swim,** held in conjunction with www.oceanswims.com, takes place annually in the middle to end of October at Heron Island and spans the island. It includes a three-kilometer and a one-kilometer swim around the island.

Half of the more than 20 dive sites are just 15 minutes from the beach, so **diving** ($70 per dive, $50 each after 5 dives) is a main attraction. Refresher dives for those who haven't dived in 12 months ($10), night dives ($99), and dive boat charters are available (prices depend on duration and number of people and dives).

Complimentary **snorkel lessons** are conducted daily at 2pm in the swimming pool. The lessons are very relaxed, and everybody is invited; the length of the lesson depends on how many participants show up and how well they get on. Organized **snorkel tours** visit Heron and Wistari Reefs (minimum age 8 years, adult $50, child $35). There are three daily snorkeling boat tours, of roughly 2-3 hours, depending on the weather.

Heron Island publishes a *Nature Calendar,* highlighting natural events happening on the island, such as the nesting and hatching of green turtles and loggerhead turtles between late October and February.

The island is mostly the home of the black noddy terns, wedgetailed shearwaters, and eastern reef egrets, but, for example, in December around 100,000 birds nest on the island, and predominantly black noddy chicks and wedgetailed shearwaters can be observed

coral colony near Heron Island

laying eggs and hatching. The resort offers complimentary nature walks, during which you'll learn about the resident birds (times depend on seasons and demand—please check with reception upon arrival).

Accommodations

The first resort on the island was established by Captain Christian Poulson in 1932, and in 1980 the current owners, P&O Australian Resorts, took over. They refurbished the **Heron Island Resort** (tel. 03/9426-7550, www.heronisland.com, Turtle Room from $318 per night, Beach House from $909 per night) in 1997, and it now caters to around 300 guests in 109 rooms and suites, plus one Beach House. The Turtle Room is the smallest of the rooms, but it is light and airy, offering both indoor and outdoor seating set in the tropical gardens. It is also available as a Family Turtle room, which sleeps up to four persons. All rooms offer coffee- and tea-making facilities, a refrigerator, hair dryer, and an umbrella for the deck. Rooms gradually get closer to the beach and include extended outdoor spaces. Several suites are even more luxurious, offering amenities such as a CD player and even larger interior and exterior spaces.

The one and only Beach House is exclusive and very private. Set within gardens, it has direct beach access and sleeps up to four persons. As in the other rooms and suites, the decor is tropical, with white and blue and green hues, wooden blinds, wicker furniture, tiled floors, colorful cushions, and the windows offering grand views of either the lush wild gardens or tantalizing glimpses of water. The resort is not ostentatious, but comfortable and relaxed, and people are here to enjoy the water, the reef, and the island, rather than insisting on the extravagant indulgences. A shop and spa plus a pool are provided on the island.

Food

There is one restaurant (part of the resort) on the island, the **Shearwater Restaurant,** which is open daily for breakfast (7:30am-9:30am), lunch (noon-4pm), and dinner (6pm-9pm, mains $30), offering a good mix of modern Australian food, local ingredients, and perennial favorites to suit all. A bar, the **Baillies Bar** (daily noon-8pm), has a veranda with great views, a couple of pool tables, a giant chess board, three TVs (which show major sports events), and a library and Wi-Fi area, and also offers all-day snacks (grilled panini $16). Please do not expect to see a lot of local fresh fish on the menu, as the island is in a fishing restricted zone, and you are supposed to look at the fish rather than eat them.

Heron Island's Pisonia Trees

The island's notorious pisonia trees are a haven for birds, because the seeds attract insects and the insects attract birds, but there is also a dark side to these pretty trees. They are also called **bird catcher trees,** as their sticky seeds get into the feathers of birds. While the tree evolved so that the larger seabirds would carry the seeds off to their distant destinations, the smaller urban species cannot cope as easily; they often get covered in the seeds and fall to the ground, only to then get even more covered in debris. If you do find a bird covered in sticky seeds, cut it loose from the vegetation (cut the plant, not the feathers) and take it to a local biologist, who will be able to help.

Getting There

Please note that all transfers—boat, seaplane, or helicopter—are arranged through the **Heron Island Resort** (tel. 03/9426-7550, www.heronisland.com) at the time of booking.

If you are arriving by plane into Gladstone, a courtesy coach departs from Gladstone Airport to Gladstone Marina, to connect with the Heron Island boat service. The catamaran departs Gladstone Marina at 11am daily and returns at 2pm. The launch trip from Gladstone to Heron Island takes approximately two hours and costs $50 per adult one way, $25 per child. All launch transfers

Heron Island

are subject to change without notice due to weather conditions.

HeliReef operates scenic helicopter transfers between the HeliReef Terminal (Curry Kenny Hangar 2, Callemondah Dr.) and Heron Island daily (excluding Christmas Day). Flights are available on request at any time (subject to availability), subject to a minimum of four passengers traveling and remaining within passenger payload (weight) restrictions. Private charters can also be arranged on request. Guests need to make their own way between Gladstone Airport and the HeliReef Terminal (a short three-minute drive; parking is only available at Gladstone Airport and not the HeliReef Terminal itself). Please allow 30 minutes prior to arrival and departure to allow for check-in procedures. The flight duration is 30 minutes, and a baggage allowance of 15 kilograms per person applies for helicopter transfers.

Australia by Seaplane operates scenic transfers between Gladstone and Heron Island daily (excluding Christmas Day) subject to availability. Flights ($291 one way per passenger) are available on request, subject to tides being permissible, with a minimum of two passengers per flight, and all flights must remain within passenger payload (weight) restrictions. All guests traveling from Gladstone to Heron Island can make their own way to the Australia by Seaplane desk, adjacent to the baggage carousel at Gladstone Airport Terminal. Please allow 75 minutes prior to arrival and departure to allow for check-in procedures. The flight duration is 25 minutes and a baggage allowance of 15 kilograms per person applies for seaplane transfers.

ROCKHAMPTON

Elegant streetscapes and imposing heritage buildings reflect Rockhampton's status as a former gold town, modern business hub, and gateway to the Queensland Outback, plus inland capital of the Capricorn Coast. By the time gold was discovered near Mount Morgan in the 1880s, Rockhampton had already found wealth as the main port for the developing Outback in Queensland, with the main export then being wool.

Today, big concrete effigies of bulls are standing guard at all the entry points into town, paying homage to Rockhampton's claim as the "Beef Capital of Australia." Many shops, motels, and other outfits throughout the city have picked up on the theme, and you'll see cows at every corner, on roofs, in traffic circles, and, of course, the real thing just outside the city limits on the farms.

Affectionately known as "Rocky," Rockhampton is home to some 100,000 people living in the greater area and enjoying a town that is at heart a country town, but is at the same time modern city and gateway to the Capricorn Coast, with all its beach, sea, and in particular Great Barrier Reef delights.

Rockhampton is set on the mighty Fitzroy River, which has the second largest catchment in Australia after the Murray-Darling, with a catchment area of around 139,000 square kilometers.

Rockhampton

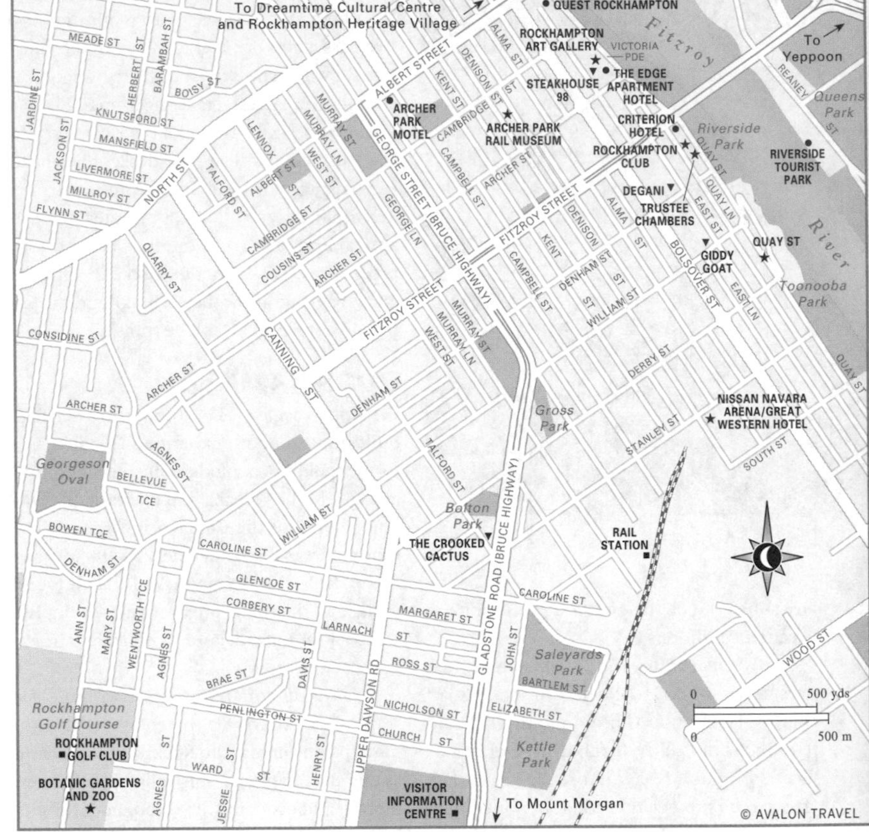

Sights

A WALKING TOUR OF HERITAGE BUILDINGS

To get the best overview of Rockhampton and the historic town, walk through the city center and enjoy the many sandstone heritage buildings. Twenty-six buildings along **Quay Street** have been included within the National Trust's classification and pay homage to the wealth in the city. Starting from Fitzroy Bridge, the three-story colonnaded **Criterion Hotel** (150 Quay St.) was built in 1858 on the site of the Bush Inn and now is reported to have a resident ghost—a chambermaid who committed suicide in room 22 with a broken heart. Colonial-style **Rockhampton Club** (166 Quay St.), which dates back to 1887, used to be an exclusive gentleman's club and is now used mostly for offices. Palm-fringed classic colonial-style **Trustee Chambers** (170 Quay St.), built in 1887, was once the private residence of Dr. William Callaghan, Rockhampton's second doctor and a surgeon at Rockhampton Hospital who had a love for thoroughbred horses and today has the honor of having the Callaghan Park Racecourse named after him.

Cattle House (180 Quay St.) is in the neoclassical revival style and dates from 1864, when it first started life as the Union Bank of Australia. Banking business used to be conducted on the ground floor, while the manager resided on the first floor. The building now, as is hinted at in its name, is home to the Cattlemen's Union. **Luck House** (182 Quay St.) was built in 1862 for general merchant P. D. Mansfield, first postmaster and second mayor of Rockhampton. Established in 1872, the **Queensland National Bank** building (186 Quay St.), in the neoclassical style with Greek Corinthian influence, housed the first and most successful of Queensland's three 19th-century banks, which held 40 percent of Queensland's deposits by 1880.

The pink-hued **Royal Bank** building (194 Quay St.), dating back to 1889, and **Archer Chambers** (206 Quay St.), a former office building, are followed by the rather impressively grand **Customs House** (208 Quay St.), which was built between 1898 and 1901 in the classic revival style; it now houses a bar and restaurant and is popular as a wedding venue. The **Heritage Hotel** (230 Quay St.) was built in 1898 in the colonial style and used to be the place to meet over a drink for the people from the countryside on their visit to the big city. At 238 Quay Street is the Victorian classical style **Goldsborough Mort** building, which used to be a private residence built for wealthy transport and livestock and mining pioneer Walter Hall in 1899. Next door, at 236 Quay Street, is the building of the neoclassical revival **Australian Broadcasting Corporation,** built just two years prior.

Parallel to Quay Street is the serene main street of **Bolsolver Street,** with grand trees shading pedestrians and further heritage buildings, such as the impressive Post Office and clocktower, dating back to 1895 and built in the classical revival style, and sandstone Court House, originally built between 1898 and 1901, which has a striking copper dome.

ROCKHAMPTON ART GALLERY

Rockhampton Art Gallery (62 Victoria Parade, tel. 07/4936-8248, www.rockhamptonartgallery.com.au, daily 10am-4pm, free) is a modern building by the river, just along from Quay Street. Established in 1967, it houses one of the finest collections of mid-20th-century Australian art in Queensland, including examples of modern and contemporary Australian and Aboriginal art, Japanese and British art, and art and artifacts of central Queensland. Regular visiting exhibitions ensure that this is a thriving art hub, with acclaim way past the Capricorn Coast's borders.

ARCHER PARK RAIL MUSEUM

Whether you're a train enthusiast or not, **Archer Park Rail Museum** (Denison St., between Cambridge St. and Archer St., tel. 07/4936-8191, Mon.-Fri. and Sun. 9am-4pm, closed Sat., adult $8.50, child 3-12 $5, family $26) is a lovely little place, set in the original, and heritage listed, Archer Park Station, built in 1899. The museum tells about the history of the station and the unique Purrey Steam Tram, which was built in and imported all the way from Bordeaux, France. There are photographs, soundscapes, and object-based exhibitions, and you can even take a ride on the restored tram (Sun. between 10am and 1pm), which is believed to be the only one of its kind in the world, dating back to 1909.

ROCKHAMPTON ZOO

Situated within the Rockhampton Botanic Gardens by the Murray Lagoon, the great little **Rockhampton Zoo** (Spencer St., tel. 07/4922-4347, www.rockhamptonzoo.com.au, daily 8am-4:30pm, free) is home to more than 50 native and exotic animals. Most animals are behind bars but in enclosures you can enter, and you'll be able to get great close-ups. Kangaroos roam free, as do some wallabies and plenty of birds, and regular feeding times ensure that you can get a close up with all sorts of animals. There is also the wombat research center, studying the seventh most endangered animal in the world, the northern hairy-nosed wombat, which is native to the Rockhampton area and has its own enclosure.

DREAMTIME CULTURAL CENTRE

Set within 12 hectares of native trees and plants, **Dreamtime Cultural Centre** (Bruce

Hwy., tel. 07/4936-1655, www.dreamtime-centre.com.au, Mon.-Fri. 10am-3:30pm, tours 10:30am, adult $14, child $6.50) is the place to learn about the traditions, culture, and history of the original occupants of this region, the Darambal. You can have a look at a replica burial site, rock art, houses, and traditional ceremonial sites. If you wish, you can try your hand at learning how to throw a boomerang. This is Australia's largest Aboriginal Cultural Centre set in natural bushland. It was originally opened in 1988 as a way for the elders of the tribe to pass on their knowledge to the younger members, but has since grown and now offers facilities such as its own motel and convention center (should you wish to stay longer or bring your work colleagues), plus a shop, kiosk, and the Torres Strait Islander Complex, which concentrates on the specific history and heritage of the peoples from there, complete with artifacts and displays, a theater, park area for picnics, and plenty of ongoing and changing exhibitions.

ROCKHAMPTON HERITAGE VILLAGE

The active township museum **Rockhampton Heritage Village** (Boundary Rd., Parkhurst, off Bruce Hwy., tel. 07/4936-8688, daily 9am-4pm, adult $10.50, child $6.80, family $30.50) is spread across over 11 hectares of bushland and charts Rockhampton and the region's history from around 1850 to 1950. Exhibits in the restored buildings include vintage vehicles, dolls, tools, homesteads, and farms. Farm animals roam free for children to get close to, and you can watch sheep shearing and enjoy many interactive displays. Several times per year there is a market, which is worth visiting. Check the local papers or ask your concierge for dates.

CAPRICORN CAVES

Capricorn Caves (30 Olsen Caves Rd., The Caves, tel. 07/4934-2883, www.capricorncaves.com.au, tour bookings essential) are believed to be the oldest tourist attraction in Queensland, discovered back in 1882 by Norwegian John Olsen, who stumbled across the entrance of the caves and continued to open them up to the public. Located some 23 kilometers north of Rockhampton, the caves were formed from ancient coral reef over 400 million years ago. While they are beautiful at any time, between December and February there are two main attractions that make a visit even more special. At dusk the tiny bentwing or microbats leave their roost to come out and feed, and zoom overhead of the visitors: thousands of small fluffy, thumb-sized bats. During December and January, the southern summer solstice brings a light spectacle that results in a single beam of dazzling sunlight entering the darkened cave through a 14-meter vertical shaft, making for a magical display.

There are several daily tours. The one-hour "Cathedral Cave Tour" (daily on the hour 9am-4pm, adult $27, child $14, minimum age 5) leads through the roots of a large fig tree into the cave system, which is set up like a cathedral, complete with benches and candlelight. This is so stunning that it is a popular venue for weddings and concerts. The "Geotour: A Journey of Discovery" (two hours, $60 pp, minimum age 6, moderate fitness essential, times depend on number of bookings) is a proper discovery tour into the geological history of the caves; you'll be visiting a Queensland Museum paleontology dig site and learning about the history of the local flora and fauna.

You can also go **adventure caving** ($75 pp for two hours, $85 pp for three hours, minimum age 16, with local guide). This is proper caving—it's not for claustrophobics or those who don't want to get on their hands and knees and have a full-on experience, but fun for those who do. For families, there is a family-friendly caving alternative that is a **guided tour** (two hours, adult $35, child $25, minimum age 6). Plus you can go **abseiling** (1-2 hours, $80 pp, minimum age 16) and use the climbing wall (1-2 hours, adult $35, child $25, minimum age 6). If you are into caves, climbing under and above ground, this makes for a great day out.

MOUNT MORGAN

The gold supply at **Mount Morgan** (Burnett Hwy., 38 km southwest of Rockhampton), said to have been the largest single mountain of gold in the world, was discovered and mined from the late 1800s. What was once a big mountain is now a big crater, in fact the largest excavation in the southern hemisphere. In around 1870, local stockman William Mackinlay had discovered that the mountain was gold-bearing, but initially kept his knowledge secret. Forming a small partnership with five other men, they mined the mountain on their own, until in 1886 the Mount Morgan Gold Mining Company was formed. The town was proclaimed in 1890, and the railway reached there in 1898. In the 99 years Mount Morgan was mined, it yielded a total of 225,000 kilograms of gold, 50,000 kilograms of silver, and 360,000 tons of copper.

Today, the historical town of Mount Morgan is well worth a visit on its own, with a railway precinct, a dam, a bridge, and plenty of heritage buildings, plus the small **museum** (corner East St. and Morgan St., tel. 07/4938-2122, Mon.-Sat. 10am-1pm, Sun. 10am-4pm, adult $4, child $0.50), which presents the history of Mount Morgan. On a small-bus tour with **Mount Morgan TMC Guided Tours** (tel. 07/4938-1823, www.tmctours.com.au, adult $25, child $10, family $60, duration roughly all morning or all afternoon, subject to bookings and weather), you can not only learn about the history of the mine and the gold findings, but also see plenty of fossils, including some dinosaur footprints on the roof of the Mount Fireclay Caves. How they exactly got onto the ceiling seems unclear.

COOBERRIE PARK

Get up close and personal with some of Australia's iconic animals at **Cooberrie Park** (Woodbury Rd., Yeppoon, tel. 07/4939-7590, www.cooberriepark.com.au, daily 10am-3pm, adult $25, child $15, family $65), some 26 kilometers (roughly a 40-minute drive) from Rockhampton, where you can hold a koala, feed a kangaroo, have a snake draped around you, or come close to a crocodile. While you are there you can enjoy a barbecue and are even allowed to jump in the pool. It makes for a great day out for the family.

KOORANA CROCODILE FARM AND RESTAURANT

If you want to get even closer to crocodiles than you can at Cooberrie Park, visit **Koorana Crocodile Farm and Restaurant** (52 Gladstone Rd., tel. 07/4934-4749, www.koorana.com.au, daily 10am-3pm, adult $27, child $12). This farm, 29 kilometers east of Rockhampton, is home to some 300 crocodiles, and you can learn everything there is to learn about these ancient-looking creatures. This is a commercial crocodile farm, not a zoo, so you can learn about the crocs, touch them, and feed them, but you can also buy crocodile leather products and find them on the menu of the restaurant. There are daily tours at 10:30am and 1pm, lasting around 1.5 hours.

Recreation

With Rockhampton being a cattle town, there is one attraction you cannot miss: bull-riding in the rodeo ring at the **Nissan Navara Arena** (Great Western Hotel, corner Stanley St. and Denison St., tel. 07/4922-1862, www.greatwesternhotel.com.au, every Wed. and Fri., prices vary, normal watching of non-professional events is free if you book a table). The Outback-styled pub is the only "hotel" in Australia (and one of only two in the world) to boast its own indoor rodeo and music arena, with seating capacity for 3,500 spectators. This makes it one of the largest indoor arenas in Australia, and there is a twice-weekly spectacle when grown men wrestle with even bigger grown bulls. Add to that regular rodeo events and a restaurant and bar, and this is one amazing night you cannot miss if you're in town. Check the website for the weekly events.

For a more sedate activity, try the **Rockhampton Golf Club** (Ann St., tel. 07/4927-3311, www.rockygolfclub.org.au). Greens fees are $30 for 18 holes, $20 for 9 holes on weekdays, and $35 for 18 holes, $22 for 9 holes on weekends. Booking is essential; club and cart hire are available.

Accommodations

A modern apartment block by the river where subtle hues are embellished with splashes of color, ★ **The Edge Apartment Hotel** (102 Victoria Parade, tel. 1800/853-224, www.theedgeapartments.com.au, one-bedroom apartments from $180) has one- to three-bedroom apartments, which are all spacious and modern and funky. Even the smallest room offers a kitchenette, while the one-bedroom apartments upwards have a dining area, balcony, and nearly a full-sized kitchen. Plus, there is a trendy lap pool.

Quest Rockhampton (48 Victoria Parade, tel. 03/9645-8357, www.questapartments.com.au, studios from $179) is a brand-new, trendy-looking, all glass and white concrete, serviced apartment facility that offers accommodations from studios to two-bedroom apartments, all with kitchen facilities, pantry shopping service, housekeeping, and baby-sitting service. All are very spacious, modern, and clean with bright color accents and views across the city.

On the main road through the city, **Archer Park Motel** (39 Albert St., tel. 07/4927-9266, www.archerparkmotel.com.au, from $120) is a great and easy, if at times a little noisy, place to stay, with comfortable rooms that have seating areas and parking right outside. The motel is serviced by an on-site restaurant (mains $25), which provides breakfast and room snacks throughout the day and is also popular with locals for dinner. The fish of the day is always a good alternative to the Rockhampton favorite steak.

Set by the side of the lovely Fitzroy River, just walking distance from the city center, **Riverside Tourist Park** (2 Reaney St., North Rockhampton, tel. 07/4922-3779, www.riversiderockhampton.com.au, unpowered site $28, deluxe two-bed cabin $120) offers campsites, caravan parking, and individual cabins. Amenities include a pool, kids' play area, laundry, and cooking facilities for those fish you can catch in the river. For the powered and unpowered sites, there are modern amenity blocks, which are serviced every day, and the cabins all have a small but clean bathroom with shower and toilet, plus a

sunset over Murray Lagoon from the Rockhampton Golf Club

small cooking area with microwave and kettle, toaster, crockery, and cutlery.

Food

Overlooking the mighty Fitzroy River, **Steakhouse 98** (98 Victoria Parade, tel. 07/4920-1000, www.98.com.au, breakfast from 7:30am Mon.-Sat., lunch Mon.-Fri., dinner Mon.-Sat., mains $28) is a simple restaurant that specializes in the region's produce, offering great steaks. Sit outside, relax with a beverage or two, and tuck into some Queensland beef.

Known across the region for its Mexican food, 30 different types of tequila, varieties of sangria, and Mexican beer, **The Crooked Cactus** (52 Gladstone Rd., tel. 07/4922-1822, daily 11am-2pm, Sat.-Sun. to 3pm, mains $23) is the place to come if you need a burrito, an enchilada, or another taste of spicy feel-good food.

Even if you are just drawn by the name, at **Giddy Goat** (128 East St., tel. 07/4921-4900, Mon.-Tues. 7am-5:30pm, Wed.-Fri. 7am-9:30pm, Sat. 8am-9:30pm, Sun. 8am-7pm, mains $15) you can still expect decent food all day long. Famed for its eggs Benedict for breakfast, this is also a good place for coffee and a decent grilled sandwich for lunch. Or try the traditional sausages with mashed potato.

Set under the colonnades of the old post office building, the little café ★ **Degani** (80 East St., tel. 07/4927-8102, Mon.-Fri. 7am-4pm, Sat. 7am-2pm) is a lovely place to relax, people-watch, and have some light bites. Try the waffles with ice cream and fresh berries ($8.50) or a grilled focaccia sandwich ($10).

Information and Services

Rockhampton Base Hospital (Canning St., The Range, tel. 07/4920-6211) is the region's main accident and emergency hospital. **AFS Chemist** (corner George St. and Denham St., South Rockhampton, tel. 07/4927-2011) is open daily 8am-8pm. There are several **banks** along the main East Street, all with ATMs accepting all major cards. The main **post office** (150 East St., Mon.-Fri. 8:30am-5:30pm) is in the center of town.

Getting There and Around

Rockhampton is a one-hour flight, a 7.5-hour train ride, or an eight-hour drive from Brisbane.

Qantas and Virgin Australia both fly into Rockhampton via Brisbane (Sydney to Rockhampton, one-way flights from $275). **Rockhampton Airport** (ROK, Canoona Rd., tel. 07/4936-8999, www.rockhamptonregion.qld.gov.au/Council_Services/Airport) is 7.5 kilometers from the city center, a 10-minute ride by taxi (**Taxi Wide Australia,** tel. 13/10-08, $10) or by bus (**Young's Bus Service,** tel. 07/4922-3810, www.youngsbusservice.com.au, adult one-way ticket from $2.40). Route 20 drops you off in the city center, although the buses run somewhat sporadically throughout the day. Phone for timetable information.

The **Tilt Train** (tel. 07/3235-2222, www.queenslandrail.com.au) leaves Brisbane's Roma Street station Sunday-Friday at 11am, arriving at 6:25pm, and at 4:55pm, arriving the following day at 12:30pm at **Rockhampton Train Station** (West St., Depot Hill), less than 500 meters from the city center.

The drive is along the Bruce Highway, up the Sunshine Coast, past the Glass House Mountains, past Bundaberg and Gladstone. It's not the most exciting part of the highway, which narrows down to one lane each way on quite a few occasions. From Bundaberg, it's 280-odd kilometers, just under a four-hour drive north; from Gladstone, it's a mere 109 kilometers, just over an hour's drive.

Within Rockhampton, **Young's Bus Service** (tel. 07/4922-3810, www.youngsbusservice.com.au, adult one-way ticket from $2.40) provides a relatively extensive network.

YEPPOON

This bustling seaside town serves primarily as the gateway to Great Keppel Island, although ferries leave from nearby Rosslyn Bay, not from Yeppoon itself. Flanked by lovely beaches, which lead northward into the rainforests of Byfield and south toward Rosslyn Bay, the main promenade is palm studded and brimming with shops and cafés. Be warned that during magpie breeding season, these rather large birds have a habit of swooping down and attacking innocent passersby seeking shade under the palms (breeding season starts in September).

For once, Captain Cook cannot be credited with the name-giving, and it is thought that the unusual name was derived from an Aboriginal word describing a place where waters join, probably referring to the mouth of Ross Creek and Yeppoon inlet.

Although popular with weekenders, by 1882 there were a mere seven buildings in Yeppoon, mostly holiday cottages and a hotel (pub). The little town didn't improve much on that over the years, but its fruit-growing region expanded in the 1970s with support from Cairns, and tourism was a mainstay, with Sunday outings to the beaches and North and Great Keppel Islands. The latter had basic cabin facilities until in 1945, when the Great Keppel Island Tourist Company set about developing the island's tourism potential. By the 1970s Yeppoon was not only growing fruit but could also call itself the largest of several small tourist settlements on the Capricorn Coast. Alas, passenger rail services ceased in the 1970s and the railway was dismantled. Yeppoon's railway station, dating back to 1909, and the war memorial in Normanby Street, restored in 2010, have since been listed on the Queensland heritage register, together with the first primary school, dating back to 1889 in Queen Street.

Yeppoon is along the Capricorn Scenic Drive (route 10), which starts just north of Rockhampton and leads to Yeppoon and Cooee Bay, where Wreck Point Lookout offers views out to sea and across to all of the major islands, including Great Keppel Island. The scenic drives continues onto Lammermoor, then Rosslyn Bay, Mulambin, Causeway Lake, and eventually Emu Bay, which is aptly named. You will, if you are lucky, spot some of these large flightless birds en route. While in Emu Bay, have a look at the Singing Ship in Emu Park, a sculpture put up in remembrance of Captain Cook at the 200th anniversary in 1970, which not only makes "music," in the vaguest sense of the definition, but most importantly sits on a piece of land allowing spectacular views across to the islands and the neighboring bays.

Some 20 minutes' drive north of Yeppoon are Byfield State Forest and Byfield National Park, which cover some 15,000 hectares, with landscapes ranging from bushland and eucalyptus forest to vast sand dunes and rugged granite pinnacles. Unfortunately, access to the forest and national park is very much four-wheel-drive only, and navigating the 15 kilometers of soft sand tracks from the park entrance to the coast may take more than an hour.

Accommodations are strung out along the coast, mostly apartments for rent or campsites. Excellent and budget-friendly options include **Island View Caravan Park** (946 Scenic Hwy., Kinka Beach, tel. 07/4939-6284, www.island-view.com.au, sites from $28, cabins sleeping four from $95), located right next to the beach under palm trees. Campsites and cabins are available, and amenities include a swimming pool and kids' activity areas. **Beaches on Lammermoor** (96-98 Scenic Hwy., Lammermoor, tel. 07/4913-8300, www.beachesonlammermoor.com.au, apartments from $195) offers spacious apartments with balconies and either ocean or garden views, two bathrooms, and full-sized kitchens. **Emus Beach Resort** (92 Pattison St., Emu Park, tel. 07/4939-6111, www.emusbeachresort.com, dorm beds from $25) has a communal kitchen, Internet café, in-house bar, satellite TV room, heated pool, and lots of fun.

To get to Yeppoon, you can catch route 20 of **Young's Bus Service** (tel. 07/4922-3810, www.youngsbusservice.com.au, adult one-way ticket from $2.40). Route 29 goes to Emu Park. Both leave from Rockhampton city center, Bolsolver Street.

GREAT KEPPEL ISLAND

When Captain James Cook first set eyes on the Keppel islands, reportedly he was unimpressed, describing the islands as having an appearance of barrenness rather than fertility. Still, he did his job naming Great Keppel Island (the largest in the Keppel group of 14 islands) and Keppel Bay after Admiral August Keppel, the first Lord of the Admiralty, and then he moved swiftly on up the coast. Matthew Flinders must have sighted the island in 1804 when he circumnavigated Australia, but it wasn't until 1847 that the first European, a naturalist named McGillivray, set foot near Leeke's Creek. Prior to the Europeans setting foot on the islands, the Woppaburra people had been using Great Keppel Island for thousands of years, leaving well-preserved middens (mounds of shells) at the western end of Long Beach. The island's first resort was established in the late 1950s and an airstrip was built in 1975.

The Keppels are a group of continental islands that offer excellent diving, with each island being surrounded by rocky reefs covered in hard and soft corals, which support a fascinating mixture of invertebrates, reef fish, and sea snakes. While the visibility might not be as good as along the Great Barrier Reef, the great number and huge variety of marine creatures present make the Keppels an excellent dive destination, and the 17 pristine beaches and lush vegetation keep guests that are happier on land satisfied.

Like most of the Queensland coast, the Keppel islands were affected badly by Cyclone Yasi in February 2011 and severe floods in the previous year, and while some resorts have closed, others are undergoing renovation and upgrades. There is even a brand-new resort under development, the Great Keppel Island Resort—the first to be built in the Great Barrier Reef for more than 20 years. But whether you are going to stay or simply visit for the day, Great Keppel is well worth a look.

Recreation

Great Keppel Island is not only a great place to snorkel, dive, and swim, it is fantastic for fishing and bushwalking as well. But there are no organized activities, unless you arrive on a day cruise. Both accommodations on the island rent equipment such as snorkeling gear, kayaks, and even motorized dinghies, but it is all very basic, and most of the time you will have to either bring your own gear or simply relax.

Great Keppel Island

Accommodations

With the swanky Great Keppel Island Resort still under construction at the time of writing, the alternative options for the moment are the Great Keppel Island Holiday Village and Svendsen's Beach.

The **Great Keppel Island Holiday Village** (tel. 07/4939-8655, www.gkiholidayvillage.com.au) offers cabins (sleeping up to four guests with en suite bathrooms), tents, and rooms with shared amenities. It is very basic, but clean and comfortable with all linens, pillows, and blankets provided. You can bring your own tent and use the amenities (from $20 per night) or book yourself into one of the fully equipped tents (from $90), multishare rooms without en suite bathrooms (from $35), or the cabins (from $150).

The little retreat **Svendsen's Beach** (tel. 07/4938-3717, www.svendsensbeach.com, from $285 for the first three nights per couple, then $80 per night per couple, cash only) offers two luxury tent bungalows, a house, and a studio, all set in lovely gardens overlooking the sea. The accommodations are basic and comfortable, but apart from drinking water and bed linen, you'll have to bring everything else, from food and drink (there is a simple refrigerator provided for keeping food chilled) to towels, flashlights, batteries, and cash. If you are not organized, you will literally find yourself stranded on a desert beach without anything, apart from a bed.

There is no **camping** allowed on Great Keppel Island, but there are facilities on North Keppel, Humpy, Middle, Miall, Conical, Pelican, and Divided Islands, all of which can be reached by private boat only. Most have very basic if any facilities, the exception being North Keppel and Humpy Islands, which have toilets, showers, and picnic tables. Permits must be obtained from the **Department of National Parks, Recreation, Sport and Racing** (www.nprsr.qld.gov.au, camping fees from $5.60 pp per night) prior to setting off.

Getting There and Around

To get to Rosslyn Bay near Yeppoon, you can catch route 20 of **Young's Bus Service** (tel. 07/4922-3810, www.youngsbusservice.com.au, adult one-way ticket from $2.40). It leaves from Rockhampton city center (Bolsolver Street) and goes via Yeppoon.

Several ferries and cruises can get you to Great Keppel Island from Rosslyn Bay. **Freedom Fast Cat Cruises** (tel. 07/4933-6888, www.freedomfastcats.com, round-trip adult $52, child $33, family $150) ferries leave daily, Monday and Tuesday at 10:30am, returning 3:45pm, and Wednesday-Sunday at 9:15am, returning 3:45pm. The 30-minute ferry service is often part of a longer day cruise around the islands, depending on the day of the week.

Funtastic Cruises (tel. 04/3890-9502, www.funtasticcruises.com, day trip adult $98, child $80, family $360) offers day cruises on a 17-meter catamaran with the day including swimming, snorkeling, and relaxing on a selection of Keppel Island beaches. Prices include equipment and refreshments.

Sail Capricornia (tel. 04/0210-2373, www.sailcapricornia.com.au) offers sunset cruises (from $55 pp) and day trips (from $115 adult, $75 children), which are spent mostly on and in the water, sailing around the island, looking out for dolphins and turtles, snorkeling, swimming, and having lunch on board. Three-day cruises (from $499 pp) travel around the Keppel Islands, with the two nights spent ashore at Great Keppel Island Holiday Village. The price includes all meals, accommodations, and snorkeling gear, but there are self-catering options available.

In addition to cruises and the ferry option, you can also fly to Great Keppel Island. **Peace Aviation** (tel. 07/4922-7055, http://peaceaviation.com) flies you from Rockhampton to Great Keppel within 30 minutes. This is a non-scheduled flight, so times and prices depend on the size of the group and the aircraft available; you can request a quote through the website.

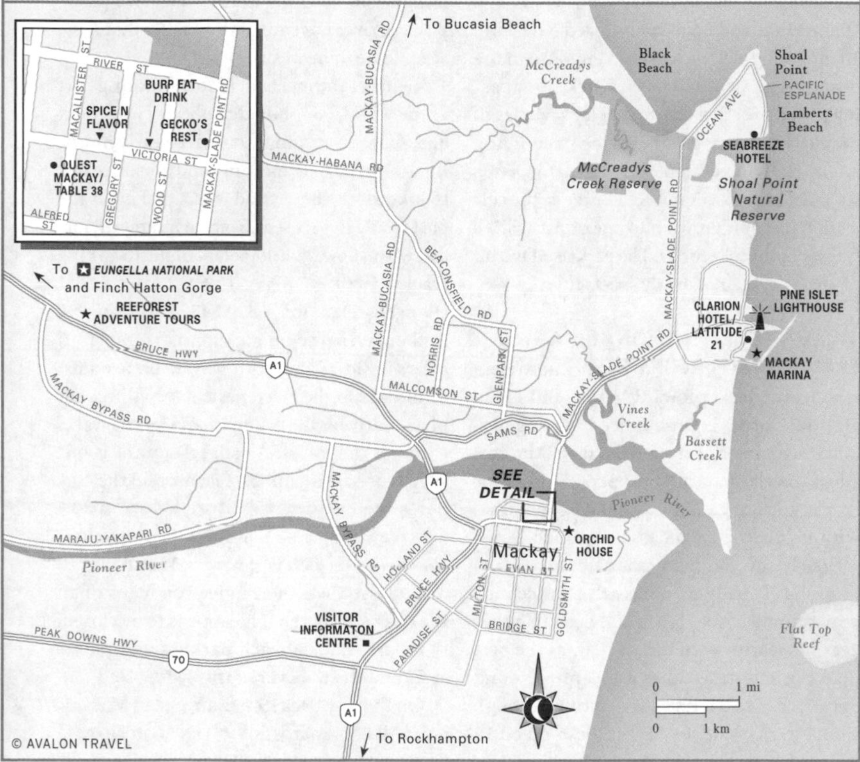

MACKAY

Straddling the vast Pioneer River and its many creeks and mangrove habitats is the mostly industrial city of Mackay. With the main factories and plants concentrated on the outskirts, the city center has a handful of pretty heritage buildings and a bustling main street (Victoria Street) full of shops, cafés, and pubs. But it is pretty obvious that Mackay is a residential and working city, not a tourist hub. Its main attractions are the modern marina north of the river, Eungella National Park, and the simple fact that Mackay is right at the southern end of the Whitsundays, with Keswick Island being closest to the city.

Sights

MACKAY MARINA

The **Mackay Marina,** north of the river next to the Mackay Harbour, is a new development with apartment buildings, fancy restaurants, and a lovely breakwater with great views across to the nearby islands, the marina, Harbour Beach, and the massive ships being filled and maneuvered out of the harbor entry. Plus it has the lovely **Pine Islet Lighthouse,** which was originally built in 1885 on Pine Islet in the Percy Group, southeast of Mackay. The chubby little white lighthouse with the red top was relocated to Mackay in 1986. The lighthouse is a still working kerosene lighthouse, the only left of its kind in the world, and it is rather picturesque.

ORCHID HOUSE

In the city, the **Orchid House** (Queens Park, Gordon St., tel. 1300/622-529, Mon.-Fri. 10am-11am and 2pm-3pm, closed Sat., Sun. 10am-2pm, free) is a lovely greenhouse in the beautiful gardens of Queens Park, showcasing a nice selection of around 600 varieties of orchid, including ground-living, tree-living and rock-living examples. With many plants supplied by park curator Ken Burgess, the collection has now grown into one of Australia's finest orchid collections. The park itself is a bit of an oasis, but not overly spectacular.

★ EUNGELLA NATIONAL PARK

Eungella National Park, 80 kilometers west from Mackay toward Mirani and Finch Hatton Gorge, is pronounced "youngella" and lies an hour's drive inland from Mackay. Australia's largest national park is famous for its platypus, the unique egg-laying mammal with its distinctive duck's bill, which is notoriously shy and rarely spotted in the wild. Eungella virtually guarantees that you see one year-round, although you will need to either get there early or later in the day, as the best platypus spotting times are 4am-8am and 3pm-7pm. Broken River, which runs through Eungella, is said to be the best place in Australia for platypus spotting, with a viewing platform built for your convenience. But even if you don't get to see an elusive platypus, the river is teeming with turtles that don't seem to be quite as shy.

To make the most out of this stunning part of the world, you should really stay overnight and allow an evening—or maybe early morning—for platypus spotting, and an entire day to hike along the myriad walks that cross the part tropical, part semitropical mountain forest, with some 22 kilometers of bushwalking tracks. **Broken River Mountain Resort** (Eungella Dam Rd., tel. 07/4958-4564, www.brokenrivermr.com.au, cabins from $130) offers basic cabins (with private bathrooms) right next to the river, perfect for falling out of bed early for the platypus, and for the walks through the forest. A café/restaurant is onsite, as are all amenities. Just around the corner is the **Eungella Visitors Information Centre** (Eungella Dam Rd., open—in their own words—Wed.-Sun. 9:30am-ish to 3:30pm-ish), which can give you maps of all the tracks, but even if it happens to be closed, there are maps at each parking and picnic stop, and the walks are easily signposted.

On the way back from Eungella to Mackay, you will come across **Finch Hatton Gorge,**

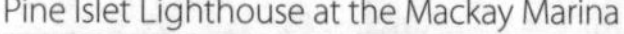

Pine Islet Lighthouse at the Mackay Marina

a short but worthwhile detour (30 minutes) from the main road. Beautiful countryside changes into forests with countless streams that are only passable with four-wheel drive in the rainy season, but as long as it has been dry, you should be fine in a normal car. You cross these fords and get deeper into the forest, before basically coming to the end of the track and having to walk on to the gorge. The stream tumbles across rounded boulders, the dense vegetation is alive with birds, and again, if you are lucky, you might well see yet another platypus, if it's the right time of day. Splash in the rock pools, seek out the waterfalls, and even stay the night at the **Platypus Bushcamp** (Gorge Rd., Finch Hatton, tel. 07/4958-3204, www.bushcamp.net), where you can either camp or stay in a rustic timber hut, adapted to fit either twin beds or dorms, by the stream (camping from $7.50, huts from $75, dorm beds from $25). While you are there, try ziplining with **Forest Flying** (Finch Hatton, tel. 07/4958-3359, www.forestflying.com, daily, weather permitting, $60 pp, weight restrictions apply), which sees you flying on a zipline up to 25 meters high across the canopy of the forest in a one- to two-hour tour.

If you are not driving, try the "A Day with a Platypus" trip with **Reeforest Adventure Tours** (Mackay and Airlie Beach, tel. 1800/500-353, www.reeforest.com.au, adult $120, child $99, family $410), which includes traveling to Finch Hatton Gorge for a cooked barbecue lunch, a visit to the Araluen Falls, a swim in Eungella National Park, and taking in the Pioneer Valley, Broken River, and hopefully a platypus or two. Tours run Tuesday, Thursday, and Saturday, with hotel pickup at 11am from Mackay.

Beaches

There are plenty of beaches around Mackay, mostly toward the north, starting with **Harbour Beach** by the marina. Patrolled year round, this beach is popular with families for picnics and fishing. Farther along toward the north is the small crescent-shaped **Lamberts Beach. Blacks Beach,** the city's longest beach, stretches for six kilometers, is lined with tropical gardens, and offers lifeguard patrols, playgrounds, and plenty of picnic tables. **Bucasia Beach** has the all-important stinger enclosure and barbecue facilities, and stretches toward the headland of **Shoal Point,** with its amazing views and long pristine beach, where even on weekends there is so much space that it feels you have it all to yourself. Bring the swimsuits and the fishing rods, as this is a perfect spot with only some rocky outcrops.

Keswick Island

Keswick Island lies some 32 kilometers north of Mackay at the southern tip of the Whitsundays. Fringed by reefs, with the water full of colorful reef fish, turtles, and even humpback whales during August and September, Keswick offers plenty of activities, such as snorkeling, swimming, fishing, and bushwalking, to keep you busy. Like the majority of the Whitsunday Islands, Keswick is mostly a national park, with approximately 80 percent of the island being protected parkland, and there are no resorts here and no campgrounds. Instead, draped across a saddle at the island's southern end is a community of about 20 people, whose houses have stunning views and who scoot around the small community and the accessible parts of the island in golf carts.

Access to the island is by light aircraft, a short 12-minute flight from Mackay (**Island Air,** Casey Ave., Mackay Airport, tel. 04/1875-7540, charters around $360 for up to five passengers one way), and the only place to stay is the **Keswick Island Guest House** (tel. 07/4965-8002, www.keswickislandguesthouse.com.au, from $550 per room per night), which sleeps eight people in four beautifully appointed and individually decorated bedrooms complete with stunning wooden decks overlooking the island and sea. All meals are included, and the guest house offers free use of snorkeling gear, kayaks, and a golf buggy to explore the rest of the island.

Accommodations

Overlooking the marina just across the river from Mackay's city center, the modern and stylish ★ **Clarion Hotel Mackay Marina** (Mulherin Dr., Mackay Harbour, tel. 07/4955-9400, www.mackaymarinahotel.com, from $285) is steps away from the water, a choice of restaurants, and the Pine Islet Lighthouse and within the bustle of the marina and working harbor. The hotel offers single rooms and suites with private balconies, all modern and comfortably furnished with plenty of space, colorful touches of cushions, and abstract paintings on the walls. A pool, playground, and proximity to Harbour Beach make this a good family option.

Voted Mackay's best accommodation in 2013, ★ **Quest Mackay** (38 Macalister St., tel. 07/4829-3500, www.questapartments.com.au, studios from $200) has spacious apartments in the city center, offering easy access to the city, marina, and roads leading out to Eungella. Modernly furnished and very roomy studio, one-, and two-bedroom apartments offer kitchenettes with stovetops and ovens, homey and elegant decor, and good service. An all-day restaurant and bar, **Table 38,** offers grill favorites as well as salads, sandwiches, and snacks. Delivery to your apartment is available.

North of Mackay, the motel-type **Sea Breeze Hotel** (72 Pacific Esplanade, Slade Point, tel. 07/4955-1644, apartments from $115) is a clean and comfortable hotel, with 36 one-bedroom units offering kitchenettes, balconies, perfect views, and a great beach location. The one-bed apartments sleep up to three people, and there is a special apartment on the ground floor with access for those with disabilities. Rates include breakfast.

Gecko's Rest (34 Sydney St., tel. 07/4944-1230, www.geckosrest.com.au, dorm beds from $28, family room $100 per night) is a clean and basic accommodation option that offers shared kitchen, rooftop barbecue area, laundry facilities, TV and game room, Internet room, and proximity to the city center.

Food

With beautiful waterfront views and elegant yet comfortable seating in dark wicker chairs, **Latitude 21** (Clarion Hotel Mackay Marina, Mulherin Dr., Mackay Harbour, tel. 07/4955-9400, mains $35) feels very tropical, offering both alfresco and indoor dining options. The food is modern and light, with daily specials and traditional favorites. If you have the time, come for a relaxed and extended Sunday brunch (11am-3pm) and linger over the setting and the food.

Burp Eat Drink (86 Wood St., tel. 07/4951-3546, www.burp.et.au, Tues.-Fri. 11am-3pm and 6pm-late, Sat. 6pm-late, mains $35) is one of the few better dining options in Mackay, offering seasonal fresh regional produce in a modern setting. Although leaning toward the steak and grill offerings, the menu also has some decent starters and seafood options. Try especially the zucchini flowers in tempura with cheese and beetroot.

An excellent Indian restaurant, **Spice n Flavor** (162 Victoria St., tel. 07/4999-9639, daily 5:30pm-late, mains $19) serves all the favorites, such as garlic naan, lamb rogan josh, butter chicken, and many more. It also offers takeout.

Information and Services

Mackay Visitor Information Centre (320 Nebo Rd., tel. 1300/130-001, Mon. 9am-5pm, Tues.-Fri. 8:30am-5pm, Sat.-Sun. 9am-4pm) is at the entrance to Mackay, alongside the Bruce Highway, and offers help with the sights, tours, and accommodations in the area. There are several large banks in the city, all of which have ATMs taking most cards. The main **post office** (137 Shakespeare St., Mon.-Fri. 8:30am-5pm, Sat. 8:30am-noon) is one of the few open on Saturday. The public **Mackay Base Hospital** (Bridge Rd., tel. 07/4968-6000) has an excellent accident and emergency department, and the pharmacy **Healthpoint Day & Night** (65 Sydney St., tel. 07/4963-0300) is open daily 8am-9pm.

Getting There and Around

Several airlines, such as Qantas, Jetstar, Tigerair, and Virgin Australia, all fly direct to Mackay. From Sydney, it is a mere 2.5-hour flight. **Mackay Airport** (MKY, Boundary Rd., East Mackay, tel. 07/4957-0201) lies southeast of the city, roughly 3.5 kilometers away. No buses stop at the airport, but several shuttles operate between the airport and the hotels and farther destinations, such as Airlie Beach. One is **Whitsundays 2 Everywhere** (tel. 07/4946-4940, www.whitsundaytransports.com), but this is a prebooking-only service, so you can negotiate where you want to go, when, and how many of you there are. Easier is a taxi service for the short distance into the city. Try **Mackay Whitsunday Taxi** (tel. 13/10-08).

The **Sunlander** and **Tilt Train** (tel. 07/3235-2222, www.queenslandrail.com.au) both offer services from Brisbane to Mackay several times per week between them, taking around 11 hours. The **train station** (Conors Rd.) is south of the city center, and with buses far and few between, a taxi is the easiest way to get into the city or to your accommodations.

Greyhound buses (tel. 1300/473-946, www.greyhound.com.au) stop at Mackay on the way up the Bruce Highway to Cairns. The journey takes around 13 hours from Brisbane, and the coach stops at **Mackay Bus Terminal** (corner Victoria St. and Macalister St. right in the city center).

If you are driving, Mackay is around 11 hours' drive north from Brisbane, or 7 hours south from Cairns along the Bruce Highway.

There are relatively good bus connections operated by **Mackay Transit Services** (tel. 07/4957-3330, www.mackaytransit.com.au, one-way adult tickets start at $2.40) within the city center and out to the northern beaches (route 7) and to the marina (route 12), but they tend to run hourly at best, and not on Sunday, so check the timetables on the website before setting off.

The Whitsunday Islands

Initially named the Cumberland Islands by who else but Captain Cook, on his epic journey in 1770, but then later renamed for the day he arrived at the group of islands, the Whitsundays are the diamond clasp in the pearl necklace that is the Great Barrier Reef. There are 74 islands altogether, with the majority of the islands designated national parks, and only seven are inhabited and outfitted with a resort—this truly is a desert island paradise. Although not on the outer barrier reef, which is still 50 nautical miles or a two-hour boat ride away, the islands offer perfect sandy beaches, coral cays, and fringing reefs that pretty much make for a perfect vacation spot. Snorkeling, scuba diving, and sailing—any water sport you can think of—are all on offer, and the laid-back Pacific-island attitude relaxes you as soon as you step on any island of the group.

Hamilton Island is the most developed island of the group, with the most choices of accommodation and recreational offerings; most likely you will either fly to that island and stay there or transfer from there to another island. If you are not on a tight budget, you are truly lucky, as you might take the helicopter straight onto Hayman Island for a luxury stay unrivaled by much else, or get the most of the entire group of islands by partaking in a sailing cruise that offers simply the best views around.

The Whitsundays are also the setting of the famed Heart Reef, the perfectly shaped heart shimmering in a variety of turquoise hues. Alas, the only way you can see it is by flying over it, as it is protected and access is barred.

The first inhabitants of the Whitsundays were the Ngaro people, and archaeological evidence indicates occupation for at least

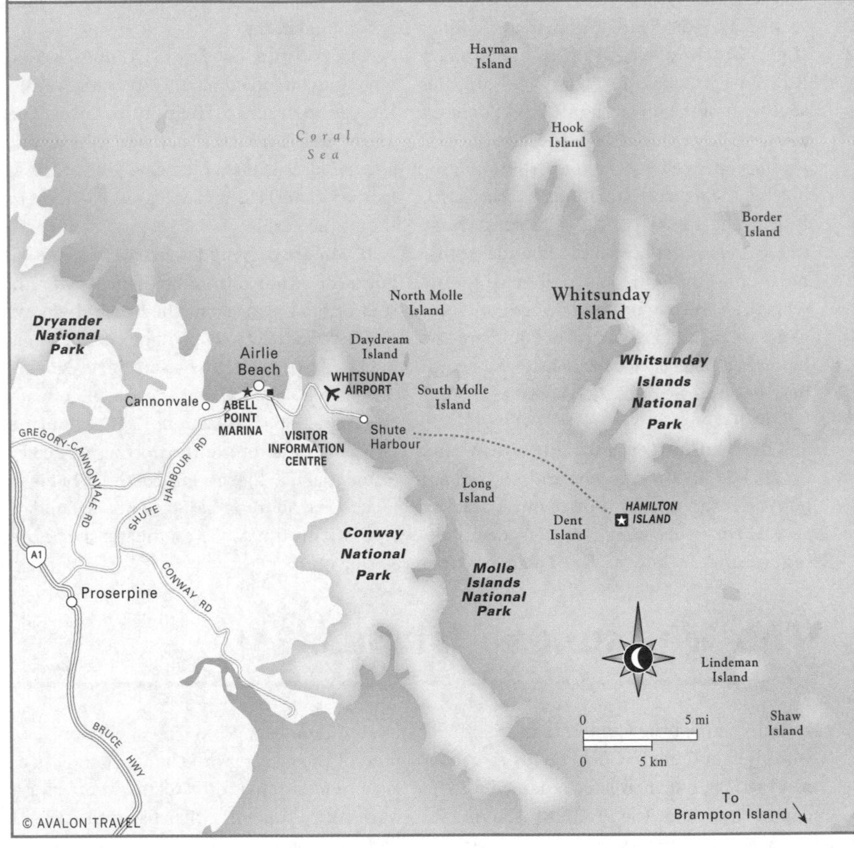

8,000 years. Although there are recordings of Aboriginal activity on most of the islands, only a few were used for full-time occupation; most were just seasonal visits, for hunting, celebrations, or culturally important events. Due to the large distances involved, there wasn't much interaction between the island and mainland tribes. During the time of the Ngaro occupation, many of the islands would have been mostly grassland rather than forest, and the grass growth was encouraged through their practice of hunting with fire, flushing out the animals. Over the last few centuries, deep forest and bushland has established itself on the islands, making the combination of white beaches and lush nature a perfect desert hideaway, times 74.

This magical combination makes the Whitsundays popular with visitors from all over the globe. The islands rely on tourism for more than 80 percent of their regional product, and contribute more than $250 million to Queensland's gross regional output. In an average year, the Whitsundays are host to nearly 500,000 domestic overnight visitors and nearly 200,000 international visitors, with day-trippers adding another 220,000. Perfect weather and setting make these islands a must-see when visiting Australia.

That said, Cyclone Yasi devastated many of

the islands in 2011, and popular island resorts such as South Molle, Hook, and Brampton are currently closed, be it due to physical destruction of the resorts or the reduced tourism following the cyclone. Regular ferry services have stopped. But while some of the resorts may still be closed, the islands are not, and as long as you can find transport, you can get to the islands and still enjoy the nature walks, the beaches, and the setting.

AIRLIE BEACH

Though not an island itself, Airlie Beach is the capital of the Whitsundays and the mainland base from where to enjoy cruises and day trips to and around the islands. A small bustling seaside community, full of shops and cafés, Airlie Beach exudes a thoroughly relaxed vacation feeling that is only emphasized by the small but perfect beach, the stunning views through the palm trees toward the sea, and the so-called lagoon, the public pool set right in the center of the beach esplanade, accessible and free to all. Nearby is a string of beaches, and on either side of the town are Shute Harbour and Abel Point Marina, small marinas from where the Whitsunday Island ferries leave and many of the sailing cruises set off.

Beaches

There are two small beaches right there in Airlie Beach along the Esplanade, complete with stinger net, if it is jellyfish season. The next beach, **Shingley Beach,** is just around the corner along Shute Harbour Road, but the clue is in the name, as it is very gravelly and small, but with nice views of Abel Point Marina.

A little farther along Shute Harbour Road, southwest toward Proserpine is **Cannonvale Beach,** a large bay with its own little island, Pigeon Island, and, at the time of visiting, a three-mast wrecked sailboat in the bay, acknowledging the sometimes treacherous sailing around this coast.

A lovely 40-minute drive through the country toward the northern tip of the headland lies **Dingo Beach.** No dingoes, but there are plenty of kangaroos nearby. The beach is wide and gorgeous and even has the **Dingo Pub** (tel. 07/4945-7153, www.dingobeachhotel.com.au) nearby for a cool refreshing drink. A couple of kilometers farther along is **Hydeaway Bay,** a huge bay with an enormous tidal range. If the tide is out, it truly is out and you can go crab hunting or spot starfish for a few hundred yards out toward the

Cannonvale Beach

sea. There is a nice campground at the entrance to the community.

Once past Hydeaway Bay the road turns into a dusty gravel track, and 10 minutes along, you'll find **Cape Gloucester Resort** (tel. 07/4945-7242, www.capeg.com.au, from $130, two-bed cabins $260), a resort and motel with cabins directly on the beach, complete with bar and restaurant, and truly hidden away from civilization.

★ Flying over the Reef

The **Heart Reef** is one of the most beautiful, iconic, and most photographed reefs in the world. Shaped like a perfect little heart, made up of pristine white sand and reef set in crystal-clear turquoise waters, this is also one of the most protected and secluded spots in the world. The only way to see it is by flying over it. **HeliReef Whitsundays** (tel. 07/4946-9102, www.helireef.com.au) offers a wide range of incredible helicopter tours, and although they're not cheap in any sense of the word, they add the "vacation of a lifetime" touch to your visit. Choose from flying over the Heart Reef plus a snorkeling stop (2 hours, from $745, including gear), diving and snorkeling at a select beach (2 hours, from $269, including equipment), or a flight over Whitehaven Beach with its swirly white sands (2 hours, from $560). In season, HeliReef also organizes whale-spotting tours.

If you are not keen on boats or helicopters, fly in a luxury seaplane with **Air Whitsunday** (Whitsunday Airport, 12 Air Whitsunday Rd., Flametree, tel. 07/4946-9111, www.airwhitsunday.com.au). A three-hour trip (adult $240, child $210) includes two hours on the beach and 30 minutes of flying time: Fly around the magnificent Whitsunday Islands, snorkel at an exclusive location inside Hardy Lagoon at the Great Barrier Reef, have a champagne picnic on world-famous Whitehaven Beach, and visit one of the islands' award-winning resorts; enjoy a scenic flight over the beautiful Heart Reef and Hill Inlet and see the islands, beaches, and reefs from above.

Other Recreation

Become a certified diver at the **Whitsunday Diving Academy** (2579 Shute Harbour Rd., opposite IGA supermarket, tel. 07/4946-4449, www.whitdiving.com). One of the best scuba diving training centers in Queensland, the academy offers extensive pool training for beginners, flexible schedules, and eLearning. There are several courses to choose from, all depending on what it is you want to learn and how much time you have. Prices for a basic Scuba Diver course start from $499, Advanced Open Water $769, Rescue Diver $1,099.

Away from the reef, there is the **Whitsunday Gold Coffee Plantation** (Bruce Hwy., just north of Proserpine, tel. 07/4945-4188, www.whitsundaygold.com, 45-minute tour $15 pp), the largest coffee plantation in Australia and bronze medal winner at the 2010 Australian Golden Bean Awards for single-origin Australian coffee. A tour through the plantation is a nice break from the beaches.

Swimming in the **Cedar Creek Falls,** between Proserpine and Airlie Beach just off the Conway Beach Road, is a relaxing experience. A lovely waterfall with a popular freshwater swimming hole, the place is secluded and perfect for a ramble and a picnic. There are turtles in the stream, so look out for them sitting on logs sunning themselves. If you are not driving, hop on a tour to the falls with **Whitsunday Getaway Packages** (tel. 04/1203-4208, www.whitsundaygetawaypackages.com.au, $39 pp, minimum two persons, transport and duration tailored to suit you); bring your own food and drink.

Whitsunday Tours

Australian Tall Ship Cruises (4 The Esplanade, Airlie Beach, tel. 07/4946-5932, www.australiantallships.com, leaves every Sat. and Tues. 7:30pm, returns Tues. and Fri. 4:15pm, three days and three nights in a double cabin $599) runs the 1902 *Solway Lass*, which was built in the Netherlands and used to be a cargo vessel. It features private double/twin cabins with teak and cedar walls along with jarrah timber trims and also offers a bar area and an outdoor dining room. In the daytime you can relax in the bow net or enter the water by rope swing. The anchorages in the three-day trip include: the western side of Hook Island, the Nara Inlet at Hook Island, Cataran Bay on Border Island, Whitehaven Beach on Whitsunday Island, Cid Harbour on Whitsunday Island, and Mantaray Bay on Whitsunday Island.

Bareboating is an option, if you are an experienced sailor and want to explore the islands without a crew on the boat. Charter a sailboat or motor cruiser with **SailFree Charters** (tel. 07/3852-2449, www.sailfree.com.au, from $400) and set off on your own.

Take the large speedboat ***Big Fury*** (259 Shute Harbour Rd., Airlie Beach, tel. 07/4946-5299, www.airliebeach.com, adult $130, child $70, family $350) out to the islands for an all-day trip without seasickness. The boat takes a maximum of 35 guests, skimming across the water at high speed, leaving more time for snorkeling, lunch, and beach relaxation. Traveling past a handful of islands to get the most out of the surroundings, the boat then stops at Whitehaven Beach, Border Island, and one or two other locations.

ISail Whitsundays (30 Airlie Crescent, Airlie Beach, tel. 1300/414-419, www.isail-whitsundays.com, from $419 pp for two days and one night) has three sailboats ranging from 10 to 12 people on board. Boats offer different cabin options, from single dorms to private doubles, some with shared bathrooms, others with private. While the crew does most of the hard work, occasionally you will be asked to help get the sails down or be allowed to take the wheel. But generally the emphasis is on the sailing experience itself, the views, and being on the water. Prices include linens, food, and equipment.

Ocean Rafting (tel. 07/4946-6848, www.oceanrafting.com.au, adult $129, child $84, family $389) offers two different tours (leaving daily at 10am from the Coral Sea Resort jetty in Airlie Beach, returning 4pm) on fast semi-rigid inflatable boats that skim across the water. The "Southern Lights" tour visits Whitehaven Beach and Hill Inlet, and includes a guided national park walk, inner fringing coral reef snorkeling, snacks and drinks, and nature talks. The "Northern Exposure" tour is pretty much the same but with a longer snorkeling time allowed by taking a slightly different route.

Southern Cross Sailing Adventures (4 The Esplanade, Airlie Beach, tel. 07/4946-4999, www.soxsail.com.au, two days and one night starting from $400) has a fleet of ex-racing yachts, such as *Ragamuffin II* (53 feet), *Southern Cross* (68 feet), Maxi *Siska* (80 feet), Maxi *Boomerang* (83 feet), and Whitbread Around the World Maxi *British Defender* (83 feet) at their disposal. You can organize a tailor-made sailing trip from three to seven days, anchoring in locations such as Whitehaven Beach on Whitsunday Island, Blue Pearl Bay on Hayman Island, Mantaray Bay, and Nara Inlet at Hook Island, and sailing past resort locations like Hamilton Island and Daydream Island.

Family-run **Whitehaven Xpress** (tel. 07/4946-1585, www.whitehavenxpress.com.au, departs Abel Point Marina 9am daily, returns 5pm, adult $160, child $80, equipment included) is a day cruise that stops at Whitehaven Beach, Hill Inlet, and Mantaray Bay for snorkeling, swimming, glass-bottom boat rides, snacks and lunch, and a bushwalk.

Whitsundays Sailing Adventures (Beach Plaza, Airlie Esplanade, Airlie Beach, tel. 07/4940-2000, www.whitsundaysailingadventures.com.au, from $89 pp for a day trip, equipment included) offers an amazing array of sailing boats, from modern catamarans to older tall ships, from single to two masters, all sailing for anything from all-day trips to weeklong cruises. There are also couples-only cruises, with privacy, romance, and even fine dining on the menu. All sailing options, apart from cruising around the beautiful islands, offer snorkeling, swimming, and on-land stops to hike around various islands and/or laze on the beaches.

Wings Diving Adventures (6 Airlie

Esplanade, Airlie Beach, tel. 07/4948-2037, www.whitsundaydive.com.au, two-night tours start at $419 pp) offers a two-day "Wings" trip on board a crewed sailing catamaran, sleeping 26 persons. Accommodations, linens, all food and snacks, tea and coffee, plus snorkel gear is included. The 3.5-day-long "Emperors Wings" tour (from $499; including unlimited dives from $840, with accommodations, food, and snorkel equipment included) takes the catamaran to the outer reef, offering superb diving at reefs that most tours don't get to. Fitting in up to eight dives for the outer reef tour, the trip is suitable for certified divers as well as offering newcomers a PADI introduction course, while non-divers can go snorkeling at every dive site. The tour travels extensively past many islands, also stopping at Whitehaven Beach.

Accommodations

Fantasea Reefsleep (book at 259 Shute Harbour Rd., Airlie Beach, tel. 07/4946-5299, www.airliebeach.com) is certainly one of the world's unique hotels, and probably one of the most isolated. It's set on a pontoon (only about half the size of a tennis court, but still the largest in Australia), some 51 nautical miles out to sea from Airlie Beach at Hardy Reef near the outer Great Barrier Reef. You will be one of six people enjoying a true close-up of the reef, overnight. Your day will start at Airlie Beach Marina (alternatively you can board the high-speed catamaran at Hamilton Island Marina or on Lindeman Island), and you will share the day on the pontoon with day-trippers until around 2:30pm, when they all leave to get back to the mainland, while you remain with the staff, the so-called reef rats.

You'll get exclusive time for exploring the reef on your own, snorkeling tours, scuba lessons, and the opportunity to see the marine life at night, under the stars. Sleeping options at Reefsleep are pretty standard with the option of the king room with en suite from $650 per person ($570 excluding scuba dive) or a bunk-style room sleeping four from $480 per person ($399 excluding scuba dive). The decor of the rooms is predictably marine inspired, with plenty of turquoise accents and reef-related artwork, while the hotel itself looks like a cross between a boat and a pontoon. Food is included in the price, and dinner is underwater, in a glass room, whose light attracts many fish to your table, so to speak.

Overlooking the rooftops of Airlie Beach to the sea and the islands on the horizon, the apartments at **Waters Edge Resort** (4 Golden Orchid Dr., tel. 07/4948-2655, www.watersedgewhitsundays.com.au, one-bedroom apartment from $225) offer luxury away from home. Options range from one- to three-bedroom apartments with pool, sea, or mountain views, and it is a brief saunter down the hill into the center of town and all its amenities. The resort has an excellent restaurant, **Déjà Vu,** by the pool.

★ **Best Western Mango House Resort** (corner Shute Harbour Rd. and Erromango Dr., tel. 07/4946-4666, www.mangohouseresort.com, from $80) is a gorgeous yet budget-friendly resort that fits right in with the general Whitsunday mood: relaxed, tropical, and stylish. All apartments are spacious, in white and blue with white shutters and tiled floors for that tropical feeling. A large living area, balcony, spacious kitchen, and other amenities make this a home from home. Try to get an apartment with a pool view for an even better experience. A supermarket is just opposite, and you are a mere two-minute drive from Airlie Beach center and seven minutes from Shute Harbour.

Shingley Beach Resort (Shingley Dr., Airlie Beach, tel. 07/4948-8300, www.shingleybeachresort.com, studio apartments from $125) is just outside the bustling center of Airlie Beach overlooking Shingley Beach and Abel Point Marina. Accommodation ranges from studios to three-bedroom apartments, making the location and size perfect for families needing a base in the area but not necessarily wanting to be right in the hub of the town. The apartments are spacious and modern with great views and all amenities close by.

Beach Court Holiday Villas (24 Beach

Rd., Cannonvale, tel. 07/4946-5316, www.beachcourt.com.au, from $190) offers basic but clean and spacious villas, sleeping four to six, set around a nice pool just a couple of minutes' walk from the lovely Cannonvale Beach, some five minutes' drive from Airlie Beach. While within reach of the town and marinas, this is a little more secluded and quiet, but with Cannonvale shopping center around the corner for all necessities.

Food

Mr Bones (263 Shute Harbour Rd., tel. 04/1601-1615, www.mrbones.com.au, Wed.-Sun. 9am-9pm, pizza $22) is known for its pizza and tapas, funky decor, and attentive staff. The little café overlooks the lagoon and beach behind and is a perfect spot for coffee, some food, or simply a cool beer.

Hidden on the first floor of Waters Edge Resort, ★ **Déjà Vu** (4 Golden Orchid Dr., tel. 07/4948-4309, www.dejavurestaurant.com.au, Wed.-Sat. noon-2:30pm and 6pm-9pm, Sun. 12:30pm-5pm, mains $32) is a smart casual boutique restaurant with views across Airlie Beach's rooftops toward the bay. Apart from great modern Australian à la carte food, such as kangaroo loin or peri-peri reef fish and prawns, the restaurant is known for its lazy Sunday lunches—between 12:30pm and 5pm, eat, drink, and listen to live music.

Fish D'Vine (303 Shute Harbour Rd., tel. 07/4948-0088, www.fishdvine.com.au, Mon.-Fri. 5pm-late, Sat.-Sun. 11:30am-late, mains $28) is just as well known for its great seafood as it is for its extensive local rum menu. A modern spacious setting at the edge of Airlie Beach's main drag, this is a favorite spot for a night out.

Salt (Beach Plaza, tel. 07/4948-0011, daily noon-9pm) is a seafood bar and grill but serves a very decent steak if you are sick of fresh fish (steak and chips $29). If you choose to eat outside rather than in, you'll have the added bonus of beach views.

Right next door to Salt is **La Tabella Trattoria** (Beach Plaza, tel. 07/4948-1888, open daily, all day for food and drinks, mains $26), an Italian restaurant specializing on pasta and risotto and other Mediterranean favorites.

If it is Mexican you crave, look no further than **Cactus Jack** (The Esplanade, tel. 07/4964-1800, Mon.-Fri. 4pm-late, Sat.-Sun. noon-late) for your nachos ($12) and fajitas ($29). Overlooking Boathaven Bay, this spot is perfect for views and people-watching.

The draw of **Sorrento** (22 Shingley Dr., Abel Point Marina, tel. 07/4946-7454, daily noon-9pm, Sat.-Sun. 8:30am-11:30am) is the location, along Bicentennial Walk within walking distance from Airlie Beach and overlooking the bay and marina. It does pizza and pasta specials daily between 3pm and 5pm, when you get two pizzas for the price of one and all pastas are only $15, instead of the usual $20.

Magnums Hotel (366 Shute Harbour Rd., tel. 07/4946-6188, daily 10am-3am) includes Party Bar, a live band venue; Sports Bar, upstairs complete with pool tables and plasma screens; and Boardwalk, the town's biggest beer garden with live music five times a week. There is no distinct decor or style; it's just fun, full of people having fun, and loud. If you crave people, music, and plenty of beer, look no further.

Information and Services

Airlie Beach itself is relatively small and does not have a wide variety of amenities, but there is Cannonvale nearby and the larger community of Proserpine a 10-minute drive away. **Proserpine Hospital** (26-32 Taylor St., Proserpine, tel. 07/4813-9400) is located in that community, but there's a well-equipped pharmacy, **ChemCoast** (277 Shute Harbour Rd., Airlie Beach, tel. 07/4946-6156), in the center of Airlie Beach. There are a couple of **banks** with ATMs in the center of Airlie Beach and a **post office** in Cannonvale (Whitsunday Shopping Center, 226 Proserpine-Shute Harbour Rd., Cannonvale, tel. 13/13-18, Mon.-Fri. 9am-5pm, Sat. 9am-12:30pm).

Getting There and Around

To get closest to Airlie Beach or any of the Whitsunday Islands, you can fly into **Proserpine (Whitsunday Coast) Airport** (PPP, Lascelles Ave., Proserpine, tel. 07/4945-0200, http://proserpineairport.com), some 40 kilometers south of Airlie Beach, with Qantas, Virgin Australia, or Jetstar, and then use one of several transfer services to get to your accommodations or tour. **Whitsunday Transit** (tel. 07/4946-1800, www.whitsundaytransit.com.au, one-way adult $18) can arrange pickup from the airport according to your arrival time and drop you off at your accommodations.

Queensland's **Tilt Train** (tel. 07/3235-2222, www.queenslandrail.com.au) offers a rail option for getting to and from Proserpine. There are two northbound and two southbound stops per week at **Proserpine Train Station** (Lot 2 Ann St., Proserpine). The trip from Brisbane takes around 15 hours, with one-way tickets from $173.40. Upon arrival, a connecting coach service can take you to Airlie Beach. **Whitsunday Transit** (tel. 07/4946-1800, www.whitsundaytransit.com.au, one-way adult $12.10) can arrange pickup from the train station according to your arrival time and drop you off at your accommodations.

The northbound **Greyhound** coach (tel. 1300/473-946, www.greyhound.com.au) has up to five daily services between Brisbane and Airlie Beach, the journey taking around 18 hours, costing from $233 one way.

When driving, leave the Bruce Highway at Proserpine and follow the signs to Airlie Beach. Proserpine is around 40 kilometers south of Airlie Beach, around a 30-minute drive.

★ HAMILTON ISLAND

Hamilton Island is the largest inhabited island of the Whitsundays, and is on private long-term lease from the Australian government. Resorts and amenities for holiday-makers have existed on the island since 1984, and although tourism is the main attraction, increasingly, residents have been buying property there to enjoy the lifestyle, often for retirement. When you arrive, be it by ferry or at the airport right next to the marina, you think you're landing in a relatively large town. But, besides some rather gorgeous private holiday residences, this is pretty much a giant resort with numerous different accommodation options. Apart from one property (the Whitsunday Apartments), all the resorts, hotels, apartments, and attractions are owned and run by one company, **Hamilton Island** (tel. 13/73-33, www.hamiltonisland.com.au). That means, with a couple of exceptions (Beach Club and Qualia), you can be staying in one hotel but use the facilities of the resort down the road. You can also pop into any of the restaurants around the marina and charge your bill to your room. Equally, you can phone other hotels, restaurants, and shops through extensions from your room telephone, as it's all interconnected. This creates a rather special resort atmosphere, where people walk around in their beachwear in the "high street" yet they are still in the resort, of sorts, and while most people stay within their chosen hotels, you can experience plenty of restaurant and pool hopping between options.

Beaches

Within the main development there is one gorgeous beach, **Catseye Beach,** right on the doorstep. Accessible through the main resort reception only, this beach offers all the activities, such as kayaking, sailing, and snorkeling, for the entire resort community, but it is large enough to handle the influx of people.

There are several other beaches around the island; for example, the private resort Qualia has a couple of secluded beaches, but these are only open to its guests. Other beaches are away from the main island center.

Wild Life Hamilton Island

Wild Life Hamilton Island (tel. 07/4946-9078, daily 8am-5pm, adult $20, child $12, or VIP entry adult $40, child $32, includes koala photo), right in the center of the main resorts, offers close encounters of the cuddly and

Hamilton Island

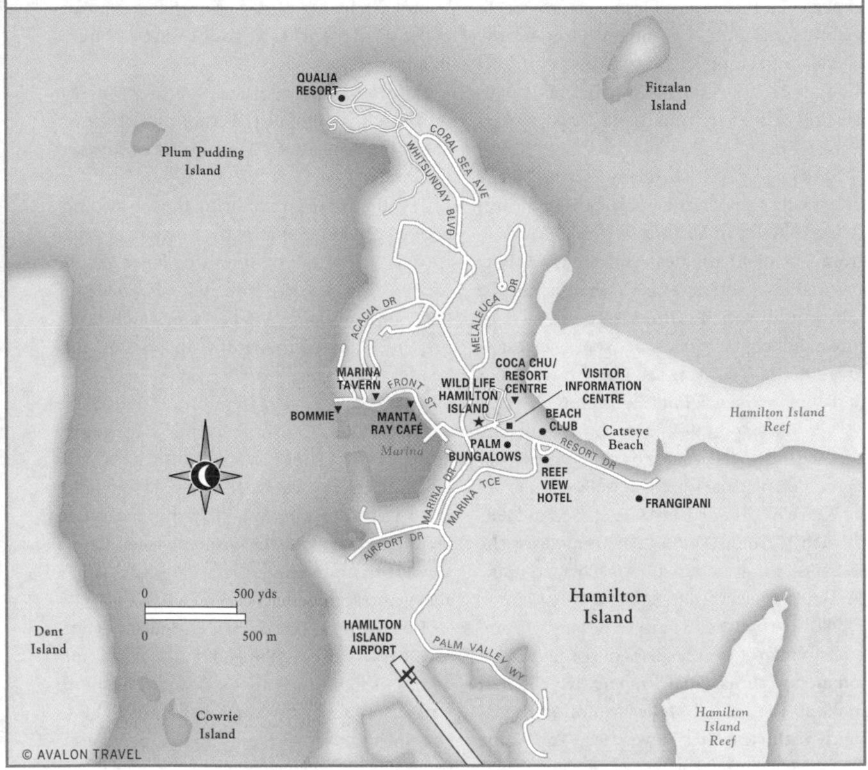

creepy kind. Daily activities include breakfast with the koalas (7am-10am, $35) and cuddles with koalas (8:30am-9:30am, $30). Tours, such as the one-hour "Park Keeper" tour (daily at 10am and 4pm), get you close to the animals. The "BBQ and Sunset Spotlight Animal Feeding" tours (Thurs. and Fri. at 6pm, adult $35, child $20) include a barbecue and nighttime visits to the nocturnal animals. Crocodile feeding takes place at 4pm on Wednesday and Saturday. The zoo is small, and the especially fun activities are the organized events, such as the breakfast or the tours, rather than the zoo itself.

Recreation

Cruise Indigo (tel. 07/4946-9664, www.cruiseindigo.com.au) offers cruises setting off from Hamilton Island Marina. Options include snorkeling trips, sunset tours, dining tours, and tailored private charters.

Be your own captain and explore the island's hidden coves and beaches in a motorized dinghy. **Dinghy hire** (tel. ext. 58305 or 07/4946-8305, from $139 per half day for up to six people, minimum age of driver 18) comes complete with fishing essentials and fuel.

Jet Ski tours (tel. ext. 58305 or 07/4946-8305, from $219 per ski, $39 for additional passenger, minimum age of driver 18, minimum age of passenger 10) give you a chance to see the island from a different perspective and have an adventure on the sea. Tours take you around the bays and beaches.

Sea kayaking tours (tel. ext. 58305 or 07/4946-8305, from $59) are a great way to experience the island. Go on an adventure paddle for a couple of hours, visiting nearby islands and stopping for a swim or snorkel along the way, or try the serene sunset paddle, kayaking while sipping a glass of sparkling wine.

Sailing the Whitsundays is simply the best sailing experience you can get. With **Adrenalin Rush Sailing** (tel. 07/4946-9664, from $75 for 40 minutes), you can try a short trip on the catamaran to get a taste and maybe follow it up with a sailing lesson or two, or hire a sailboat for a group of experienced sailors. Alternatively, you can go with a skipper and explore the neighboring islands.

Become a spectator of stunning sailboats descending on the islands during August's famous **Hamilton Island Race Week,** started by Keith Williams in the 1980s. Hundreds of yachts, from 30-foot boats rented for the week to billion-dollar super yachts, compete in some serious racing.

Walking trails (daily 6:30am-5:30pm, pick up map at your resort) cover some 20 kilometers of the island. Climb up to the Resort lookout, the second highest point on the island, with stunning views; head to Escape Beach at low tide with a picnic; or find Coral Cove Beach with views across to Lindeman Island. There are plenty of options. You can order picnic lunches at your resort 24 hours in advance.

Audio tours (free, ask at your resort desk) will teach you about the island's history or about the nature you'll encounter on the set bushwalk.

If you want to go exploring the resorts and activity centers, and want the freedom of driving yourself rather than waiting for the shuttle, look into **buggy hire** (tel. ext. 58263 or 07/4946-8263, from $45 per hour). Golf carts are the standard mode of transport on the island.

Quad bike tours (tel. ext. 58305 or 07/4946-8305, 15 minutes from $109 adult, $32 child 6-14) are available for kids and adults. Drivers must be 16 years old and hold at least a learner's permit. With the quad bikes you can set off along the bushland trails across the island and enjoy otherwise inaccessible views and secluded nooks.

Have fun on the purpose-built track for **Go-karts** (tel. 07/4946-8305, from $47 for 10 minutes, minimum age 11 and minimum height 140 cm, duo karts minimum age 4 years with adult) at Hamilton Island's Palm

Hamilton Island

Valley. Take the wheel on the exhilarating outdoor track, reaching speeds of up to 45 kilometers per hour.

Playing **golf** (tel. ext. 59760 or 07/4948-9760, from $100 for 9 holes and $150 for 18 holes, $90 for professional lesson) in the Whitsundays includes a trip to the neighboring Dent Island, either by boat or helicopter. But once you're there, it offers a championship course, par 71, measuring 6,120 meters. Private lessons, a driving range, club house, and pro shop are all available on the island, making for a great day out.

The purpose-built 9-pin (not 10-pin) **bowling alley** (tel. ext. 58440 or 07/4946-8440, 1 hour $59) offers a bit of a challenge, with seven lanes, an amusement arcade, a licensed bar, food and snacks, and glow-in-the-dark lanes at night.

Art classes (tel. ext. 59657 or 07/4948-9657, adult $69, child $39) can be arranged at the dedicated space, the Art Gallery. Learn how to capture the beauty of the islands and work on a special souvenir. Classes can be adult only, for children, or even for families. All materials are supplied.

There are also daily activities organized by the resorts, such as spin classes, mini-golf championships for kids, buggy rallies, trivia evenings, and countless others, some at extra cost, a lot of them free to resort guests. You can also hire snorkel equipment at Catseye Beach, get windsurf boards and paddle boards and much more, all free for guests.

Accommodations

There are around a dozen or so accommodation options, all part of the main resort, plus also private apartment hires. Here is a selection of some of the best.

Qualia Resort (tel. 1300/780-959, www.qualia.com.au, from $975 per night, Beach House from $3,650 per night, minimum guest age 16) is a premium luxury resort on its own gated headland away from the main hub. Fifty-nine one-bedroom private villas nestle among the natural beauty of the island, with the 60th villa being the ultimate luxury retreat of the two-bedroom Qualia Beach House, with its own guest quarters, lap pool, and breathtaking views. The rooms are held in sublime water colors—tasteful, modern, and comfortable—with private verandas overlooking the sea. It is serenity and luxury personified. The resort offers every facility, including two infinity-edge swimming pools, a library, two restaurants, a private gym, and quintessential Australian treatments at Spa Qualia.

The only resort within the main hub that is directly on Catseye Beach, the **Beach Club** (tel. 07/4946-8000, www.hamiltonisland.com.au, from $570 per night, minimum guest age 18) offers guests access to all of the island's facilities (except Qualia's), but the hotel is closed to other resort guests and is an exclusive, romantic retreat for adults only. All rooms at the Beach Club have a private courtyard or balcony looking onto palm-fringed beach and the Coral Sea, with the interior designed to reflect the ocean's proximity, full of light woods, wicker furniture, turquoise hues, and open spaces creating an atmosphere that is light and airy.

The apartments at **Frangipani** (tel. 07/5641-4004, www.frangipani204.com.au, from $550 per night, three-night minimum stay) are close to the beach and the main hub but are nestled at the end of the main road and close to the forest, ideal for bushwalks. Three bedrooms, three bathrooms plus the use of two golf buggies make this ideal for groups or a large family.

Choose from a range of rooms and suites at the four-star **Reef View Hotel** (tel. 07/4946-9999, www.hamiltonisland.com.au, from $360 per night). One of the few high-rise buildings on the island, the hotel has breathtaking views from the upper rooms. All rooms are spacious and well appointed, with a furnished balcony, Internet access, and bathroom with separate bath and shower. Garden View rooms have leafy views and ocean glimpses, while each Coral Sea View room has spectacular views over Catseye Bay and nearby Whitsunday Island. A huge pool and special deals allowing children to stay and eat free make this a very family-friendly option.

Nestled among the lush greenery, ★ **Palm Bungalows** (tel. 13/73-33, www.hamiltonisland.com.au, from $340 per night, sleeping up to 3) has no ocean views, but does have plenty of character. The free-standing bungalows are in a style akin to a Balinese or African retreat, with wooden floors, pointed thatched roofs with rafters and ceiling fans, plenty of cushions and comfy couches, and a balcony or terrace overlooking palm trees. A kitchenette includes fridge and coffee/tea-making facilities. A two-minute walk from the beach and other resorts' amenities, this is a family- and budget-friendly option, with kids under 12 years old staying for free.

Hamilton Island Holiday Homes (tel. 02/9433-0444, www.hihh.com.au, apartments from $315) has a website with a wide range of private homes for rent, from studios to five-bed properties to Yacht Club villas. There is a wide choice and something to suit everybody. Many properties even have a golf cart in the garage for use on the island.

Right next to the Reef View Hotel, **Whitsunday Apartments** (tel. 07/4946-9865, www.wahi.com.au, from $299) offers spacious one-bedroom apartments, with a separate bedroom, dual-access bathroom, and a large living area, which can sleep more people, if required. Large balconies overlook Catseye Beach and the sea, or the gardens.

Food

A must-do is to have **breakfast with the koalas** at **Wild Life Hamilton Island** (tel. 07/4946-9078, daily 7am-10am, $35 for breakfast, an extra $30 for cuddles and picture). Choose from hot and cold buffet food and meet an array of critters while you eat.

Right at the entrance to the marina, opposite Dent Island, ★ **Bommie** (Hamilton Island Yacht Club, tel. 07/4946-9999, Thurs.-Mon. 6pm-midnight, mains $39) has views spanning across Hamilton Island itself and the sea, with the busy marina's boats coming and going. The architecturally interesting building, hinting at ships and whales, has simply the best location on the island. Views aside, the trendy restaurant and bar offers delicious fine dining with fresh regional ingredients on the menu. The modern Australian cuisine is presented like little pieces of artwork on your plate, fresh and seasonal. The seafood is fantastic. And did I mention the views?

Located right in the heart of the resort overlooking the beach, the modern Southeast Asian restaurant **Coca Chu** (Resort Center, tel. ext. 58580 or 07/4946-8580, daily 5:30pm-late, mains $26) allows children under 12 years to eat for free if you are staying at selected accommodations, such as Reef View Hotel, Palm Bungalows, or accommodations booked through Hamilton Island Holiday Homes. The open-plan setting is relaxed, under a high pointed roof with rafters, and you can watch the chefs in the open kitchen prepare your fresh and light food.

Manta Ray Café (tel. ext. 58213 or 07/4946-8213, daily 10:30am-9pm, pizza takeaway noon-10pm, mains $23) is the place for gourmet pizzas on the island, but they also do coffee and cake during the day. Pizza takeaway and delivery are available.

Within the main resort center, overlooking the pool and the beach, **Sails Steak & Seafood Grill** (tel. ext. 58562 or 07/4946-8562, daily 7am-late, mains $20) is the best place for steaks and fresh fish, although it is open for breakfast, lunch, and dinner. And, again, kids eat for free if you are staying in selected accommodations.

Marina Tavern (tel. 07/4946-9999, ext. 58213, no booking required, daily 11am-late) is a no-frills pub-style tavern where you can eat inside or alfresco, looking out over the marina and the hustle and bustle around you. Family favorites include fish and chips, chicken parmigiana, and pasta and burgers.

Information and Services

There are a couple of **banks,** one opposite the Hamilton Island Outrigger Resort (Mon.-Fri. 9:30am-3pm, closed Wed.-Thurs.

11:30am-12:30pm) and one in the marina. The **post office** (Mon.-Fri. 8:30am-4:30pm) is opposite the ferry stop in the marina, and the **Medical Center** (tel. 07/4946-8243, Mon.-Fri. 8:30am-noon and 2pm-4:30pm, Sat. 9am-noon, closed Sun.) is next to Reef View Hotel. A **pharmacy** (tel. 07/4946-9053, Mon.-Fri. 8:30am-6pm, Sat.-Sun. 8:30am-4pm) is in the marina. For **emergencies** call 555 from your hotel phone.

Getting There and Around

You can fly directly into **Hamilton Island Airport** (HTI, tel. 07/4946-9999) from Sydney with Qantas, Jetstar, and Virgin Australia (from around $129 one way, flight duration 2.5 hours). From the airport, there are free shuttles to all the resort accommodations.

Alternatively, **Cruise Whitsundays** (tel. 07/4946-4662, www.cruisewhitsundays.com) has at least one ferry per hour leaving both Abel Point Marina and Shute Harbour to Hamilton Island, with transfers taking 30-60 minutes, depending on which connection you take, as connections are available via Daydream and Long Islands. A one-way ticket from the mainland to Hamilton Marina is $48 per person. Ferry timetables are available online and at all visitor information stalls.

Once on the island, you can either hire a **buggy** (tel. ext. 58263 or 07/4946-8263, from $45 per hour) or use one of the three free shuttle buses that leave regularly and stop off at all points of interest and accommodation options. Some go clockwise and others counterclockwise, so it might be faster one way rather than the other, but the entire circle takes around 20 minutes, so it really is not that important which one you take.

DAYDREAM ISLAND

Undoubtedly the island with the best name, Daydream Island is the only one that has dedicated the entire island to its resort. The **Daydream Island Resort & Spa** (tel. 07/3259-2350, www.daydreamisland.com) is popular with families and wedding parties who stay on after the ceremony for the honeymoon. At first the resort comes across as a bit of a theme park, with statues of mermaids, dolphins, and even a giant octopus by the main restaurant. There are lagoons within the island with fish, coral, and even stingrays, and the activity centers are bright and colorful and at first can look a little too much aimed at younger visitors. But when you add it all up, the resort offers peace and quiet, as well as plenty of things to do for the entire family; it has beaches, pools, a wellness spa, a small aquarium, bowling, miniature golf, and water sports and is within a 25-minute ferry ride from the mainland.

Recreation

This island takes its fun seriously. Free activities include paddle-boarding, kayaking, catamaran hire, water polo, volleyball, tennis, walks, fish-feeding shows, marine talks, open-air cinema, giant chess, trivia evenings, and various daily activities. On a daily basis there are kids' activities organized, anything from face painting to sandcastle building, while scavenger hunts, bingo, yoga, and naturopathy workshops keep the adults busy.

Other activities available at a fee include: Jet Ski hire ($55 for 15 minutes, $190 per tour), parasailing (from $65), boat rental (half day $149), crazy golf (adult $10, child $6, family $25), glass-bottom boat tours ($110 half-day), and waterskiing lessons (from $89).

Accommodations

Daydream Island Resort & Spa (from $119 pp if booked 72 hours before stay) is relatively large, with several two-story building wings strung along the resort, facing either the beach or the bush side of the island, but due to the low-rise design and palm trees overshadowing the buildings, it doesn't get cramped or too bulky. Accommodation options move from standard rooms and suites to the Grand Ocean suite and the Honeymoon suites, with family rooms and other options in between. The spacious standard rooms are outfitted with modern furniture, seating areas comprising a comfy chair and couch, en suite bathrooms, and coffee-making facilities; larger rooms and suites have private balconies looking out over the sea, the jetty, the pool, or the garden, depending on whether you are in the Coral, Marina, Daydreamer, or Rainforest wing, respectively.

Food

The main restaurant is **Mermaids Restaurant** (daily 11:30am-2:30pm, mains $22, from 5:30pm on select evenings according to the daily resort schedule, mains $33), where you can get lunches and dinners in a lovely setting by Mermaids Beach. Other options include the Waterfall Restaurant (breakfast daily from 6:30am), Splashes Pool Bar, Lagoon Bar, Gilligans Bar and Health Hut, the Boathouse Bakery, the Coffee Bean café, and the Fishbowl Tavern. They offer plenty of choices, from your fish of the day to healthy salads, from burgers and fries to pizza, from coffee and cake specials to freshly squeezed juices and smoothies.

Information and Services

There is an ATM on the island, but you can charge all activities and food, shopping, and outings to your room, so cash is not really necessary.

Getting There and Around

Cruise Whitsundays (tel. 07/4946-4662, www.cruisewhitsundays.com) has nearly hourly services to Daydream Island, from both Shute Harbour and Abel Point Marina, with frequent connections on from the island to Hamilton and Long Islands. The trip takes around 25 minutes.

Once on the island, you can walk from one end to the other within 10 minutes at the most, although they do have a long, limousine-style golf buggy that gets dressed up for wedding parties. There is a lounge for new arrivals and departures, where you get briefed, your luggage is taken care of, and you'll get to know the island and what it offers.

LONG ISLAND

Long Island is a hilly island approximately nine kilometers in length, covered with dense forest. It is one of several islands that form the **Molle Islands National Park.** Contrary to today, the first European visitors to Long Island did not arrive at the island by choice, but landed there after their ship, the *Valetta,* was damaged on a reef off Scawfell Island in 1825. Following repairs they set off again, but further trouble led them into the calm waters of Happy Bay on the same island. Here the

Daydream Island Resort & Spa

crew of 57 set up huts and tried to repair the vessel again, with no luck. They lived here until another vessel came by three months later and rescued them.

Long Island changed hands many times in the 1800s but remained basically unused until 1921, when Carl Alderman moved onto the island and grew bananas, and eventually built the first resort on the island. Although closed during World War II, the resorts soon started changing hands again, and today two resorts invite guests to quietly enjoy the island.

Accommodations, Food, and Recreation

Today there are two main resorts on the island—technically three, if you count Long Island Resort's backpacker option at the back of their existing resort, although it is only used when the resort itself is filled to capacity.

Long Island Resort (Long Island, tel. 1800/075-125, www.longislandresort.com.au, from $90 pp per night including breakfast) is reached with the Cruise Whitsunday ferries from Abel Point Marina and Shute Harbour on the mainland. A budget resort, the buildings are a little on the neglected side, but it's popular with young families who simply want to relax, enjoy the surroundings, and not spend too much on accommodations or eating out in fancy restaurants. All-inclusive packages start at $149 per person. The simple rooms all have balconies or terraces facing the sandy beach. Amenities include a pool plus a separate lap pool, playgrounds, and a restaurant (three-course dinner $30). The backpacker lodge (from $30) offers dorm rooms with bunk beds sleeping up to four, and guests enjoy the some facilities in the resort. With tennis and basketball courts, crazy golf, fish-feeding areas, and an activity desk organizing daily action (such as karaoke, lorikeet feeding, mixology classes, batfish feeding, and live music), there are plenty of activities to keep everybody busy. There are several nature walks on the island, including short and easy walks, such as Humpy Point (600 meters); various walks to nearby bays with secluded beaches; a Round Hill circuit of 2.1 kilometers; or the longest walk, to Sandy Bay (4.4 kilometers), for which you can pick up maps in the resort.

Paid activities include turtle and reef kayak safaris ($30 for 1.5 hours), sunset kayak tours ($25 for 1.5 hours), Jet Ski rental (from $55 for 15 minutes), fishing (from $15 per day for a rod, $50 per hour for a boat), coral reef ecotours ($25 for 1.5 hours), tube rides ($25 pp), and much more.

Paradise Bay Resort (South Long Island, tel. 07/4946-9777, www.paradisebay.com.au, all-inclusive from $1,100 pp, plus $760 helicopter transfers round-trip) is also on Long Island, but at the other end, separated from Long Island Resort and the ferry jetty by lots of thick national park forest. The resort is exclusive, with a maximum of 18 guests, very luxurious, and much more difficult to get to, with the only way to get there being by helicopter. Individual wooden eco-lodges directly on the beach have solar-powered lighting and rainwater showers. Ceiling fans and sun loungers keep things comfortable. There are no telephones, virtually no mobile phone reception, and no computers, basically forcing you to relax and enjoy the island and your lovely lodgings, which, despite the eco-approach, are luxurious and comfortable.

The restaurant in the resort offers buffet breakfasts, gourmet picnic lunches, and top-notch fine-dining dinners, prepared by a chef trained in celebrated restaurants on the mainland, and champagne on arrival and cocktails daily at sunset are pretty much obligatory. Soft drinks and house wine at dinner are also included, as are snacks throughout the day.

Activities can include treatments at the house spa, yoga classes by the pool, and all water sports. Boat excursions and hire of all equipment, such as snorkel gear, paddle boats, kayaks, Hobie cats, and more, are included.

Getting There and Around

Cruise Whitsundays (tel. 07/4946-4662, www.cruisewhitsundays.com) has nearly hourly services to Long Island, but only to the Long Island Resort jetty, from both Shute Harbour and Abel Point Marina, with frequent connections on from the island to Hamilton and Daydream Islands. The trip takes around 25 minutes. For Paradise Bay Resort, helicopter transfers will be arranged upon booking.

HAYMAN ISLAND

One of the top resorts in Australia, private Hayman Island gives new meaning to luxury. Closest of the Whitsunday Islands to the outer barrier reef with its spectacular diving and snorkeling sites, this little island is not as large and densely overgrown as some of the other islands, but it does offer a small population of the rare and endangered Proserpine rock wallaby, and there are prospering resort gardens. The well-tended and -stocked 16-hectare gardens have 33,000 new plants designed and planted by master gardener Jamie Durie in an overhaul following cyclone destruction, and the garden now showcases palms, vines, and at times nearly overpoweringly sweet-smelling tropical flowers, especially lovely jasmine.

The opulent resort is one of only four Australian members of the prestigious Leading Hotels of the World consortium, and it is Australia's most awarded five-star resort. It is far from its origins as a fishing getaway in the 1930s and '40s. In 1947, Reg (later Sir Reginald) Ansett bought it for £14,000, said to be based on a rate of £10 for every wild goat on the island. Now, the garden overhaul alone cost $4 million. And, to give you an idea of the service, or experience, you can expect: The staff on the island move via underground tunnels that connect separate buildings to make them less obvious and to ensure that things like moving trolleys and tradespeople do not affect the guests.

Recreation

Hayman Island is one of the few resorts that combine utter luxury with a lot of recreational activities. Of course, you can simply lounge by the pool or on the beach, but if you are bringing kids, or you are feeling restless, there is plenty of fun to be had. Not all activities are complimentary, though, and prices depend on what packages you are booking. As a general rule, all motorized activities will incur a fee. (For example, motorized water sports such as waterskiing and wakeboarding cost $70 for 30 minutes and $120 for 1 hour.)

Complimentary catamaran sailing, windsurfing, and paddleboarding are available from Hayman Beach, and you'll even get

the Long Island Resort jetty

instructions, if you are unsure on what to do. Then there is snorkeling, which is possible from the beach, but you can hire a private guide to show you some secluded spots. Or join a small group for the walk'n'snorkel, which is, as the name suggests, a guided five-kilometer walk across the island, with fantastic views over the resort, to another beach.

A PADI dive center on the island offers shore dives and dive trips for certified divers, refresher courses, and introductory and three-day courses to get fully qualified, with gear rental possible from the dive center.

If you'd rather swim, beautiful Blue Seal Bay is a five-minute boat ride or slightly longer walk away. It's better for swimming than snorkeling. Or you can relax and/or swim in the large pentagonal pool flanked with sun loungers and umbrellas, not too far from the bar.

On land, you can take part in golf lessons (or take the helicopter to nearby Dent Island for an 18-hole round); play tennis, squash, or croquet; get fit with Boxfit, Zumba, Pilates, or aqua fit; or start the day with morning yoga classes.

The resort offers excursions by helicopter and seaplane, from snorkeling trips to scenic flights or a private picnic at Whitehaven Beach. Private yacht and helicopter charters can also be arranged.

Amenities include a spa, shops, and, during Australian school holidays, a program for kids 5-12. In addition there are several purely kid-oriented activities, such as wildlife encounters, special diving programs, a behind-the-scenes kitchen tour, and various arts and crafts workshops. Baby-sitting services are also available.

Like most islands along the Great Barrier Reef, Hayman also has a nature calendar and schedules events according to, for example, turtle hatchings or whale sightings.

Accommodations

While the **One & Only Hayman Island resort** (tel. 07/4940-1838, http://hayman.oneandonlyresorts.com) does not come cheap, there is a range of accommodations available, all utterly modern and stylishly tropical. There are three distinct areas to the resort, plus the luxurious penthouses.

In the **Hayman Wing** on the eastern side of the resort, set within gardens and overlooking the lily lagoon, are the Hayman Lagoon, Hayman Ocean View, and Hayman Premier Ocean View rooms and the Hayman Suites, plus the family rooms and suites. These are beautiful rooms, with romantic mosquito nets over the four-poster beds, ample seating, and relaxation space, but they're also relatively (and this is relative to the rest of this uber-luxurious resort) "normal" rooms, where there is no need to feel inadequate or out of place. Families and young couples settle in these modern and stylishly tropical rooms, but if you need more space, there is the **Pool Wing,** which houses the Pool Suites, which are larger and feature double balconies and pool views.

Then there are the **Hayman Penthouses.** The Owner's Penthouse accommodates up to six adults in three separate bedrooms, with a kitchenette and bar, plus a large sitting room. The "normal" penthouses can be either one- or two-bedroom, with complimentary snacks and in-room bar. The DvF Penthouse has been styled by Diane von Furstenberg, in her typical monochrome patterns complementing the seaside hues, with personal touches such as private photos by the designer. This penthouse has two bedrooms and two bathrooms, with a large living area and a secluded balcony.

The jewels in the crown, though, are the **Beach Villas,** of which there are eight, all with around-the-clock service, private veranda and pool, and all possible technology and amenities; no children under 13 years old are allowed in the villas. And then there is the **Beach House.** A dream of luxury indulgence, this house comes with butler, private courtyard, large veranda, and access to the beach, infinity pool, refreshment bar full of sparkling water and sparkling wine, a media room complete with iPads and iPods, and Apple TV.

Hayman Lagoon rooms cost from $730 a

night, while one-bedroom Pool Suites start at $1,790 a night. The Beach House costs from $3,700 per night, and the Owner's Penthouse starts at $10,600 per night. Rates include buffet breakfast for up to two guests; the Owner's Penthouse includes breakfast, selected dining, launch transfer, and butler service.

Food

There are seven permanent restaurants and bars, with many more special events and private dining possible on occasion, or at request. Gourmet picnics allow you to put together a box to take to the beach or on a trip, offering anything from smoked salmon to rosemary lamb cutlets and the most sinful chocolate brownie. **Pacific** is the relaxed place where you get your buffet breakfast and, on certain evenings, have something from the grill. The resort's signature restaurant **Fire** (mains $45) offers fine-dining, modern Australian cuisine with an emphasis on fresh seafood. **Amici** (mains $35) is a relaxed alfresco Italian place where you can get pizza and pasta. **Bamboo** (mains $35) offers a mix of Thai, Chinese, Korean, and Indian cuisine with a garden setting. **On the Rocks** is a poolside bar where you'll find dishes such as a burger and fries ($30) and a salad Niçoise ($28). Family-friendly **Aquazure** serves up Spanish-influenced fare. The **Bar Fifty** is the place for a drink, plus a game of pool or sitting down with a book.

The **Chef's Table** is part of regular foodie events that include bringing in celebrity chefs to the island for gourmet experiences and interactive courses. There is also private dining, in the rooms or somewhere secluded in the garden for a romantic occasion.

Getting There and Around

All major airports around Australia offer direct flights to **Hamilton Airport** (HTI, tel. 07/4946-9999), the flight from Sydney being a mere 2.5 hours. Guests will wait in the private Hayman Lounge at the airport for the transfer to Hayman, which can either be by **seaplane** (tel. 07/4946-9111, reservations@airwhitsunday.com.au, from $790 one way for 6-seater aircraft), **helicopter** (tel. 07/4940-1730, helitours@hayman.com.au, 1-2 passengers from $660 one way or $1,320 round-trip), or **launch** (adult $145, child $72.50). The launch transfers are sweetened by canapés and champagne, and take a maximum of 50 minutes.

WHITSUNDAY ISLAND

Whitsunday Island is the largest of the Whitsundays, and it is home to famous **Whitehaven Beach,** probably one of the most iconic beaches in Australia, and the **Hill Inlet,** a much-photographed mosaic of turquoises and white sands that emerges with every changing tide. There is no development on the island because it is part of the **Whitsunday Islands National Park,** but the beauty of the island's beaches is such that cruises and day trips visit the island extensively.

There are several reasons to visit Whitsunday Island, the main one being Whitehaven Beach, which is an absolute stunner and reportedly the most photographed beach in Australia. The perfect curve, coupled with gleaming white sand and the pristinely colored sea, makes it hard to beat, although the myriad motor- and sailboats and various cruise operators constantly dotting the bay make it best appreciated in the early morning or later afternoon, after the visitors have left and only campers remain. The beach alone is spectacular enough really, but it shows off what it can do at the northern end, where Hill Inlet is a swirl of whites and turquoises, when the sands shift with the changing tides. The spectacle can best be viewed from Tongue Point, a higher ground lookout on the island. Try to time your arrival at the lookout to coincide with low tide to fully experience the beautiful fusion of colors that emerge, and keep your camera at the ready.

There are several **campgrounds** on the island, with maximum capacity ranging 6-12 persons each. All of them provide basic amenities, such as composting toilets and picnic tables, but there is no development of the island, so you will have to bring your own water, food, and equipment and take all your garbage away with you again when you leave. Permits can be obtained through the **Department of National Parks, Recreation, Sport and Racing** (tel. 13/74-68, www.nprsr.qld.gov.au, camping from $5.60 pp per night).

Getting There and Around

A lot of tour operators visit Whitsunday Island, mostly to enjoy Whitehaven Beach. The island is accessible by private or charter boat, seaplane, or helicopter only. There is secure anchorage off Cid Harbour.

SOUTH MOLLE ISLAND

Unfortunately, South Molle Island Resort is one of those that has fallen afoul of the cyclone. The resort is still pretty much intact, apart from the rooms falling into disrepair, and the pool and other buildings are all still there, with a caretaker looking after them. But you can no longer stay on the island, as the resort is closed, with currently no intentions of reopening it. The island, however, is still part of a national park, so the government looks after the nature walks, and if you can find a way of getting to the island, it is well worth bringing a picnic, your swimsuit, and your walking boots, as the tracks around the island are beautiful, as are the beaches. One option is to hire a sailboat or motor yacht, crewed or bareboat, from **Sail Free** (tel. 1800/911-244, www.sailfree.com.au), where a 36-foot Clipper motor yacht starts from $420 per night, sleeping up to eight people.

HOOK ISLAND

The second largest of the Whitsunday Islands, Hook Island lies between Whitsunday and Hayman Islands. Because it's quite large and remote, nature had a good chance to establish itself, and the birds and wildlife are plentiful. Hook Island boasts **Hook Peak,** which rises to 450 meters above sea level, and the **walk to Nara Inlet** is a perennial favorite. Alas, the resort is another one that has closed after Cyclone Yasi hit the islands, and it has not reopened. So, you cannot stay on the island, nor can you take the ferry there anymore, but if you can find a way of getting there, then the walks on this island are well worth it. You can hire a sailboat or motor yacht, crewed or bareboat, from **Sail Free** (tel. 1800/911-244, www.sailfree.com.au).

Whitsunday Island's Whitehaven Beach

On the walk to the Nara Inlet on the eastern shore, you will pass a cave that is thought to have been occupied by the Ngaro people during their fishing expeditions around the island, with some remaining Aboriginal artwork present. The track continues on past the cave, where there are several good lookouts offering fine views down Nara Inlet and the nearby anchorages, which always feature some stunning sailboats.

LINDEMAN ISLAND

This is another Whitsunday Island resort that is currently closed. The Club Med Resort has changed hands, and the current owner is still contemplating as to whether a resort will be built and opened for tourism in the near future. And while Lindeman Island does have an airstrip, it is not in use for the public at the moment, with access to the island's walks and camping areas by boat only.

But once you are there, several bushwalks offer great views and a vast variety of natural vegetation and wildlife. Try the **Mount Oldfield walk,** setting off from the airport hut near the former resort, a walk that covers 7.2 kilometers round-trip, taking around 3.5 hours at a moderate level. You can make the easy to moderate walk to **Coconut Beach,** 5.4 kilometers round-trip, taking two hours through eucalyptus forest to the resort dam, which is a great place for bird-spotting. It then descends to the sandy beach through fringing scrub, giving the beach a secluded feel. Or try **Gap Beach,** another moderate 5.4-kilometer round-trip hike winding through eucalyptus forest and dry rainforest before emerging at a pebbly beach with spectacular views of nearby Pentecost Island.

If you want to spend the night, there is a **campground** at Boat Port on the northwest side of the island, approximately 25 kilometers southeast of Shute Harbour. Limited to a maximum of 12 people, the campground is on sand with the forest nearby, and there is a toilet and a picnic table. Get permission before you go, as access is limited during certain months due to bird nestings, from the **Department of National Parks, Recreation, Sport and Racing** (tel. 13/74-68, www.nprsr.qld.gov.au, camping $5.60 pp per night).

BRAMPTON ISLAND

The southernmost island of the Whitsundays, Brampton Island is closer to Mackay than to Airlie Beach. Known simply as "M" on the charts of the region until 1879, a few

South Molle Island

years later the Queensland Agricultural Department, in a program to help shipwrecked sailors, planted coconut palms on a large number of islands, including Brampton, hoping the coconuts would provide food for the sailors. In 1916, Joseph Busuttin, his wife, Sarah, and five children became the island's first European settlers. The family remained on the island, establishing the first resort in 1933. Joseph Busuttin's sons did not leave the island until 1959, when they sold the resort. In late 1997 the resort was purchased by P&O Resorts, who promptly spent $3 million on refurbishment and decided that the traditional day-tripper market from Mackay should be halted, with the island kept for resort guests only. At the time of writing, the resort is closed, but with possible redevelopment in the future.

Most of the 770-hectare Brampton Island is designated national park, resulting in seven unspoiled and idyllic beaches that are, even for an island, isolated and pristine. The three-meter tidal range offers a different perspective at different times of the day.

Brampton is characterized by great variation of vegetation, with stands of hoop pine, sections of tropical rainforest, and coastal mangroves, making bushwalks one of the main land-based recreational activities. The seven-kilometer **National Parks track,** which circumnavigates most of Brampton, is perfectly constructed and maintained, with changes in grade that are subtle enough that even those who find anything other than lazing on the beach a chore can complete it in a leisurely couple of hours. Encounters with plenty of birdlife and gray kangaroos keep the animal lover busy.

There are additional walks to the **Cape Hillsborough Lookout** and to both **Oak Bay** and **Dinghy Bay West.** You can even reach the small uninhabited sister island, **Carlisle Island,** on foot at low tide.

For things to do in the water, try the **snorkeling safaris** exploring Brampton's coral gardens, or sail a **catamaran,** take out a **paddle ski,** or simply laze in a beachside hammock and savor the tropical setting.

Camping is not allowed on the island, but Carlisle Island has a campground at its southwestern edge, Neils Camping Area, overlooking Brampton Island. A maximum of 12 people are allowed to camp on this sand and grass site, with basic amenities of pit toilet and picnic tables provided; everything else needs to be carried on you. Permits need to be applied for and displayed from the **Department of National Parks, Recreation, Sports and Racing** (tel. 13/74-68, www.nprsr.qld.gov.au, camping $5.60 pp per night).

Getting There and Around

With the resort closed, at present the only way to access both Brampton and Carlisle Islands is by private boat. At low tide it is possible to walk from Brampton Island's Sandy Point to the campground at Carlisle Island. Check tide times and always leave enough time for the return trip to Brampton Island.

Bowen

Located halfway between the major towns of Mackay and Townsville, nearly an hour's drive north of the Whitsundays' hub of Airlie Beach, little Bowen is often overlooked. It is famous for mangoes, something that is made more than obvious by the **Big Mango** along the Bruce Highway, not only officially one of the "Big Things" in Australia, but which also doubles as a visitors center. But you really do not need a map for Bowen. Drive through the town and you will be surprised when told you just passed through the main street—it's difficult to tell. It's a sleepy little town that does not seem to offer visitors anything, really. At first sight.

When Australian director Baz Luhrmann was scouting out locations for his epic film *Australia*, he discovered and settled on little Bowen, took over the place, turned it into Little Hollywood for a while, and left. The locals didn't seem fussed either way, and today you don't find a single reference to that close brush with fame anywhere. But it does tell you that there is something hidden behind Bowen's outwardly sleepiness that is worth stopping for. And that is the beaches.

There are several main beaches, as well as many small coves and inlets that reward exploration, and each one is prettier than the next. Ranging from a tiny little cove to a long sandy stretch, there really is a beach for everyone, but only a handful of hotels and campgrounds, proving that Bowen is still a hidden little gem.

Head straight for **Flagstaff Hill** to get an overview of the little town and its beaches, and the nearby Poole, Thomas Stone, North, Middle, Gloucester, and Holbourne Islands. Then check out the beaches a little further.

BEACHES

Horseshoe Bay is the most popular beach because of its proximity to hotels, campgrounds, and restaurants. During filming of *Australia*, it was reportedly the backdrop for an endless series of paparazzi stakeouts of Hugh Jackman, who regularly took his children bodysurfing in the gentle waves. Then there is the long and lovely **Queens Beach,** where the rocks and small pools that cradle each end of the five-kilometer stretch offer plenty of diversions in the way of marine life. **Rose Bay** is the perfect tiny bay, flanked by rounded boulders, white sand, and a handful of palm trees. It's simply stunning. Snuggled between Horseshoe Bay and Rose Bay is **Murray Beach,** which is wind-protected, making it perfect for swimming and snorkeling even on windier days. **Gray's Bay** is popular with anglers, as is Horseshoe Bay. If you're staying at Horseshoe Bay Resort and Caravan Park, they provide you with snorkeling equipment for a small fee.

ACCOMMODATIONS

To stay right next to pretty Rose Bay, choose **Rose Bay Resort** (2 Pandanus St., tel. 07/4786-9000, www.rosebayresort.com.au, studio from $150). It's in a cul-de-sac, so there is no traffic, and it's literally a skip to the beach. The resort offers studios, one-bed to two-bed apartments, and a penthouse, which has two bedrooms and two bathrooms. All apartments have balconies looking out toward the sea, kitchen facilities, and tiled floors to keep the heat down.

Horseshoe Bay Resort and Caravan Park (1 Horseshoe Bay Rd., tel. 07/4786-2564, www.horseshoebayresort.com.au, cabins $68-170) offers the cutest brightly colored wooden cabins a brief walk from the beach. Each cabin has two bedrooms, with a queen and a bunk bed, and a lounge that can be converted to sleep two; there is also a small kitchen, air-conditioning, and en suite bathrooms. All linens are provided. The campsites (from $35 per night) all have access to three

"Big Things" of Australia

Wherever you go in Australia, you'll see at least one "Big Thing." They're gigantic sculptures of common everyday objects, designed to draw your attention and get you to pull off the road and stop for a while. Usually these sculptures are found by the side of main roads, along highways, at entrances to towns, or outside museums or other attractions that might just make for an interesting break during a road trip. Some are dating back to the 1960s, when kitsch was all the rage, while others are more recent additions; most are advertising some sort of product, animal, or merchandise the place is famous for.

And once you've happened upon one, usually quite by chance, it can turn into a bit of an obsession, and people tend to start "collecting" Big Things. There are maps (car rental companies such as East Coast Car rentals issue maps listing sites), lists, and picture websites of all the Big Things.

Connoisseurs are at loggerheads as to what a truly authentic Big Thing is, tending toward the earlier 1960s and 1970s icons, and deeming the more modern ones lesser additions. According to one count, there are around 150 Big Things dotted all across Australia, with the most famous being the Big Banana at Coffs Harbour. Connoisseur or dilettante, when you are driving through Australia, where the roads can be days long at a time, it is great to have a little target every now and then along the way: a destination, a photo op, another Big Thing for your collection.

You'll have the chance to spot a few on your way around Sydney and Queensland, and maybe you'll accumulate a photo series to impress friends with, something that differs ever so slightly from your average beach and kangaroo picture.

Here are some of the ones you might come across on your trip:

- **Big Banana** (Coffs Harbour, NSW)
- **Big Wine Bottle** (Pokolbin, Hunter Valley, NSW)
- **Big Merino Sheep** (Goulburn, on the way to Canberra, NSW)
- **Big Barrel** (Bundaberg, QLD)
- **Big Rum Bottle** (Bundaberg, QLD)
- **Big Bulls** (Rockhampton, QLD)
- **Big Mango** (Bowen, QLD)
- **Big Brolga** (bird; Townsville, QLD)
- **Big Cassowary** (Mission Beach, QLD)
- **Big Golden Gumboot** (Tully, QLD)
- **Big Marlin** (Cairns, QLD)
- **Big Captain Cook** (Cairns, QLD)
- **Big Barramundi** (Daintree Village, QLD)

amenity buildings, laundry, camp kitchen, and fridges.

Just up the road from the colorful beach huts, **Coral Cove Apartments** (2B Horseshoe Bay Rd., tel. 07/4791-2000, www.coralcoveapartments.com.au, from $690 for three nights) offers more modern amenities, including a good restaurant, The Cove Restaurant, within its premises. On a headland jutting out over Gray's and Queens Bays, the one-, two-, and three-bedroom apartments and penthouses are very spacious, with large living areas, kitchens, amazing views, and access to a large pool, making them perfect for families and maybe a longer stay. Please note that generally a three-night minimum stay applies, but at times special offers waive this requirement. Please check the website.

FOOD

At **360 On Flagstaff** (1 Margaret Reynolds Dr., tel. 07/4786-6684, Tues.-Fri. 9:30am-2:30pm, weekends 8:30am-2:30pm, some evenings open for dinner, depending on demand, mains $18), the food is café food, easy comfort food such as burgers, sandwiches, salads, and other snacks. What draws people here is the stunning setting with, as the name suggests, 360-degree views of the surrounding coast.

Food Freak (1 Starboard Dr., tel. 07/4786-5133, Wed.-Fri. 10:30am-2:30pm and 6pm-8:30pm, Sat. 10:30am-2:30pm, Sun. 9:30am-2:30pm, mains $18), at the Yacht Club, is a bistro-style café offering simple, fresh, and seasonal fare, such as open sandwiches and steak.

GETTING THERE AND AROUND

Proserpine (Whitsunday Coast) Airport (PPP, Lascelles Ave., Proserpine, tel. 07/4945-0200, http://proserpineairport.com) is some 80 kilometers south of Bowen. Qantas, Virgin Australia, and Jetstar fly to Proserpine. **Bowen Travel** (tel. 07/4786-1661, www.bowentravel.com.au) organizes door-to-door transfers for the one-hour journey according to flight arrivals.

Queensland's **Tilt Train** (tel. 07/3235-2222, www.queenslandrail.com.au) offers a rail option for getting to and from Bowen. From the stop there are courtesy taxis taking passengers to the taxi office on Williams Street in the center of town. The trip from Brisbane takes around 16 hours, with one-way tickets from $179.40.

The northbound **Greyhound** coach (tel. 1300/473-946, www.greyhound.com.au) has up to five daily services between Brisbane and Bowen; the journey takes around 19 hours, costing from $233 one way.

Drivers should leave the Bruce Highway at Bowen; you'll see the Big Mango at **Bowen Visitor Information Centre** (Bruce Hwy., tel. 07/4786-4222, weekdays 8:30am-5pm, Sat.-Sun. 10:30am-5pm), and the turnoff is just after that.

Bowen Transit (tel. 07/4786-4414) offers buses to Horseshoe Bay and Rose Bay (route 3) and Queens Beach (route 1); one-way tickets start at $2.60, though the schedule is sporadic at best.

Townsville

Like most places along the Queensland coast, Townsville was first visited by Europeans when the intrepid Captain Cook traveled up the coast, reached the area in 1770, and named Cleveland Bay, on whose coast Townsville was eventually built. This was a busy stretch of coastline, and a number of maritime explorers stopped off at Cleveland Bay, such as Admiral Phillip Parker King in 1819 and Captain John Wickham in 1839. These explorers weren't too interested in settling the area, but in 1861 businessman Robert Towns asked his employee, John Melton Black, to select a suitable site for a port on the northern Queensland coast, where Towns had considerable holdings and was eager to create a port that would serve not only his interests, but the whole region.

Little did Towns realize that the site chosen by Black on Cleveland Bay would, over the next century, serve the soon-to-be mining interests of the regional gold-mining towns of Charters Towers, Mary Kathleen, and Mount Isa, as well as the agricultural proceeds across the region. Townsville was initially known as Castletown, but it was officially declared a port and renamed after its founder, Towns, in 1865. As chance would have it, no sooner had the port been established than gold was discovered at nearby Ravenswood, and the area around the port boomed with the discovery of gold, the growing of sugar, the establishment

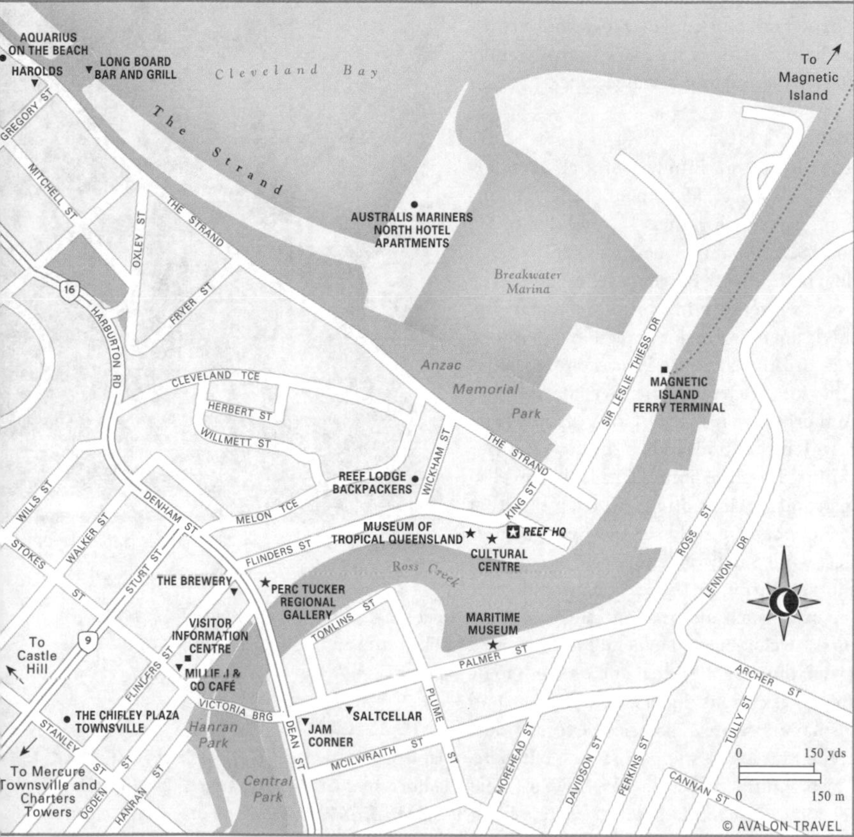

of meat works, and the growth of pastoral industries in the hinterland. A railway from the port moved out into the hinterland, reaching Charters Towers in 1882, then Ravenswood in 1884. Townsville was successfully built on business.

Located some 1,371 kilometers from Brisbane, Townsville today is a city of great charm and style, reflecting its historic riches. It is not overwhelmed by tourism; even the premier attraction for visitors, Reef HQ, is relatively low-key. Acknowledged as the capital of tropical northern Queensland, with a population approaching 200,000 it is the largest city in tropical Australia. That said, there are not so many large cities north of the Tropic of Capricorn—only Cairns on the east coast, and then Darwin in the north and Broome in the west.

SIGHTS

The Strand

The Strand stretches for 2.2 kilometers along the city's coastline, providing a superb beach promenade space between the beach and the city, designed not only to be stunning, but to be enjoyed by visitors and residents of all ages. Features include a tidal pool, park areas complete with picnic and barbecue spots, stinger enclosures on the four beaches, playgrounds, a water play park, exercise equipment (including equipment teaching you how to learn to surf), a fishing platform at the Rock Pool, a basketball half court, and various art installations. This is the place to really enjoy Townsville and its glorious weather.

★ Reef HQ

Reef HQ (2-68 Flinders St., tel. 07/4750-0800, www.reefHQ.com.au, daily 9:30am-5pm, closed Christmas Day, adult $26.50, child $12.80, family $66.50, tickets valid all day) is the Great Barrier Reef on land. The world's largest living coral reef aquarium, this is not only a major attraction for visitors, it is also the National Education Centre facility for the Great Barrier Reef Marine Park Authority, where marine biologists study and research the thousands of living creatures calling this place home. This is the only living coral reef in captivity, which means that visitors can actually see the Great Barrier Reef while safely on land. Even on a dive or snorkel trip out on the reef, you would never see quite such an amazing range of creatures, so close up and in detail, accompanied by vital information that you tend not to be able to ask about underwater. In one small display there are 12 species of coral alone, giving you a mere snippet of what's out there. The bioluminescence display shows off what seem like evil comic-book characters floating around in the dark, fish that live in the dark yet show off features of themselves to those who can see them. Inspiring, and really amazing, this is a must for those who do not like to get wet but still want to see what the Great Barrier Reef is all about and those who, despite already having gotten wet, still cannot get enough information about the wonders of the underwater world.

Daily tours and talks include the "Predator Dive Show" daily at 10:30pm, where you can talk to a diver who is underwater with the sharks; the "Turtle Talk," daily at noon and 3:30pm, where you learn about the plight of the marine turtle; "Shark Feeding" (Tues., Thurs., Sun. at 2:30pm); and the "Animal Feeding Tour" (Mon., Wed., Fri. at 2:30pm). The tours and talks are included in the ticket price.

Townsville's main shopping street, Flinders Street

The Cultural Centre

In the same building as Reef HQ, the Aboriginal **Cultural Centre** (2-68 Flinders St., tel. 07/4772-7679, www.cctownsville.com.au, Mon.-Sat. 9am-4:30pm, adult $5, child $2) promotes indigenous culture through art, with a gallery showcasing works in various media, plus there are exhibits of historical artifacts, weapons, and tools. In the visual pods, you can sit and are surrounded by audio and visual images from elders of Aboriginal and Torres Strait peoples telling their stories, and an interesting picture wall shows the many faces that make up the Aboriginal and Torres Strait Islander people.

Museum of Tropical Queensland

Right next door to Reef HQ and the Cultural Centre, the **Museum of Tropical**

Queensland (70-102 Flinders St., tel. 07/4726-0600, daily 9:30am-5pm, adult $15, child $8.80, family $38) is a great museum, a mix of history, nature, geology, Australiana, zoo, botanic garden, and interactive fun. In here there is pretty much everything you need to know about tropical Queensland, from its very beginnings to its recent history, from its unique flora and fauna to the story of the HMS *Pandora*, the ship that was sent after the *Bounty* to capture its mutinous crew. In addition to the many permanent exhibits, there are always temporary exhibitions covering a wide range, far extending the realm of tropical Queensland to military life in Afghanistan and even private collectors' treasures, such as a Dalek from the famous TV series *Doctor Who*.

Castle Hill

Not quite Uluru (Ayers Rock), Castle Hill is still an impressive pink granite monolith towering over the city, rising up to a height of 286 meters. Offering 360-degree views over Townsville, Magnetic Island, other smaller islands, and the floodplains, it is a great place to find your feet, get an idea of where everything is, and, at the same time, maybe get some exercise? You can walk or run up the goat track, or drive up to the top, where you can park and enjoy the setting. There are even pretty restroom amenities, including shower cubicles, provided to refresh you. Do come up once during the day and once at night; the difference is amazing and well worth taking in. There is a marker and an observation bunker built by the Americans during World War II.

Perc Tucker Regional Gallery

Opened in 1981, the **Perc Tucker Regional Gallery** (Denham St., tel. 07/4727-9011, Mon.-Fri. 10am-5pm, Sat.-Sun. 10am-2pm, free) is named after a former mayor of Townsville and is housed in one of the city's lovely heritage buildings in the center of town. Its collection, numbering more than 2,000 works of different genres, is displayed in subsets forming one major exhibition annually. Focusing on works that relate to the geographical location of north Queensland, the works encompass Contemporary Art of Tropical Queensland, Historical Art of Tropical Queensland, Aboriginal or Torres Strait Islander Art, Contemporary Art from Papua New Guinea, Popular Art, and Ephemera.

Maritime Museum of Townsville

As you'd expect, there is quite a bit to learn about the region's maritime history, as it all started with a busy port. The little **Maritime Museum of Townsville** (42 Palmer St., tel. 07/4721-5251, www.townsvillemaritimemuseum.org.au, Mon.-Fri. 10am-3pm, Sat.-Sun. noon-3pm, adult $6, child $3, family $15) has a great collection of memorabilia from the coast's most famous wreck, the SS *Yongala*. There are also plenty of model boats, military models, a shiny brass U.S. Navy diving helmet, other instruments, galleries showcasing photographs and model boats, and even a lighthouse.

Royal Australian Air Force Townsville Museum

The **Royal Australian Air Force Townsville Museum** (Ingham Rd., Garbutt, tel. 07/4752-1712, Tues. and Thurs. 9am-noon, Sun. 10am-4pm, free) has a small collection of models, aircraft, personal belongings, and photographs, all telling the history of the regional RAAF. Next to the still-active RAAF base by Townsville Airport, the museum is staffed by volunteers, all of whom have some personal connection to the place and the history it tells.

Townsville Heritage Centre

Spread across three beautifully restored and furnished heritage buildings, the **Townsville Heritage Centre** (5 Castling St., tel. 07/4771-5873, Wed. 10am-2pm, Sat.-Sun. 1pm-4pm, adult $8, child $2) gives visitors a chance to see what life was like in the days before modern conveniences. A residential house, a worker's cottage, and a farm building allow you to snoop into the earlier settlers' lives, complete with furnishings, utensils, knick-knacks, and books.

The Palmetum Gardens

Townsville's answer to everybody else's botanic gardens is **The Palmetum Gardens** (Nathan St., Annandale, tel. 07/4727-8929, daily sunrise-sunset, free). It is a lovely display of, yes, palm trees, and other plants. In the world, there are some 300 species of palm; in Australia alone, there are 60 species, many of which are represented here. You get fluffy ones, smooth ones, tall ones, short ones, and everything in between. In short, this is an enjoyable celebration of all things palm tree.

Billabong Sanctuary

If you want to get up close and personal with some of the regional wildlife—hug a snake, feed a croc, pat a wombat, and snuggle up to a koala—the **Billabong Sanctuary** (Bruce Hwy., about 20 minutes south of Townsville, tel. 07/4778-8344, www.billabongsanctuary.com.au, daily 9am-4pm, adult $32, child $19, family $85) is the place to do it. Beautiful parkland, wetland, and bush are teeming with the local critters. Regular feeding and display times allow you to do the honors as well, so you will get your money's worth. There are talks, feeding times, and experiences on at least every 30 minutes. The most popular, the koalas and wombats, are on thrice daily, at 10:30am, 11am, and 3pm.

Charters Towers

Charters Towers lies some 135 kilometers (a 90-minute drive) southwest from Townsville along the Flinders Highway (A6). The drive is comfortable and scenic, with plenty of kangaroos and even camels to spot along the way. Just take care in the early morning and later in the day, around dusk, when the wildlife comes out to play and often sits in the middle of the road. There are also road trains (trucks with three trailers that can be some 50 meters long) along this road, and they don't slow down unless they absolutely have to.

Arriving in the little town of Charters Towers is a little like stepping back in time, if it weren't for modern signage. The main road could be in any 19th-century country town, and you wouldn't be surprised at all to see a horse tied up outside the pub. Instead you'll probably find a four-wheel drive, but the sense is definitely there. Charters Towers' modern history began in 1871, when a 12-year-old horse boy named Jupiter Mosman discovered gold at the foothill of Towers Hill. Before you knew it a gold rush started up, and the gold in this region proved to be double the grade of that found in the Victorian goldfields and 75 percent more than the Western Australian goldfields. Between the years 1872 to 1917, 200 metric tons of gold had been mined. By 1890 Charters Towers was Queensland's second largest town, with a population of 30,000, and it was lovingly and unashamedly called "The World." In 1907 the town was proclaimed a city, but the population has dwindled to a meager 8,000 today.

The central precinct of Charters Towers is now classified as a conservation area, with 60 buildings listed on the Australian heritage register. Some of the best-preserved Victorian buildings can be found in this central one-mile square. When you arrive, head for the **Charters Towers Visitor Information Centre** (74 Mosman St., tel. 07/4761-5533, www.charterstowers.qld.gov.au, daily 9am-5pm) and get yourself a heritage walking map and a *Centenary of Federation Heritage Sculpture Trail* map. Both are easy saunters through town, stopping off at the important buildings and the sculptures (sometimes a little odd), all depicting the city's history.

Although mining continues to be an important part of life in Charters Towers, the old-fashioned crushers have long since been silenced, but links to the gold rush days of mining can still be explored by joining the "Ghosts of Gold" heritage trail, also a self-guided tour, which includes a trip to Australia's largest surviving battery relic, the **Venus Gold Battery** (Milchester Rd., tel. 07/4761-5533, tours daily 10am, 11am, noon,

Historic Shipwrecks Along the Coast

Where there's a reef, there's a wreck. Where there's some 300,000 square kilometers of reef, there are plenty of wrecks. Just as beautiful as the Great Barrier Reef is to look at, it is as treacherous to navigate. Many sailors without intimate knowledge of the reef's many secrets have fallen afoul of the coral outcrops. Today, some 30 wreck sites are known and provide some of the best diving spots around the reef.

One of the best-loved shipwrecks is the **SS *Yongala,*** which sank during her 99th voyage, just off Townsville during a cyclone in 1911, taking the lives of all on board, 121 people in all. The *Yongala* was an early-20th-century interstate coastal steamer whose history supplies a snapshot of Edwardian life in Australia. It is now not only a historical site, but also a substantial artificial reef that supports a great diversity of fish life, with 122 recorded fish species in an established community around the wreck. **Yongala Dive** (www.yongaladive.com.au) runs dive trips here from Townsville.

Discovered in November 1977, some 186 years after its loss, the **HMS *Pandora*** was a 24-gun post ship, best known as the ship sent in 1790 to search for the *Bounty* and the mutineers who had taken her. She struck an isolated crop of coral and sank in 1791, within the now-called Pandora Entrance, approximately five kilometers northwest of Moulter Cay. This sand cay is on the outer Great Barrier Reef, approximately 140 kilometers east of Cape York, on the edge of the Coral Sea. Several expeditions have since managed to secure artifacts that can be viewed in the Queensland Museum in Brisbane. (Due to its distance and depth, this is not a wreck covered by local diving companies.)

The ***Lady Bowen,*** originally built in 1864 as an iron twin-engine paddle steamer but converted into a luxury 220-foot (70-meter) four-mast schooner by a Sydney businessman in 1888, struck the Kennedy Shoal off Dunk Island in 1894. She has since taken on a new role once again, as a dive site for advanced divers and a home for giant groupers, lionfish, sea snakes, turtles, sharks, and huge rays.

The **HMSC *Mermaid,*** a 21-meter wooden vessel built in India, was well known in Australian waters in the late 1820s, having circumnavigated the continent on a voyage of exploration under the command of Lieutenant Phillip Parker King, but failed to return from its final voyage when it hit Flora Reef, some 13 kilometers east of the Frankland Islands off Cairns. The site is in shallow water on the southern side of the reef and is dotted with interesting items, such as an anchor chain clump, pulley sheaths, compass components, and barrel rings. (No organized tours run here.)

Dive the Reef (tel. 1800/101-319, U.S. tel. 800/207-2453, www.divethereef.com) offers flexible dive charters—you decide where you want to go, for how long, and whether to do it in luxury or stick to a budget. They are an American online outfit with Australian connections, so arrangements are organized by phone or online.

1pm, 2pm, 3pm, adult $15, child $7.50, family $32). It used to crush ore. Follow the small brown signs with the gold history symbol throughout the town and outside, and you can trace some of the golden history.

You'll see the **Columbia Poppet Head,** a timber structure that used to stand at a mine's entrance, when you are heading into town. The **Historic Ambulance Centre** (157 Gill St., tel. 07/4787-1478, open sporadically, $1) houses a collection of old ambulance vehicles. The tiny **Miner's Cottage** (26 Deane St., tel. 04/1496-7369, $5) is a restored miner's home, giving background on the life and work of miners in the gold rush era. Like most local attractions, this is staffed by volunteers, so check opening times on the day.

For a food break, head to the old **Stock Exchange Building,** where you'll find the **Stock Exchange Café and Restaurant** (76 Mosman St., tel. 07/4787-7954, breakfast and lunch Mon.-Sat.), which sells "the best coffee in the World" and also a good assortment of snacks.

BEACHES

Despite the near perfect beach on Townsville's doorstep, you might want to head north on the Bruce Highway for additional beaches, most of them absolutely deserted and peaceful.

It starts with **Bushland Beach,** around a 25-minute drive north, which is hemmed by mangrove habitat on either end, not only attracting plenty of birds but making it a perfect spot for fishing (bring your own gear). There is even a beach bar serving drinks and snacks, plus a playground.

A little farther up the road lies **Saunders Beach,** with its Wulgurukaba Plant trail, named after the original inhabitants of the region, which teaches you about the local plants and their importance for food and medicine use. After Cyclone Yasi, which destroyed much of the coastal area, the plant trail was replanted to act as a natural buffer zone. There is a car park with some basic amenities where you can stop and stay in your camper van.

Toolakea Beach is not really worth it as it has no camping or any other facilities, and it has an enormous tidal range that makes the water difficult to reach at low tide. **Toomulla Beach** has a campsite for your camper van, with a few facilities next to a small mangrove forest. A tree trail has signs explaining what each tree is and its importance, and there's a boat ramp. The beach itself is more a creek breach than a sandy access to the sea, although it is okay for swimming at high tide.

Balgal Beach, some 50-odd kilometers north of Townsville, stretches itself past a small residential community and has another car park-cum-camper van site with a few amenities and a beach restaurant. Picturesque **Rollingstone Creek,** hemmed by mangroves, is perfect for fishing.

RECREATION

With **Adrenalin Snorkel & Dive** (252 Walker St., tel. 07/4724-0600, www.adrenalindive.com.au), certified divers can go out to the famed SS *Yongala* wreck for the day. Various packages are available; a day trip with two dives for a certified diver and full equipment hire is $285, including morning tea, lunch, and afternoon coffee. Adrenalin Snorkel & Dive also has diving courses.

Want to get up close and personal with a ghost? **Townsville Ghost Tours** (tel. 04/0445-3354, www.townsvilleghosttours.com.au, 2.5-hour tours adult $69, child $49) takes you to some of the city's most eerie and haunted sites in a ghostly bus (no spoilers given). You can even sign up for an overnight stay in a haunted house ($250 pp).

Jupiters Casino (Sir Leslie Thiess Dr., tel. 07/4722-2333, www.jupiterstownsville.com.au, over 18 years only) has more than 320 gaming machines and over 20 tables, so if you fancy a night out trying your luck at gambling, then this is the place to head to.

Red Baron Sea Planes (Breakwater Marina, Mariners Dr., Townsville, tel. 04/1289-6770, www.redbaronseaplanes.com.au, flights from $365 for two people) features an aircraft, a historical Grunman Sea-Cat, that is itself a genuine movie star, having starred in movies such as *The Phantom,* and human stars such as Billy Zane and Catherine Zeta Jones have flown in it. It's the only two-passenger, open cockpit biplane on floats in the world, and it's a great way to explore the region or Magnetic Island.

This being cattle country, why not spend a day as a cowboy or cowgirl? **Woodstock Trail Rides** (Jones Rd., Woodstock, tel. 07/4778-8888, www.woodstocktrailrides.com.au, half/full-day trail rides $80/150, cattle musters $150) gives you the chance to do just that on a working ranch. You can muster cattle on horseback through the Australian bush and then have a go at whip cracking, sheep shearing, drafting cattle, and maybe branding calves (seasonal). The ranch lies some 40 kilometers inland, west of Townsville.

If you'd like to **fish** at the Rock Pool on The Strand or at Bushland Beach, there are plenty of tackle shops in town: **Tackle World** (Shop 8, Domain Central, Duckworth St., tel. 07/4725-1266) is one of the largest.

ACCOMMODATIONS

If you are looking for location, you don't get any better than ★ **Australis Mariners North Hotel Apartments** (7 Mariners Dr., tel. 07/4722-0777, www.australiashotels.com.au, from $200). On a tiny peninsula jutting into the sea between the marina and The Strand's beach, this apartment building has views that are simply stunning, and is within minutes of the city center, the museums, and the Magnetic Island ferries. The two- and three-bedroom apartments are all privately owned, and are all individually furnished and outfitted, but are huge and offer everything a home would. Considering the price for a night, the space and location are incredible.

Mercure Townsville (166 Woolcock St., tel. 07/4725-2222, www.Mercure.com/Townsville, from $129) has a quiet garden and lake setting that feels a million miles from the bustling town center, yet is mere minutes from all the amenities and within easy access from the airport. Set in the residential area of The Lakes, the resort is a family-friendly yet corporate hotel that offers large comfortable rooms, a pool, and gardens filled with birds that flock to the lakes. The award-winning cosmopolitan **Celsius** restaurant and bar makes this a destination on its own.

The Chifley Plaza Townsville (409 Flinders St., tel. 07/4772-1888, www.theplazahotel.com.au, from $108, not including breakfast) is conveniently located just off Flinders Street, literally seconds from the shops, bars, restaurants, and art galleries, and within walking distance to The Strand and Magnetic Island ferries. The rooms are compact but with everything you need, including TV, Wi-Fi, coffee- and tea-making facilities, and a fridge. There is cooked and buffet breakfast in the mornings and a restaurant on the ground floor for dinner.

Townsville doesn't have many high-rises, and one that stands out is **Aquarius on the Beach** (75 The Strand, tel. 07/4772-4255, www.aquariusonthebeach.com.au, from $99). Right on the beach, the building might be a bit of an eyesore, but you can't beat the views the rooms have because of it. Trendy and modern, the hotel has that resort feeling, being a hop and skip from the beach, with beachside restaurants and a pool that also overlooks the beach, and with all that, it's affordable.

Reef Lodge Backpackers (4-6 Wickham St., tel. 07/4721-1112, www.reeflodge.com.au, dorm beds from $22) is a cool, funky, and very relaxed backpackers' lodge right in the center of town. Large kitchen, book exchange, huge DVD library, game room, barbecue, laundry facilities, Internet, and tour bookings—it's all there.

FOOD

Townsville has several "food streets," each with its own character.

Palmer Street on the city's south bank has a range of international food options and award-winning restaurants, such as excellent **Jam Corner** (1 Palmer St., tel. 07/4721-4900, www.jamcorner.com.au, Sun.-Mon. 7am-3pm, Tues.-Sat. 7am-10pm, mains $35), which specializes in locally sourced modern Australian cuisine, and **Saltcellar** (13 Palmer St., tel. 07/4724-5866, www.saltrestaurants.com.au, Tues. 6pm-10pm, Wed.-Fri. noon-3pm and 6pm-10pm, Sat. 6pm-midnight, mains $35), which also offers modern Australian cuisine, but with a hint of Italy.

Gregory Street near The Strand has a village flair with individual boutiques and international restaurant cafés that offer a destination in themselves. Try **Gyo Japanese Tapas** (48 Gregory St., tel. 07/4771-5155, www.gyojapaneserestaurant.com.au, Tues.-Sun. 11:30am-2:30pm and 5:30pm-9:30pm, 8 pieces of sushi $28) or **Long Board Bar and Grill** (80 Gregory St., tel. 07/4724-1234, www.longboardbarandgrill.com, daily 11:30am-10pm, burgers $18).

The Strand itself is right on the beach and offers people a choice of relaxed bistro places, ice cream parlors, and snack bars. Try **Harolds Seafood** (The Strand, corner of Gregory St., tel. 07/4724-1322, www.haroldseafood.com.au, daily 7am-9pm, mains $18) for fresh reef seafood and legendary fish and chips.

Flinders Street East is right in the center of the city and offers a wide variety of places to sit, eat, and drink. **The Brewery** (252 Flinders St., tel. 07/4724-2999, www.townsvillebrewery.com.au, daily 9am-late, mains

$25) consists of a pub and several restaurants within the old post office building. For decent coffee and midday snacks, try **Millie J & Co Café** (Flinders Square, just by the footbridge, tel. 07/4724-4028, weekdays 6am-4pm, weekends 7am-2pm, sandwiches $12).

INFORMATION AND SERVICES

Townsville Visitor Information Centre (Flinders Square, tel. 1800/801-902, Mon.-Fri. 8:30am-5pm, Sat.-Sun. 9am-1pm) has information on the attractions and sights within Townsville, the region, and Magnetic Island and can book tours right there. The **post office** (Office Plaza, Sturt St., tel. 13/13-18, Mon.-Fri. 8:30am-5:30pm) offers money transfers and currency exchange on top of postal services. There are several banks along Flinders Street, all with ATMs.

Internet on Flinders (324 Flinders St., ground floor, Holiday Inn Hotel, tel. 07/4721-5444, www.Internetonflinders.com.au) offers Internet access, scanner, laptop access, and Skype facilities from $2 an hour.

The Townsville Hospital (100 Angus Smith Dr., Douglas, tel. 07/4433-1111) has an emergency unit and is open 24 hours; the hospital also has a pharmacy on-site.

GETTING THERE

Townsville Airport (TSV, corner Halifax Ave. and Stinson Ave., Garbutt, tel. 07/4727-3211), just five kilometers west of the city center, is easily reached from many major airports around Australia, such as Sydney (2.5 hours), with Virgin Australia, Qantas, and Jetstar all offering regular services. Connections from the airport to the hotels or the ferry to the islands can be arranged prior to booking (**Con-x-ion,** tel. 1300/266-946, www.con-x-ion.com, transfer direct to accommodation roughly $20, online pre-booking required). Routes 205 and 215 on the local **Sunbus** (tel. 07/4771-9800, www.sunbus.com.au, fares within the city starting at one-way $1.80) can also take you into the city center. All major car rental companies are represented at the arrivals terminal, as are taxis (**Townsville Taxis,** tel. 13/10-08). If you are driving, the airport is just off Bundock Street, which, with Warburton Street, Saunders Street, and Woolcock Street, forms a loop around Castle Hill in the center of the city and takes you to most of the accommodations with 15 minutes' drive.

The **Sunlander** and **Tilt Train** (tel. 07/3235-2222, www.queenslandrail.com.au) operate 2-3 times per week from Brisbane, taking around 18 hours from Brisbane (one-way tickets from $189). The **Townsville railway station** (4-8 Charters Towers Rd.) is just at the start of Flinders Street, which leads into the city center, a mere 10 minutes' walk away.

By bus, the **Greyhound** route (tel. 1300/473-946, www.greyhound.com.au) stretches along the Bruce Highway all along the coast, with a stop in Townsville.

Townsville lies on the Bruce Highway stretching along the Queensland coast. If you are driving up from the south, it's 275 kilometers from Airlie Beach, taking about 3.5 hours. If you are coming from the north, Townsville is 350 kilometers from Cairns, a four-hour drive.

GETTING AROUND

The local **Sunbus** (tel. 07/4771-9800, www.sunbus.com.au, single-trip fares within the city starting from $1.80) has an extensive route system, and fares are low. In addition to single-trip tickets, there are daily passes (from $3.60) and weekly passes (from $14.40).

Islands off Townsville

★ MAGNETIC ISLAND

It can't have been easy for Captain Cook, traveling up along the coast of a brand-new continent, having to name everything in sight. Once you have depleted the names of king and country, then you have to get a little bit more imaginative. Thus Magnetic Island, named after the fact that the ship's compass went a little wonky when they sailed past. Why exactly it happened, nobody knows, but fact is, there is no more magnetic activity on this island than anywhere else. Still, the name stuck. Or to be precise, this being Australia, it has since been lovingly abbreviated to "Maggie" and is simply called Townsville's Island Playground.

Magnetic Island came into its own when Townsville was founded and provided coral, stone, and timber, which were collected as a source of building materials for the nearby city. Local legend has it that at some stage gold was mined on the island, too. And while in 1875 Magnetic Island was set aside as a quarantine station, it had always been a popular spot with Townsville residents to pop across for a picnic. Robert Hayles, an English migrant, was the first recorded settler of Magnetic Bay and started it off on the road to tourism. He bought four and a half acres in Picnic Bay in 1899, then built a jetty and the island's first resort in the bay, which is still popular for picnics today.

During World War II Townsville became a major base for the military, and its harbor, Cleveland Bay, was an important assembly point for shipping. In 1943, a signal station and coastal battery were completed on Magnetic Island for defense of the harbor, and two 3,000,000-candle-power searchlights, capable of spotting aircraft at 30,000 feet, were placed in Horseshoe Bay and Florence Bay; the Forts Walk, which takes in some of the old fortifications, now is a popular track with panoramic views and opportunity for koala spotting.

More recently the island has gained some notoriety as Julian Assange's childhood home. It's also a thriving artists' community and the place where you can roam free in trendy little Mini Moke vehicles, akin to beach buggies,

getting around Magnetic Island in a tropical beach buggy

Magnetic Island

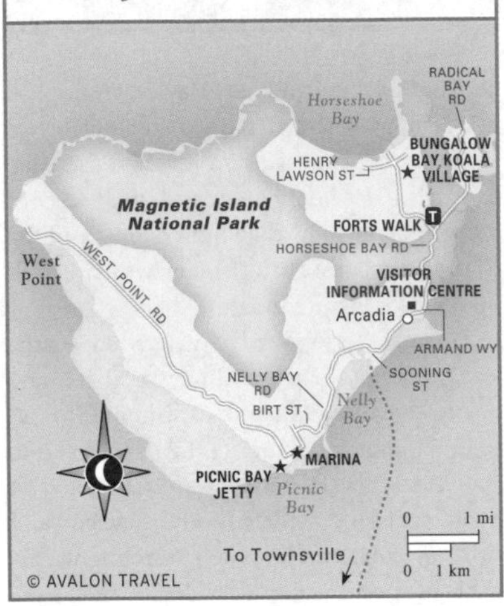

lending the place its rightful laid-back beach lifestyle.

Beaches

There are 23 beaches and 22 bays officially named on Magnetic Island, so there is one at every turn. The most popular are Nelly Bay, Horseshoe Bay, Picnic Bay, and Radical Bay.

Nelly Bay is where the ferries arrive and where the main "village" is located. A handful of shops, restaurants, and accommodations are all there, with the beach offering a great locale for windsurfing, catamaran sailing, and snorkeling on the fringing reef, mostly available through the resort. The crescent-shaped, golden-sand beach of **Horseshoe Bay** is easily the best of the island's accessible beaches, and its largest bay: Not only is it stunning, but there is a patrolled swimming area, seasonal stinger enclosure, water-sports equipment for hire, a row of cafés, and a good pub. Everything you need for a day out on the beach, really.

Alma Bay is a little bay with a perfect beach bounded by Magnetic Island's famous boulders and is a perfect little setup for families, with a playground by the beach. There is water sports equipment available to rent. Next door is **Geoffrey Bay,** offering great views across to Townsville. It has a large stretch of fringing reef, making it perfect for snorkeling and for reef walks at low tide. The *Moltke* wreck lies just off the old barge ramp and makes for a good dive spot. At dusk the wallabies descend on the northern end of Geoffrey Bay, **Bremner Point,** making for great photo opportunities.

Florence Bay is studded with scenic boulders and is a popular anchorage point for day-trippers, whereas **Picnic Bay,** where it all started, has the historic jetty, which is a good vantage point for a spot of fishing. There are plenty of beach hotels where you can grab some lunch.

Arthur Bay is said to be one of the best snorkeling spots on the island, as it is undeveloped and has a good freestanding coral reef, whereas **Radical Bay** is great for swimming and simply relaxing on the beach. It once housed a resort, and a replacement is in the pipeline. From there you can walk across the headland to Horseshoe Bay, taking a detour down to the unofficial nudist beach of **Balding Bay.**

Bungalow Bay Koala Village

The two-hour tours and shows at **Bungalow Bay Koala Village** (40 Horseshoe Bay Rd., tel. 07/4778-5577, www.bungalowbay.com.au, tours daily at 10am, noon, and 2:30pm, adult $21, child $12, family $62) allow you to hold a koala, crocodile, snakes, and lizards. Learn about the natural environment, culture, and history of Magnetic Island. This is the sister sanctuary of Billabong Sanctuary outside Townsville, and they work hand in hand protecting the local animals and making sure those in captivity are looked after in the best way to delight visitors and make the animals happy.

Recreation

Walking is the best way to see the island, and there are several walks for all fitness and enthusiasm levels. The most recommended is the **Forts Walk,** which is a scenic four-kilometer,

1.5-hour round-trip starting from the Radical Bay turnoff that goes past the searchlights and batteries. It's a moderate trail, though at times steep. **Hawkins Point Track,** from Picnic Bay, is a short and easy 1.2-kilometer round-trip, with spectacular views across Rocky Bay over the island toward Townsville.

The **Picnic Bay to West Point** bush track is an easy, but longer 16-kilometer walk, approximately five hours in total, that takes you across the bays on the western side of the island, which has noticeably different flora and fauna from the rest of the island. See tidal wetland, mangroves, paperbark swamps, and savanna grassland.

Self-guided **snorkeling trails** are available in Nelly Bay and Geoffrey Bay. You can pick up laminated swim cards from numerous outlets on the island (Magnetic Island Post Office, Nelly Bay; Arcadia Newsagency; Koala Village at Bungalow Bay, Horseshoe Bay; Foodworks, Horseshoe Bay; and others). These cards offer you guidance as to where to snorkel and what to see and help with identification of marine life. For a $5 donation, you are asked to enjoy the cards and then pop them back into provided boxes at the beaches, for others to reuse them. **Pleasure Divers** (10 Marine Parade, Arcadia, tel. 07/4778-5788) rents out snorkeling gear (from $7 per set for 4 hours, $12 for a full day).

Fish'n N Fuel'n (36 Mandalay Ave., Nelly Bay, tel. 07/4778-5126, open daily) rents and sells fishing rods and other fishing gear, crab pots, lures, and all sorts of things you will need for a day's fishing. Please note that fishing is not allowed in Geoffrey, Alma, Florence, Gowrie, Radical, and Balding Bays, as these are Marina National Park green zones.

Pleasure Divers (10 Marine Parade, Arcadia, tel. 07/4778-5788, www.pleasuredivers.com.au) offers introductory dives, courses, and packages for certified divers with outer reef and SS *Yongala* wreck dive tours available. Dives start from $50 for certified divers, with equipment hire extra.

Jet Ski Hire Magnetic Island (Boat Ramp, Horseshoe Bay, tel. 07/4758-1100, www.jetskihiremi.com.au, from $95 for 30 minutes) rents Jet Skis that seat one, two, or three people and explore the bays of the island from the water. No license is required.

At **Magnetic Island Sea Kayaks** (tel. 07/4778-5424, www.seakayak.com.au) you can either hire a kayak for the day ($75) or go on a 4.5-hour tour around the island with a guide (from $85 pp, but options are available, from double kayaks, accompanying children, etc.). No experience is necessary as full instruction is provided.

The tall ship ***Providence*** (Peppers Blue on Blue Marina, Nelly Bay, tel. 07/4778-5580, http://providencesailing.com.au, from $65), a 62-foot gaff-rigged schooner, brings romance to sailing with lunch sails, afternoon trips, stops for snorkeling, and even a sunset cruise with a glass of champagne.

With **Horseshoe Bay Ranch** (38 Gifford St., Horseshoe Bay, tel. 07/4778-5109, www.horseshoebayranch.com.au, 2 hour tours at 9am and 3pm daily, $100 per rider), you can go horse riding along the beach and into the sea, an ideal way to enjoy the island. You start off in the bush, crossing creeks and heading toward Horseshoe Bay, where you then have the option to strip to your swimsuit and take the horse off the beach into the sea.

Magnetic Island Country Club (Hurst St., Picnic Bay, tel. 07/4778-5188, www.magneticislandgolf.com.au, daily from 8am, greens fees 9 holes $25, 18 holes $35) is not necessarily a championship course, without sand bunkers to contend with, but instead strategically placed patches of longer grass protect some greens. It is a pretty 18-hole course where social playing is key.

Shopping

Shop at the Horseshoe Bay Sunday markets on the beach, every last Sunday of the month 9am-2pm, or the weekly markets in Arcadia, every Friday 6pm-9pm and Saturday morning 8am-11am. There you can pick up everything from art to jewelry, clothing, and knick-knacks, from fresh produce to cooked food.

Accommodations

Peppers Blue on Blue (123 Sooning St., Nelly Bay, tel. 07/4758-2400, www.peppers.com/blue-on-blue, from $140, two-bed apartments from $250), Magnetic Island's fanciest resort (relatively speaking, considering the island's bohemian relaxed approach to life), has accommodations ranging from hotel rooms and studio apartments to contemporary two- and three-bedroom apartments, some with private plunge pools. Decorated in light hues, cool light wood, and turquoise, the furniture is modern and comfortable, and the setting of this two-story block along Nelly Bay makes the most of the great views.

Why rent a beach shack or apartment, if you can rent the stunning **Lotus House** (20-1 Pacific Dr., Horseshoe Bay, tel. 07/4778-5955, www.lotusonmagnetic.com, from $5,600 per week) instead? This three-bedroom house sleeping six is arguably one of the entire island's nicest properties, with its pool, pond, manicured lawns, and tropical interior, which has high ceilings, wooden floors and rafters, gigantic couches, a perfect outdoor deck, and space to spare.

Hotel Arcadia (7 Marine Parade, Arcadia Bay, tel. 07/4778-5177, www.hotelarcadia.com.au, from $99) is basic but fun. Rooms inside the pub are comfortable and clean, but the draw, for those who don't necessarily want peace and quiet, is that there is always something on downstairs: cane toad racing on Wednesday, bingo on Friday, live music on the weekends. Add swimming pools, market stalls, and a pizzeria, and fun is pretty much guaranteed, even if sleep is not.

Beautiful two- and three-bedroom apartments steps away from the beach are available at **Maggies Beachfront Apartments** (Horseshoe Bay seafront, tel. 07/4778-5955, www.bestofmagnetic.com, from $260). They have a modern design, open-plan styling, large private wooden decks, and balconies. Amenities include a pool, Jacuzzi, and secure parking.

★ **Bungalow Bay Koala Village YHA** (40 Horseshoe Bay Rd., tel. 07/4778-5577, www.bungalowbay.com.au, camping from $12, dorm beds from $28, en suite double huts from $90) is a magical and very budget-friendly place offering basic campsites, dorms, and separate huts that range from basic to en suite double rooms. It's all set among lush forest, a five-minute walk to the beach, with a small restaurant and bar on-site and plenty of animals to go around, wild and behind fences.

Food

The **Champagne Bush Tucker Breakfast** at **Bungalow Bay Koala Village** (Horseshoe Bay Rd., tel. 07/4778-5577, www.bungalowbay.com.au, breakfast every Wed., Fri., Sat. 8:30am-10am, adult $28, child $15, family $80) features Outback dusted lamb, lemon myrtle reef fish, and other cooked-to-order favorites, such as pancakes, bacon, and eggs, along with fresh local honey. While you are eating, you get the chance to make friends with the koalas, crocodiles, lizards, snakes, and Shadow, the black red-tailed cockatoo. (A photo with a koala is an extra $15.)

Stage Door Theatre Restaurant (5 Hayles Ave., Arcadia, tel. 07/4778-5448, www.stagedoortheatre.com.au, $84 pp, 6:45pm-10:15pm) offers dinner with something a little different. Every Friday and Saturday night (check website for seasonal changes), entertainers Bernadette Smith and Phill Stephens regale the diners with their ever-popular comedy cabaret dinner shows. The three-course dinner is not necessarily the reason to come, but the evening as a whole is good fun.

On the beach esplanade, **Sandi's** (7 Pacific Dr., Horseshoe Bay, tel. 07/4758-1673, breakfast, lunch, and dinner daily) is a favorite place for lunch and dinner. Lunchtime offers include $20 for a main course and beer or wine, choosing from steak, burgers, schnitzel, fish, pasta, or pizza. Dinner offers the best of surf and turf (mains $28). This is relaxed alfresco eating.

★ **Nourish** (6 Pacific Dr., Horseshoe Bay, tel. 07/4758-1885, breakfast, lunch, and dinner daily, sandwiches around $13.50) is the healthy option on the beach, where you can get fresh juices, smoothies, salads, and sandwiches, but also rather sinful cakes and big, cooked breakfasts.

Barefoot (5 Pacific Dr., Horseshoe Bay, tel. 07/4758-1170, Mon. and Thurs.-Sat. 11:30am-3pm and 5:30pm-9pm, Sun. 9am-4pm and 5:30pm-9pm, mains $30), next door to Nourish, is a unique blend of good food and art, with Australian artists exhibiting their work in this modern-setting restaurant/bar famous for its steaks.

If you'd rather drink than eat, head straight to **Marlin Bar Tavern** (3 Pacific Dr., Horseshoe Bay, tel. 07/4758-1588, daily 11am-10pm, mains $20), a large pub that offers a nice cold beer and other select beverages, but also decent pub food, usually in the shape of a rather well-proportioned steak.

Picnic Bay Hotel (Esplanade, Picnic Bay, tel. 07/4778-5166, daily 9:30am-midnight, mains $18) is another large pub with a sports bar, where you can either watch sports channels or have a go on the pokies (poker machines). The food is bar snacks and items brought over from the restaurant adjoining the pub, R&R.

Next to Picnic Bay Hotel, **R&R** (Esplanade, Picnic Bay, tel. 07/4778-5166, daily 9:30am-9pm, lunch $20, dinner mains $28) serves homemade muffins and good coffee, plus a nice selection of eats for lunch, before turning itself into a relaxed fine-dining restaurant at night.

Information and Services

Magnetic Island has a **post office** (98 Sooning St., Nelly Bay, Mon.-Fri. 9am-5pm, Sat. 9am-11am) and a **pharmacy** (Sooning St., Nelly Bay, tel. 07/4778-5375, Mon.-Fri. 9am-5:30pm, Sat. 9am-1pm). **ATMs** can be found at the Queensland Country Credit Union, Nelly Bay; Picnic Bay Hotel, Picnic Bay; Horseshoe Bay Store, Horseshoe Bay; and Foodworks, Nelly Bay.

In an emergency, contact **Rescue Services** (tel. 07/4778-5270), **Magnetic Island Health Service** (tel. 07/4778-5107), or the **Poison Information Center** (tel. 13/11-26, daily 24 hours).

Getting There and Around

To get to Magnetic Island from Townsville, hop on the **SeaLink ferry** (tel. 07/4726-0800, www.sealinkqld.com.au/magnetic_island.php). It runs from 5:30am (Sun. 6:30am) to 10:30pm every day, at least once every hour (adult round-trip $32, child $16, family $74). There is also a car ferry (**FantaSea,** Ross St., tel. 07/4772-5422, www.magnetic-island.com.au/car-ferry.htm, Mon.-Fri. 5:20am-6:05pm, Sat.-Sun. 7:10am-6:05pm) that runs roughly every two hours and costs $178 for the round-trip with your car.

Once there you can either rent a car (**Magnetic Island Car Hire,** tel. 07/4778-5955, www.bestofmagnetic.com, from $49 per day) or hire a Mini Moke (**MI Wheels,** tel. 07/4758-1111, from $65 per day, all manual transmission). Those little cars are more akin to a beach buggy, seating four people, and are more fun than a serious car.

The four main settlements are around Picnic Bay, Nelly Bay, Arcadia, and Horseshoe Bay, which are linked by a regular bus service, **Sunbus** route 250 (tel. 07/4778-5130, www.sunbus.com.au). It also stops at the Bungalow Bay Koala Village. The buses run around every 30 to 40 minutes, and a day ticket for unlimited use costs $7.

Magnetic Island is ideal for cycling. Most places to stay rent bikes for around $15 a day. **Magnetic Island Bike Hire** (tel. 04/2524-4193, www.islandbike.com.au) charges the same, with free delivery.

For a cab, call **Magnetic Island Taxi** (tel. 13/10-08).

ORPHEUS ISLAND

Orpheus Island lies 80 kilometers northwest of Townsville, next to **Palm Island** and **Fantome Island,** both of which are rich in history, although a somewhat disturbing history. Palm Island was described as an "open-air jail" for Aboriginal Australians during much of the 20th century, while Fantome

Island was a leper colony for Aboriginal people from 1939 until 1973. Kept secret by the state government, the colony was Queensland's solution to stopping the disease by taking indigenous Australians from their families, confining them to this lonely outpost, and slowly eradicating the disease. When the colony was closed, it was purged by fire and is now the eerie site of more than 200 graves. You can take part in day trips to Fantome Island from Orpheus Island and be shown around by a local guide who lost family on the island, making the visit even more poignant.

On a much lighter note, Orpheus is a gorgeous island, brimming with lush vegetation set in the pristine and crystal-clear waters, edged by picture-perfect beaches. The resort's buildings are nearly completely hidden from sight.

But while utterly luxurious, Orpheus is a working island quite a distance away from the mainland, with food delivered to the island once a week by barge. It is famous for putting its guests to work, helping with the fishing and harvesting the little veggie patch so the chefs can prepare some magic. Once dinner is sorted, activities include a **water sports and dive center,** a forest full of **hiking and biking trails,** and daily **fishing** trips, as well as **snorkeling** and **nature walks** around the accessible areas of the island. A protected giant clam farm is located at the other end of the beach, where daily walks are taken with the head chef to collect oysters and smaller clams, plus anything else he and the guests can find, to cook up for that night's gourmet dinner.

Orpheus Island is a unique mix of relaxation, luxury, and getting close to nature, and has attracted many a celebrity.

Accommodations and Food

Nestled in the sheltered Hazard Bay on the western side of the island, the lodge of **Orpheus Island Resort** (tel. 07/4777-7174, www.orpheus.com.au) is laid along a ribbon of pristine beach and features, apart from the accommodations, a main pavilion bar and alfresco-style dining area, a restaurant, a reading room, an infinity pool, and a sustainable veggie patch among the gardens. The resort accommodates just 34 guests in 17 rooms and suites in three arrangement types: room, villa, or suite, with eco-tents in the planning to be available soon for a night out under the stars. It is nearly impossible to spot the resort from the water, or indeed the helicopter, as the buildings are snuggled into the trees.

Inside, understated elegance is the main theme, with clear-cut lines and subdued but light hues of white and gray. All rooms are spacious and bathrooms very generous. The outdoor decking sublimely made of dark wood holds sun loungers facing the stunning view onto the ocean. The villas come complete with living room, kitchenette, bedroom, and large bathroom. Rooms and suites range from $1,400 for a room to $2,800 for a villa per night for two, with the villa sleeping up to four. Specials are regularly on offer, such as five nights for the price of four. Cost includes use of all water sports equipment, excluding diving ($250 for a reef dive); all meals and house beverages; and day trips, such as the one to Fantome Island.

There is a signature dining villa for special events and occasions, such as the Monday night deluxe barbecue and "Dining with the Tides," a private dinner in a romantic setting at the end of a fire-lit pier.

Getting There

Qantas flies to Townsville and to Cairns from most Australian capital cities from $120. Transport to Orpheus Island is arranged by the resort; this may be helicopter, seaplane, or boat. A private 25-minute helicopter transfer from Townsville costs around $572 per adult and $291 for children under 11 years old; from Cairns, the one-hour trip costs $550 per adult and $275 per child.

HICHINBROOK ISLAND

The largest island national park in Australia, Hichinbrook Island is basically two large islands joined by a long sand isthmus, which has developed so there is a narrow sandy beach facing south, then a few substantial dunes and a vast, impenetrable mangrove swamp cut by sinuous channels. At 52 kilometers long and 10 kilometers wide, it covers an area of 37,379 hectares, making it the largest island on the Great Barrier Reef.

Hinchinbrook is a magnet for walkers, with its 32-kilometer-long Thorsborne Track challenging hikers from all over the world. But even if you are not a dedicated hiker (or at least not quite dedicated enough to commit yourself for five days), Hinchinbrook is also for people who enjoy the quietness of virgin rainforest and pristine beaches, all 11 of them. The channel between the island and the mainland is a flooded river valley and is notable for its extensive areas of mangroves, and Hinchinbrook rises spectacularly like a floating mountain range just offshore from the industrial town of **Lucinda.** While Lucinda itself is not really worth stopping at, it enjoys the accolade of having the world's longest pier, stretching a massive 5.76 kilometers into the sea, and it is the place from where to reach Hinchinbrook the easiest.

Recreation

The **Thorsborne Track** generally takes around four to five days to complete. Hikers must carry all their supplies, as there are no facilities on the island. The trail will allow you to experience cloud-cloaked mountains, jungle-like rainforest, melaleuca swamps, and unspoiled white beaches, and there's myriad wildlife, from colorful butterflies and birds to crocodiles, sea turtles, dugongs, dolphins, and armies of small blue soldier crabs that scuttle along the beach. The island is a true wilderness, and the walk only for the experienced walker, as the path is neither graded nor hardened, and can be difficult to traverse in places. Recommendations are to walk in either direction, camp in any of the seven designated sites, and remember to "leave no trace." Only 40 people can walk the trail at any one time, so booking is essential through the **Department of National Parks, Recreation, Sport and Racing** (www.nprsr.qld.gov.au). Planning and following safety guidelines is vital, and the best time to walk is during the cooler months from April to September.

Increasingly, Hinchinbrook is becoming a favorite with kayakers, who either come on their own or as part of tours. It's an easy crossing from the coastal towns of Lucinda and Cardwell, and you can circumnavigate the island, camping along the route and enjoying the manifold marine wildlife as you go. It is not unknown to see dolphins and even the elusive dugongs along the way.

Week-long kayaking trips along Hinchinbrook Island are operated by **World Expeditions** (tel. 1300/720-000, www.worldexpeditions.com), **Southern Sea Ventures** (tel. 02/8901-3287, www.southernseaventures.com), and **Coral Sea Kayaking** (tel. 07/4068-9154, www.coralseakayaking.com). All offer the same trip from $1,970 for seven days, including all food, camping and kayaking equipment, and transport from Mission Beach.

Accommodations

The accommodation option on Hinchinbrook Island is **camping.** But your do have the choice of seven sites, some with facilities such as composting toilets and picnic tables, others without any facilities at all. Sites can be booked through the **Department of National Parks, Recreation, Sport and Racing** (tel. 13/74-68, www.nprsr.qld.gov.au, camping $5.60 pp per night).

Getting There and Around

Lucinda is about 140 kilometers north of Townsville, roughly a two-hour drive, and is the closest mainland connection to Hinchinbrook Island. That said, **Cardwell,** some 60 kilometers farther north from Lucinda, is easier to get to if you are not driving. Virgin Australia, Jetstar, and Qantas fly to Townsville and Cairns from Sydney (from $179). From either Townsville or Cairns you can take the **Tilt Train** (tel. 07/3235-2222, www.queenslandrail.com.au), operating several weekly connections either north- or southbound, taking around three hours from Townsville and four from Cairns, with tickets roughly $49 either way. Cardwell is small enough that the distance from the train to the ferry to Hinchinbrook Island is walkable.

By bus, the **Greyhound** route (tel. 1300/473-946, www.greyhound.com.au) stretches along the Bruce Highway all along the coast, with a stop in Cardwell, roughly two hours from Townsville, three from Cairns.

If you need to transfer between Cardwell and Lucinda, there are buses (**Ingham Travel,** tel. 07/4776-5666, roughly $30 one way), which provide two daily transfers from the train station (Mon.-Fri. 7:15am and 10:50am). Ingham Travel also provides transfers from Townsville to Hinchinbrook Island; the price depends on the number of people, the time of year, and availability, please telephone for information.

You can get to Hinchinbrook Island by ferry from Lucinda with **Hinchinbrook Wilderness Safaris** (Lucinda Boat Ramp, tel. 07/4777-8307, www.hinchinbrookwildernesssafaris.com.au, round-trip $70) for the short trip across the eight-kilometer crossing, or by water taxi from Cardwell with **Hinchinbrook Island Cruises** (Cardwell Visitors Center, 142 Victoria St., tel. 07/4066-8601, www.hinchinbrookislandcruises.com.au); the water taxi fare depends on the number of people and the day of transfer but is roughly $60 one way.

Tully and Mission Beach

This little area along the Queensland coast, pretty much right in the middle between Townsville and Cairns, is often overlooked by visitors as it is not very touristy, very developed, or much written about. But that is exactly its appeal. Tully takes a couple of minutes to walk from one end to the other, and there are no fancy restaurants or resorts, but plenty of laid-back backpackers come and stay, work the fields during the week, and ride the Tully River or chill on the beach during the weekends. And, hey, who wouldn't want to see a gigantic gumboot?

Mission Beach and its outlying Dunk Island have a similar approach to life: relaxed, laid-back, taking it easy. Yes, there are a couple of fancier places to stay and eat, and a handful of little boutiques in which to spend some money, but otherwise it's all about enjoying the beach and the weather and going with the flow. Oh, and driving through the countryside hoping to spot a cassowary, a bird that looks as if it were friends with the dinosaurs. It might not be the easiest place to get to, but when you're there you can't do much but relax.

TULLY

The town of Tully's main claim to fame lies in the dubious honor of being the wettest place in Australia. The **Big Golden Gumboot** (one of Australia's famous "Big Things" dotted around the continent) gives you a clue as to the best attire when visiting this little place at the foot of the Cardwell Range. Living about 1,557 kilometers north of Brisbane, 240 kilometers north of Townsville, and 180 kilometers south of Cairns, the 2,500 people who call Tully home work mostly on the many banana and sugarcane farms dotted throughout the region. The town itself is overshadowed by a huge sugar mill and, of course, the gumboot.

The main drag, **Butler Street,** has a few nice examples of Art Deco buildings, but you will need to look past and above the drab shops to spot them. The main attractions along Butler Street now seem to be a couple of hotels (a.k.a. pubs), and in that respect not much has changed since 1925. The story goes that the first hotel licensed in the brand-new town of Tully was the Mullins Brothers' Hotel, opened in 1925 by Pat and Mick Mullins. Tully was a little rough around the edges, a true frontier town, and on the night the hotel opened, there were some 36 fights ongoing at the same time, as legend has it. Ambulance officers attended to 65 men. A marker on Butler Street commemorates that successful celebration of the opening of the pub, and it went down in history.

Nowadays, most people who visit Tully are either on the way to somewhere and are simply stopping briefly, or are backpackers on a working vacation. But while Tully might not be that exciting, the nearby Tully River offers reportedly the best white-water rafting in all of Australia and, if you believe the hype, even New Zealand. This is not necessarily surprising considering all the rain that is swelling the river.

Sights

Tully Visitor and Heritage Centre (Bruce Hwy., tel. 07/4068-2288, Mon.-Fri. 8:30am-5pm, Sat.-Sun. 9am-3pm) is a small but informative center where you can get directions and ideas on forest walks and activities in the region. Before you set off anywhere, be sure to check for weather warnings, as the rainfall is infamous and can get quickly out of hand, and there are sometimes issues with flash floods.

The **Golden Gumboot** (daily 9am-5pm, free) stands an impressive 7.9 meters tall, a figure that represents the amount of rainfall recorded in Tully in the year 1950. There is a spiral staircase inside the boot, and from the top you get a good view across the town and the sugar mill opposite.

Tully Sugar Mill (tel. 07/4068-2288, tours Mon.-Fri. at 10am, 11am, and 1:30pm, Sat.-Sun. at 11am during crushing season, June-Nov., adult $17, child $11, family $42, no children under 7) gives a good insight into what happens to all the sugarcane grown in the region, transported to the mills on the intricate web of narrow rail tracks that crisscross every road. On the tours (1.5-2 hours) you can experience the intense smell and be impressed by the immense size of the mill and the different machines inside.

Tully Gorge Forest Park (Tully Falls Rd., Koombooloomba, tel. 13/74-68) is the place to go for white-water rafting. The state park encompasses 80,600 hectares of rainforest with some eucalyptus areas. Within the forest, there are a few waterfalls and plenty of creeks, making for a lush setting

Tully Gorge Forest Park

that encourages a mind-boggling diversity of flora and fauna. Take your time looking around, and take a picnic along. There is a great vantage point to watch the rafters hurtling down the river at Cardstone Weir (reportedly the best viewing time is 1pm-1:30pm), and there are more great views to be had from Flip Wilson Lookout, just down a bit from Cardstone Weir.

Accommodations

Tully's Hotel (5 Butler St., tel. 07/4068-1044, www.hoteltully.com.au) is a working hostel, a clean backpackers' place; the staff helps guests find jobs in the nearby fields. Laundry and high-speed Internet are available 24 hours a day. Facilities and amenities are cleaned daily. Sheets, cutlery, and towels are provided on check-in. All rooms are air-conditioned. A bed in a four-person dorm is $100 per week without bathroom en suite, $120 per week with bathroom.

Banana Barracks (50 Butler St., tel. 07/4068-0455, www.bananabarracks.com.au) is a setup similar to Tully's Hotel just on the other side of the street, with slightly more upmarket accommodations available in the form of recently upgraded bungalows, complete with LCD flat-screen TV, but also the usual dorm accommodations with air-conditioning, fans, and linen provided. Bungalows are $40 per night, $175 per week; space in an eight-share dorm with en suite bathroom is $28 per night, $145 per week. There are all the usual facilities—a shared kitchen and a laundry—and even fax, Internet, and printing facilities.

Food

The pubs associated with the backpacking accommodations serve daily hearty, homemade food, ranging from burgers to pies. There are a few takeout places for fish and chips and pizza, and the **Flametree Café** (24 Butler St., tel. 07/4068-2207, Mon.-Sat. 9am-3pm) offers a drinkable cup of coffee, cakes, and a quite decent Barra Burger (fish burger) as a special for $12.50.

Getting There

Queensland Rail (tel. 07/3235-2222, www.queenslandrail.com.au) operates several weekly connections either north- or southbound, taking around four hours from Townsville and three hours from Cairns, with tickets roughly $49 either way. If you have accommodations booked in Mission Beach, they generally offer transfers from the station, or there are taxis (**Mission Beach Taxis,** tel. 07/4066-2091) waiting for the arrival of the trains, and passengers often share, as it brings the price down.

By bus, the **Greyhound** route (tel. 1300/473-946, www.greyhound.com.au) stretches along the Bruce Highway all along the coast, with a stop in Tully's town center on Butler Street, roughly three hours from Townsville or three hours from Cairns.

MISSION BEACH

The signpost to "Mission Beach" (the name derives from an Aboriginal mission that was established in 1914 but destroyed soon after by a cyclone) is a little misleading, as there are four individual beaches and residential settlements making up the 14-kilometer-long stretch commonly known as the one Mission Beach: South Mission Beach, Wongaling Beach, North Mission Beach, and Bingil Bay. To get to Mission Beach from Bruce Highway, you will first have to drive through **cassowary** country. These large relatives of the emu are shy, but when you see one, you know it, as they have a bone-plate on their blue head and are tall (males are around 1.5 meters tall, females up to 2 meters). If you see a bird with chicks in tow, that would be a male, as they are the rearing birds. But make sure not to approach the birds because they have a temper, especially when they have chicks with them, and can easily attack you.

Starting from the south, **South Mission Beach** is mostly residential and very quiet, with a pristine stretch of beach allowing great views all the way to Hinchinbrook Island and Dunk Island, just across from Mission Beach. The clusters of smaller islands in between are the Bedarra Islands. Next along is **Wongaling Beach,** the closest point to Dunk Island and the place where you'd catch the water taxi to go across (**Mission Beach Dunk Island Water Taxi,** tel. 07/4068-8310, depart from 71 Banfield Parade, Wongaling Beach, daily at 9am, 10am, and 11am, return noon and 3:30pm, $35 round-trip). **North Mission Beach** is where most of the action is, with restaurants and shops lining the main road. Beachside restaurants, galleries, Internet cafés, interior design stores, and clothes boutiques make up this lovely small beachside community. A little farther on, at **Bingil Bay,** things become more quiet again, this being a small residential arts community with a beautiful beach neighbored by the lush green rainforest.

Recreation

Mission Beach Travel Center (Shop 3, Cassowary Shopping Village, tel. 07/4068-8699, www.missionbeachinfo.com) books accommodations, tours, day trips, and activities in the region. The helpful staff advises on what activities are available and takes you through the booking process.

Tully River white-water rafting is one of the best activities here, and **Experience Oz** (tel. 1300/935-532, www.experienceoz.com.au, tours from $159, plus $30 rafting levy, minimum age 13) offers a couple of tours, which include pickup, some five hours of white-water rafting, and a barbecue lunch. No experience is necessary as instructions are given and safety gear is included. But do bring your swimming costume, as you will get wet.

Think you know your fruit? **Mission Beach Tourism** (tel. 07/4068-7099, www.missionbeachtourism.com) hosts regular fruit presentations and tasting sessions at the visitors center, showcasing the tropical and ultra-tropical fruit growing in the region. Check for dates and times and enjoy a sweet treat.

Jump out of a plane in tandem with **Skydive Mission Beach** (Bali Hai Skydive Resort, Banfield Parade, Wongaling Beach, tel. 07/4068-9291, www.skydivemissionbeach.com). Reportedly Australia's highest skydive, the jumps come in three categories: 9,000 feet/25 seconds free fall ($249); 11,000 feet/40 seconds free fall ($310), and 14,000 feet/over 60 seconds free fall ($334). In addition there are plenty of DVD and photograph packages available, recording your daredevil stunts.

Half-day local paddles to seven-day **sea kayak tours** to Hinchinbrook and the Family Islands can be booked through **Coral Sea Kayaking** (tel. 1800/787-718, www.coralseakayaking.com, half-day paddle plus snorkeling, nibbles, and instructions $77 pp, plus $5 Great Barrier Reef Marine Fee; or $1,970 for seven days including camping gear, equipment, all meals, fees, and a full-time guide).

Shopping

The Cassowary Shopping Centre (Tully to Mission Beach Rd., Wongaling Beach) is a small and somewhat uninspiring shopping plaza. You can get essentials or grab a bite to eat (a handful of restaurants offer eat-in and takeout food), and shops include a pharmacy, Internet café, newsagent and DVD rental, beauty salon, an excellent visitors center, and booking agents for all the activities in the region.

Helen Wiltshire Gallery (The Village Green, Porter Parade, Mission Beach, tel. 07/4068-7280) carries gorgeous jewelry, accessories, clothes with a difference, and beautiful knickknacks and artwork.

The Beach House (Shop 3/47, Porter Parade, Mission Beach, tel. 07/4088-6115) lets you indulge in the fantasy of owning your own beach house and decorating it with lovely marine-inspired accessories. While you are there, pick up some scented candles, a colorful caftan to throw over your bikini, some accessories, and gifts. You won't leave without a little something.

Accommodations

Absolute Backpackers (28 Wongaling Beach Rd., tel. 07/4068-8317, www.absolute-backpackers.com.au) has clean, basic accommodations available in up-to-10-person dorms ($23) or double rooms en suite ($58). Amenities include a pool, barbecue area, laundry facilities, sporting equipment (fishing, badminton, volleyball), and something on every night, be it quiz night, movies and popcorn, or pool competitions. Emphasis is on fun, with the booking of adventure tours and activities available in-house.

Beachcomber Coconut Caravan Village (Kennedy Esplanade, South Mission Beach, tel. 07/4068-8129, www.beachcombercoconut.com.au) is a large site with tent spaces ($32 one person, $35 two people), standard cabins (sleeping up to four, from $80 per night), en suite cabins (sleeping up to four, from $110 per night), and two- to three-bed en suite villas with Jacuzzis (sleeping up to seven, from $160). A pool, playground, tennis court, boat rentals, and water taxi to Dunk Island make this a perfect family getaway.

A beautiful resort right on the pristine beach, **Castaways Resort & Spa** (Pacific Parade, Mission Beach, tel. 07/4068-7444, www.castaways.com.au, from $265 per night) has all the amenities a resort should have: day spa, pools (including a lap pool), beachside dining, elegant sun lounges under shade-giving umbrellas, and a choice of hotel-style elegant and airy rooms and apartments.

The gorgeous four-bedroom residence ★ **Horizons on Mission** (Explorer Dr., Lugger Bay, tel. 07/4088-6699, http://missionbeachluxuryaccom.com/horizons.html, from $450 per night, no children under 10) is set on top of the exclusive Lugger Bay Estate, overlooking Mission Beach, the bay, and Dunk Island. With three bathrooms and an outdoor shower and pool, the residence sleeps up to eight and offers all the amenities a couple or family requires, plus a Playstation 3, several TVs, a pool table, DVD player, even a wine fridge. Luxurious and spacious, with a deck for relaxing and views that are stunning, this is a perfect grown-up summer retreat.

The name is a little misleading, as **Mission Beach Resort** (Wongaling Beach Rd., Wongaling Beach, tel. 07/4088-8288, www.missionbeachresort.com.au, from $130) is not on the beach but about 10 minutes' walking distance from the coast. Accommodations are basic, but amenities include a selection of pools, a Jacuzzi, an à la carte restaurant and bar, and a game room.

Mission Beach Retreat YHA (49 Porter Promenade, Mission Beach, tel. 07/4088-6229, book through www.hostelworld.com, rates from $22 per night for a nine-bed dorm, $55 for double room with shared bath) is a lovely hostel, with rooms light and open and nicely decorated. There's a pool, and meal deals cost $14 for a meal and a drink, including beer and wine every night. If you book a 14,000-foot skydive through them, you even get to stay the night for free. There are always special deals, and the hostel has a great location, right next to shops and restaurants.

Food

There is not much in the way of entertainment and food in Bingil Bay, but family-run **Bingil Bay Café** (39 Bingil Bay Rd., Bingil Bay, tel. 07/4068-7146, daily 7am-10pm, mains $18) covers it all. This little gem serves up decent food, good comfort home-style cooking, but particularly great cakes and cookies. While you're there, check out the local artwork, swap some books or DVDs, get the daily newspaper, and book yourself in for the fortnightly quiz night.

★ **The Fish Bar** (7 Porter Promenade, Mission Beach, tel. 07/4088-6419, daily noon-9pm), an open seaside bar, does exactly as it promises, providing lots of local seafood and a great selection of drinks. It serves good food at good prices; at lunchtime there are always specials from $10, at dinner from $17. It offers a relaxed and easy atmosphere, great people-watching and fresh food—perfect for when you are hungry from spending the day on the beach.

The New Shrub (44 Marina Parade, Mission Beach, tel. 07/4068-7803, Mon.-Fri. 10am-midnight, Sat.-Sun. 7am-midnight, mains $25) is a beach bar as it should be: right on the beautiful beach, under palm trees and decorated as if you were in the South Seas.

With local fresh seafood, plenty of cocktails, live music on Sunday, gorgeous views, and great atmosphere, there's something for everybody.

Right by the beach, **Millers Beach Bar** (1 Banfield Parade, Wongaling Beach, tel. 07/4068-8177, www.millersbeachbar.com.au, Tues.-Fri. 3pm-late, Sat.-Sun. noon-late, mains $35) offers slightly more upmarket dining than most of the restaurants in and around Mission Beach, with entrées such as cured yellowfin tuna ($16) and spiced fish of the day ($32), and decent steaks. It also offers a gluten-free menu.

Scotty's Bar & Grill (167 Reid Rd., Wongaling Beach, tel. 07/4068-8676, daily 5pm-late) is a popular place for drinks and dinner, serving basic favorites such as burgers and lasagna. There are regular specials when a football game is on and for karaoke or disco night.

Zenbah (39 Porter Promenade, Mission Beach, tel. 07/4088-6040, Tues.-Thurs. 4pm-midnight, Fri.-Sat. 4pm-2am, Sun. 4pm-midnight, mains $25) is a colorful and exotic restaurant with a great and somewhat eclectic menu, from tasty Moroccan meatballs, falafel, and hummus to the local grilled barramundi and Australian rump steak, and a good array in between. I'd opt for the Moroccan and Lebanese goodies, which make a nice change from modern Australian.

Getting There

If you are driving, and coming north from the direction of Townsville, turn right off the Bruce Highway just north of Tully, following the sign to Mission Beach. It's about 26 kilometers from the highway to Mission Beach. Please drive carefully, as you might well encounter a cassowary, a very large flightless bird, which has the habit of crossing the road at the most inconvenient times.

Queensland Rail (tel. 07/3235-2222, www.queenslandrail.com.au) operates several weekly connections either north- or southbound, taking around four hours from Townsville and three hours from Cairns, with tickets roughly $49 either way. If you have accommodations booked in Mission Beach, they generally offer transfers from the station, or there are taxis (**Mission Beach Taxis,** tel. 07/4066-2091) waiting for the arrival of the trains, and passengers often share, as it brings the price down.

By bus, the **Greyhound** route (tel. 1300/473-946, www.greyhound.com.au) stretches along the Bruce Highway all along the coast, with a stop in Mission Beach (at the Cassowary Shopping Village at Wongaling Beach), roughly 3.5 hours from Townsville, 2.5 from Cairns.

DUNK ISLAND

The largest of the Family Islands, Dunk Island is a granite island covered in a variety of dense rainforest, with an idyllic sandspit sticking out at one end, forming a perfect little beach. Other small beaches are strung around the perimeter, while the dense forest is home to countless birds, reptiles, butterflies, and mammals. Protected, as all islands in and around the Great Barrier Reef are, the environment here is as lush and natural as it should be, with both flora and fauna thriving.

Sadly, in February 2011, Cyclone Yasi completely destroyed the elegant beach resort on the island, and also much of its wildlife and plants; while nature is quickly recovering, the resort is still completely ruined, with no plans for rebuilding it in the near future.

It's possible to camp on Dunk Island, but the bulk of visitors are day-trippers, arriving either by water taxi or kayak to explore the island, snorkel along its coastline, and enjoy the secluded beaches.

Recreation

Coral Sea Kayaking (tel. 1800/787-718, www.coralseakayaking.com, $128 pp, plus $8.50 park fees) offers organized full-day trips on sea kayaks, complete with guide, snorkeling gear, lunch, and necessary instructions.

There are two **island walks** of moderate difficulty. One is to the summit of Mount Kootaloo (7 km round-trip, around 3 hours, steep at times). The other is the island circuit (9.2 km round-trip, around 3 hours). Signs are provided to guide you around.

Accommodations

Camping is popular on Dunk Island, with basic amenities available, although no food or water, so you will need to bring everything with you (bring plenty of water) and, at the end of your stay, take everything back with you. There are nine campsites to choose from. Four family sites on the beachfront along each side of the spit are equipped with picnic tables and tent space. Tariffs are $5.45 per night per adult or $21.80 per night for a family group. (A family group is two adults and up to six children under 18 years old.) To book, contact **Dunk Island Camping** (tel. 04/1787-3390).

Getting There

The **Mission Beach Dunk Island Water Taxi** (71 Banfield Parade, Wongaling Beach, tel. 07/4068-8310, www.missionbeachwatertaxi.com) is $35 round-trip, departing daily at 9am, 10am, and 11am, returning at noon and 3:30pm. Other times may be arranged. The same company does a "Fozzy's 3 Hour, 3 Island Tour," taking in Dunk Island and some of the smaller Family Islands, every Monday, Wednesday, and Friday for $50 per person, departing at Wongaling Beach at 12:30pm.

Cairns and the Northern Reef

Look for ★ to find recommended sights, activities, dining, and lodging.

Highlights

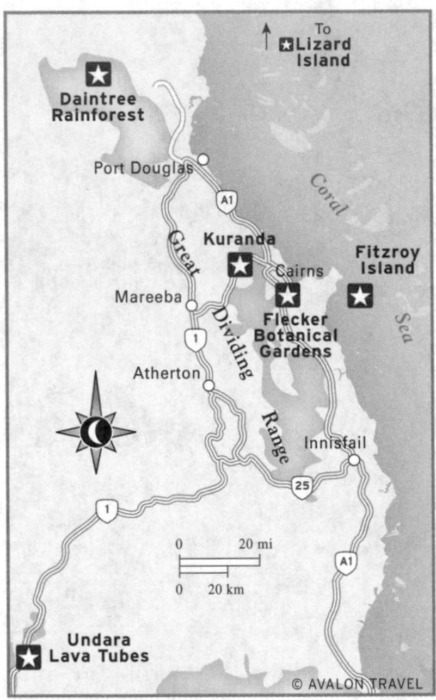

★ **Flecker Botanical Gardens:** Imagine walking from a bustling city center into a wild and luscious rainforest within 30 minutes. The botanical gardens are slightly more manicured and not as wild as the forest farther up the coast, but that means that you can safely walk along boardwalks taking in the incredible plants that grow here, view special exhibits, and stop for coffee, all without worrying about the indigenous wildlife eating you while you are in the jungle (page 217).

★ **Kuranda:** Take a cable car up over the rainforest's canopy, see the cockatoos sitting on the treetops, then visit colorful markets in Kuranda over lunch and get back to the starting point in a historic train that trundles past waterfalls and across gorges—this is quite simply one of the region's best days out (page 238).

★ **Undara Lava Tubes:** Just when you think nature could not get any more impressive than the magnificent Great Barrier Reef and the luscious tropical rainforest, then you'll walk through a maze of enormously large tubes that were formed from lava flow some 190,000 years ago. Add to that a hike around a crater and toasting your morning bread at a bush breakfast, and you get an all-round Outback experience that is hard to beat (page 249).

★ **Fitzroy Island:** After a mere 45 minutes on the ferry from Cairns, you are on a (nearly) deserted island offering self-guided walks through the rainforest, a white sandy beach that is flanked by giant boulders, and the possibility of encountering green sea turtles when snorkeling. But this desert island also comes with a beach bar and snacks (page 265).

★ **Lizard Island:** The only continental islands close to the outer Great Barrier Reef, an hour's flight from Cairns, the Lizard Island group offers pristine water, easy access to the colorful reef, untouched beaches, and a true desert island experience. The star of the islands is Lizard Island and its award-winning five-star luxury resort, where celebrities come to take advantage of the combination of unspoiled nature, luxury amenities, and utter seclusion (page 268).

★ **Daintree Rainforest:** Covering some 1,200 square kilometers north of Cairns, the World Heritage-listed Daintree is the largest continuous rainforest area in Australia. At an estimated 180 million years old, some tens of millions of years older than the Amazon rainforest in South America, it is also the oldest rainforest in the world, containing examples of fauna and flora that are not found anywhere else on the planet (page 271).

It doesn't matter for how long you are up in tropical northern Queensland; there are two things you will need to see and experience: the Great Barrier Reef and the Daintree Rainforest. This is the only place in the world where two UNESCO World Heritage listed natural wonders come together so closely, in certain places mere steps away from each other.

The first European visitor known to have laid eyes on this stunning landscape was Captain James Cook. The nearby forests and mountains had been inhabited by Aboriginal tribes for tens of thousands of years when Cook sailed up the coast near Cairns in June 1770. His journey was a treacherous one, navigating unknown waters, especially the reefs in the region, but he managed to nevertheless name numerous landmarks, such as the Trinity Inlet, now the starting point of most ferries taking visitors on cruises around the Great Barrier Reef, and also Cape Tribulation and Weary Bay, the names being somewhat of a historic reminder of how he and his crew felt when sailing along these shores.

No further Europeans visited the region again until gold was discovered at the Palmer River, east of Cooktown, some 260 kilometers north of Cairns, in 1872. Gold called thousands of prospectors to the region in the coming years.

Trinity Inlet became known for its excellent natural harbor when George Dalrymple explored the coastline in around 1873. But Cairns was not officially established until October 1876, when settlers arrived on board the SS *Porpoise*. Cairns was originally known as Thornton, after the collector of customs in Brisbane, William Thornton; and then Dickson, after the colonial treasurer at the time. The town was eventually named Cairns after the first governor of Queensland, Sir William Wellington Cairns.

Settling the region was not easy. Mostly swamp and wetlands, Trinity Inlet and its surrounding countryside were flat land that was loved by birds but pretty much inaccessible and too unstable for humans. Yet the early settlers were a determined lot, and in October 1876, the Esplanade, or the

Previous: getting ready to go scuba diving on the Great Barrier Reef; one of the beautiful beaches on Fitzroy Island. **Above:** kauri tree, which can grow up to 50 meters tall.

Cairns and the Northern Reef

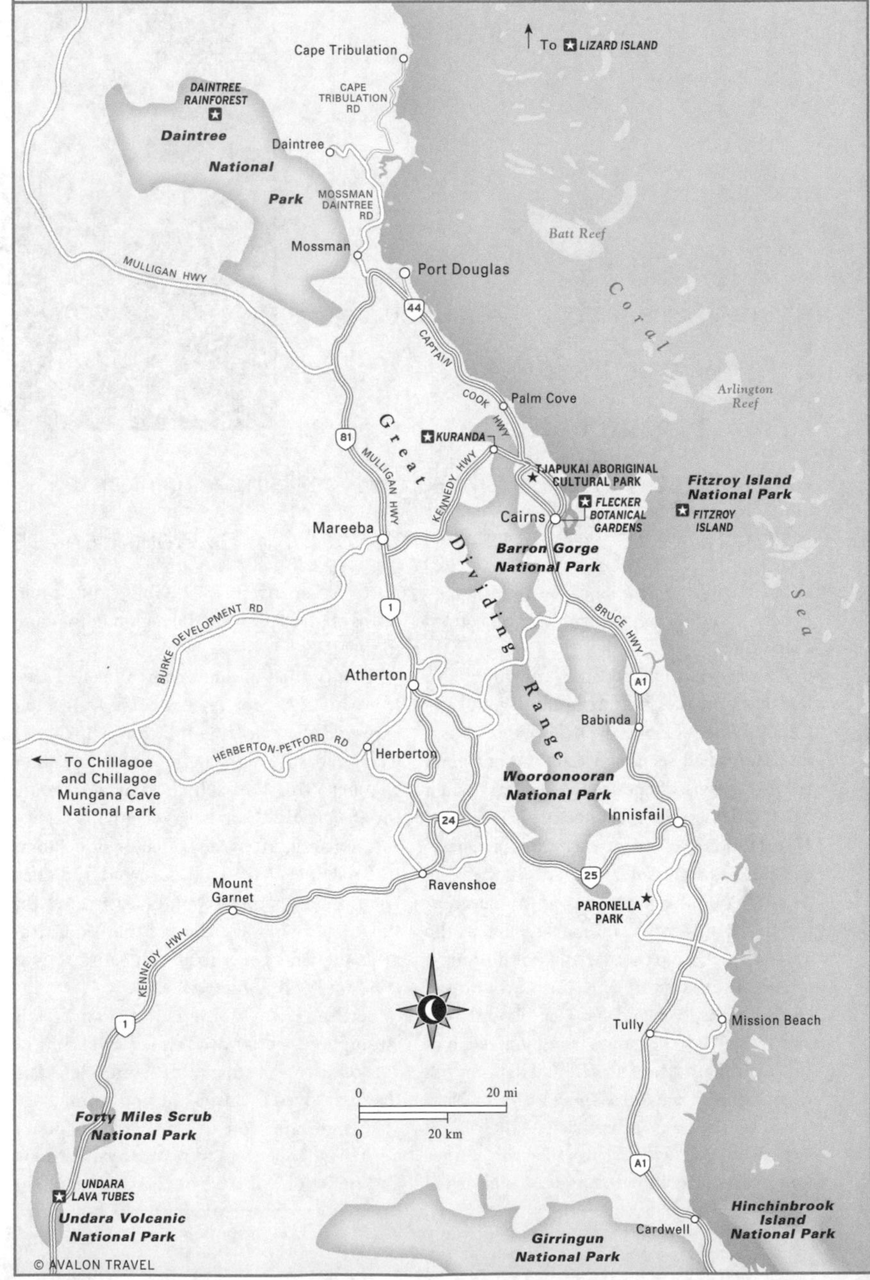

Troughton Esplanade as it was originally known, was the first surveyed street in young Cairns. Permanent buildings were slow to be erected, with most settlers living in tents, while building priority was given to wharves and storage sheds. The outlook was bleak—the growing city competed with richer Port Douglas, established in 1877, and was going broke. By early 1882, Cairns was in the depth of a depression, with only 90 people on the official electoral roll. Light at the end of the tunnel came from the building of the railway line that was to connect the interior Atherton Tablelands through the rainforest and mountain range with Cairns. It was an unbelievable feat of engineering that can still be appreciated today with a trip on the Kuranda Scenic Railway, which follows exactly the historic tracks.

With the revenue from the railways also came the onset of agricultural wealth from the fruit- and dairy-farming tablelands and the sugarcane industry. Cairns prospered and continued to grow. By the early 1900s, the tent city had developed into a town of 11,000 people.

Progress continued steadily, and in World War II the Cairns region played a big part supplying the Allied Forces. After the war, the tourism industry started taking off, but it was not until 1968 that the first passenger jet service started up between Brisbane and Cairns, allowing easier access to the wonders of this previously very secluded region. Currently more than 79 percent of land in Cairns and the Great Barrier Reef is protected, including areas in the Daintree and Cape Tribulation rainforests of the north, the tropical Atherton Tablelands to the west, and Mission Beach to the south.

PLANNING YOUR TIME

If you are utterly time-deprived and are planning to jet in and out for a single day, then the only option you have to experience both reef and lush forest is to cruise to either Fitzroy Island or to Green Island. Both islands offer snorkeling and diving to discover the magnificent underwater world with its colorful reef fish, turtles, and sometimes even whales, and both have a crop of dense forest that, if not the Daintree Rainforest per se, still gives you an idea of the lush vegetation and the amazing on-land animals (particularly birds) this kind of vegetation attracts. Fitzroy Island is a little closer to Cairns and is more sedate, with a quiet resort, a house reef, some kayaking, and a couple of beautiful beaches. Green Island, on the other hand, is a full-on tourist attraction, which can turn into a bit of a circus, but if you have kids to entertain and a saunter along the beach or hike through the forest with a sedate lunch just won't cut it, this is your option. There's snorkeling, diving, swimming, glass-bottom boat touring, an observatory, a small weird museum, nature walks, a bar, barbecues, pontoons, and more to keep everybody happy and make for a fun- and people-filled day.

However, it would be best to dedicate a little more time to this part of the world. A minimum of three days, maybe a week would be good, and more would be better.

This region is not explored on foot, although hikes and boardwalks take a high priority when it comes to closely experiencing it. You will need to choose a base and take day trips from there, be it by car or via organized tours. Everybody vaguely connected with tourism in Queensland is aware of this, and the number of tour operators and the combinations they offer is mind-boggling. So, your base should either be Cairns or Port Douglas. Cairns has the airport on the doorstep; Port Douglas is an hour's drive farther north. Cairns is young, bustling with a clientele of backpackers and lots of local and Asian tourists. Fast food restaurants line the Esplanade, live music thumps out of pubs all evening, and there is always something on. Port Douglas is popular with western tourists, many Europeans and Americans. There are no traffic lights and no fast food outlets, although you can get a burger or taco in town; rather, the emphasis is on fine—if relaxed—dining, and it's a quieter stay all around. Both places offer access to all the day trips, but Port Douglas is an hour closer to the Daintree.

Once you have the base, choose your trips. Obviously you will need to spend at least one day on the reef and then one day in the forest, so a day trip to Cape Trib, as it is affectionately called, maybe combined with some croc spotting and a guided nature walk, is in order. If you can spend a night at the Undara Experience, then you could leave your base in the morning, take a leisurely drive through the Atherton Tablelands, get to Undara in the late afternoon in time for sunset. Spend the night, explore the tubes, and head back to base taking a different route through the tablelands.

Depending on what you want and need out of this trip, and whom you are traveling with, the region offers a plethora of thrill-seeking activities, be it bungee jumping, ziplining, or wild-water rafting, as well as more serene ways of spending the day, such as taking the cable car to Kuranda, doing some shopping in the market, and taking the scenic railway back.

Always bear in mind that this is the tropical north of Australia, and a rainforest doesn't get its name without some precipitation around. The temperatures are never really cold, with summer (Nov.-Feb.) temperatures between 24 and 33 degrees Celsius (75 to 91 degrees Fahrenheit), and in winter (July-Sept.) between 14 to 26 degrees Celsius (57 to 79 degrees Fahrenheit). The summer is the wet season, the so-called "green season," stretching from the onset of the monsoon (usually in November) and ending in May. The rain makes it hot and humid, at times uncomfortable, and can hamper the excursions, although places such as the Undara Lava Tubes adapt to the seasons and, if the tubes are filled with water, offer snorkeling excursions instead of the boardwalk.

The dry season; i.e., the southern hemisphere winter, is the high season up here, drawing more visitors and inviting higher prices. Australian schools have generally a two-week vacation in early July and another in September, and there are some Europeans around on long excursions throughout the season. If you can plan for August, or the fringe times, you should not be overrun with people and should be able to enjoy some of the 300 days a year of sunshine without being too hot.

The water is warm enough to swim in all year round, but keep in mind that box jellyfish populate the shallow waters from October to May. These are nasty critters, giving bad stings, but most popular beaches offer "stinger nets"—netted areas on the beaches to swim in safely. Do check about the conditions before you head to the beaches.

Cairns

Today, Cairns is among to the top 10 fastest-growing towns in Queensland, with a population growth rate at 3.2 percent. By 2012, the population of Cairns had increased to almost 166,000.

Cairns is often not perceived as a destination in its own right. It is the hub to the Great Barrier Reef and to the tropical rainforests—the gateway to the many incredible sights to be visited in tropical northern Queensland. And there is no doubt that few people linger in the town. You notice it by just walking down the street during the day: After the mass exodus in the morning when nearly every visitor leaves either by ferry to the reefs and islands, or by bus or car to the tropical forests, waterfalls, and inland attractions, Cairns is empty. Come midafternoon and people start to trickle back, and by early evening the Esplanade is filled with people eating and drinking, and, often, booking further sightseeing tours that will take them away from the town again the next morning.

Although Cairns's sights are not comparable to Sydney's, neither is its size, and for its size it has plenty to keep guests busy who may not want to leave on day trips every single day. Cairns itself does not have a beach adjoining the Esplanade, but for those who may just want to soak up the sun near some water, most hotels offer pools in relaxing settings; some are proper resorts with pool bars and play areas. A swimming lagoon right in the middle of the Esplanade offers a free pool for all. For those who want a little historical and cultural background on the town and region, options include the museum, art galleries, and heritage buildings. And for those who love animals and plants, this is sheer heaven. Wander down the Esplanade any time of the day, and you'll see pelicans, curlews, sandpipers, egrets, and many more birds; walk (carefully) under the banyan trees in Aplin Street next to the Cairns City Library and you see and hear countless fruit bats hanging around, chatting very loudly indeed. Enter the Flecker Botanical Gardens and you enter an enchanted forest, like a slightly tamed version of what you find farther north, and with safe walkways and the odd café. But the plants, enormously huge and rich, cannot be anything but awe-inspiring. And all that is just in the town itself. Venture farther out, and the region is no doubt one of the most varied and exciting in the world.

SIGHTS

Cairns Museum

The **Cairns Museum** (corner of Shields St. and Lake St., tel. 07/4063-2656, www.cairnsmuseum.org.au, Mon.-Sat. 10am-4pm, adult $5, child $3 child) is located on the first floor of a corner shop, so you'd be forgiven if you walked right past the museum without noticing it. This is a little gem packed full with artifacts and historical information that will help you understand Cairns a little better. From WWII reminders to Aboriginal weapons and utensils, from a corner exhibiting Chinese artifacts to details of the local railway construction and displays of antique bottles, suitcases, and information on the local dentist who was the first person to diagnose malaria in the region, the exhibits document the history of Cairns and the surrounding region through the ephemera of bygone times. Quirky and unique, the museum, for the price, is worth an hour of your time.

Cairns Regional Gallery

Housed in a heritage building, the **Cairns Regional Gallery** (corner of Abbott St. and Shield St., tel. 07/4046-4800, www.cairnsregionalgallery.com.au, Mon.-Fri. 9am-5pm, Sat. 10am-5pm, Sun. 10am-2pm, adult $5, child under 16 free) is a beautiful space, well worth visiting just for the red-brick building, completed in 1936 in the neo-Grecian style complete with a columned entrance reminiscent of that of a temple. Regular exhibitions range from the traditional to the modern, from sculptures to paintings. Exquisite choices of artists, such as New Zealand-based Dame Lynley Dood and Tasmanian landscape artist Philip Wolfhagen, and their work, together with the setting, make this a must-see attraction within Cairns. Make sure you also visit the shop, as it has a superb collection of greeting cards, books, and souvenirs, such as the pretty "Little Building Company" heritage house sets.

Cairns Zoom & Wildlife Dome

The **Cairns Zoom & Wildlife Dome** (35-41 Wharf St., on top of the Pullman Reef Hotel Casino, tel. 07/4031-7250, http://cairnszoom.com.au, daily 9am-8pm, prices for Wildlife Dome plus one activity such as the PowerJump or Dome-Climb start from $45 pp, going up to $75 for all available activities) is a two-in-one destination for the younger members of the family. It is a wildlife center with numerous feeding sessions throughout the day of birds, marsupials, reptiles, and the rest of the 400 animals calling the dome home. You can even have your picture taken with Harvey the Koala. The tickets are valid

Cairns

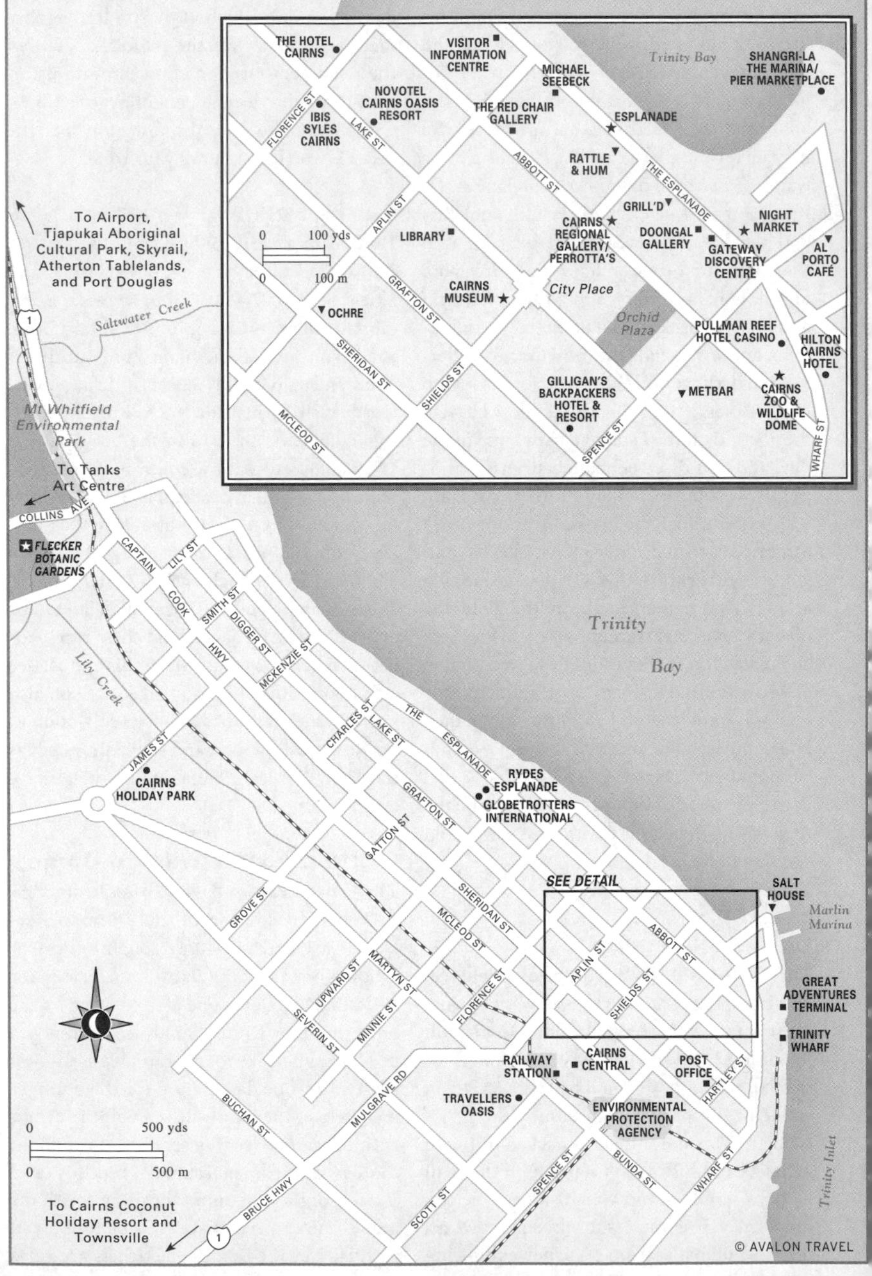

Trinity Bay
THE HOTEL CAIRNS
VISITOR INFORMATION CENTRE
MICHAEL SEEBECK
SHANGRI-LA THE MARINA/ PIER MARKETPLACE
NOVOTEL CAIRNS OASIS RESORT
IBIS SYLES CAIRNS
THE RED CHAIR GALLERY
ESPLANADE
RATTLE & HUM
GRILL'D
CAIRNS REGIONAL GALLERY/ PERROTTA'S
DOONGAL GALLERY
GATEWAY DISCOVERY CENTRE
NIGHT MARKET
AL PORTO CAFÉ
LIBRARY
CAIRNS MUSEUM
City Place
Orchid Plaza
OCHRE
PULLMAN REEF HOTEL CASINO
HILTON CAIRNS HOTEL
GILLIGAN'S BACKPACKERS HOTEL & RESORT
METBAR
CAIRNS ZOO & WILDLIFE DOME
FLORENCE ST
LAKE ST
ABBOTT ST
THE ESPLANADE
APLIN ST
GRAFTON ST
SHERIDAN ST
SHIELDS ST
MCLEOD ST
SPENCE ST
WHARF ST
0 100 yds
0 100 m
To Airport, Tjapukai Aboriginal Cultural Park, Skyrail, Atherton Tablelands, and Port Douglas
Saltwater Creek
Mt Whitfield Environmental Park
To Tanks Art Centre
COLLINS AVE
FLECKER BOTANIC GARDENS
CAPTAIN COOK HWY
LILY ST
SMITH ST
DIGGER ST
MCKENZIE ST
Lily Creek
Trinity Bay
CHARLES ST
LAKE ST
THE ESPLANADE
JAMES ST
CAIRNS HOLIDAY PARK
RYDES ESPLANADE
GLOBETROTTERS INTERNATIONAL
GRAFTON ST
GATTON ST
SHERIDAN ST
SEE DETAIL
SALT HOUSE
Marlin Marina
GROVE ST
MCLEOD ST
ABBOTT ST
APLIN ST
SHIELDS ST
UPWARD ST
MARTYN ST
FLORENCE ST
GREAT ADVENTURES TERMINAL
TRINITY WHARF
SEVERIN ST
MINNIE ST
RAILWAY STATION
CAIRNS CENTRAL
POST OFFICE
HARTLEY ST
TRAVELLERS OASIS
ENVIRONMENTAL PROTECTION AGENCY
BUCHAN ST
MULGRAVE RD
0 500 yds
0 500 m
SPENCE ST
BUNDA ST
WHARF ST
Trinity Inlet
BRUCE HWY
SCOTT ST
To Cairns Coconut Holiday Resort and Townsville
1
© AVALON TRAVEL

for five days to give you a chance to catch as many feeding sessions as possible during your stay. Then, above the wildlife habitats, recreational opportunities include a zipline, rope courses, and dome climb. The difficulty level varies, ensuring everybody can have a go at exploring the habitats from above.

Esplanade

The five-kilometer-long art-studded **Esplanade** (Marlin Marina to Lily St.) is Cairns's life-line. Stretching from Marlin Marina all the way along the bay with a signposted walk extending it to the Flecker Botanical Gardens and Tank Arts Centre, the wide wooden boardwalk is a hub for residents and visitors alike. Fitness enthusiasts find regular fitness points along the way; bird-watcher guides point out the local and migratory wildlife; those interested in the history and important facts about Cairns and the Great Barrier Reef can stop and read information boards in regular intervals. Families are drawn by playgrounds, tourists by the views across the sea (all the way to Green Island on a clear day), and those who want to go swimming can do so, too.

Although Cairns does not have a beach as such—only mudflats that are a haven for plenty of birds, but not suitable for swimming—there is a large seawater swimming lagoon right on the Esplanade that is perfect for all water enthusiasts. In a leisurely and lively atmosphere, the lagoon offers 4,800 square meters of safe swimming, sandy edges where children can build sandcastles, timber decks, and shade trees. Saunter along toward Pier Point and rest on one of the benches to watch the sunset over the mountains behind the city before heading off to one of the many restaurants and bars settled along the way. Regular concerts and events extend daytime activities well into the night.

Cairns Night Market

Aimed unabashedly at tourists, the **Cairns Night Market** (71-75 The Esplanade, daily 5pm-11pm) sells anything from Australian bush ranger hats to opals, from candy to kangaroo jerky, from toys, clothing, and accessories to kitschy souvenirs. Some 130 stalls and numerous (mostly Chinese) food kiosks ensure that every night this place is buzzing with people. The variety is enormous, the prices are acceptable, and the food tempting.

★ Flecker Botanical Gardens

It is hard to believe that the **Flecker Botanical Gardens** (Collins Ave., tel. 07/4032-3900, Mon.-Fri. 7:30am-5:30pm, Sat.-Sun. 8:30am-5:30pm, free) were created in 1886, and by now the 71-acre park is so lush and has grown to represent a slice of rainforest near the city. Wooden boardwalks guide you through the dense foliage, with flowers that take your breath away and gigantic versions of plants you try and nurture toward growth in pots back home, such as the rubber plants and orchids. There is even an exhibition in a greenhouse entitled "Sex and Death," full of orchids and carnivorous plants. It is a delight to walk around the gardens, get lost in the wetlands and the swamp forest, and simply be enchanted by greenery that will not be held back. If you are lucky, the world's largest flower, *Amorphophallus titanium,* also known as carrion flower due to its smell, might be in bloom. It last flowered to worldwide acclaim in February 2012, and can reach over two meters in height. There are also some 170 recorded bird species in the gardens and surroundings.

Walk for four kilometers along the Esplanade to get there, or take bus service 131 from the city center. If you are stopping for lunch, try the hidden-away **Botanic Café** (third entrance from main along Collins Ave., tel. 07/4053-7087, daily 7am-4:30pm, mains $10-18), not the big restaurant by the main entrance. Here you sit on basic chairs in what feels like the middle of the rainforest and can feast on the soup and bruschetta of the day, fresh focaccia, and refreshing salads—try the roasted chicken with macadamia nut. They also do fresh waffles.

Cairns's Heritage Buildings

Cairns City Library

Cairns has a number of lovely heritage buildings that often get overlooked when wandering through town and looking into shop windows rather than at the facades. Particularly beautiful buildings on Abbott Street include the **Cairns City Library,** housed in the former inter-war classical building of the Cairns City Council Chambers (dating back to 1930), and the **Cairns Post building,** completed in 1908 and extended in 1924, which still houses the newspaper offices of the city. The **Cairns Regional Gallery,** on Shields Street, was formerly the Public Curator's offices and State Government Insurance office; it dates back to 1936. **Boland's Centre** on Spence Street was built in 1912 for the trader Michael Boland and still retains most of its original form and function. Even the **Cairns & Tropical North Visitor Information Centre** on the Esplanade is a little gem of its own.

Tank Arts Centre

Part of the botanical gardens, **Tank Arts Centre** (46 Collins Ave., tel. 07/4032-6600, www.tanksartscentre.com, Mon.-Fri. 9:30am-4:30pm, admission varies according to events) is an unusual facility that combines art exhibitions, workshops, and multi-use venues, all housed in three concrete fuel storage tanks built for the Australian Navy in 1944, to be used during World War II. Camouflaged by the lush rainforest of Mount Whitfield, the Tank Arts Centre and the botanical gardens were placed on the state heritage register in 2006. Regular exhibitions in Tank 3 showcase local and touring artists in an unconventional setting. On the last Sunday of every month from April to September, there is Market Day (9am-2pm), full of stalls featuring arts and crafts, knickknacks, local produce, and other food, plus live music and entertainment.

Tjapukai Aboriginal Cultural Park

Tjapukai Aboriginal Cultural Park (next to Caravonica Skyrail Station, tel. 07/4042-9900, www.tjapukai.com.au, daily 9am-5pm and 6:45pm-10pm, day admission adult $36, children $18, family $90; night admission adult $99, child $49.50, family $247.50) is a designed-for-tourists destination managed by Aborigines belonging to the Tjapukai people, with earnings going back directly to tribe members. There is a lot to do and see, so allow around three hours minimum, especially if you arrive with kids. Upon arrival you will be presented with an itinerary and information

Flecker Botanical Gardens

card, which tells you about the history of the people and their region. You will have schedules of dance and storytelling performances to attend. You can learn to play the didgeridoo, find out about bush tucker, and try your hand at boomerang and spear throwing. The kids can have their faces painted in the traditional way. And there is a restaurant and shop on-site as well. While this is set up for tourists and at times can feel artificial, the lessons you'll learn are truly interesting and unique—this is after all the original culture of Australia, and without story-telling and passing the messages on, it will be lost, if we're not careful.

There is also nighttime entertainment coupled with a buffet dinner, all outside by the lake, with plenty of dances, eerie music, and fire-making. During the evening you can be as involved as you wish, and even try your hand at traditional dancing on stage.

RECREATION

Bird-Watching

Bird-watching is a must in northern Queensland. Home to some 450 species and visiting place of many migratory species, the many national parks are literally teeming with birds. Either explore some of the parks by yourself (check www.birdingtropicalaustralia.com.au, and download the app from the site to give you pictures and details about the birds) or join some professional tours and cruises. Check www.closeupbirding.com.au, www.finefeatherstours.com.au, and www.daintreeriverwildwatch.com.au for inspiration.

One of the easiest-to-reach locations for spotting a fair number of birds is the Esplanade. The most obvious ones are the pelicans, but there are also curlews, kingfishers, plenty of exotic migrants, and a huge number of parrots at sunset. If you have a rental car, don't miss the chance to spot a cassowary near Mission Beach or around Cape Tribulation. These huge flightless birds are truly unique and spectacular to look at, although difficult to spot, as they live in the dense undergrowth of the rainforest. But they do cross the road, and that's when a car comes in handy.

If you are a serious birder and would like to spend several days making the most of what Australia has to offer, check out the tours arranged by **Close-up Birding** (Cape York, tel. 07/4094-1068, www.closeupbirding.com.au). Some tours last several days and are arranged on specific dates to coincide with special events, such as migration or breeding. There are, for example, 11-day "Gulf and Outback Birding Adventures" ($5,150 pp, including transport, accommodations, guide, food, and access to habitats), but there also are day tours in and around Cairns ($235 pp for a full day, including morning tea and lunch, 4WD transport, pickup, and a guide). In addition, if you are after something specific, the guides can arrange personalized tours that suit your interest and timeframe.

Cairns Bird Tours (Yorkeys Knob, tel. 04/2431-7764, www.cairnsbirdtours.com, day tours $230 pp, minimum two people) tailor tours to your interests and vary their set tours according to what birds are best to spot at what time of the year. Trips include the Atherton Tablelands as well as the diverse habitats around Cairns, ranging from mangrove mudflats to grassland, from urban habitats to bushland. Tours include snacks, lunch, transport, access to reference books, and telescope, but it's recommended that you bring binoculars yourself.

Biking

The region of Cairns and northern Queensland is a great place to ride a bike, be it pedal-powered or motorized. Whether you want to ride along the Esplanade to enjoy the views and explore the relatively flat city and nearby beaches, or head toward the tablelands and mountains for more of a challenge, there are dedicated loops that you can ride without the need for an organized tour. To search for rides that suit your time allowance and abilities, check out http://cairnstrails.com/trails.

Cairns Mountain Bike Tours (Bike Stop Espresso, Shop 13 Campus Shopping Village, 5-21 Faculty Close, Smithfield, tel. 04/1876-9762, www.cairnsmountainbiketours.com, half-day tours from $149) caters for groups of 1-6 riders, using a network of trails in the Cairns Mountain Bike Park. Trips go through the local forest and are available at all skill levels. They supply bikes, helmet, gloves, and hydration packs. Alternatively, you can rent a bike for self-touring from $95 per day.

Dan's Mountain Biking (Earlville, Cairns, tel. 07/4032-0066, www.dansmountainbiking.com.au, half day $85, full day $165, all equipment included) offers a selection of tours starting from different points according to destination. They cover all terrains and all fitness levels. Some tours offer optional extras, such as a crocodile show or overnight stays at additional cost.

Cairns Scooter & Bicycle Hire (3/47 Shields St., Cairns, tel. 07/4031-3444, www.cairnsbicyclehire.com.au, bicycles from $15 for four hours, scooters from $35 for two hours) is a family-run business offering bicycles and motorized scooters and motorbikes for hire on hourly to daily rates. There is a wide range of bikes.

Adventure Sports

Need a thrill other than tropical fish? **AJ Hackett Cairns** (McGregor Rd., Smithfield, tel. 07/4057-7188, www.ajhackett.com.au/cairns), some 15 kilometers north of Cairns, offers **bungee jumping** (one jump from $159) from its bungee tower, which has been open since the 1980s and has operated over two million safe jumps overlooking the rainforest and reef in the distance. Children over 12 years of age and a minimum weight of 45 kilograms are allowed to jump. If you can't face it alone, you can even jump tandem.

Also located at AJ Hackett is the **Minjin Jungle Swing** ($99 pp), the only multi-person jungle swing in Australia. The swing swoops through the rainforest from 45 meters down to one meter in 3.5 seconds, reaching speeds up to 120 kilometers per hour. It's great fun, and safe for nearly all ages. Safety gear is provided and door-to-door pickups are available.

Fishing

Whether you are into reef or bottom fishing, light tackle sports fishing, heavy tackle game fishing, or river fishing, **Fishing Cairns** (60 Collinson St., Westcourt, tel. 04/4856-3586, www.fishingcairns.com.au, half-day estuary fishing from $95, ocean fishing charter around $1,980 per day for two people) can help you organize a charter that meets your needs. Charters include all equipment, lures, tackles, light refreshments, beverages, and transport. They work with several operators in the region that offer trips to a variety of locations, ranging from estuaries (Trinity Inlet is a natural harbor with calm waters) to reefs to open-ocean fishing (out in the Coral Sea past the reef islands). You can try to land your favorite fish, anything from the estuarine barramundi to a marlin or tuna.

Whale-Watching

The Great Barrier Reef attracts several species of whale, humpback whales and minke whales in particular, during the southern hemisphere winter months. **Experience Oz** (tel. 1300/935-532, www.experienceoz.com.au, tours July-Sept. only, adult $99, child $79, family $277) will take you out to the greater reef for some 3.5 hours, and they even give you a whale-sighting guarantee: If you don't see one on your trip, you will be able to go again for free.

Reef Magic Cruises (1 Spence St., Cairns, tel. 07/4031-1588, www.reefmagiccruises.com, adult $99, child $79, family $277) offers 3- to 3.5-hour-long cruises to watch the seasonal whales, including detailed information of the biology and behavior of the humpback whales. They use spotter aircraft to locate whales, making sure you'll see some. Drinks and cookies are included, and a bar for further purchases is on board.

River Tubing and Rafting

Cairns has three rivers in its surroundings that lend themselves to white-water rafting: the Tully, Barron, and Russell Rivers. The closest river to the city is the Barron River, offering Class II-III rapids. The Tully River has rapids graded Class IV, and the Russell River has a range of grades from I to IV.

Everything Cairns (www.everythingcairns.com, online booking only) offers a range of rafting tours, such as the half-day "Barron River Raging Thunder" tour, which offers two hours of rafting, pickup and drop-off at your hotel, all safety equipment, in rafts that carry seven passengers ($133 pp, minimum age 13).

For river tubing, go down the Mulgrave River rapids in twin-chamber tubes (giant rings you sit in) and take in the scenery as you go. This is safe for children upward of five years, and a fun, if wet, day out. **Foaming Fury** (19-21 Barry St., Cairns, tel. 1800/801-540, www.foamingfury.com.au, half-day adult $69, child $49) offers half-day tours that include free pickup from the hotel and allow for two hours of tubing. The company does river rafting on the Barron River as well (from $129 half day).

Waterskiing

Because waterskiing is not encouraged around the coral reefs, you will have to go and cable-ski in a lake by the Kuranda Mountain Range, just north of Cairns. **Cable Ski Cairns** (Lot 5 Captain Cook Highway, Smithfield, tel. 07/4038-1304, www.cableskicairns.com.au, adult $39 per hour, child $34) is one of only four cable-ski parks in Australia. You can water-ski, wakeboard, and kneeboard here, with tuition (i.e., instruction) available, and all equipment is provided. There is even a beach with umbrellas, sun lounges, and a barbecue area for afterwards.

Sugarworld Waterpark

Ten kilometers south of Cairns, you can find water fun somewhat different to snorkeling among tropical fish. At **Sugarworld Waterpark** (Hambledon Dr., Edmonton, tel. 07/4055-5477, www.sugarworld.com.au, weekends and school holidays 10am-4pm, adult $15, child $12, families $48) there are slides, tunnels, raft rides, a pool, and all sorts of wet interactive fun. A licensed food kiosk keeps the kids' bellies full.

Golf

Open year-round, **Half Moon Bay Golf Club** (Wattle St., Yorkeys Knob, tel. 07/4055-7884, www.halfmoonbaygolf.com.au, 18 holes $38, 9 holes $25) is an 18-hole, 5,129-meter, par-70 golf course that offers all the facilities you need for a round of social golf: club hire, motorized cart, pro shop, teaching pro, and a lovely setting together with a clubhouse offering local pies. Visitors are welcome, but bookings are essential.

Land Tours

If you want to get into the saddle, be it on a horse or a quad bike, **Blazing Saddles** (Captain Cook Hwy., Edge Hill, tel. 07/4055-7400, www.blazingsaddles.com.au, horse riding from $125, quad biking from $130), located on a working sugar farm, makes for a fun day out for the entire family. Ride through the farm, into the rainforest, through mangroves, and in native bushland, where you might just spot some local animals along the way. A number of tours are available, from half-day horse riding to all day horse riding and quad biking combination tours, suited to all experience and skill levels. The minimum age for horse riding is 4 years old; for quad biking, it's 12 years old. Pickup from hotels can be arranged.

For motorized biking tours, **Fair Dinkum Bike Tours** (Shed 7, 170-182 Mayers St., Manunda, Cairns, tel. 07/4053-6999, www.fairdinkumbiketours.com.au) takes you out on tours ranging from one-day rainforest trail rides ($510 pp, including bike and safety equipment plus fuel) to eight-day tours all the way up the coast (Cape York Ride, $5,450, including accommodations, food, guides, and equipment). Experienced guides and a selection of bikes offer enthusiasts a wide range of experiences exploring the region on two wheels.

Air Tours

It is difficult to appreciate the reef and the setting of reef together with the coastline of beaches and rainforests unless you see it from above. **GBR Helicopters** (Cairns Airport, tel. 07/4081-8888, www.gbrhelicopters.com.au) offers aerial tours. Whether you simply want a 10-minute thrill to see Cairns and its surroundings ($159 pp), or you want to indulge in a 60-minute reef and rainforest extravaganza ($599 pp), this is undoubtedly the most thrilling way to appreciate this unique environment.

To see the surroundings a little more tranquilly and slowly than in a helicopter, why not try a hot air balloon? **Hot Air** (tel. 07/4039-9900, www.hotair.com.au, prices from $235 adult, $160 child) offers pickups from Cairns, Palm Cove, and Port Douglas, and depending on where the wind takes you, you'll float above Cairns, the Atherton Tablelands, Kuranda, and the reef.

ENTERTAINMENT AND EVENTS

Nightlife

A party and live music venue, **Gilligan's Nightclub** (57-89 Grafton St., tel. 07/4040-2777, www.thegspotcairns.com), also known as The G Spot, is one of Cairns's biggest and most popular nightspots for the young and young at heart. The lineup of DJs and live bands changes daily, offering anything from electro to retro, from techno to lounge. The cover charge varies with events, but it's free if you are staying in the hostel.

The Woolshed (24 Shields St., Cairns, tel. 07/4031-6304, www.thewoolshed.com.au, Sun.-Thurs. 7pm-3am, Fri.-Sat. 7pm-5am, cover charge varies) is backpacker party heaven. This large venue parties through the night with weekly events that include bikini competitions, wet T-shirt competitions, trivia contests, dance offs, and more.

If you are a bit of a gambler or sports fanatic, then **Reef Hotel Casino** (35-41 Wharf St., Cairns, tel. 07/4030-8888, www.reefcasino.com.au) is a great place to spend a couple of hours. You'll find this complex underneath the iconic dome on Cairns's skyline, where numerous gaming tables offer up blackjack, roulette, and even a local variant called Reef Routine. The Casino Sport Arena Bar there upstairs has a dozen or so TV screens, including reportedly the largest LED screen in Queensland, showing games going on live all across the globe.

Vibe Bar & Lounge (39-49 Lake St., Cairns, tel. 07/4052-1494, www.vibebarcairns.com, Wed. 11am-midnight, Thurs. 11am-1am, Fri. 11am-3am, Sat. 5pm-3am, Sun. 5pm-1am, no cover) is a relaxed bar and lounge with comfortable couches and small tables. Open for lunch and dinner, it has separate rooms available for hire for parties. On weekends, DJs invite you to the dance floor from 10pm, offering a variety of lounge and dance music.

Festivals and Events

Cairns Airport Ironman Cairns (www.ironman.com) is an incredible show of fitness, featuring a 1.9-kilometer swim, a 90-kilometer bike course, followed by a 21.1-kilometer run. You can either take part or simply watch as the athletes compete. The event usually takes place in early June.

The **Cairns Blues Festival** (www.cairnsbluesfestival.com.au) is an annual weekend event usually held in mid- to late June. It brings together Australian bands in a number of venues.

Cairns Indigenous Art Fair (www.ciaf.com.au) was started in 2009 to showcase Aboriginal arts and cultures. The three-day event, usually held at the end of July, is a great opportunity to learn about the local peoples' art, buy some examples yourself, or simply marvel at the exhibits.

Cairns Festival (www.cairns.qld.gov.au/festival) was started back in 1961 and is a weeklong annual community event usually held in early September. It starts with a Grand Parade, with floats making their way down the Esplanade, followed by fireworks on the first evening. Throughout the week special children's programs take place, and there are live performers and concerts, arts and crafts, and sporting events. The finale is the Parade of Lights the following weekend, with the entire community pitching in.

SHOPPING

Being the largest city in northern Queensland, Cairns has all the shops one needs. The shops along the Esplanade and the city's center are often tourism focused, but with a handful of nice art and picture galleries and specialist stores. Along Spence Street at the corner of Abbott Street you'll find higher end stores, and both Abbott Street and Lake Street offer stores covering all necessities. Due to the sunny location you'll find plenty of beachwear and accessories, plus vacation-related offerings, from kids' beach toys to underwater cameras. Bear in mind, though, that while Cairns is the largest city in the area, it is still a relatively compact city, so if you need anything specialized, it might be best to buy it in Sydney.

Shopping Center

Cairns Central (1-21 McLeod St., tel. 07/4041-4111, www.cairnscentral.com.au, Mon.-Sat. 9am-5:30pm, Thurs. until 9pm, Sun. 10:30am-4pm) is the region's largest mall, offering all the Australian high street fashion shops, such as Sportsgirl, Forever New, and Sussan; department stores such as the Australian favorite Myers and budget shop Target; general stores ranging from books and toys to sports equipment to jewelry; and a supermarket.

Art Galleries

The Red Chair Gallery (70 Abbott St., opposite Cairns Library, tel. 04/1965-7553, Mon. 10am-8pm, Wed.-Thurs. 10am-4pm, Fri. 10am-8:30pm, Sat. 10am-9pm) may look a little dilapidated from the outside, but it houses an eclectic mix of local art, drawings, prints, and gifts from over 30 local artists at reasonable prices.

If you like photography but your efforts to capture the incredible local countryside don't quite cut it, try **Michael Seebeck** (85/87 Esplanade, tel. 07/4041-5353, http://michaelseebeck.com, Mon.-Fri. 5pm-9pm, Sat.-Sun. noon-9pm), whose photographs are simply stunning.

For superb examples of Aboriginal artwork, mostly paintings, check out **Doongal Gallery** (49 The Esplanade, tel. 07/4093-9999, www.doongal.com.au, daily 10am-5pm).

Specialty Shops

For good quality and honest advice on the local gemstone, opal, try **Evert Opals & Fine Jewellery** (26 Abbotts St., tel. 07/4051-2576, Mon.-Sat. 9am-10pm), and remember that you can shop tax free.

For local fresh produce, you cannot go wrong with **Rusty's Markets** (57-89 Grafton St., Fri.-Sat. 5am-6pm, Sun. 5am-3pm).

For clothes, check out **Annie's** (Boland's Centre, 14 Spence St.), selling colorful ladies fashion; **Tommy Bahama** (4 Spence St.) for tropical beach clothes just right for the location; **DFS Galleria** (Spence St., next to the Cairns Post building, daily noon-8pm), where Gucci nestles next to Louis Vuitton and major designer brands are on sale tax free for that special treat.

If you need a souvenir of the local sports—an AFL or rugby T-shirt—then head for **Canterbury Sports** (Boland's Centre, corner Lake St. and Spence St., tel. 07/4031-4783, daily 10am-6pm, Sat. to 8pm), where all sorts of sporting articles are on display.

Should you wish to take underwater photos or need some extra camera accessories to get the most out of the stunning scenery, then go to **Calypso Reef Imagery Centre** (next to Reef Fleet Terminal, 1 Spence St., tel. 07/4041-5581, http://calypsoproductions.com.au, daily 7am-11am and 2:30pm-7pm), where you can rent cameras or buy underwater housing for existing cameras and get all sorts of photographic accessories.

ACCOMMODATIONS

Cairns has three quite distinct accommodation areas: the luxury five-star hotels tend to be near the Reef Fleet Terminal on the west side of the city center, the midrange hotels are on or near the Esplanade in either the first or second row of streets, while the backpacker accommodations and budget stays are mostly located centrally along Sheridan Street and also slightly farther outside the center.

Under $100

Gilligan's Backpackers Hotel & Resort (57-89 Grafton St., tel. 07/4041-6566, www.gilligans.com.au, bed in six-bed dorm from $29 per night, twin room up to $129), slap-bang in the center of the city, is not a place to stay the night, but to party the night away. Yes, it is a hostel, but it is legendary for its parties and facilities. Most rooms are dorm rooms with four or more beds, fully equipped with en suite bathroom and air-conditioning, and there are even private twin rooms; linens are provided. Deluxe rooms come with TVs and refrigerators, and some have private balconies. But mostly what Gilligan's offers is a live concert every night, along with karaoke competitions, foam parties, jelly wrestling, the chance to bungee jump within the resort, a large pool, and an even larger bar.

On the outskirts of Cairns, the ★ **Cairns Coconut Holiday Resort** (23-51 Anderson Rd., Woree, tel. 07/4054-6644, www.coconut.com.au) is a large family resort with the emphasis on family. Playgrounds, water fun, and children's activities rule the day, and the resort is so large that it offers cabins and villas in all sizes to suit families of any number. Accommodations are in cabins, all with cooking facilities, bathrooms, lounges, dining facilities, TVs, and outdoor seating; small cabins sleeping up to four start at $85, and larger villas sleeping up to eight by the lagoon pool are around $260. Activities include, but are not limited to, various pools and playgrounds, outdoor movies, snorkeling lessons, tennis, mini golf, barbecue areas, and beach volleyball. The resort offers a courtesy bus into the city and a tour desk. If you have a family and want to enjoy time out rather than "just" traveling and sightseeing, and you need to keep younger kids happy while trying to stick to a budget, this is the place for you.

Cairns Holiday Park (12-30 Little St., tel. 07/4051-1467, www.cairnsholidaypark.com.au, campsites from $15 pp, en suite cabins from $77 for two) is a lovely campground just outside the city limits, minutes away from the airport and the Flecker Botanical Gardens, with easy access to the beaches in the north of Cairns. The campground has a pool, open-air camp kitchen, TV room, tour desk, laundry facilities, regular activities, free Wi-Fi and Internet room, and a free vegetable garden. Overall it's a very pleasant place to camp, with easy access to the city and surrounding sights. Cabins with private bathrooms come complete with small fridge, coffee-making facilities, indoor and outdoor seating area, and double bed; linens are provided.

Globetrotters International (154-156 Lake St., corner Upward St., tel. 04/1974-4431, www.globetrottersinternational.com.au, dorm bed $26, private single room with bathroom and kitchen $60) is a small and relatively quiet hostel (compared to, for example, Gilligan's), offering comfortable and clean bedrooms, ranging from single rooms to four-bed dorms. Amenities include a small pool, free Wi-Fi, free movies and book exchange, and several communal areas. It's a mere 50 meters from the Esplanade.

Travellers Oasis (8 Scott St., tel. 1800/621-353, http://travellersoasis.com.au, dorm bed $26, private deluxe double $74 per room) is more a large bed-and-breakfast than a hostel. Friendly, colorful, and clean, this homey hostel offers a small pool, two shared kitchens, TV room, and free Wi-Fi, and the deluxe room even comes with a balcony and plasma TV, although not a private bathroom. Travellers Oasis is on the main road through Cairns, handy for city and airport and all facilities.

$100-150

★ **The Hotel Cairns** (corner Abbott St. and Florence St., tel. 07/4051-6188, www.thehotelcairns.com, from $100) is a lovely little hotel, an airy white building with shutters and palm- and bamboo-fringed gardens, in the tropical plantation style. A little shabby around the edges, with the decor in the hallways and corners of the bathrooms wearing a little thin, the rooms, however, are lovely and light, with stylish understated decor, cool tiles, TV, desk, balcony, and coffeemaker. The pool is small but nevertheless inviting, and you can rent a little car from the reception for a mere $45 for 24 hours, perfect for exploring the surroundings.

Just slightly away from the hustle and bustle of the city center, the **Rydges Esplanade** (209-217 Abbott St., tel. 07/4044-9000, www.rydges.com/esplanade, from $105) provides a comfortable stay, with all the amenities, but without too many frills. The rooms are comfortable and spacious, and amenities include a pool with a swim-up bar and gym facilities shared with the apartments next door. Rooms higher up have lovely views across either the city or the sea. A mere 10 minutes from the center and the airport on either side, the location is great for exploring the surroundings of Cairns.

Ibis Styles Cairns (10 Florence St., tel. 07/4053-8800, www.ibis.com/Cairns, from $104, family rooms and Loft Room $134) is a simple but comfortable hotel near the Esplanade, the marina, and the shops. Rooms are decorated in modern browns and greens, complementing the plantation-style building and palm-fringed pool; some rooms have private balconies. Family rooms have a queen bed and three singles, and the chic Loft Room, set on two levels, sleeps two and has a large private balcony and hot tub.

Over $150

★ **Novotel Cairns Oasis Resort** (122 Lake St., tel. 07/4080-1888, www.novotelcairnsresort.com.au, from $154) immediately gives you that vacation feeling, even though it is not on the beach. The pool area is palm-fringed, with a beach bar in Balinese style, and you can imagine spending a day by the pool rather than dashing out every day on trips. The amenities are basic, but all there: an Internet lounge, travel desk, and a restaurant and bar. Four buildings are set around the pool, some with pool and sea view, others facing the city; the rooms are not huge but perfectly adequate, including desks and coffee-making facilities. Centrally located, it is minutes from the Esplanade and the central shops and sights. Reef Terminal is around a 10-minute walk away.

Shangri-La The Marina, Cairns (1 Pier Point Rd., tel. 07/4031-1411, www.shangri-la.com/cairns, from $175) has undoubtedly the best location in Cairns, right at the end of the pier overlooking the marina, cruise terminal, and the end of the Esplanade. The sea-facing rooms overlook the Trinity Inlet, and the hotel is surrounded by restaurants and bars, making eating out very easy. While some Shangri-La hotels around the world are opulent and overly luxurious, this one is more understated, with the typical-for-Cairns simple furnishings and decor keeping things unpretentious and cool. You'll still see all the little luxuries and details to attention expected from a Shangri-La. All rooms have private balconies, and amenities include a fully equipped gym, a stunning pool with separate kids' pool, a Jacuzzi, a sauna, and a small mall.

The ★ **Pullman Reef Hotel Casino** (35-41 Wharf St., tel. 07/4030-8888, www.reefcasino.com.au, from $209) is a five-star hotel with a distinctive dome rising above the skyline, making it easy to find. Tasteful decor in a tropical style mixed with understated elegance, as well as the slight anonymity that often accompanies luxury hotels, makes this a very comfortable place to stay. More a city hotel rather than a resort where you might want to linger for the day, this is a hub that is a few minutes' walk away from the cruise terminal, the Esplanade, and the city center, making it perfect for a brief stay in Cairns when you are out all day exploring. Four restaurants, bars, a nightclub, the casino, and the Cairns Zoom & Wildlife Dome are all under the same roof, making entertainment and eating easy.

Hilton Cairns Hotel (34 Esplanade, tel. 07/4050-2000, www3.hilton.com, from $152) is a stylish, luxurious hotel that balances city hotel with resort thanks to elegant and spacious rooms and an inviting outdoor pool (in addition to the indoor one), with wooden decks and comfortable sun loungers. A business and leisure hotel, it has a range of facilities that make life very convenient, from a fully equipped business center to a florist and convenience store, from foreign currency exchange to special family services, including babysitting and cribs. Just around the corner from Reef Fleet Terminal, it's ideally located for day trips to the reef. Unlike many hotels, the Hilton Cairns is also fully equipped to accommodate guests with mobility problems.

FOOD

Cairns overall has a food scene that is more convenience oriented, with plenty of casual restaurants allowing travelers who have been out and about all day to relax and grab a bite to eat without having to dress up or sit through a long degustation menu. Aimed at the young crowd, emphasis is on a fun and beachy atmosphere, especially along the Esplanade. That said, there are a handful of excellent fine-dining restaurants for special nights.

★ **Ochre** (43 Shields St., tel. 07/4051-0100, Mon.-Fri. noon-3pm and 6pm-9:30pm, Sat.-Sun. 6pm-9:30pm, mains $35) offers modern Australian cuisine with an Asian twist. The restaurant is the brainchild of chef Craig Squire. After stints in some of Europe's finest restaurants, he opened Ochre to serve food that is locally sourced, healthy, and sustainable. Australian wood, ochre-toned walls, and tiled floors make for a welcoming and unpretentious setting. The staff is knowledgeable and friendly, and the food is quite simply the best in Cairns. The Queensland Bugs (small crayfish, not creepy-crawlies) are award-winning, and the crocodile and prawns, lightly fried with pickled Vietnamese vegetables and spicy sambal, are divine. All ingredients are Australian, the majority from Queensland; all are fresh and prepared to the highest standard. To save you making a decision on what to choose, there is the six-course taster menu ($90), which can also be paired with a selection of Australian wines ($130). Don't miss it.

Built right next to and partially on the water, at the end of Marina Point, is ★ **Salt House** (6/2 Pierpoint Rd., tel. 07/4041-7733, Mon.-Fri. noon-midnight, Fri.-Sat. 7am-2am, Sun. 7am-midnight, mains $35). The menu offers many regional specialties, such as the fish of the day, locally reared lamb, and a lovely Australian cheese platter, as well as a decent steak. It also has a mix of Asian and Italian-inspired dishes, such as a delicious sesame-encrusted tuna tataki starter and pappardelle with smoked chicken and pancetta for a main dish. Make sure you leave some space for the absolutely decadent dessert of macadamia baklava with local fresh figs and cinnamon ice cream.

Grill'd (77 Esplanade, tel. 07/4041-4200, daily 11am-9:30pm, $10) is an Australian burger outlet that prides itself on serving healthy burgers. Using only fresh, locally sourced ingredients, the aim is to serve nutritious and delicious meals. Grass-fed free-range beef, lamb, and chicken burgers are filled with anything from beetroot to carrots, served with chutneys and sauces and an optional side of crispy thick fries. Try the grilled chicken burger with beetroot; it's a great burger without the guilt.

Al Porto Café (1 Spence St., tel. 07/4031-6222, www.alportocairns.com, daily 6:30am-2:30pm) is right next to the Reef Fleet Terminal, where all the ferries to the reef leave in the morning. Al Porto not only brews a decent cup of coffee but also sells things for your day out: sandwiches ($7), cookies (try the gluten-free almond biscotti, $2.50), and small bottles of water ($3.50). It also has many of the other last-minute things you may need, such as sunscreen, hats, mosquito repellent, and all sorts of other nibbles and drinks.

Rattle & Hum (65/67 The Esplanade, tel. 07/4031-3011, www.rattlehum.com.au, mains $14-30) is a buzzing saloon-style place, a typical Aussie pub, large and unpretentious, where good food and drink doesn't cost much and you don't need white tablecloths either. Its iconic emu peers back at you from napkins, coasters, and menus, and there's even one standing outside the entrance. A large wood-fired pizza oven sits right next to the front door, giving you a clue as to their specialty, but there also are flame-grilled burgers, fried calamari, steak sandwiches, pasta, and good-for-you salads. And for dessert: death by chocolate. Right on the bustling Esplanade, this place is always hopping, and whether you sit inside or out, it's a large place with enough space for everybody, and you are in the middle of it all.

★ **Perrotta's at the Gallery** (38 Abbott St., tel. 07/4031-5899, daily 8:30am-11pm, breakfast $18, dinner mains $37) is a lovely restaurant café that is open for breakfast through to dinner. Right next to the entrance of the Cairns Regional Gallery, the restaurant continues the arty theme with trendy metal chairs and tables on a wooden deck as well as inside. The varied menu covers breakfast until 3pm, with tempting morsels such as buttermilk ricotta hotcakes or baked eggs with chickpeas and ciabatta toast. For dinner you can order the fantastic porcini dry-rubbed angus sirloin with Tuscan potatoes.

Tamarind (35-41 Wharf St., Reef Hotel Casino, tel. 07/4030-8888, daily 6pm-10pm, mains $40) is a chic, contemporary restaurant that sets a romantic mood with candlelit ambience. Woven lampshades and bamboo-floor lights, together with exotic flower arrangements and a Bali-esque entrance, set the scene. The food is unashamedly pan-Asian, but using local ingredients: try the excellent chili butter north Queensland tiger prawns or the Penang curry duck. Tamarind also offers a superb five-course taster menu for $90 per person, giving you a chance to work your way through the favorite dishes.

INFORMATION AND SERVICES

Tourist Information

The **Cairns & Tropical North Visitor Information Centre** (51 Esplanade, tel. 07/4051-3588, www.cairnsgreatbarrierreef.org.au, Mon.-Fri. 8:30am-6pm, Sat.-Sun. 10am-6pm) is worth visiting just to see its pretty heritage building, but the visitors center is also a treasure trove of brochures, maps, tours, and ideas of what to see and do in the vicinity. The staff is friendly and extremely knowledgeable, helping you choose the right excursions for what you want and booking it all right there.

Every hotel has a travel desk and a wall full of brochures about trips and cruises. Most of the time you can book them yourself right there in the lobby.

For savings on many attractions, accommodations, restaurants, and basics, pick up a "Savings Passport" in many public places, or download coupons directly from the website at www.adlinkmedia.com.au.

Hospitals, Emergency Services, and Pharmacies

Cairns is well-equipped with emergency facilities. For emergencies the best place to go is **The Cairns Base Hospital** (165-171 The Esplanade, tel. 07/4226-0000). The **Cairns**

24 Hour Medical Centre (corner Grafton and Florence St., tel. 07/4052-1119, www.thedoctors.com.au) handles general emergencies for vacationers and also provides dive medicals to assess your fitness for diving. For general inquiries, try **Cairns Day Surgery** (156-160 Grafton St., tel. 07/4051-5454, Mon.-Thurs. 6:30am-6:30pm, Fri. 6:30am-4pm) or **Cairns Family Medical Centre** (120-124 Mulgrave Rd., tel. 07/4051-2755, Mon.-Fri. 7am-6pm).

Medical centers and hospitals often have smaller pharmacies attached to them, but there are also plenty in the town center. **Cairns Apothecary Pharmacy** (156-160 Grafton St., tel. 07/4031-8411, daily 7am-11pm) is the one with the longest hours.

Money

In Cairns the main banks are **Bank of Queensland** (27 Lake St., tel. 07/4048-0530) and **ANZ** (Shop 41 in Cairns Central Shopping Center, 1 McLeod St., tel. 13/13-14). Hours are generally weekdays 10am-4pm. To exchange currency, you can go to the banks, the larger branches of which all offer exchange rates; to one of the many currency exchange shops along the Esplanade; or to the larger hotels.

Postal Services

The **Cairns Central Post Shop** is at 1-21 McLeod Street (Mon.-Fri. 9am-5pm, Sat. 9am-12:30pm). Additional offices can be found at 38 Sheridan Street (Mon.-Fri. 8:30am-5:30pm), 58 Lake Street (Mon.-Thurs. 6:30am-6pm, Fri. 6am-6:30pm, Sat. 7am-4pm), and 115 Abbott Street (daily 9am-9pm). The phone number for all regional post offices is tel. 13/13-18.

Internet and Telephone

Cell phones' compatibility with U.S. phones can be a problem, but even if yours is working abroad, the costs of international roaming can easily spiral out of control. If you feel you will absolutely need a cell phone, stop off at the Optus shop in the airport, or any mobile phone shop in the city, and get yourself a local SIM card or an Australian starter kit. Telstra, Optus, and Vodafone all have prepaid mobile systems that are easily available and quick to set up. The kits start from around $30. Try **Optus** (corner McLeod St. and Spence St., shop 136, Cairns Central Shopping Centre, tel. 07/4051-2233) or **Telstra** (shop 105, Cairns Central Shopping Centre, tel. 07/4031-7000); both are open daily 9am-5:30pm. For international phone cards, try **The Good Guys** (285 Mulgrave Rd., tel. 07/4046-7900, daily 9:30am-5:30pm).

Internet and Wi-Fi are widely available, although sadly, in most hotels you still have to pay for Wi-Fi/Internet access. Often you can get free access in the lobby, but to be safe, allow for Internet fees in your budget. That said, the majority of backpacker hostels, such as Globetrotters International, usually offer free Wi-Fi and access to laptops. Many cafés and fast food chains, such as McDonald's, offer free Wi-Fi hot spots throughout the city, and the Esplanade has recently launched several free Wi-Fi hot spots near its lagoon and adjoining seating areas.

GETTING THERE

Air

The flight from Sydney to **Cairns International Airport** (CNS, Airport Ave., tel. 07/4080-6703, www.cairnsairport.com) is just over three hours, so this is the chosen way to arrive in this northern part of the country. Budget airlines such as Tigerair charge from $70 one way without check-in baggage (an extra $24 gets you an allowance of 20 kg) and are a quick, cheap, and comfortable way to travel between the cities. Other airlines flying between Sydney and Cairns are Jetstar (fares from $149 one way, without check-in baggage); Virgin Australia (from $169 one way), and Qantas (from $389 one way), and it is easy to connect to Cairns from most larger cities in Australia and along the Queensland coast.

Cairns Airport, a mere seven-minute drive from the city center, is easy to maneuver, with one international and one domestic terminal connected by a five-minute walkway. Several car-rental companies have offices at the domestic terminal. A taxi into Cairns city center charges around $25. A bus right outside arrivals goes straight to the city center but also stops at hotels along the way, as long as these have been booked by passengers (**Sun Palm Transport Group,** tel. 07/4087-2900, www.sunpalmtransport.com.au). The fare to the city center is adult $14, child $7, and prebooking is required; the schedule coincides with arrivals of flights. You can take the bus as far as Port Douglas, a 30-minute trip (one-way $40 per adult). Many hotels can arrange airport pickups for you.

If you are driving, head out of the airport along the only road, and turn left at the intersection with Sheridan Street. Most hotels will require a left turn off Sheridan Street toward the Esplanade.

Rail

CountryLink trains (tel. 13/22-32, www.countrylink.info) run a daily service from Sydney's Central Station to Brisbane's Roma Street station, from where **Queensland Rail** (tel. 07/3235-2222, www.queenslandrail.com.au) can connect you to Cairns. Leaving Sydney in the afternoon, the trip is an overnight one, arriving in Brisbane in the morning. Fares start from $92 one-way (economy seating only) and rise to $217 for a sleeper. Three times per week the **Sunlander** train between Brisbane and Cairns, a luxury all-inclusive service with fine dining and first-class accommodation options, can carry you onward. This service takes 32 hours and costs from $115 one-way (seating only) to $366 (single or twin sleeping berths). Twice a week the **Tilt Train** also runs a service between Brisbane and Cairns, a 25-hour journey without sleepers; fares start at $215 for a discount fare and $359 for a standard, more flexible fare. There is a Motorail (take your car) option on the Sunlander train, but not between Sydney and Brisbane. Cairns Railway Station is off Spence Street, close to the city center.

Bus

Greyhound (tel. 1300/473-946, www.greyhound.com.au) provides several daily services to Cairns from Sydney's Central Station and the international and domestic terminals at the Sydney airport, changing coaches in Brisbane. With a Mini Traveller Pass ($410), you can hop on and off wherever you want to, although travel is allowed in only one direction. The pass is valid for 90 days, and the trip from Sydney to Cairns via Brisbane takes around 50 hours, dropping you off at the corner of Abbott and Shields Streets in the city center. Alternatively, you can use the coaches between cities along the coast, such as Townsville and Cairns; there are usually three or four daily departures. The trip between Townsville and Cairns would take around 5.5 hours, with fares starting at $55 one way.

Car

Cairns is a long way from anywhere, so unless you are on an extended vacation, it is more likely that you will be renting a car from the airport or in the city rather than driving up from the south. In the arrivals hall of the airport, all the major car-rental firms are represented, but convenience such as that comes at a price. It is usually a lot cheaper to rent a car from a firm in the city and use their free shuttle service to pick you up at the airport and take you to their offices. **East Coast Car Rental** (tel. 07/4031-6055, www.eastcoastcarrentals.com.au), for example, is a reliable company that is positioned on Sheridan Street and sends a shuttle bus to pick you up at the airport free of charge. All you need is a current driver's license, your passport, and a valid credit card and you're off. A small four-door car costs around $120 per week, plus insurance and gas, but special deals are to be had if you book early enough or are flexible with the various options.

Should you wish to hire something a little larger to go touring in, then try **Jucy** (55 Dutton St., Portsmith, tel. 1800/150-850, www.jucy.com.au), an established camper-van rental company that has branches all across Australia. A relatively large camper van that sleeps up to four in two double beds, complete with gas cooker, refrigerator, and DVD player, costs around $80 per day. For a luxury six-berth camper van with showers and toilet, three double beds, kitchen, and water tank, you will be looking at around $220 per day, although prices vary depending on number of drivers, mileage allowance, insurance, age of vehicle, etc.

Driving in northern Queensland itself is easy, but roads are limited. The Bruce Highway winds its way all the way up the east coast from Sydney to north of Cairns, and turnoffs become less and less frequent the farther north you get. While there are plenty of forests and wetlands, the roads are paved in the vast majority of cases, so driving is relatively smooth. That said, the north is prone to serious flash-flooding, and you will need to be aware of daily forecasts during the wet season, which is during Australia's summer months, roughly between December and April. If in doubt, check the website of the **Bureau of Meteorology** (www.bom.gov.au/qld/forecasts) for warnings.

If you are time-rich and would like to drive all the way up the eastern coast, make sure you appreciate the vast distances involved in driving in Australia. Sydney to Cairns along the Bruce Highway is around 2,607 kilometers, which without stopping is estimated to take around 34 hours in good road conditions. From the southern tip of the Great Barrier Reef, Bundaberg to Cairns is around 1,357 kilometers (17 hours); from Townsville to Cairns it's around 348 kilometers, taking roughly 4.5 hours.

GETTING AROUND

Getting around Cairns is easy. Not only is the city center compact and walkable, but the **Sunbus** (www.sunbus.com.au) has several routes that take you from the city center to many of the attractions. It is easiest to catch a bus from The Pier, from Abbott Street or Spence Street. Check the website for routes and schedules. Fares depend on distance: A single adult fare within zone 1, which covers the city to the outskirts, is $2.30, or a daily ticket within that zone for unlimited trips is $4.60.

Although some beaches, such as Yorkeys Knob, can be reached by bus, for other attractions it is usually easier to get a taxi (city center to Skyrail approximately $25). The region is a tourist hub, and most visitors do not have access to transport, so the vast majority of tours, attractions, and activities offer a pickup and drop-off service from your hotel, usually at a competitive extra fee.

The easiest way to get around is by driving, if you are planning to go exploring and will get use out of the car. Some of the beaches around Cairns, such as Yorkeys Knob, Machans, and Holloways, are accessible by bus (routes 112, 113, and 120), but others are off the public transport route or simply too far out. However, if you are going to go on organized tours and trips, then a car would simply be a waste of funds. I would suggest to organize trips with pickup and drop-off at the hotel, and then maybe have a car for a couple of days to get to the more secluded places.

Beaches Around Cairns

While Cairns itself does not have a beach, outside the city limits there is quite a selection of sandy beaches. Bramston Beach is the only one featured south of Cairns, as the distances involved are longer than if you search farther north. The one with the best vacation feeling to it out of this selection is Trinity Beach, with its beach bars and walkable esplanade, but the best resort-type beach is undoubtedly Palm Cove, with its small village vibe, relaxed atmosphere, and a lovely beach literally on the doorstep of the hotels and restaurants.

BRAMSTON BEACH

Just 60 kilometers south of Cairns, 18 kilometers off Bruce Highway through cassowary country, the beach you'll find is farther off the beaten track than the distance from Cairns suggests. This is a purely residential setting, with one campground, the **Bramston Beach Caravan Park and Camping Ground** (96 Evans Rd., Bramston Beach, tel. 07/4067-4121, non-powered site 1-2 adults $20). At the time of writing, the lone motel was closed and up for sale, and there is not much in terms of man-made amusement.

A tiny café-cum-convenience store, **Bramston Beach Café & Store** (67 Evans Rd., Bramston Beach, tel. 07/4067-4129) has only sporadic opening hours, so check before you rely on it. The beach therefore is peaceful and relaxed, flanked by greenery that reportedly gets taken over by laughing kookaburras every sunset hour. Bring your own entertainment, food and drink, and a tent or camper van if you want to spend the night.

YORKEYS KNOB

Heading north past Cairns International Airport, signposts direct you first to **Machans Beach,** then, one exit farther on, to **Holloways Beach.** Machans Beach, a 10-minute drive from Cairns, neighbors protected Redden Island (an excellent birding location). Not strictly speaking a beach, it's more a residential suburb, albeit with seafront views. There's a small bistro, **O'Sheas Restaurant** (169 O'Shea Esplanade, tel. 07/4055-0010, Wed.-Fri. 4pm-late, Sat.-Sun. noon-late), and that is pretty much it.

Drive on to Holloways Beach, a couple of minutes down the main road, which is a secluded tropical beach. During the high season, the beach is protected from box jellyfish through "stinger nets," and there are lifeguards on duty during busy times. Although the suburb is mostly residential, there are some smaller beachside cafés and bars, and some accommodations offer activities and entertainment in-house.

The best beach in close proximity to Cairns, though, is **Yorkeys Knob.** An upmarket suburb of Cairns, around 15 minutes north of Cairns, it has a marina and boating club, a small local shopping center, golf, and beach activities. The 18-hole, par-70 **Half Moon Bay Golf Club** (66 Wattle St., Yorkeys Knob, tel. 07/4055-7884, http://halfmoonbaygolf.com.au) also offers accommodations. The beach is famous for **kite surfing:** try **Kite Rite Australia** (Shop 9, 471 Varley St., tel. 07/4055-7918, www.kiterite.com.au, 1-hour kite lesson $79, 2-day certificate course $499) for lessons.

Incidentally, the name Yorkeys Knob is quite legendary, with several reports being utterly unconfirmed: One story claims it was Yorkshire man George Lawson who named the "knob," the promontory jutting out from the bay; another says it was named after a Norwegian fisherman's nickname.

Accommodations

At Holloways Beach, the four-star **Australis Cairns Beach Resort** (129 Oleander St., Holloways Beach, tel. 07/4037-0400, www.australishotels.com.au, apartments from $150) is a family-oriented resort offering apartments sleeping up to four people, not even one minute from the beach. All rooms have modern furnishings, tiled floors, and en suite baths and are equipped with kitchenettes, coffeemakers, fridge, microwave, and toaster. The resort has a pool with sun loungers, barbecue facilities, and a tour desk where you can book tours to all attractions in and around Cairns.

At Yorkeys Knob, most accommodations are in the form of vacation-rental apartments. Some of the best can be found at the **Golden Sands Beachfront Apartment Resort** (12-14 Deauville Close, Yorkeys Knob, tel. 07/4055-8033, www.goldensandsresort.com.au, one- to two-bedroom apartments from $145 per night), a small four-story modern resort with a pool and all facilities in the rooms. Airy rooms in white have plenty of wicker furniture, tiled floors, and a simple but stylish decor. Another great option is **Half Moon Bay Beach Resort** (101-103 Wattle St., Yorkeys Knob, tel. 07/4055-8059, www.halfmoonbayresort.com.au, apartments from $125 per night), part of the golf club. It's a modern, two-story block fringed with palms and lush gardens, with 12 self-contained one-bedroom apartments overlooking either the saltwater pool or the gardens, with all the facilities and a restaurant accessible via the golf club. The apartments have a small bedroom and a larger living area with a comfy sofa, wicker chairs and tables, TV, private balcony, and off-street parking.

TRINITY BEACH

Together with Trinity Park a few hundred yards farther south, Trinity Beach, a 20-minute drive north of Cairns, is an award-winning beach with a lovely beachfront, the **Vasey Esplanade,** which invites families to walk and play under its almond trees. Plenty of small restaurants and bars line the quiet road, and the atmosphere is distinctly one of beach vacation. It's not overdeveloped with high-rises, but there are plenty of lower-key resorts and apartments, situated among gardens alongside the beach.

At each end of Trinity Beach are twin headlands. These are popular spots for fishing or walking or simply sitting and taking in the tropical mornings and evenings, and views stretch to Double Island with its two humps, off the coast of Palm Cove a little farther north. Activity wise, there is not anything available here that isn't available at any of the other travel hot spots along the coast, but if it's small-time relaxation and quiet you're after, you might want to check this beach out.

Accommodations and Food

Stay at **Vue** (78-86 Moore St., tel. 07/4058-4400, www.vuetrinitybeach.com.au, one-bedroom apartment from $225 per night, three night minimum stay), a sleek apartment block with a huge pool overlooking the beach and backing onto Vasey Esplanade. The luxury accommodations range from one-bed to four-bed apartments, all with large balconies, kitchens, laundry, free Wi-Fi, large plasma screens and DVD, walk-in showers, and bathtubs. The floors are tiled to keep things cool, and the decor is clean and modern with lovely accents of color and pieces of art.

Set on a large corner plot, **L'Unico Trattoria** (75 Vasey Esplanade, tel. 07/4057-8855, www.lunico.com.au, daily noon-9:30pm, mains $25) offers stunning views along the esplanade and across to the beach and the Coral Sea. The food is modern Italian with plenty of antipasti, pasta, *pesci* (fish) and *carne* (meat), made using local fresh ingredients. Try the pasta with the local "bugs" (crayfish) in a garlic chili sauce.

All the restaurants along Vasey Esplanade offer a takeout service, catering to the many apartment dwellers here on vacation.

PALM COVE

It was, of course, Captain Cook who was the first European "tourist" on this coast and also named the nearby Sweet Creek, for the fresh water it proffered his parched crew. But the first proper tourists were Adam Hamilton and Tom Veivers, who bought the land alongside the beautiful bay of Palm Cove and built a hut to be used by their extended families as a vacation home. That was back in 1918. The first road was not built until the 1930s, and Palm Cove's claim as a great vacation spot finally took off when the Veivers family sold a plot in the late 1930s, and the first resorts were slowly built for those seeking respite from a life that cannot have been easy in this region in those days.

In more recent years, Palm Cove was voted to be among the top 10 beaches in Australia, and the small village has never looked back. Now a premier destination for visitors, Palm Cove has also added the accolades of "Queensland's Cleanest Beach" and "Far North Queensland's Friendliest Beach" to its name. A half-hour drive north, some 27 kilometers from Cairns, the village is nestled between the Coral Sea and the rainforest. Although small, it has a myriad of attractions, activities, and accommodations, yet manages to maintain its laid-back beach village atmosphere. The main drag, **Williams Esplanade,** is lined with majestic white tea trees, or melaleuca trees, which grow up to a height of 40 meters, with a girth of up to 10 meters. These trees not only add grandeur to the already lovely esplanade but are also still the level of buildings, as no buildings are allowed to be built higher than the tallest melaleuca tree, keeping the village's charm intact.

Sights

Located on six hectares of tropical landscaped gardens, **Cairns Tropical Zoo** (Captain Cook Hwy., Clifton Beach, tel. 07/4055-3669, www.cairnstropicalzoo.com.au, daily 8:30am-4pm, adult $33, child 4-15 $16.50) has the largest, most comprehensive wildlife collection in tropical north Queensland, with snake displays, monitor lizards, komodo dragons, lizards, crocodiles (saltwater and freshwater varieties), cockatoos, parrots, emus, cassowaries, koalas, wombats, dingoes, possums, and many more. With many of Australia's animals being nocturnal, the zoo also hosts an evening event—Cairns Night Zoo.

Cairns Night Zoo (Captain Cook Hwy., Clifton Beach, tel. 07/4055-3669, www.cairnsnightzoo.com, Mon.-Thurs. and Sat. 7pm-10pm, adult $138, child $69 including hotel transfers from Cairns) literally makes a night of it, starting off with a typical Aussie barbecue, complete with steaks, sausages, shrimp, baked potatoes, salads, and sinful desserts. Then it's off on a guided walk through the zoo by torchlight to spot the creatures of the night. Get up close to the possums and kangaroos,

Double Island, off the beach at Palm Cove

and examine the amazing southern hemisphere constellations in the clear sky, all while enjoying a cold beer or wine. The guides are knowledgeable, and it's an all-round enjoyable evening for the whole family. Booking in advance is essential.

Hartley's Crocodile Adventures (Captain Cook Hwy., Wangetti Beach, tel. 07/4055-3576, www.crocodileadventures.com, daily 8:30am-5pm, adult $35, child $17.50, family $87.50) is not merely a crocodile park where you can get up close to the local estuarine crocs. It's also a wildlife park where you can take a cruise on the lagoon and see other regional wildlife, such as the famous cassowary, which lives in the rainforest but is very rare to spot in the wild; watch feeding times of the crocs, cassowaries, and the cute koalas; enjoy a snake show; and even feed a crocodile yourself. A walkway leads through the forest, where you can discover the local fauna and flora, and you can attend talks to learn more about the animals and the environment.

Michaelmas Cay

Michaelmas Cay is a beautiful sand cay (a sand island on or next to a reef, pretty much a beach in the middle of the ocean) that is accessible from Palm Cove and offers great snorkeling, diving, and bird-watching, with the cay being a bird sanctuary for some 20,000 migratory seabirds. Full-day excursions are organized by **Viator** (www.viator.com, from $219 per adult, with one dive $274) and include lunch, snorkeling trips and equipment, a trip on a semisubmersible submarine, and wildlife presentations.

Double Island, off the beach at Palm Cove, is an obvious attraction, with its two humps beckoning to potential day-trippers. Alas, the lovely island is privately owned, and although there used to be a popular luxury resort on the island, the current owner has so far made no move to redevelop or reopen the facilities.

Recreation

Get picked up from your hotel in Cairns or the northern beaches and take a 14,000-foot jump with **Jump the Beach Cairns** (various locations, tel. 1800/800-840, www.jumpthebeach.com.au, tandem jump $369). You'll have over 60 seconds of free fall to enjoy either sunrise or sunset over the lovely Palm Cove beach. You have the option of a tandem or solo jump and get rewarded with either a champagne breakfast or canapés and cocktails in the evening.

Treat yourself to a spa day. Palm Cove is the spa capital of the tropical north, so book yourself in for a super-duper treatment before you get back on the plane. Try the **Angsana Spa** (1 Veivers Rd., tel. 07/4059-5529, www.angsana.com, 60-minute massage $140) or the **Salt Spa** at Peppers Beach Club & Spa (123 Williams Esplanade, tel. 07/4059-9200, www.peppers.com.au, 60-minute full-body massage $110).

Accommodations

Resorts, apartment rentals, and other accommodations are available in and near Palm Cove. Luxury boutique accommodations are provided by the lovely ★ **Reef House Boutique Resort & Spa** (99 Williams Esplanade, Palm Cove, tel. 07/4080-2600, www.reefhouse.com.au, from $149). The plantation-style 69-room hotel has a luxury colonial charm yet a relaxed, chic beach-house ambience. White timber buildings provide a perfect foil to turquoise pools and tropical gardens of fragrant frangipani, red hibiscus, and pink bougainvillea vines. Rooms are beachy in decor, with romantic mosquito nets over the beds, lots of white interspersed with fresh tropical colors, wicker furniture, tiled floors, and slatted doors and shutters. Amenities include three swimming pools, two spa pools, an award-winning day spa, and an open-air signature restaurant and bar with views of the water. This is a relaxing retreat where you can chill after a busy day full of tours.

★ **Peppers Beach Club & Spa** (123 Williams Esplanade, tel. 07/4059-9200, www.peppers.com.au, from $239) is a lovely resort that tempts anybody simply not to leave. Rooms and suites, outfitted with squashy couches and rattan furniture, all have private balconies overlooking the palm-fringed pool. There is even an entire section of suites with private access to a secluded pool, surrounded by what feels like the rainforest. The beach is a mere hop across the esplanade away. The relaxing day spa offers specialized treatments, such as hot and chilled stone treatments, Vichy treatments with exfoliation and rehydration rituals, and others just right for sun-kissed skin. Peppers also has several relaxed fine-dining restaurants directly on the doorstep.

Paradise Palms Resort & Country Club (Paradise Palms Dr., Kewarra Beach, tel. 07/4059-9999, www.paradisepalms.com.au, from $132) is not only a resort, but part of one of Australia's top 100 championship golf courses (and also one of the most picturesque). Accommodations come in form of a resort room or as apartments with one to two bedrooms, complete with kitchen. Decor is modern and comfortable, and the emphasis is on being out on the course, with packages available that combine accommodations and golf.

Villa Paradiso Apartments (111-113 Williams Esplanade, tel. 07/4059-8800, http://villaparadiso.com.au, one-bedroom apartments from $235) are right on the Esplanade overlooking the beach and offer spacious living and sleeping accommodations, featuring one to three bedrooms, with fully equipped kitchens and balconies, cots and highchairs for rental, and full wheelchair accessibility.

On the budget front is **Ellis Beach Oceanfront Bungalows** (Captain Cook Hwy., Ellis Beach, tel. 07/4055-3538, www.ellisbeach.com, camping from $32, bungalows from $95), just north of Palm Cove. Accommodation types range from unpowered tent sites at the campground (which nevertheless offers an amenities block and a kitchen with refrigerator, gas cooker, and coin-operated barbecue) to ocean-front bungalows with a deck overlooking the sea (with bathroom, TV, air conditioning, kitchenette, and linens).

Food

Palm Cove's Williams Esplanade has one restaurant snuggled up to the next. From Greek to burgers, from fish and chips to pizza, there really is something for everybody and for every occasion. One of the best restaurants is ★ **Nu Nu** (1 Veivers Rd., tel. 07/4059-1880, www.nunu.com.au, daily 11:30am-11pm, tasting menu $110 pp, with wine $175, mains $27, light snacks $10), just in front of Peppers Beach Club & Spa. The chef is an artist who uses fresh local ingredients according to the season and then mixes them up to come up with something completely new. Try the heart of palm with melon, pickled shallots, and young coconut for a fresh starter; or the delectable smoked red emperor, a local reef fish, with a peanut and papaya relish and salmon pearls all wrapped in the local beetle leaf, which is crunchy, slightly peppery, and full of flavor. The dishes are all presented beautifully and the portions are just right for the weather—light and not too much. Instead of a soup of the day, here you can get a juice of the day—ask for the orange, melon, and mint, which is perfectly refreshing.

Lime & Pepper (123 Williams Esplanade, tel. 07/4059-9200, www.peppersbeachclub-spa.com.au/dining, daily 11:30am-11pm, mains $28), literally next door to Nu Nu, is Peppers Beach Club's signature restaurant, serving up modern Australian cuisine. ★ **Il Forno** (upstairs, 111-117 Williams Esplanade, tel. 07/4059-1666, www.ilfornopalmcove.com.au, daily 5pm-9:30pm, mains $22) has great pizzas, or try **Beach Almond** (145 Williams Esplanade, tel. 07/4059-1908, www.beachalmond.com, daily 5pm-9:30pm, Sun. from noon, mains $30) for excellent Southeast Asian fare.

Apres Beach Bar & Grill (119 Williams Esplanade, tel. 07/4059-2000, www.apres-beachbar.com.au, daily 11am-9:30pm, mains $20) offers fun entertainment, live music, pub quizzes, karaoke, and easy alfresco food ranging from steak to curry, mixed with plenty of beer. Make sure to stop at the **Numi** ice cream van, usually parked by the jetty—all the ingredients are sourced locally and it's simply gorgeous ice cream.

Reef Cruises from Cairns

A wide variety of cruises are available along the Great Barrier Reef. They range from ferries taking you to purpose-built moored platforms anchored above the outer reefs, offering myriad activities, to sleek motor yachts and beautiful sailboats taking you away from the mainland. Here is a small selection, all of which conveniently leave from Cairns's Reef Fleet Terminal at the end of the Esplanade; hotel pickups are available, at approximately $16-20 per person.

With **Great Adventures** (tel. 07/4044-9944, www.greatadventures.com.au, adult $238, child $122, family $604) you cruise to a multilevel reef activity platform just off **Green Island,** a 45-minute ride away, with full bar facilities, a swimming enclosure for children, change rooms with freshwater showers, sundeck, and scuba diving facilities with a semisubmerged platform. The round-trip air-conditioned fast catamaran cruise includes morning tea, coffee, and cake, served until departure from Cairns; three hours at the platform, with a reef education presentation, hot and cold buffet lunch, semisubmersible coral reef viewing tour, and guided eco-reef talk in the underwater observatory; afternoon tea and coffee available while at the platform; and cheese and biscuits on the return journey. Snorkeling equipment and buoyancy vests are included. Optional activities include introductory dives ($150), certified dives including equipment ($107), and guided snorkel tours (adult $54, child $27).

Sunlover Reef Cruises (tel. 07/4050-1333, www.sunlover.com.au, adult $190, child $80, family $460) runs daily catamaran trips to the pontoon anchored at **Moore Reef,** leaving at 9:30am (8:30am check-in) and returning to Cairns at 5:30pm. The day's activities include four hours at the outer reef with snorkeling (gear included), glass-bottom boat tours, semisubmersible (a half-submersed boat) tours, a safe swimming enclosure for children; tropical buffet lunch including hot and cold dishes, and tea and coffee prior to pontoon departure. Extra activities include a Seawalker platform helmet dive ($140), introductory scuba dive ($125), certified scuba dive ($80), and guided snorkel safari ($39), all equipment included. Bar facilities are available on the pontoon. You can also book a two-day cruise (no overnight stay), with the first day spent at the pontoon at Moore Reef and the second on Fitzroy Island (adult $219, child $97).

Reef Magic (tel. 07/4031-1588, www.reef-magiccruises.com, $190 adult, $90 child, $470 family) has an all-weather platform anchored out by a reef catering for all activity levels.

Travel time in the fast catamaran is around 90 minutes to cover the 50 kilometers out to sea, and time spent on the platform is five hours. Included in the fee are snorkeling, tours on the semisubmersible with commentary, glass-bottom boat tours, marine biologist presentation, hot and cold lunch buffet, tea, coffee, and water throughout the day, and access to a children's swimming enclosure. Additional paid activities include introductory diving (1st dive $120, 2nd $70), certified diving (1st dive $60, 2nd $30), helmet diving (1st dive $120, 2nd $70), and snorkel tours (30-minute tour $35, 50-minute tour $45). All equipment is included.

Passions of Paradise (tel. 07/4041-1600, www.passions.com.au, adult $159, child 4-14 $109, family $489) is a state-of-the-art catamaran with which you can dive, sail, and snorkel the Great Barrier Reef. The 25-meter high-performance crewed catamaran with air-conditioned salon sails daily from Cairns to two unique locations, the stunning **Michaelmas Cay** and the exclusive **Paradise Reef,** where you can dive, snorkel, swim with turtles and colorful fish, and see an amazing variety of coral. A dedicated snorkeling instructor provides free tuition (i.e., instruction), and there's a 10-minute scuba diving demonstration as well as an onboard marine naturalist presentation on coral and bird life. A tropical buffet lunch of hot and cold dishes is prepared on the boat by a chef, along with freshly brewed coffee, muffins, and a cheese platter for afternoon tea. Diving and snorkeling equipment is included in the fee, along with flotation vests to aid nonswimmers. Optional costs include introductory and certified dives (1st $70, 2nd $45) and a glass-bottom boat tour (adult $20, children $10).

The 20-meter luxury cruiser **Ocean Freedom** (tel. 07/4052-1111, www.oceanfreedom.com.au, adult $185, child $100, family $517) visits the surrounding reef of **Upolu Cay** and the so-called "Wonder Wall" on the outer edge of Upolu Reef. The tour includes six hours on the reef at two reef destinations, a smorgasbord lunch, snorkeling instruction, a snorkeling tour with a marine naturalist, a reef talk by a marine interpreter, and a glass-bottom boat tour. Tropical fruit, cheese, crackers, and assorted cakes are served during day. The fee includes snorkeling and diving equipment, buoyancy snorkel vests, and Lycra suits or wet suits (depending on the season). Optional costs include an introductory dive (1st $105, 2nd $50) and certified dives (1st $70, 2nd $35).

The gorgeous yacht **Ocean Free** (tel. 07/4052-1111, www.oceanfree.com.au, adult $140, child $90, family $418) sails you leisurely to Pinnacle Reef, an exclusive mooring on the eastern lee of Green Island offering excellent coral coverage and vibrant marine life. Ocean Free limits its daily guests to just 35, ensuring a truly personalized and unforgettable Great Barrier Reef experience, with maximum comfort and space. After a leisurely sail to Green Island with coffee and tea, you can dive and snorkel on the reef, and after lunch transfers to Green Island offer a beach experience. Introductory dives are charged at $85 for the first, $35 for the second; certified dives cost $65 for the first, $20 for second. Check in at the Ocean Free/Ocean Freedom desk (both are run by the same tour operator) inside Cairns's Reef Fleet Terminal from 7:15am, with boarding at 7:30am for an 8am departure; arrive back in Cairns between 5pm and 5:30pm.

Down Under Cruise and Dive (www.downunderdive.com.au, adult $159, child up to 16 years $80, family $418) offers a cruise on a very sleek motor yacht that includes five hours of snorkeling, a hot barbecue lunch, and onboard musical entertainment. An adult diving package ($189) includes the cruise fee plus one dive, saving you money on separately booked dives: Introductory dives are charged at $65 for the first, $45 for the second, and certified dives are $65 for the first, $20 for the second. The tour also offers a free glass-bottom boat trip, large air-conditioned lounges on board, and spacious sundecks for sunbathing. The cruise departs Cairns at 8:20am and returns at 4:45pm.

Inland Excursions from Cairns

Tropical northern Queensland is an incredibly diverse part of the state, and although the main draw for tourists is the Great Barrier Reef, there is no getting away from the fact that there is so much more to see than "just" the sea. Rainforest, tablelands, mountains, and volcanic wonders all form part of the natural attractions that have developed over millennia in this region. Add to that the man-made attractions—villages, trains or cable cars, quirky ruins, or simply places that have arisen because of said natural wonders—and visitors can enjoy the diversity of what Queensland has to offer. This is a region of Australia that will leave you breathless, not just from trying to see it all, but simply from its beauty and variety.

★ KURANDA

Quaint colorful Kuranda is a day trip worth its while. Nestled in the mountain range separating Cairns from the tableland, this little village is bustling and brimming with things to do and see. From art galleries to markets, from animal experiences to hikes, Kuranda is like a vacation from your vacation. And it's not just a destination—the journey there and back is just as exciting. Going on a cable car across the mountains, looking down on the canopy of the rainforest and even spotting a crocodile sunning itself by the river, is a treat in itself, but if you take the cable car to Kuranda, you'll get two treats in one. Then there is the historic railway, which also goes to Kuranda and back to Cairns, making it a three-in-one day trip.

I suggest taking the cable car on the way out before it gets too sunny and hot; you might still get the mist settled above the canopy. On the way back you can relax on the train journey, have a drink, have a snack, and enjoy the views down the steep embankments. Mixing it up and taking both the cable car and the train as modes of transport makes your day out extra special.

The village is a hive of activity between 9am and 3pm; after that, shops and cafés close, and tourists drift away. Originally settled by the Djabugay people, who called the place Ngunbay, or "place of the platypus," Kuranda was first surveyed in 1888 for the building of the railway and road that were to connect the new seaport of Cairns with the people across the mountain range.

With the establishment of the railway, Kuranda soon became a vacation and honeymoon hot spot for local couples, who took the train through the forest and stayed in the pretty village and visited the Barron Gorge. Alexander Graham Bell spent a vacation here back in June 1910. As the president of the National Geographic Society, he tried to promote an understanding of distant lands through pictures in an age when travel—especially to a far-flung place such as Australia's tropical north—was a privilege of only a few.

Tourism truly took off in 1915 and reached its peak in the 1930s. In the 1960s, "hippy" communes flourished in the region, so abounding with natural beauty that made it easy to pursue an alternative lifestyle. Today's artistic community is left over from that time and has established a thriving art hub that attracts visitors from around the globe.

Art is prevalent all over the village. Look out for pavement art, interesting benches and street signs, and sculptures dotted around the village. Even the fences are decorated.

Skyrail Cableway

Although you can drive or take a coach tour to get to Kuranda, by far the best way to go is by **Skyrail** (www.skyrail.com.au, one-way adult $47, child $23.50, family $117.50, daily 9am-5:15pm in 15-minute intervals, round-trip 2.5 hours). The privately owned Skyrail cableway is as spectacular as is the location it is trying to show off: the rainforest beneath the cables. It took the owners years to get the permissions in place to build the rail, promising to go above (as opposed to through) the rainforest but with still several clearings having to be cut for the towers. True to their endeavor to protect the environment, all plants that were removed to allow construction were put in a national park nursery and replanted as close as possible to their original growing place. And the effort to promote an environmentally conscious tourism attraction makes the trip such a special one.

The cabins seat six people each, and because there is no standing in these gondolas, and it's comfortable seating, everybody gets great views all around.

The journey starts at the Caravonica terminal outside Cairns, and the trip is broken into three sections. **Red Peak,** the first station, is a 10-minute "flight" across the treetops, showing off not only the canopy of the rainforest with some eucalyptus thrown in the mix, but also views across to Cairns and the sea. On a clear day you can even see Green Island, some 27 kilometers out to sea from Cairns. At the Red Peak stop, regular free 15-minute tours take you along the wooden boardwalk to the site of a **timber cutters' camp** in the 1800s. The tours set off regularly, once enough people have exited the cabins, and while you can walk along the boardwalk on your own and read the signs, this short tour is well worthwhile for the extra information you'll get from the ranger. The guide will explain which plants to look out for, give some of the history of the area, and point out any animals, such as the ubiquitous brush turkey, along the way.

Fifteen minutes on, the next stop is **Barron Falls,** a spectacular waterfall, more impressive in the rainy season but still strikingly beautiful at any time of the year. A viewing platform allows you the perfect photo opportunity. At this stop you can also go on the **Djabugay Aboriginal Guided Tour** ($20 for 45 minutes), where you learn about the culture of the indigenous people of this region (including their traditions, the way they lived in the forest, and what plants were of special importance to them), hear stories from dreamtime, and lots more. This tour is led by an Aboriginal guide who really brings the stories, information, and culture alive, and is happy to answer all your questions along the way, so if you have the time and budget, it's well worth opting for this tour along the way.

The last part of the trip, a brief five-minute journey, takes you across the **Barron Gorge** with its river far below, where on the sandbanks you can sometimes see crocodiles, before landing at **Kuranda terminal,** from where it is a five-minute walk into the village.

Caravonica terminal, the starting point for the Skyrail trip, is at the corner of Cairns Western Arterial Road and Captain Cook Highway in Smithfield, some 15 minutes by road from Cairns city. Skyrail offers a regular bus service to the station from most hotels in Cairns, the northern beaches, and Port Douglas. If you would like to take advantage of these transfers, make a note during your booking. Coach transfers take 20-30 minutes and cost $11.50 per adult, $5.75 per child.

Kuranda Scenic Railway

Kuranda Scenic Railway (Coondoo St., Kuranda, tel. 07/4036-9333, www.ksr.com.au) is the best way to return to Cairns after the long day of excursions in and around Kuranda. Give yourself some time before boarding the train to enjoy the picturesque **Kuranda Railway Station.** Built upon the completion of the railway line in the late 1880s, it was often known as the "Honeymoon Station" and has won numerous awards for its colorful gardens and plant displays. It also has a little café and a souvenir shop where train enthusiasts are bound to find something unique.

The railway line, constructed between 1882 and 1891, is even by today's standards an engineering feat of tremendous magnitude. Hundreds of men were employed to battle against the natural perils of the rainforest and build the 15 hand-made tunnels and 37 bridges across breathtakingly deep gorges. They stand as monuments to the pioneers of tropical north Queensland who lost their lives while working on the railway. The train has beautifully restored carriages and two colorful engines decorated with the local tribe's artwork.

Two classes are offered on the train: **heritage class** (adult one-way $49, child $25) and **gold class** (one-way adult $97, child $73). (There are three classes, really, but royale class is for group bookings of 15 persons or more.) Heritage class has refurbished leather benches seating up to three passengers and offers a water cooler and refresher towel but no food and drink. Gold class has individual comfy armchairs, and you'll be served refreshments, snacks, and alcoholic beverages and get a nice souvenir pack to take home. If you can, spoil yourself with gold class. You are welcomed with a glass of local wine (sparkling, white, or red) or a cold beer. This is followed with a nibble of macadamia nuts, a cheese platter showcasing three locally produced cheeses, some mango sorbet as a refresher, and tea and coffee. All this food, though, cannot distract from the truly awe-inspiring scenery outside the windows. Just five minutes into the trip, you have a 10-minute stop at the **Barron Falls station,** with a platform giving the best views across the gorge, then onward through tunnels and across a selection of incredible gorges, clinging onto the rock face, making you wonder how this line was ever built. Ask your waiter for a copy of the book *Tracks of Triumph* to read while you trundle along—it describes the history of the railway with some stunning photographs and in incredible detail.

When, after 90 minutes, you get to the Freshwater station, you can either alight for a bus transfer back to the Skyrail station ($8 one way) or sit tight for another 20 minutes until Cairns. There are two trains in the morning, leaving **Cairns Railway Station** (Bunda St., tel. 07/4036-9333) at 8:30am and 9:30am, returning from Kuranda at 2pm and 3:30pm. Gold class is only available on the 9:30am departure from Cairns and the 3:30pm return from Kuranda.

You can combine the entire day's excursions, Skyrail and Kuranda Scenic Railway, within one ticket, giving you a one-way trip on Skyrail and a return on the railway (heritage class only) for $105.50 adults, $53.25 per child, and $264.25 for a family. Transfers from and back to your hotel can be arranged through the same channels as the Skyrail transfers.

Kuranda Scenic Railway

Kuranda Wildlife Experience Pass

Three of the main animal attractions in Kuranda, the **Australian Butterfly Sanctuary, Birdworld Kuranda,** and **Kuranda Koala Gardens,** and offer visitors a bumper pass, saving on the individual tickets. The pass costs $46 per adult and $23 per child, allowing you entrance to all three attractions while saving $7 per adult and $3.50 per child when compared to the individual ticket prices. Alternatively, you can opt for a Friends of the Rainforest ticket, which includes entry to both the Koala Gardens and Birdworld for $29 per adult and $14.50 per child. The Butterfly Sanctuary, for some reason, is not included in any other deals.

Sights

The **Australian Venom Zoo** (Coondoo St., tel. 07/4093-8905, daily 10am-3pm, adult $16, child $10) showcases everything that freaks out the average adult and delights nearly every child: snakes, scorpions, gigantic spiders, and centipedes. The zoo breeds many of the resident animals for the extraction of their venom, which is then sent to research labs around the world, who use it for medical research and the preparation of medicines. Considering that many life-saving medicines are being developed from venoms, this is a worthwhile undertaking, and checking these creatures out is creepy fun. While the number of creatures in the zoo is quite impressive, they are relatively small, so going around the facility shouldn't take more than 30 minutes.

Head straight from the venomous underworld into the colorful fluttering of the **Australian Butterfly Sanctuary** (8 Rob Veivers Dr., tel. 07/4093-7575, www.australianbutterflies.com, daily 9:45am-4pm, adult $19, child $9.50, family $47.50), just across the road from the zoo. This is the largest live butterfly exhibit in Australia, with over 1,500 tropical butterflies and moths in residence. Look out for the electric blue Ulysses butterfly, which lives in the local rainforests, and the world's largest moth, the Hercules moth, which is sometimes on display.

Birdworld Kuranda (Heritage Market Place, tel. 07/4093-9188, www.birdworldkuranda.com, daily 9am-4pm, adult $17, child $8.50) houses some 80 species of birds from around the world. Even though theoretically you should be able to spot most of these birds in their natural habitat outside, the waterfalls, ponds, and natural plants make this a birdlovers' and photographers' delight, as you can watch the colorful birds and get some decent close-up pictures. Some even come and land on your shoulders.

Kuranda Koala Gardens (Heritage Market Place, tel. 07/4093-9953, www.koalagardens.com, daily 9am-4pm, adult $17, child $8.50) is dedicated to arguably the world's cutest marsupial, the snub-nosed koala. You can watch them, take pictures, and even hold one. In most states in Australia, only trained professionals are allowed to handle koalas, but Queensland still allows the general public to cuddle koalas, although the experience may not be around for much longer. It comes at a price ($19 per picture), and you only get to hold one briefly, without any interaction, as the law is very strict about not stressing these critters out too much. They feel like slightly matted woolly sweaters, in case you are wondering. And after that hug, there are other fellow marsupials on display: kangaroos, wombats, wallabies, and some other wildlife.

Recreation

A few **rainforest walks** are linked and signposted, so you can mix and match walks through the forest, river walks, and Kuranda Village. The **Jum Rum Creek** walk is an easy one-hour round-trip of around three kilometers starting at the visitors center, going across the main street down Jum Rum Creek and through forest to the riverside, then back again past the railway station. The **Rainforest Canopy** walk is shorter, an easy 40-minute circuit, covering one kilometer of boardwalk and path to Barron Falls Lookout, from where you have spectacular views across the gorge and the waterfalls.

Or you could quite simply stay in the village and follow the **Kuranda Art Trail,** which starts at the railway station just next to the Skyrail station and takes you along Coondoo Street, which on both sides of the road is decorated with pieces of art ranging from sculptures to signposts; the benches are decorated, as are the pavement tiles. Make sure you look up, down, and closely at all normal day-to-day items, as in Kuranda, they are certainly all small pieces of art. A detailed map with information on each display can be picked up at the visitors center.

The **Kuranda Riverboat** (pier by the train station, tel. 04/1215-9212, adult $15, child $7, family $37, departs daily 10:45am, 11:45am, 12:30pm, 1:30pm, 2:30pm) takes you along the river past truly awesome natural scenery. Spot the estuarine crocodiles sleeping on the logs and the birds on the trees, and sit back for 45 minutes of natural beauty.

Shopping

If you need some souvenirs, Kuranda is the place to shop. Colorful markets (Heritage Market and Kuranda Markets, off Therwine St., 7-minute walk from Skyrail and railway stations, daily 9:30am-3pm) sell everything from local knickknacks to paintings, from jewelry to sarongs for the beach, from local mango wine to macadamia nuts, all interspersed with food stalls and cafés. Many stalls on the markets are manned by local artists, who are displaying their various disciplines, from paintings to sculpture, from caricatures to quirky knickknacks.

There are also art galleries along the main street. Try **Australis Art Gallery** (40 Coondoo St., tel. 07/4093-8572, daily 10am-3pm) for examples of fun ceramics, colorful glass, and vibrant paintings. It's not too expensive, either.

Accommodations

Most people do not stay overnight, as Kuranda pretty much closes down after 3pm, but if you are planning a stopover and moving on the next day, there are a few options. **Platypus Springs Rainforests Retreat** (19 Platypus Close, tel. 04/3893-0770, www.platypusprings.com.au, two-night minimum stay, $299 per night per couple) is aimed at honeymooning couples, with cozy accommodations in a self-contained house, twin rain showers, in-house spa services, private outdoor pool, and seclusion in the rainforest.

Kuranda Birdwatchers' Cabin (25 Butler Dr., tel. 07/4093-9154, www.kurandabirdwatcherscabin.com.au, $110 per night for two guests) is a tiny secluded stilt cabin with en suite bathroom and kitchen, set within luscious gardens at the edge of the rainforest and a grassed area that attracts anything from birds to kangaroos, to possums and the odd snake.

Slightly out of Kuranda, on the way to Mareeba, lies the **Cedar Park Rainforest Resort** (250 Cedar Park Rd., tel. 07/4093-7892, www.cedarparkresort.com.au, from $125 pp, no children under 14). The beautiful building, featuring gothic brick arches, serene lighting, and the closeness of the forest, makes this resort not unlike a fairy-tale castle. The rooms are equally gothic, with burnt orange walls, brick arches above the beds, chunky furniture, and exposed brickwork adding to the atmosphere. The small resort offers a help desk full of information of nearby walks and activities, a roaring open fire in the colder months, a library, a fully licensed restaurant and bar, and even a carafe of port wine in the rooms, included in the price.

Food

There are many cafés and food stalls throughout Kuranda Markets, but a café worth seeking out is **German Tucker** (Therwine St., tel. 07/4093-7398, daily 10am-2:30pm), which sells simply the best *wurst* in the region. For around $6 you get a genuine German sausage hot dog with sauerkraut that is delicious.

If you want to spend a little time resting away from the hustle and bustle that is Kuranda during the day, pop into **Village**

Vibe (5 Coondoo St., tel. 07/4093-7184, daily 7:30am-3pm, mains $15), where you can get a light lunch in the shape of sandwiches made to order with fresh ingredients and a choice of breads, warmed panini, and healthy salads, all washed down with an excellent selection of teas or a decent cup of coffee. The sofas and walls are colorful, and inside, away from the stream of people that wander the main street in Kuranda, you can sit undisturbed and get your strength back.

The **Kuranda Rainforest View Restaurant** (28 Coondoo St., tel. 07/4093-9939, www.rainforestview.com.au, daily 8am-4pm, mains $20) is a larger restaurant just on the main street but with decking out back looking out across the rainforest. The food is international, with all the favorites, including pancakes, pizza, pasta, and burgers. You can also try kangaroo and crocodile, if you so wish.

Information

The **Kuranda Visitor Information Centre** (corner Coondoo St. and Therwine St., tel. 07/4093-9311, www.kuranda.org) is open daily 10am-4pm.

Getting There

Kuranda is some 30 kilometers inland from Cairns. The roughly 30-minute drive is a scenic one, along winding roads up the mountains. Take the Captain Cook Highway (Hwy. 1) north out of Cairns past the Caravonica Skyrail terminal. Keep left at the Smithfield traffic circle, following the signs to Kuranda. The road turns into the Kennedy Highway but remains road 1. After a steep ascent, turn off the road onto Rob Veivers Drive into Kuranda. There is an all-day carpark behind Coondoo Street.

Alternatively, use the **Trans North** bus and coach service (www.transnorthbus.com, tel. 07/4095-8644, adult one way $6.50, child $4.50), departing Cairns from the Central Station at 6:50am, 8:35am, 11:35am, and 1:35pm daily, arriving in Kuranda 40 minutes later. Returns to Cairns leave at 7:30am, 9:15am, 2:30pm, 2:15pm, and 4:10pm.

The Skyrail and Kuranda Scenic Railway are other options. They might take longer but add to the overall experience of the day trip.

BABINDA

A small town just 57 kilometers south of Cairns, Babinda might just have the prettiest visitor information building in Queensland. Painted bright blue, the **Babinda Information Centre** hails drivers from the side of the Bruce Highway.

Turning off the highway toward the inland sights Babinda has to offer is a worthwhile excursion. Babinda's name is probably a corruption of the word *binda*, which meant "waterfall" in the dialect of the indigenous people. This name might well have been referring to the waterfalls in the nearby Bellenden Ker National Park, or the annual rainfall, which is a massive 4,218 millimeters. Either way, the masses of water make for a few great treks around the nearby countryside.

Start at **The Boulders.** A brief, easy, seven-kilometer trip from the highway, this is an enchanting place full of myth and legend teamed with natural beauty. The boulders refer to several large rocks that were smoothed over the years by water erosion and look like giant marbles littering the stream. Small pools gather and look inviting for a dip, but beware; many a visitor has fallen foul of the slippery rocks and strong currents. A Yidinydji tribe story warns of the beautiful young maiden named Oolana, who beckons visitors into the creek's raging wet season flow, never to be seen again. Since 1956, more than 15 people have died tragically in this picturesque spot. This shouldn't deter you, though, from following the signposted walking track, which leads to Devils Pool Lookout (940 meters roundtrip). There are conveniently provided picnic tables, so bring some food and spend a couple of hours enjoying the environs.

A little farther south of Babinda, along the Bartle Frere turnoff from the Bruce Highway, are the probably most beautiful falls in this region (and there are many), the **Josephine Falls.** Regularly used in TV commercials, these falls are wide rather than high and tumble down various steps in the landscape. There is a 700-meter picturesque walk from the car park to the falls and the reportedly safe swimming area. From Josephine Falls, you can take a two-day hike and climb up Queensland's highest peak, the 1,622-meter-high **Mount Bartle Frere** (www.nprsr.qld.gov.au). The two-day trail, spanning 15 kilometers, is for the fit and experienced, but there are plenty of other hikes in the area for all fitness levels.

Getting There

FNQ Travel (tel. 07/4044-9792, http://active.fnqtravel.com.au, adult from $116, child from $82, depending on meal options) offers a day tour to Atherton Tablelands, Lake Barrine, Millaa Millaa Waterfalls, Paronella Park, and Babinda Boulders. The bus leaves Cairns in the morning around 8:30am. There's an option to go swimming along the way. There are two meal options: You can go for lunch, morning tea, and afternoon tea or simply have afternoon tea and bring your own lunch.

Take a comprehensive day trip via minibus with **The Tour Specialists** (tel. 07/4059-2654, www.thetourspecialists.com, $178 pp) that covers the Mamu Canopy Tower, Misty Mountains, Babinda Boulders, Josephine Falls, national parks, and Johnstone River Crocodile Farm and includes lunch.

PARONELLA PARK

Just over an hour's drive, 106 kilometers south of Cairns, alongside the old Bruce Highway lies the enchanting **Paronella Park** (1671 Jappon Vale Rd., Mena Creek, tel. 07/4065-0000, www.paronellapark.com.au, daily 8:30am-4pm, adult $40, child 5-15 $20, includes nightfall tour Tues.-Sat. at 6:15pm). It was the brainchild of José Paronella, a young man from Spain who left Catalonia in 1913 to sail to Australia to earn money for his impending marriage. The buying and development of the five-hectare parcel of land, complete with waterfall, took years of hard toil, a lot longer than José had originally anticipated. He worked hard and earned a small fortune, more than enough to buy this plot of land. After 11 years, he finally went back to Spain to collect his bride, only to find that she'd married another. But he could not blame her, as he had neglected to write to her for some seven years and her family had assumed his death or at the very least his disinterest. Long story short, he brought his former fiancée's younger sister back to Australia with him, and with her in mind he

Babinda Information Centre

built a fairy tale castle, fountains, and gardens to rival no other. Their fantasy home was made purely of enduring concrete that could withstand the humidity of the land, and included a ballroom; a movie theater; an avenue of gigantic kauri trees, planted in 1933, that live for a thousand years and can grow up to 50 meters in height; 7,500 varieties of plants; and the first hydroelectric plant, powered by his very own waterfall, providing electricity not only for Paronella Park but also the neighbors.

The park today is a mix of botanical garden, wildlife park, and historical site. A guidebook provided when you enter the park explains the many signed and listed plants you will encounter along the paths. Plenty of small brush turkeys huddle through the undergrowth, and bats fly overhead. The many buildings are now ruins, but beautiful, moss-covered ruins that still capture the romance of the place to perfection. By the waterfall there is a lake where you can feed the fish (food is provided with your ticket), but be careful not to go for a quick dip, as there are also crocodiles resident. Guided 45-minute tours leave every 30 minutes and explain the history of José Paronella and the execution of his dream. The tours are well worth taking, if just for the guides' sheer enthusiasm and love for the place. From Tuesday to Saturday, in the evening, take advantage of the special one-hour nightfall tour guiding you through the floodlit gardens and fountains, making the place even more magical.

Accommodations

Paronella Park (tel. 07/4065-0000, www.paronellapark.com.au) has a handful of newly built timber cabins ($85 per night, maximum occupancy two people) on-site, beautifully decorated and fully equipped with a queen-size bed or twins, a bar fridge, coffeemaker, air-conditioning, flat-screen TV, and a small patio with table and chairs to enjoy the surrounding rainforest at night. Bathroom facilities are shared in another cabin.

Food

The **Paronella Park Café** serves lunch and snacks during the day, anything from salads to sandwiches—basic fare, but just right for a light lunch. If you are staying the night, a five-minute walk across the road is the small village of Mena Creek, where the **Mena Creek Hotel** (1 Mena Creek Rd., tel. 07/4065-3201, daily noon-8pm, mains $18) serves pub-style food for dinner, with pastas and steaks featuring heavily on the menu.

Getting There and Around

From Cairns, head south along the Bruce Highway for around 90 kilometers until after Innisfail, where you will turn right onto the old Bruce Highway toward Mena Creek. There are signposts all along the way, but there is also a visitors center just south of Innisfail, just before you turn off the main road; ask for directions there, if you are unsure.

Alternatively, there are guided bus tours from Cairns, which take you to Paronella Park and offer a few other worthwhile stops along the way. **Tropical Horizons** (tel. 07/4035-6445, www.tropicalhorizonstours.com.au, adult $161, child $113) offers a "Waterfalls, Wildlife & Paronella Park" tour, which leaves Cairns in the morning and drives through the tablelands to volcanic crater Lake Barrine. After a stop for tea and scones, you will take a wildlife cruise followed by a boardwalk stroll through the forest to see the giant curtain fig trees and maybe even catch a glimpse of an elusive platypus. Lunch is provided atop the stunning Mungalli Falls, before heading off to Paronella Park in the afternoon, with another stop for coffee and cakes provided.

ATHERTON TABLELANDS

The Atherton Tablelands region is 32,000 square kilometers. It soars to heights of almost 1,300 meters in places and consists of mostly rural, agricultural landscapes surrounded by mountain ranges, full of rolling hills, wetlands, savanna, forest, and lush fields growing anything from sugarcane to peanuts, from avocados to coffee. Dotted throughout the region are small towns and villages, lakes, and historic stop-offs. Coming across the Great Dividing Range from the tropical beaches and the Great Barrier Reef, the first glimpse of the tablelands is reminiscent of Switzerland. The air is clean and the temperatures are more temperate. You'll see cows munching on the green grass, and there are signs to coffeehouses and teashops everywhere. From Port Douglas, the first town you will hit is **Mareeba,** whereas if you are coming from Cairns, you'll go past **Kuranda** and then onto **Atherton.**

It's an ideal region to explore by driving, climbing through the mountains separating the coastline from the tablelands, then descending onto the plains and stopping off at the many sights, villages, and cafés along the way. There is one main road, the Kennedy Highway (Hwy. 1), threading its way through the mountain range past Kuranda and linking most of the other towns, such as Mareeba and Atherton.

If you are planning on staying in the area to explore it at your leisure, make Atherton your base, as it is central to all the region's attractions. Alternatively, if you are interested in driving to the lava tubes in Undara, use the drive through the tablelands as a welcome diversion. It is lovely just to drive and enjoy the scenery, but an overnight stay will be more relaxing and will give you a chance to sample a few of the regional attractions.

Mareeba

Mareeba is a rural town famed for its wetlands, which are liberally sprinkled with gigantic termite hills and home to some 200 species of birds. (Load the app "Birding Tropical Australia" for free on your smartphone to help you identify some of the species.)

Mareeba and surroundings is also where over 70 percent of Australia's coffee crop is grown, and where you can find Australia's oldest commercial coffee plantation, situated on the rolling hills and huge rock formations behind the town.

To have a look at how coffee is grown, and more importantly, brewed, go to **Jacques Coffee Plantation** (232 Leotta Rd. via Gilmore Rd., off Kennedy Hwy., tel. 07/4093-3284, www.jacquescoffee.com.au, daily 9am-5pm, tours every 45 minutes, adult $15, child $8), where you can learn all about the region's beans and taste some of the product, too.

If you'd rather have something stronger than coffee, head for **Mt. Uncle Distillery** (1819 Chewko Rd., Walkamin, tel. 07/4086-8006, www.mtuncle.com, daily 10am-4:30pm). Mt. Uncle Distillery is north Queensland's first and only distillery, and it produces a range of real 100 percent spirits and liqueurs on-site. It also makes more than 50 types of teas. Set on an avocado, banana, and macadamia plantation, the surroundings alone are worth stopping for.

The **Mareeba Heritage Museum and Tourist Information Centre** (345 Byrnes St., Mareeba, tel. 07/4092-5674, www.mareebaheritagecentre.com.au, daily 8am-4pm, free) is a fantastic assortment of local history and heritage. The museum tells about the region's Aboriginal heritage and the initial settlers' history, and has many displays about more recent history, including a railway ambulance carriage. And while you are there, you can get information on the rest of the tablelands' attractions.

Atherton

Atherton was named after 19th-century pastoralist John Atherton and is 30 kilometers south of Mareeba. Atherton is the hub for the region's communities, bustling with shops and restaurants. If you are planning on staying in the area to explore it at your leisure, make Atherton your base, as it is central to all the region's attractions.

The attractive **Lake Tinaroo,** as the locals tell those who ask, was named by John Atherton, who in 1875 stumbled across a deposit of alluvial tin and, somewhat excited, exclaimed: "Tin! Hurroo!" The lake, estimated to be around two-thirds of the size of Sydney Harbour, is popular with locals and visitors alike and offers opportunities not only to swim and watch the local birdlife, but to fish for the ever popular barramundi, and maybe even spot a shy platypus. The lake and its surroundings have not yet been exploited by tourism and the pace here is slow. The region is rural, and for exploration, driving is the easiest—consider combining it with your drive to Undara through the tablelands.

The township of Tinaroo counts around 210 people, although weekend trippers swell that number somewhat. The favorite pursuit is fishing. **Lake Tinaroo Cruises** (Tinaburra boat ramp, Yungaburra, tel. 04/5703-3016, www.laketinaroocruises.com.au) offers private charters for fishing, from $300 for a half day, up to four people, including tea and coffee, barbecue facilities, bait, and tackle; fishing permits need to be obtained prior to cruise through the Queensland government (www.smartservice.qld.gov.au, weekly permit $7.70). The same outfit also organizes wildlife and bird cruises through private charter, with a two-hour sunset cruise costing $200 for up to four people. Cruises include a local skipper.

Crystal Caves (69 Main St., Atherton, tel. 07/4091-2365, www.crystalcaves.com.au, Mon.-Fri. 8:30am-5pm, Sat. 8:30am-4pm, Sun. 10am-4pm, adult $22.50, child $10) is a collection of all things shiny and crystal. The sprawling manmade "cave" (actually a shop/museum) houses the world's largest amethyst geode, which is enormous; detailed Chinese carvings in lapis lazuli; and an entirely purple room home to an amazing number of amethysts. You'll even have the opportunity to crack open your own geode, hoping to strike it rich.

The first Chinese came to the region in the 1800s, when gold was found, and left their legacy on the tablelands, such as introducing peanuts and litchis as agricultural crops. Pretty much all that remains of Atherton's once-busy **Chinatown** is the **Hou Wang Temple** (86 Herberton Rd., Atherton, tel. 07/4091-6945, www.houwang.org.au, Wed.-Sun. 11am-4pm, adult $10, child $5, family $25). The museum and temple complex tells the history through interactive displays and restoration of the original community's heritage.

Herberton

Herberton lies just down the road from Atherton's Chinatown and is a pretty little village with a handful of quirky shops, a large pub, and two main attractions.

The **Herberton Historic Village** (6 Broadway, Herberton, tel. 07/4096-2002, www.herbertonhistoricvillage.com.au, daily 9am-5pm, last entry 3:30pm, adult $26, child $12, family $65) is an amazing reconstruction of the old Herberton mining village, with more than 50 historic buildings, ranging from the Grocer's Store to the Tuition Room, and from the *Herberton Times* office to the Suspension Bridge. The buildings are filled with genuine artifacts from the times, anything from costumes to children's toys, machinery, and vehicles. Take a couple of hours at least to have a snoop around.

Then head to the **Spy & Camera Museum** (49 Grace St., Herberton, tel. 07/4096-2092, www.spycameramuseum.com.au, daily 10am-4:30pm, closed Feb., adult $15, child $5, family $40) in Herberton itself. This small place in a small village has an amazing collection of cameras and gadgets, all thoughtfully brought together to tell the complete story of photography.

A little farther out are the **Chillagoe Caves** (Burke Development Rd., Chillagoe, ranger-guided tours adult $23, child $11.50, family $57.50). Various tours can be booked via **The Hub** (tel. 07/4094-7111, www.chillagoehub.com.au). Once an ancient coral reef, the caves are now an amazing system of limestone structures that exhibit not only the relatively common stalagmites and stalactites, but also a beautiful variation in color. The Chillagoe Caves are a warren of over 560 known caves, the largest having over 11 kilometers of passages. Selected cave systems are accessible with tour guides; some are more difficult to maneuver than others. **Doona**

Cave (daily at 9am, duration 1 hour, involves 200 steps inside cave), **Trezkinn Cave** (daily at 11am, 45 minutes, 80 steps), and **Royal Arch Cave** (daily at 1:30pm, 1.5 hours, flat) are all spectacular. The difference is that the first two are electrically lit, while the Royal Arch tour requires you to carry lights while going through the flat caves (no steps to negotiate), which makes it a little more adventurous than the others.

Accommodations

There are plenty of down-to-earth, family-friendly boutique bed-and-breakfast accommodations. Try the homey **Atherton Blue Gum B&B** (36 12th Ave., next to Halloran's Hill Leisure Park, Atherton, tel. 07/4091-5149, room and breakfast from $130 per couple). The rooms offer basic but comfortable accommodations with plenty of warm wood decor, and amenities include a huge terrace overlooking the countryside, a communal kitchen area, plus a small pool. The owners are very knowledgeable about the region and can help you decide on what to see.

Perfect for bird-watching, the **Jabiru Safari Lodge** (Pickford Rd., Biboohra, tel. 07/4093-2514, www.jabirusafarilodge.com.au, cabins from $215 pp, twin share, all meals inclusive) has African safari-style tented cabins with individual private verandas. They are small but comfortably outfitted. An en suite bathroom, fridge, and fan make this a luxury "glamping" experience right in the bushland. Included in the rate is a daily wildlife safari and canoeing in the lagoon on-site.

The uniquely beautiful **Crater Lakes Rainforest Cottages** (Lot 17 Eacham Close, Lake Eacham, tel. 07/4095-2322, www.craterlakes.com.au, from $240 per night) offers four individually styled wooden cabins set right in the bushland. The decor is homey and warm, with individual touches evident throughout, complete with books, fresh flowers and candles, squashy couches, big beds, and kitchen and dining areas—basically a home away from home. There is a laundry facility and communal deck set near a mini-waterfall.

Larger accommodation options include the **BIG4 Atherton Woodlands Tourist Park** (141 Herberton Rd., Atherton, tel. 07/4091-1407, www.woodlandscp.com.au, one-bedroom cabins from $110), a large campground with wooden cabins in all sizes, from one-bedroom en suite cottages sleeping two, to two-bedroom family villas sleeping four. All cabins have private outside seating, kitchenettes, and fridge, plus TV. The park offers outdoor areas, pool, and playground and has easy access to walking trails.

A little farther on from Atherton, past Malanda, the eco-friendly houses at **The Canopy Treehouses** (Hogan Rd., Tarzali, tel. 07/4096-5364, www.canopytreehouses.com.au, from $169 per night, depending on length of stay, for 1-4 persons) are set high in the rainforest canopy on the banks of the flowing Ithaca River, in the middle of amazing opportunities to spot wildlife. There is also an in-house spa.

Getting There

Leave Cairns toward the north and, after around 10 minutes, take a left toward Kuranda. You are now on the Kennedy Highway (Hwy. 1), which will take you through the Barron Gorge National Park to a turnoff either right to Mareeba or left to Atherton. Allow around one hour to Atherton from Cairns. If you are coming from Port Douglas, head north until just before Mossman, then turn onto the Mulligan Highway past Lake Mitchell toward Mareeba; from then on you are on the Kennedy Highway to Atherton.

Trans North bus service (tel. 07/4095-8644, www.transnorthbus.com, adult one way $24.60, child $12.30) has a route between Cairns and Atherton (leaves Cairns Central Station Mon.-Fri. at 8:45am, 3:20am, and 5:45pm, Sat. at 8:45am and 3:20pm, Sun. at 3:20pm and 5:45pm). It arrives in Atherton after 1 hour and 40 minutes (returns to Cairns Mon.-Fri. at 6:15am, 9am, and 3:30pm, Sat. at 6:15am and 9am, Sun. at 9am and 3:30pm).

There are plenty of tours that collect you at your hotel and take you around most of the attractions in the Atherton Tablelands. **Cairns Visitor Centre** (tel. 07/4036-3341, www.cairnsvisitorcentre.com) organizes a **"Tablelands, Outback, and Chillagoe Caves" day tour** (Mon., Wed., and Fri., departs 7am, adult $200, child $145, family $595). A full-day tour in a comfortable four-wheel drive includes morning tea, lunch, and stops at the Mareeba wetlands, the Chillagoe Caves with tour, Chillagoe Smelters, and Mt. Uncle Distillery, with a naturalist driver as your guide.

Tropical Experience (tel. 07/4051-1120, http://tropicalexperience.com.au, departs Cairns 7:30am, returns 5:30pm, adult $220, child 145, family $690) combines Skyrail, Kuranda, and Atherton Tablelands into a tour that includes a lunch stop at a coffee plantation. Get picked up at your hotel and travel to Kuranda either by Skyrail or train, visit the Kuranda markets, and travel across the mountains in a coach, stopping at Barron Falls and several lookouts, sampling some regional fruit, and returning by Skyrail or scenic railway.

Greyhound Australia (tel. 1300/473-946, www.greyhound.com.au, from adult $85) offers a full-day tour by coach that combines the Atherton Tablelands with Lake Eacham, and both the Millaa Millaa and the Josephine Falls, without lunch but with midmorning and afternoon tea provided.

Uncle Brian's (tel. 07/4033-6575, www.unclebrian.com.au, $119 pp, departs every Mon., Tues., Wed., Fri., and Sat. around 7:45am) simply takes you through the Atherton Tablelands in a minivan, stopping at waterfalls (Josephine and Millaa Millaa Falls) to swim, relax, and try to spot a platypus at Yungabarra. Further stops include Lake Eacham, a volcanic crater, and the Babinda Boulders. The tour includes lunch, music, and plenty of fun.

Billy Tea Safaris (tel. 07/4032-0007, www.billytea.com.au, adult $205, child $150, family $605) does a day tour to the Chillagoe Caves, including Mt. Uncle Distillery and Mareeba wetlands with a brief cruise and morning snack at Jabiru Safari Lodge. The all-day tour includes lunch, guided cave tour, Chillagoe Smelter, and hotel pickups, all in a four-wheel-drive vehicle rather than a large coach.

★ UNDARA LAVA TUBES

Undara National Park is not simply a national park, but a volcanic national park. It boasts the world's largest and best-preserved lava tube system, with a geological history dating back millennia.

Undara, an Aboriginal word meaning "long way," is just that—a long way from Cairns. Some 275 kilometers southwest of Cairns, it is a four-hour drive through the Atherton Tablelands and then extending into the beginnings of the so-called Outback of Australia, where space and distance are changing all meaning, and you could easily keep on going on the same road for several days until you reach the west coast. Chances are, you'd meet only a few people along the way.

But, luckily, before the drive becomes too long, you're there and can start enjoying the Outback, with its plenty of animals, such as the mob of kangaroos that comes every afternoon to feed on the grass by the pool, pretty-faced wallabies that sneak into the place at night and ogle you when you emerge in the morning, and kookaburras that steal your food if you don't hold on to it. And those are only a few of the native residents. Then there is the distinctive bushland, scraggly trees, lots of grass, and undergrowth, all held together by a sky that simply seems larger out here, away from the cities. An amazing 164 extinct volcanic craters dot the landscape, adding something different to the walks you can take all around the national park.

Undara is not just a place where you can view some of nature's quirky creations; it is an all-round experience that adds enormously to any visitor's understanding and enjoyment of Australia. Don't be put off by the distance and the fact that you should stay the night to really get the most out of the trip—it really is worth it.

The **Undara Experience** (tel. 07/4097-1900, www.undara.com.au)—i.e., the entire

Volcanic Australia

Although today one of the most seismically stable places on Earth, Australia has an extensive volcanic history that dates back some 10 million years. One of the most recent volcanic explosions was here, in Undara, more than 190,000 years ago, when an estimated 233 cubic kilometers of 1,200-degree Celsius (2,192-degree Fahrenheit) hot lava flowed from the main crater at a rate of 1,000 cubic meters per second. Reportedly, a lava flow of that magnitude could fill Sydney Harbour within six days.

As the lava spread across the landscape, the streams started to cool. Not cool as we understand cool—for lava to cool, it takes only a few degrees of difference to stop it from being completely liquid. Hard crusts started to form on the outside, while underneath the lava continued to pour out. Eventually the lava flow stopped, and tunnels were left with ceilings sometimes up to 15 meters thick, underneath which was nothing: a lava tube or tunnel was formed. Some are up to 160 kilometers long, some have collapsed a long time ago, and others form perfect archways that are open for exploration. More than 300 roof collapses have led to the identification of 68 separate sections of lava tube, the largest measuring more than 21 meters wide and 10 meters high. The tubes are dry for most of the year but can fill to a certain level with water during the wet southern hemisphere summer season. All the accessible sections are utterly mind-blowing when it comes to what nature has formed so long ago and left us to marvel at.

operation, from access to lava tubes to accommodations, and the only way to explore this part of the country—is a family-run business, set up by the Collins family, who were the first white settlers in the region back in the 1860s, and who opened their amazing land to the public in the 1990s. Working closely with the national park authorities they work hard to make the entire operation have as little impact on the environment as possible, and they have won many awards indicating that they are doing well in their endeavors. You are most likely to meet Gerry Collins at the bush breakfast; he is a dab hand with the billy can.

Tours

The only way to see the lava tubes is with a trained guide. The Undara Experience offers many tours of varying lengths, such as the two-hour **"Archway Explorer" tour** (departs daily at 8am, 10:30am, 1pm, and 3:30pm, subject to numbers and availability, adult $52.50, child $26.25, family $157.50), which takes in three sections of lava tube—including the largest piece, the so-called archway, which stretches like a man-made bridge across some local plants found only in the fertile recesses of the lava tube—and the surrounding countryside. This tour is along good tracks, boardwalks, and steps, and requires only a low level of fitness. The **"Active Explorer" tour** (departs May-Sept. daily at 8am, 10:30am, 1pm, and 3:30pm, subject to availability, adult $52.50, child $26.25, family $157.50) also takes around two hours and involves some climbing over rocks and walking on uneven surfaces. You see three different sections of lava tube and the surrounding countryside and wildlife.

The **"Wildlife at Sunset" tour** (departs between 5pm and 6pm, depending on sunset, adult $60, child $30) is the perfect tour to take on the day you arrive, as it eases you into the surroundings, cheers you up after a long drive with some cheese and biscuits and sparkling wine, and allows you to appreciate the sun setting across the plains. You will see kangaroos, wallabies, wallaroos, birds, snakes, and, most importantly, at sunset, hundreds of thousands of tiny little microbats flying out of the lava tubes for their nightly feeding spree. Absolutely amazing.

The longest tour available is the **"Volcano Valley" tour** (departs at 8am, adult $95, child $47.50). This four-hour tour is longer, but of an easy-to-moderate fitness level, with mostly boardwalks but also a climb onto a rocky

bush breakfast at the Undara Lava Tubes

outcrop to appreciate what the lava fields and tunnels look like from above. Refreshments are included in this tour.

All tours set off from Undara Lodge by bus to cover the distance to the main tubes. Maximum capacity is 20 people, and early booking is essential to ensure you do not drive all this way and not see the lava tubes.

Hiking

Although you can explore the lava tubes only with the help of a local guide, there are many self-guided walks you can set off on from the lodge. Regulations require you to sign the guestbook and state which walk you are going on, so that in case of an emergency, or if you don't return in due time, the rangers have at least an idea of where to start searching. The land here is vast and lonely, and cell phone reception not available. There are eight recommended treks, ranging from an easy 25-minute **Bluff Walk** (1.5 km round-trip) to the slightly harder six-hour round-trip (12 km) to take in the **Rosella Plains.** Details and directions for each walk are available at reception.

One must-see is the **Kalkani Crater,** to which you can either drive (20 minutes one way) or walk (2.5 kilometers, 1 hour). Then climb up and trek along the rim of the old crater. Australia doesn't have many craters, so this is quite a unique sight and experience. Signage will give you directions and some historic and geological information along the way.

Other Recreation

The lodge (the main building where the restaurant and small shop are located) also has an outdoor **pool** to cool you off, where you can mingle with the kangaroos in the afternoon. After dinner, in the evenings from 8pm, there is always a **campfire** going; stories are told about the local culture, the history of the region, and the animals and plants that live in this isolated part of the world.

Accommodations

Accommodations at Undara include powered and unpowered caravan and camping sites, permanent tents, a handful of en suite cabins, and a selection of restored train carriages.

The **caravan park** is basic, with 29 powered sites and an amenities block with hot and cold water (unpowered site $12 per adult per night, powered site $17.50 per adult per night). Each site has a campfire pit or barbecue, and firewood can be purchased from reception. Collecting wood from the bush is not allowed.

Swags Tent Village consists of permanent, off-the-ground tents with bunks ($45 per night, 1-2 adults), cooler boxes, and electric lights. Most tents have an adjoining undercover kitchenette with a gas barbecue, fridge, picnic tables, and chairs. There is a separate amenities block with hot and cold water. Linen is available at an extra cost.

The **Pioneer Cabins** are basic but cozy wooden huts set in the bushland around the main building and offer private bathrooms, a veranda, linen, coffeemakers, and a small fridge. In the mornings you'll find wallabies right next to your veranda, nibbling the shrubs.

Then there are the 25 lovely turn-of-the-(previous)-century **railway carriages** ($85 pp) from the original Sunshine Express, which used to run from Brisbane to Cairns. The carriages were saved from certain destruction in the late 1980s, relocated to Undara, and refurbished as multi-cabin accommodations. Most are very basic, although you have the choice of twin or queen beds, and it is possible to link several "rooms" together for families. But there are only fans instead of air-conditioning, bathroom facilities are shared, and there's no fridge. That said, there are a couple of carriages with private bathrooms ($170 for 1-2 people sharing), and the carriages are beautiful, with their old leather seats intact and the baggage nets above, all joined by a wooden deck and with plenty of quirky original features. You have a bench outside your carriage, from where to enjoy the wallabies and nature before lights-out.

Food

Lunch and dinner are served at **Undara Central** (mains $25), which is a huge sheltered area with a bar/bistro and restaurant, which carries on the railway theme with the Saloon Bar and some dining areas set up in the old railway carriages. The menu is basic (no fine dining here), but the food is hearty, and there is a reasonable selection of fish, meat, and other dishes, such as a rather good kangaroo fillet. There is usually soup for starters, and something chocolaty for dessert. The fare is not cheap, but unless you are cooking for yourself and have come prepared, you're pretty much at their mercy.

One of the highlights is the **bush breakfast** ($12 pp), which is served at the Ringers Camp, a short stroll from Undara Central. Stumps of trees are used as tables and chairs. Coffee and tea are served from billy cans straight out of the log fire, and you'll have to toast your own bread in the other fire. Take care, as it only takes a few seconds to get them very brown indeed. Fried eggs and bacon are provided too, but you don't need to cook them yourself. If you do not hold onto your plate, chances are that the cheeky kookaburras and butcher birds will snatch said toast from you before you even know what's happening.

Information and Services

Being quite a distance from so-called civilization, the Undara Experience tries to meet most visitors' basic needs. There are a couple of gas meters, supplying unleaded gas and diesel for those who either have run out or are willing to pay extra for the convenience. (The nearest gas station back on the way to Cairns is in Mount Garnet, one hour's drive from Undara.) There are laundry facilities, and a shop sells basic food supplies, maps, and some souvenirs, plus ice, firewood, and gas refills. There is no ATM, but reception accepts credit cards.

Cell phone coverage is limited to nonexistent, but there are two phones behind reception. Phone cards are required and these can be purchased at reception or the Saloon Bar. Supposedly there is Wi-Fi available, but the server is temperamental, and it's better to assume that you will be out of contact with everybody for the duration of your stay.

Water at the resort is drawn from a natural aquifer and passes through a filtration unit, purifier, and settling tanks, but it is not treated with chlorine or fluoride.

Getting There

Most people drive to Undara, as the distance is too far for day trips by coach from the coast. Driving to Undara from Cairns, you should allow four hours, but leaving Cairns early and traveling leisurely through the Atherton Tablelands along the way makes the trip much nicer, and you kill two birds with one stone, as they say. Leave Cairns toward the north and, after around 10 minutes, take a left toward Kuranda. You are now on the Kennedy Highway (Hwy. 1), which you stay on until just after Forty Mile Scrub National Park. But let's take it one town at a time. From Kuranda head toward Atherton; you could stop at historic Herberton or take the slightly faster route directly to Ravenshoe. Head onward to and through Mount Garnet, and after Forty Mile Scrub National Park, turn right toward Mount Surprise. The turnoff to Undara is 18 kilometers along this road. Turn left and follow the private road for around 15 minutes until you reach the lodge.

Alternatively, the **Savannahlander** train (tel. 07/4053-6848, www.savannahlander.com.au, adult $1,200, child $1,165) offers extended three-day tours from Cairns to Undara, also taking in the Chillagoe Caves and the Cobbold Gorge along the way. It is a unique, if pricey, way to see and experience the Outback in style. The train departs Cairns every Wednesday between March and December, returning Saturday. The price includes accommodations, breakfast, and dinner, plus tours.

Another option is to book the **overnight coach tour** (adult from $405, child from $273, depending on the season and type of accommodations) organized by the **Undara Experience** (tel. 07/4097-1900, www.undara.com.au), a complete package including coach pickup and return to your hotel, lunch, sunset tour, dinner, accommodations, bush breakfast, lava tubes tour, and another lunch before returning to Cairns.

Port Douglas

As with so many places around the world, Port Douglas's modern history starts with gold. The said gold was found in 1873 by James Venture Mulligan inland by the Palmer River. The spit on which Port Douglas is located today was called Island Point by explorer George Augustus Frederick Elphinstone Dalrymple, and was deemed a suitable site for a port for the Palmer River goldfield. Initially the harbor was named Port Owen, but it was also known by the monikers of Terrigal, Owenville, White Island Point, and Salisbury before it was finally settled on Port Douglas, after the then Queensland premier, John Douglas, in 1877. Although at first thriving, the establishment of Cairns and the Kuranda Railway sent Port Douglas into steep decline, and in 1901 the population of Port Douglas totaled a meager 331, with 6,000 in the entire district, many of them sugarcane farmers. When the Captain Cook Highway along the coast between Cairns and Mossman was opened in 1933, it bypassed Port Douglas, and by 1960, the population was registered as some 100 people.

Port Douglas ended up having the last laugh when cruises to the Great Barrier Reef started up in the late 1970s, and tourism took off. The permanent population is still a small and manageable 1,500 people, roughly, but this quadruples with vacationing guests pouring into the small town.

Driving up to Port Douglas from Cairns along the Captain Cook Highway is undoubtedly one of the most beautiful road trips in Australia. The road hugs the coastline for most of the way, and the views of the rainforest spilling down the mountainside to meet the sea in a necklace of deserted white beaches are magnificent. Although the highway still bypasses the town, this is really what people are coming here for—the seclusion and exclusiveness, away from the highway. The small but bustling little town offers visitors everything they could possibly need when away from home: a four-mile beach, small shops, plenty of good restaurants, easy access to some of the world's most stunning scenery, and, of course, having two World Heritage listed sites on the doorstep—the Great Barrier Reef with its beautiful Agincourt Reef, and Daintree Rainforest. There are no traffic lights, parking meters, or fast food outlets, nor buildings higher

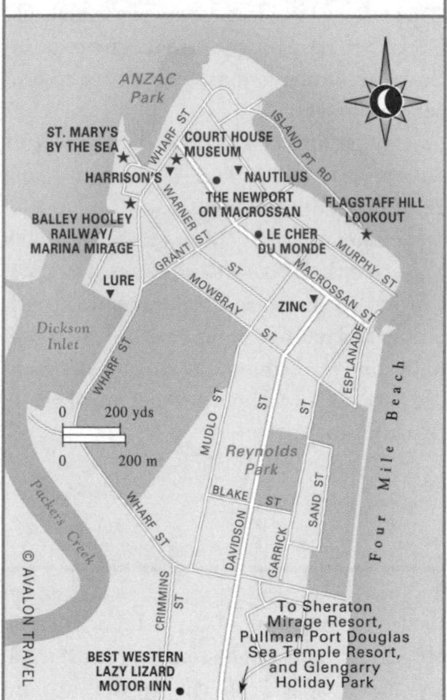

than the tallest palm tree, ensuring the village atmosphere remains as it originally was, making it a welcoming and relaxing place for all.

SIGHTS

Port Douglas is a small settlement that mostly attracts visitors with its long beach and the handful of day cruises taking off from here. Its historical sites are far and few between, mostly due to the town having been devastated by a 1911 cyclone and the existing sites having been refurbished or rebuilt. But those sites that are there are interesting and pretty, especially the lovely St. Mary's by the Sea church. Because it's a much quieter town than younger and louder Cairns, activities need to be sought out rather than being obvious. But overall, Port Douglas makes a relaxing base from where to hop on day tours and see the surrounding country and its attractions, and a base for chilling rather than partying through the night.

Rex Lookout

Rex Lookout (along Captain Cook Hwy., between Palm Cove and Port Douglas) is a mere stop along the highway, but worth it for the vistas. This is a favorite spot for hang gliders, adding some color to the scenery. Want to go up on a hang glider yourself? Tandem hang gliding with **Airplay Hang Gliding** (call Greg, tel. 04/1200-0797, www.airplayhang-gliding.com) takes off from Rex Lookout for flights from 20 minutes to 40 minutes ($155 and $195 respectively). You can even sign up for an entire course to become a licensed pilot yourself, if you are in the area long enough ($2,500).

Port Douglas Court House Museum

The oldest structure in Port Douglas, dating back to 1879, **Port Douglas Court House Museum** (25 Wharf St., tel. 07/4098-1284, Tues., Thurs., Sat., and Sun. 10am-3pm, $2) is also the second oldest timber courthouse in Queensland, and merely the size of a small family home. There is an interesting exhibit about Ellen Thomson, the only woman ever to be legally hanged in Queensland (and the emphasis seems to be on "legally"), upon confessing to the murder of her husband at this courthouse. Other exhibits include details on the Chinese community, WWII details, and some naval displays. For $2, you can't go wrong.

St. Mary's by the Sea

Dating back to 1878, the original building of this pretty church, then called simply St. Mary, was destroyed by a cyclone in 1911, which left only seven out of 57 houses in Port Douglas standing. In the 1980s, when Port Douglas was being heavily redeveloped, the rebuilt church was once again in danger of destruction, but in 1988 it was saved, restored, and moved to the current site by the sea among the palm trees and renamed **St. Mary's by the Sea** (6 Dixie St., tel. 04/1845-6880). St. Mary's by the Sea is now one of the oldest buildings in Port Douglas and undoubtedly the prettiest, in a lovely setting. This nondenominational place of worship conducts weddings, christenings, memorial services, and funerals. It is open during the day, so you can just wander in. Although it is the size of a garage, with a plain interior, it offers tropical views through the back window and an all-round gorgeous setting.

Flagstaff Hill Lookout

On top of Port Douglas's hill and right at the end of the peninsula lies **Flagstaff Hill Lookout** (end of Island Point Rd.), where the stunning four-mile beach can be appreciated. Go for an energetic walk uphill, or drive, but leave your trailer behind, as it probably won't make it up. Stop on the way where you see a small brown Lighthouse sign and sneak along between two residential houses to the little lighthouse, a lovely secluded place with a gorgeous view.

ANZAC Park

ANZAC Park (Wharf St.) is a lovely park that starts next to St. Mary's church and stretches round along the coast. Marked by a monument to the unknown soldier, the park is not only a lovely place to take in Port Douglas and the background of the Coral Sea but also the hub for the Sunday Markets. Established in the mid-1990s, **Port Douglas Sunday Markets** (Sun. 8am-1:30pm) provide locally made hand-crafted goods. Back in 1998 the city council decided that the Port Douglas Sunday Markets would be a "cotters market," thereby ensuring that goods offered for sale were made by the stallholder or their immediate family.

Bally Hooley Railway

The **Bally Hooley Railway** (Marina Mirage Station, Wharf St., tel. 07/4099-1839, www.ballyhooley.com.au, adult round-trip ticket $10, child $5) is a narrow-gauge sugarcane railway originally owned and operated by the Mossman Sugar Mill. It has operated off and on as a tourist railway since the early 1980s. The journey is but a brief one, from the marina to St. Crispin's Station, but it offers a unique and fun way to explore Port Douglas. You'll go through mangroves, past bushland, and by a tidal lake near St. Crispin's where there are local crocodiles that can sometimes be spotted from the train. With this little train, it is the journey that's the most fun, rather than the destination. Trains run on Sunday only, leaving Marina Mirage Station at 11am, 1pm, and 2:30pm. The entire round-trip takes an hour.

St. Mary's by the Sea in Port Douglas

Wildlife Habitat

Wildlife Habitat (Port Douglas Rd., tel. 07/4099-3235, http://wildlifehabitat.com.au, daily 8am-5pm, prices from adult $32, child $16, family $80) offers eight acres of land full of the regional flora and fauna and gives you a great insight into the variety of animals and plants in Australia. Follow the boardwalk through the forest on your own, or join a guided tour. Have breakfast or lunch with the birds (breakfast daily 8:30am-10:30am, lunch daily noon-2pm, $45, includes park entry), join one of the many daily presentations, get up close to a cuddly koala or a slithery snake, and chat with the many wildlife experts on hand. A "Wildlife Care Behind the Scenes" tour is offered daily at 1:30pm ($20). You will certainly meet many animals you didn't even know existed.

Mossman Gorge

Mossman Gorge (off Captain Cook Hwy., just before Mossman village, www.mossmangorge.com.au) is a beautiful part of the Mossman River, with swimmable pools strewn with smooth boulders, nature walks aplenty, and an abundance of plants and animals. However, access is no longer easy. Whereas before you could drive up to the small parking lot and take your walks from there, now the road is blocked and you have to stop at **Mossman Gorge Centre** (212 Mossman Gorge Rd., tel. 07/4099-7000, daily 8am-6pm), a large several-million-dollar investment that houses information, an art gallery, a shop, and a basic restaurant. Most importantly, this is where you either start your walk to the entrance of the gorge (around 4.5 kilometers) or hop on the shuttle bus. The shuttle bus leaves every 15 minutes but charges $6 per adult for the round-trip (child $3, family $15). Once there, you can embark on several walks. The shortest self-guided walk is around one kilometer, taking you to a lookout point that gives you a good idea about the stunning surroundings. The picnic site has restrooms, and there's access to the crystal-clear water of the river, where you can swim (the water is what the locals call "refreshing"—otherwise known as freezing cold, but nice on a hot day).

Other activities are guided walks and include the **"Dreamtime Gorge Walk"** (adult $50, child $25, family $125, around 1.5 hours, departs daily at 10am, 11am, 3pm), which starts you off with a traditional smoking ceremony (no, you don't have to smoke) before you set off through the forest, learning about plant and animal uses and traditions of the Kuku Yalanji tribe. Go for a swim in the natural river pools (optional) before refreshments and more lessons on Aboriginal traditions.

There is also the **"Dreamtime Legend Walk"** (adult $70, child $35, family $175, around 2.5 hours, departs daily at 1pm), which again starts with the smoking ceremony and takes a small group to sacred sites on Kuku Yalanji land, where you see traditional huts, hear dreamtime stories, learn about traditions, watch performances, and finish off with refreshments.

Please note that if you are going on a guided tour, the price of the shuttle bus is included.

BEACHES

Four Mile Beach

This is the only beach in Port Douglas, but if you have four miles of pristine sea front with white powdery sand, then what more do you need? Apart from building sandcastles or playing in the waves (make sure you stay between the flags to ensure the attention of the lifeguards), you can also turn up for **Yoga on the Beach** (every morning 8am-9am, $15, bring a towel) or hire a sun lounger and umbrella for the day right there on the beach (two loungers, cushions, and umbrella, $40), or maybe try your hand at surfing (rent a board from the same vendor, with prices starting at $5). The beach attracts many local runners and walkers, as it is perfect for exercise, but an equal number of families are just there for the fun. The esplanade has a couple of cafés, but the main drag of Macrossan Street (the corner of which is also the main access to the beach) starts at the top end of the beach for a choice of venues.

RECREATION

Walking Tours

Walking around tiny Port Douglas is the best way to see it, and the historical walking tours from **K-Star Walking Tours** (call Kevin, tel. 04/3437-2040, www.kstartours.com.au, adult $20, child $5) will give you anecdotes, history, and facts as you go. Starting every day at 10am and 3pm, the 1.5- to 2-hour tours tend to be small friendly groups.

Alternatively, you can guide yourself by following the brown signs by the side of the road, put in place by the **Douglas Shire Historical Society** (www.douglashistory.org.au): 22 stops take in everything from the oldest pub in town to the tiny lighthouse on the steep climb to the lookout spot on top of the hill.

Air and River Tours

Enjoy the incredible scenery of Port Douglas and the Four Mile Beach via **Port Douglas Microlights** (tel. 07/4099-3046, www.users.on.net/~mort, 30 minutes $166, 1 hour $251). Tandem flights are available for 30-minute or one-hour flights over the surrounding region, giving you not only a bird's-eye view but also a thrilling adventure.

A sedate river cruise on the small paddle steamer the ***Lady Douglas*** (tel. 07/4099-1603, www.ladydouglas.com.au, adult $30, child $15, family $80) is a historical experience, much quieter than some of the bigger cruises. Travel up the Dickson Inlet and see crocodiles in their natural habitat, spot sea eagles, ospreys, and kingfishers, and learn about the habitat from the knowledgeable skipper. Cruises leave the marina at 10:30am, 12:30pm, 2:30pm, and 4:30pm for 1.5-hour cruises. This is a seasonal operation, and not all cruises are available all week or weekend, nor all year round. Please check the website or call before traveling.

Snorkeling and Diving

Snorkeling on the Opal Reef off Port Douglas means clear water and a small group of fellow snorkelers.

Calypso Snorkel and Dive (tel. 07/4099-6999, www.tropicaljourneys.com, adult $200, child $160) takes a maximum of 38 snorkelers at any one time, and the full-day cruise includes one hour of snorkeling at three different sites, morning and afternoon tea plus buffet lunch, transfers from your hotel, equipment, marine biology talks, and showers. Bring your own drinks (including water), towels, and some cash for potential reef fees ($3.50 pp).

Wavelength (Shop 20, Marina Mirage, Wharf St., tel. 07/4099-5031, www.wavelength.com.au, adult $235, child $175, family $730) offers full-day snorkeling tours to three snorkeling sites, including the Opal Reef, on its modern motor yacht. All equipment, a reef talk, a gourmet lunch and afternoon tea, and pickup from your hotel are included in the price.

Blue Dive Port Douglas (Reef Adventure Centre, corner Grant St. and Macrossan St., tel. 04/2798-3907, www.bluedive.com.au) organizes full-day (for two divers $430 pp, including transfers and all equipment) and overnight diving adventure tours for certified divers to Agincourt Ribbon Reefs and Opal Reef, offering twilight, night, and sunrise dives ($1,100 for two days, $50 for equipment, $6 per day reef fees, includes up to seven dives) from a luxury catamaran.

Silver Series (Meridien Marina, tel. 07/4044-9944, www.silverseries.com.au, all-day dive tours from $214 adult, $150 child, $45 for certified dive, $65 introductory dive, all gear included) allows for five hours on the reef sites, including Agincourt Reef. You sail on a modern catamaran, with unlimited snorkeling, morning and afternoon teas, lunch, and transfers to and from your hotel.

The **Low Isles** are two coral cays, Low Island and Woody Island, with pristine beaches and perfect snorkeling (you can snorkel right off the beaches). Reportedly one of the best places to see green sea turtles, there is also an attractive lighthouse on the larger isle of the two, Low Island, and a research station. Incidentally, the lighthouse was erected in 1878, and the original lens for the light is on display in the Port Douglas Court House Museum.

You can organize day trips from Port Douglas on a lovely catamaran with **Sailaway** (Shop 18, The Reef Marina, Wharf St., tel. 07/4099-4200, www.sailawayportdouglas.com, full-day trip adult $215, child $130, family $620), complete with hotel transfers, lunch, equipment, snacks, and glass-bottom boat rides, spending 4.5 hours on the isles. Alternatively, if you are prone to seasickness, try traveling to the Low Isles on the **Reef Sprinter** (tel. 07/4099-6127, www.reefsprinter.com.au, departures daily at 9am, 11am, 1pm, and 2pm from Marina Mirage, adult $120, child $100). This speedboat takes a mere 15 minutes to the reef and, due to its skimming across the water, does not cause nausea, although it may not be the best option for the very young, pregnant, or frail. Short trips allow you to spend some 1.5 hours snorkeling, but there are also half-day trips to the outer reef, with slightly longer transfers of 45 minutes each way but a longer time, two hours, snorkeling ($200 per seat).

Land Tours

Learn about the Kuku Yalanji people with a cultural habitat tour from **The Bama Way** (tel. 07/4098-3437, www.bamaway.com.au, adult $75, child 5-15 $45, two hours, departs daily at 9:30am and 1:30pm). Drive to Cooya Beach just north of Port Douglas and learn how to spearfish on the mud flats and mangroves with brothers Linc and Brandon Walker of the Kubirri Warra people. You can also learn how to throw a woomera (an Aboriginal spear) and can ask countless questions about their people, their culture and heritage, and the wildlife. Back at base camp, you can cook and eat your catch of the day, be it mangrove mussels, crabs, scallops, or even the supposedly very healthy green ants right off the tree. Alternatively, go night-spearing for a couple of hours with a small group (maximum three people, $150 pp). Transfers from your hotel can be arranged for $30 per person for each tour.

Go mountain biking through the rainforest along the so-called Bump-Track, reportedly one of the 10 best mountain-bike rides in Australia. **Back Country Bliss Adventures** (tel. 07/4099-3677, www.backcountryblissadventures.com.au, half day $135 pp, full day $250 pp) offers half- and full-day tours for medium levels of fitness, including bikes, safety gear, gloves, and hydration packs, plus lunch and snacks. Or opt for the heli-biking tour, organized through the same outfit, which flies you up, and you simply ride down ($375 pp for 1-3 people, $369 pp for 4+ people).

SHOPPING

Most shopping in Port Douglas is along **Macrossan Street,** which offers anything from fashion, resort wear, and bookstores to small supermarkets and smaller specialized stores. **Marina Mirage** (74 Seaworld Dr., Main Beach, tel. 07/5555-6400, daily 10am-6pm) is a small mall attached to the marina. It offers some souvenir, resort wear, and sporting shops, selling basically everything you will need for a day out on the reef, and there is a small shopping center at the entrance to Port Douglas, with a larger supermarket and pharmacy and specialist stores.

On Sunday morning, the place to shop is in ANZAC Park at the local **Sunday Markets** (end of Macrossan St., Sun. 8am-1:30pm). If you are in town on a Wednesday, check out the **Sunset Markets** at Port Douglas Marina (Wed. 2pm-7pm).

If you are heading to Mossman, stop at **Janbal Gallery** (5 Johnston Rd., tel. 07/4098-3917, www.janbalgallery.com.au), a gallery run by Aborigines for Aboriginal art, not sponsored but independent and excellent. They also run workshops and classes, either individual or in groups.

ACCOMMODATIONS

There are scores, if not hundreds of accommodation options in Port Douglas, ranging from five-star resorts and lodges to lower-budget apartments and camping sites. The main thing to bear in mind is that, apart from two (Sheraton Mirage Resort and Pullman Port Douglas Sea Temple Resort), none of the accommodations have direct access to the beach. Many line the main road off the Captain Cook Highway, on both sides, and tout themselves as resorts, but that does not necessarily mean beach access. However, the stretch of land is small and the beach is within easy walking distance from anywhere in Port Douglas.

Under $100

The Newport on Macrossan (16 Macrossan St., tel. 07/4099-5700, www.thenewport.com.au, from $89) offers budget accommodations right in the middle of the town with restaurants and shops on the doorstep. Basic, clean, no-frills accommodations range from studios to two-bedroom apartments, all with private bathrooms, either coffeemakers or kitchens, and basic amenities. Larger apartments have private balconies overlooking the pool and forest.

Whether you want to camp, stay in a cabin, or rent a two-bedroom villa, **Glengarry Holiday Park** (70 Mowbray River Rd., tel. 07/4098-5922, www.glengarrypark.com.au, campsite from $36, cabin from $108, family villa from $160), just before the turn off to Port Douglas on the Captain Cook Highway, offers a choice of budget accommodations and is as popular with backpackers as it is with families on a budget. Accommodations range from simple grass camping sites to campsites with private toilet and shower facilities, to a range of cabins, all with private bathrooms, from small ones sleeping two to two-bedroom villas sleeping up to six. Amenities include a pool, water slides, playground, free Wi-Fi in hot spots, camp kitchen, TV lounge, and regular events such as live music.

$100-150

★ **Best Western Lazy Lizard Motor Inn** (121 Davidson St., tel. 07/4099-5900, www.lazylizardinn.com.au, from $131) is along the main road into town and is a 20-minute walk from the center of Port Douglas. Basic, but spacious, clean, and comfortable, this is a perfect stop for those who are driving themselves and don't intend to spend days in resorts but rather be out and about all day. The studios come with a kitchenette, and there is a pool for a quick dip. The owners, Jim and Penny, are extremely helpful and keen to look after you. There's free Wi-Fi throughout.

Le Cher du Monde (34 Macrossan St., tel. 07/4099-6400, www.lecherdumonde.com.au, apartments from $99), a little apartment hotel, is a bright turquoise hacienda-style building right on Macrossan Street, not even a stone's throw from the shops and restaurants. The apartments have kitchens and private balconies or verandas overlooking the pool. This is a budget-friendly stay for guests who want to stay out, walk everywhere, and don't mind a little bit of noise in the evening. That said, everything shuts quite early in Port Douglas.

Over $150

A sprawling resort and country club, the ★ **Sheraton Mirage Resort** (Port Douglas Rd., tel. 07/4099-5888, www.sheratonportdouglas.com, from $173) has been popular since the 1980s. It is the grande dame of Port Douglas and still retains an aura of decadent glamour after all these years, when the rich and famous came to party. You could be splashing in the same pool as Kylie Minogue, Mick Jagger, or even Bill Clinton. This resort has absolutely everything, from several pools, 14 sea- and freshwater lagoons, the highly coveted direct beach access (rare in Port Douglas), golf club, restaurants, shops—everything you need for an extended family resort stay. Rooms are airy and light, with a lot of light wood accents, shutters, and blue hues, adding to the resort feeling.

The luxurious **Pullman Port Douglas Sea Temple Resort** (10 Mitre St., tel. 07/4084-3500, www.pullmanhotels.com, from $219) is set around a large palm-fringed pool and has direct beach access. Spacious modern yet comfortable accommodations range from studios to three-bedroom apartments, including swim-out apartments, which connect you directly to the pool via private access. An 18-hole championship golf course, day spa, and fine-dining restaurant make you never want to leave the resort to explore outside, but with shuttle buses into the town center ($9) and a travel desk, the hotel is also in a great position for exploring the region.

FOOD

Port Douglas is a foodie heaven, with no fast food chain in attendance, but instead plenty of the famous local seafood and locally sourced meats, vegetables, and fruit. There is a dazzling mix of chic fine-dining establishments and restaurants that have a more casual vacation-vibe setting, plus eateries for the entire family covering the usual favorites from pizza to burgers, from ice-cream parlors to cookie stores. Macrossan Street comes alive at night with all restaurants offering alfresco dining, and there are plenty of places for a few pre- and après-dinner drinks.

Right on the Marina Mirage, **Lure** (Shop 15-16, Port Douglas Marina, tel. 07/4099-5201, www.lurerestaurant.com.au, daily 7am-6pm, mains $16) is the best place to watch the marina come to life with day-trippers going out to the reef in the mornings, or to spend a peaceful afternoon by the water. They serve up great breakfast options and easy, family-friendly food, such as burgers, fish and chips, and pasta.

A long-time favorite with locals and visitors, even celebrities (check out the signed plates from Bill Clinton and Nicole Kidman), **Salsa Bar & Grill** (26 Wharf St., tel. 07/4099-4922, www.salsaportdouglas.com.au, daily noon-midnight, mains $33) is an open-plan restaurant overlooking ANZAC Park and little St. Mary's church and offers food with a difference. Try the twice-baked spinach soufflé, the tempura barramundi, and the spicy Creole seafood jambalaya, all served in a relaxed setting.

An award-winning fine-dining restaurant, ★ **Harrisons** (22 Wharf St., tel. 07/4099-4011, www.harrisonsrestaurant.com.au, daily noon-2:30 and 6pm-10pm, two-course lunch $35.50, mains $39, to share plates $76) is snuggled under a tree canopy, which is lit with fairy-lights at night, making for a lovely romantic setting. The modern Australian food has been awarded one-hat status by the renowned Australian Good Food Guide, with a Michelin-starred chef at the helm, and offers specialties such as miso-blackened salmon with wild rice, black fungus, and oyster beignets in a star-anise consommé. In accordance with the romantic setting, some dishes are solely to share, such as the hay-smoked pork with smoked mashed potatoes, fennel, and applesauce.

An institution, **Sassi Cucina Bar** (9 Grant St., tel. 07/4099-6744, www.sassi.com.au, daily 11am-9:30pm, mains $25) has been a family-run Italian restaurant since the mid-1990s. The typically Italian approach to enjoy good food with friends is reflected in lots of sharing dishes, from crispy fried small shrimp in aioli, zucchini fritters, and whitebait to pizzas and pasta, all washed down with a good wine from the Sassi Bar next door.

If you are in town for a special occasion, then ★ **Nautilus** (17 Murphy St., tel. 07/4099-5330, www.nautilus-restaurant.com.au, daily 6:30pm-midnight, no children under 8, mains $40) would fit the bill for a special setting and grand food. Off the main road, with a secluded pathway through luscious rainforest, literally in the middle of the town but seemingly a million miles away, the atmosphere is truly unique. On the menu is lots of local fresh seafood, presented in unusual form, such as tiger prawn spring rolls or whole coral trout dusted in spices and served with a green papaya salad and chili jam. It's not cheap, but it is special.

★ **Zinc** (53-61 Macrossan St., tel. 07/4099-6260, www.zincportdouglas.com, daily 10am-midnight, mains $25) is a contemporary coffee shop cum leisurely restaurant, with comfortable couches perfect in the daytime or for a leisurely evening, offering a great place to people-watch over a refreshing drink. It's a modern setting for lunch and dinner offering something a little different, such as coral trout and cashew spring rolls with wakame and bean sprout salad for starters, and pan-fried barramundi with crushed citrus potatoes and a champagne butter sauce for mains. Zinc also offers good traditional food, such as spaghetti Bolognese. All dishes are light, fresh, and tasty. And please do use the restrooms, as there is a great big aquarium stretching between the ladies and gents, saving you a snorkeling trip.

For a dining experience like no other, try **Treehouse** (Silky Oaks Lodge, Finlayvale Rd., Mossman, tel. 07/4098-1666, www.silkyoakslodge.com.au, daily from 7pm, no children under 12, mains $36)—it's luxurious, tasteful, extravagant, and set above the gurgling Mossman River in the middle of the rainforest. You will have to book in advance and hope there is space, but it is worth the effort. Not only is the setting spectacular, but the food is, too. The restaurant produces unusual dishes that are fresh Australian with an Asian twist, such as the crocodile cheesecake, which is not a cheesecake at all but a mix of smoked barramundi, crocodile, and tarragon; Tasmanian oysters three ways, which are delectable; and mains such as Cape Grim beef tenderloin served with roasted garlic polenta chips and béarnaise sauce, or grilled prawns and crispy nannygai (fish) with spiced greens. For dessert opt for anything to do with chocolate or ice cream—everything is made in-house.

★ **Flames of the Forest** (Port Douglas, tel. 07/4099-5983, www.flamesoftheforest.com.au, $180 pp) is a truly enchanting experience—having dinner under the stars in the rainforest, with fire and pretty lights illuminating the tented venue and the forest and river behind it, creating a magical setting. On Saturday night you can opt for a romantic fine-dining dinner, with excellent Australian specialties paired with regional wines (please note that the dinner is not suitable for vegetarians). On Tuesday and Thursday you can go for the cultural experience, watching Aboriginal dances and listening to their ancient tales, all while enjoying a special dinner. It's not cheap, but it's worth it. Just make sure you bring the insect repellent. The restaurant offers bus pickups from your hotel for $13 each. Children are welcome but not specially catered to.

For something a little different to be enjoyed by the whole family, how about a good old steak, combined with some fun—karaoke or cane toad racing, anyone? The rustic family restaurant **Ironbar** (5 Macrossan St., tel. 07/4099-4776, www.ironbarportdouglas.com.au, daily lunch-late, mains $20) features chunky wood-hewn furniture, burgers and steak, plenty of kid-friendly choices on the menu, and live music, fun, and games. From 8pm onward you can watch the giant cane toads racing against each other and can cheer on your favorite.

If you are after a simple but hearty breakfast or a lunchtime or picnic sandwich, ★ **The Little Larder** (40 Macrossan St., tel. 07/4099-6450, daily 7:30am-3pm, sandwiches $12.50) is the place to go. It offers a great selection of freshly made-to-order sandwiches and other light snacks, all using sustainable ingredients; they are affordable, filling, and easy.

Tortilla's Cocina Mexicana (43 Macrossan St., tel. 07/4099-4199, daily early-late, mains $14) offers tex-mex cuisine, including tacos, nachos, quesadillas, burritos, and all the Mexican favorites. The restaurant's ambience is akin to a fast food place. The huge menu is all available as takeout as well, in case you want to go on a picnic or eat in your apartment.

INFORMATION AND SERVICES

Tourist Information

The **Port Douglas Tourist Information Centre** (23 Macrossan St., tel. 07/4099-5599, daily 8:30am-7pm) provides a wealth of information, and the **Marina Mirage** (74 Seaworld Dr., Main Beach) is where the local cruise companies have their offices, allowing you to book tours right there.

Hospitals, Emergency Services, and Pharmacies

There are a number of smaller medical centers in the town, such as the **Port Village Medical Centre** (Port Village Shopping Centre, Shop 17, 11 Macrossan St., tel. 07/4099-5043, Mon.-Fri. 8am-6pm, Sat.-Sun. 9am-noon) and **Port Douglas Medical Centre** (33 Macrossan St., tel. 07/4099-5276, Mon.-Fri. 9am-1pm and 2:30pm-5pm).

In nearby Mossman, you'll find the **Mossman Medical Centre** (37 Front St., tel. 07/4098-1248, Mon.-Fri. 9am-5pm) and **Mossman Hospital** (Hospital St., tel. 07/4084-1200, daily 24 hours), which deals with accidents and emergencies.

Money

There are several banks along Macrossan Street, with access to ATMs. The main banks are **Bendigo Bank** (11-17 Macrossan St., tel. 07/4099-4231) and **Westpac Bank** (5/43 Macrossan St., tel. 07/4030-4977), and they offer currency exchange.

Postal Services

There is a main post office down Owen Street, just off Macrossan Street, which deals with all postal services (Mon.-Fri. 8:30am-5:30pm, Sat. 9am-noon).

Internet and Telephone

There are a handful of Internet cafés along Macrossan Street, and many coffee shops, restaurants, and hotels have free Wi-Fi access.

GETTING THERE AND AROUND

Port Douglas is around one hour, or 69 kilometers, north of Cairns International Airport. The scenic route along Captain Cook Highway, with the forested mountains on one side and the Coral Sea fringed with beautiful beaches on the other, is one of the most beautiful drives in Australia.

Most hotels offer a pickup service from the airport, or there is the fun **Port Douglas Bus** (www.portdouglasbus.com, adult round-trip $56, child $30, family $155 from the airport), a regular service in a small minivan between Cairns and Port Douglas, which also stops in Trinity Beach and Palm Cove along the way.

Northern Reef Islands

The northern part of the Great Barrier Reef is as studded with beautiful islands as the southern part. Unspoiled islands and sand cays lie across the reef, ranging from relatively close to Cairns, such as Green Island, to far up north in the Coral Sea, such as Lizard Island. To mention them all would take another entire book, so we have a few selected individual ones as a taster.

GREEN ISLAND

Pretty little Green Island is the closest coral cay island to Cairns, which makes it also the most popular and most overrun with visitors. The island is surrounded by white sandy beaches and reefs teeming with life and snorkelers. When Captain Cook first named it, not for its tuft of green vegetation but for his resident astronomer, Charles Green, the pretty spot was mostly used by the local Gungandji and Mandingalbay people for fishing and manhood initiation ceremonies. It was later discovered by bêche-de-mer (sea cucumber) fishers, who built a bêche-de-mer smoking station on the island.

As early as 1890, pleasure cruises started arriving at the island, and by 1906 Green Island was declared a recreational reserve under the Cairns Council. By 1937, Green Island was declared a national park, and the world's first glass-bottom boat was launched in 1948 for tourists to marvel at the wonders beneath the surface, together with a research facility being built on the island, and so the island's development progressed. By the 1940s the popularity of the island was such that the facilities were expanded to make available tents and huts for visitors and researchers, as well as a guesthouse. The world's first underwater observatory, built in 1954, was probably the most important innovation and piece of history for the region for its time. The observatory was manufactured in Cairns and towed to the island on a float made from empty 44-gallon drums. The drums were then pierced and the complete structure was sunk at the end of the pier, where it still stands today.

Still stunning, with gorgeous beaches and fantastic snorkeling and diving spots, the island has, however, been completely given over to tourism. The long jetty reaching out into the sea across the shallows points the way to permanently moored platforms used by myriad cruise organizers, bringing in some 400,000-plus annual visitors from the mainland, making it one of the single most visited islands in the Great Barrier Reef. Catamarans, helicopters, cruise ships, parasailers, dive pontoons, speed boats, and other vessels, complete with plenty of people enjoying the water, turn this island into a bit of a circus during the daytime. However, it is a mere one-hour cruise from Cairns, and it offers entertainment for the whole family, plus access to the stunning underwater world. Once your head is underwater, the hustle and bustle above does seem a million miles away. If you are staying the night, after 4pm the area magically empties and you'll have the island to yourself, give or take a few other resort guests.

Literature buffs might be interested in finding out that Green Island was the setting for an innocent premarital holiday for the characters in Nevil Shute's 1950s novel *A Town Like Alice.*

Sights

The world's first **underwater observatory** sits at the end of the jetty (tel. 07/4044-9944, www.green-island.com.au, daily 9:30am-4pm, adult $10, children free with an accompanying adult) and is a great way to see what the Coral Sea has to offer as well as a great piece of history, with it having been built back in 1958, a complete novelty and innovation in those days of early tourism. Today it may look a little dated, but it gives great views of the underwater world, with some signs to help you identify the fish outside, and is quite a historical rarity.

Green Island

Marineland Melanesia (tel. 07/4051-4032, www.marinelandgreenisland.com.au, daily 9:30am-4pm, adult $16.50, child $7.50) is a family-owned museum with collections brought together by retired crocodile hunter George Craig. Several aquariums showcase what lives on the reef nearby, as well as turtles and crocodiles, including the ancient Cassius, who, as legend has it, is over 100 years old and the largest crocodile ever caught in Australia. Other exhibits detail some unusual Melanesian tribal art.

Recreation

The best way to get your bearings and see the island is to follow the **circuit track** leading around the island. Pick up a map from the information center when you land at the island's jetty and enjoy learning about the wildlife. The walk is less than two kilometers long and takes about 50 minutes. You can enjoy the scenery and try to spot some of the more than 60 different species of birds, including egrets, doves, ospreys, sea eagles, silvereyes, and wood swallows, plus many local plants.

Always wanted to get up close and personal with a parrot fish? Meet Gavin, the photobombing tropical fish who seems to like the attention he's getting from people enjoying the unusual method of going underwater offered by **Seawalker** (tel. 04/0758-1096, www.seawalker.com.au, adults and children over 12 $160, around 55 minutes altogether, 20 minutes underwater). Rather than scuba diving or snorkeling, you don one of those old-fashioned-looking diving outfits, complete with big helmet, and you'll walk under water, on the bottom of the ocean, enjoying all the coral and reef fish around you, including Gavin. This is a great option for those who are reluctant to go diving or snorkeling, as you can enjoy the underwater world without having to undergo serious training, or even getting your hair wet. You can also wear your glasses.

There are obviously the usual culprits of snorkeling and using the beach. You can snorkel right off the beach. Bring your own gear, or hire whatever you need for the day at the kiosk, with rates around $16 per person. You will have to leave either a deposit of $20 or your ID.

Accommodations

Green Island Resort (tel. 07/4031-3300, www.greenislandresort.com.au, from $650 per night for two people sharing) is nestled within the rainforest away from the day-trippers. Forty-six spacious suites with private balconies overlooking either the forest or the pool area are dotted around the secluded part of the island and enjoy all the facilities you'd expect from a five-star resort: laundry, Internet, a private pool, pool bar, a lounge equipped with books, board games, Playstation, DVDs, and concierge service to organize the day's activities. Shops on the island offer a wide range of souvenirs, resort wear, and necessities.

Food

The restaurants are all within the resort but are open to day visitors 9:30am-4pm.

Emeralds Restaurant offers fine dining with specialties including fish of the day, lobster, and other fresh seafood, and also meaty options such as beef tenderloin and rack of lamb. The emphasis is on fresh and seasonal, and a range of fusion cuisines is always available. In the daytime, the **Canopy Grill** offers snacks such as burgers and fries, whereas the **Greens Buffet** offers a hot and cold foods including fresh fruits and salads.

Additional options include an ice cream parlor and a pool snack bar. Private beach dining can be arranged via the resort.

Getting There and Around

Arrive by helicopter, seaplane, or fast catamaran, or indeed on one of the many Green Island cruises available from Cairns.

Big Cat (tel. 07/4051-0444, www.greenisland.com.au, from adult $85, child $42, catamaran), **Great Adventures** (tel. 07/4044-9944, www.greatadventures.com.au, from adult $84, child $42, family $210, catamaran), and **Ocean Free** (tel. 07/4052-1111, www.

oceanfree.com.au, from adult $140, child $90, two-mast sailing yacht) all offer half- and full-day excursions to Green Island, all including free snorkeling, glass-bottom boat tours, and snacks. All depart from Cairns.

Once on the island, you can reach everything easily on foot.

FRANKLAND ISLANDS

The Frankland Islands National Park consists of five uninhabited continental islands some 45 kilometers south of Cairns by the mouth of the Russell-Mulgrave River. Beach-fringed, rainforest-topped, and limited to 100 persons per day, the islands are pretty much deserted, offering pristine water conditions, untouched reefs, and sightings of green turtles, occasional manta rays, giant clams, and many tropical fish and coral. Russell Island is a roosting site for flying foxes, and the islands are always busy with migratory birds. You'll find peace where other islands might offer a tourism circus, but on the other hand, there are no amenities, cafés, or shops, so you will have to come prepared with everything.

Accommodations

Camping is allowed on two of the five islands, **High Island** and **Russell Island.** Only 11 campers are allowed on High Island at any one time, and there are no facilities and only very limited mobile phone coverage. On Russell Island there are three basic campsites, with a composting toilet, but no other facilities and also very limited cell phone coverage. Get permission from the **Department of National Parks, Recreation, Sport and Racing** (tel. 13/74-68, www.nprsr.qld.gov.au, camping fees from $5.60 pp per night).

Getting There and Around

No regular ferries or water taxis have a scheduled service, but there are several day-trip cruises. **Diving Cairns** (tel. 07/4041-7536, www.divingcairns.com.au, adult $159, child $89, family $417) offers a day trip that includes pickup from your hotel in Cairns, morning and afternoon teas, lunch, snorkeling gear and instruction, and park fees. A certified dive with gear hire adds another $100, and an introductory dive costs $130.

Cruise & Dive Frankland Islands (tel. 07/4031-6300, www.franklandislands.com.au) offers a day cruise from $149, with all the above included as well, plus optional scuba diving (introductory dive $122, 2nd dive $89; certified dive $89, 2nd certified dive $69, including equipment). This day trip also includes a cruise down the Mulgrave River.

Both Diving Cairns and Cruise & Dive Frankland Islands can arrange transfers for campers.

★ FITZROY ISLAND

When some 8,000 years ago the sea levels rose, Fitzroy Island was created. Keeping its luxurious cover of dense rainforest, with its diverse assortment of flora and fauna, it also over time grew a fringing reef around the island, and broken coral and rocks formed a selection of beautiful beaches on its shore. While it is not strictly speaking on the outer Great Barrier Reef, Fitzroy Island is the closest continental island and probably the most easily accessible from the mainland, being a mere 45 minutes by ferry from Cairns. It offers everything guests expect from a reef island and more. Day-trippers coming out to either walk and discover the secrets of the island or simply laze on the beach and enjoy the colorful underwater world are as welcome as resort guests who wish to stay a little longer. There is even a **Little Fitzroy Island,** little more than a rock off the northeastern end of Fitzroy Island, that has been home to several lighthouses over the years, and which today houses an automated lighthouse.

Sights

The island is essentially a rainforest-covered rocky outcrop with a handful of beaches and bays and the resort snuggled into one of the bays. To get about, a few tracks have been created through the forest, and the island's sights are only reachable via those—it is not only not allowed (because this is protected land) but also not possible (due to the dense vegetation) to get off the tracks. The emphasis on Fitzroy Island, as on all the other islands and national parks along the Great Barrier Reef, is on nature and protecting it, and visitors will have to always stick to the tracks.

The lovely, albeit now decommissioned, **lighthouse** can be reached via the Lighthouse Road, a 3.6-kilometer round-trip that takes around two hours via a steep concrete road that leads toward the northeastern end of the island. The track is undulating, with regular ascents and descents, but not only is the lighthouse pretty, it is also a good vantage point with 360-degree views across the island. If a ranger is on duty, you can get a brief introduction to its maritime history.

The highest point of the island at 269 meters, **The Summit** is another great hike of around 2.6 kilometers, taking around three hours through the forest. The views are spectacular.

A track leads not to but through the **Secret Garden** that is the rainforest. The walk is around one kilometer round-trip, taking roughly 45 minutes. Regular signs provide information about what you see and experience.

Nudey by name (reportedly after an otherwise anonymous Captain Nudey), not by nature, **Nudey Beach** is spectacular and well worth the 1.2 kilometers round-trip. Covered in coral, sided by huge boulders creating a Seychelles-like ambience, this beach is popular for bathing and snorkeling.

Please note that while the distances of these walks don't seem far for the time given, these tracks tend to be very steep in places, asking you to clamber across boulders, go up and down precipitous steps, and trek through the forest. It is possible to do these walks in flip-flops, but slightly more sensible shoes are advisable for the longer treks.

Recreation

Although Fitzroy Island is relatively close to the mainland, it is still the Great Barrier Reef's magic that is king on the island: scuba diving, snorkeling, kayaking, and watching and feeding the reef fish, all designed to allow guests to get the most out of their experience. But there are also some other things to keep guests busy on land. Please note that all activities are organized through the resort.

A first look at **scuba diving** in the pool is free, then an introductory dive in the ocean is $100 for the first dive and $65 each for subsequent dives, with night dives $85. A day on the outer reef by boat, including two dives for

Little Fitzroy Island

certified divers, is around $170, including dive gear (including wet suits and dive computers), lunch, and tea and coffee.

Snorkeling at the fringe reef literally two meters from the beach is sufficient to see myriad fish and even turtles and dolphins (mask, fins, and snorkel can be hired for the day for $15, individual items for $5 each per day), but a snorkeling trip to the outer reef is still a different experience. A day on the boat including gear and lunches costs from $99.

Kayaks with Perspex viewing panels to enjoy trips around the big island and also Little Fitzroy can be hired from $20 per hour for a single and $25 for a double.

Fish feeding from the jetty happens twice daily, at 11:30am and 4pm, with guest participation encouraged, and there is a branch of the **Cairns Turtle Rehabilitation Centre** on the island, with daily free tours to learn more about these beautiful but threatened sea creatures.

For those who would like to see the fish but don't like to get too close, the **glass-bottom boat** (adult $25, child 4-14 $10, child under 4 free, 30 minutes) is an ideal alternative, with twice daily tours departing at 10:30am and 2pm.

The main building of the resort has a full-fledged cinema, a small library, a playroom for smaller kids, and a video-game arcade for teenagers.

Accommodations

When approaching the island from the sea, the **Fitzroy Island Resort** (tel. 07/4044-6700, www.fitzroyisland.com) is totally hidden amongst the palm trees. No higher than three floors, the buildings blend into the background, making the merging of rainforest and ocean near perfect. With a western approach, the resort is sheltered from the winds and bad weather that can over hang over the nearby mainland, and it generally has better weather than Cairns.

Reopened in 2010 after a complete overhaul, the resort sells itself as 4.5 stars. The decor and facilities are first class, aimed at families and couples. Options include ocean suites with two bedrooms and a fully equipped kitchen, resort studios, and a handful of beach cabins nestled on the ocean's fringe facing the sunset. The rooms are decorated in understated elegance in browns and beiges, wood, and tile, with the kitchens being very modern in wood and stainless steel. All rooms and cabins face the sea. Room rates start at $132 per night for a studio or $183 for an ocean suite if a three-night stay is booked; rates are slightly higher if staying only one night. Beach cabins start at $300. Rates do not include breakfast or activities.

There is a beach literally in front of the resort, and Nudey Beach is a worthwhile 20-minute walk through the forest. A pool with an indulgent swim-up bar and sun loungers is perfect for days when you don't want sand. With only 99 rooms in the entire resort, there is, even at full occupancy, never a scramble for the beach or the pool. People spread out along the beaches and the pool, taking part in the many activities, and the only time you might see the same faces is over drinks or dinner in the evening.

Part of the resort is also a small **campground** (tent space $35 per night), just a little farther along from the main building, but out of sight and with separate facilities. The maximum stay is seven nights.

An ATM in the lobby takes most bank and credit cards, and there's a small convenience store.

Food

There are two food outlets within the resort. **Foxey's Beach Bar** (daily 10am-7pm or 10pm, depending on the season, mains $18) is a wooden cabin, open to the elements, offering simple salads, burgers, and snacks throughout the day, with daily specials, such as a succulent "barra burger" (barramundi is the favorite local freshwater/estuarine fish). The bar has plenty of cocktails perfect for sunset.

Zephyr (daily 7am-10:30am and 6pm-9pm) is the resort's fine-dining restaurant, where booking, even for guests, is essential (book through reception). The menu is classic, with favorites such as seared scallops or tuna sashimi for starters ($17), and the mains tempt with steak and fish options, daily specials, and local offerings such as kangaroo fillet ($30). The menu is seasonal and changes regularly, but it always offers enough variation for even long-stay guests to enjoy the food daily.

Getting There and Around

The **Fitzroy Island Ferry Fast Cat** (tel. 07/4044-6700, www.fitzroyisland.com, 45-minute ride) leaves Cairns Reef Fleet Terminal at 8am, 11am, and 1:30pm daily, and returns at 9:30am, 12:15pm, and 5pm. Round-trip fares for resort guests are $69 ($34 for children). Arrive at the ferry a minimum of 20 minutes prior to departure to ensure safe stowing of your luggage. On the ferry you can buy a selection of snacks and drinks.

★ LIZARD ISLAND

The name Lizard Island was bestowed in 1770 by Captain James Cook, who climbed to the island's highest point to look for a safe passage for his vessel, away from the treacherous reefs. On Sunday, August 12, 1770, he wrote in his journal about the island:

> The only land Animals we saw here were Lizards, and these seem'd to be pretty Plenty, which occasioned my naming the Island Lizard Island.

Maybe his accompanying naturalist, Sir Joseph Banks, had the day off, as the most conspicuous of the island's 11 species of lizards are Gould's sand monitors (*Varanus gouldii*) or, as they are locally called, goannas, which grow up to 1.5 meters in length, have a forked tongue, and live in burrows in the sand, but are generally quite harmless if not threatened—and certainly are more impressive than mere "lizards."

Today, the lizards, large and small, are still there, and happily mingle with two other types of rare creature, the enthusiastic marine biologist and the shy celebrity drawn to the luxurious Lizard Island Resort.

It's the only continental island close to the outer reef, 240 kilometers north of Cairns and 27 kilometers from the mainland, and the waters around Lizard Island are generally clearer than elsewhere in the Great Barrier Reef, allowing for great snorkeling and diving. The island is quite secluded and not as easily reached as some others along the coastline. Again, this makes Lizard perfect for the reclusive traveler and the serious scientist. The Lizard Island Research Station is a coral reef research facility that is owned and operated by the Australian Museum. It attracts marine biologists and researchers, including postgraduate students from all over the world, who are busy conducting about 100 different research projects each year. From the research work conducted at Lizard Island, more than 1,200 scientific publications have been produced by Australian and international researchers since the station's inception in 1973.

The island is a national park (strictly speaking the Lizard Island National Park includes Lizard Island and five smaller nearby islands), the waters surrounding it are a marine park, and the resort is often awarded a spot in the Top Hotels in the World list—Lizard Island is really quite something special.

Sights

The sights on Lizard Island are mostly of a natural kind, with the resort publishing a *Nature Calendar*, alerting guests to seasonal goings on, such as sighting green sea turtles in May, humpback whales in June and July, minke whales in September, various birds nesting throughout the year, and even special star constellations in the sky. You can apply upon booking to go on a guided tour of the **Lizard Island Research Station** (tel. 07/4060-3000, scheduled tours $40 pp) and learn about ongoing projects and long-term research being carried out; **Nature Slide Presentations** are ongoing throughout the week, with resident naturalists explaining the flora and fauna above land and under water.

Beaches

With 24 sand beaches around the island, it is nearly guaranteed that you'll find one just for you. The resort even gives guests dinghies and gourmet picnic baskets and sends them on to find their own desert island beach for the day.

The beaches include some secluded sandy coves with great names, such as: **Mermaid Cove,** named after the dugongs sometimes seen in the seagrass and mistaken for mermaids once upon a time; **Turtle Beach,** where regular sightings of green sea turtles, loggerhead, and hawksbill turtles are reported; and **Sunset Beach, Pebbly Beach,** and **Hibiscus Beach,** all named for their own obvious reasons. Then there is **Watson's Beach,** which recalls the sad story of Mary Watson, who with her husband, Robert, and their Chinese staff were bêche-de-mer fishers, collecting sea cucumbers in these parts in the 1880s. In a tragic and somewhat ironic drama, Aborigines visited the island for initiation ceremonies on a day when the husband was away from the island and killed one servant, causing Mary to take her young son off in a floating water tank, making it to the next island, only to then die of thirst. Near Watson's Beach, ruins remain of the Watsons' stone house, which is believed to have been built on a sacred Aboriginal burial ground and thus thought to have caused the attack.

Recreation

There are more than 10 **dive/snorkeling sites** off Lizard Island, all within a 30- to 60-minute boat ride away. The most famous site is probably the **Cod Hole,** where two friendly potato cods, Cuddles and Grumpy, together with Delicious, a resident Maori wrasse, are always delighted to greet divers. **Watson's Bay** is well known for its clam gardens, which can be easily explored snorkeling. The resort also organizes twilight snorkeling ($85), beach dives ($95), and night dives ($185), plus sunset wine and cheese cruises ($85).

Included in the stay at the resort are snorkeling lessons and equipment, catamaran usage, and glass-bottom paddle skis (paddle boards with a window in them so you can see the fish); glass-bottom boat tours; star-gazing sessions; and six motorized dinghies guests can use to explore the island's 24 beaches (gourmet picnic hampers to take with you are included in your room rate).

The island can be explored via various **nature walks,** one to the island's highest point, **Cook's Look,** 359 meters above sea level, a very steep, 2.5-hour walk. Others include the **Chinamans Ridge** (680 meters round-trip, 40 minutes, moderate); **Watson's Walk** to Watson's Bay (1.4 kilometers, 1-hour round-trip, easy), and the **Blue Lagoon** walk (900 meters, 80 minutes round-trip, easy).

The resort's Azure Spa delivers a range of therapeutic spa treatments.

Accommodations

The **Lizard Island Resort** (tel. 1300/863-248, www.lizardisland.com.au) is one of the world's most exclusive resorts and has been frequented by celebrities such as Ellen DeGeneres, Portia de Rossi, Russell Crowe, and many more, who chose the resort for its inaccessibility and luxurious pampering. Room rates start at $1,235 per night for a single garden room, including all meals, wine, cocktails, and gourmet picnic hampers

The rooms, suites, and villas are all decorated with tropical comfort in mind, with open-plan living, large comfortable couches, and expansive glass doors; wooden decks with lounges, daybeds, and/or hammocks; and huge bathrooms complete with stone-tiled showers, double basins, and space for all your bits and pieces. Utter luxury can be had at The Pavilion, a private villa with personal plunge pool and a private path, offering total privacy. The more affordable family garden suites offer two separate sleeping areas, sleeping a maximum of four. Amenities for all types of accommodations include a spa offering Li'Tya indigenous products and massages; a pool; tennis court; and a guest lounge with TV, DVD player, and computers with Internet.

Even though it's a true getaway from daily life's stresses, be assured that you get all the mod cons you may require, and some you probably never even thought of, but overall this place is all about location. And that it has in spades.

Another way to stay on Lizard Island is by **camping** at the Watson's Bay camping area. But this is a far cry from the luxurious getaway offered by the resort, although obviously the beauty of the island is just as impressive—and a lot cheaper from there. Visitors arriving by plane must carry all their gear 1.2 kilometers from the airstrip to the camping area. No supplies are available on the island. Campers are welcome at the Marlin Bar, a resort bar at the eastern end of Anchor Bay, although the bar is not open every day.

At the campsite, toilets, picnic tables, and gas barbecues (burners only, no hot plates) are provided. Open fires are not allowed. Bore water can be obtained from the hand-pump located 250 meters from the camping area. This hand pump may be unreliable at times. If it fails, water can be collected from a tap outside the Marlin Bar (approximately a 40-minute walk from the camping area). Bring water containers suitable for carrying water this distance, and treat all water before drinking.

Camping fees are $5.45 per person per night or $21.80 per family group per night plus airfare. A family group is up to two adults and accompanying children under 18, up to a total of eight people. Children under five are free. Book online with the **Department of National Parks, Recreation, Sport and Racing** (tel. 13/74-68, www.nprsr.qld.gov.au).

Food

There is only one restaurant on Lizard Island, but that one is five-star luxury fine dining and haute cuisine. **Osprey** is an airy veranda space with lazily undulating fans. It has a colonial tropical atmosphere, luxurious yet easy-going and laid back. The food is fresh, seasonal, and light, but all with a fine-dining twist, making even a humble salad into an experience worth savoring.

For pre-dinner or simply drinks, there is the **Lizard's Bar & Lounge,** where local and imported wines, beers and spirits, plus a selection of cocktails, sweeten any sunset.

Guests can also book a special seven-course degustation menu set up on a private beach.

Getting There and Around

Hinterland Aviation flies from Cairns to Lizard Island, flights taking around one hour. Round-trip flights cost $590 and can be arranged by **Lizard Island Resort** (tel. 1300/863-248, www.lizardisland.com.au).

Daintree Air Services (www.daintree-air.com.au) organizes private charters on request and arranges day trips to Lizard Island (from $690 pp). You will be picked up from your hotel and taken to Cairns International Airport. The low-level scenic flight to Lizard Island departs at 8am, with everyone getting a window seat. The flight takes in the wetlands of the lower section of Cape York Peninsula as well as lovely aerial views of Port Douglas, the Daintree Valley, Daintree River, Cape Tribulation, Bloomfield, Cooktown, the Endeavour River, and the silica sands of Cape Flattery. Once on Lizard Island guests have around six hours to explore the island, its beaches, and its nature walks and snorkel along the reef, returning to Cairns by early evening.

Daintree and Cape Tribulation

Daintree and Cape Tribulation are the northernmost regions covered in this guide, and two of the most exciting. Where two UNESCO World Heritage listed sites (the Great Barrier Reef and the Daintree Rainforest) meet is a special place indeed. With a history dating back several hundred million years and a natural beauty that is probably the most distinctive and beautiful found anywhere on Earth, the Daintree region has drawn visitors since the first settlers set foot on this continent. Getting here then, however, was nearly impossible, as the name Cape Tribulation, coined of course by Captain James Cook, suggests, and it is still not easy to this day. Initial entry is by ferry only; no bridges are crossing the Daintree River, even though it is one of the longest rivers on Australia's east coast. A slim tarmacked road leads up to the secluded beaches of Cape Tribulation, but then it turns into a gravel track on which four-wheel-drive vehicles are preferable and rental cars are forbidden (do check with your rental company before you set off).

Visitors, however hampered in their efforts to progress up north, are a major mainstay of the minuscule population of this northern region. Apart from a few farmers and loggers, most residents eke out a living from tours coming into the region, be it on day trips or for a short stay. And come they do. Plenty of tours allow visitors to experience this unique environment. The Daintree has the world's most complete history of the evolution of plant life, dating back to the beginning of life on Earth some 3.5 billion years ago. Visitors marvel at the prehistoric-looking crocodiles and cassowaries, and at the myriad birds, which renowned naturalist David Attenborough was particularly impressed with on a well-documented recent visit to film footage of this exceptional habitat. There are pristine beaches (even though they come with a crocodile warning), secluded campsites, and, most of all, a nearly overwhelming abundance of utterly unspoiled nature.

★ DAINTREE RAINFOREST

Daintree Rainforest is the world's last remaining example of tropical rainforest from the time of the Gondwanaland supercontinent. Around 180 million (million!) years older than the Amazon rainforest, Daintree is one of Earth's natural treasures. This area, or 900,000 hectares of it, was granted international protection through its addition in 1988 to the World Heritage list, an agreement signed by more than 100 countries and designed to preserve areas of ecological importance. Although the Australian continent today is quite diverse and includes vast stretches of desert and bushland, it was once covered by lush rainforests. As the climate became more arid, the rainforests began to die, but the Daintree Cape Tribulation region was warm and humid, which was the ideal climate for supporting a rainforest. Covering 1,200 square kilometers between Mossman Gorge and the Bloomfield River, north of Cairns, the World Heritage-listed Daintree is the largest continuous rainforest area in Australia, and the oldest in the world. Not only a botanical treasure, the Daintree is a living museum that catalogues the evolution of plant life on Earth, containing living examples of ancient plant lineages that are found nowhere else on the planet. It also contains 30 percent of all frog, marsupial, and reptile species in Australia, 65 percent of Australia's bat and butterfly species, 20 percent of bird species, and around 12,000 species of insects alone. All of this diversity is contained within an area that takes up 0.2 percent of the landmass of Australia.

Scientists claim that the age and relative stability of the Australian continent have enabled the Daintree Rainforest to survive intact, with the area having remained practically

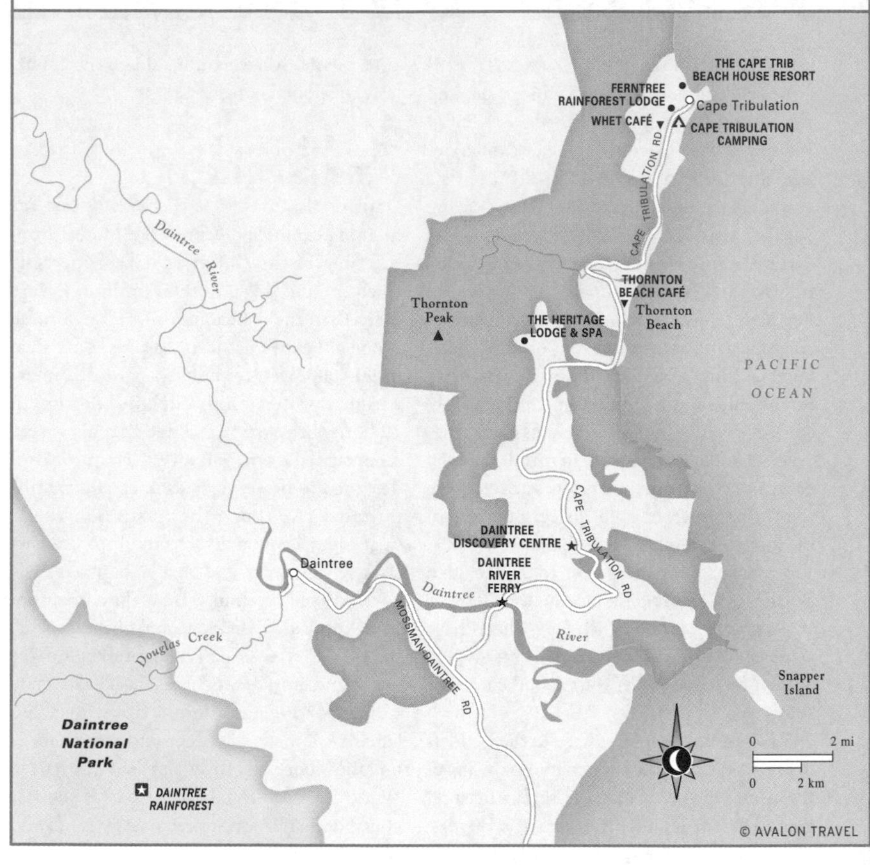

unchanged since the formation of the Great Dividing Range some 180 million years ago. The Daintree Rainforest can be perceived as a time capsule of plant development. There are towering examples of king ferns (*Angiopteris evecta*), the largest living fern, which are the size of trees, whose "family tree," if you forgive the pun, can be traced back some 300 million years. Some plants (for example, *Idiospermum australiense*, or idiot fruit tree) are found nowhere else on the planet and were not long ago considered to be extinct. And to the local people, the Kuku Yalanji, the forest has always been a highly revered source for food, medicine, building materials, and much more—not merely a breathtaking forest, but a pharmacy, supermarket, hardware store, and church all in one.

Just driving up along Captain Cook Highway, you can feel the change in the plant life, and the farther north you travel, the stronger the feeling gets. It is incredible just to be there, to walk around and marvel at the enormity of the plants and the entire ancient region. But to go with an experienced guide, who may even be of the tribe of people who call this place home, and to learn about the plants and animals—and have your eyes opened to so many little things we outsiders simply are not aware of—is a true treat.

The tourism industry up in tropical northern Queensland has found a rare balance between sharing their incredible natural wonders with the world while still managing to protect them.

Daintree Village

The Daintree is a place where nature plays first fiddle and people live in small pockets, remote from the hustle and bustle of metropolitan life. Daintree Village is pretty much the last village before Cooktown in the far north, the last village before you cross the Daintree River toward Cape Tribulation, but even so it is only a small village. (The Daintree River, incidentally, was named for a friend of explorer and later politician George Elphinstone Dalrymple, geologist Richard Daintree, back in 1873. The river shares the name with the village, the national park, and the region as a whole.) The village, 100 kilometers north from Cairns, about a 90-minute drive, is home to some 100 people. Daintree Village was first settled in the 1880s, mostly by people working on the nearby farms and in the timber industry.

The village has a small school, a couple of coffee shops, a small tour operator organizing local croc trips on the river, a resident artist with a bijoux gallery, a tiny market, and a large barramundi, which points to the best barra burger ($8.50) in town. Add a campground, **Daintree Riverview** (tel. 04/0962-7434, www.daintreeriverview.com, campsite $10, lodge $99), and public restrooms, and you've pretty much got it. There is a short **self-guided walk,** set up by the Douglas Shire Historical Society of Port Douglas (www.douglashistory.org.au), which you can follow to make sure you haven't missed anything. Taking in some of Daintree's history, it leads past the Red Mill House, the Hash House, the old Butter Factory, and the Wharf. Download the guide at the website.

Daintree Discovery Centre

Daintree Discovery Centre (Cape Tribulation Rd., about 10 km from the ferry, tel. 07/4098-9171, www.daintree-rec.com.au, daily 8:30am-5pm, adult $32, child $16, family $78) is the ideal place to find out more about the region and the forest, to learn about ecotourism, and to get information about local nature walks. Grab an audio set for a self-guided tour, and enjoy the in-situ attractions. The facility is a self-contained information and activity center—it is not like a tourist information center, where you simply get your brochures and head off again, but a place to pay the entrance fee and spend a few hours looking around, gathering information and learning about the rainforest.

The center offers visitors access to the 23-meter-high Canopy Tower, which gives incredible views across the tall canopy of trees, giving you an idea just how dense the forest is; the mid-canopy Aerial Walkway, which leads to the tower and allows a sneak view across the life going on underneath (you may even see a cassowary); and an all-round comprehensive Display Centre. Established in 1989, the center has been widely recognized as a leader in the field of ecotourism and provides an excellent introduction to the wonders of the Daintree.

CAPE TRIBULATION

Cape Tribulation officially starts where you land off the Daintree River Ferry. Once you've crossed this wide, serene (albeit teeming with crocodiles) river, you are entering another world. The road (the one and only road) gets smaller, steeper, and more winding, the plants more dense and imposing; prehistoric-looking birds cross the road, and on the pristine isolated beaches, there is nothing but a sign warning you about crocodiles. Soon the gregarious vegetation takes over, the road turns into a track, and civilization has been well and truly left behind. There are no villages, let alone towns, for hours, and the change from bustling Cairns could not be more pronounced.

Beaches

There are plenty of idyllic beaches all along the coast: Cow Bay Beach, Thornton Beach (with its small Struck Rock island, which you can walk to at low tide), Coconut Beach, Myall Beach, and Cape Tribulation Beach. All are pretty much deserted and your chance to step fresh out of the dense vegetation onto the pristine white coral sand. Most beaches have a small parking area, often a picnic facility, and many have access to a self-guided nature walk with signs guiding you along, pointing out certain plants or highlighting some historic or interesting fact about the local Kuku Yalanji people.

Recreation

There are plenty of self-guided boardwalks through the forest and along the beaches. One of the most popular is the 1,200-meter **Dubuji Boardwalk** (Myall Beach); it takes around an hour for the round-trip through rare tropical lowland forest, home to the interesting peppermint stick insect, which lives on the pandanus palms. The **Kulki Boardwalk** (near Myall Beach) is a brief 400-meter walk to a lookout with great views to the mountains. The **Mardja Botanical Walk** (Oliver Creek) wanders in a 1,200-meter loop and is studded with signposts teaching you about rainforests and mangroves.

You can go sea kayaking with **Paddletrek Kayak Adventures** (Cape Tribulation Bay, tel. 07/4098-0062, www.capetribpaddletrek.com.au, half day $79) or ziplining with **Jungle Surfing Canopy Tours** (Snake House, Lot 2, Cape Tribulation Rd., tel. 07/4098-0043, www.junglesurfing.com.au, $90 pp, 1.5-2 hours).

Horse riding is available with **Cape Tribulation Horse Rides** (tel. 07/4098-0030, www.capetribhorserides.com.au, from $89 pp) as a 3.5-hour tour, with pickups from your Cape Tribulation accommodations. It's not suitable for children under 13, and the weight limit is 102 kilograms (225 pounds). No previous experience is necessary.

Crocodile spotting is available on the Daintree River, where you get up and close to not only crocs but also other reptiles, birds, and butterflies on the **Crocodile Express** (tel. 07/4098-6120, www.crocodileexpress.com, adult $25, child $13), a hop-on river cruise service from the Daintree River Ferry stop or from Daintree Village.

Accommodations

There is limited accommodation, and most of that is camping. Without a village or town, there is no concentration of places to stay;

Cape Tribulation

rather they string along the Cape Tribulation Road, set into the forest or near the beaches. For a mix of family and hostel accommodations, try the **Ferntree Rainforest Lodge** (Lot 36, Camelot Close, tel. 07/4098-0000, www.ferntreerainforestlodge.com.au, dorm bed $28, private cabin $130). Featuring a quite swanky hostel, with four-bed dorms, and separate lodges for families and couples, Ferntree Rainforest Lodge is set around a pool, right in the middle of the forest, yet minutes away from the beach. There is also an on-site restaurant, The Cassowary Café, along with a bar.

The **Heritage Lodge and Spa** at Cooper Creek (236 Turpentine Rd., tel. 07/4098-9321, www.heritagelodge.net.au, cabins from $280) is the most established higher-end accommodation north of the Daintree River, with different sized single lodges, big enough for two or for a family. There is even a small spa offering local treatments and ingredients.

The **Cape Trib Beach House Resort** (Cape Tribulation Rd., tel. 07/4098-0030, www.capetribbeach.com.au, dorm bed from $26, cabin from $130) offers a wide range of accommodation options, from dorm rooms to a beachfront villa and cabins of various sizes to suit your party. The villa, Kulki Beach House ($600 per night, minimum stay three nights), sleeps up to seven people and is a mere 20 meters from the beach.

Cape Tribulation Camping (Lot 11, Cape Tribulation Rd., tel. 07/4098-0077, www.capetribulationcamping.com.au, unpowered tent sites and powered motorhome sites $40 for two people, safari tents $70 for two people) is a great site, right on the beach, with camp kitchens, barbecues, and laundry facilities, as well as a tour booking desk with options of kayaking, horse riding, and even massages on the beach. For "glamping," try a safari tent, more akin to a little hut, with linen and towels provided, and decking in front of the tent.

Food

Mostly the few food places along the road are associated with the campgrounds and lodges, although there are couple of standalone outfits.

Basic and simple, **The Sandbar** (Cape Tribulation Camping, Lot 11, Cape Tribulation Rd., tel. 07/4098-0077, daily lunch and dinner, hours depending on demand) is a small place that serves a decent wood-fired pizza, even a dessert pizza with caramelized bananas on it. Pizza is $20, but big enough to share.

Laid-back **Whet Café and Bar** (Lot 1 Cape Tribulation Rd., tel. 07/4098-0007, www.whet.net.au, daily 11am-8:30pm, mains $26) offers a bit of a surprise in the middle of the rainforest, with some stylish yet low-key menu options, such as the garlic and lime tiger prawns steamed in a whole fresh coconut with fragrant rice. In addition, the café has a small **cinema** (tickets $10) on-site with showings at 2pm, 4pm, and 8pm.

Thornton Beach Café (90 Cape Tribulation Rd., tel. 07/4098-9118, breakfast, lunch, and early dinner daily, breakfast $15, fish and chips $16) has a perfect location with tables literally on the beach, and is one of the few places along the road that is open for breakfast. It's very basic, but the setting makes up for a lot it may miss. At least stop for coffee and the view.

INFORMATION AND SERVICES

Services and facilities are extremely limited up here, but there is an ATM at Daintree Discovery Centre, a couple of small supermarkets alongside the road, and one gas station at Cow Bay.

GETTING THERE

Driving up from Cairns will take you a little over two hours up Captain Cook Highway, turning right toward Cape Tribulation before Daintree Village. The **Daintree River Ferry** is the only way to cross the river and operates between 6am and midnight. The round-trip for a car is $23; for a trailer it's an extra $8. The ferry crosses continuously, and even if you miss one, it'll only be 10 minutes before it is back to pick you up. Stay in your car during the crossing. If you are the first off the ferry, consider pulling over and letting everybody go before you follow, as it is a small winding road with plenty of lookout and stop-off points, and you might not want to drag a line of cars behind you.

Alternatively, take a day-trip tour with **Back Country Bliss Adventures** (tel. 07/4099-3677, http://backcountryblissadventures.com.au, $155 pp, small group). The tour includes pickups from your hotel, Daintree River Ferry, optional jungle surfing (a.k.a. zip-lining, not included in price, $90 pp), lunch, and a river cruise.

Rainforest Tours

Tropical northern Queensland is covered in dense rainforest, most of which is uninhabited, inaccessible, and protected, so even if you could venture in, you are not allowed to. But to travel all this way up to the northern tip of Australia without experiencing this incredible feat of nature is not an option. Luckily there are plenty of tours that take you out for the day or several days to show you this remote part of the world. Here is a selection of options.

TOURS FROM CAIRNS AND PORT DOUGLAS

FNQ Travel (tel. 07/4044-9792, http://active.fnqtravel.com.au) has a long list of day and overnight trips on their books. For a tour that the kids will enjoy, try the "1 Day Cape Tribulation & Daintree Rainforest with Wildlife Habitat" tour (adult $170, child $90, minimum of 4). It picks up from your hotel (in Cairns, the beaches, or Port Douglas) from 7am onward and starts off with a guided tour at Wildlife Habitat in Port Douglas; wander along elevated boardwalks and observe a huge range of flora and fauna as birds fly and roam freely. See rare animals such as the endangered southern cassowary and the Lumholtz's tree-kangaroo. A cruise on the Daintree River allows you to spot crocodiles, tree snakes, water birds, and other wildlife going through mangroves along the crocodile-infested river. A forest walk is followed by a cable-ferry crossing of the river. Lunch and morning tea are provided. The tour returns between 5pm and 6pm.

Jungle Tours (tel. 07/4041-9440, www.jungletours.com.au) specializes in budget options, such as the "Go Troppo Overnight Tour" (prices vary depending on activities chosen and accommodations), with lots of stops. Accommodation choices and optional activities on the second day make it very flexible. The tour picks up from either Cairns or Port Douglas, with pickup times varying between hotels. First-day stops include Port Douglas, the Wildlife Habitat, Daintree River Ferry, Alexandra Lookout, Dubuji Boardwalk, and a beach at Cape Tribulation, with arrival at the accommodations (either dorm rooms or 3.5-star beach resort) around 4:30pm. The next day's available activities include horse riding, kayaking, jungle ziplines, snorkeling, and night jungle safaris. On the second day you will arrive back at your hotel at approximately 4:30pm.

Tropical Horizons Tour (tel. 07/4035-6445, www.tropicalhorizonstours.com.au) offers an all-day eco-certified Daintree tour (adult $180, child $120, family $580) that includes highlights such as Daintree National Park, Mossman Gorge Centre, Ngadiku Aboriginal Dreamtime Walk, Daintree Village and Timber Museum, tropical restaurant lunch, tropical fruit demonstration and tasting, one-hour Daintree River wildlife cruise, and a Port Douglas tour including Flagstaff Hill Lookout and Four Mile Beach, plus tea and coffee and entrance fees to all Daintree National Park areas.

Eco Resorts

Apart from hotels, motels, and apartments, tropical northern Queensland offers eco resorts for guests who appreciate keeping in tune with the awe-inspiring environment of the region. The resorts are designed to make the most out of their respective settings while making the least impact on nature, giving guests the best of both worlds: luxury at a low carbon footprint.

Located between Palm Cove and Port Douglas, **Thala Beach Lodge** (private road, Oak Beach, Port Douglas, tel. 07/4098-5700, www.thalabeach.com.au, from $226) sits atop a private peninsula with several different habitats not only for the native flora and fauna, but also the guests: accommodations range from suites to eucalyptus bungalows. Built eco-sensitively, the decor is light and tropical, with rattan furniture, wooden floors and decking, and plantation-style shutters. The lodge offers an award-winning restaurant, in-house spa, and nature walks, talks, and experiences, led by local habitat experts—making this a perfect combination of beach and rainforest hideout.

Placed right in the rainforest, with the tag line *nature, nurture, culture,* **Daintree Eco Lodge & Spa** (20 Daintree Rd., Daintree, tel. 07/4098-6100, www.daintree-ecolodge.com.au, from $380) is proud of its combination of location, spa and wellness programs, and closeness to Aboriginal culture. Only 15 rainforest houses are nestled into the forest, close to nature but still protected, with micro-screened balconies and an undercover swimming pool. The spa offers many traditional ingredients and approaches to wellness, and on site Aboriginal guides explain the surroundings and their culture to those who want to know.

Snuggled into the rainforest that lines the peaceful Mossman River, **Silky Oaks Lodge** (Finlayvale Rd., Mossman, tel. 07/4098-1666, www.silkyoakslodge.com.au, from $308) offers closeness to nature with a boutique-style approach to luxury. Thirty-nine river houses and treehouses, named after their distinct locations, offer sensational living accommodations, spectacular views and surroundings, and practically no carbon footprint. Add to that swimming in the river with freshwater turtles and a resident platypus, and a spa that was awarded a "Best in Australia" accolade, and you won't want to leave.

TOURS FROM PORT DOUGLAS ONLY

Tropical Journeys (tel. 07/4099-6999, www.tropicaljourneys.com) offers some off-road four-wheel driving that reaches parts coaches simply cannot reach. The day-long "Bloomfield Track" tour (adult $190, child 4-14 $170, starts at 7:30am) picks you up from your accommodations and heads across the Daintree River toward Cape Tribulation. After morning tea, you go off-road on the Bloomfield Track to Stingray Bay and secluded Cowrie Beach. After a tropical picnic lunch, it's onward to cruise the Cooper River to spot the crocodiles, followed by sampling local Daintree ice cream and a drive to Alexandra Lookout, allowing views across Daintree River, Snapper Island, and Port Douglas.

Daintree Discovery Tours (tel. 07/7098-2878, www.daintreediscoverytours.com.au) offers half-day tours, if you are pressed for time. The morning tour (7:30am-12:30pm, adult $90, child $70, family $275) includes a Daintree River cruise followed by a trek in an open-top four-wheel drive and a short walk to the Cassowary Falls, where you can swim under the waterfall. Morning tea is included. The afternoon tour (1:15pm-5:30pm, adult $90, child $70, family $275) includes a Daintree River cruise followed by a swim in Mossman Gorge and a trip along an elevated boardwalk, spotting the local wildlife. Afternoon tea is included.

Daintree Specialised Tours (tel. 07/4098-7897, www.daintree-specialised-tours.com) operates a classic Land Rover safari wagon, specializing in small groups (maximum six). Please note that these safaris are generally totally flexible, with a tour group of 1-6 passengers being able to choose where they want to go and what they want to see. There are suggested day-long itineraries, but emphasis is on flexibility, with prices of around $700 for a group of six, including pickup and drop-off. One suggested tour is the Bloomfield Falls tour, where you cross the Daintree River, go for a short introductory bushwalk learning what is edible and which plants to avoid due to their unfriendly tendencies, and sample bush tucker. After lunch on the banks of a deep river pool and a dip, you end up at beautiful Bloomfield Falls.

Wildlife Guide

Sea Life

On the Great Barrier Reef alone, you'll find some 400 species of coral, 5,000 species of mollusk, 1,500 species of fish, 14 species of sea snake, six species of sea turtle, a reasonably healthy population of dugongs, and 30 species of whales, dolphins, and porpoises. This is a tiny sample of what you might see.

Angelfish (various species)

The Pomacanthidae family consists of seven genera and around 86 species and should not be confused with freshwater angelfish. With their vibrant colors and deep, laterally compressed bodies, marine angelfishes are some of the more conspicuous residents of the reef. The largest species, the gray angelfish *(Pomacanthus arcuatus)* may reach a length of 60 centimeters, while some of the smaller species do not exceed 15 centimeters. The angelfish changes color as it reaches maturity, and can also change sex if the male in the group disappears. If this happens the dominant female in the group will then become the male. The female angelfish releases its eggs to float with the plankton until hatched.

WHERE TO SEE THEM

Angelfish are found at all levels of the bommie fields (stand-alone coral structures), from the surface to the base of the reef formations and the seabed. The nice thing about angelfish is that they are inquisitive rather than shy and tend to come out to look at you just as much as you look at them.

Blue Starfish *(Linckia laevigata)*

One of the most auspicious inhabitants of the reef, the blue starfish is easily spotted. With five cylindrical arms in usually a bright blue color, but sometimes in different shades, the starfish is predominantly a scavenger, living on dead organisms within the coral reef and on rocks, but it also feeds on algae and microbes. It has an eye at the end of each arm but can only see light and dark.

WHERE TO SEE THEM

They are found on nearly every reef among the coral. On islands such as Lady Elliot and Lady Musgrave, they are very commonly spotted by snorkelers and at low tide.

Cardinalfish (various species)

When most fish on the reef seem to put on their gaudiest colors to impress the divers, the cardinalfish (family Apogonidae) is more one for understated elegance. Their colors are quite subdued, with relatively large eyes. Notable for having their dorsal fin separated from a single protrusion into twin fins, probably the prettiest species is the Banggai cardinalfish *(Pterapogon kauderni)*, which is gray and black with white spots like beads threaded along the fins. In cardinalfish, the male fertilizes and cares for the eggs inside of his mouth.

WHERE TO SEE THEM

Cardinalfish are nocturnal and typically bury themselves within gaps in coral or caves during the daylight hours before emerging at night to get their fill of their typical shrimp- and crab-based diet. So a night dive might be in order.

Clownfish *(Amphiprion ocellaris)*

The one fish everybody knows is Nemo, the clownfish or anemone fish. These orange and

Previous: kangaroos at the beach; koala.

white fish with black details live in groups nestled into the seemingly soft anemones, which they use as protection against their plentiful predators. They are immune to the anemone's stings. What exactly the anemone gets out of the relationship is still unknown. There are actually 328 species of clownfish, and not all look like Nemo; they come in all sorts of different colors and even shapes, and the black and white ones are quite common. Clownfish inhabit a single sea anemone in groups that include the breeding male and female and a number of younger male clownfish. Interestingly, all clownfish are born male and develop female reproductive organs when needed. When the female in the sea anemone group dies, the dominant male becomes female and breeds with one of the males inhabiting the same sea anemone.

WHERE TO SEE THEM

The clownfish is very widely spread across the world's oceans and will be one species you will see for sure when you snorkel or dive, or even during a glass-bottom boat ride along the Great Barrier Reef.

Cone Snails (various species)

Out of the up to 600 species of the Conidae family, about 166 occur in Australian waters, with 133 of those recorded in Queensland. The snails are active predators, typically "hunting" at night. Their teeth are modified into elongated, hollow barbs shaped like harpoons, with a venom gland supplying poison to inject into the flesh of the prey, which may be worms, other mollusks, or fish, immobilizing them. As cone snails tend to have pretty shells, beachcombers often pick them up and can then be harmed. If you have been "bitten" by a cone snail, please alert the nearest lifeguard immediately and ask for medical assistance.

WHERE TO SEE THEM

They are quite common on the beaches, although they come out mostly after dark. If you do see a shell, please don't pick it up unless absolutely certain there is no animal still living inside. They are very poisonous.

Coral Trout *(Plectropomus leopardus)*

A favorite on regional seafood menus, the coral trout in turn ranks fairly high on the reef's food chain itself, with a diet that includes many other smaller fish (with damselfish being a particular favorite). One of

blue starfish

Above: cardinalfish. **Below:** clownfish.

dwarf minke whale

the most visually stunning attributes of the coral trout is the male's ability to instantly change its color when putting on displays of courtship, such as showing off a stunning green polka dot pattern on a red background. Depending on species, coral trout typically grow anywhere from 70 to 120 centimeters in size, and thus are one of the larger common denizens of the Great Barrier Reef.

WHERE TO SEE THEM

Not technically a reef fish, coral trout prefer the open spaces around the coral to hunt. But because they do prey on crustaceans and smaller reef fish, you are likely to see them shoot around at speed chasing the little ones.

Damselfish (various species)

The favorite snack of coral trout, damselfish (family Pomacentridae) are some of the prettiest members of the reef gang. Electric blue, sometimes with splashes of yellow, or entirely yellow, they are stunning and tend to hang out in groups above large clumps of coral. Recent research has shown that juvenile damselfish grow larger fake "eyes" toward the rear of their bodies to direct any potential attacks from predators away from their heads. Young damselfish have lightly colored bodies and grow the conspicuous eyespots on their rear dorsal fin, which fade away as individuals grow older.

WHERE TO SEE THEM

They are probably the most abundant of the reef fish and easily spotted. They tend to hang suspended above a formation of coral and, if you come too close, pop back into the coral in one swift motion.

Dugong *(Dugong dugon)*

Dugongs or sea cows are plant-feeding mammals that are more closely related to elephants than to other marine mammals such as whales and dolphins, but their closest living aquatic relatives are the manatees. Large, up to 400 kilograms heavy, and very gentle creatures, they are teetering on the brink of extinction. Human-related threats to dugongs include being hit by boat propellers, incidental capture in fishing nets and marine debris, and habitat degradation due to coastal development and declining water quality.

WHERE TO SEE THEM

The Great Barrier Reef region supports globally significant populations of dugongs. This is one of the reasons the area was given World Heritage status. There are reportedly some 10,000 individuals living in and around the Great Barrier Reef, and you might just be lucky around the Whitsunday Islands.

Dwarf Minke Whale *(Balaenoptera acutorostrata)*

These whales are a black/purple or gray color, with a length up to seven meters, and their bodies are generally dark gray or black with a white band underneath. Dwarf minke whales, commonly regarded as subtypes of the northern minke whales, are still quite a new species, having first been described in the mid-1980s, after they attracted attention from scientists for frequently approaching waters in the northern Great Barrier Reef, disrupting swimmers. They feed on krill, lantern fish, and other small fish and are utterly harmless to humans as they have no teeth.

WHERE TO SEE THEM

Minke whales are very common along the Great Barrier Reef, and all along the reef whale-watching cruises give you the opportunity to dive and swim with these inquisitive mammals. The best time to encounter them is between May and September.

Giant Grouper *(Epinephelus lanceolatus)*

Giant grouper, sometimes spelled groper, along with the marlin species and swordfish, is one of the world's largest bony fish and the aquatic emblem of Queensland. The species can grow as large as three meters long, weighing up to 600 kilograms. Juveniles have irregular black and yellow markings, while adults are green-gray to gray-brown with faint mottling with small black spots on the fins. The grouper has a large mouth and a rounded tail, and it can expand its mouth to create a strong suction, which allows it to engulf its unsuspecting food.

WHERE TO SEE THEM

While numbers are declining, there are still plenty of those gigantic fish around the reef, and most diving guides know a place where you can spot at least one, so check before a diving trip if you are particularly interested in spotting a grouper.

Green Turtle *(Chelonia mydas)*

Adult green turtles have a smooth, high-domed carapace (shell), are olive green in color, with occasional brown, reddish-brown, or black highlights. Hatchlings have a black carapace with white margins around the carapace and flippers. They grow up to 150 centimeters in length and up to 130 kilograms in weight. The proportion of a green turtle population that nests each year is highly variable and is influenced by variations in the El Niño Southern Oscillation (ENSO) Index. Green turtles are the only species of marine turtle for which this correlation has been shown, and it may be based upon nutrition. Adult green turtles are the only truly herbivorous marine turtles.

WHERE TO SEE THEM

These are the most common turtles around the Great Barrier Reef. There is a popular breeding ground on Heron Island.

Hawksbill Turtle *(Eretmochelys imbricate)*

The hawksbill, which owes its name to its tapered head ending in a pointed bird-like mouth, has two claws on each flipper, along with a heart shaped carapace when young, which turns into a more elongated shape when they get older. Its carapace is serrated, unlike other turtles, and overlapping plates give it a distinctly reptilian appearance when viewed from above. The hawksbill is omnivorous, although it mostly consumes sea sponges. Interestingly, they can also devour food poisonous to other creatures, such as the Portuguese man o' war and the jellyfish-like hydrozoan.

WHERE TO SEE THEM

Unfortunately the hawksbill turtle is a critically endangered species, as their shells remain popular for decorative purposes, and they are one of the rarer species seen on the reefs.

Humpback Whale *(Megaptera novaeangliae)*

Not the largest of whales, with a length of up to 15 meters, humpbacks get their name from the "humping" motion they make when diving back down below the surface after a usually very acrobatic display. Large-scale whaling in the 1940s, '50s, and early '60s is thought to have reduced the population of humpback whales in the Great Barrier Reef Region from around 25,000 animals to

Above: giant grouper. **Below:** hawksbill turtle.

between 200 to 500 individuals, but they can be seen regularly along the Queensland coast when they migrate.

WHERE TO SEE THEM

Each year between April and November, the whales move along the coast and can be spotted off the coast of Port Douglas and Cairns, and farther south as well.

Humphead Maori Wrasse *(Cheilinus undulate)*

Adult humphead Maori wrasses have a relatively deep body, a rounded caudal fin, and a hump on the forehead. The fish is green with wavy lines on the body and two lines behind both eyes. It's the largest species in the family Labridae; it can grow up to 2.3 meters in length, weighing in at a hefty 190 kilograms.

WHERE TO SEE THEM

These wrasses are found in inshore waters and on coral reefs, with larger individuals often near steep outer reef slopes at depths below 10 meters.

Manta Ray *(Manta birostris)*

With a wingspan up to five meters and weighing several hundred kilograms, the manta ray is the next largest marine species on the Great Barrier Reef following the whales and the whale sharks. Often seen "flying" through the deeper columns of water amongst the reef, they are magnificent animals to see when snorkeling.

WHERE TO SEE THEM

They prefer open water but often come close to the reefs around the islands. They are studied off Lady Elliot Island, so you might be lucky there.

Parrot Fish (various species)

Found at every reef, this colorful green turquoise fish (family Scaridae) with the slight overbite is one of the prettiest there is. One of its unique characteristics is how it sleeps; the fish excretes a sleeping bag-like mucous, which surrounds it and offers protection from predators. This sleeping bag also contains antibiotic properties that greatly benefit the fish. Something else to think about: Some scientists say around 30 percent of the coral sand you see at the reef is parrot fish poo. This poo is believed to create small islands while contributing to the profusion of sandy beaches.

manta ray

Above: parrot fish. **Below:** whitetip reef shark.

WHERE TO SEE THEM

Although parrot fish can be found on nearly every coral outcrop, one particularly friendly specimen, called Gavin, can be found on Green Island, where he regularly photobombs the Seawalkers.

Stinger Jellyfish (various species)

The stinger season generally runs from November through to May/June. During this period, the dangerous jellyfish are of particular concern, but most popular beaches have stinger nets in place, within which it is safe to swim. Marine stingers include the most common box jellyfish *(Chironex fleckeri)* and Irukandji *(Carukia barnesi);* however, other stingers include the bluebottle *(Physalia physalis),* hair jelly *(Cyanea capillata),* jimble *(Carybdea rastoni),* fire jelly *(Morbakka fenneri),* and little mauve stinger *(Pelagia noctiluca).*

WHERE TO SEE THEM

This will probably be the first species you will come across, but hopefully only on warning signs along beaches, and not in person. If you do meet them in person, every beach has a vinegar emergency station; pour it on liberally and call the lifeguards for help.

Triggerfish (various species)

A truly picture-perfect fish with a black top, black-and-white spotted belly with yellow accents, and a pointy mouth, triggerfish (family Balistidae) are tidy individuals. To make their nests, the triggerfish lie on the sandy ocean bottom and blow water out of their mouths to create a small crater. They clean the sand of any rubble by picking it up with their teeth and discarding it over the edge. The triggerfish lay their eggs on the bottom and become fiercely protective of them.

WHERE TO SEE THEM

One of the several species can be found on nearly every reef outcrop around Cairns and the various islands.

Whitetip Reef Shark *(Triaenodon obesus)*

This slender shark, around 1.6 meters long, has a short, blunt snout and a brownish-gray color, with scattered dark gray spots on the sides of the body. The tips of the first dorsal fin and upper caudal fin lobe are, as suggested in the name, brilliant white.

WHERE TO SEE THEM

This shark is found in tropical marine waters often associated with coral reefs or lying on the bottom in caves and under ledges; many divers have described this phenomenon as looking like a bunch of logs lined up side by side. While the whitetip reef shark is a curious species that often approaches divers, it is not considered dangerous to people.

Land Mammals

Marsupials evolved in North America, then found their way to South America before arriving in Australia via Antarctica when the southern continents were still joined as the big continent Gondwana. Once there, they diversified to fill many niches. Most of the 140 species of marsupials in Australia are found nowhere else in the world, and the vast majority of the world's marsupials do live in Australia.

A marsupium or pouch is one of the features that characterize marsupials, although not all have a permanent pouch and a few have none at all, while others have theirs open at the bottom rather than the top, such as the wombat. Marsupials are similar to other mammals in being covered in fur and bearing live young that are suckled by the mother, but in marsupials the gestation period is very

dingo

places in the world where you can see the range of mammals, with their little quirks that make them so special and different from each other.

Dingo *(Canis lupus dingo)*

The dingo is a medium-sized dog with a bushy tail and red to yellow coat. Dingoes are not native to Australia but are thought to have been brought to the continent some 15,000 years ago by the Koori people. An alternative theory suggests that they were introduced to Australia by Asian seafarers about 4,000 years ago. Their origins have been traced back to a south Asian variety of gray wolf *(Canis lupus lupus)*, and they have been known to breed with domestic dogs. Dingoes do not bark like dogs, but they do howl.

WHERE TO SEE THEM

Dingoes are mostly absent from New South Wales, Victoria, the southeastern third of South Australia, and the southernmost tip of Western Australia, but you might see one in the bush in Queensland.

short, resulting in the birth of extremely undeveloped young. Minute (baby kangaroos—joeys—are the size of a jellybean when first born), blind, without fur, and with hind limbs only partially formed, these tiny newborns have well-developed forelimbs with claws that enable them to make their way into the pouch and attach to a teat and continue the rest of their development, which can take several long months.

Apart from the large group of the marsupials, the very unusual monotremes and other mammals also call Australia home. Out of the five living species of monotremes in the world, two are found in this country: the platypus and the short-beaked echidna. Like all mammals, both are warm-blooded, have fur, and produce milk for their young, but instead of giving birth to live young, they lay eggs, which makes them unusual, with debates still ongoing as to their exact taxonomy. Other mammals in Australia include a myriad of bats, from large flying foxes to tiny microbats. Australia is one of the few

Flying Fox (various species)

There are several species of flying fox, or fruit bat, in Australia, such as the spectacled flying fox, the grey-headed flying fox, and the black flying fox. They are the largest bat species in Australia, and the vegetarian bats are seen as important pollinators and seed-dispensers for many plants. Common in Queensland and with a large population in Sydney and surroundings, they generally live high in the tree tops, living off native fruits such as figs and feeding on nectar and pollen from flowers. Flying at a rate of around 23 kilometers an hour (with a good tail wind up to 60 kilometers an hour), they tend to forage within a radius of 20 kilometers from their camp, but satellite tracking has shown some individuals to travel 24,000 kilometers in a year, visiting many camps along the east coast of Australia. Late in the dry season, the female gives birth to a single pup.

WHERE TO SEE THEM

The easiest place to spot these large bats is right in the center of Sydney. They roost during the day within the Royal Botanic Gardens and at night fly across the water and over the Sydney Harbour Bridge, making quite a spectacle. They are extremely common in Sydney, and in Cairns there are a handful of trees along Aplin Street where huge numbers roost during the day.

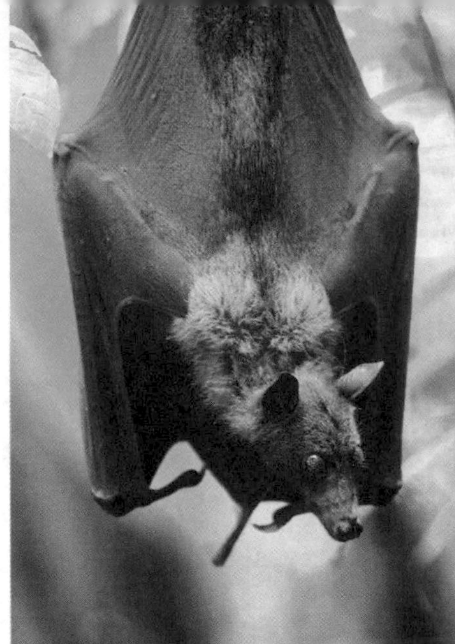

flying fox

Kangaroo *(Macropus spp.)*

There are 60-plus species belonging to the family Macropodidae (*macropod* meaning "great foot"). The family includes kangaroos, wallabies, wallaroos, pademelons, tree-kangaroos, and forest wallabies. Kangaroos are herbivorous, eating a range of plants. Most are nocturnal but some are active in the early morning and late afternoon, and they tend to rest in the daytime as part of large mobs (groups) in the shade under trees. Kangaroos are one of the few animals that are not able to move backwards easily, and this is why they are used on the Australian national emblem. To keep cool they pant like dogs, dig shallow holes in sand and rest there, and lick their forearms to cool their circulating blood.

WHERE TO SEE THEM

If you are outside the city limits in the morning or afternoon, it is difficult not to see kangaroos. They gather in clearings, grazing on fresh grass and shoots and often can be found on golf courses, grassy areas of campsites, and by the side of the road. Unfortunately you will see a lot of dead kangaroos by the side of the road, as they often stop in the middle of the road without fear of traffic.

Koala *(Phascolarctos cinereus)*

Koalas are tree-dwelling, herbivorous marsupials that average about nine kilograms in weight. The koala gets its name from an ancient Aboriginal word meaning "no drink" because it receives over 90 percent of its hydration from eucalyptus leaves, although it is a myth that they don't drink, especially during hot summers and droughts. Ironically, one of the problems they face, together with road deaths and land clearing, is the increasing number of swimming pools in which they drown when trying to take a drink. Koala populations are declining, and if the drop continues at the current rate, they could be extinct within the next five years.

WHERE TO SEE THEM

If you want to hug a koala, Queensland is the only state in Australia where that is still allowed, and any wildlife park will, for a fee, take a picture of you holding a koala. But if you want to see them in their natural habitat, Magnetic Island has one of the largest wild populations in Queensland. On the Fort Walk, look out for their furry little behinds wedged between branches up high in the eucalyptus trees.

Lumholtz's Tree-Kangaroo *(Dendrolagus lumholtzi)*

Unlikely as it sounds, there are kangaroos that

live in trees. Smaller than their ground-dwelling cousins and highly adapted to their lofty life, these are also the only kangaroos that can actually walk backwards and have arms and legs of roughly the same length. The very long tail is not used as an extra limb, but for balance. They are primarily browsing herbivores but can be considered omnivores, as they occasionally consume small birds and eggs.

WHERE TO SEE THEM

Lumholtz—and Bennett—tree-kangaroos are found in patches of northern Queensland's rainforest in the Atherton Tablelands and the surrounding hills, such as the forest near Kuranda, but they are nocturnal, extremely shy, and rare to the point of being listed as endangered, so to see one in the wild would be a true treat.

Microbats (various species)

In Australia there are six families of microbats in the suborder Microchiroptera, containing 58 species. Microbats derive their name from the tiny size they all have in common, with their body weight varying from a minute two grams to a still rather small 170 grams. Microbats form large colonies in summer when their young are born and tend to roost in dense clusters. Particularly in winter they can be inactive for several days and nights, but normally they spend their days in a meditative state and become active at sunset, when they leave their roosts to find food. They prefer to eat flying insects and can eat up to 500 individual insects within an hour, consuming an equivalent to half their body weight in one night.

WHERE TO SEE THEM

Many microbat species live in Sydney and surroundings, with further species living in the rainforest, open forest, coastal scrub, mangroves all along the Queensland coast, and farther inland. A great place to see them in huge numbers is at the Undara Lava Tubes, especially during the sunset tour, when you will be positioned outside a cave, just when they are all leaving for the night. The noise is incredible.

Platypus
(Ornithorhynchus anatinus)

When the first platypus specimen was brought back to Europe by British naturalists, they thought it was a joke: an egg-laying mammal covered in fur, with webbed feet and a duck's bill. Semi-aquatic and mostly nocturnal, this very shy solitary monotreme feeds on insect larvae, worms, or other freshwater insects, with an ability to consume its own body weight in food in 24 hours. It can be found in freshwater lakes and streams in eastern Australia. The males have a venomous spur behind each hind ankle, with enough venom to kill a small dog or cause excruciating pain in humans. The females lay two eggs during the dry season in a burrow and feed their young for up to five months. And if you are wondering about the plural of platypus, there seems to be no definite rule: Most say platypus, others try platypuses, while sticklers of ancient Greek insist that it should really be platypodes.

WHERE TO SEE THEM

The best place, with a near guarantee, to spot a platypus in the wild is in Eungella National Park, an hour's drive from Mackay. At Broken River there is a platform dedicated to platypus spotting; for your best chance, though, you'll need to be there 4am-8am or 3pm-7pm.

Possum (various species)

Australia's possums are arboreal marsupials belonging to the suborder Phalangeriformes. The common brushtail possum is the most widely distributed large possum species. Roughly the size of a house cat with a bushy tail and pointy ears, the common brushtail is usually silvery gray in color with a black band across the snout and a white to brownish-yellow belly. Adults weigh around 1.5-4 kilograms. Brushtails come out after dark to feed on flowers, fruit, buds, and leaves. They are very inquisitive and often come down from a tree to have a look at you, but refrain from touching them, as they can have a nasty bite. Much smaller than the brushtail possum, the common ringtail possum weighs up to one kilogram and is around half the size of a cat. The tail is sleek with a white tip and is prehensile, meaning the possum can use the tail when climbing on branches, like a fifth limb. Gray-brown in color, ringtails are also nocturnal and tend to live off eucalyptus leaves.

kangaroo

WHERE TO SEE THEM

Mainly inhabiting areas of woodlands and open forests, common brushtails are also often found in parks and suburban gardens, where they make a home in a tree hole, roof, or shed. Go to any park in Sydney after dark and you'll see plenty of them everywhere. Like the brushtails, the ringtails have pretty much invaded city parks and suburbia, and they clamber around the trees soon after sunset.

Short-Beaked Echidna *(Tachyglossus aculeatus)*

These spiny ant-eaters, one of four species of echidna, are, together with the platypus, the only monotreme animals on Earth. They exhibit many features that are reptilian in nature, such as egg laying, legs that extend outward then downward, and a lower body temperature than other mammals. Echidnas can grow up to 45 centimeters in length, weighing around 3.5 kilograms, and the body, except for the underside, face, and legs, is covered with cream-colored spines. They eat mostly ants and termites, although they will also eat grubs, larvae, and worms, and they use their strong forepaws to open up the ant or termite nest and get the ants out with their extremely long tongue.

WHERE TO SEE THEM

Echidnas are slow movers and are often spotted at night when they waddle across country lanes. If you move slowly and carefully you can approach them. To get them off the road, hold them underneath, as their belly is soft.

Wallaby (various species)

There are some 30 species of wallaby (family Macropodidae) found in a variety of habitats throughout the Australian continent. The habitats of wallabies are so diverse that wallaby species are often named after their habitat, such as the rock wallaby, while others are named after their size and appearance, such as the pretty-faced wallaby. With wallabies and kangaroos belonging to the same family, what is the difference? Mostly size. Kangaroos are generally larger and have more height between their ankles and knees, which makes their legs seem out of proportion to their body. Then there is the coloring: A wallaby's coat is usually brighter, with two to three different colors. There is also a difference in their teeth, although that one is difficult to tell from afar.

WHERE TO SEE THEM

Wallabies are found in nearly all habitats. If you are heading to the Undara Lava Tubes, you'll meet plenty of rock and pretty-faced wallabies; on Magnetic Island there are also

Above: koala. **Below:** platypus.

Should You Cuddle a Koala?

It is the most iconic souvenir picture any visitor to Australia can bring home: the one of you holding a little koala. After all, everybody will immediately know you've been to Australia. But should you get that photo? And will you actually get to hug the animal?

Picking up a koala is actually against the law in all states bar Queensland. You can get near a koala in most wildlife parks; all of the park managers are very aware that these are the most-loved animals, the ones that overseas visitors want to get close to, so they arrange feeding schedules and talks about them. In some wildlife centers you can get into the enclosure and stand next to the koala perched in its tree and get your photo done. It comes at a price—usually quite a steep price, of around $20 each and more. But even then you do not get to hold the koala, although sometimes you are allowed to stroke one gently on the back.

There is a controversy as to whether you should be able to hold a koala. After all, this is not at all natural for the animals, even if it feels like the most natural thing to us. Is it stressing them too much, is it a marketing ploy at the cost of the animals' well-being? If you are an ardent animal lover and conservationist, then the answer should be not to hug any wild animal.

But on the other hand, the koalas offered up for the picture experience are not wild, nor have they even lived in the wild, generally; the money made on the photos is generally put back into caring for the koalas in the center and in the wild, and these stunts are very well organized. The time with them is strictly limited, the koalas get rest days and are never used two days in a row, and you are under the strictest instructions when you do get close to one. You must stand like a tree, arms out, and no grabbing hold of the animal. The koala will be placed on you, and your arms are gently positioned so it is comfortable for the koala, not necessarily you. No squeezing, tickling, or cuddling of any kind is allowed. Even standing like a tree, however, the experience is quite magical, with this little creature clinging onto you with its funny-toed feet and hands and its fluffy little ears sticking out in front of your face. But just to put an end to two myths: They don't smell bad (there's a little eucalyptus breath as if they've been sucking a throat lozenge), and they are not as soft as you might think—more like a well-worn fleece, slightly matted, but nice and warm.

So should you cuddle a koala? Obviously it's up to your conscience, but if you really can't resist, here is a selection of wildlife centers where you can get up close and personal to a koala:

- **Wildlife Habitat,** Port Douglas (Port Douglas Rd., tel. 07/4099-3235, http://wildlifehabitat.com.au)
- **Cairns Tropical Zoo,** Palm Cove (Captain Cook Hwy., Clifton Beach, tel. 07/4055-3669, www.cairnstropicalzoo.com.au)
- **Cairns Night Zoo,** Palm Cove (Captain Cook Hwy., Clifton Beach, tel. 07/4055-3669, www.cairnsnightzoo.com)
- **Kuranda Koala Gardens,** near Cairns (Heritage Market Place, tel. 07/4093-9953, www.koalagardens.com)
- **Cairns Zoom & Wildlife Dome,** Cairns (35-41 Wharf St., on top of the Pullman Reef Hotel Casino, tel. 07/4031-7250, http://cairnszoom.com.au)
- **Bungalow Bay Koala Village,** Magnetic Island (40 Horseshoe Bay Rd., tel. 07/4778-5577, www.bungalowbay.com.au)
- **Billabong Sanctuary,** Townsville (Bruce Hwy., about 20 minutes south of Townsville, tel. 07/4778-8344, www.billabongsanctuary.com.au)

wallaby

lots of rock wallabies, and you'll spot numerous species across the countryside, especially during early mornings and late afternoons.

Wombat (various species)

There are three species of wombat in Australia: the common wombat, also called the bare-nosed wombat, which is quite common all over Australia; the southern hairy-nosed wombat; and the northern hairy-nosed wombat, which is endemic to Queensland and severely endangered, with at most a mere 400 individuals said to be left in the wild. All of them are marsupials with their pouches opening toward the hind legs, to prevent dirt from getting into the pouch while digging burrows. All are primarily nocturnal. They are cousins of the koala, with a hard pad on their backsides with which they compact the walls of their burrows, which can be up to 30 meters long. The average wombat is about one meter long and weighs about 25 kilograms, living off mostly grasses and roots.

WHERE TO SEE THEM

Unless you are out on a secluded campsite at night or driving in rural areas at night, it is unlikely that you will see a wombat in the wild. But to meet one and learn a little more about their plight, especially of the northern hairy-nosed wombat, head to Rockhampton Zoo in the Rockhampton Botanical Gardens, which has a research facility dedicated to them, or the Koala Sanctuary on Magnetic Island, where you can meet the two resident wombats.

Reptiles and Amphibians

An amphibian is often regarded as an evolutionary link between fish and reptiles, and they are dependent on water to some degree, more so than most reptiles. Types of amphibians include frogs, toads, salamanders, and newts. Only the frogs occur naturally in Australia, although one species of toad, the cane toad, has been introduced and is now widely distributed. Australia is home to two species of crocodiles, several species of turtle, and many species of snakes and lizards.

Cane Toad *(Bufo marinus)*

In the 1930s cane-growers in Queensland had their crops severely threatened by a near epidemic of beetles, and the Queensland Department of Agriculture looked into possible solutions. Trying not to use environmentally damaging chemicals, they thought of a "less destructive" approach and imported cane toads, which were thought to increase yields in sugarcane crops by eating said beetles. The rest is history and the toads a true pest, with no local predators. These huge toads can grow up to 26 centimeters and 2.5

kilograms, and they produce a cocktail of highly toxic, physiologically active substances concentrated in their "warty" skin. Their toxins are very dangerous if eaten or rubbed into the skin or the eyes.

WHERE TO SEE THEM

Cane toads are found in open forests, grasslands, swamps, beach dunes, farmland, and suburban areas. Not widely spread through rainforests, they can still be found in these areas along roads and walking tracks. They are often encountered on roads at night and around outdoor lights that attract nocturnal insects.

Carpet Python *(Morelia spiiona)*

A common and very beautiful snake, the carpet python is totally harmless despite its potential to reach lengths of up to 3.5 meters. It is usually active at night and spends most of the day coiled up in a tree or rafters, or stretched out basking in an open area. They are quite tolerated by people living in suburbia because they tend to keep the rat population down, but if you keep birds in a cage outside, you're bound to find a snake showing interest in them sooner rather than later. Despite that, they are quite maternal for reptiles, with the female helping her eggs to maintain temperatures at an optimum level for embryo development by coiling around them, occasionally shivering to adjust the temperature.

WHERE TO SEE THEM

Carpet pythons can be found in habitats ranging from tropical rainforest in the northeast of Australia to arid and coastal regions. If you are staying in accommodations in the countryside, ask a local resident, as they are bound to know where there is one living nearby.

Common Green Tree Snake *(Dendrelaphis punctulata)*

Beautifully adapted to its habitat, the tree snake is often bright green with a lighter, yellowish belly, but it can also be more gunmetal gray, depending on its habitat. It has a sleek body and head and lovely big eyes. Nonvenomous, it moves at speed and likes to eat lizards and frogs. Growing up to one meter in length, they only have small teeth and no fangs, but if threatened or handled, they can emit a nasty smell from their anal glands.

WHERE TO SEE THEM

Green tree snakes are very common in Brisbane and the surrounding area, but they

cane toad

Crikey! The Legend of Steve Irwin

Wildlife warrior and television personality Steve Irwin became known around the world through his documentary *The Crocodile Hunter*, his enthusiastic exclamations of "Crikey!" (an utterance of surprise and admiration in Australia), and as the owner of Australia Zoo, north of Brisbane.

Although he was named Queenslander of the Year 2003 and the State of Queensland celebrates Steve Irwin Day every year on November 15, Steve Irwin was actually born in Upper Fern Tree Gully, Victoria, in 1962. He moved to Queensland with his parents when he was seven years old and developed his special bond with and interest in reptiles through his parents' Beerwah Reptile and Fauna Park. He helped his father to capture problem crocodiles and look after them before they could either turn on people or be shot by poachers.

Over the years, he became a dedicated advocate for crocodiles and other reptiles and in the early 1990s took over the running of his parents' wildlife park, which by then had been renamed Queensland Reptile and Fauna Park. He met American tourist Terri Rains in 1991, and they married in 1992. The same year, they traveled and filmed a wildlife documentary, which was soon turned into the successful series *The Crocodile Hunter*.

Dividing his time between making documentaries about Australia's amazing wildlife, getting up very close and personal throughout all his encounters, and his conservation work, plus running the now renamed Australia Zoo, Steve became a household name throughout the world and became synonymous with the (stereo-)typical lively outgoing Australian in khakis chasing crocodiles around the place.

Sadly, in 2006, while filming a documentary off the coast of Cairns, he was killed in a freak accident involving a stingray. His wife and two children are still running Australia Zoo, with his teenage daughter Bindi becoming a TV-documentary star in her own right, speaking out for the animals and carrying on the Crocodile Hunter's legacy.

are notoriously difficult to spot because they blend in perfectly with their environment. If you are going to the Undara Lava Tubes, you will hopefully see some either during the sunset tour or in the trees by the tubes' entrance. Get the ranger to point them out to you.

Coastal Taipan *(Oxyuranus scutellatus)*

The coastal taipan snake is highly venomous and probably Australia's most dangerous. They are extremely nervous and alert snakes, and any movement near them is likely to trigger an attack. Like any snake the taipan prefers to avoid conflict and will quietly slip away if given the chance; however, if surprised or cornered it will ferociously defend itself. The head has a distinct angular shape, with the mouth and face generally paler than the body, which ranges from a uniform pale brown to nearly black, with the belly lighter with orange spots and blotches.

WHERE TO SEE THEM

Although called coastal, the taipan can be found in dry forest land, grassy and shrubby areas, and sugarcane fields. It's mostly found around Brisbane, along the coast from temperate to tropical regions, although it is a little less common in tropical northern Queensland. Coastal taipans are active throughout the year; however, they are most commonly encountered in late winter and spring (of the southern hemisphere).

Eastern Bearded Dragon *(Pogona barbata)*

The eastern bearded dragon occurs along the length of the Great Dividing Range and is replaced in more arid areas by the central bearded dragon. Bearded dragons are named for the distinctive flap of skin below their jaw. When threatened, these lizards assume a defensive posture, opening their mouths and pushing their throat skin forward to make this "beard." This, combined with the strong

Above: carpet python. **Below:** eastern bearded dragon.

spikes lining the lizard's throat and the side of its body, serves as a deterrent to would-be predators. Although they are predominantly gray in color, color change can occur, depending on their emotional state.

WHERE TO SEE THEM

They are a common sight along the Queensland coast, up to Cairns. They're terrestrial and sun-loving, so it is not uncommon to see them basking in the sunshine on the roadside, on fenceposts or logs.

Estuarine Crocodile *(Crocodylus porosus)*

Estuarine, or saltwater, crocodiles (or simply "salties") have not noticeably evolved in the last 60 million years, being perfectly adapted for their lifestyle and having no natural predators except for humans. Because of hunting, they were on the verge of extinction in the 1970s, until the government intervened and they became a protected species. Now the population has shot up to more than 200,000 in the wild. Especially in northern Queensland, the ubiquitous warnings by the sides of rivers, wetlands, and the sea need to be taken seriously.

They are remarkable creatures: They can hold their breath for up to eight hours, cutting off circulation to their legs and tail; they live for some 70 to 80 years, and the males can grow up to six meters in length and more than 1,000 kilograms in weight.

The females are extremely protective of their young, helping them to hatch by rolling the eggs in their mouths and looking after the babies for some two months after they hatch, something unheard of in the reptile world.

WHERE TO SEE THEM

In tropical northern Queensland you will come across increasing numbers of warning signs the farther north you go. The Daintree River is one of the easiest places to hop on a croc tour and see them in their natural habitat.

Freshwater Turtle *(Cheluidae spp.)*

There are two basic body forms found in the 14-odd species of freshwater turtles in Queensland: short-necked and long-necked—long-necked turtles fold their necks sideways under the protective edge of the shell. All have clawed, webbed feet, and most species have distinct barbels on the chin. Some of the

green tree frog

short-necked turtles have the dubious ability to breathe through their backsides because their cloaca is lined with numerous finger-like projections that act in a similar manner to the gills of a fish. By breathing like this, the turtle can satisfy much of its oxygen needs and needs to surface much less frequently than others.

WHERE TO SEE THEM

They live in the streams, rivers, and lagoons along Queensland's coast, and if you go platypus-spotting in Eungella National Park, you will see plenty of them sunning themselves on logs and boulders.

Green Tree Frog (*Litoria caeruiea,* plus other species)

The common green tree frog is a large species, growing to 11 centimeters, with a bright to dull green color and a quite rounded head with a fleshy skin fold above the ear. The tree frog's diet includes spiders, crickets, lizards, other frogs, and cockroaches, and it seems the green tree frog is a natural insect repellent, with secretions from its skin reportedly being lethal to blowflies. The green tree frog is distributed through the eastern and northern parts of Australia.

WHERE TO SEE THEM

Although these are tree frogs and they can actually climb trees, they prefer cool damp places and, particularly in more arid areas, will often use human habitation for shelter. They are well known for their habit of hiding under the rim of outback toilet bowls, and you'll probably find some sitting in the public toilets around picnic areas.

Lace Monitor (*Varanus varius*)

This is a great lizard in so many ways: Growing up to two meters long, this slender lizard has strong claws and can climb trees effortlessly, and it is the only lizard to have a forked tongue. Monitors live off birds, insects, bird eggs, reptiles, and small mammals, but will readily feed on carrion, including road-kill. The female will lay up to 12 eggs a year, often into termite mounds found in trees, excavating a hole on the side of the termite mound, laying the eggs, and then leaving the termites to reseal the eggs inside the nest. It is believed that the female is aware of when the eggs are due to hatch and returns to the nest to open it up to allow the baby monitors to escape.

WHERE TO SEE THEM

The lace monitor lives along the Queensland coast and tablelands and most of the islands. Much of its time is spent up fairly large trees, although they usually come down to the ground to forage for food, and as they are learning to investigate picnic sites for tidbits, you will most likely encounter some on island campsites.

Birds

There are more than 820 native species of bird, ranging from coastal birds to tropical parrots, from your common sparrow to the elusive cassowary. Queensland in particular is a bird-lover's paradise, with the state not only having a wealth of native birds, but also being a favorite stop-off for many migrating species from Asia and beyond.

Australian Bustard (*Ardeotis australis*)

The Australian bustard is one of Australia's largest birds. It is a mainly gray-brown bird, speckled with dark markings, with a pale neck and black crown, with a slight crest and a white eyebrow. There are bold black and white markings on the wing. The female is slightly smaller than the male. Newly hatched

Australian king parrot

chicks are striped dark and light. Bustards are unique among Australia's birds in that they exhibit what is known as an "exploded lek" mating system. Leks are tight aggregations of males that come together to display in specific areas, in order to attract females. Usually, among lekking species, it is the larger, more elaborate males that are most successful at attracting mates.

WHERE TO SEE THEM

Bustards live in grasslands, grassy woodlands, and low shrub lands, and you'll see them walking slowly and erectly across the grasses, often turning to look back at you if you stop for them.

Australian King Parrot *(Alisterus scapularis)*

Bright red plumage and green wings and back, and in the females a green head as well, make Australian king parrots some of the most conspicuous birds in Australia. It takes nearly three years for the male king parrot to develop his full colored feathers; before that he resembles the predominantly green female. Mostly traveling in pairs, the birds are found in coastal forests, preferring humid and rainy regions, but they are more and more often found in urban areas as well. They feed on seeds of eucalyptus and acacia trees, fruit, berries, nuts, nectar, blossoms, leaf buds, and insects and their larvae.

WHERE TO SEE THEM

You will see flashes of the colors along the coast of Queensland, especially when they fly to their roosting trees at sunset.

Australian Magpie *(Gymnorhina tibicen)*

Magpies are basically a black and white crow. They are everywhere, in cities and the countryside, living in groups, although you do see just a couple of them at a time in parks. They are extremely loud, with their shriek sounding something like a broken water pipe, although reportedly they have one of the most complex songs in the world. When they breed, they can turn extremely vicious, attacking passersby before they even realize that they might be near a nest. Many places put up warning signs, for example at Yeppoon Esplanade, to try to limit the damage these quite large birds with very solid beaks can do to unsuspecting humans.

WHERE TO SEE THEM

Pretty much everywhere.

Australian Pelican *(Pelecanus conspicillatus)*

There are seven species of pelicans in the world, all similar in shape and, with one exception, primarily white in color. The most characteristic feature of pelicans is the elongated bill with its large throat pouch; the Australian pelican's bill is up to 50 centimeters long and is larger in males than females. With a wingspan of up to 2.5 meters, these are impressive birds. During the courtship period, the bill and pouch of the birds change color dramatically. The forward half of the pouch becomes bright salmon pink, while the skin of the pouch in the throat region turns chrome yellow. Parts of the top and base of the bill change to cobalt blue, and a black diagonal stripe appears from the base to the tip. This color change is of short duration, with the intensity usually subsiding by the time incubation starts.

WHERE TO SEE THEM

They can be found in the coastal and estuarine waters along the Queensland coast, with groups living in most marinas and creeks. Walk along Cairns's Esplanade and you'll see them on the mud banks.

Australian White Ibis *(Threskiornis molucca)*

This bird looks just like its mummified Egyptian ancestors, with white plumage, black legs, and black, naked head and neck and curved long beak. A wading bird, the white ibis is found anywhere where it's not bone-dry, as their range of food includes both terrestrial and aquatic invertebrates and human scraps. The favored foods are crayfish and mussels, which the bird obtains by digging with its long bill. Mussels are opened by hammering them on a hard surface to get to the inside.

WHERE TO SEE THEM

In Sydney, look no further than the Royal Botanic Gardens, and do watch your fish and chips on Bondi Beach, as you will have least one ibis looking for scraps. They are also common in northern Queensland, anywhere along the creeks, estuaries, and wetlands.

Brush Turkey *(Alectura lathami)*

The Australian brush turkey, or just brush turkey, scrub turkey, or wild turkey, is unmistakably black in color, with the head and neck skin red and a red-and-yellow wattle around the neck. They scratch around the undergrowth for food. The most amazing thing about them is the enormous leaf and plant matter mounds the dominant males build for the incubation of their eggs. The turkeys are up to 60 centimeters in size, but their mounds can be two meters in diameter, with as many as 30 eggs, laid by several females, in one mound. The decomposing plant matter gives off heat, saving the birds having to sit on them, and the chicks are immediately self-sufficient upon hatching.

Australian white ibis

emu

Females lay 3-5 large, olive-green eggs, generally between June and October. That done, the eggs are incubated by the male, who raises the chicks alone. The young start fending for themselves at about 8-18 months old, when they are chased away by the male.

WHERE TO SEE THEM

There are pockets of cassowaries near Mission Beach and around Cape Tribulation, where plenty of signs will warn you about the birds. Sadly, the best chance of spotting them is when they are crossing the road, but many of the roads through their territory are equipped with speed bumps, slowing you down to safer speeds. When you do see one, don't get out of the car to get close to them, because they have a temper and turn vicious very quickly.

Cattle Egret *(Ardea ibis)*

Similar to other egrets, the cattle egret is quite small and stocky, with brilliant white feathers and a yellow beak, which turns orange during breeding season. Although classified as a water bird, this egret likes to eat grasshoppers, frogs, cane toads, lizards, and some small mammals.

WHERE TO SEE THEM

Being cattle egrets, they like to inspect cattle for ticks, making them easy to spot when they are perching on the backs of grazing cattle along the Queensland coast or at least mingling with the livestock in the fields. They also follow tractors plowing fields and flock around wetlands and meadows. Thanks to the many working farms in northern Queensland, you'll see lots of these birds.

Emu *(Dromaius novaehollandiae)*

The emu is the world's third largest bird. The ostrich, living in Africa, and the cassowary, living in tropical northern Queensland, take the top positions. They stand 1.5-2 meters tall and on average weigh 36 kilograms. They have three toes and long legs, which allow them to run extremely fast. In this species, the female

WHERE TO SEE THEM

Brush turkeys live in close forests or dense vegetation pretty much throughout northern Queensland, with pockets in New South Wales, and even though numbers have been depleted due to shooting, they are still plentiful. You will most likely spot them on any of the nature walks anywhere in Queensland, and even in the gardens of lodges and hotels, if slightly out of town.

Cassowary *(Casuarius casuarius)*

Up to two meters in height, with a high helmet-like protrusion on its head, a vivid blue neck, and long drooping red wattles, the southern cassowary looks like some prehistoric animal. Found only in the tropical rainforests of northeast Queensland, Papua New Guinea, and some surrounding islands, this bird is extremely rare and utterly unique. The heaviest of Australia's flightless birds (the emu is taller), the cassowary lives right in the dense forest, rarely coming out into clearings.

is larger than the male and, after breeding, wanders away and leaves the male to perform all the incubation. Sometimes she will find another mate and breed again. The male takes his job seriously and incubates the eggs without drinking, feeding, defecating, or leaving the nest.

WHERE TO SEE THEM

Interestingly enough, the first specimen collected in 1788 by Europeans was from what is now the inner suburb of Sydney, Redfern. Today, emus are absent from heavily populated regions, especially along the east coast, but you might spot them a little farther inland. A good spot to try to see then is in Emu Park, north of Yeppoon, which must have been named for obvious reasons, as there still is a population living by the coast.

Galah *(Eolophus roseicapillus)*

Also called the rose-breasted cockatoo, this stunning bird has a pink head, chest, and neck with gray wings and tail. The galah is one of the most abundant and familiar of the Australian parrots, occurring over most of Australia, including some offshore islands. They spend much of the day sheltering from heat in the foliage of trees and shrubs, with large and very noisy flocks of birds meeting up at sunset to roost together at night. Galahs form permanent pair bonds, although a bird will take a new partner if the other one dies, and they have been recorded breeding with other members of the cockatoo family, both in the wild and captivity.

WHERE TO SEE THEM

Galahs are very common, and if you go to any of the larger parks around sunset you will first hear them, then see huge flocks of pink birds descending on the trees.

Laughing Kookaburra *(Dacelo novaeguineae)*

Due to this bird's call, which sounds like raucous laughter, you will usually hear a kookaburra before you see one, usually at the inconvenient time of 5am in the morning. According to an Aboriginal legend, the kookaburra's famous chorus of laughter every morning is a signal for the sky people to light the great fire that illuminates and warms the earth by day. It's the largest bird in the kingfisher family, with a thick beak and a very fluffy brown and beige body. Unlike its kingfisher cousins, the kookaburra is sedentary and occupies the same territories the year round. Before spring breeding season, when family groups adjust their boundaries, keen ornithologists can easily locate the individual territories by listening to the noisy choruses at dusk as each group calls in turn and awaits the replies of neighboring groups.

laughing kookaburra

WHERE TO SEE THEM

Kookaburras are common in most habitats, even in the cities' parks and gardens. They tend to swoop down and harass picnickers, trying to steal scraps of food to add to their diet of snakes, lizards, rodents, and the odd small bird, although they mostly live on various insects and other invertebrates. Their method of hunting, perch and pounce, is typical of kingfishers, so watch out.

Magpie Lark *(Grallina cyanoleuca)*

The conspicuous magpie lark, also called peewee, is nearly as common as your average sparrow, but a lot prettier. It's relatively petite, at least when compared to the Australian magpie, and the black and white plumage helps distinguish males from females, with the male having a black throat and a black face with a white stripe above the eye, and the female a white throat and white around her beak.

WHERE TO SEE THEM

They are common throughout Australia and you'll see them in urban areas and parks.

Rainbow Lorikeet *(Trichoglossus haematodus)*

The rainbow lorikeet is unmistakable with its bright red beak and colorful plumage. Both sexes look alike, with a blue or lilac head and belly; green wings, tail, and back; and an orange or yellow breast. They are often seen in loud and fast-moving flocks or in communal roosts at dusk, as they are strongly gregarious and usually travel in parties of a few dozen, with even larger flocks congregating where there are is plenty of food. They have a brush-tipped tongue, an adaptation for feeding on pollen and nectar.

WHERE TO SEE THEM

The rainbow lorikeet is found in a wide range of treed habitats, including rainforest and woodlands, in coastal regions across northern and eastern Australia, as well as in well-treed urban areas. If you are in the Rockhampton Botanical Gardens, the wild lorikeets tend to come to the zoo to get some food usually laid out for them.

Sulphur-Crested Cockatoo *(Cacatua galerita)*

These large, extremely vocal, and utterly stunning birds can be found throughout Australia's northern and eastern mainland and are common in urban parks. The popularity of the sulphur-crested cockatoo as a cage bird has increased its range, as these birds either escape or are released deliberately in areas where they do not already occur. The species has become a pest around urban areas, where it uses its powerful bill to destroy timber decking and paneling on houses.

WHERE TO SEE THEM

At any urban park around sunset you will hear the distinctive loud screech of the sulphur-crested cockatoo, ending with a slight upward inflection. Then you'll see flashes of white clouding the sky, usually descending on palm trees.

Wedge-Tailed Eagle *(Aquila audax)*

In the early 1900s bounties were paid for the destruction of these eagles, as it was believed they were detrimental to the sheep industry. In one year in Queensland 10,000 bounties were paid, and between 1927 and 1968 in Western Australia another 150,000. It has since been realized that these birds only attack sick or injured animals, and today they are protected in all states. With a wingspan of up to 2.74 meters, the wedge-tailed eagle is the largest raptor in Australia.

WHERE TO SEE THEM

The eagles are commonly seen gliding over forest and open country on plains and mountains throughout mainland Australia. Head off inland from the cities and you'll soon spot them, often hovering above roadkill.

Insects and Spiders

Insects comprise 75 percent of all animal species that scientists have named and described, and the key to their global triumph over most species is their ability to survive on land and take to the air. It is estimated that Australia has over 300,000 insect species, but only 160,000 have been named or described. As for Australian spiders, they are the most widely distributed venomous creatures in Australia, with an estimated 10,000 species inhabiting a variety of ecosystems. Luckily, records show no deaths from spider bites in the country since 1979.

Cairns Birdwing *(Ornithoptera priamus)*

The Cairns birdwing is the largest endemic butterfly in Australia, with a wingspan of up to 18 centimeters. In addition to its size, its beauty makes these difficult to overlook. Shimmering gold and green tones are made even more vibrant by sunlight. Sadly, once hatched, the Cairns birdwing butterfly has only four to five weeks of life, and those are busy with courtship and mating. Interestingly, given their short life span, courtship can take up to 36 hours.

WHERE TO SEE THEM

Cairns birdwing butterflies are abundant in tropical northern Queensland from Mackay north up to Cooktown, and you can spot them tumbling along clearings in the rainforest, in the gardens, and parks. The males often come out early for their so-called "morning patrol" in search of a female.

Funnel-Web Spider *(Atrax robustus)*

The male of this species is Australia's most dangerous spider, and one of the species is indigenous to Sydney, of all places. Sydney funnel-web spiders are large black spiders with big powerful fangs, which can be up to 7 millimeters long. The body of the female is about 3.5 centimeters long, while the male is smaller and about 2.5 centimeters long. Their bodies are covered with fine hairs and they have shiny legs. They

Cairns birdwing

live in small, neat holes lined with a collar of silk in parks and suburban gardens. The holes are made in shady places under rocks, shrubs, logs, and leaf litter, with silk threads leading away from the entrance to the burrow to trap small animals such as beetles, cockroaches, insect larvae, snails, millipedes, and sometimes even small frogs and lizards.

Be careful with the funnel-webs, as the males are very aggressive if disturbed in any way. An antivenom has been devised, so if you are bitten call the Poison Information Centre (tel. 13/11-26, daily 24 hours).

WHERE TO SEE THEM

Funnel-webs, with their various subspecies, are found mostly on the east coast of Australia, predominantly in moist wooded areas and highlands. So, while they are well known for living in Sydney, with species that are only found there, their genera can be found as far north as northern Queensland.

Golden-Orb Weaving Spider *(Nephila spp.)*

Golden orb spiders are huge, with females of the species growing up to a hand span's width, but the males are tiny in comparison. There are several species, but they all have their web-making abilities in common. Enormous webs, up to one meter in diameter, are made of strong silk that shimmers golden in the light. They tend to spread between trees, across paths, and the female spider tends to be there waiting at all times. The webs can be so strong that they trap small birds, even bats. Luckily, these are nonvenomous spiders.

WHERE TO SEE THEM

Golden-orb weaving spiders are found in dry open forest and woodlands, coastal sand dune shrub land, and mangrove habitats. Sometimes you will see them on verandas and balconies, with the webs being really rather pretty and the spiders hanging motionless waiting for victims.

Green Tree Ant *(Oecophylla smaragdina)*

Green tree ants, also called weaver ants, live in colonies in trees. They build nests from living leaves, pulling leaves together and "gluing" them tight with silk from their own larvae. To reach the leaves, ants form chains of up to 12 centimeters long to bridge the gap between the leaves, anchoring themselves in position using tiny hooks on their feet. Green tree ants have long been used as so-called bush tucker, with the Aboriginal people utilizing the ubiquitous ants to make refreshing drinks and potions to cure headaches, as a cold remedy, and as an antiseptic.

WHERE TO SEE THEM

The ants are very common in tropical northern Queensland, and they can be seen in many campsites, parks, and forested areas. Look for round shapes in the trees; once you spot one, you'll soon see more.

Hercules Moth *(Coscinocera hercules)*

Growing from stunning pale-blue caterpillars of some 12 centimeters long, the females of the Hercules moth have a wingspan of up to 27 centimeters and the largest wing area of any moth in the world. Males have the rear corners of the hind wings stretched into long tails. They are absolutely stunning but very short-lived, as the adult moths do not feed because they do not have mouth parts, and the females die after mating and laying their eggs.

WHERE TO SEE THEM

Hercules moths can be found in tropical northern Queensland and are most commonly seen around the bleeding heart tree, as the caterpillars like to feed on those leaves. A good spot to try to see them is around the Barron River Hydro Power Station, whose floodlights attract the moths at night.

Huntsman Spider *(Sparassidae spp.)*

There are several species of huntsman

spiders, also called giant crab spiders because of their crab-like hairy legs, and they are all rather large and can reach an adult's hand-span width from leg to leg. They live in the countryside and urban areas, and do come inside houses. But however intimidating they might look and behave, they are nonvenomous, and even if you do get bitten, you should be able to get away with just some swelling. The interesting thing about them is that they do not build webs: They hunt, and they do that at an astonishing speed.

WHERE TO SEE THEM

Common in the countryside and in cities, huntsman spiders tend to prefer to hide in leaves such as ivy. Given their size, they are surprisingly timid and tend to run off if challenged. If you really do want to see one, go out at night and look around on houses' walls, garden fences, even up at the ceilings if you are staying somewhere in the countryside.

Peppermint Stick Insect *(Megacrania batesi)*

Pale green to bright turquoise blue in color, this up-to-15-centimeter-long stick insect lives in the prickly leaves of certain pandanus trees on which they feed. When disturbed, they emit a strange milky substance that smells strongly of peppermint. With a long but flattened body and short wings, they tend to come out at night.

WHERE TO SEE THEM

Due to their preferred food source, they are limited to a few coastal regions in northern Queensland, but you should come across them on various islands, such as Lady Musgrave, Lady Elliot, Heron, and Wilson Islands, and others.

Ulysses Butterfly *(Papilio ulysses)*

One of the most distinctive butterflies in Australia, if not the world, the royal blue Ulysses butterfly, also known as the blue mountain butterfly or the blue mountain swallowtail, is the emblem of Queensland Tourism. With a wingspan of over 100 millimeters, the butterflies create a blue flash in the dark forest but are virtually invisible when the wings are closed. They live between two and four weeks, and in their haste to breed, a male Ulysses may try his luck by landing on any blue object. They are said to be able to spot anything blue from a distance of some 30 meters away, due to the thousands of lenses in each eye.

WHERE TO SEE THEM

They are a common sight in northern Queensland, especially at the end of the wet season. You'll come across their flirtatious and colorful dance within parks and in the canopy of the rainforest. If you are going to Kuranda by Skyrail, you might spot them on top of the trees.

Background

The Landscape

Australia is the world's only island continent, seemingly at the other end of the world from whichever way you look at it. From Sydney, the nearest country is New Zealand, a four-hour flight away, and besides the small island nations of the South Pacific, it is eight hours flying time to Southeast Asia and 13 hours to the United States.

In addition to its isolation, Australia is totally dry, except for the Mediterranean climate around the extensive coastline. Seventy-five percent of the population lives within 80 kilometers of the Pacific or Indian Ocean. Although the interior is dry, it is loaded with mineral wealth and a growing agriculture industry, based on irrigation, primarily in wheat, sheep, and cattle.

Overwhelmingly, the most important coastline is the southeast. The coast from Brisbane in the northeast to Adelaide in the central south is well-populated and was the first area to be settled by nonnatives. This part of Australia remains the financial and population hub of the country, and Sydney, Melbourne, and the national capital, Canberra, are the most important centers.

The country as a whole is roughly the size of the United States without Alaska. It consists of plateaus in the west tapering off to the Indian Ocean, a series of massive interior deserts second only to the Sahara in size, and on the east coast a fringe of mountains, called the Great Dividing Range, that shelter the humid subtropical coast from the desert winds. Amid the Great Dividing Range are pockets of temperate rainforest that contain the most extensive variety of unique Australian birds and plants. But Australia's famed and unique wildlife, especially the kangaroos, is found throughout the country in areas away from population centers.

CLIMATE

Australia is split in half by the Tropic of Capricorn, and generally speaking, anything north of it is part of the tropics, and below it is temperate. This doesn't quite work out perfectly in the real world, but the farther north you go, the warmer it gets, and farther south you experience four seasons with hot and cold spells.

Central Australia is pretty much all desert, with some grasslands surrounding it. The southeast is temperate, with the mountains in Victoria and New South Wales even getting enough snow to produce some good ski resorts. The southwest and northeast are subtropical, and the north is tropical and equatorial.

That means that Australia has something for everyone. The continuous warm weather you may see on television is typical of Brisbane; in the south you will need to dress warmly in winter. And while Australia is the driest inhabited country in the world, its various regions get their fair share of rain. The temperate regions, including Melbourne and Sydney, have some rain every month and a pretty steady flow throughout the year, but subtropical Perth and Brisbane are subjected to annual rainy seasons.

In general, Canberra and Hobart are the coldest places to live, surrounded by mountains in the south, and except for absolutely scorching Alice Springs and Darwin, Brisbane and Perth are the hotter cities. Sydney is generally said to have perfect weather, and Melbourne is famous for its "four seasons in

Previous: Bondi Beach; Australian white ibis grazing in the Royal Botanic Gardens in Sydney.

Great Barrier Reef Facts and Figures

- The Great Barrier Reef (GBR) was listed as a UNESCO World Heritage site in 1981.
- Extending over some 2,000 kilometers and covering around 348,000 square kilometers, it is the world's largest World Heritage property.
- The Great Barrier Reef Marine Park is larger than the entire area of the United Kingdom and Ireland combined.
- It is so large it can be seen from outer space.
- The GBR is the world's biggest single structure made by living organisms, containing the world's largest collection of coral reefs, with approximately 400 species of coral.
- The GBR is not one continuous reef, but around 2,900 individual reefs, 760 of which are fringing reefs along the mainland or around islands.
- The GBR is not "just" a reef; it also includes over 900 islands, all within the jurisdiction of Queensland, and about half have been declared national parks.
- There are some 32,000 described species of fish worldwide; 4,400 of those species are found in Australian waters, and 1,500 along the GBR alone.
- There are 4,000 types of mollusk, 1,500 species of sponges, and about 800 species of echinoderms (starfish, sea urchins).
- Then there are also around 125 species of shark, stingray, skates, or chimera, along with 17 species of sea snake.
- The GBR is home to over 30 species of mammal, including the dugong, which is listed as vulnerable, and six of the world's seven species of threatened marine turtle.
- The reef is a breeding area for humpback whales that come from the Antarctic to give birth in the warm waters.
- The islands and sand cays support around 215 bird species, many of which have breeding colonies there. Most nesting sites are on islands in the northern and southern regions of the GBR, with more than 1.5 million birds using the sites to breed.
- In addition to the fauna the reef supports, it is also home to 2,195 known plant species; three of these are found only on the Great Barrier Reef.
- The GBR is of great cultural importance and has been for some 50,000 years and more, containing many archaeological sites of Aboriginal or Torres Strait Islander origin, including fish traps, rock quarries, story sites, and rock art.
- The fishing industry throughout the reef is strictly controlled by the Queensland government, making sure the reef can sustain both human and fish life alike, with the industry being worth around $1 billion annually and employing approximately 2,000 people.
- Tourism is the region's largest commercial activity; the Great Barrier Reef and associated activities generate over $4 billion annually.
- More than 1.6 million people visit the reef every year.

one day" experience with the weather, when you have to learn to dress in layers.

GREAT BARRIER REEF ECOLOGY

Consider an animal that is nearly too tiny to be seen with the naked eye, and then consider that this tiny animal has formed colonies with its fellow species so large that they are visible from space. One individual tiny polyp floating around the sea looking for somewhere to settle usually ends up attaching itself to submerged rocks, wrecks, or any hard surface it can find alongside the edges of islands or landmasses. The polyps themselves are invertebrates—creatures without a backbone, or indeed any skeleton whatsoever, similar to anemones and jellyfish—yet they have the capacity to build some of the world's largest limestone structures, such as the Great Barrier Reef. The tiny polyps use calcium carbonate (i.e., limestone from seawater) to build themselves a hard, cup-shaped skeleton, which protects their soft, fragile body. Coral grows at different rates depending on species, water temperature, salinity, turbulence, and the availability of food. Some fast-growing coral are said to add an astonishing 15 centimeters (6 inches) to a reef per year, whereas the slowest-growing species grow a mere 5-25 millimeters (0.2-1 inch) per year.

Coral polyps are usually nocturnal, meaning that they stay inside their skeletons during the day, but at night they come out of hiding, and with their pretty and delicate fan-like tentacles they feed on either zooplankton (including minute fish, squid, or other animal larvae) or planktonic algae called zooxanthellae. These algae normally live within the corals, photosynthesizing just like plants on land do, and give the coral some of their spectacular colors.

There are three types of commonly occurring reefs: fringing, barrier, and atoll. **Fringing reefs,** which are the most common, project seaward directly from the shore, forming borders along the shoreline and surrounding islands. **Barrier reefs** also border shorelines, but at a greater distance. They are separated from their adjacent landmass by a lagoon of open, often deep water. If a fringing reef forms around a volcanic island that subsides completely below sea level while the coral continues to grow upward, an **atoll** forms. Atolls are usually circular or oval, with a central lagoon.

The **Great Barrier Reef** (GBR) is the world's largest barrier reef (the world's second largest barrier reef is in Belize, which is also the longest in the northern hemisphere), and it is also its youngest, formed only some 10,000 years ago by trillions of these tiny polyps, all belonging to some 400 different species of coral. To say it's one large structure, though, is inaccurate, as some 3,000 individual reefs make up the vertebra-like mega-structure that stretches along the Queensland coast and occupies an incredible 350,000 square kilometers. Parts of the reef are 400 kilometers offshore, and there are some 600 to 900 islands in the system, depending on how they are counted.

Corals have been building reefs for more than 65 million years, although some sources say that geological records have been indicating that coral reef structures have been formed as early as 250 million years ago, and are fragile yet adaptable creatures that can cope and adapt to certain degrees of change and challenges. Over the millions of years, reefs have been completely destroyed by natural phenomena such as cyclones, and others disappeared under the water's surface due to changes in sea levels, but they have always rebounded and continued to grow. Mostly, the living top layer of a reef is like a veneer on top of thousands of years of layers of dead coral underneath. But their pervasiveness and stubborn persistence to return, however, was before the evolution of humans to our current sophisticated and dangerous level.

Whereas natural threats (such as outbreaks of the crown-of-thorns starfish, which graze on coral to an extent that they drive them into extinction in places) happen regularly, they are thought to be a natural way of controlling the fast-growing acropora coral, to give slower-growing, less competitive coral a chance. Over the years, man-made threats to the GBR have included limestone mining and drilling for oil in the 1960s and 1970s, followed by water pollution from agricultural run-off. Now the direst threat comes from climate change and especially the resultant coral bleaching and ocean acidification.

Ocean acidification is seen as the most significant impact of a changing climate on the GBR ecosystem. The oceans absorb carbon dioxide from the atmosphere and are estimated to have absorbed about half the excess carbon dioxide released by human activities in the past 200 years. But reportedly, if all our fossil fuel was burnt, the oceans' surface waters' pH would shift by an estimated 0.7 of a pH unit, turning it almost, if not quite, into acid, making the world's inhabitants, in the water and above, ripe for extinction.

Coral bleaching occurs during times of warm water and high light conditions, which cause chemical reactions ending in the eviction of the zooxanthellae algae. Events of bleaching have occurred in 1998 and 2002. In 1998, the temperatures in some parts of the GBR were between 1 and 2 degrees Celsius above normal; some 42 percent of shallow water coral was affected, and 2 percent died. In 2002, the largest event to date, 55 percent of coral was affected and 5 percent died. Just a 1 degree Celsius rise in temperatures could see more than 80 percent of the GBR bleached, 2 degrees Celsius could result in 95 percent, and 3 degrees Celsius would result in total devastation. While the initial occurrence of bleaching might result in more colorful coral, due to the changes in the algae, the reef eventually bleaches to a white skeleton. A bleached reef can recover, but only if the adverse conditions do not persist for too long.

The rise in temperature has already resulted in the change in longevity of some fish, who have survived some winters when normally they would not, and probably should not, have done so. It is expected that the minimum threshold winter temperatures will be increased steadily over the coming decades, changing the habitats, ecosystem, and the status quo of the GBR forever.

To try and preserve one of the world's natural wonders, the GBR is managed by the **Great Barrier Reef Marine Park Authority** (GBRMPA, www.gbrma.gov.au), a Commonwealth agency responsible for protecting the marine park, allocating and enforcing zoning areas, allowing only certain activities in those zones, and overseeing scientific research programs.

PLANTS

When the Australian landmass broke away from the southern supercontinent Gondwana some 100 million years ago, it took with it some unique flora and fauna and the conditions to evolve and nurture some more. Eighty percent of plant and animal species found in Australia are seen nowhere else in the world. Due to its range of climates, you can find a wide variety of life: mangroves and palm trees, dense million-year-old rainforest and impressively tall eucalyptus trees, unique flowers and gigantic evergreens.

You will notice in Australian gardens that all those plants you have carefully nurtured in pots around the house back home grow like weeds here. The variety of plants is simply mind-blowing, and although most people will cite the tall eucalyptus and the bottlebrush as the most iconic plants in Australia, the cheerful yellow daisies growing in abundance by the side of the road, the cherry blossoms in September, and the imposing Moreton Bay fig trees are also striking. The wide range and variety of greenery make Australia a dream for gardeners and those who simply enjoy gardens.

ANIMALS

Utterly unique and enchanting, many of Australia's animals could be from a fairy tale. Apart from the scientific marvels such as the monotremes, or egg-laying mammals, which include the platypus and the prickly echidna, there are the marsupials, mammals that carry their underdeveloped young around in a cozy pouch until they are ready for the world, along with vast colorful birdlife and a few creepy crawlies thrown in for good measure.

You know you have arrived in Australia when at sunset flocks of cockatoos perch near you, making an incredible noise; possums clamber around the electricity wires outside your room at night; and maybe, if you are very lucky on a drive through the country, you spot an elusive koala nestling in the fork of a tree, or indeed see a kangaroo powerfully propelling itself through the bush. Yes, there are nasty spiders and dangerous snakes in this country, but generally they stay out of your way and are not really interested, unlike the possums. They actively come down from the trees to have a good look at you, and while it is illegal to hug a koala in most states, you can—if you can't find one in the wild—get a close look at these eucalyptus-munching cuties in any nearby wildlife center and appreciate that you are truly in Australia.

Introduced Fauna

The rabbits by the side of the road, the camels ruminating in the desert, those poisonous toads that scare everybody—none are native to Australia, but they are very common and are usually a pest. Those cute button-nosed bunnies were imported by a farmer from Britain because he wanted to have something to shoot at in the back garden. Not many years later those 20 or so rabbits had produced uncountable new generations that literally changed Australia's landscape from shrubby undergrowth to desert. The introduction of the myxomatosis virus decreased the numbers, but only for a while, until new generations had become immune to it. The camels were imported because they suited the large desert regions in Australia, and now they have gone native and are so prolific that they are exported to the Middle East. The cane toads were introduced to combat an epidemic of beetles that were munching on the sugarcane harvests, and while they managed to get rid of the beetles, they are now a pest themselves without natural predators. Even the iconic dingo didn't initially belong here, introduced thousands of years ago by the Aboriginal people, who had dogs. Since then, the dingoes have thrived; they thieve from farmers to such a degree that a 5,400-kilometer-long dingo fence, reportedly the world's longest fence and one of the world's longest structures, was built between South Australia up to Queensland, trying to keep the dingoes and farm animals apart. Probably the best-known nonnative species is sheep, brought from South Africa by some of the first British settlers to establish the wool industry. And where would we be today without the famous Australian sheepskin boots and Australian lamb?

History

Australia's post-European settlement history is documented extremely well. The cities are replete with many grand old buildings and residents can go to the bronze plates at Darling Harbour and find their ancestor's name and ship they came over on. Older historical information, especially Aboriginal history, is harder to find, because a lot of it has been lost over the years.

Looking farther back, Australia's indigenous population is one of the oldest on the planet. The Aboriginal people have always been seminomadic and connected to the land, rather than builders of great pyramids or temples. The lack of structures led early European visitors to believe Australia was mostly uninhabited, but people have roamed this continent for at least 50,000 years. And even in the brief 200 years that Europeans have been here, Australia has grown from a penal colony through peaceful independence from Great Britain into a continent-sized federation.

The ancient as well as the more recent history of this continent has shaped its people, their attitude, and their choices in life. Just like everywhere else on this planet, history is what we build on, and in Australia, there are plenty of building blocks to choose from.

BEFORE EUROPEAN CONTACT

When the Australian landmass broke off from the supercontinent Gondwana and became a continent some 15 million plus years ago, it was indeed the *terra nullius* or empty land the Europeans thought they had found only a few hundred years ago. But despite the vastness and the seemingly uninhabitable landscapes, people eventually came to populate the island continent. The original inhabitants of Australia are called Aborigines, from the Latin *ab origen,* meaning "from the beginning." They arrived some 50,000 years ago either by boat via the shallow northern seas or perhaps via land that was then still joined to New Guinea, today submerged under the Torres Strait.

In splendid isolation, the many different tribes lived a seminomadic lifestyle. They brought their dogs, today's dingoes, and hunted three meter-tall kangaroos, marsupial lions, tigers, and the hippopotamus-sized *Diprotodon.* They remained hunter-gatherers, never turning to farming, and were often hostile toward other indigenous groups. By the time of European contact, there were between 350 and 750 distinct indigenous languages in Australia, of which only around 100 survive today. The Aboriginal people never developed a writing system, passing along their history and stories orally and via dance and song. Like the languages, songs varied widely, although similar styles can be seen in their visual art, which is generally acknowledged as the longest continuous art form still in use and still understood anywhere in the world.

Sadly, after European settlement, the Aboriginal people were dispersed, killed, and put on reservations designed to contain the "wild tribes" of Australia. They lost much of their sense of tradition, their skill of telling about the dreamtime (meaning the time of the great ancestors when all life forms, human and animal, were connected), and their sense of identity; along with this went any opportunity to trace their history and ancient culture. While the traditional storytelling skills are once again increasingly being nurtured and encouraged, most descriptions of ancient history have already been lost.

Among the original inhabitants' innumerable contributions to modern Australian life were their names for animals, plants, and places, which are in wide use today, plus their unique hunting and musical tools, such as the boomerang and the didgeridoo, and beautiful art that is revered the world over.

FIRST EUROPEAN SETTLEMENTS (1788-1850)

While Malay fishing vessels regularly visited the northern shores of Australia, it wasn't until Dutch sailors first began making contact on voyages from Cape Town to Indonesia via the west coast of Australia in the early 1600s that the Europeans took notice. More and more expeditions were sent "down under" to discover and chart the great land, of which nothing was known.

Australia and its surroundings were gradually explored. Portuguese explorer Luís Vaz de Torres proved that he was either a very lucky navigator or already knew about the Torres Strait between New Guinea and Cape York in the north of Australia when he sailed past the main continent. The Dutch navigators Anthony van Diemen and Abel Tasman discovered Van Diemen's Land, now Tasmania, in 1642 and charted the western Australian coast, which they named New Holland. The French came, explored, took some kangaroos and other specimens, and left again. But Australians generally date the first proper European contact to April 29, 1770, when Captain James Cook, commanding the HMS *Endeavour* on a mission of exploration,

Sir Joseph Banks: Captain Cook's Naturalist

Sir Joseph Banks (1743-1820) was the British explorer and naturalist who sailed with Captain James Cook along Australia's east coast between 1768 and 1771, discovering, exploring, and naming so many of Australia's unique flora and fauna along the way. Today, some 75 species bear his name, and he is credited with the introduction to the west of the eucalyptus, acacia, and mimosa, as well as the genus named for him, the Banksia.

Born in London to a wealthy family, Joseph Banks developed a passion for botany while at Oxford University in the early 1760s; it was a time of discovery and revolution in many fields of science, and Banks set out to become a botanist. He soon established his name by publishing the first Linnaean descriptions of the plants and animals of Newfoundland and Labrador.

He was elected to the Royal Society and appointed to a joint Royal Navy/Royal Society scientific expedition to the South Pacific Ocean on the HMS *Endeavour*. This was the first of James Cook's voyages of discovery into that region, and of huge importance to Australia's history.

They set off and sailed via Brazil and other parts of South America, Tahiti, New Zealand, before finally reaching the New South Wales region of Australia. The time in Australia led to Banks's second great passion, the British colonization of that continent. He was to be the greatest proponent of settlement in New South Wales, as is hinted by its early colloquial name: Botany Bay. The identification could have been even closer, as the name "Banksia" was reportedly proposed for the region by Linnaeus. In the end, a genus of *Proteaceae*, a flowering plant, was named in his honor as Banksia.

For his services to the crown and to science, he was made a baronet in 1781, three years after being elected president of the Royal Society. The latter position he would hold for a record 42 years. He played a large part in directing the course of British science for the first part of the 19th century. He was directly responsible for several famous voyages, including George Vancouver's to the Pacific Northwest of North America and William Bligh's voyages to transplant breadfruit from the South Pacific to the Caribbean Sea islands; the latter brought about the famous mutiny on the HMS *Bounty*.

During much of this time, Banks was an informal adviser to King George III of the United Kingdom on the creation of Kew Gardens, a position that was formalized in 1797. Banks dispatched explorers and botanists to many parts of the world; through these efforts Kew Gardens became arguably the preeminent botanical gardens in the world, with many species being introduced to Europe through them.

He died in London at the age of 77.

landed at Botany Bay, adjacent to modern-day Sydney.

Cook's meticulous charts of the eastern Australian coast were highly valued by the Royal Navy and the British government, but it was the 800 specimens of Australian flora collected by Joseph Banks, the ship's botanist, and tales of the fantastic Australian animals that caused a sensation in London. The discovery of the region also soon provided Britain with much-needed relief for a domestic problem.

Prior to 1776, convicts were transported to America for 7-year, 14-year, or life terms to relieve overcrowded prisons and provide low-cost labor to American business. With the outbreak of the Revolutionary War in 1776, English prisoners sentenced to "transportation" had nowhere to go and were held in rotting ships in English harbors, a situation that reached crisis proportions by 1786. Prime Minister William Pitt's government ordered a fleet of ship-borne convicts sent to the new land under the command of Captain Arthur Phillip. The convict fleet arrived in Botany Bay on January 26, 1788, and although the colony was called New South Wales, and the continent itself was not named Australia until 1824, today, the date is celebrated as Australia Day.

After realizing that Botany Bay did not offer sufficiently good land for farming and lacked fresh water, Captain Phillip moved north to what is now Port Jackson or Sydney

Harbour, globally recognized as one of the great natural harbors of the world. This move is seen as the best thing Captain Phillip ever did. He landed at Sydney Cove, today's busy ferry port Circular Quay, and named the settlement for Britain's Home Secretary, Lord Sydney. Convict transportation continued until 1850, peaking after 1800 when a second penal colony was established at Hobart, in Van Diemen's Land, in 1803.

The cities of Melbourne, Brisbane, Adelaide, and Perth were successively settled. The colony of New South Wales passed briefly from the command of Captain Phillip to Captain Bligh, of *Mutiny on the Bounty* fame, who found himself the object of a coup d'état staged by disgruntled army officers. A governor named Lachlan Macquarie was sent to straighten out the situation, and he cleaned up the administration, brought the military into line, improved agriculture, and sponsored exploration. Macquarie continues to be a byword for "quality" in Australian life, and institutions, streets, towns, and enterprises routinely take the Macquarie name as a branding strategy.

The cities themselves continued to be named for British officials and members of the royal family. Thomas Brisbane (a colonial secretary), the Duke of Newcastle (a prime minister), Lord Melbourne (also a prime minister), and Queen Adelaide all were honored. The colonies of Queensland and Victoria acquired their names during the long reign of Queen Victoria in the 19th century. A good working knowledge of the history of the British cabinet and royalty is invaluable in roughly calculating the age of a given neighborhood or street in Australia.

The period of convict history was marked by a considerable social divide between the military and gentry and the descendants of the convicts, many of whom stayed on after completing their sentences; they were granted land, got married, and had children. These class distinctions have ebbed through the generations since the end of transportation in 1850, but there are two distinctive Australian dialects to this day, and there continue to be subtle yet broad divisions in Australian society between the gentry and the laboring class. The gentry tends to speak with a light Australian accent, using mostly standard English, while the laboring class has traditionally had a much thicker accent and draws heavily on slang (often rhyming slang) and the dialect known as Strine, which is how "Australian" is pronounced in Strine.

ESTABLISHING COMMONWEALTH AND CULTURE (1850-1901)

With the end of transportation, Australians began to lobby Great Britain for a stronger role in determining their own affairs. The British, learning from their mistakes in the American Revolution, wisely devised the so-called dominions, nations that retained allegiance to the British crown and had common defense and foreign policy but were internally self-governing. New South Wales, Victoria, Tasmania, Queensland, South Australia, Western Australia, and New Zealand began a decades-long evolution toward self-government at the colonial level and ultimately federated in 1900, with the notable defection of New Zealand. The transition happened in stages that echo in Australia's current political system: An appointed royal governor with full powers eventually gave way to a strong governor advised by an appointed legislative council. Eventually that appointed council became the upper house, with the election of a legislative assembly, from which a colonial premier and cabinet were elected. Ultimately, the royal governor was limited to a largely ceremonial role.

This period was remarkable also for the commercial development of Australia. Massive gold strikes at Ballarat, near Melbourne, made Melbourne one of the richest and fastest-growing cities in the world in the 1850s. This coincided with the era of the great clipper ships that would ride the hard-blowing westerlies from Cape Town to Melbourne before crossing the Pacific to the

United States. During this period, Melbourne eclipsed Sydney, and a good-natured rivalry between the two cities has been a central point of Australian life ever since. The presence of large amounts of money in the colonies resulted in a massive increase in "bushranging." The traditional English highway robber transformed into the Australian bushranger with distinct overtones of Robin Hood, and several bushrangers, including Ned Kelly and Mad Dog Morgan, became folk heroes.

In this period of the nation's growing economic importance, the Australian Outback was opened for sheep and cattle ranching on a massive scale, and a mythology grew up around the hard life of the drovers managing the sheep; jackeroos (trainees, typically sons of "connected" families) working as cowboys on the gigantic stations (ranches) that could be more than 200,000 hectares in size; and wandering shearers who would travel the Outback from station to station and engage in famous shearing contests, which were the subject of significant betting at the time.

EARLY 20TH CENTURY (1901-1945)

The great issues of the 1890s for Australia had been labor-capital challenges caused by a worldwide collapse in commodities prices and the fight over the terms of federation into a single commonwealth. New Zealand opted out of the federation altogether; several of the states and sections of society were uneasy about the concept of federation and the constitution that had been hammered out. With the return to prosperity and the debut of the commonwealth, these issues mostly faded, and Australia enjoyed a golden period that was shattered by the onset of World War I.

Although formation of the commonwealth had given Australia control over its own foreign policy, broadly speaking the public and the government were pro-British Empire, and Australia dutifully followed Great Britain into the war in 1914. They were in for a shock. Respect for the Australian military was low among the Allied command, and initially Australian units were used only as replacements in existing British divisions. Australia was initially denied any role in charting the direction of the war in the strategy rooms or on the battlefield. Public uproar led to the combining of the Australian and New Zealand forces, the Australia New Zealand Army Corps (ANZAC), but not to autonomous command. The initial major force was sent to the Gallipoli Peninsula, in modern Turkey, to fight under British generals in a combined army-naval attack on Constantinople (now Istanbul), the capital of the Ottoman Empire.

The invasion of Gallipoli on April 25, 1915, is celebrated today in Australia as ANZAC Day, and most Australians believe the nation was forged in that battle. The attack itself was a bloodbath and resulted in defeat, massive casualties, and eventual withdrawal. The defeat profoundly shocked the nation; Australians would never again participate in large-scale operations under direct British field command, although they served loyally under overall Allied command.

For most Aussies, the British disregard for essential preparations at Gallipoli was due to a general British disregard for the Australians and their country, and although Australia had the second-highest volunteer rate among the nations of the Empire, a split emerged in Australian society over loyalty to Great Britain. This debate is still ongoing today, with a small but highly organized pro-monarchy faction still fighting to keep the British monarch as Australia's monarch, while republican forces have been gathering strength since 1915; in 1999 they almost ousted the monarchy in a national referendum.

Aussies owe a sense of national identity as Australians to World War I, for at Gallipoli they served for the first time not as members of the colonies but as a united national army. Gallipoli also fostered the cultural values of the "fair go"—the idea that people need to be given a fair chance. In the popular perception, a fair go was exactly what the slaughtered ANZAC forces were denied at Gallipoli. It was an idea that existed in the society long before Gallipoli, but it was seared into the fabric of the culture thereafter. Even today, governments have fallen with more than a little credit given to the idea that the other party deserves a fair go at running the country. Corporate, academic, and diplomatic culture is suffused with the fair go concept, which, blended with the general egalitarianism of Australia, makes people somewhat suspicious of certain aspects of economic competition and free enterprise.

Following the war, Australia assumed a role in administering a number of former German colonies in the South Pacific and had its first taste of colonial administration. The postwar period was significant not for international events but rather for the great rise in the popularity of Australian sports. Rugby, cricket, and Australian Rules football began to be played in large stadiums before massive crowds. The general prosperity of the times sparked an Australian love of sports that was already profound but now reached epic proportions, where it remains today. Emblematic of the rivalry between Sydney and Melbourne, which reached a peak during this period, Sydney embraced rugby and Melbourne embraced Aussie Rules football. In politics, the two cities could not agree on which would serve as the national capital, so the city of Canberra was established between the two to serve as a neutral location for the government.

The heady prosperity of the 1920s gave way to the devastating Great Depression, in which the effects of the worldwide economic collapse were greatly magnified by another collapse in worldwide commodities prices. With the slump came searing and widespread poverty, and political radicalism soared. Tensions reached a peak in 1932 when a pro-fascist military officer interrupted the opening of the Sydney Harbour Bridge by riding up on a horse and slashing the bridge-opening ribbon so that the radical New South Wales premier Jack Lang would not have the honor.

Most ordinary Australians were profoundly shocked by radicalism, the massive poverty and economic dislocation that caused it, and by a growing sense that the British Empire would be unable to provide for Australia's defense owing to its own economic woes. But nevertheless, Australia again loyally followed Britain into World War II in 1939.

The war went very badly for the British in the first 18 months, and there were few resources that could be diverted to the defense of Southeast Asia. Further, the European colonial system had long sunk into a polite form of despotism that led to the Japanese being hailed as deliverers when they successfully invaded Malaysia, the Philippines, Indonesia, and South Pacific islands in 1941 to 1942. Great Britain attempted to mount a defense of Malaysia and Singapore but was rapidly and comprehensively defeated, and in early 1942 the Australians found themselves on the retreat and in the clear path of the Japanese advance.

The American-British war strategy placed a priority on defeating Germany. Accordingly, Australia, though still a small nation of 10 million in population, played a leading role in the South Pacific War. Supported by the American fleet, the Australians led the counteroffensive in New Guinea that stopped the Japanese advance. The sacrifices were heavy, but after the end of the war, Australia had earned international credibility to play an important role in the formation of the United Nations and organizations such as the Southeast Asia Treaty Organization (SEATO) and the Australia, New Zealand, United States Security Treaty (ANZUS).

Australia had faced its darkest economic times before and during the war, but it returned to prosperity in 1945 and achieved a new level of international prominence and total independence from Britain. Australians continue to acknowledge a debt of gratitude to Americans for their support in the war (especially the older generations), and Australian-American trade cooperation and investment rapidly intensified during the postwar period.

MODERN AUSTRALIA (1945-PRESENT)

Since 1945, in many ways Australia has brought its individual historic threads together into a new and exciting culture and economy that preserves the Australian concepts of mateship, dinkum, and the fair go, along with a new sense of multiculturalism that reflects significant postwar immigration as well as the country's belated but genuine attempts to address the gulf between mainstream Australians and the Aboriginal Australians.

Although Australia has generally followed the United States' lead in international affairs, supporting the United States with troops and logistics in the wars in Vietnam and Iraq, the country engaged with China earlier, and in many ways more successfully, than the United States, and has also participated positively in the postcolonial transition of Africa. After a great resource boom in the 1950s and 1960s that led writer Donald Horne to dub Australia "The Lucky Country," Australia found itself in a tougher economic state in the 1970s and early 1980s, and has substantially diversified and globalized its economy since that time, generally reducing governmental controls and regulations to enable the free market to operate with less friction.

The 1940s and 1950s were a period of tremendous investment in infrastructure projects, much of it aimed at irrigation projects to expand the range of land under cultivation. Significant diamond, iron, oil, and uranium discoveries in the postwar period have continued to fuel Australia's economic dependence on resource exports. To provide a labor force for the resources boom, Australia had to alter its traditional emphasis on allowing only "white" immigrants, and the "White Australia" policy was substantially reformed with a resulting huge influx of southern European immigrants. The policy was abolished altogether in the 1970s, resulting in substantial Asian immigration. The end result today is a highly multicultural society with decidedly British roots but an increasingly internationalized urban population.

In cultural terms, Australian literature and cinema went through a renaissance in the 1970s and 1980s, with filmmakers such as Peter Weir *(Gallipoli, Picnic at Hanging Rock, Witness)*, Bruce Beresford *(Breaker Morant, Driving Miss Daisy)*, and George Miller *(Mad Max, Babe, Happy Feet)*, and such outstanding Australian films as *Priscilla, Queen of the Desert, Muriel's Wedding,* and *Strictly Ballroom*, which achieved near cult status. Australian musicians and actors such as the Bee Gees, Mel Gibson, Olivia Newton-John, Keith Urban, Russell Crowe, Toni Collette, Rachel Griffiths, Nicole Kidman, and many more have also become internationally known in their fields.

In the 1980s, with the ascendancy of the Labor Party after a long period of domination by the center-right Liberal-Country Party coalition, there was a new level of commitment to opening doors for women and Aboriginal Australians, in the latter case culminating with National Sorry Day in 1998. On this day the nation observed a national apology to the Aboriginal Australian people to acknowledge, in particular, that 100,000 Australian children were forcibly removed from their homes between 1915 and 1969 and raised in orphanages and camps.

Since a steep but brief period of recession in the early 1990s, Australia has experienced nearly continuous economic expansion. In particular, Sydney has reached world-class status among global cities, although Melbourne continues to present itself as a compelling alternative to Sydney's brashness. Regional cities such as Brisbane, Perth, and Adelaide have developed highly attractive economies and are quickly growing in population.

The 2000 Olympic Games gave Sydney in particular and Australia in general a lift in prestige, and Australia's continued remarkable success in Olympic competition gives the nation a quadrennial focal point as well as a surging sense of national pride and confidence. Yet Australian confidence, tempered by its own "tall poppy" dislike of cockiness, is appealing rather than annoying. Australia has entered the 21st century with some issues in the environmental arena as a leading resources nation, but in all other respects as a remarkably integrated country where the lessons of the past have paid dividends in the present.

Government and Economy

GOVERNMENT

One continent, one country, six states—New South Wales, Victoria, Tasmania, South Australia, Western Australia, and Queensland—along with two main territories, the Northern Territory and the Australian Capital Territory, plus a few so-called external territories, such as the Australian Antarctic Territory, and numerous islands and countless smaller divisions all make up Australia. Size-wise, Western Australia and Queensland are the largest states, followed by the Northern Territory, South Australia, New South Wales, Victoria, and Tasmania. The national capital, Canberra, is situated in the smallest territory, the Australian Capital Territory, which is self-governing but not independent from Australia as a whole.

While there is one federal government and some national administrative organizations, such as the Australian Federal Police, most decisions are made at the state or municipal level. Officially each state is subdivided into counties, municipalities, and shires, although you rarely hear mention of those. Typically each city has smaller "cities" or parishes, formerly independent little towns that are now suburbs, each with an often splendid town hall, integrated into the larger cities. For example, people say they live in Mosman or Paddington instead of simply saying they live in Sydney. On the surface these seem mere suburbs, but they still wield plenty of political power and run their divisions sometimes completely differently from their neighbors, even if the outward indicator of that is only the color and size of the trash cans.

Federal Government

The Commonwealth of Australia is of relatively recent vintage, founded in 1901, and the framers of the Australian Constitution had the opportunity to integrate aspects from the American, British, and Canadian constitutions that they admired, plus a few inventions of their own. Consequently, the Australian system of government is primarily British in character but has significant features borrowed from the United States. In addition, some features are historical remnants of the development of the country from its colonial roots.

Australia is a constitutional monarchy, which means that Queen Elizabeth II reigns as monarch of Australia, and Prince Charles is heir apparent. In the constitution, her royal powers are nearly absolute, but in practice they are "reserve powers" to be exercised only in a national emergency; those powers are vested in the governor-general appointed by the queen based on the recommendation of the prime minister. In 1975 Governor-General John Kerr sacked the elected Labor government when it could not pass its money-supply bills in the Senate, so it's not without precedent that the governor-general takes political action, but by and large the "GG" is a ceremonial figure, usually popular and more seen than heard.

The federal government is composed of a Senate and a House of Representatives. An equal number of senators are elected from each of the six states, and House members are elected in proportion to the population: In this way, the Australian legislature is like that of the United States.

Unlike in Britain, it is common to have members of the cabinet from the Senate, although by convention they rarely serve in the most senior posts. Only one senator, John Gorton, has served as prime minister, and in his case he resigned his Senate seat to obtain a House of Representatives seat as soon as he became prime minister. In addition to the cabinet, the prime minister appoints junior (noncabinet) ministers to run minor departments.

Supporting the government is a permanent bureaucracy of departments, each department headed by a nonpolitical permanent secretary. In addition, Australia has a High Court headed by a chief justice. They are life appointees, and the High Court closely resembles the U.S. Supreme Court.

The most famous omission from the Australian Constitution is a Bill of Rights. Australia simply doesn't have one, and many controls over private property and private conduct are just as perfectly constitutional in Australia as they are perfectly unconstitutional in the United States. For example, in Australia it is legal to have randomized breath tests and to use cameras to photograph speeding vehicles, with the result of fewer road casualties.

Australian governments are voted on at least every four years, in which elections for half the Senate and all the House seats are contested. The government can seek an earlier election date, but not a later one. Also, under special circumstances, the government of the day may be granted a double dissolution, in which all the Senate seats in addition to the House are contested: This is intended to be used in cases where the government's program has been defeated in the Senate, but in practical terms it's used to maximize electoral opportunities.

In Australia, voting is compulsory for citizens age 18 and over, with fines levied against those who fail to vote. Australia uses a preferential voting system. In this system, voters rank candidates in order of preference. If one candidate does not receive a majority of the votes, then the lowest vote-getter is eliminated and his or her votes distributed to the voter's second preference. In this way, candidates add to their vote tallies until one candidate reaches a majority. Voters cast one vote in their House race but in the Senate race cast as many votes as there are seats up for election in that state.

The federal government collects all state and national taxes and shares the revenues with the states in a negotiated split. Another difference between the United States and Australia is that sales tax (the Goods and Services Tax, or GST) is collected federally instead of by the states, and there is one consistent nationwide rate.

The federal government operates a national health scheme, Medicare, and also owns several important national industries, such as stakes in the airline Qantas and Telstra, a phone company. The federal government also oversees the Australian Capital Territory, which is the area surrounding Canberra and a small coastal enclave at Jervis Bay.

State Government

The state governments are structured in essentially the same format as the federal government; the governor-general of a state is a governor, the prime minister is a state premier, and the upper house is known as the Legislative Council. Queensland does not have an upper house.

State governments obtain their funds from the national income tax via revenue sharing. A key role of the state government is responsibility for schools, police, zoning, roads, and the extensive public transportation in major cities.

Municipal and Shire Government

Municipal governments obtain funding from local property taxes and other local fees on businesses and residents for services. In some locations, shire (county) government replaces the municipality as the local government. In Australia, local government provides garbage collection, local police, local development and zoning, child services, elder care services, and beach and sports facilities.

In Australia, cities are often exceedingly

small geographic areas with limited populations. The Lord Mayor of Sydney, for example, presides over only the Sydney Central Business District, which has approximately 100,000 residents.

Legal System

In Australia, there are four types of federal courts and three types of state courts (although Tasmania has two levels of local courts, and Western Australia has four).

The federal courts include the High Court, which has final right of appeal and hears constitutional cases; the Federal Court, which oversees most corporate, copyright, industrial, customs, immigration, and bankruptcy aspects of federal law; the Family Court, which oversees divorce, custody, and child support cases; and Federal Magistrates Courts, which hear less complex cases that otherwise would be heard by the Federal Court or the Family Court.

The state courts include the State Supreme Court, which oversees appeals, and in the case of Tasmania, oversees the work handled by District Courts elsewhere; the District Court, which oversees most criminal trials and major civil suits; and the Magistrates Court, which oversees smaller civil suits and petty matters such as driving offenses.

Political Parties

The major political parties are the Australian Labor Party (ALP), Liberal Party, National Party, the Greens, and the Australian Democrats. The Australian Labor Party is the oldest party, founded in the 1890s. In addition to representing the interests of organized labor, it represents the center-left of Australian politics. The Labor Party is typically either in government or leading the opposition. In recent years it has had conspicuous success at the state level, but less so federally, where it has been in opposition more than 65 percent of the time since World War II.

The Liberal Party was founded in the 1940s to replace the United Australia Party as the leader of the center-right. It has formed a coalition with the National Party during its entire existence, including arrangements regarding contesting seats.

The National Party was founded as the Country Party in the 1910s and has been the junior partner in coalition with the Liberal Party since the 1940s. The National Party represents the interests of rural Australia and is generally more conservative than the Liberal Party.

The Greens are the newest party of significance, gaining Senate seats in the federal legislature in the last decade or so. It represents environmental causes and in general is the most left-wing party.

The Australian Democrats were formed in 1977 to provide a middle road between the Liberal-National coalition and the ALP. The Democrats have held the balance of power in the Senate on many occasions and have used their power as a brake on the most extreme left- or right-wing ambitions of the governments of the day.

ECONOMY

The Australian economy is primary-resource intensive and goes through boom-and-bust cycles because of this. In recent decades the economy has diversified, and the effects of boom-and-bust are less now than in the past, but the economy still booms when its resource prices are high, and since 2000 this has generally been the case. Despite a high degree of dependence on primary resources, 75 percent of Australia's workforce is employed in the service sector, roughly equivalent to the United States. Inflation is generally low, less than 3 percent for most of the 2000s.

The gross domestic product in 2010 was US$1,242.2 billion or US$55,341 per capita. This makes Australia one of the 20 largest economies in the world, and its per capita income is in the top 10 worldwide. The Australian dollar is the fifth most widely traded currency in the world, valued for its stability and for the hands-off nature of the Australian government toward currency manipulations. Major trading partners include

The Best Job in the World

Following on their first initiative of "Best Job in the World" back in 2009, when the job to be had was an island caretaker in the Great Barrier Reef, Australian Tourism re-launched the initiative in 2013 with six jobs up for grabs: chief funster in New South Wales, Outback adventurer in the Northern Territory, park ranger in Queensland, wildlife caretaker in South Australia, lifestyle photographer in Melbourne, and taste master in Western Australia. The six jobs—as diverse as the country they are offered in—each come with an attractive six-month salary package worth $100,000, including living costs.

The campaign targets travelers between 18 and 30 years of age in Australia and overseas, with particular focus on international markets eligible for Australian working holiday visas, including the United Kingdom and Ireland, the United States and Canada, Germany, France, Italy, Sweden, Hong Kong, Taiwan, South Korea, and Japan. Tourism Australia Managing Director Andrew McEvoy said the competition provided an excellent platform to entice more young people from around the world to come to Australia to holiday but also to work, helping to fill many unfilled tourism jobs across Australia, a key challenge for the industry.

"We've taken one of the most successful tourism campaigns in recent times—Best Job in the World—and made it bigger and better by coming up with a competition which represents the very best of our country—our breathtaking landscapes and scenery, our unique nature and wildlife, great food and wine, and, of course, our huge sense of fun," McEvoy said.

McEvoy said the competition was expected to appeal to youth travelers' sense of fun and adventure. "The youth market contributes more than a quarter of all Australia's international arrivals. These are visitors who tend to stay longer, disperse widely, and often come back again, with their families, later in their lives. For many young people, Australia's working holiday visa programs provide the economic means to fund travel plans, and this is at the heart of our new campaign," he said.

During the first campaign's six-week application timeframe, 34,684 people from almost 200 countries uploaded their video applications onto www.islandreefjob.com and YouTube, providing an independent promotion for the Great Barrier Reef and Queensland viewed by more than 8.6 million people. In 2013 some 330,000 people from 196 countries applied for the various jobs, but there wasn't an Australian among the final contenders, even though more than 40,000 Australians originally applied. Of the final 18, there were five from the United States, two each from England and France, and one each from Belgium, Afghanistan, Brazil, Canada, Germany, Hong Kong, Ireland, Scotland, and Taiwan. Eventually, the six lucky ones taking up one of the best jobs in the world were an American finance graduate, a Brazilian travel photographer, an Irish Internet entrepreneur, a French tourism graduate, an English film costume designer, and a Canadian adventure tour guide.

the United States, China, Japan, Singapore, Germany, South Korea, India, and New Zealand.

Australia is becoming friendlier to entrepreneurs, but it remains a country where big business and multinationals have been the rule rather than the exception, primarily resulting from the capital-intensive nature of Australian industry. Accordingly, relationships are very important to the conduct of business, and the "old school tie" still opens many doors in Sydney and Melbourne. Dominant multigenerational family enterprises run by the Murdochs, Packers, Holmes à Courts, and others are common in Australia. Media ownership, in particular, has been concentrated in the hands of a few families.

Australia is known for high wages and for a strong trade union movement, which is the mainstay of the Australian Labor Party in political terms and, through the Australian Council of Trade Unions, is a powerful negotiator of rights and benefits for workers.

The country has a strong commitment to building and maintaining infrastructure and strong historical support for electricity, telecommunications, and transportation projects. Internet access is widespread. A national highway system has been in place for many years, and the national ring road around

Australia is being upgraded to include more divided, limited-access, high-speed corridors.

The country is less regulated than comparable countries in Europe but has strong regulatory oversight compared to the United States.

Major Industries

The major natural resource industries are uranium, bauxite, iron, diamonds, coal, and oil. Key agricultural industries are wool, beef, and wheat. Australia is a major food exporter and is nearly energy self-sufficient. Sydney is home to world-class banking, legal, and finance industries. Sydney and Melbourne are the centers of the communications industries.

Melbourne is home to primary industry. The automotive and wine industries are based in Adelaide. Mining is based in Perth and to a lesser extent in Brisbane, while Brisbane is home to the tourism industry. Canberra, as the capital, is home to the government.

In terms of pace and reputation, Sydney is often described as the New York or Los Angeles of Australia, while Melbourne is described as more similar to Chicago. Perth is a mining city, Brisbane a tourism and agriculture town, and Adelaide has a heavy industry focus, including much defense-related contracting. Two regional industrial cities in New South Wales, Wollongong and Newcastle, focus on heavy industry, including paper, oil, gas, and coal; Tasmania is mostly agricultural, with some mining and primary industries and a small specialized industry serving Antarctic activities.

People and Culture

POPULATION

Australia is the sixth largest country in the world and has some 22 million inhabitants. The population averages two people per square kilometer, making it also the least densely populated country in the world. Considering that Australia is also the driest inhabited country in the world, it is hardly surprising that some 90 percent of people live within 120 kilometers from the coast, and in Tasmania 99 percent live within 50 kilometers of the coast. More than 70 percent of the overall population lives in cities, but conversely, some 70 percent of the Aboriginal or Torres Strait people live outside urban areas.

According to the Australian Bureau of Statistics, the 2011 census showed that 26 percent of Australians were born overseas, and a further 20 percent have at least one parent who was born overseas. Add to that some 550,000 citizens of Aboriginal or Torres Strait Islander origin and you have a pretty diverse bunch living here, with plenty of short-term and long-term expatriates from all over the world thrown into the mix.

ETHNICITY AND CLASS

Australians are ethnically highly diverse, with the roots of the "true" Australians in the small surviving number of Aboriginal Australians who arrived some 50,000 years ago. Centuries later came an influx of English, Scottish, Welsh, and Irish settlers who emigrated between 1780 and 1850 as convicts, soldiers, bureaucrats, or land grantees. The gold rush period of the 1850s through the 1870s brought a further inflow of Asians, Americans, and other Europeans, including the first sizable German immigration, and the railroad-building era brought some southern Europeans and more Chinese to the country. A major expansion in immigration started after World War II, when a wave of immigrants arrived from southern and eastern Europe to help with major public works projects such as the Snowy River hydroelectric scheme, and for a period Melbourne had the third-largest Greek-born population in the world. Asians began arriving in great numbers after the Vietnam War in the 1970s, along with many Middle Easterners. Today, the vast majority of Australians have at least one ancestor who arrived after 1900, and Australia is truly a land of new arrivals.

While the high percentage of immigrants can create more tension than in countries that have fewer expatriates and migrants, Australia has a mostly tolerant culture that generally embraces diversity and shuns direct confrontation.

Historically, Australia has been beset by issues of tolerance not only of foreign cultures but of its own Aboriginal Australian population, which has been the victim of rampant discrimination in past generations. The indigenous Australians, nearly wiped out in the 19th century not only by European diseases but the Europeans themselves, have made a modest comeback in numbers, but their lack of access to education, employment opportunities, and medical care has restricted their presence in the cities, except in lower-income areas. It wasn't long ago that the Australian government issued an apology to the Aboriginal people for their treatment, and events that recognize the treatment of indigenous people, such as National Sorry Day, have encouraged a growing rapprochement between the cultures, though the issue continues to be a sensitive matter.

Australia faces lingering class divisions that go back to the days of the convicts versus the free settlers. There is a lingering establishment in Australia, primarily comprising white Anglo-Saxon Protestants who continue to dominate high-earning or high-visibility professions such as medicine, law, politics, and finance, and who live in highly affluent circumstances and socialize within a tight circle of the "right" people. The influence of the establishment dwindles on a daily basis, but it remains a fact of life. In recent years, an encouraging trend has been that people from a much wider range of cultural and ethnic backgrounds have been gaining access into the so-called Australian elite.

The countryside and the cities produce quite different characteristics and accents. Rural Australians love their pioneer culture, and the archetypal characters in famous Australian ballads and stories are bush-based, often from the 19th century, and exhibit a blend of tolerance, a streak of mischief known as larrikinism, and a healthy disrespect for authority. Outlaw figures such as bushranger Ned Kelly are openly admired by many, despite their nefarious careers, and sporting figures are widely idolized. On the other hand you have more educated urban Australians who pride themselves on their cosmopolitan outlook and interest in art and sniff at the old Australian ways.

RELIGION

From the number of churches and faith-affiliated schools around Australia, you would think that Australians are a religious bunch, but that's not necessarily the case. Only 10 percent of the population attend weekly religious services, and about 20 percent say they go monthly.

The main churches in Australia are the Anglican Church (Episcopalian), the Roman Catholic Church, and the Uniting Church (a fusion of Presbyterians, Methodists, and Congregationalists). There are small Jewish, Islamic, and Buddhist communities in the cities, with a large Jewish community in and around Balaclava in Melbourne. A strong Pentecostal movement is the fastest-growing segment in Australian religious life.

CULTURAL VALUES

Australia is a proud nation and fiercely patriotic. Migrants applying for residency have to agree to the "Australian Values Statement," which pretty much lists everything Australians so fiercely believe in. It states that Australian society values respect for the freedom and dignity of the individual, freedom of religion, commitment to the rule of law, parliamentary democracy, equality of men and women, a spirit of egalitarianism that embraces mutual respect, tolerance, fair play, and compassion for those in need, and pursuit of the public good. With such a diverse cultural and religious background to the people of Australia, these are not just values but staples that bind the society and make it work.

In Australia's pioneer days, conditions were so harsh beyond the sheltering coastal ranges that cooperation was essential to survival, much like self-reliance was essential in the American West. Looking out for your mate is a major Australian cultural value that cannot be underestimated and permeates every aspect of city and country life. Also, Australia's history as a penal colony, during which thousands were brought to here for extended prison terms for offenses as minor as stealing food to feed families impoverished by the industrial revolution, has made Australia a society that values the "fair go" more than others might. That history has also fostered a general suspicion of sophistication and power.

Australian Contradictions

If you are of a certain age, you may remember Crocodile Dundee, that leathery-skinned, loud, and enthusiastic big-hearted Aussie who wore the hat with corks dangling off the rim and, of course, chased crocodiles for a living. Yes, you will probably find one or two of those types around somewhere in the north (minus the hat), but they are just as likely to exist as the beer-swigging German or the overweight ill-informed American. Yes, they all exist, but mostly, they don't.

Australians come in just as many variations as people from every country. When you say that all Australians are sports-mad, you are partly right, but look around and you'll find plenty of arts, literature, and culture festivals with plenty of support. Recently, Australia appointed its first female prime minister, who has now been replaced, but ask some red-blooded Aussie males and they'll tell you a woman's place is in the kitchen. Australians are proud of not having a class system, yet the gap between the haves and have-nots is wide and frequently complained about, and people often work three jobs to put their kids through upmarket private schools. Aussies love the outdoors, camping, and roughing it in the fresh air, yet 80 percent live in the cities, and five-star luxury lodges are springing up everywhere in the Outback.

Tall Poppies and a Fair Go

One of the most important social values is the concept of the "fair go." The fair go, or giving someone a chance, is extremely important in Australian culture, and Australians and newcomers who ignore this do so at their peril, whether it applies to family, friends, colleagues, or public figures. This concept is connected to the "tall poppy syndrome," meaning that touting your own accomplishments or not being modest is frowned upon. According to gardening wisdom, a poppy that grows too tall needs cutting down. Public figures have experienced this in the public forum; an actor who recently claimed to have outgrown Australia found herself cut down in the media for weeks.

A corollary of the tall poppy syndrome is the generally accepted idea that in Australia there are no class distinctions. Although Australia has no traditional aristocracy or caste system, there are at least two distinct classes: those who have a solid education and money, lack a thick accent, and tend to succeed in life, attending the "right" schools; and those of the working class, less educated, less fortunate, and a lot more vocal when it comes to cutting down those tall poppies. There are people who work hard in order to leave their working-class roots behind and send their kids to the "right" schools in order to get closer to the "better" class. In the media and popular culture, it is clear that there is a distinct disdain for those of the wealthier class; these people get cut down regardless of whether they were born into it or got there through personal achievement. So elements of the tall poppy syndrome reflect the sincere desire of the working class that there really be no class distinctions.

Mateship

Mateship means many things but originates in the era when people had to rely on each other when settling in a hostile land. The term is also discussed in connection to the devastating Gallipoli campaign during World War I that galvanized Australia's national psyche. Today it may involve having a few beers at a barbecue with your mates, or leaving the family behind on Saturday to concentrate on sports and fun instead of on obligations. Mateship is fundamental to the Australian way of life, and a basic understanding of it will take you a long way in understanding Australians. For a lighthearted look at the meaning of the word "mate," have a look at the videos at www.themeaningofmate.com.

LANGUAGE

Spend even a brief time on a bus, train, or tram and you'll truly appreciate the variety in the Australian language. You'll barely understand some people, with the thick accent, distinctive drawl, and slight upward inflection at the end of sentences that sounds like they might be asking a question. Others have a barely noticeable accent, and most people are somewhere in between. Like anywhere, differences in language use are usually connected to education and social class, even though Australians will insist their society has no class differences. One thing most Australians have in common is the almost inevitable shortening of every expression. An avocado becomes an "avo," a U-turn is a "yewy," and football is "footy."

Aside from the Australian dialect itself, which can vary among cities and states and by social class, Australia has three types of language differentiation: slang expressions that are common to nearly all Australians; rhyming slang, which crosses social and geographic boundaries and is virtually impossible to comprehend; and Strine, the "ocker" accent and vocabulary that at times feels like a whole new language, replete with unique expressions and words.

Slang

Not all Australians use Aussie slang extensively. You may have to wait to hear your first "g'day," and as with all slang, phrases common in one generation do not always carry over to the next. Aussies do not really call each other "cobber" except on rare and often ironic occasions, despite the universal presence of the word in dictionaries of common Aussie slang. "Righto" is also fading out, although it has been popular for several generations.

But understanding slang is essential for following even average-length conversations of moderate complexity. Get a decent online or printed dictionary of slang and read it through once, have a giggle, and familiarize yourself with the sound of the phrases and words. A good example is Koala Net (www.koalanet.com.au/australian-slang.html).

In general, the use of Australian slang words by new arrivals is a no-no; it's just too difficult to understand the nuances, and a well-meant phrase can easily be offensive. Even the use of diminutives and basic words like "g'day" could be misinterpreted as insulting.

Certain words in common usage elsewhere should not be used in Australia: "fanny," "root" (as in "root for the home team"), and "bung" (as in "I bunged my car right into the wall"). These have vulgar meanings in the Australian idiom.

Rhyming Slang

The prevalent rhyming slang of Australia needs to be explained to be understood. For example, to "have a Captain Cook" is rhyming slang for "have a look." Rhyming slang is often combined with the diminutive: "Yank" rhymes with "septic tank," which becomes "seppo," a derisive slang term for Americans. "Trouble" becomes "rubble," then "Barney Rubble," which becomes "barney," so that a "friend in barney" needs your help. A "bone," from "dog and bone," is a phone; a "Noah," from "Noah's Ark," is a shark; and so it goes in ever-increasing circles. It is colorful and is only learned by example.

Strine

Beyond Australian slang, which is common

to most Australians, there is an extensive vocabulary and a strongly drawled accent known as Strine. Someone who speaks Strine is an "ocker" (OCK-ah). Strine is known as Broad Australian English and generally reflects the working class. The classic ocker says "yous" for the plural of "you," "good on ya" for "well done," and "me" instead of "my" as in "tie me kangaroo down, sport."

SPORTS AND RECREATION

There is hardly anything more important in Australia than sports. Whether it is the Olympics, the footy, the tennis, a host of other exciting professional events, or just a game of professional or backyard cricket, nothing unites and rivets Australians like sports.

The biggest crowds come out for **football,** which comes in four flavors—soccer, Rugby Union, Rugby League, and Australian Rules football—to divide the focus. Australian Rules football is the most different from games played in other countries and is the most popular. Aussie Rules is the sport of choice in Melbourne, Perth, and Adelaide; rugby is more popular in Sydney and Brisbane.

The truly unifying national game is **cricket,** and the 11 members of Australia's national team are household names. Cricket is a relative of baseball and is the main summer sport. Innumerable families and kids play backyard cricket, which supplies a stream of players to local clubs, who in turn supply the state teams and the national team. The national team plays five-day matches, called tests, against the top nine other cricketing nations. These events grip the nation on television, radio, or live at legendary cricket grounds such as the Sydney Cricket Ground.

In addition to the main spectator sports, **golf, tennis, surfing,** and the **Olympics** are highly popular. In golf, legends such as Greg Norman, Stuart Appleby, Ian Baker-Finch, and Steve Elkington have been noted winners of major championships, while numerous Australians have achieved tennis fame at Wimbledon and other grand-slam events, including John Newcombe, Margaret Court, Evonne Goolagong, Pat Cash, Patrick Rafter, and Lleyton Hewitt.

To many Australians, personal sports are of far more importance: surfing, skiing, running, windsurfing, sailing, climbing, tennis, golf, and backyard cricket. Australians are generally relentlessly fit and eager to participate in a wide variety of sporting activities. It is often the glue that holds families and neighborhoods together, if not in participation then at least in cheering for a team.

THE ARTS

Literature

Most people will be hard-pressed to name an Australian author, but you may be surprised to hear which well-known authors actually are Australian, including Markus Zusak *(The Book Thief)* and Peter Carey *(Oscar and Lucinda)*. Patrick White is the only Australian to have been awarded the Nobel Prize in Literature, but other authors worth reading include Tim Winton *(Cloudstreet)*, Steve Toltz *(A Fraction of the Whole)*, Kate Grenville *(The Secret River)*, Geraldine Brooks *(Years of Wonder)*, and, of course, well-known best-selling authors such as James Clavell, Thomas Keneally, and Nevil Shute. Both Sydney and Melbourne hold annual Festivals of Literature, when acclaimed writers visit and talk about their work.

Music

If you are of a certain age, you will know bands such as Midnight Oil, the Bee Gees, the Seekers, Crowded House, Split Enz, AC/DC, and INXS. Others include Kylie Minogue, Olivia Newton-John, Savage Garden, Delta Godrem, Keith Urban, and plenty more. The variety of musicians reflects the diversity to be found in Australia, and new bands are constantly springing up.

Film

Australia was "discovered" in the 1970s

when influential film directors such as Peter Weir, Bruce Beresford, and George Miller arrived on the scene. Weir's *Picnic at Hanging Rock* (1975) started an art-house revolution that brought wide attention to the national film industry, which was receiving government support. Bruce Beresford's *Breaker Morant* was the first Australian film to win widespread acclaim as well as an award at Cannes. The postapocalyptic *Mad Max* introduced Mel Gibson to international audiences, and *Crocodile Dundee* was an international comic hit for actor Paul Hogan. Excellent films such as *Priscilla, Queen of the Desert, Strictly Ballroom,* and *Muriel's Wedding* made people sit up and take note of Australian movies.

Owing to the absence of government financial support for film, budgets are low and work is scarce, and talented actors and producers generally make the move to the United States. Guy Pearce, Cate Blanchett, Toni Collette, Nicole Kidman, Judy Davis, Geoffrey Rush, Hugh Jackman, and Heath Ledger are among the best-known emigrant Australians, and several of them have won Oscars. Baz Luhrmann *(Moulin Rouge, The Great Gatsby)* and Gillian Armstrong *(My Brilliant Career)* have had notable success in Hollywood.

Essentials

Transportation

GETTING THERE

Sydney's **Kingsford Smith Airport** (SYD, Airport Dr., tel. 02/9667-9111, www.sydneyairport.com.au), eight kilometers from the city's Central Business District (CBD), is the busiest airport in Australia. With direct connections to most regional airports, it is usually the first stop for U.S. visitors arriving in Australia.

The flight to Australia is a long one from almost anywhere, and your first day will consist of simply getting here, particularly if you are arriving from Western Europe or the U.S. east coast. Typical itineraries involve a connection in Los Angeles (LAX). Qantas is a good airline to fly on this trip, but Air New Zealand (ANZ), Air Tahiti Nui, and United also fly this route; ANZ connects via Auckland, and Air Tahiti Nui connects via Papeete. Qantas connects with American Airlines to Sydney from many major cities nonstop, and to Brisbane from Dallas and LAX, so you may not have to face two connections, which take time and drain energy levels. Qantas is also a good way to start acclimating to Australian accents, vocabulary, and etiquette.

Flight time from LAX to Sydney is around 13 hours, but you lose a day crossing the international date line; you get it back on the trip home. These flights are often overnight, allowing you to arrive first thing in the morning, with connecting flights at the ready. Fares range from $1,500 round-trip in economy to $5,000-10,000 round-trip in business class, and at least an extra 50 percent more for first class. From New York City, deals can be had for around $1,500 round-trip, with the trip taking around 22 hours; more comfortable business class costs from $7,000 round-trip.

If you can fly business or first class (this is a good time to use those frequent flyer miles you've been saving up), you can use the Admirals Club Lounge in LAX to freshen up, get Internet access, or even take a shower or get a meal, which will help ensure that you arrive a little fresher and more enthusiastic than you might otherwise.

GETTING AROUND

Air

Most larger towns have small regional airports, and, due to the distances involved, flying is the most time-efficient way to connect around Queensland. The largest hub in Queensland is **Brisbane Airport** (BNE, 11 The Circuit, tel. 07/3406-3000, www.bne.com.au), which connects Sydney with all the small regional hubs, such as Bundaberg, Gladstone, and Rockhampton. **Cairns Airport** (CNS, Airport Ave., tel. 07/4080-6703, www.cairnsairport.com) is the northernmost airport, ideal for the northern reef and the Daintree Rainforest. **Proserpine (Whitsunday Coast) Airport** (PPP, Lascelles Ave., Proserpine, tel. 07/4945-0200, proserpineairport.com) and the tiny **Hamilton Island Airport** (HTI, tel. 07/4946-9999) are the hubs for the Whitsunday islands.

A handful of competing domestic budget airlines occasionally have fare wars. **Tigerair** (www.tigerairways.com.au) and **Jetstar** (www.jetstar.com.au) are cheap domestic airlines that forgo comfort and always sell one-way tickets. Prices vary by airline and destination, and regular fare sales show lively competition. As a rough guide, if you shop around and are willing to fly at the less popular times of day, you'll spend a maximum of $150 for flights between Sydney and Brisbane (two hours). Booking online allows

Previous: Sydney's bustling Circular Quay; the Australian flag.

you to compare prices more easily at a glance. Websites such as **WebJet** (www.webjet.com.au) and **Flight Centre** (www.flightcentre.com.au) have fare deals from Australia.

Taxis

Taxis are widely available, especially at airports. The cost will be about double what you are used to if you are living in a U.S. city outside of New York City, but the trip is short from Sydney's Kingsford Smith International Airport to most hotels in the Central Business District (CBD) or the airport area. In general, taxis are an acceptable and common option to get to and from the Sydney airport, costing around $30 for a trip into the city center, but they are less reliable for getting around the city and are not as cost effective. It's better to use public transportation if you are not renting a car.

There is one Australia-wide taxi company, 13Cabs, and countless state-governed local companies. Taxis are either yellow or white, easily identified by the lettering on the sides and the For Hire sign on the roof. Most taxis can be hailed from the side of the road, and there are taxi stands outside major venues, such as airports, stations, the CBD, and ferry terminals. All taxis are registered and have driver registration, meters, and satellite tracking systems. Taxi fares vary with the hour and the company, but you can get an estimate of costs and travel times at **TaxiFare** (www.taxifare.com.au).

Private Transportation

Chauffeured private cars are widely available, especially to and from airports, but it is an expensive and unusual way for egalitarian Aussies to get around, and using private cars is not recommended. Stretch limos are very rare; private cars tend to be less conspicuous sedans.

Car

Car-rental pickups are usually done at the airport, as in all major cities. It's best to book a car through your travel agent, although major global brands such as Avis and Hertz are in most locations. Cars, by the way, tend to be much smaller outside the United States. You do not need a special driver's license to drive while you are in Australia.

Australians drive on the left, and the driver is on the right-hand side of the car, so you have to shift gears with your left hand. It takes a little getting used to, but it sounds harder than it actually is. The pedals are configured the same as in the United States, but the gears are typically reversed, so you shift differently when putting the car into reverse in a manual. Save yourself some trouble by getting an automatic transmission so that all you have to focus on is driving on the left. You will find that it is quite easy to follow the flow of traffic while driving, or even changing lanes. The biggest danger is in turning, when you may habitually drift toward the right side of the road, which will put you up against oncoming traffic. It's easy to learn; just make sure you concentrate fully on your turns rather than thinking about directions or the kids in the back seat.

Australia is freeway-challenged, and you will find yourself more often than not on crowded urban arterials. It's not too tough—just allow for extra time for urban transit.

Speed limits and distances are expressed in kilometers per hour (kph) and kilometers. Generally speaking, you will be driving at 50-60 kph on city roads, 80 kph on highways, and up to 130 kph on freeways. For an exact conversion, divide miles by five and multiply by eight to get kilometers or kilometers per hour (do the reverse to determine miles from kilometers—divide the kilometers by eight and multiply by five). Or for a quick calculation, halve the miles and multiply by three. But then, your car's speedometer will be in kph, so just keep an eye on your speed; you'll quickly get used to it.

The blood-alcohol limit for drivers in Australia is 0.05 percent. On weekend nights police often set up roadblocks and perform breath tests randomly, handing out immediate penalties.

Apart from stringent alcohol limits, low speed limits, and strict penalties on breaking either one, most traffic rules are the same as in other countries, with common sense, defensive driving, and good manners being most important.

Along the Bruce Highway, the long stretch of highway winding itself up along the coast between Sydney and northern Queensland, gas stations are available in regular intervals. All small and larger towns have a choice of gas stations—there is no shortage. Once you head farther inland, though, toward the Outback (the rather strange name for the inner region), then make sure you stop whenever you see a gas station as they become rarer and rarer. They are there, but in intervals more suitable for the large road train-trucks, so if you have a small hire car with a small tank, you could easily get caught out. Most hire cars take unleaded gas, which is available at every station.

Public Transportation

Statistics show that Australians, at least the city-dwelling ones, use public transportation more than people in most countries, especially those that have a highly decentralized population. Typical options in most cities are buses and light rail systems, although the coastal cities have ferry systems; Sydney's is an important part of getting around the inner harbor area. In each city, there are multiday transit passes available from ticket offices, usually at main rail and bus stations, and these cannot be recommended strongly enough for reducing the cost and aggravation of public transportation. In Sydney, for example, you will need to buy a MyMulti card before you step on many buses and especially trains, as you can no longer buy tickets onboard. Major rail stations and ferry and bus hubs have easy-to-use vending machines for one-way or multiday and longer-term tickets; they also offer ticket, route, schedule, and fare information, but the best way to get information is via each state's transportation authority page, as transit is controlled at the state rather than the metropolitan level.

In Sydney and surroundings, **NSW Transport** (tel. 13/15-00, www.transport.nsw.gov.au) covers all eventualities, and there is even an app you can download, helping you to catch exactly the right combination of public transport to get you to the right place.

In Queensland, the public transport availability is more sporadic. In larger cities, such as Townsville and Cairns, the local **Sunbus** (www.sunbus.com.au) has good route networks; in smaller towns, public transport is not as frequently available as visitors might wish for.

TRAIN

As I keep mentioning, Australia is a large country, a continent even. Distances are enormous and as such are much easier covered by plane rather than any other means of transport. Within Sydney, there is a fantastic network of trains, operated by **Sydney Trains** (www.sydneytrains.info), but once you are trying to traverse distances between Sydney and Cairns, the duration of the journey is only suitable for travelers with a lot of time on their hands: We're talking around 2.5 days, plus having to change in Brisbane. But, when you consider the distances covered, the prices are effective and the journey pleasant.

A ride from Sydney to Brisbane (from $69) takes around 14 hours on **CountryLink** (www.countrylink.info), a rail company that connects various parts of New South Wales and Brisbane, Canberra, and Melbourne. From Brisbane you can get onto the Sunlander or the Tilt Train, both of which are operated by **Queensland Rail** (tel. 07/3235-2222, www.queenslandrail.com.au) and have several services per week stopping off at most towns and cities mentioned in this guide between Brisbane and Cairns.

BUS

Buses and commuter public transportation are regulated at the regional or state level. Every city has an extensive network of buses, and in larger cities like Sydney, buses run around the clock. On some lines you buy tickets before you enter the bus, and others have ticketing onboard, but this varies from city to city and even within the same city.

There is also interstate bus travel on so-called "coaches," which are comfortable buses, with restrooms, that are designed for longer journeys. The main operator is **Greyhound Australia** (www.greyhound.com.au), offering overland coaches connecting most major cities, although you may have to change and reconnect. Greyhound does not serve all destinations but partners with local operators to get you there eventually.

Traveling by Greyhound coach tends to be economical and offer more stops than the trains. With Greyhound's Mini Traveller Pass ($410), you can hop on and off wherever you want to, although travel is only allowed in one direction. The pass is valid for 90 days, and the trip from Sydney to Cairns via Brisbane takes around 50 hours.

FERRY

Ferries in Sydney feed into other modes of public transportation and tend to start at 5am or 6am and in most cases run until after midnight. Like other modes of public transportation, ferry timetables are widely publicized, tickets come in single-ride to annual passes with many other options, and there are discounts for students, people with disabilities, and senior citizens.

Ferry fares vary the length of the ride; for example, the regular Manly ferry in Sydney Harbour costs $7 one-way, while the fast Manly ferry costs $9 one-way, with the fast one being quicker than any comparable bus trip. Generally speaking, if you have a ferry stop near you in Sydney, it can be quicker and more economical than the bus, and certainly more fun.

The Sydney ferries are also covered through **Transport NSW** (tel. 13/15-00, www.transport.nsw.gov.au), and you can use the MyMulti passes too. The ferries offer a very cheap way to do some of the sightseeing in the harbor, and when the weather is fine, there really is no better and cost-efficient way to travel and enjoy the harbor, its islands, and its surrounding sights and city views.

Visas and Officialdom

VISAS AND PASSPORTS

From a tourist's perspective, obtaining an Australian entry visa is not much trouble, but you do have to remember to obtain a visitor's visa in advance. Travelers from most countries can obtain an Electronic Travel Authority (ETA), which takes about five minutes to obtain online and costs $20, payable by credit card only (Visa, Mastercard, or American Express).

An ETA is equivalent to a visa, but it doesn't appear in your passport. Airline staff will be able to access your record at check-in time. You can apply at www.eta.immi.gov.au if you live in the United States, Canada, or most Western European countries. A full list of eligible nationalities is found at www.eta.immi.gov.au/ETAAus1En.html.

If you do not live in an ETA-eligible country, you can find the right office to contact at www.immi.gov.au/contacts/overseas, and you will make a traditional visa application through a visa office or an authorized third party. Allow up to one month to process a visa application via the traditional channels.

An ETA or traditional visa will permit you to stay in Australia for up to three months at a time; it is valid for 12 months and for multiple stays of up to three months per visit, although you are not allowed to work. If you are planning to combine some business meetings with your vacation trip, make sure you apply for the short-validity business ETA, which has the same time frame.

CUSTOMS

Australia is an island and has an ecosystem that could be harmed severely by introduced diseases and pests, which could be as tiny as a bacterium—things we are not even aware of carrying on us. Therefore, there are plenty of prohibited and restricted items on the import list for Australia. Here are some to be aware of:

- Pharmaceuticals, unless prescribed (and accompanied by a letter from your doctor) or clearly over-the-counter
- Animals (plan on leaving your pet at home)
- Animal products
- Any food items, fresh or dried
- Plants, soil, seeds
- Untreated wooden items

You will have to declare any items made from wood, animal parts, shells, or other natural materials such as rattan, as well as any food items that you haven't gotten rid of. You will also need to declare anything of a value above $1,000 and anything new, such as still-boxed electrical items, for example—should you be planning to travel with some newly purchased gadgets, it's best to unwrap them first.

A full list of prohibited items is available from **Australian Customs** (www.customs.gov.au). If you are unsure, it is generally a good idea to declare whatever you have on you; you may be allowed to take your item with you.

Your duty-free exemption is $900 worth of goods ($450 for people under age 18), excluding alcohol and tobacco products; 2.25 liters of alcoholic beverages; and up to 50 cigarettes or 50 grams of other tobacco products for travelers age 18 or older.

EMBASSIES AND CONSULATES

U.S. Embassies and Consulates in Australia

- **Embassy of the United States:** Moonah Place, Yarralumla, ACT 2600, tel. 02/6214-5600, fax 02/6214-5970, http://canberra.usembassy.gov. Office hours: 8am-5pm Monday-Friday. *Note:* U.S. passports (including lost/stolen passports) and visa services are *not* available at the embassy.
- **U.S. Consulate-General, Sydney:** MLC Centre, Level 59, 19-29 Martin Place, Sydney, NSW 2000, tel. 02/9373-9200 or 02/4422-2201 (after hours), fax 02/9373-9184, http://sydney.usconsulate.gov. Office hours: 8am-5pm Monday-Friday.

Canadian Embassies and Consulates in Australia

- **High Commission of Canada, Canberra:** Commonwealth Avenue, Canberra, ACT 2600, tel. 02/6270-4000, fax 02/6270-4081. Office hours: 8:30am-12:30pm and 1pm-4:30pm Monday-Friday.
- **Consulate General of Canada, Sydney:** Level 5, 111 Harrington Street, Sydney, NSW 2000, tel. 02/9364-3000, fax 02/9364-3098. Office hours: 8:30am-4:30pm Monday-Friday for general inquiries; 9am-noon Monday-Thursday for immigration and visa inquiries.

Accommodations and Food

ACCOMMODATIONS

Australia is well-equipped when it comes to accommodations and offers everything from luxury five-star suites to camping on deserted islands. One thing to note, something most first-timers in Australia fall foul of, is that a "hotel" is not necessarily a hotel as you know it. A "hotel" in Australia is often a pub or low-key bar. So, if you search the Internet for "hotels in Cairns," for example, you might well get a listing for pubs (which may or may not offer accommodations). Search for "accommodations in Cairns" to be on the safe side. Another use of words that may confuse visitors is "spa." While most of us think of spas as relaxed places where you can get pampered with a facial and a massage, in Australia, quite often a "spa" is nothing more than a hot tub. So, if you book a "spa suite" that could simply mean that you have a Jacuzzi in your bathroom. If, however, your accommodation is titled "resort and spa," it is safe to assume that there is an on-site day spa.

One thing to keep in mind is that Australia generally is very expensive, and that goes double for Sydney. Accommodation rates that look as if they should get you the presidential suite usually don't. If you are visiting during the high season (i.e., the season when it simply is the most pleasant to visit), you get hit with even higher rates. High season is roughly between January through to April and again in October through to mid-December, with the time over New Year's Eve in Sydney being the priciest of all. May to August, in the cooler months, is low season and you get a little more bang for your buck, but expect to pay top dollar for accommodations in Sydney.

The good news is, once you are out of Sydney and heading north to Queensland, you get a lot more for your money. It's still relatively pricey but a lot more affordable. The even better news is that in Australia, generally speaking, most accommodations come with tea- and coffee-making facilities, and quite often with a mini-kitchenette, with a small fridge, maybe a microwave or hot plate, allowing you to occasionally eat in, rather than splashing out on restaurants all day long.

Room prices quoted in this guide are usually for the most basic double room, low-season, without breakfast unless mentioned.

Resorts

Australia's mainland has a total coastline length of 35,876 kilometers (22,292 miles) with countless beautiful beaches and stunning islands, and there are just as many inviting resorts. One thing to note is that the majority of Australian beach resorts don't necessarily have direct and private access to the beach (though most have at the very least a public road between them and the sea). Quite often something is called a beach resort when it is nowhere near the beach, but in a beachside town or village. Take Port Douglas in northern Queensland as an example: Alongside its famous four-mile beach there are countless beach resorts, but only two have direct access to the beach, and in no case is the beach a private one secluded from the public. For that, you will have to get onto one of the private resort islands on the Great Barrier Reef, and even then you may well have to share with day-trippers.

Hotels

As discussed above, be aware of the definition of "hotel." Don't assume that because a place is called a hotel you will be able to stay the night there—you might only be able to grab a few drinks and snacks. That said, in the cities, most hotels are indeed hotels, and come in ratings from budget to five-star.

Motels

Motels are very popular in towns and cities outside major metropolises such as Sydney and provide a generally clean and cheap option to spend the night. By definition, they are designed for you to drive up and leave your car outside your room and are as such mostly located on major throughways. They are generally convenient if you are, say, driving yourself along the coast of Queensland and are counting on a quick getaway in the morning, they can be noisy and sometimes a little dingy. But they are always better for a limited budget than anything closer to the city center.

Holiday Parks

Holiday parks in Australia are a favorite with families. Usually offering spaces for tents and motor homes, powered and unpowered, they often also offer a variety of chalets from one-bed cabins to good-size villas. More often than not these parks are located outside the city center but are generally filled with amenities such as swimming pools and playgrounds. Quite often they provide regular shuttle buses into the city or the beaches. This is always a budget and family-friendly option, especially if you are traveling in groups larger than two people.

Camping

Camping is synonymous with travel in Australia and the only way to stay in and on certain parts of the country. Many of the most beautiful parts of the land and coast are designated national parks and world heritage sites, hampering the development of resorts in favor of protecting the sites, but quite often campgrounds (referred to in Australia as "campsites") can be found on even the remotest islands, with facilities ranging from nonexistent to reasonably good. Check the website for **NSW National** (www.nationalparks.nsw.gov.au) or **Queensland National Parks** (www.nprsr.qld.gov.au) and take it from there.

More often than not, if you are camping on a remote beach or island, you are required to carry everything with you on the way in and out (water, cookwares, bedding, etc.), and on the way out take all your garbage. There can be camping restrictions during certain times of the year, such as breeding seasons for birds or turtles, and also you might encounter complete fire bans during bushfire season, meaning no open barbecues. Bushfire season, officially, is during the summer, October-March, but fires can occur during dry and hot spells at any time during the year.

FOOD

Australian food is often mistakenly thought of as consisting of the so-called bush tucker—witchetty grubs and green ants—and you can experience those tastes if you travel to the Outback on a special tour. But try and get anything like that in your average Australian restaurant, and you'll be disappointed. Australian food generally is as diverse and cosmopolitan as its people. You get plenty of Asian food, excellent Greek and Italian restaurants, decent Indian and Thai curries, and, say, Ethiopian fare, and pretty much everything in between. Obviously you'll get a little less diversity in the countryside, but generally Australia is made up of many nationalities, and all are keen to show off their cuisines.

Plenty of restaurants call themselves "modern Australian"—actually, most restaurants that do not specifically cater to one country's cuisine are just that: modern Australian. With modern Australian, there is an emphasis on seasonal and local or regional ingredients, and menus tend to change accordingly. You will be able to taste local Australian fare in many places; do not shy away from kangaroo meat, as it is probably one of the healthiest and environmentally friendly meats around by not being farmed and being utterly lean. There is often emu on the menu, as well as the strangely named Moreton Bay bugs, which are shellfish like small crayfish and are very good. The favorite and most ubiquitous fish is the barramundi, an estuarine fish that is best pan-fried or grilled with a crispy skin.

On the daily faster food menu, you'll find that Australians have a taste for savory pies, usually with "sauce" (ketchup), and fish and chips. Burgers often come with a slice of beet. Other than that, you'll find that all tastes are generally catered to.

DRINK

There is nothing unusual about what Australians drink, although it is often quite a lot, especially after a successful football, cricket, or rugby game. Where alcohol is concerned, Australian wines are varied and fantastic, Bundaberg Rum is known to connoisseurs across the globe, and beer comes in so many guises that, if you are an aficionado, you should visit a local bottle shop to marvel at the variety.

The only thing you might stumble over is ordering coffee. There are several Starbucks branches across the country, but any other café will probably not know what you mean if you order "black" or white coffee, or an Americano, or whatever your tipple is. The easiest choices to remember are that a "long black" is a black coffee with two shots of espresso per cup, and a "flat white" is a coffee with a lot of warm milk in it, similar to a latte, with some foam on the top.

Travel Tips

CLOTHING

Outside of hotels and major businesses, Australian buildings have fairly rudimentary heating and cooling systems because of the mild climate, and in the extremes of winter and summer there can be episodes of humid heat or cold that can be a bit of a shock for those accustomed to modulated temperatures. If you are planning a visit to Australia July-August or January-February, plan to dress in layers. Heavy jackets or parkas are advised if you are coming in the winter months (July to September) and are planning to visit the elevated mountain areas, but leather jackets, a light rain shell, and a cardigan also come in handy. Think "layers" and you can't go too wrong.

Generally, Australian society is highly informal and tolerant when it comes to clothing, so light and casual travel attire is always acceptable as day wear. For restaurants, smart casual is typical.

If you are attending a formal event, such as a theater opening night, or dining at a very upscale restaurant, suits and cocktail dresses are typical, but casual dress is the norm for most nightlife that caters to travelers.

SMOKING

Smoking is rapidly declining in Australia, from 45 percent of men and 30 percent of women in the 1970s to 23 percent of men and 19 percent of women in 2008, with rates at present around 15 percent, one of the lowest in the world. Smoking is banned in all enclosed public places and offices, and only a few pubs and hotels still allow smokers a secluded enclave. Legislation differs from state to state, but since December 2012 all cigarette packaging is a uniform olive color with large and dramatic health warnings on them with the brand's name in small generic lettering. It is hoped that this change in advertising will further push the percentage of smokers below 10 percent.

GAY AND LESBIAN TRAVELERS

The experiences of gays and lesbians in Australia are in many ways similar to those in the United States, where general acceptance in educated urban areas is balanced by diminishing but still common cultural hostility in other regions and demographic groups. Homosexuality is legal in all states except Queensland, where limited bans on homosexual sex are not generally enforced. Same-sex marriage is prohibited at the federal level, but all states and territories recognize same-sex civil unions. Gays and lesbians are allowed to serve in the military.

Gender reassignment has been legal nationwide since 2006.

While legal discrimination is fading, gays and lesbians will face a typical range of social discrimination similar to in the United States. Anti-gay humor is not acceptable in the mainstream media but lives on at the conversational level, and Aussie tolerance should not be mistaken for active acceptance. In general, Australia tends to be more tolerant than the United States, but some of the political parties oppose the expansion of rights for gays and lesbians, and the path to full equality is not yet mapped out.

Australian gay men and lesbians are socially and politically well organized and are especially visible in Sydney and Melbourne. In Sydney, the heart of the gay scene is Darlinghurst and Paddington on the eastern edge of the CBD, along with the inner west suburbs of Newtown, Erskineville, and Glebe.

Fishing Licenses

Keen to do some angling while in Australia? You might need to get a recreational fishing license, depending on your destination.

NEW SOUTH WALES

In New South Wales, a three-day license costs $7 and covers spear fishing, hand lining, hand gathering, trapping, bait collecting, and prawn netting or when in possession of fishing gear in, on, or adjacent to waters, both saltwater and freshwater. You can get the license online from the **NSW Department of Primary Industries** (www.dpi.nsw.gov.au/fisheries/recreational/licence-fee).

QUEENSLAND

Anglers do not require a license to fish recreationally in Queensland, except if fishing in some stocked impoundments, where operators will let you know and/or the license is included in the trip.

ACCESS FOR PEOPLE WITH DISABILITIES

In general, most Australian public facilities are well equipped when it comes to accessibility for those with mobility difficulties. Parking, toilets, and ramp accesses are well marked and plentiful, and all major cities and many states produce maps and websites listing their services. Local governments issue parking permits for the disabled, but you are allowed to use your current and valid disabled license when parking, as long as you put it on display where it can easily be seen. Facilities and assistance vary from state to state; check with the local government for details. Another good website is the **National Information Communication Awareness Network** (www.nican.com.au), which aims to give full information on recreation, tourism, sports, and the arts for people with disabilities.

Health and Safety

HOSPITALS AND CLINICS

In Australia there are public and private hospitals, with the public hospitals funded jointly by the federal government and state or territory governments, and administered by those regional governments. Generally speaking, the health care system is the same throughout the country, but regional variations exist.

In the public hospital sector, large general hospitals cover anything from maternity and pediatrics to infectious diseases and geriatrics. Some hospitals and clinics may specialize further in pediatrics, oncology, eye problems, and the like.

The quality and quantity of good hospitals and clinics depend on where you are. Cities are exponentially better equipped than the less densely populated regions of Australia, and there are many of those. There is a severe shortage of qualified staff willing to move to more isolated regions—so much so that the government is actively inviting and importing qualified staff for those areas, such as Western Australia or the Northern Territory, plus some of the more remote areas of Queensland.

Many people depend on the famed Royal Flying Doctor Service, which provides medical services in the most remote areas, either on the spot or to evacuate patients to the nearest hospital by plane.

SUN INTENSITY AND AIR QUALITY

Australia is famous for its Slip, Slop, Slap campaign (slip on a shirt, slop on sunscreen, and slap on a hat) and the dire statistic that Australia has the highest skin cancer rate in the world. This is partly due to the depletion of the ozone layer above the Antarctic, and while it is tempting to soak up the sun, especially after some gray days, always wear sunscreen and reduce the amount of time you spend in direct sunlight, avoiding the sun between noon and 3pm in particular. You will burn much faster here, so step up the screening factor above what you are used to. If you typically wear SPF 15, wear SPF 30 in Australia. Also, a good pair of "sunnies" (sunglasses) is a must, and a good hat is strongly recommended. If you feel like assimilating into the Australian look, buy and wear an Aussie Akubra hat, the iconic slouch hat available from **Akubra** (www.akubra.com); just leave the corks behind.

As a whole, Australia continuously ranks high among nations for clean air, but this is partly due to it being one of the least densely populated countries in the world. When you look at Sydney and Melbourne, Australia's most populous cities, the statistics are slightly less impressive, and subject to seasonal variations, with air quality worse in winter, due to temperature inversions and popular wood-burning ovens that raise the amount of particulate matter in the air. Sydney has also been called the allergy capital of the world, probably attributable to the voluminous green spaces and parks everywhere, which increase the pollen count at certain times of the year to uncomfortable levels for sufferers. Parkland also offsets air pollution, however.

FIRES AND EMERGENCIES

In Australia, fire and paramedic services are combined into individual state emergency response systems, accessible via the national **emergency numbers: 000** from landlines, **112** from cell phones, and **106** for TTY, teletypewriter, or text phones for the hearing or speech impaired. It is not possible to contact emergency services using text messaging (SMS).

Fire is taken very seriously in Australia, with an average of 52,000 bushfires per year, some 50 percent of which are found to have been deliberately lit or suspicious. In late October and early November 2013 (late spring, and not yet official fire season), vast bushfires raged within the city limits of Sydney. Many homes and tourist attractions in the Blue Mountains were destroyed, and the skies over the city and Bondi Beach were colored red and brown from the smoke. And in 2009 Victoria experienced the worst bushfires in Australia's history, leaving entire communities wiped out and 209 people dead. Bushfire is an annual threat that kills people and animals and destroys homes, businesses, and farms. There are daily warnings in the summer season, when people living in or near the bush, even on the outskirts of towns and cities, are encouraged to have a fire plan in place and be ready for evacuation if necessary.

You'll need to be aware, especially when driving on your own, so it's a good idea to keep up with local news during the season, and double-check if there is any doubt. Warnings are issued through TV and radio, and the hotel concierge will know what's going on and which regions to avoid. Tour operators will be aware and reschedule tours if necessary.

SURF AND SAIL RESCUE

Going into the water in Australia can be a dangerous undertaking, with strong riptides, undertows, and a wide variety of nasty creatures. This is where the famous Aussie lifeguards come into play. The Surf Life Savers are a mix of paid lifeguards and enthusiastic volunteers organized in 310 clubs with more than 158,800 members throughout Australia. They have saved more than 600,000 lives since 1907, and aided countless victims suffering from shark bites, jellyfish stings, and other painful encounters with not-so-cuddly creatures. Surf Life Savers also runs Westpac Life Saver Rescue Helicopters, the world's longest-serving search-and-rescue helicopter service, with helicopters stationed in every state. The helicopters are also used for shark patrols during the southern summer months (October-April), scanning the waters in particularly affected regions but also watching out for other dangers. Given that Australia has threatening wildlife and riptides on the coast, drowning is a very real danger, and it is advisable to swim only at patrolled beaches between the flags.

POISON CONTROL, BITES, AND STINGS

Australia has some of the most poisonous spiders, snakes, and toads in the world. Why exactly Australian beasties have evolved to be so toxic and vicious is not completely understood, but it pays to be alert. In the cities you are generally a lot safer than in the countryside; the riskiest places are in bush with plenty of undergrowth. But one of the most poisonous spiders, the funnel web, is indigenous to Sydney. In the outer suburbs you may have snake encounters, and once you leave the relative safety of the cities, be wary. The best way to protect yourself is to know your enemy. While it might not be great bedtime reading, get a book on local spiders and snakes and learn to recognize them, because once you have been bitten, time is of the essence. Call the **Poison Information Centre** (tel. 13/11-26), state your emergency, and they will provide you with antivenin. Don't panic—of all the countless spiders in Australia, only three can actually kill you (the funnel web, red back, and white tail), and not a single person has died from a spider bite since 1979.

CRIME

Like every country, Australia has crime, and at times it can seem that this is all that is covered in the news. But when properly analyzed, the rates are generally better in Australia than in the United States, and much better when it comes to serious crimes such as murder (1 in 100,000 in Australia, as compared to 4.8 per 100,000 in the United States). Robberies are reported at 56 in 100,000 in Australia, compared to 114 in 100,000 in the United States.

Common sense should be applied: Don't leave your handbag or cell phone unattended; lock your car; avoid walking the streets late at night; and look after your belongings even more carefully when visiting tourist areas.

Information and Services

MONEY

Note: Prices in this guide are quoted in Australian currency unless otherwise noted. The Australian currency is the Australian dollar, which in recent years has been near parity with the U.S. dollar. Coins come in denominations of 5, 10, 20, and 50 cents and $1 and $2, and bills are in denominations of $5, $10, $20, $50, and $100. Each note is a different color and size to allow the visually impaired to distinguish them.

The good news for travelers to Australia is that the country is highly adapted to electronic payment systems—more so than just about any country on Earth—and establishments of almost any size will accept credit cards such as Visa and Mastercard. ATMs are available in every suburb within a two-block radius of the main train or bus stop, and most shops that cater to tourists accept debit cards.

However, it's always a good idea to carry Australian cash, and you would be well advised to invest in a money holder, because Australian coins are large and heavy compared to those of most other countries. Because there are no $1 or $2 bills, only coins, you can accumulate a lot of change in your pocket. The size of Australian paper money differs depending on the denomination, and the $100 bill is significantly larger than the $5 bill; it will not fit in a standard wallet. If you don't mind a bit of heavy jingle in your pocket, a standard money clip will do just fine for the bills.

If you want to minimize the risk of losing your cards and your cash, try using an international debit card, which you can load with money before your trip. It can also help you stick to a budget.

Tipping

You don't have to leave tips in cafés and restaurants. While the personnel will always appreciate it, it is not expected. Unlike in the United States, your bill will include service charges and the service staff is paid competitive wages, making them independent from the reliance on tips. That is not to say that in fine dining restaurants, or anywhere where you were pleased with the service, you shouldn't leave something to show your appreciation. Often you can simply round up the bill, or a tip of up to 10 percent is absolutely sufficient.

For cab drivers, round up the fare, or give a tip of about 10 percent.

If you are going on a day trip, and your guide and driver were great, then leave them something on the way out of the bus (roughly 10 percent, or even just a $10 or $20 bill), but you will not need to do so on harbor cruises or other paid-for activities.

It's not necessary to tip hotel staff, but it's a nice gesture if they have been helpful.

MAPS AND TOURIST INFORMATION

The best maps of Australia, covering pretty much every up until now discovered inch of it, are **Hema maps** (www.hemamaps.com.au), available at all good bookstores, many gas stations, and often in the local visitors centers.

When it comes to visitors centers, Australia is extraordinarily well prepared. There is hardly a village or small town that doesn't have a small visitors center on its outskirts, usually signposted well in advance and staffed by local volunteers who are brimming with information and enthusiasm. Many of the centers have small websites adding to the information.

In Sydney there are two main branches of the **Sydney Visitor Centre,** one in The Rocks (corner Playfair St. and Argyle St., tel. 02/8273-0000, www.therocks.com.au, daily 9:30am-5:30pm) and another at Darling Harbour (33 Wheat St., behind Starbucks and IMAX Cinema, tel. 02/9211-4288, www.darlingharbour.com, daily 9:30am-5:30pm), with three additional kiosks: outside the Town Hall (George St.), at Circular Quay (corner Pitt St.

and Albert St.), and in Haymarket (Dixon St. near Goulburn St.).

In Cairns, there is the **Cairns & Tropical North Visitor Information Centre** (51 Esplanade, tel. 07/4051-3588, www.cairnsgreatbarrierreef.org.au, Mon.-Fri. 8:30am-6pm, Sat.-Sun. 10am-6pm), which can give you information on the rest of Queensland as well.

For the whole of the country, an excellent website is www.australia.com, which covers pretty much all locations and eventualities.

COMMUNICATIONS AND MEDIA

Internet

The Internet is easily accessed in Australia's main cities, such as Sydney, but the farther inland you go, the more difficult it becomes. That said, the regions covered in this guide are generally connected, with most cities and large towns having a number of Internet cafés, Wi-Fi zones in public spaces, and business centers in hotels. Bar some of the more remote islands, you have access available throughout the resorts on the Great Barrier Reef as well. In cities, most libraries have free Wi-Fi and computers available where the web can be accessed at minimal charge.

Sadly, most hotels still charge for Wi-Fi and Internet connections, with some notable exceptions, such as Best Western, which, although a budget accommodation option, always offers free Wi-Fi to guests.

Generally speaking, Australia and its businesses and services are very well connected, with statistics showing that the accommodation sector is 94 percent online, with more than 85 percent having their own websites; the dining sector is 60 percent online; and the tourism sector, such as tours, facilities, and recreational sources, is more than 90 percent online. So booking and researching Australia on the web is an easy and comprehensive option.

Phones

AREA CODES

For telephone calls, Australia has a short and easily remembered system of calling codes. Area codes are organized by state, with some exceptions around border areas. Mobile phones have their own code, 4. When dialing from inside Australia, you add a 0, so that Sydney phone numbers are dialed using 02. In addition to the area code, which you don't have to dial if you are within the area (an exception is the mobile phone code), there are generally eight digits to a phone number.

- 2—Central East: New South Wales, Australian Capital Territory, parts of northern border areas of Victoria
- 3—Southeast: Tasmania, Victoria, and parts of southern border areas of New South Wales
- 4—Digital GSM mobile phones
- 7—Northeast: Queensland
- 8—Central and West Region: South Australia, Northern Territory, and Western Australia

The prefix 1800 denotes a toll-free number when dialed from a landline, but some 1800 numbers may incur a charge; numbers with a 190 prefix are often used for premium rate calls, such as competitions or announcements, whereas numbers with the 1300 prefix are charged at a roughly local rate.

MOBILE PHONES

For mobile calling, Australia has three networks that work with a wide variety of devices: Optus, Telstra, and Vodaphone. Your U.S. device may work if you have an international roaming plan; check with your service provider.

Australia uses the same 900 MHz and 1800 MHz GSM (Global System for Mobiles) technology used in most of the world except North America and Japan. Some American GSM phones designed for 1900 MHz can handle standard GSM. Both 3G and 4G services are also in use, via Telstra.

A typical CDMA (Code Division Multiple Access) phone from the United States will not work here, although some will—check with your individual manufacturer. The good news is that GSM is getting more and more popular in the United States, so there's a good chance that a handset will work in Australia if it's unlocked.

If you have an iPhone, whether it will work in Australia depends on whether it is GSM or CDMA.

For your visit, **Telestial** (www.telestial.com) offers an Australian SIM card, with free incoming calls and local-rate outbound calls, all prepaid and with no contract. It gives you a local Australian number, and you start with US$10 airtime credit. Minutes cost US$0.49. **Optus** (www.optus.com.au), which has shops in larger airport arrival terminals, also offers local SIM card packages that can be used with most unlocked 4G phones. Double-check the 4G compatibility of your phone, as not all 4G devices are compatible with the Optus 4G network.

Skype

For long-distance service, most travelers choose to use **Skype** (www.skype.com). It is a VOIP (Voice Over Internet Protocol) service that offers free, unlimited computer-to-computer calling and cheap calls from your computer to a landline (as low as a mere $0.03 per minute). Most computers these days have microphones and cameras built in, or you can buy a small USB camera-microphone set. Apple users can use iChat, similar to Skype.

Postal Service

The postal service, Australia Post, has improved its services from the dreadful state of years past.

The cost of postage is incredibly complex, determined based on size, weight, thickness, and destination distance. Sizes come with unusual codes: DL (110 by 220 mm), C6 (114 by 162 mm), C5 (162 by 229 mm), C4 (324 by 250 mm), and B4 (353 by 250 mm). A standard envelope, the DL size, of standard thickness, weighing 20 grams (or 3 ounces), and traveling within Australia costs $0.60 for nonguaranteed first-business-day service, or $5.55 for express mail that is guaranteed the next business day. Internationally, a postcard will cost $1.65 and will arrive in 3-10 business days.

Packages over 20 millimeters (0.75 inch) thick, weighing more than 500 grams (1.1 pounds), or larger than 260 millimeters by 360 millimeters (12 by 14 inches) are considered parcels. A 500-gram package that is a small standard package-size of 22 by 16 by 7.7 centimeters (roughly 8 by 6 by 3 inches) will travel Sydney to Melbourne in up to three business days for $6.60, or $9.55 for Express Post, guaranteed next day.

FedEx services are available for international shipments only.

WEIGHTS AND MEASUREMENTS

Australia uses the metric system, with distances in kilometers, weights in kilograms, and volume in liters.

Electric Converters

Australia runs on 240 volts, which means that appliances made for 110-volt countries such as the United States may not work when plugged into Australian electrical outlets. The shape of the standard prongs is tantalizingly similar but crucially different. Devices that can handle variable voltage (such as laptops, iPods, or cell phones) need a simple plug adapter, which you can buy at airports or in the travel section of major retailers. For other appliances, check the instruction manual or contact the manufacturer; they may advise you to get a small transformer that steps the voltage down.

Clothing and Shoe Sizes

In Australia, dress sizes are numbered two sizes larger and shoe sizes are numbered a half size smaller than in the United States. For example, a size 10 dress in the United States is a size 12 in Australia; a size 8.5 shoe in the United States is a size 8 in Australia.

Resources

Glossary

arcade: small shopping area, usually in the CBD
arvo: afternoon
Aussie: Australian (pronounced "Ozzie")
avo: avocado
barbie: barbecue
barrack: to cheer
barrister: trial lawyer
battler: someone who struggles valiantly, typically financially
beaut/beauty: fantastic
bikkie/biscuit: cookie
bingle: accident
bloke: guy
bloody: very
bonnet: hood of a car
bonza: great
booze bus: police vehicle used for catching drunk drivers
bottle shop: liquor store
bub: baby
bum: fanny ("fanny" is a vulgarity in Australia; do not use)
bush: anywhere beyond the city
BYO: bring your own (e.g., wine at a restaurant)
CBD: central business district; downtown
chemist: pharmacist
chips: French fries
chook: a chicken
cooee: literally, within hearing distance; figuratively, far away ("he's not within cooee of Sydney")
courgette: zucchini
cozzie: swimsuit
crook: sick ("I feel crook")
cuppa: cup of tea
dag: nerd
daks: trousers
dead set: true
dear: expensive
dill: a foolish person
dinky-die: the real thing, genuine
dobber: informer
dobbing/dobbing someone in: informing, tattling
drongo: a foolish person
dunny: toilet
entrée: starter, appetizer (not a main dish)
esky: ice chest, drinks container
fair dinkum: genuine
fair go: a fair chance
flat: apartment
g'day: hello
gobsmacked: astonished
good on ya: well done
greengrocer: fruit and vegetable store or department
grog: liquor
gumboots: rubber boots
gum tree: eucalyptus tree
hotel: pub
I reckon: Yes, I agree.
jersey: sweater
John Dory: local white fish
lolly/lollies: candy
Maccas: McDonald's
mains: main dishes; what Americans would call entrées
mateship: loyalty

mate's rate: discount for a friend
middy: small beer glass in New South Wales
milk bar: takeaway food shop
mince: ground beef
mobile: cell phone
nappy: diaper
Never Never: the Outback
no worries: no problem, you're welcome
ocker: an Australian who speaks Strine
Outback: the hot, dry interior
Oz: Australia
pav/pavlova: classic dessert made from meringue topped with cream and fruit
petrol: gasoline
pissed: drunk
plaster: Band-Aid
pom, pommy: an English person
post code: zip code
pot: small beer glass in Queensland and Victoria
pozzy: position ("get a good pozzy at the football stadium")
prawn: shrimp
prezzy: present, gift
pudding: dessert
Rack off!: Get lost!
return: round-trip (a return ticket)
rissole: sausage-filled pastry
rort: fraud
roundabout: traffic circle
rubbish (noun): garbage
rubbish (verb): to criticize
schooner: large beer glass
seppo: American
serviette: napkin
sister: registered nurse
snag: sausage
solicitor: commercial lawyer
Southerly Buster: the cooling afternoon breeze in Sydney
spill: battle, often used with respect to political leadership contests
spit the dummy: get upset
sprung: caught
sticking plaster: Band-Aid
strata unit: condominium
strides: trousers
Strine: Australian dialect
sunnies: sunglasses
surgery: doctor's office
ta: thank you
takeaway: takeout food
tall poppies: very important people (often sarcastic)
tea: dinner
tin: can
togs: bathing suit
tosser: a foolish person
Tresca: Sprite
tucker: food
uni: university (pronounced "YOU-knee")
unit: apartment
ute: utility vehicle, pickup truck
veggies: vegetables
wardrobe: closet
whinge: complain
wog: illness
wuss: coward
yakka: work
yewy: U-turn
yobbo: a foolish person
yonks: ages

Suggested Reading

GENERAL

Bryson, Bill. *In a Sunburned Country.* Sydney: Broadway, 2001. This fact-filled, anecdote-filled cornucopia of Australiana is from perhaps the best-known travel humorist.

Horne, Donald. *The Lucky Country.* Sydney: Penguin, 1967. This brilliant exploration of Australian culture was written in the 1960s but is applicable today.

Hughes, Robert. *The Fatal Shore: The Epic of Australia's Founding.* Sydney: Penguin, 1967. An acclaimed art critic turns his eye to the convict story. His vivid writing resulted in a book considered a masterpiece on early Aussie history.

Jacobson, Howard. *In the Land of Oz.* London: Bloomsbury Publishing, 2011. Booker Prize winner and humorist Howard Jacobson is a Brit who is not necessarily PC about his intrepid travels through Oz in his younger years.

FICTION

Anderson, Jessica. *Tirra Lirra by the River.* Sydney: Picador Australia, 2007. An old woman looks back on an extraordinary life in Queensland and London.

Carey, Peter. *Oscar and Lucinda.* New York: Vintage, 1997. A Booker Prize winner in 1988, this is one of the most acclaimed Aussie novels ever. A love story and much more.

Franklin, Miles. *My Brilliant Career.* Sydney: Bibliobazaar, 2007. This acclaimed turn-of-the-20th-century classic was made into a landmark film in 1979 by Bruce Beresford.

Grenville, Kate. *The Secret River.* Melbourne: Text Publishing, 2005. Historical novel about a 19th-century Londoner transported to young Sydney for theft. Brilliant insight on what the first settlers had to deal with.

White, Patrick. *Voss.* New York: Viking, 1957. In the generally accepted masterpiece of Australia's only Nobel Prize winner, romance between an explorer and a young woman turns into dark obsession.

Winton, Tim. *Cloudstreet.* Sydney: Picador Australia, 2002. This is Australia's most admired work of fiction, according to http://Bookworm.com.au. Two rural families begin again in the big city.

LANGUAGE

Lauder, Afferback. *Let Stalk Strine.* Sydney: Australia in Print, 1989. This is a classic and hilarious study of the Australian dialect. Followups include *Nose Tone Unturned, Fraffly Well Spoken,* and *Fraffly Suite.*

O'Grady, John. *They're a Weird Mob.* Sydney: Ure Smith, 1965. This 1957 classic is about an Italian journalist who takes a job as a bricklayer to learn about Australians and speaking Strine. Hilarious.

CHILDREN'S BOOKS

Gibbs, May. *The Complete Adventures of Snugglepot and Cuddlepie.* Sydney: HarperCollins Publishers Australia, 2010. The charmingly illustrated adventures of two little gumnut babies and other bush characters were first published in 1918 and have not been out of print since.

Lindsay, Norman. *The Magic Pudding.* Sydney: Dover, 2006. This classic children's tale features Bunyip Bluegum, an itinerant Aussie koala traveling at the turn of the 20th century in Australia.

Pedley, Ethel. *Dot and the Kangaroo.* Sydney: Echo Library, 2008. This classic children's tale was made into a film in the 1970s. A little girl becomes lost in the Outback.

Thiele, Colin. *Storm Boy.* Sydney: New Holland, 2004. Classic young adult fiction about a boy, his pelican, his father, and an indigenous Australian man.

Suggested Films

Australia. Directed by Baz Luhrmann. 165 minutes. 20th Century Fox, 2008. Big-budget epic starring Nicole Kidman and Hugh Jackman, telling the story of an English aristocrat inheriting a large cattle station, the battle with thieving cattle barons, the cattle drive through the unforgiving Outback, the bombing of Darwin in World War II, and the romance with a rather handsome drover. Great photography shows off the Outback at its best.

The Castle. Directed by Rob Sitch. 98 minutes. Village Roadshow, 1997. A classic Aussie cult film, virtually unknown outside of Oz but beloved at home, this is the story of a family whose home in the suburbs is threatened by an airport expansion. The father refuses to move, setting off a series of comic incidents in a send-up of Australian culture (or lack thereof).

Crocodile Dundee. Directed by Peter Faiman. 98 minutes. Paramount, 1986. This comedy classic introduced famed Aussie comic Paul Hogan to the world. He plays a crocodile hunter, naturally, who gets in any number of comic and romantic entanglements.

Mad Max. Directed by George Miller. 99 minutes. Village Roadshow, 1979. In this vaguely futuristic film about biker gangs and the lone policeman who takes revenge on them, Mel Gibson's voice was dubbed for the American market because producers thought his thick Aussie accent would not be understood. Amazing car chases and stunts. The sequels, *The Road Warrior* and *Mad Max Beyond Thunderdome,* were even more popular.

Muriel's Wedding. Directed by P. J. Hogan. 106 minutes. Miramax, 1995. Toni Collette's breakthrough film is a classic comedy about an ugly duckling who leaves behind a small town to explore life in the city.

My Brilliant Career. Directed by Gillian Armstrong. 100 minutes. Blue Underground, 1979. This is a coming-of-age film about a spirited young woman, expertly played by newcomer Judy Davis. It was Davis's breakthrough film, as well as Gillian Armstrong. She went on to helm *Little Women* and *Oscar and Lucinda.*

Picnic at Hanging Rock. Directed by Peter Weir. 115 minutes. Atlantic, 1975. Peter Weir's atmospheric mystery is about a picnic at a girls' school that results in the disappearance of three girls. It's widely considered one of the breakthrough films that propelled the renaissance of Aussie films in the 1970s.

Sunday Too Far Away. Directed by Peter Faiman. 98 minutes. South Australian Film, 1975. Jack Thompson stars in the story of an Australian sheep station in the 1950s as bonuses disappear and nonunion laborers show up. Shearers' wives used to say of their husbands, "Friday night too tired; Saturday night too drunk; Sunday too far away," which gave the movie its title.

The Year of Living Dangerously. Directed by Peter Weir. 115 minutes. MGM, 1983. This moody romantic thriller made an international star out of Mel Gibson and showed that Sigourney Weaver could do more than fight off aliens. A Sydney journalist is sent to Jakarta as the 1965 coup unfolds and discovers his capacity for love and betrayal (both good and bad) through his encounters with a diminutive man named Billy Kwan (played by Linda Hunt), fellow journalists, the government, the communist conspirators, and a beautiful British intelligence agent.

Internet Resources

www.australia.com
This is the official website of the Australian tourism industry. It allows you access to pretty much everything and anything about Australia you would every wish to know: facts and figures ranging from climate to animals; culture and history, covering early Aboriginal Australia as well as details on the Australian obsession with sports; and detailed information about each major city, territory, and region. There are all the facts you'll need to know about where you might want to go and how to get there, plus the nitty gritty you need to achieve it.

www.australiantraveller.com
This is Australia's best-loved travel magazine and a monthly inspiration to all who want to explore this vast country. Excellent firsthand travel reports from some of the country's writers inspire, guide, and inform anybody who wants to get a little deeper and learn about personal experiences, new accommodations and restaurants that have been reviewed anonymously, and nuts and bolts travel on this continent.

www.cairns-greatbarrierreef.org.au
This is a great compilation of facts and figures, places to see, and things to do, including tours and events in Northern Queensland and off shore.

www.nprsr.qld.gov.au
At the official website of the Queensland Government Department of National Parks, Recreation, Sport, and Racing you can get information on where to camp, how to obtain a license, and further information on each campground within a national park, plus alerts on fires and floods.

www.state.gov
Statistics and up-to-date travel information about Australia are provided by the U.S. Department of State. The site also offers information on entry and exit requirements, medical resources, and whom to contact in case of emergency.

www.sydney.com
This is the official website of Sydney, listing attractions, accommodations, things to do, and most importantly all the big annual events and festivals months by month, with links to the events' respective websites, so you can get dates and tickets before your trip.

www.transportnsw.info
Make your trips on public transport in Sydney really easy. Just type in where and when you want to go and the site will offer you simple solutions, be it a no-change trip or using a combination of types of transport; if you have to walk in between connections, it gives you directions. It also offers time estimates and alternative ways of getting to your location, and it's available as an app.

www.willyweather.com.au
This is a comprehensive website giving five-day weather forecasts, sunset and sunrise timings, and details of high and low tides around Australia, making it a great planning tool for trips that might depend on any of the above.

Index

A

B

G

H

N

OP

QR

S

T

UV

WXYZ

List of Maps

Photo Credits

Title page photo: © strangerview/123rf.com

All photos © Ulrike Lemmin-Woolfrey except page 6 (top right) © Giovanni Gagliardi/123rf.com; page 7 (top) © Joanne Weston/123rf.com; page 10 © strangerview/123rf.com; page 13 (top right) © strangerview/123rf.com; page 18 © Irina Tischenko/123rf.com; page 22 © ivogoetz/123rf.com; page 69 © chaiwat leelakajonkij/123rf.com; page 71 © Rita Melville/123rf.com; page 72 © Heewon Seo/123rf.com; page 73 © rorem/123rf.com; page 81 © Anthony Ngo/123rf.com; page 90 © Thorsten Rust/123rf.com; page 126 © andesign101/123rf.com; page 136 © andesign101/123rf.com; page 147 © strangerview/123rf.com; page 149 © Anna Orlyanskaya/123rf.com; page 154 © John Casey/123rf.com; page 157 © Stephen Gibson/123rf.com; page 172 © Nick Kempt/123rf.com; page 176 © Alan Benge/123rf.com; page 181 © Andrey Bayda/123rf.com; page 182 © Ilia Torlin/123rf.com; page 234 © Paul Kennedy/123rf.com; page 263 © junichi suzuki/123rf.com; page 266 © Jason Ross/123rf.com; page 279 (top) © kummeleon/123rf.com, (bottom) © Viktor Cap/123rf.com; page 281 © Giovanni Gagliardi/123rf.com; page 282 (top) © Matt Caldwell/123rf.com, (bottom) © cbpix/123rf.com; page 283 © Joanne Weston/123rf.com; page 285 (top) © strangerview/123rf.com, (bottom) © Cigdem Uzun/123rf.com; page 286 © shihina/123rf.com; page 287 (top) © Joe Quinn/123rf.com, (bottom) © Andrey Golubev/123rf.com; page 289 © Chris Putnam/123rf.com; page 290 © Kitch Bain/123rf.com; page 292 © kjuuurs/123rf.com; page 293 (top) © Viktor Cap/123rf.com, (bottom) © Johan Larson/123rf.com; page 295 © Kitch Bain/123rf.com; page 296 © Johan Larson/123rf.com; page 298 (top) © petervick167/123rf.com, (bottom) © Ina van Hateren/123rf.com; page 299 © Christopher Ison/123rf.com; page 301 © Melissa Armstrong/123rf.com; page 302 © Ina van Hateren/123rf.com; page 303 © Velislava Yovcheva/123rf.com; page 304 © feathercollector/123rf.com; page 306 © Johan Larson/123rf.com

MOON SYDNEY & THE GREAT BARRIER REEF

Avalon Travel
a member of the Perseus Books Group
1700 Fourth Street
Berkeley, CA 94710, USA
www.moon.com

Editor and Series Manager: Kathryn Ettinger
Copy Editor: Deana Shields
Graphics Coordinator: Darren Alessi
Production Coordinator: Darren Alessi
Cover Design: Faceout Studios, Charles Brock
Moon Logo: Tim McGrath
Map Editor: Kat Bennett
Cartographer: Stephanie Poulain
Indexer: Greg Jewett

ISBN-13: 978-1-61238-828-1
ISSN: 2376-1954

Printing History
1st Edition – March 2015
5 4 3 2 1

Front cover photo: An aerial view of the stunning coral formations of the Great Barrier Reef © Michele Falzone / Alamy

Printed in Canada by Friesens

All recommendations, including those for sights, activities, hotels, restaurants, and shops, are based on each author's individual judgment. We do not accept payment for inclusion in our travel guides, and our authors don't accept free goods or services in exchange for positive coverage.